ARHAT YOGA

A Complete Description of the Spiritual Pathway to the Sambhogakaya Yoga Attainment

WILLIAM BODRI

Copyright © 2021 William Bodri. All rights reserved. No part of this book may be used or reproduced in any manner whatsoever the without written permission of the publisher, except in cases of brief quotations in articles and reviews. However, the chapter Arhat Yoga may be freely reprinted without copyright permission, as well as edited for corrections and commented upon with addendums, as long as there is correct attribution of the initial text to William Bodri and this book. For information write:

Top Shape Publishing LLC
1135 Terminal Way Suite 209
Reno, NV 89502

2021 First Edition
January 2022 Second Edition
March 2022 Third Edition

ISBN: 978-0-9998330-5-6
Library of Congress Control Number: 2021938296

DEDICATION

Students in every spiritual school are seeking *Moksha*, salvation, liberation, or enlightenment. This book was written for these individuals as it will greatly help all seekers of enlightenment or self-realization regardless of their spiritual tradition, especially those in the monastic traditions who are trying to improve their practice, or just want to figure it out. It primarily relies on the vocabulary of Hinduism and Buddhism to make matters clear but its contents and message are non-denominational.

Please take a yellow marker and mark anything that strikes you in this text because this is the one book that explains the common spiritual guidance provided by religions that can guide you to attaining the Tao of spiritual ascension and illumination, and you will probably reference this information frequently over the years. As stated, it is especially written for those devoted to spiritual practice, especially yogis and monastics.

This is only the first chapter from *Bodhisattva Yoga*, an even more elaborate and detailed anthology of selected writings on the cultivation practices necessary for attaining enlightenment and the stages of the spiritual path. Enlightenment actually entails not just mental attainments but the development of a collection of connected transcendental spiritual bodies – composed of ascending levels of energy - that together are called the *sambhogakaya* attainment.

For more details on spiritual cultivation techniques (especially inner energy work), please reference *Neijia Yoga*, *Nyasa Yoga*, *Buddha Yoga*, *Bodhisattva Yoga*, *Color Me Confucius*, *The Mystical Path of Christian Theosis*, *Visualization Power*, *Sports Visualization* and *Meditation Case Studies*.

Especially recommended are *Neijia Yoga*, *Buddha Yoga* and *Color Me Confucius* as well as several other related works for the cultivation path: *Detox Cleanse Your Body Quickly and Completely*, *Look Younger Live Longer*, and *Culture, Country, City, Company, Person, Purpose, Passion, World*. For life guidance: *Move Forward* and *Quick, Fast, Done*.

CONTENTS

	Preface	i
1	The Fundamental Substratum of the Universe	1
2	The Primal Constituent – The Primordial Universal Substratum	5
3	Evolutes – Manifest Existence	8
4	Impermanence Characterizes Phenomena	17
5	Infinite Interdependent Simultaneous Co-Arising	22
6	Consciousness & Knowledge – The World We Experience is a Mind-Only Mental Representation	44
7	Mastering One's Consciousness and Perfecting Consummate Conduct	112
8	The Physical Body and the Four Transcendental Bodies	225
9	Generation of the Higher Spiritual Bodies	234
10	The Stages of Spiritual Attainment	242
11	The Three Requirements for Cultivation Success	251
12	Meditation Practice	282
13	Self-Improvement, Spiritual Values and Virtuous Conduct	328
14	General Principles for Qi/Prana Internal Energy Practices	344
15	Mental and Physical Phenomena Arising Due to Spiritual Practice	413
16	Arhats, Bodhisattvas and Buddhas	419
17	Comprehending *The Heart Sutra* & *Bhagavad Gita*	429
18	Summary	499

PREFACE

The Buddhist, Hindu and Taoist traditions are usually taken as the primary guides to enlightenment theory and practice, yet all genuine religions (such as Christianity, Islam, Judaism, Shinto, Shugendo, Jainism, Confucianism, Sikhism, etcetera) lead ardent practitioners to achieve the spiritual body attainments that constitute *Moksha* or spiritual enlightenment along with liberation from the lower realms of birth and death.

This book explains this cultivation pathway but much of the material will seem revolutionary to the spiritual seeker, including: (1) a comprehensive description of principle of interdependent origination that defines manifest reality according to the *Hua Yen* view, (2) the *Diamond Sutra* teachings about our true self-nature and our ultimate origins, (3) an explanation of the goal of *sat, chit, ananda* (the subjective experience of the ultimate unchanging reality) and how this necessitates a dualistic mind-body cultivation system entailing physical exercise, devotion to intensified inner energy practices, mental mindfulness of one's thoughts and behavior with the purpose of self-rectification, and meditation practice, (4) revelation of the five spiritual body achievements within the *sambhogakaya* attainment and the five cultivation stages that denote one's spiritual progress, and the (5) principles of Yin and Yang Qi/Prana cultivation inherent in yoga, martial arts and all spiritual cultivation practices, (6) how to set up an emptiness meditation routine and a more complete routine that incorporates emotional cleansing practices and other techniques, (7) how to cultivate a new personality or character, replete with virtues, so as to merit a better life, better subsequent incarnation, the spiritual enlightenment bodies, and so that you can execute Bodhisattva vows, and more.

This should be a perennial guide to spiritual cultivation efforts in your life by shedding illumination on many topics. Although it doubtless has errors, the information should help revolutionize your cultivation work, and over time I hope that others will flesh out more details and corrections for you. Philosophy is used to attain a certain goal in life, so it is the orientation that is important rather than whether some minor fact or thought is wrong. Does this information put you in a better position and direction? It should.

Chapter 1
THE FUNDAMENTAL
SUBSTRATUM OF THE UNIVERSE[1]

The primordial fundamental substrate, substance, essence, foundation, substratum or ground state of the universe is its fundamental nature, and is known by many names such as the source nature, primordial essence, Supreme Reality, Ultimate Reality, "Highest, Clearest, Purest," absolute essence, original nature, fundamental essence, Source, Ultimate, true nature, absolute nature, self-nature, absolute purity, the Unmanifest, Suchness, the Supreme Beatitude, Self or True Self. This is the fundamental substance-essence that composes all things, and which somehow through differentiation gave birth to the manifestation of everything in existence.

In religious terms It is sometimes called Parabrahman, Brahman, Nirguna Brahman, Shiva, *Purusha*, God, Father, Ein Sof, Ik Ongkar, Supreme Ultimate, ground state, Great Perfection, primal divinity, *dharmakaya*, Buddha-substrate, *nirvana*, *Anama*, Allah, beingness, true existence and many other names that suit various faiths. It is the true original existence-substance from which everything else originates.

Being the original essence-substance that is the most fundamental and primal universal substrate, logic necessitates that It must be uncreated, self-so, pre-existing or beginningless. Being the most primal substrate or substratum It cannot come from anything else so there is nothing prior to

---

[1] See *Traditional Theory of Evolution and Its Application in Yoga* (Gharote, Devnath, Jha), *Maya in Physics* (N.C. Panda), *Avadhuta Gita of Dattatreya* (Swami Chetanananda), *The Ribhu Gita* (translated by Dr. H. Ramamoorthy), *Astavakkra Samhita* (Swami Nityaswarupananda), and *Avadhuta Avadhuta Avadhuta Dasbodh* (Shri Samartha Ramdas).

It. Because It has no prior, It has no coming into being, and thus is unborn. Because It is beginningless It is the primal, primordial, fundamental, foundational substance or substratum before myriad other universal things were created, and Itself is pre-existing rather than born. If It was created than its own source would have been some other primordial essence, but It *is* the primordial essence or ground state of beingness. The best way to think about It is to consider It as something like empty space or a great void lacking attributes within which all things have somehow arisen.

Since Its existence does not come from any prior causes or conditions It is therefore self-so, uncreated, intrinsic, inherent, self-sufficient, and present before the creation of the universe of myriad things started. It is their primordial substance or essence, infinite and all-pervading, immanent and omnipresent because It is present in all things since they are born of It. It is everywhere at all times. It is neither limited nor bounded and constrained. Only phenomena are limited and bounded.

This primordial essence/substance, or original nature of the universe, is the only independent thing while everything else is dependent upon Its existence. It is their support and ultimate composition since they all come from It – "they owe their existence to God's existence." All other things are conditional constructions of Its essence that are temporary, transient, ever-changing and therefore undependable due to their quality of impermanence. Their true nature is this unchanging primordial essence-substance.

This primordial essence, energy, ground state, beingness or substance must, by logical inference, be a solitary singleness of one primal unity that is unmanifest into anything else. It is without any qualities. As the primal-most essence It exists only as pure Oneness and Aloneness, a pure being Itself that is a "One Without A Second." It is the One Without Another, the Solitary One, the Pure One, the Immaculate One without divisions or differentiation.

Since It is the only primal existent, Its immaculateness necessitates that It cannot have anything else beside It so Its nature is empty of manifestations other than Itself, and thus it is called the Void or Empty One or Emptiness. It must be a single solitary whole that is alone (perfectly pure) rather than two or more things since being just Itself It is a oneness that has never entered into differentiation. The term "one" or "oneness" means that things are not-to-be-distinguished within It because they are non-existent.

This original essence must also be infinite – endless, All, everything – because being limited by having borders would mean It transforms into something else at its boundaries, and then there would be two things instead of a single fundamental substratum. Therefore It is infinite, endless, partless, an unbroken infinite whole of single purity that does not undergo modifications such as by possessing any attributes (which would constitute impurities within It).

It cannot be superseded by a more transcendental reality because It is the original foundational substrate. It is the foundational, fundamental, primordial base of Creation – the only reality that is *real* (true and unchanging) in every respect. Being absolutely pure in being only Itself without any differentiation, It is therefore without attributes and without changes, without marks or signs, unsullied and unclouded by phenomena so It is continuous and everywhere the same, present in entirety everywhere. Being homogenously pure and changeless since It is foundational and infinite, It has no precedent stage nor consequent stage, no increase nor decrease, no coming into being nor transformation into anything else. Being perfectly pure It *cannot* change into anything else (because there are no causes within It to transform) so It *doesn't* change unto anything else but always remains what It is, hence It is *forever unmanifest* into anything else. There can be no question of its birth as being eternal it has a permanent existence. It is the primordial Unmanifest Aloneness since it is unmanifest into anything else, for True Reality must be changeless and everlasting.

It is always just Itself and only Itself – immutable, pure, infinite, eternal. It is everlasting due to Its changelessness, and thus It is the sole unchanging Reality. It is the ground truth, the ground state of Reality, the motionless real nature of all things. No matter what may happen to the universe, the foundational substratum will always be there and always has been there due to its permanence. It is what is *real and dependable* in life because It is always there, and It is therefore your source nature or core self, your True Self. It is the essence of your self, your true beingness. Thus It is your true self-nature, what you are in the most genuine, truest absolute sense. At the center of your being is This One, your True Self, your changeless fundamental nature that is empty of all things.

For understanding's sake It is sometimes described as formlessness, void or Emptiness without attributes (qualities or marks or phenomena), and thus akin to empty space. Its comparison to undivided endless empty space is because It is also pure, changeless, motionless, and without attributes or differentiation inside It. Just as space cannot be destroyed, It cannot be altered.

Moses Maimonides wrote, "you must understand that God has no essential attribute in any form or in any sense whatever (like empty space), and that the rejection of corporeality implies the rejection of essential attributes." In other words, God is this fundamental substrate that lacks corporeal forms, and in being empty of phenomena God is essentially without any attributes just like empty space. Any changeable entity, on the other hand, has a beginning and an end as well as attributes that can be described.

What is a change? It is the appearance of another characteristic when a previous characteristic has disappeared. A mutation or transformation is a change. Any changeable entity has a beginning and end and must therefore decay, whereas the primordial essence never changes since It is infinite, eternal, immaculately pure, motionless and without any divisions or attributes. Without borders It must be infinite. Immaculately pure, It must be a homogenous oneness or perfection without differentiations and thus changeless. Changeless, It must be eternal and motionless. Pure and infinite in being, It is beyond all description.

This is the fundamental substratum. When people think of It they often compare It to an infinite emptiness like space since empty space fits many of these characteristics, but It is not space because space can be bent and twisted by gravity (such as the great mass of black holes) so space is a fabric of form that can be affected by energy. Most spiritual schools ask adherents to contemplate this fundamental nature, which is called a form of "emptiness meditation."

Chapter 2
THE PRIMAL CONSTITUENT – THE PRIMORDIAL UNIVERSAL SUBSTRATUM

All things, at their most fundamental level, must be (and are) composed of this primordial essence. Therefore their composition, in its most absolute aspect, is only this fundamental substance-essence-nature-substratum-ground state. It is the omnipresent, *real part of you* that can never change or be eliminated and thus is your truest Self or genuine self-nature. It is immanent – always there – and because It lacks forms (which would be attributes) It is transcendent to all created things.

Ultimately there is only this original, primordial, fundamental essence and nothing else since all things are composed entirely of only this. Being all-pervasive, It is neither near nor far. It is always present. It is the *essence of our beingness*.

You are essentially this fundamental natural substratum. At the core of your body and mind this is your True Self, your self-nature, your non-evolving inherent Self. This is what you are, and It is what atoms are. *Everyone and everything* is this same primordial substrate, the foundational substance, the original nature, the True Self, the fundamental substratum. The most real "I" in you is this unchangeable self-nature that is your utmost unchanging Self, and this means that your own nature is infinite and never-ending.

You are nothing different from this original essence. Somehow your manifest form and being has evolved out of It. You are actually this one self-nature that is in All, that is everything, that is *the one universal soul-self*. You are It, It is you, you are one of Its aspects, attributes or functions. Wholly being It, which is the ground state of the universe, you are no different from the rest of the universe, which is also the rest of you. You and It are no different from one another as is also the case with all other things. Being It you were never born and will never die. That is your true nature. Therefore, you are ultimately beyond birth and death.

Just as gold can be made into various ornaments, those golden ornaments are in their primal essence only gold. From gold's standpoint, they are all just itself, namely gold, because gold sees no differentiation into anything that is other than itself. If gold changes shape it is still gold. When clay becomes a jar the name "jar" arises but it is still only the material of clay. A jar is only a modification, transformation or change in appearance of the clay. As ocean waves, bubbles and foam are still just the ocean, so the universe that emanates from the absolute substratum is not anything different from It. The ground state universal substratum is the only substance composing the universe, and the forms and attributes of objects we classify as Its multiplicity are mere superimpositions we make upon It because we do not penetrate through the appearances to perceive the ultimacy of this clear nature. What seems to exist outside of It is merely illusion.

Given this understanding, from the standpoint of the fundamental nature there is nothing else in existence despite all the apparent forms we see and the different names we give things. Thus the saying, "The infinite variety of appearances and manifestations and numberless distinctions are all His shapes, His qualities, His modes of existence."

There are no phenomena at all because there is only the one fundamental essence underlying all things, permeating them and composing their absolute construction. In the universe there is just the original nature - just Itself. All subsequent evolutes (energies, forms and phenomena) are just Itself no matter what their shapes, forms, attributes, functions or appearances. They are only It. The universe is this pure existence only.

The fundamental ground nature is therefore the Ultimate Source, the Ultimate Self, the true self-nature of all things. It is their foundational substratum, primal nature, fundamental substrate, their fundamental substance, their ground state of being, their innermost Self, their absolute self-nature or True Self. All things, at their ultimate compositional breakdown, have This as their absolute essence or substrate (substance).

A spiritual saying goes, "Although He existed in many forms He was single. He was there in all the elements and was all the elements." Thus the primordial essence is often called the source nature, fundamental nature or primordial substratum that becomes all things. It is the Self inside us that is the Self of All. Ultimately there is only one entity, this fundamental Self and the universe is Its manifestation into apparent form. Our true beingness is this one eternal nature.

Chapter 3
EVOLUTES – MANIFEST EXISTENCE

Being totally pure as a single unified substrate the universal ground state is changeless and therefore eternal, being changeless It can never transform into anything else, and therefore It can never give birth to anything. Yet the universe is here, so what a paradox is that!

By a process therefore unknown, which Buddhism terms "Ignorance" since we don't know how it happened, this solitary essence somehow gave rise to evolutes that in turn gave rise to further transformations and even more evolutes. Hinduism says that the "desire" of the absolute caused It to give birth to manifestation, or the "will" or "play" or "whim" or an "urge" of the absolute moved It into giving birth to manifest reality but the fundamental substrate is an inanimate substratum without consciousness. Basically, no one knows how it happened, which some schools call an "overflow," so these are just words used to anthropomorphize the appearance of Creation.

In Judaism, from the perspective of the manifested realms Creation takes place as *Yesh me-Ayin*, "something from nothing." From the perspective of the Divine or fundamental substratum (God), only God has absolute existence so Creation is only an apparent existence or appearance that is *Ayin me-Yesh*, "nothing from something (the real nature)." Even so, God alone is and God alone exists for all time.

Taoism explains that within the Great Ultimate, quiescent and pure, arose something like a movement.[2] It maintains, "The Tao from Emptiness and

---

[2] See *Buddha Yoga* for a recap of the many ways in which various religions describe Creation.

Non-being generated the One Breath," which means that primordial energy or Shakti was somehow generated from an empty ground state that lacked all things. The one original nature somehow gave birth to Shakti (Nature, the cosmos or the universe of manifest existence), which as the first emanation or evolute is still entirely the primordial essence, and then from this Shakti the process of producing all other elements of the universe started. Hinduism thus explains that the Ultimate Reality of *Nirguna* Brahman (the absolute existence without attributes) gave birth to *Saguna* Brahman (existence with form and qualities) that then generated the rest of the universe. Through complex interactions of cause and effect, the evolutes through continuing transformations produced innumerable subsequent energies, forms and phenomena. This is the process of Creation.

During the process of gold being formed into jewelry the substance of gold never changes at all, only its outer form or appearance changes. There is nothing separating one piece of gold jewelry from another when you are just looking at the absolute substance of gold. Analogy: all the various forms of the world are still nothing but the all-pervading fundamental substratum appearing in various forms. The primordial essence is indivisible and cannot emanate into something other than Itself.

No one can conceive of a cause at the stage of Creation since the Original Purity never leaves Its state of purity, yet a state of apparent diversity or multiplicity somehow arises in Ultimate Oneness that produces the forms of Creation. This diversity of apparently separate independent forms is an illusion because they are all still only a single emanation (Shakti) rather than a multiplicity of particularities, and they are only the one absolute foundational substrate. They are not the independences they appear to be and thus the saying, "In all forms, in all diversity and disparity is He alone." Only one fundamental substrate (one "Divine Identity") alone is everywhere.

The evolutes in aggregate are called Creation, Shakti, *Prakriti*, karmic formations, *Saguna* Brahman, Manifestation, Triple Realm, Logos (the Word), universe, cosmos, all things, attributes, forms, Indra's web, the Primal Illusion, Maya, Mara, *samsara*, and many other names. They are generated by the process we call creation, generation, production, birth, emanation, manifestation, mutation, change, or transformation and in essence they are always the original nature.

Evolutes are constantly in a state of movement, flux, transformation, change, interaction, fluctuation, no-rest or vibration as opposed to the motionless original nature that doesn't move because of its changeless immutability. The fact that It is the one single essence in existence means there is no change possible within It, so the appearance of changes is compared to an illusion superimposed upon it.

Due to constant vibratory change, the manifest realm of evolutes is characterized by transience and impermanence. What appears to be solid and unchanging is just a monotonous illusion that hides the qualities of incessant change and impermanence. The realm of Creation is a grand illusion populated by objects that look firm but lack solidity just like the images within a dream. They look like they are a solid and *slowly* changing reality but they are not – objects are mostly empty space and changing every moment. They are like the reflection of the moon in water that looks firmly real but is insubstantial and cannot be grasped. The images we see are an apparent reality of solidity and changelessness that disguise the real nature of how things actually exist. To understand how things really exist is called an awakening of understanding, or a "realization."

On the surface phenomena may appear solid, still, and unchanging but due to the limitations of consciousness and the media of our sensory apparatus what we see around us is a blurred vision of the universe, an approximation that is a simplified, abbreviated, limited incorrect perspective. What we see of the outside world within our minds is nothing like the true manifest reality that is out there but instead is a magnificent illusion created within our consciousness. The world we see within us is a representation we mentally create within our minds because of our sense organs and anatomy. If we perceived the world with a different set of senses then we would see it in a different way. What we see inside us of the outside world is a cognitive algorithm, a similitude of perceived qualities that are quite limited and at times incorrect, but that perceptual view has developed over the millennia as adaptations to the challenges of existence. They developed due to the needs of evolutionary fitness (survival needs) rather than as truthful representations that embody the greatest possible fidelity to the external world. In the same way, over the course of millions of years of natural selection we have as a species also developed certain psychological characteristics in addition to our physical ones.

Evolution has shaped us to generate a perceptual world that allows us to survive, but those perceptions hide from us stuff we don't need to know to survive, including the way the universe actually is. Our mental images of reality do not give us a true or complete picture of phenomenal reality, whatever the reality of the outside world might be. However, we can accurately conclude that the true reality of phenomenal existence is far, far larger than the limited pictures painted within our minds.

We cannot see all the attributes of objects but only what our eyes allow us to see. If we cannot see all parts of the electromagnetic spectrum such as ultraviolet or infrared light then we cannot see the entire picture of reality. In fact, we're missing most of the physical world and don't know what physical reality really is. In our minds we construct a reality that doesn't have to exactly represent actual reality, but we can be convinced that the outside world works in a certain way (operates according to facticity) as long as the illusion we construct within consciousness offers consistencies that are sufficient for survival. Objective reality is very far from the reality we experience within our mind which tries to simulate it. We are interacting with reality, but what we perceive to be that reality is not the way it really is. What we see within our consciousness as a picture of the world is simply an abstraction meant to represent the world but it is imperfect, incomplete, inaccurate.

If our sense of smell isn't good enough to distinguish millions of odors then we cannot experience a complete aroma picture of reality. If we cannot hear very quiet sounds then we cannot experience a complete picture of the environment too. If we have cataracts in our eyes then our vision cannot create an accurate picture of what other people normally see. If we fall for optical illusions such as mirages then we interpret reality incorrectly. Everyone experiences the same reality but experiences it differently not only due to anatomical differences, but also due to mental conclusions, values and emotions that each of us superimposes upon those experiences. Each of us wears a different set of distorting lenses that distances us from direct, accurate knowledge of the world and reality. In the great game of life we must recognize what is wrong with our perceptions and compensate for those errors.

Whatever data we perceptually acquire about the objective external world of things-in-themselves out there will always be a partial approximation because that information will be acquired through our limited perceptual systems. We're never in direct cognition of reality. Whatever we perceive is simply a construction of our mind – a blurred image that avoids details – that allows us to work with the world in a useful way that supports our survival (with adaptive behavior), but our worldview is actually very different from the fullness of objective reality.

What we see of the universe is only the projection of the mind. We create a coherent world within our brains that we extrapolate from sensory interactions with the world that register, but it is just a simple subjective similitude due to cognitive algorithms that by necessity is incomplete while including simplifications and thus errors. Furthermore, the experience will be polluted by whatever values, emotions and so forth that naturally arise from within our minds to wrap around the processing of that raw information.

We might perceive the calm surface of a lake, but our limited vision prevents us from seeing its rapid dance of myriads of miniscule water molecules and even smaller energetic interactions. Hence our perception of the world is different from its actual temporal structure. We cannot see the true granularity of existence but need instruments to transcend our physical senses at the smallest scale. As stated, we cannot see all wavelengths of light and can only hear sound in a narrow range of frequencies, so it is easy to understand that we never perceive the world in all its glory through our senses, nor register the fine details of the true nature of the conventional world or even see its macrocosmic structure. We do not perceive quantum fluctuations so we think of spacetime being as rigid as a rock, and we do not see galaxies and superclusters so we think our small world is large.

The actual universe of Shakti is so much more than what appears within our minds. We may even misperceive the world due to faulty sense organs and on occasion we might suffer from perceptual illusions such as by seeing a mirage, or mistaking a rope for a snake. In short, what we envision within our minds is not the true reality of the external world of Shakti, but an illusion that is an approximation of Shakti that is not really accurate, yet it is a useful worldview that humans have mentally developed through the course of evolution so that we might as a species survive. Nature, through evolution, has produced consciousness for "living objects" to enable them to navigate, survive and replicate in unpredictable environments, so consciousness is a design principle for extending the continuance of existence for living objects. Natural selection has not only shaped the bodies of living beings (providing sensory apparatus and other attributes) and produced consciousness within living beings to do this but has also shaped their psychological dispositions. Nature, through evolution, has produced the characteristics of countless species of conscious agents.

As to the absolute essence or ground state, we can never ever perceive the formless original nature either. You can think about the original nature, but any images you make in your mind of It are wrong since the foundational essence lacks attributes. As soon as you create an image of It, the images includes attributes so are incorrect. You cannot create a similitude of the fundamental essence in your mind since It lacks all attributes, and thus all images of It are incorrect. Mental fabrications (thoughts) cannot duplicate

It. You cannot attribute any descriptions to It other than It is not this or that. It is therefore said that God's *essence,* being free of all attributes (like empty space) is thus unfathomable, unapproachable, and incomprehensible whereas God's energies and attributes (forms and phenomena) are readily accessible to us. None of those appearances, however, are similar to God's essential nature since It lacks all forms and attributes.

When the wind flows in the sky it does not distort the sky in any way. With the arising of wind you can in no way say that space becomes broken. There is no distortion in the sky if it becomes pervaded by darkness or light either. Similarly, when evolutes arise within the original nature there is no change or distortion within It. Nothing can produce an effect on It and so It remains ever changeless. However, new appearances within It do somehow arise just as the wind somehow appears in a vast empty sky.

These evolutes, energies, effusions, forms and phenomena (subtle elements) comprise what we can call various planes/levels of existence in the cosmos, which are also known as *realms of being,* and they are populated by innumerable diverse beings and phenomena that comprise the multidimensional universe. Living beings are also objects, forms or phenomena within the universe. We denote them as "living" to characterize them as having the special attribute of life, and "sentient" to denote that they have the special property of consciousness.

Many spiritual schools maintain that the earthly plane has evolved from a gradual condensation, solidification, crystallization or emanation of higher non-physical energies and essences, with the ultimate foundation being our ground truth - the changeless original nature. Mass, for instance, is an emergent property due to the confinement of energy; mass is the condensation of energy - a masquerade of energy as form that in terms of levels is the least degree of real being. Religions, and especially spiritual cultivation schools, typically talk about five planes of existence in additional to the primordial original essence. However, there are many more despite the abbreviated discussion.

The causeless cause – the original essence – is in no way associated with whatever pervades It as part of It, meaning these realms. All phenomena, energies, forces and so forth are inseparable from It, meaning that It omnipresently pervades all evolutes with immanence because they are, in their essential nature, It. Whatever exists in the universe is pervaded by It. The primal essence is therefore the "I," True Self or absolute self-nature of all things since It is permanently there. It is impossible for phenomena to escape from being It through some type of independence for It is the composition of their absolute essence. Being the only existent, It is All. Shakti, Its Creation, is the All of Manifestation but It is a greater All since It is the Unmanifest substratum within which Shakti appears. These two realms of the Manifest and Unmanifesting substrate inseparably pervade one another as "There is no place empty of Him."

Everything is the fundamental primal substrate. Evolutes, emanations, forms, appearances or manifestations are Its physical, corporeal, non-transcendental aspects, functions, or attributes. They are what we call *conventional existence*, an ephemeral realm of continuous constant change. Shankara said, "The universe is truly Brahman, ... for that which is superimposed (the universe) has no separate existence from its substratum (Brahman). Whatever a deluded person perceives through mistake is Brahman and Brahman alone."

The two principles of the original nature (Brahman) and evolutes (Shakti) have no control over each other. The original nature is not involved in the evolution of Shakti or the transformations within Shakti since being perfectly pure, motionless and changeless It does not cause anything and thus is not the cause of any evolute, which is why Moses Maimonides wrote, "There is, in truth, no relation in any respect between God and any of God's creatures." No change whatsoever ever occurs to It just as there is never any distortion in the sky when darkness or light pervades it. It does not perform any actions whatsoever, so it is up to us to create significant change and meaning in the world as we deem fit.

Nevertheless the universe has arisen and It always exists everywhere and in everything as the ever-present existential support. So no changes ever happen to It; changes only happen in the field of Creation, emanation or manifestation that we can call Shakti the universe. In other words, evolution only happens to Shakti. It is from Shakti that all is evolved, and all that is evolving is Shakti only, which is in turn the original essence. In *Purusha* (the primal essence) nothing ever happens. Shakti (*Prakriti*), however, is constantly in an evolving state of flux and transformation, and so its phenomena are characterized by incessant change and impermanence.

The primordial essence is hence a causeless cause in birthing the universe and It is in no way associated with whatever appears within It. It is inseparable from everything, pervading everything, but the two principles of Parent and Offspring, Host and Guest, Mother and Son, primordial original substance and Shakti have no control or influence over each other.

Purusha, the original essence, is not involved in evolution since It does not create anything. It does not cause anything and so is not the cause of any evolute because changes never occur to It. All changes only happen in Shakti, the field of emanations. Evolution only happens to Shakti, *Prakriti* or Creation, from which all is evolved. The original nature is not different from Shakti and yet Shakti appears to be different from It, but yet the two are identical because Shakti is It and It is Shakti.

Our mind (consciousness) is also one of the many phenomena of the universe, a working process of matter and energy dependent upon a brain that through its internal processes lets us know things. It creates Knowledge for a living object Knowledge-knower (us). When the mind arises (creates thoughts) it creates all things, and when the mind stops birthing thoughts then all things disappear such as in the states of deep sleep, anesthesia, a coma or non-existence. The universe doesn't exist for inanimate objects because for them there is no knowing, knower, and objects known. The existence of the universe is only recognized because of knowingness, or Knowledge. This is the function of consciousness.

Since Knowledge is ultimately the original essence that is empty of everything, such as phenomena, even Knowledge does not truly exist as an absolute. It is basically an illusion we construct because it is a subjective opinion or point of view rather than an absolute truth. Knowledge, knower and the knowable do not exist in reality. Why? Because the original nature does not contain a single thing, so all such differentiations do not exist within It. In other words, the underlying nature of All things is in an absolute state of purity, Aloneness, non-transformation, or Suchness. In It there are no phenomena, no knowers, no Knowledge, no processes, no anything. Everything is Itself. In the absolute sense, there is no such real thing as a living sentient being.

What we experience within ourselves is a transient apparent reality, an illusion that is ultimately nothingness because that is what we are, which is an emptiness of all forms and phenomena. Our consciousness is also at times inaccurate and we often act against conscious rationality, but with all its faults consciousness still creates a conventional world and gives us a remarkable miraculous gift - the experience of life. Let us make the best use of consciousness to enjoy reality and try to experience happiness in life, feel our active inner vitality that makes us alive, and savor the overall bliss of living. But let us not be coarse animals in this enjoyment, but strive for a measure of elegance and refinement above our animal nature. Let us reach for nobility and spirituality and then rise to a level of transcendence.

From the standpoint of the evolutes, we must say that the manifestation of each and every phenomenon of the cosmos proceeds and is governed by universal laws of cause and effect. All production, emanation, manifestation, transformation, mutation, evolution, generation or creation of phenomena has to be understood as a relationship between cause and effect. The cause and effect laws of transformation/generation may be as yet unknown, but all things arise and transform into new states through definite laws of cause and effect, stimulus and consequence, provocation and result. Cause and effect rules everything except the fundamental substrate, which is free of cause and effect because there is only Itself. Within It there is no such thing as cause and effect because there is only Its solitary self that lacks any attributes.

As to phenomenal cause and effect, entities that are themselves evolutes serve as the cause for subsequent entities to appear within Shakti. As sentient beings with minds we have the ability to investigate and then understand some of the causative/transformation processes behind the appearance of phenomena (Nature), and when we learn these principles and patterns we can then make use of them to our own benefit. This is a necessity in order to live, so should we not also use this ability to make situations and circumstances as good as possible? How wonderful it is to learn the natural course of Nature and then put yourself in harmony with its transformations by taking the path of least resistance for your ends.

With consciousness we experience the world, but we can also use our sentience to improve our world experience to decrease our suffering, increase our pleasure or comfort, and maximize our well-being. Thus, we should master the capabilities of our consciousness in order to improve our lives, such as for improving our health, increasing our longevity and maximizing our chances for continuity. Such mastery requires learning the principles of Nature (developing wisdom or understanding) so that we can shape it for our convenience, and mastering the skillfulness in our activities and behavior.

Chapter 4
IMPERMANENCE CHARACTERIZES PHENOMENA

All the constituent forms of Shakti that make up the universe (phenomena, energy, forces, etc.) are always in a continuous state of flux. Ultimately composed of energy, they are always continuously fluctuating with vibrations in motion. Since the world is in a constant state of flux, Heraclitus said, "Everything is on fire." Thus the apparent natures of phenomena (those which we experience) are impermanent, transitory or temporary. Because they each lack a fixed, unchanging stable identity they lack an *inherent* identity. They arise and pass away, and therefore are unstable formations lacking a concrete phenomenal identity. They lack a constant core or unchanging "self," a solid underlying inherent identity that is a fixed nature free of ceaseless transformations.

Because they are birthed from prior causes and conditions, they also lack a self-so or *intrinsic* identity because they are dependently produced. Every single phenomenon in the universe exists only because of an infinite interdependence of causes and effects defining it within the body of Shakti, so even the seemingly stand-alone existence of what appears to be an independent phenomenon is actually an existence dependent upon everything else in existence, and upon everything else in the past that has brought the universe to this very present state. The entire net of reality works together to produce a single phenomenon, which is why Maimonides said, "Know that this universe, in its entirety, is nothing else but one individual being." All events and phenomena interpenetrate. There is nothing with own-nature or own-beingness, meaning that an object exists purely in-and-of itself. Only the fundamental substrate exists that way.

All things are bound together by an infinite interdependence of mutual support that as a whole manifests the entire web of phenomenal existence.

In other words, things manifest because of a compendium of causes and effects where every element of existence enters in some measure into everything else that is a cause. This means that all things are dependent upon each other to exist instead of there just being a simple linear relationship of singular causes and effects. Every single phenomenon exists because of the totality of everything else, so all phenomena have a "conditional nature" or "dependent nature" rather than self-so intrinsic nature. All phenomena exist dependent upon all others so you are in everything and everything is in you. Phenomena, including individuals, are all conditional constructions dependent on innumerable causes and conditions that are themselves dependent on innumerable causes and conditions within an infinite network of co-dependencies. Since all those dependencies are always wavering with movement, how can they create something fixed, stable or permanent for even an instant?

All things are manifested by conditionedness (cause and effect) rather than by being independent existences with an own-nature. The most important aspect of their conditionedness is that they have no singular metaphysical substrate for manifestation other than the fundamental essence; they are conditional constructions that arise due to a conglomeration of infinite sources (causes). However, ultimately the primal substrate that is an unborn eternal, uncreated and indestructible, non-composite and unchanging, and which is beyond the network of dependent origination is their foundational support.

All the phenomena within Shakti are therefore termed "unreal" because they don't exist on their own in the way that we view them to be as standalone independent entities with the limited set of attributes we ascribe to them. They are impermanent rather than lasting, and causes define them. They are conditional constructions, composed of a myriad of other things, and not absolute existences with their own self-nature; they are composite constructions that lack an absolute existence. They lack their own-nature, so are only apparent constructions that seem to exist locally, yet their composition stretches out into the entire universe. Their appearance as a *separate* singularity within space is an illusion that you conceptually construct by seeing the world incorrectly. Paramount, we incorrectly perceive them as possessing some kind of intrinsic existence and identity.

The world of appearances is an illusion of limitations (separate objects or individualities separated by space) we create with our minds. The view is therefore unreal/incorrect, but the view is a conventional reality that works for us due to its predictable facticity. With our unique human way of perceiving the world we have - as living objects that replicate through sex while requiring food and protection for the continuance of our survival – successively been able to maintain the continued existence of our species until now.

Phenomena are seamlessly united with the whole of Shakti, thus so are we, and phenomena are actually the unchanging original substratum rather than independent phenomena. They lack being a "true reality" or "dependable existence" because they never remain the same identity for even an instant whereas the original nature remains eternally present in a state of changelessness, motionlessness, stability and reliability. Our True Self is the dependable genuine reality, and thus True Reality, whereas phenomena, since they are changeable, are like unreliable dream objects. Phenomena never remain stable appearances because their existent identity continuously changes from one interaction to another, thus altering their form.

There are no persistent stable identities, no eternal universals nor independent particulars within Shakti, and hence nothing you can rely on. You therefore need to learn how to adapt to change to survive, and how to control change to prosper. There are no crisp borders for phenomena or states because the forms of things are constantly changing and their causality bleeds into their surroundings. All phenomena are like fire in that they are a form of energy that is constantly moving, and yet look to be the very same element despite continuous change. All phenomena also lack borders in that there is not demarcation between them and Nature.

There is no thing within Shakti that exists solely because of just itself, whose existence is due only to itself, and since Shakti is all of Creation or Manifestation there is nothing (manifest) outside of Shakti either. Entities are all impermanent components of a shimmering, dancing, fluctuating ephemeral "Grand Illusion" we call the universe and cannot be grasped as anything solid, constant, or dependable. Vibrating and changing constantly, phenomena are like a moving mirage within a universe that is itself a roiling, seething froth.

This lack of an enduring identity for phenomena, which have ephemeral existences, has important implications for the condition of human suffering. It gives us the possibility of becoming liberated from suffering because our conditions can change. Because phenomena, conditions, circumstances or states of being are impermanent and flexible, marked by conditionedness, we can change them by influencing their nature, the conditions that produce them, or their trajectory. Because we have consciousness we are superior to inanimate matter in that we can learn how to master the transformations of phenomena to create and enjoy better states of being.

We do not simply exist but can decide what our existence will be. We can create happiness, prosperity, fulfillment, well-being or success. This capability is due to having consciousness whereas inanimate phenomena cannot change their states of being, conditions or attributes at will, and the changes we can bring about in the universe are only limited by our wisdom, skills and efforts.

All together the myriad individual phenomena of the universe comprise one single body, Shakti, whose most fundamental essence is the eternal original essence. Each phenomenon within this whole, or you can say the whole itself (All or Shakti), is constantly changing, mutating, fluctuating, roiling, vibrating or flowing because of infinite interdependence – infinite interlinked dependent conditions causing ceaseless transformations everywhere every moment. Shakti's essential nature is to transform. A single ripple in the tiniest of phenomena actually affects the entire universe, which means that the entire cosmos and all phenomena within it are continuously vibrating. The universe is constantly changing; for survival and flourishing we need to learn the pattern of changes and make best use of them for our thriving. Then we can attain prosperity and pleasure from the world.

Each entity that appears within the cosmos arises due to all previous and present ones, meaning that each form or phenomenon arises conditionally in the form of a *dependent origination*. Despite what seems like a myriad of separate individualities the whole universe comprised of everything should be considered an effervescent, scintillating appearance that is just one body. It is just one macrocosmic body that is a unity of apparent diversity rather than a soup of separate multiplicities. Although in continuous flux, Shakti-cosmos must be considered one single whole. Transcending Shakti is the original nature, for underlying all forms, all changes, all forces, all matter, and all spirit is the One that never changes and always endures, the absolutely pure substrate and substratum that is the support of All always, everywhere and in everything.

As an individual you are part of the single unified body of Shakti or Logos, and thus you form a unity with all the other myriad things of the universe, including all other life. They are essentially your greater body surrounding you, and you are just a composite of conditions within this whole connected to everything else. You can rightfully say, "All phenomena – they are all me, and as events they are all mine." Because you are connected to everything else within the cosmos, how you act and behave and even what you think (because thoughts are part of Shakti) will affect the greater universe, which is your true manifest body. How then should you conduct yourself? Spiritual cultivation provides the answer.

Beyond your apparent form you are essentially your True Self, your self-nature or "True I," but localized as a small apparent self within the cosmos you appear to have limited attributes and functions. One attribute is that you possess the ability to fashion present conditions *and the future* in any way you want if you proceed skillfully with wisdom, daring and determination.

What do you ultimately want to achieve as a consequence for yourself and for your greater body, which is your greater self that involves the lives of others? Your actions will produce consequences in many directions, so you should undertake training that helps you master your consciousness, body and your behavior to produce the results you ultimately want in life. First you must determine your goals using your *values*, second use your *reason* that (free from passion and bias) evaluates and determines the best course of action that leads to their achievement, and third you must rely on your *desires* to serve your highest goals by pushing you forward and rely on your *will* to strive with determination to execute that plan to achieve them. All phenomena and conditions are impermanent rather than fixed, so this gives you a possibility or opening to create something new that you truly want to achieve for yourself or for someone else.

The unity of Heaven (the cosmos) and man constitutes one all-pervading whole, so how will you devote your sentient actions within this one unity? What is worthy of you spending your time and vitality? What are you willing to sacrifice for in order to create it? In which directions do you want your efforts to be applied? What highest excellence do you want people to reside within that you are willing to work to create?

There will always be consequences for whatever you think, say and do. Why not choose efforts whose consequences will uplift mankind and the world?

Chapter 5
INFINITE INTERDEPENDENT SIMULTANEOUS CO-ARISING

The creation of a phenomenon is called its appearance, manifestation, birth, arising or development. Its continuance is called its continued existence, sustained existence, sustainment, sustention, survival, preservation or maintenance. Its dissolution is called its death, departure, disappearance, disintegration, disposition or settlement. In Hinduism these three phases of existence are symbolized by Brahma, Vishnu and Shiva.

There are laws that control the three phases of generation, sustention, and dissolution for each phenomenon. These are the laws of cause and effect (such as the laws of physics, chemistry, etcetera) that rule or guide the transformations, interactions, mutations, evolution, or changes of phenomena. All things arise and disappear due to cause and effect, which means that arising entities are "expressed conditionally" since they appear due to previous entities. When we cannot fathom the reasons for an event or entity appearing it is simply because we are ignorant as to the ultimate causes, but causes are there. Nothing appears without a set of causes. In fact, the causation necessary for the arising of a single phenomenon is actually the entire network of the universe.

The existence of each singular phenomenon actually depends upon all other phenomena in the entire universal whole. This is because all phenomena in the cosmos are interlinked in an infinite web of simultaneous interdependent intertwining that is an immense interweaving of co-dependent causes and conditions. This web excludes absolutely nothing. All phenomena are infinitely interconnected to one another within the fabric of Shakti because they are all Shakti and Shakti is a single unity. Everything is connected and ultimately one. In other words, each phenomenon has an existence that all other phenomenal parts of Shakti participate in. This causes all things to "simultaneously arise" due to each entity or factor of existence playing a role in co-defining everything else, and in total they produce the one singular phenomenon the Shakti (the universe) that is always shimmering, vibrating or fluctuating due to all the co-linked changes inside it. In other words, each universal phenomenon or element enters in some way into everything else that is and therefore there is, or because there is, a single unity or oneness, a fact that Sufism calls "comprehensiveness." The fabric of the universe is one whole, one existence, and all elements within the universe compose that single fabric. Therefore the arising of a singular phenomenon is not the creation of a singular object but a transformation within the one body of Shakti due to all its parts.

The interconnections between all things in the universe is called "Indra's net," which refers to an infinite web or net of glittering jewels wherein each jewel in each "eye" of the infinite net contains within itself the reflection of all the other jewels in the netting. If we were to inspect one of these jewels we would find on its polished surface the reflection of all the other jewels in the net, infinite in number, and in each reflected jewel we would also find the reflections of all the others, and so on ad infinitum. Thus they all enter into each other as all phenomena enter into one another; within each jewel are present all jewels. Similarly so, within each phenomenon of the universe are actually all the other phenomena of the universe that enter into it to compose it. There is a connection amongst all things; all points in space and time are connected.

This means that everything in the universe arises in dependence on everything else; each individual thing is a "dependent arising" dependent on the infinity of conditions rather than on just a limited set, although we use just limited sets when making predictions or calculations. However, all things, elements, entities, forces or phenomena actually arise and disappear in a magnificently great net of cause and effect relationships that spans all things and rules all changes, and absolutely nothing in the universe is independent of it including consciousness and your body. Everything in the universe is part of the single fabric of the universe, which is a scintillating ocean of energy in constant movement, a fluid-like body of energy fields that takes a particular value at every point in space that changes over time, and which ripples and sways in strange and interesting ways.

Every thing has an existence that is dependently or conditionally defined, meaning that the existence of every entity depends on everything else in existence and *on the past*. In other words, all parts of existence are linked together and interchange their influences, producing one giant shimmering whole whose "components" have existences rooted in reciprocity. Of course this is just a way of speaking, for who can say what "giant" is since there is no comparison of size against anything else, and who can say what "shimmering" is also?

No phenomenon has an existence of its own – meaning an intrinsic self-so inherent existence of own-beingness – but always comes into existence in dependence upon *all other things* via an infinite network of causality that comprises all phenomena in infinite interrelationships. So every thing is nothing on its own since all other things compose it – it doesn't have its own self-nature (it lacks a own-nature) – and hence does not actually exist as a "thing" but as a localized appearance that seems separate but is not.

Within the All of Manifestation everything exists that exists, but nothing "exists on purpose," including you. Every thing exists through transformations due to laws of cause and effect that produce evolutes within Shakti, and so the universe created you without any plan or purpose for your existence. Therefore you must create your own purpose for existence and create your own life goals and objectives in a way that provides you with personal meaning! *Things only exist due to interdependent origination; every entity exists due to all other things co-defining it rather than that there is an ontological ultimate purpose for this or that.* We are the ones who come up with such interpretations, and such conclusions are imaginative illusions, or you can say delusions. The presence of all other things connected together creates a phenomenon, and so they all share in its beingness. It has no purpose other than apparent existence. For your individual life you must therefore derive a personal purpose and significance for its existence that encompasses specific aspirations, pledges, vows of commitments.

There is nothing there that is a "thing" or "entity" other than a localized appearance due to multiple intersecting conditions, so in actuality there is no single thing anywhere at all. Rather, there is everything that is just one entity, and that macrocosmic entity of a single fabric is an illusion since its true nature is itself the absolute foundational substrate that is absent of phenomena. There is no such thing as a single thing except for Shakti itself, (the entire universe), and Shakti is in turn an illusion or Mara. Interdependence means there is only one thing – the universe – rather than a multiplicity of many different things, and that one thing is actually the underlying substratum that is the absolute Truth of the universe.

Therefore, everything is actually a one thing (the universe or Shakti) that is actually a "no thing (there)" since it is essentially the fundamental substrate. As to individual entities, you cannot say a phenomenon is a singular or separate thing because it is defined by and connected with everything else. A single phenomenon is a manifestation of infinite simultaneous conditions that exclude nothing, and so the conditions of an unknowably beginningless past and universal present come together to create it. A "thing" is a derived condition that is defined by or descended from innumerable, uncountable present and past conditions and have also already defined a future. A self is therefore not an independent thing but an intersection of interacting interdependencies.

Thus one can say that "each phenomena contains the entire universe" since the entire universe is involved/participates in the creation (birth) and maintenance (existence) of every single thing as well as its transformation into something else (its destruction, death or disappearance). If you grab a "thing" you are grabbing the entire universe in your hand since that phenomenon holds the entire universe within it. Each thing within the universe *is* the (entire) universe because it holds within itself the entire universe and cannot be parted from the All; by grabbing a corner of a book you hold the entire book, by squeezing a drop of water within the ocean you hold the entire ocean, and by grabbing a tiny iota of the universe you hold the entire universe.

Every iota is therefore not a part of the universe but the entire universe itself. The entire universe is found in a drop of the universe. In other words, the center of the universe is really everywhere. It is within each one of us. Every tiny thing is the center of the universe and every moment is its most important moment. Every moment is now, and the universe is always present in that now.

Mindfulness is paying close attention to the nature of our experience – what it is like to be you moment by moment. Mindfulness is non-judgmentally paying living attention to the moment of now, being aware of whatever your experience is in a sustained way and accepting whatever is arising within your experience. It is being aware with full knowing without any moment of thought coming and transforming you in any direction through entrainment. Mindlessness, on the other hand, is the same as being out of touch, which is not being present. It is a state where you are non-attentive to your beingness because you are abiding in thought rather than your witnessing function of awareness.

The implication of this is that you should pay attention to every present moment, and therefore your awareness needs to become more engaged with reality in the present moment so that you can inhabit the moment with freedom and authenticity. The ideal is to exist only in the present moment with clarity and full engagement/immersion, and in a positive mental state that lacks anxiety, fear, selfishness or desire. Your focus and attention need to be deeply involved with the present moment so that you can connect with reality and experience real living rather than a mentally unclear, foggy and almost robotic existence. Meditation trains you to live in a mode of full focused awareness with shine and flow.

The circumstances of your life do not need to become arranged in a way good enough for you to say "this moment counts" while others do not. Every moment should have attentiveness to your being. Circumstances do not have to be perfect enough to demand your attention in a way that is fulfilling or makes you sharp, clear, blissful or happy. Your life does not have to significantly change so that you have an excuse to be here in a captivating present moment. You never need defer your sense of "this is it" in life because every moment counts, so *you need only recognize when you are out of sync with the feeling of presence and then correct yourself.* This requires the necessity of alive awareness, non-foggy awareness, a pristinely aware beingness that is fully clear and engaged with the present moment rather dulled via a robotic or hypnotic engagement with life. In clear awareness you are never stepping over the thing you are seeking, which is the feeling of being alive in the present moment of existence. However, as the Mongolian saying runs, "There are men who walk through the woods and see no trees," which is because their awareness of the present moment is lost in a hypnotic stupor without a master of the mind-stream being present. They don't see anything of the world around them because their head is filled with thoughts without a pristine awareness— a type of sleepwalking without presence.

Every moment is your awareness and life. Every moment is "it." Ordinary activities are the Tao simply because you have the great treasure of sentient awareness. You don't need a good enough reason to be happy, or just to be present with your mind. There's no preparation required for living or reason for every feeling that "you haven't quite arrived." You can learn to enjoy the immediate experience, which is life existence and consciousness, if you let yourself. You can be happy in the present moment while ablaze with crystal clear awareness, which is what life is about. Your awareness *is* the present moment and it should be captivated by the present moment, literally sinking into it. Every moment should be a peak experience of clarity rather than an experience of a wandering, oscillating, robotic, foggy or distracted mind. The universe has given you a body vehicle with consciousness, and the ability to recognize a world of qualities is your great miracle of existence. Every thing you do is the center of the universe, and every moment of your existence is the most important moment of the universe.

The entire universe does not just produce the existence of a "thing," but also participates in the transformation of every single thing into something else. The *Yi Jing* calls this change, Taoism calls this transformation, Buddhism calls this impermanence, Hinduism calls this movement (dancing), Kashmir Shaivism calls this vibration, physics calls this the laws of cause and effect, and Islam calls this complex interaction. The universe and all its parts, states, fields, forces, energies and phenomena are ruled by cause and effect interrelationships, which is called the "rationality" or orderliness of the universe in that it is regulated by principles we can uncover. The transformations within it are not chaotic or random but form patterns and regularities that can be codified and then used, and when we learn how to use those patterns people say we are "wise" or skillful. Those relationships in their entirety determine the transformations or "trajectories" of events and phenomena within the universe.

Simply put, the existence of each and every apparent thing is due to an infinite network of causes and effects, an infinite simultaneous co-dependence, so no single thing exists separately on its own. Each thing lacks a substantive existence, a self-so inherent existence all on its own that is an ultimate or absolute existence of own-beingness in some sort of fundamental way. Rather, it only exists through infinite other conditions generating it just as the gravity experienced by a single object is governed by the totality of all masses in the cosmos. And since you too are a phenomenon without an intrinsic self that only finds existence through interrelationships, as beingness without your own body you should strive to find a portion of your significance, purpose and happiness in life through reference to groups of relationships. After all, the texture of your beingness is through and through relational so you can find meaning in reference to your relationships with others. Acts of kindness and service to others can develop within you feelings of internal contentment and happiness while also winning you the praise, friendship and esteem of others, and therefore produce within you a type of happiness connected to your self-concept that is derived from helping members of your relational groups.

Nothing in the universe has an independent self-nature, an underlying self-so existence whose beingness or existence is independent of all universal forces. The universe creates it; the multiplicity factors of the universe cooperate to produce it as a composite creation rather than it being a creation all on its own, namely self-created. Nothing exists independently; all things exist conditionally, meaning dependently (they are dependent upon other things for their birth and existence). They all have conditionally defined natures, existences that manifest because of infinite contributing causes, and the primary support that they all depend upon is the existence of the primordial nature Parabrahman. They are actually Parabrahman, the supreme ground state or fundamental substratum (which Christianity calls God), in their absolute essence. Their absolute composing substance or essence is Parabrahman, the foundational fundamental substratum, so everything is and everything is not.

All things, because they are defined conditionally due to the intersection of infinite other conditions, are therefore said to arise, appear or manifest because of all others. We also say that they *participate in each other*. In other words, all objects, forces or events in the cosmos *have a constant participation in one another*. Furthermore, if one single object in the universe changes, then the entire universe as a single whole simultaneously changes its manifest nature, which is why it is called a scintillating, roiling, fluctuating, vibrating or shimmering whole subject to constant changes, movements, transformations or vibrations.

Everything is "dependently arisen" because of being dependent on everything else, and each and every thing is therefore devoid of inherent existence, a self-so nature, an existence by itself, a solitary nature or independent existence. Instead, everything is a dependent arising. All things look like they have permanent essences, but are actually conditional appearances that are always being subjected to forces of constructive and destructive interference. If they had their own essential natures they would never change, and thus would not be ruled by cause and effect or ruled by dependent origination.

Things appear to exist as singular discrete objects in space, but how they appear to us masks their true nature as composite creations that flow into everything else. So how they appear to us, how we "see" reality, is entirely different from how things really are. What we see is an illusion, delusion, mirage or similitude rather than the truth of manifest reality, and we make this mistake simply because we don't have the sensory capabilities to experience all the forces permeating objects and don't use our minds to fathom the truth of things correctly. It is an illusion of your mind to perceive objects as independent individuals. To understand the true nature of objects is considered a form of enlightened understanding or spiritual realization.

How things appear to us is therefore very different from what is actually there in front of us. We think of the world as made up of things, phenomena, objects, and entities but we should think of it as being made up of processes, events, fields, forces, interconnections, interrelationships, happenings, energies or occurrences. From the standpoint of the ground state substratum there is nothing there at all. Whatever appears to us through our imperfect senses as an entity or object is actually our focusing on an appearance formed from the conjunction of innumerable processes within an infinite field that is undergoing continuous transformations, and that limited entity we create within our mind actually lacks solidity, borders and temporal permanence.

This dependent arising of phenomena where they are a mixing of all things is alternatively called simultaneous arising, infinite interdependence, interdependent generation, dependent origination, Indra's net, linked interdependence, simultaneous co-arising, codependent origination, conditional existence, dependent construction, and many other names. The terms mean that an infinite networked chain of cause and effect is responsible for the appearance of any single phenomenon in the universe (Shakti), although for practical use we always limit networks of causality, or chains of cause and effect, to a smaller set of conditions. For instance, in your mind you may will to perform a particular action due to a cause (or thought) that is determined by another, and this again by another, and so on to infinity. Naturally you only explained that you did something due to a smaller set of causes.

To master cause and effect relationships, we reduce this infinite immensity into a more simplified set of principles that limits the number of things we must consider. Reducing infinity down to a smaller set of conditions to consider makes it much easier to understand causality and learn how to manipulate it to our favor. Our goal in understanding causality is that we can use an understanding of cause and effect, and its regular patterns of predictability, to manage situations, "control Nature," "control natural forces," "control material reality" or "guide (master) the changes of phenomena." We want to control Nature and domesticate it so that it comes under human control, and thus becomes manageable, predictable, more beneficial to us and much less frightening. We investigate to discover the laws of Nature and its various transformations in order to use that information to improve our lives. Consciousness lets us do this.

What this truth about the infinite causation behind a singular phenomenon essentially means, however, is that one entity or evolute cannot serve as the sole cause for a subsequent entity to appear, but normally we assume this is the case so that we can simplify our navigation through the process of living. Actually, however, there is no such thing as a single cause or single evolute being solely responsible for the appearance of any manifesting phenomenon in the universe. Because of infinite interdependence, *when anything within the universe manifests the entire cosmos gets into the act.* Those manifestations or phenomena are furthermore sustained only so long as their sustaining factors remain. Basically, *all events interpenetrate,* a*ll phenomena interpenetrate.* The personal implication of this is that we are all interconnected, and thus your life and what you do is also connected to every other life in society and with what everyone else does. Should we not then be careful in what we think, say and do because of the possible effects on every one else? How can we act to make things better for all?

Every tiny configuration within the universe is effectively created from the participation of its entire body. Everything is responsible for the manifestation of everything else, which is infinite interlinkage and infinite co-dependence. Everything is therefore the way it is because everything else was the way it was before everything became the way it is now; the present moment is the outcome of all cause and effect relationships everywhere in the universe. When one iota of the universe changes the entire universe changes, and when one part changes it is because the entire universe got into the act and caused it to change. This is called karma. What we have now is a result of everything that came previously.

Hence, the consequential changes within your own life are also sometimes called "karma," which is an experience you have as a consequence of all these prior causes and conditions coming together to produce the present *for you.* Karma just means that whatever manifests in the universe does so because all past and present conditions have come together to produce it, and you experience a certain configuration in your life because it is *your karma.* Your life is karma and the events of your life are your karma.

Karma is another word for the results of causality. The result or consequence of prior causes you set into motion that rebound to you are called karma, and of course consequences require a lot of supporting conditions to manifest. Everything happens due to cause and effect, and "cause and effect" is the manifestation mechanism of karma. As for your life, an abbreviated meaning of "karma" is that whatever manifests in your life does so because all your past and present actions come together during conditions to produce your present circumstances, but this also entails *the entire past history and current conditions of the universe.* Everything happens the way it does in your life, and in the universe, not only because of your actions but as a consequence of everything else in the universe as well, so your karma is not due solely to your own efforts and actions but to everyone else's as well. There is therefore a need in the world for everyone to become wiser, kinder, more compassionate and wiser in their actions.

Everything that happens to you is really a consequence of everything in the universe coming together to produce that result, but essentially your surrounding circumstances and your network of past actions or the actions of people in your sphere of relationships starting with smaller wholes and working up to larger wholes – your family, friends, coworkers, community, society, state, country, world and then universe. In other words, any consequence/event in your life is due to a totality of circumstances and conditions, some of which you are not directly responsible for, but especially due to your prior actions in this life and also due to your merit from prior lives that has given you a certain body, personality, family, society, environment and the like.

The entire universe gets into the act to produce the events and circumstances that you will experience in life. Therefore you cannot just say blindly that your misfortunes are a past debt that must be repaid or is deserved due to unwholesome previous acts. Sometimes bad experiences or circumstances simply happen to you as a result of infinite other factors working together, and they produce your life events within a tapestry of universal outcomes where you are just a single jewel in the net reflecting the effects of all the other jewels (events, phenomena, conditions, etcetera) within the netting, and you don't directly deserve what happens to you in any way, shape or form. What happens to you is then a *consequence* rather than karmic debt.

Hence, there are both uncontrollable and controllable factors to consider when you want to put order into your life to achieve a goal or prevent unfortunate outcomes (such as painful incidents that involve loss and suffering). The task within life is to learn how to identify and manage the controllable factors, for which individuals need wisdom and skillfulness. As to unpredictable or uncontrollable factors you must try to take precautions for prevention. This is why we study cause and effect relationships. That knowledge or understanding (wisdom) can help guide our thinking and actions. Wisdom allows you to improvise technique according to principle, and skillfulness allows you to execute techniques with efficacy.

Wisdom is the ability to judge rightly in matters relating to phenomena, life and conduct, and so it entails the science or understanding of principles and pattern regularities such as actions and their usual results. It includes the understanding or knowing of dependable patterns and regularities, namely reliable cause and effect relationships. How to behave according to principles that reflect this knowledge is also called wisdom. For living you need to study wise ways of thinking, speaking, doing and being to be most effective and successful in life. Wisdom or understanding, which comes from your thinking, learning, training and experience, guides you through to the behavior that will get you more of what you want to experience in life and avoid what you don't want. It involves understanding the likelihood of short-term, intermediate-term and long-term results due to actions within particular circumstances, and then guides you to act accordingly.

Since the only things you can control in life are your mind and your actions (which are your thoughts expressed) but not the results of those actions, wisdom ultimately involves mastering/perfecting your mind and behavior (thought, speech and deeds) so that you can create better outcomes in life for yourself and others with a higher likelihood than from just acting according to emotions or impulses like animals. Plato argued that a person was like a charioteer and his emotions, irrational impulses and desires were like horses that pulled him in conflicting directions. By transcending your animal nature through better thinking and acting you take the very steps necessary to elevate the conditions of your existence. In striving to become the best possible version of yourself this principle can take you to greatness.

Since the net total causes, conditions and circumstances that produce the birth-generation (or dissolution) of anything are actually infinite, meaning that everything is conditionally defined through an infinite crisscrossing of filiation relationships that cause appearances, this also means that things are not distinctly apart from one another. They appear to have separate appearances/existences but actually interpenetrate, and only appear separate entities in space because we think in simplified concepts meaningful or useful to us that appear on a certain scale. All things actually flow into one another, and even seemingly sharp borders are fuzzy with blurring. It is hard to then say where one thing ends and another begins because of being co-dependently linked in the grand unity of interconnected energy field relationships; there is no demarcation line between any single thing and the cosmos. It is almost as if cause and effect are synonymous in some way – that an effect is latently present in a cause. Zen Master Fazang therefore said, "Cause and effect are not different, and beginning and end interpenetrate." However, if one insists that things are the way they are simply because they are that way rather than attributing results to causality, this is incorrect.

The implication then is that we ourselves are therefore really nothing - no inherent thing - since our bodies and selves are a bundle of causes that stretch far outside us. We are in no way entirely independent entities but just a configuration of processes that are localizing into a somewhat stable limited appearance where we ignore its vast composition. Our attributes do not include an intrinsic nature so we (and all other phenomena) are just empty appearances, but our worldly appearances persistently remain until they no longer do due to the changing causes once again.

While the original essence has an existence that does not derive from anything else, our own existence is derived from everything else ... and its ultimate support is the fundamental ground state of the universe that is always and ever present in everything. We are then nothing at all other than localized appearances (without intrinsic, self-so, inherent identities) that arise due to infinite causal processes, and are actually part of everything in existence since everything participates in defining us. Within us there is nothing that is specifically us at all. Instead we are everything there is, or you can say we are beingness without a body. This is the meaning of no-self or selflessness. Thus your actions truly do affect the entire universe, and one should therefore learn how to act most wisely.

Because of the intertwining of causes and effects, the destruction or disappearance of something in the cosmos must be viewed simply as a transformation into something else, just as is stipulated by the conservation of energy law. A cause never perishes, but continues existing through transformation by becoming an effect, which thus is simply a change in function, name and appearance. This is all due to the fact that the universe has nothing to interact with except itself, and has only a fixed total energy. It is therefore useful to ponder/meditate on whether an effect is not somehow within its cause, or existent in its causes, because things are never purely themselves but only exist by incorporating other influences or elements, which are the non-entity, in their composition. There is always around us the ever-present truth of infinite interdependent origination, infinite simultaneous arising. Since all things interpenetrate this is why there is no such thing as perfectly pure Yin or pure Yang in the universe, and the composition of anything called a "pure element" is therefore polluted because it contains (is comprised of) non-element factors within it.

This vast crisscrossing of filiation relationships is actually a singleness in total. Shakti is a single oneness or unity of complete comprehensiveness that internally appears (in the phenomenal sense) as a vibrating flux of multiplicities. In order that we can conveniently identify things and handle affairs, our minds subject the unified cosmos of oneness to fragmentation. At the fundamental level each fragmentation is vibrating and thus its properties are fuzzy, uncertain, undetermined as the Heisenberg uncertainty principle suggests. Even so, we conceive of the world by segmenting it, fragmenting it and grouping it as best we can in ways that are stable to us so that we can understand it and interact with it more easily. This is the function of consciousness, and evolution has given us a consciousness that has faults and produces errors in understanding but which is good enough for our continuation of existence. In a complex world of infinite interconnections the notion of a singular pure "cause" becomes suspect, but we fragment infinite causality into primary causality for the sake of predictions.

Our minds segment out particular configurations within Shakti and thereby mentally produce limited, discrete phenomena even though this is not the way things really exist. We simplify this immensity of oneness by mentally cutting out localized phenomena. Things in themselves are only temporary events or processes that for a while seem stable and monotonous. For a brief amount of time they seem to be stable and hold their shape and maintain their equilibrium before changing into something else (a new state), or disintegrating entirely. Things ("*dharmas*") have only momentary existence and then are substituted by other things (*dharmas*), but the constant termination and substitution provides a false appearance of continuity. To change situations or circumstances to your liking you will have to learn how to master these changes, which is the Great Learning of developing your intellect, wisdom and skillfulness to control/manage the phenomena of Nature. It is how you act and behave and maneuver – rather than your situations, conditions and circumstances alone – that will ultimately determine the events of your life.

Since the appearance of any single phenomenon is determined from infinite prior causation with the whole cosmos getting into the act, in Buddhism this dependent arising is described as "this arises from that because of prior causes and conditions." The appearance of anything is completely dependent upon causes and conditions. A phenomenon occurs because of the mutual interpenetration of all phenomena in infinite realms upon realms, mutually containing and interacting with one another in inter-causal relationships. The appearance of any one thing is an *unfoldment* of cause and effect that fully encompasses the entire universe into a localized enfoldment, but we don't normally think this way even though this is the truth of manifest reality. We normally only see a localized space (rather than infinite components) where our mind identifies a phenomenon, but we can correctly say that the entire universe *enfolds* to produce that entity, event or phenomenon.

The fact that phenomena affect one another is called *mutual perfuming* or mutual interpenetration. This is the *Hua Yen*, *Avatamsaka Sutra* or Flower Ornament view of Buddhism, which is that all phenomena are transitory and have apparent existences dependent entirely upon other factors, infinite in number. Those factors depend functionally upon each other, or you can say they all enter into each other. In Confucianism this is described in the reflexivity phrase, "Man affects the Heavens and the Heavens affect (interact with) man." It is not just that all phenomena are in each other (each phenomena enters into every other) but also that the fundamental substance is in all and all are in the fundamental substance. Hence, each individual is the essence and reality of all things, our foundational self-nature ground state substratum, and all things exist in It and of It.

To better understand this *Hua Yen* view of interpenetration and dependent origination, imagine an infinite ocean and that we take out one iota from this limitless ocean. This tiny iota of water, *while in* the limitless ocean, is the ocean itself before separation. In other words, every iota or drop of the ocean, when not seen as a separate drop, is the infinite ocean itself. However, when an iota of the ocean is separated from the infinite ocean then this iota only then obtains an independent existence as a drop, and begins to look like a finite existence rather than the boundless ocean. However, the process of separation is impossible. With Shakti, it is impossible to remove any drop from within it to be placed elsewhere as an independent separate existence, for all new locations or circumstances are still within Shakti! There is always a total interpenetration or interfusion of all phenomena within Shakti, and nowhere else to go. Every phenomenon is Shakti, and Shakti itself has no separate existence apart from its self-nature, which is the fundamental universal substratum. How can anything become independent or separate? Where would it go to be that way?

A living being looks like a separate entity different from its surroundings due to a superficial analysis of seeing it separately in space that ignores it flowing into everything else. Its existence is actually within the ocean of Shakti and its appearance comes about because of the innumerable interdependencies within Shakti that define it. Hence, a living being, soul or entity is not some self-so independent or inherent entity, but *is* Shakti. It is a localized space within Shakti whose form and appearance is caused by infinite conditions enfolded into that region that interpenetrate it, but you just cannot see them because your sense organs and consciousness have not developed to enable this.

Since Shakti is essentially the fundamental substrate, you must cognize the primordial Self as your ultimate true nature. You don't exist in reality but only in appearance. In other words, you may harbor the illusion that you are separate from God just as you harbor the delusion that you are an independent entity in space, but you are God. Humans harbor the illusion of separation from Nature (the universe) and God (the fundamental substratum).

You can only come to know these facts through thinking and understanding, and that understanding is the view of enlightenment – understanding the true nature of your existence, which includes understanding your self-nature (the nature of your self) and the nature of your consciousness. Since this understanding provides you with the correct view of your body, soul or self, understanding these facts is called understanding your self-nature, realizing your true self-nature, or becoming enlightened as to the truth about your real self-nature. This knowledge is an aspect of self-realization.

On the apparent plane phenomena certainly seem limited and different from one another, but at their core they share the same essential identity because they are all Shakti that, in turn, is the changeless source nature. The Tibetan master Tsong Khapa thus said of phenomenal identities, the world of "interdependent manifestations of appearing phenomena are emptiness lacking any inherent existence."

A living being unfolds into all of Shakti because it is Shakti, and Shakti is an appearance within the original essence. For an *atman*, *jiva*, soul, individual, being, entity or phenomenon this truth always remains the same. Furthermore, just as Shakti is ultimately the fundamental essence this means that an *atman*, soul, self or sentient entity is also essentially the fundamental essence that is empty of all phenomena. Hence, just as the *Diamond Sutra* states there is no such true thing as an *atman*, *jiva*, soul, individual, self or living being. The idea of a self is only a convention – you have the idea that you are person but this is only an idea. What the self is isn't really what we assume it to be.

In the Buddhist *Milanda Pandha* a King Milanda asks the sage Nagasena his name, and the sage replies: "I am called Nagasena, O great king but Nagasena is nothing but a name, a designation, an expression, a simple word. There is no person there." The name "Nagasena" does not designate a person, but a collection of relations, processes or events. However, we simplify matters and say that it designates a person, which is a conventional way of speaking while there is no real person there. In other words, there is no intrinsic entity there, there is no independent entity there, there is no autonomic entity there, there is no self-so inherent entity there, there is no person or soul there with independent own-beingness. There is only a collection of intertwined processes and interrelationships that have combined with each other to form a local appearance within a great tapestry of infinite appearances that are all just one thing. The idea of a self is only a convention.

What we call "Nagasena" is only a name that we give to the consequence of a relatively stable localized appearance that we have mentally cut out of a unified whole. "Nagasena" is only an event or process that for a while seems stable and monotonous, but which is actually a collection of infinite processes and events that are always, always changing but appear limited, stable and unchanging. Ibn 'Arabi referred to all things as "instantaniations," which is what they are since they only appear/exist for an instant despite stable appearances that mask incessant changes. They are always transforming into new states every instant.

You are actually *the whole primal essence Itself, and you are also the whole of Shakti itself*. An ornament of gold remains gold despite being formed into a new shape or appearance, and so Shakti remains the foundational substratum of manifest nature despite having a different appearance from its own fundamental essence. Similarly, when clay becomes a jar, having changed only its shape, the name "clay" is lost and the name "jar" arises, but it is still only clay just the same. You, being part of Shakti and wholly the original nature, despite being called a "person" are only the original nature. There is not a single anything within you that is a real inherent thing. You are not some unique, separate, independent soul with an inherent nature of your own nor do you have anything permanent and unchanging as your core. You are a constructed composite entity without a single thing within your structure/composition that is wholly, inherently you. And, you are also the universal substrate because there is no existence other than the absolute Self itself.

Another way of saying it is that wholes depend upon their parts for their existence, their parts are infinite in number, and parts owe their existence to all other parts so that all things interpenetrate and arise simultaneously in oneness. Within the universe there is not a single thing that is independently arisen or has a self-so intrinsic nature. And, those perceived multiplicities are actually just the one fundamental substance of the universe, which is your True Self.

Now, because of the infinite interdependence connecting all things that begets simultaneous arising, one might say that causes and effects within Shakti are neither absolutely different from one another nor absolutely identical with one another. Because everything is interlinked or "defined through an infinite web of causality" we cannot clearly say where one thing ends and another begins. No one can then say where karma originates. All things interpenetrate, so you are in all beings and all beings are in you, which has definite implications for how we should treat one another. Since this also means that everything in the world is part of you too it has implications for how we should treat the environment (nature) as well.

"All things share in the existence of any single particular thing" also means that objects do not cease when you turn your back on them and they are no longer perceived by your mind. The lack of consciousness on your part or in the universe in total does not wipe out (invalidate) the reality/existence of the physical world. Known or not known it is still there. There is the beingness of the universe (Shakti) before the awareness of an individual being can arise. The conscious mind particularizes objects and creates a world of qualities, but if there weren't consciousness in the universe the universe would still exist and has always existed otherwise it couldn't develop to the point where it is now has produced consciousness. Only recognition of the universe disappears when there is no consciousness; objects still exist without consciousness finding them. There would just be no one who knows it if there was no sentient life, yet that does not negate existence or the prior chain of interdependent origination that has evolved to this present moment in time that includes your presence. Without that long chain of prior events you and your consciousness would not be here, so you cannot say that the universe does not exist if there is no consciousness. The configuration of the universe exists even if unobserved. The overall patterns of causality stand with constancy regardless as to whether or not there are living beings who see them. Objects not observed are still defined by an infinity of conditions that includes the necessary continuity of those objects when you do not view them. However, "when there is no mind then objects are not there" is true in terms of your personal perceptions, but not their existence. It is not that the universe/Shakti is just mind *but that your experience of the universe is just your consciousness.*

All things arise within the One original nature. The One foundational substrate not just permeates everything but comprises All Things as their ultimate source substance-essence that doesn't transform, so from Its aspect no things or phenomena ever appear at all – It remains solely Itself throughout all of the transformations of manifest existence. *Nirvana* and *samsara* are therefore inseparable and interdependent; there is no difference between *samsara* and the realm of enlightenment. The All melts into a single whole, and the Unity is Shiva and Shakti, *Purusha* and *Prakriti*, God and Creation. This is a union like empty space and the matter-energy emanations that appear within it which, when decomposed, are found to be the same empty space that supports those appearances. Basically, Shiva and Shakti, *Purusha* and *Prakriti* or God and the Logos (Creation) are the same.

Purusha the ultimate non-moving ground substratum and the ever-moving Shakti are an identity. Shakti in some spiritual schools is even called the "ocean of all languages" because it is a single body (ocean) characterized by these innumerable kinetic vibrations.

Christianity says, "In the beginning was the Logos (Shakti), and the Logos was with God, and the Logos was God. The same was in the beginning with God. Through Him all things were made; without Him nothing was made that has been made" (John 1:1-3). "Logos" means Word, so the Logos represents sound, vibration or energy. Logos is therefore another term for Shakti, Creation, emanation or manifestation. "God" on the other hand means the underlying absolute nature rather than a Creator-being. The Bible says that the Logos (Shakti) and God, the unmoving primordial substrate that is absent of qualities such as Creation, are the same thing. All created things (energy) don't actually proceed from God (who cannot change) but proceed from the Logos Ocean of Energy – Shakti - that has its inexplicable beginning in God. Christianity does not say that the Logos is beginningless but that the beginning of Creation initially starts with the Logos and through the Logos all else is created. This accords with the teachings of all the other spiritual schools and is the principle within Hinduism that Nirguna Brahman never moves or changes, so it is Saguna Brahman that gives rise to Creation.

Ramana Maharshi commented, "Iswara, the personal God, the supreme creator of the universe really does exist. But this is true only from the relative standpoint of those who have not realized the truth, those people who believe in the reality of individual souls. From the absolute standpoint the sage cannot accept any other existence than the impersonal Self, one and formless." In other words, only the original nature truly exists and It is the true status of God. If you want a personal God who is a Creator then you have to proceed to an emanated level, which is an evolute that serves as the Mother of all Creation. Thus Shakti, Ishvara, Saguna Brahman, or the Womb Matrix would be the Creator God if you want to assume there is a Creator being. However, the absolute nature is actually inanimate.

In the absolute reality there is only the single oneness of the pure primordial substratum. So whatever you now perceive because of having consciousness (illumination or comprehension) is actually *That alone* despite your experience of apparent multiplicity. Within Alonehood (the One Without a Second) arises an appearance of diversity, but the apparent multiplicity is nothing but an illusion superimposed on the single, indivisible, attributeless fundamental nature, thus screening It. You see diversity but you are seeing an illusion superimposed on the unchanging absolute substratum that is empty of attributes like space. You misidentify the world as something else other than what it truly is.

Although the fundamental substance seems to exist in many forms It is singularly one. The universe has no separate existence from its substratum that is its absolute substance, and whatever a person perceives is the fundamental substratum and substratum alone despite appearances. The name "universe" is superimposed on the fundamental substratum, but what we call the universe is nothing but the fundamental substrate. To call it the universe is just a way of speaking for convention's sake. It is manifested through mere name (labels, phenomena, marks, signs, etc.), meaning that we need consciousness to recognize It through the multiplicity of phenomena which we do so through mental differentiation that references the contents of our own internal neural organization, our own subjective principles. That multiplicity misidentifies the world as something else other than true reality.

Because we have a mind, we can discern these truths. Insentient phenomena lack mental illumination, and primitive organisms or animals lack sufficient neural capabilities, so they cannot have such realizations. Understanding these facts is called *prajna* transcendental wisdom. We can reason as to the origins of phenomena and understand their ultimate true (transcendental) nature as well as conventional attributes and functions. We are conscious life and can discern the apparent multiplicity of phenomena and also discover the principles of cause and effect that rule them. We can then use our knowledge of these causal relationships to our favor, guiding phenomenal changes and complex interactions to make things the way we want.

Guiding the changes of phenomena to manage them and create the situations we want requires training, wisdom and skillfulness, which are factors you must cultivate in life. This is the Buddha and Bodhisattva way, which is to develop a high understanding and skillfulness in using cause and effect principles to create desired change within Shakti, navigate Shakti better, and perfect our lives. This is only possible because we possess consciousness and its abilities of learning and comprehension. We can use consciousness to investigate and learn and then our accumulated wisdom can be used to create better states of the future.

The principle that things are inherently empty of fixed natures and always changing means they are free to evolve as well as open to improvement by our efforts. We are conscious beings that experience life and can guide phenomena, and this power of change is what gives us the fundamental potential to transform matters in the directions we want to better our lives and futures. We have life and we have consciousness, and because of these miraculous gifts we can experience our inner vitality and the bliss of life. We can decide what our existence will be. As conscious beings we possess a body, we also have the ability to manipulate conventional reality to produce outcomes that we have imagined in our minds, and thus we are an antidote to chaos and no-meaning because we can create an intended order of desired results. There are no absolute purposes in the universe, nor does it hold any specific meaning. However, because we have minds we can create meaning for ourselves and can create patterns and arrange matters to experience within our consciousness feelings of significance, well-being and states of mental-physical bliss. We can do this for our selves and others.

Consciousness has the property that we need not be robotically enslaved in a mechanistic straightjacket to absolutely follow our present train of thoughts or fatalistically follow our previous conditioning that has become our psyche. You don't have to remain a hostage to the emotional and behavioral imperatives of your thoughts. Most of your life you are a bit on autopilot using subconscious rules of prior conditioning that you automatically follow. Your actions run on autopilot because you are not being mindful of your mind and behavior. You tend to sleepwalk throughout life when you don't center within mindful awareness where you are fully present, fully alive and fully creative in every life moment. Mindfulness puts satisfaction in your own hands. The bliss and joy of life is found in flow where we are fully engaged in what we are doing and experiencing the beauty of the present mindful moment. It's a time where we can appreciate being alive because we feel the (blissful) vitality of our being while our awareness is clear and our mental narrative has quieted down so that it does not distort the moment.

We have an independent mind that doesn't have to have an inner narrative talking all the time nor follow its thoughts with fusion or our prior conditioning like clockwork. Through mindfulness or self-observation we can learn how to detach from our thoughts, emotions, mindset-attitudes and impulses that would normally impel us, can refuse to follow our learned patterns of behavior, and can even reprogram our thinking and behavioral processes to be entirely different so that they consistently produce much better results. We can learn so we can expand our horizons to enlarge our worldview and go beyond any current prejudices or limits we've developed. We can learn, grow, and develop. We can improve, develop or cultivate ourselves to become whatever we want to be, unlike insentient matter. We can cultivate our bodies to better states of health and well-being, and cultivate our consciousness to produce better mind-streams within us (we can purify and elevate our inner psychology), improve our intellectual and cognitive abilities, and achieve more effective behavior in the world.

We can rise above all our prior mental patterning and thus transcend the preconditioning within us that automatically produces predictable behavior and "fated" fortunes. We can, because of mental powers of self-observation, view thoughts as mental objects rather than commands that must be strictly followed. We can thereby defy our own strong behavioral tendencies that are our personal characteristics like the attributes of an inanimate object. Through study, training, self-cultivation and effort we can reconfigure our personalities, thinking patterns, habits and behaviors and work to transform our surrounding environment and circumstances in any way we want. No inanimate object can do this. It must remain the way it is, subject to laws of transformation that proceed according to its attributes.

We can change our attributes and create a new character, new life and new future. We can produce for ourselves health, happiness and prosperity. Guided by knowledge of the principles of cause and effect, through the artful manipulation of phenomena we can also put some new good into the world and create personal, global and universal results that are better for ourselves and for society. The results of any efforts will manifest as conditions allow for we cannot perfectly control the outcomes or consequences of our efforts; we can only control our efforts (and our minds). Since our actions always result in consequences that might sometimes vary from what we want, we must learn to be wise and skillful in our efforts to adaptively produce the results we desire with the highest likelihood of outcome.

What we presently experience in our lives is the result of the total past deeds of man and Nature within a grand unity of man and the cosmos that also includes our own personal history of past deeds and actions. The world we have made has therefore helped to make us. Each of us has had and presently has our own individual effect on the world, and this effect on the world surrounds and influences us in turn. Each of us has experiences due to the aggregate of our past actions (karma) as well as due to the influences from our family, friends, community, state, country, and world. We absorb those influences into us as social and mental conditioning just as a clear crystal takes on the color from the object that is nearest to it.

All worlds and realms, including the residences of the heavens, are produced by the complex interactions of affiliations or relationships. They are transformed into new states of existence with different characteristics by the actions of living beings interacting with each other and phenomena.

We produce the world we inherit that manifests according to the quality of our consciousness. We build or transform its nature according to the aggregate of our actions that are the result of our thoughts (consciousness) and states of mind, which give rise to those actions, and thus the world is a functional result of our consciousness. It is a dependent arising based on the interaction between the state it is and the consequences of all sorts of phenomena along with the actions and behaviors of sentient beings. Since our world and environment is really our physical body of manifestation (as our true body is Shakti because we are Shakti, we are derived from the substance of the universe) we have a common responsibility to improve things within the world for the better.

Chapter 6
CONSCIOUSNESS & KNOWLEDGE[3] - THE WORLD WE EXPERIENCE IS A MIND-ONLY MENTAL REPRESENTATON

Of the countless phenomena that have appeared within this infinite web of interdependence called Shakti, which is the manifest universe, one is called life. Life evolved because the right causes and conditions eventually came together. Some forms of life have sentience and some forms of sentient life, such as ours, are capable of higher consciousness and great cognitive skills. Higher consciousness with complex cognitive skills is only possible when a living being possesses an anatomical structure with an advanced nervous system. Without a body there can be no such thing as consciousness, without advanced anatomy there can be no such thing as higher consciousness, and without culture that consciousness cannot develop to its very best.

The functional operations of consciousness exist because of the anatomical structure of our nervous system composed of a special pattern of molecules and energy. Our nervous system includes our sensory organs, brain, nerves, neurons and their contents, and also our subtle life energy. Together these elements produce internal mental perceptions from the five senses as well as the processes of thinking, emotions and will. Whatever you experience of the external world has only one place in which it can appear, which is within your consciousness. It is the only thing you have. Your life *is as your consciousness is* each moment – all you have is your experience.

Consciousness creates empirical Knowledge that consists of object recognition/identification, reasoning skills of analysis and apprehension

---

[3] See *Inside Vasubandhu's Yogacara* (Connelly), *Color Me Confucius* (Bodri), and Chapter 4 "Life Purpose" from *Buddha Yoga* (Bodri).

(understanding), body-mind coordination skills and many other capabilities. Its skills can be of the mind alone, or of the mind and body conjointly. It creates frameworks that allow it to respond consistently to the world, and it stores memories of its operations.

Consciousness means knowing and perceiving, which is the ability to generate Knowledge via thoughts and perceptions that are then stored in memories used to name, label, identify, categorize or differentiate mental phenomena via pattern recognition to produce a frame of reference for human cognition. Consciousness therefore involves discrimination, which in turn requires having a memory along with comparison or reasoning abilities. Discrimination basically means the knowing of differences between two or more things, which requires making comparisons. You absolutely cannot do this unless you have memories that can be used for pattern matching predispositions. Discrimination – which includes the abilities of recognizing, understanding and reasoning – basically means the ability to generate Knowledge.

Consciousness thus means the ability to cognize, which is mentally differentiating, discriminating, understanding or comprehending by giving meaning (names and conceptual labels) to phenomena that arise within the mind. Our mental operations that involve memory make it possible for us to cognize objects out of a field of formless chaos, which is one type of comprehension or Knowledge generation.

What are the types of Knowledge we typically generate from these processes? There are *perceptual experiences* such as smells, tastes, sounds, and sights as well as your body's own *physical sensations* such as pains, irritations and comfortable feelings; *imaginative experiences* such as mental rehearsals or imaginative scenarios we mentally create of future actions; general *mental states with emotional tones*; and *streams of conceptual thought* where we experience an internal dialogue thinking "in words" or "in images" that is centered around an overt sense of an I or inner being.

This I-sense, concept of selfhood or I-thought, which is considered the experiencer of your perceptions, is the central theme around which consciousness is based and is itself a mental construction formed from a collection of diverse thoughts linked together. Those thoughts create the seat of consciousness in that they create the sentient being or I-self of the mind, a sense of presence that is a direct experience of our self. The "mind of me" that sports the feeling of egoism is the I-self, the instinctive notion of "I am," or seat of consciousness and self-awareness.

In order for a discrimination of beingness (a recognition of conscious existence) to manifest within a living being there must be the discrimination of a self – the recognition or identification of being an "I." The feeling of egoism, I-hoodness or the I-sense (a natural instinctive notion of "I am") is this recognition. You cannot give rise to the idea of being a self unless there is also an idea of others as opposed to the self, which helps to congeal the idea of being a limited self. In other words, the self-identity of I-hoodness can only arise if there also arise concepts of not-self (things that aren't the self). There cannot be anything external without there also being a direct awareness of ourselves as the experiencer of the thing. In other words, anything I know includes knowledge of myself at the same time.

For a sentient being to be able to cognize its beingness (self-existence) it must be able to discriminate some other state as juxtaposed to itself ("others" or "not-I"), otherwise it cannot fathom that it is an existent I and that there are others (objects) which are "not-I." It cannot simply assert "I am" without there being some sort of juxtaposition, comparison or differentiation to others which you might call the world. This is how the I-thought arises out of oblivion. Those activities probably occur within the recticular brainstem that contains the prerequisites for I-consciousness to be able to appear. All consciousness is dependent upon brainstem consciousness.

As stated, a sentient being becomes conscious of its entityhood existence as subject-only "I" in part by knowing (differentiating) objects or "others" out of the one seamless, infinitely interconnected, undifferentiated soup of Shakti, which assumes there are independent, unconnected objects standing in space. It goes without saying that the identity of being an "I" exists in your mind only; the universe doesn't think of you as a person at all because you are just another ripple within the single fabric of Shakti, a wave in the ocean of being. You are just another process within space-time seamlessly connected with everything else and functioning in a special way according to your properties. In other words, the I-concept only exists *because you have a mind* since without consciousness you would just be an insentient, inanimate object, and in terms of the universe there isn't any real such thing as being a sentient living being at all.

In order to be able to say "I am not this" or "I am that" there must be an "I" to say it, which is the ego-self, self-identity or I-thought that is the center of the inner narrative. That I-thought or self-thought where you identify yourself as a subject isn't a simple single conception because its generation is developed on the basis of many mental processes coming together. However, we usually refer to it as a single thought. The inner sense of being a witness or self becomes one with every form or thought that is witnessed/known. After the rising up of this I-thought by whatever mechanism produces it (such as when you wake up after sleep) all other thoughts can then start arising, so it is actually the root thought. To say "something is" the "I" must be there first. If the "I" (self-thought) is not there you cannot differentiate anything because there is no conscious self, so the I-sense of beingness must be there before anything else is recognized in the mind.

To put it another way, to become self-cognizant or aware of its existence, the consciousness of a living entity must develop the sense of being an individual I which entails generating a self-notion, subject-notion, ego-concept, I-sense or I-thought in its processes of consciousness. In the *Diamond Sutra* this is described as the thought of being a self, person, *atman*, living being or individual. The *Diamond Sutra* also states that this is an incorrect false thought or conclusion, but evolution has developed our body vehicle and energy matrix that causes this to arise within us for the purposes of survival – so that we can continue our existence. Only with such an idea can a sentient being develop a self-awareness of self-existence ("I exist" or "I am"), which also requires thoughts that others are "not-self."

If there is an *I-thought* of I-hoodness then there is always a sense of *other*. Further, only if there is an I-self can you even recognize the existence of others, which enables you as a being of consciousness to navigate the world and survive. We identify a special pattern involving our thoughts, emotions and sensations within the mind and call it the "I" when *the true "I" is none of those identities*. The true I within you must be something unchanging at your core that is really you since it is permanent. This must be the fundamental substance of the universe since It is there at your core, never leaves you, and is not a composite being that is your True Self. A living self, composed of a body with consciousness, is really just a small agglomeration of countless parts within the ocean of Shakti and composed from the convergence of an infinite number of Shakti conditions. Thus it is a dependent construction within Shakti rather than a separate sovereign entity or own-being that stands apart and exists independently of all else. It is part of the soup broth of the one ocean of the cosmos, and as a member of Shakti lacks an unchanging core manifest I.

Humans typically view their I-self as an independent, intrinsic entity but this is a false view, an errant perspective, a misperception of reality. The true I is your fundamental substrate since it is permanent, everlasting and never changes. It is an unbecoming Is-ness, the Unmanifest nature of the universe. Nevertheless, the nexus of processes that comprise an apparent self naturally gives rise to a mental notion within its consciousness that it is a self-so independent I-self when it is just a temporary dependent construction (or process) operating within Shakti having certain qualities or attributes, one of which is consciousness.

People do not know any better because they don't normally think about these things unless they cultivate an understanding of their true self-nature. You are like a dream body/person within Shakti without an intrinsic nature, and your true unchanging self-nature is your True Self. You are not an independent self but a dependent construction of It – an apparent sentient being, "fake being" or function/attribute of the fundamental nature. When you realize what you and consciousness ultimately are then *this is the view of enlightenment or self-realization!* This is the rare enlightenment view because you realize the true nature of your self and consciousness. By understanding the nature of Shakti, our limitations of perception and conception, and what we ultimately are you understand the true nature of your existence.

The individual self and the Supreme Self (universal substratum) are identical. Microcosm (individual self) and macrocosm (Shakti) are also one. Advaita Vedanta sums it up by saying, "I am That, All of this is That" to denote the fact that you are Shakti, which in turn is the primordial essence, so you are the fundamental substratum (That) and so is everything else. When you ask yourself, "Who is this 'me'?" the answer is the primordial substratum, and the apparent you that you see in the mirror is a transitory conditional construction, which always changes, composed of innumerable interlocking conditions within the one field of Shakti. Shakti is a oneness of emanation – a giant ball of energy-matter – that is in turn the fundamental substratum or substance. Everything is It! In everything and everybody is but the One Itself.

This is the view of enlightenment, the understanding of self-realization where you realize the true nature of your apparent self and True Self and the nature of your consciousness/sentience. You understand the true nature of existence. Consciousness is inherently the absolute ultimate substratum as well that is empty of constructions or contents. The fundamental substrate is present in all states of mind and modes of existence.

This understanding is called *prajna* transcendental wisdom because your understanding transcends the conventional world by gaining comprehension of what you truly are - you comprehend your manifest beingness as lacking a core unchanging or intrinsic self (no-self), that you are ultimately nothingness, but that being composed of energy you are also the All of manifestation. You arise out of nothing and eventually go back to the void, which is another aspect to the emptiness of the self. Nature, through a long process of evolutionary trial and error, has developed this central concept of an I-self within humans and many other sentient species with consciousness in order that the sentient species survives. The self-thought within us is an evolutionary product attendant with consciousness that is a necessity for our survivalist ability to navigate the world. It is a design principle of consciousness for extending a living being's continued existence. The universe doesn't care if you survive or not, but this object called a sentient living being is one of many types of living objects that have developed within the universe and this is part of its mechanisms for maintaining the continuity of existence, otherwise it would have died out. Through the abilities of consciousness can you ponder, reason and discover the truth of what you ultimately are and thereby discover your true self-nature.

Without an I-self there can be no knowledge at all, and then you have insentience or no-self which is just the same as inanimate objects, insentient beings, non-existence or the state of sleeping. In these states there is no cognizance of a self.

The other meaning of no-self is that you have no intrinsic, inherent nature of your own because you are a blob of processes infinitely connected to all else within Shakti that cause your appearances. This state of no-self (not being an inherent self with an own-nature) means that your being/existence is God's being and existence, which is ultimately the existence of the fundamental ground state that is the fundamental substance of the cosmos. God's being and existence must therefore be your existence, so you are not an intrinsic soul-self but are God. Your I-self is an artificial condition not having a true identity because it is a false creation of the mind – it is Knowledge within a mind that assumes your real nature is an apparent self rather than the True Self.

Created beings are nothing in themselves for they are truly only God the Creator (the receptacle of the universe) *and* Creation (through perfect interdependence) as well as the ground state fundamental substratum. The standard meaning of "no-self" is that the ground of the soul (person) and of God are one and the same. They are a fused identity because they are both the Ground, the foundational substrate of reality. You don't have a self-so intrinsic self because you are God, the ultimate substratum that has no parts. There is no difference between God and man, between you and God. Therefore there is no such true thing as an independent self. You arise out of nothing and eventually go back to that nothingness, which is another aspect to the emptiness of the self.

As to the workings of consciousness, basically if there is no "I-witness" there is no self-awareness or awareness of others. The knowledge of being a self necessitates the presence of memory in order that an I-thought can discover its beingness or existence through a juxtaposition against "others" that are "non-self." Basically, memory is necessary for identifying, distinguishing, differentiating, classifying and comparing patterns that are "others." Reality, for us, can therefore be formed only because we have mental processes that reference an I-self and memories.

Higher knowledge absolutely necessitates the existence and usage of an I-thought and memories to make sense out of our conceptual processes. Memories provide names and labels to phenomena, namely meaning and order, that then lead to a recognition (or building) of a world. Our mind contributes features and attributes to objects through the definitions of memory (patterns), which make it possible for us to experience objects as objects. Otherwise there is only chaos within the field of experience, and chaos means that there are no such things as distinct entities or qualities of any type. A conscious experience means that *the experience is structured*, it is a oneness where all the sense inputs are turned into a single unified perception, and you cannot decompose it into non-interdependent parts.

The temporal structure of the world formed in our minds is found in our ways of thinking and perceiving that in turn rely on memories. The pattern matching capabilities of our mind and memory enable us to construct a recognizable world within our consciousness where the moment of experience lasts anywhere from about fifty milliseconds to one-tenth of a second – a different amount of time for the neural integration process depending on the kind of information being processed. "Time slices" consisting of the unconscious processing of stimuli can last for several hundred milliseconds and are immediately followed by a conscious perception of events that lasts for a much shorter block of time – the fifty milliseconds. In other words, we take the world in through our senses and analyze it in a process called microgenesis (to develop a fully formed sensory experience), and then in a moment of clarity consciously perceive the world (stimuli) that our senses have detected. Some say that the *now that you are aware of* (the *experienced moment* of *subjective presence* rather than the neural moment of functional processing) lasts on average many hundreds of microseconds as your brain fuses what you are experiencing into a psychological present. Hence, experts argue that the duration of an instant of consciousness ranges from a few tens of milliseconds to a few hundred milliseconds. Basically, the experience of actual now is momentary, and reality is experienced in a series of quanta time slices where each moment that comes into existence is replaced by another at a specific refresh rate, but they are fused into a unitary whole that seems like a seamless continuous experience.

How is an object recognized during our awareness? A potential takes shape and is then known in the mind as a form or object due to the discriminative powers of consciousness that reference memories during their functioning. Without the presence of consciousness and memories there is no such thing as the knowing of names, forms or objects, and thus no pattern, phenomena or object in existence. Then there is only chaos, or formlessness rather than a world of meaning. We experience meaning because we are a type of functioning within the universe that has developed consciousness (a mind) that produces cognition and discrimination and memories and provide us with perceptions and thoughts.

There needs to be a mind in order for anyone to discern a form, pattern, object, mark, name, label or phenomenon. Thus, in some sense we might say that mental chaos – mental functioning without a recognition of the I-thought or others – is insentience even though there might be neural biochemical functioning going on as with plants. In that case there is only functioning or activity, but not the cognizance of self-consciousness. There might be ions traversing through holes in neural membranes but no recognizable conscious activity. An undifferentiated mass of brain activity lacking objective differences or distinctions (such as within a coma or during anesthesia,) is certainly a chaotic state of ignorance or non-cognition, and thus not really consciousness at all in the sense that we take the word.

Thus, memories are being accessed with every recognized experience, and there is also a sense of I-self going on behind (underlying) every such experience. However, conceptualization, cognition, consciousness or the intellect within a living being is actually just a natural process going on without any truly definite, separate, self-so living entity being involved in the generation process. It is a process producing Knowledge, where no being is involved, which is just happening within a localized area with highly specific qualities. We call these phenomena of sentient beings within Shakti "sentient beings" as a manner of speaking but there is no such true thing. No sentient being is an intrinsic independent entity but just a ripple within seamless Shakti that is in absolute nature just the fundamental substrate. Conventionally, living beings are just collections of forms and processes within Shakti that we call "sentient beings," but none has the intrinsic nature of being a separate self-entity our own-being even though it believes itself to be an independent sentient I. This illusion is a mistaken notion of consciousness that has not thought through matters correctly, which is why it is called a "false thought" within Buddhism.

The I-thought or I-sense is something that naturally arises/occurs within the human mind due to the body's anatomical structural design. Brain activity (consciousness) creates the I, but what we take the I to mean is really an errant view (misunderstanding) about the way things *really are*. To hold such a view is to cling to Ignorance and be unenlightened as to your true nature. What really has arisen is Knowledge within the consciousness of a physical body that is itself an intersection of countless conditions and processes, and Knowledge is not an I-self entity. Knowledge is just Knowledge - a point of view.

It is not a person but Knowledge that is actually the true experiencer of everything. Knowledge experiences Knowledge, and there is understanding via an apparent self, empty of true nature, who is also just Knowledge. The I-thought of a doer or experiencer is just Knowledge and this is what "understands." There is no true inherent, self-so soul or entity within the process experiencing the understanding. It is just another inanimate process going on within Shakti, an apparent self, but we call that life "animate" for the sake of making distinctions. So there is Knowledge and understanding but no person involved with the process, and yet understanding is there. Deeds are done, but there is no doer.

There is no fixed, unchanging self because what you think you are at present is totally different than what it was years ago. You are not a unified ego but instead an ongoing and constantly evolving process of aggregation – an assemblage of causes and conditions – and so there is no core unchanging spirit within your self. You are not a self-sustaining, causally independent and permanent identity that exists through own-being. There is just Knowledge automatically being generated in an ever-changing body vehicle and this body of Knowledge is doing everything, even thinking the wrong thought, "I am an independent sentient being with knowing." That whole body unit, called a sentient being, is just another phenomenon interwoven within the fabric of the universe with the special characteristic that it automatically generates Knowledge within itself as part of its functioning. We call it an "independent sentient being," but it is certainly not independent nor intrinsic, and it is really just the production of Knowledge within it that is doing everything rather than a "being."

This is the lesson transmitted within the *Diamond Sutra*. Conventionally we call ourselves a living being, self, person, *atman, jiva*, and so on whereas we are just another "neutral" phenomenon within Shakti that is ultimately the original nature. We are part of the fabric of the universe without any fixed borders; there is no demarcation line between our body and the cosmos. We call ourselves living or beings but what part of Shakti is animate? It is all Shakti and there is no such real thing as "livingness." There is no such real distinction. We make that distinction with our minds for our own sake of differentiation. It is all due to consciousness that we can even have such thoughts.

Conventionally we are an effusion that is connected to everything else in existence, like a bit of soup wiggling within a grand soup that doesn't actually compose anything (any special pattern). We cannot see all the energetic connections of magnetism, electricity, gravity and other fields and forces that compose us through infinite interconnections of permeation, but they are there. Essentially we are just energy, and some of that energy has condensed into quanta, atoms, particles or "simples," but ultimately they too are just energy and energy is ultimately the fundamental substratum that has somehow birthed itself into becoming energy. No one knows how but here we are. We are a small section connected to everything else within a gigantic soup of energy – Shakti or the universe – and its ultimate substrate is what everything ultimately is.

It is therefore impossible to unravel the total causes and effects for our existence because they are infinite. Since we lack a self-so nature our *individual essence* is a nothingness. You, as the absolute, are none of the qualities of existence, and as religious practice you should stabilize in that state since it is your true nature. Or, you can say that your individual essence is *all things*, namely the ocean of totality itself. In religious terms you would say that God's existence must be your existence and God's beingness must be your beingness so you are not an intrinsic soul-self but are God. You must try to stabilize in that realization as a spiritual practice. Similarly, each part of the cosmos contains the whole universe through infinite interconnections and therefore represents the entire macrocosm because everything is internally related to everything else through infinite interpenetration – the universe is just one thing (Saguna Brahman or Ishvara) without parts. This means that when you hold up an empty palm you can say that you hold the entire universe in your hand. *Each thing is in all things, all things make up each individual thing.* In other words, each thing is defined by the existence of all other things, which is how we are connected to all things and all beings. Every man has within himself the entire universal condition. And, through infinite interdependence everything disturbs everything all the time so that the universe is a continuously vibrating whole. A single atom shakes the cosmos, the dance of the cosmos turns it into an effervescent dream without reality.

The interconnectedness of the universe exists at a fundamental level where nothing then is a purely local phenomenon or event. *When there is a "local event" it is the entire universe having an event.* This is because Shakti is an undivided whole of oneness rather than a collection of apparent (seeming) multiplicity. Interdependence also means that every location is the center of the cosmos since everything gets into the act, and every moment is the most important moment.

Self-delusion means to be confused about these matters. It means being confused about the nature of the universe and your self, being confused about the *true nature of our apparent existence.* It means not recognizing that we are not really a permanent, independent, separate, inherent, intrinsic, underlying, innate self-so entity-being – a self-sufficient and substantially real master in charge of the body-mind complex – which is what everyone out of ignorance and with foggy thinking assumes us to be. There is no inherent or fixed self (soul, *jiva, atman,* person, living being, entity or individual) within what we take as our limited borders – no innate, inherent, essential, absolute or everlasting soul or being. There is no inherent self amid everything that arises in a moment of consciousness either because the Knowledge producer is not an inherent being. It's just a process.

There is also no "absolute" or "real" (meaning independent, separate, fixed or inherently self-so) self-entity within the universe of manifestation we call Shakti, universe, cosmos, the All, Manifestation, Creation or Triple Realm. As the *Diamond Sutra* states, there is no such thing as a living sentient being within Shakti. There is only Shakti - non-living Shakti, insentient Shakti, neutral Shakti, inanimate Shakti whose portions large or small – having or not possessing consciousness – are just Shakti. It is through the possession of consciousness, which is definitely an illusion but an attribute good enough for the survival of our species (even though fraught with errors such as mistakes and misperceptions) that we discriminate Shakti into portions that we call objects or living beings. We have the idea that we are an inherent, intrinsic person but this is only an idea.

The "consciousness" within a "living being" is Shakti too and not anything separate from its fabric that transcends it. It is just another flickering within Shakti's overall fabric. However, we can also call our consciousness the "consciousness of Shakti" since we are portions of Shakti; Shakti (the cosmos) is our body and our consciousness is therefore its consciousness. We are part of Shakti's one consciousness that is a collection of all consciousnesses. We are part of the universal consciousness, the sentience of the cosmos and our mind is ultimately the organ of our world's own process of self-revelation. Thus, each of us is a portion of the voice of the universe. Furthermore, all the contents of our consciousness are the Supreme Self or original substance; all consciousness is consciousness that belongs to the self-nature so our mind is the consciousness of our True Self or self-nature. We are the consciousness of our True Self.

If just one living being within Shakti attains consciousness then that living being is the consciousness of Shakti. When many parts of Shakti become living beings that attain consciousness they are then all (part of) the consciousness of Shakti. Who knows what other things Shakti has also developed within it that are even greater than the great treasure of consciousness? The funny thing is that consciousness is the great miracle of the universe, and it is also an illusion. Nonetheless, it is ours and gives us the precious experience of life where inanimate matter experiences nothing. We can refine it to experience higher and better states of experience and well-being, and his we should do. How will we shape society so that we live better lives and are taught to become masters of our prize of consciousness and its capabilities, such as the ability to regulate our emotional mind or control the forces of Shakti (Nature) for our benefit? This is the question of life and in particular of spiritual cultivation since you are cultivating your spirit. What will be your creative participation within Shakti?

Consciousness is part of Shakti, an illusion that seems to independently transcend Shakti by superimposing a Maya of multiplicity upon a unity. Together with the I-thought and the inadequacies of our sensory organs, this is the inherent illusion provided by consciousness. This being the case of faulty consciousness, the ultimate question comes down to how you will choose to use your consciousness since it has inherent errors but is what you are. What will you do with it? Can you purify it of frequent interpretational errors or unwanted psychological afflictions (such as addictions, anxiety, worry, depression, anger or fear)? Can you correct for its implicit biases and inaccurate approximations that distort judgments? Can you use it to elevate your physical health? Can you use it to enhance your physical capabilities? Can you use it to improve your cognitive and intellectual abilities? Can you use it – by devoting yourself to a gradual path of self-cultivation - to reshape your neural patterns so that you can achieve higher and longer lasting states of happiness, flourishing and well-being? Can you develop its many abilities, and which of those abilities would you especially focus on mastering? *Mastering consciousness and its expression into behavior is the gist of the spiritual path.* You cannot control the results of your actions, but you can control your actions/behavior and the thoughts that give birth to your behavior. This is the Great Learning of life, and involves mastering our consciousness.

The I-self or ego-notion is a mental fabrication you produce within your consciousness that is within your body-mind, and you take it as your self-identity or self-nature. That I-self notion of I-hoodness is created within your mind due to the mental processing algorithms that operate within your brain. It is the notion of being a unified, solitary self. This notion is not just errant but at times also quite fragile since it can be easily changed, such as when you use psychedelics and lose the touch stones of self-identity.

The I-notion, constrained by neural limitations, helps to construct a view of the world from experiences, and is attached to learned prejudices and incorrect/false views. Too often the I-self notion assumes that the I is a homogenous entity separate from the elements that make it up, which is essentially all of Shakti, but the I-self concept that assumes limitedness and homogeneousness is incorrect and false. It is a false notion that does not reflect the way things really are. However, the self-notion has developed within living beings in order that living object-species may proliferate and survive within the universe. Without it most species of living agents would not have been able to adapt to changes and would have died out.

You are not an independent being that just happens to be visiting or living in Shakti in some independent fashion. Shakti has created you out of its fabric and through interconnections of fields and forces Shakti defines your very existence within the structure of its being. Your I-thought that develops inside you is part of the total natural (inanimate) processes within the one fabric of Shakti that has formed your body too. In some sense, the self-notion mechanically arises within a certain type of body structure and the miracle is that it produces awareness of a world of qualities, the thought of being a self, and a feeling of the vibrancy of life. It gives us the miracle of knowing existence and feeling alive.

Regardless of who or what we are, *we should use our great miracle of consciousness to reduce the problems we face in life and to enjoy life to the fullest.* Life isn't perfect and is filled with pain and suffering but it's still a gift. Unfortunately, most people live their lives in unsatisfactory conditions hard to exit (suffering) and in robot-like mental states where they have deadened their vitality and suppressed their fullest capacities of awareness. Many spend their time in a state of dimmed awareness akin to foggy muddled thinking, hypnosis or "waking sleep" where they exist but don't "live." The spiritual path is to awaken ourselves (our consciousness) despite any conditions of suffering or deficiency to a vibrant full awareness that is accompanied by a tinge of bliss. The spiritual path is for us to achieve our full conscious potential by purifying our consciousness of afflictions, irritations and unwanted elements; perfect its operations so it produces whatever we want; master as many of its abilities as we can; and master our environment, life circumstances and Nature to produce better living conditions for our happiness and well-being. With the mastery or perfection of consciousness we can use its abilities to seek solutions to our problems so that we can experience better states of happiness, elevation, comfort, meaning, flow and bliss.

Any mental concepts that the I-self spins are accomplished within a mind that we say is owned by an I, ego, self, soul, personality, *atman*, *jiva*, living being, personality, sentient entity, etcetera. These are merely convenient terms used to indicate a small ripple within the fabric of Shakti. They do not refer to any really intrinsic entity but to a composite living structure, entangled with an inherent subtle body also made of components, that all exist due to countless processes and conditions internal to and external to itself. It is a "conscious entity" composed of a large agglomeration of non-self components and conditions.

The mental processes of the I-self view usually produce subjective rather than objective mental fabrications (thoughts) that are often blemished by flaws and errors. They are usually conditional or relative truths rather than objective truths. They are thoughts, feelings and stories that color reality due to the automatic reflexes of our mind ... subjective, imagined creations prone to bias and error rather than absolute realities. Since they are not purely objective they are sometimes termed "false thoughts," "false views" or "false perspectives" in Buddhism when incorrect, wrong or errant.

Even our perceptions of the external world, since they are not direct cognitions but incomplete mental approximations of the world, are also imaginations, unrealities, illusions or falsities since they are inaccurate representations or similitudes of what's out there. Being representations within yourself that are shared by no one else they are actually personal subjective fantasies of how the world really is, and yet they are good enough for you to use them to maintain your existence because they create a world of conventionalities you can use for the purposes of survival, thriving and well-being. Even what you experience as "now" is something false because it happened tens or hundreds of milliseconds in the past and it took your brain that long to combine all the relevant inputs that give to you your present perceptions.

A purely objective reality can never be experienced through the mind, so all you ever experience of the world is a figment of your imaginative capacities of approximation, and thus an illusion or Maya that is classified as delusion, "false thoughts" or "unreal thoughts" in Buddhism. It is not that the world is not a reality of facticities (empirical facts) ruled by cause and effect, but that what you see of the world is an illusion, a simplified abbreviation, an imagination, a similitude or approximation. You build your idea of the world that exists only in the (mental) realm of name and form. You never experience the world directly and fully (validly) but only through the thoughts and images within consciousness, which are best guess approximations of external appearances. They are erroneous imaginations or approximations of genuine appearances because the world does not exist in the limited way that they portray, yet that is how we take the world to be because of the operational consciousness of our species. Your perceived picture of the world is also incorrect because many of the qualities you project onto phenomena are only in your mind. An example of flawed thought processes is when you make a mistake in interpreting an optical illusion.

Thoughts are just a creation of the mind, which only exists due to the presence of a living body capable of sentience, that is in itself a creation of inanimate atoms and energy coming together in a specific pattern or structure called "sentient life." The laws of nature describe human life and its pattern on a fundamental level. All of these components are ultimately processes within the one single fabric of inanimate Shakti, which is ultimately the original nature that has somehow enfolded into a functional living form that has consciousness. A living being gives birth to thoughts that spin a realm of reality in that body's brain (a world of qualities we call experience), and that world image is ultimately incomplete/partial, certainly conditional, a representation that is often incorrect, and thus an illusory delusion. And yet consciousness creates a conventional world that *works* due to its predictable facticity. In spiritual cultivation you actually want to construct a view of the world that is as correct as possible in order to correct the mistaken notions that you regularly form in your brain, and should want to start interpreting events and situations in more accurate ways without biases due to developing a higher wisdom or understanding.

Precisely, the world you see is all a relative illusion of yours, a simplified approximation or representation of the real world. You are living inside a mental dream, an illusionary fantasy, but you don't recognize this fact because you don't have the wisdom of enlightenment – the understanding of your true self-nature that is self-realization, which includes the fact that your consciousness produces just a representation of the world. For instance, somehow your brain has created a picture of the world inside consciousness and then inverts it so that it seems to appear outside of you. You don't even think about this fact, or wonder how it happens. It must be illusory for this to happen since consciousness happens only inside your brain, and yet you see the external world outside you. Cognition is like a magical illusion. Nonetheless, you operate in a shared consensual illusion with others of like mental properties – humans – and therefore the human worldview is an apparent reality shared by human beings. You possess the great magical treasure of consciousness – the ultimate prize of existence – that has somehow come about in the cosmos, and because you don't develop a transcendental understanding of who and what you ultimately are you hold onto the illusion of your separate beingness and existence as an intrinsic, independent, absolute entity transcending Nature. Such an idea is a false thought, an incorrect view, an unreality, a falsity. Nature is the parent and humanity is the child who inseparably lives within it as part of it.

You must realize who and what you truly are, and that understanding is called "self-realization." You must also see/evaluate situations that you encounter in life by what they truly are and not by what you want them to be, which is "being realistic" in terms of conventional affairs. Wisdom entails figuring out the *truth* of situations, and transcendental wisdom means comprehending the true nature of your being and that your existence as an apparent self actually has no intrinsic self, you are ultimately the ground state of existence that lacks phenomena, but in manifestation you are not just a localized entity but the All of manifested energy-matter. To use consciousness correctly you must not distort facts or clear thinking because of likes, dislikes, preferences, biases and prejudices that reflect unconscious influences on your mental states. Emotions, for instance, tend to completely color your experiences and you become those emotions if you are not careful. If you close your mind to the truth or to self-correction when evidence proves you wrong on some topic these are also errors of consciousness. These are some of the many, many rules for using consciousness properly.

Although the self-concept itself is just a mental fabrication within your brain, and another experience like all others, it is *the basic one that makes other conceptions possible* due to there being an (imagined independent non-connected) self at their center that produces a first person point of view within any inner dialogue narration (thinking). In other words, we think ourselves into existence as an I-self – one day awakening as an "I" – and that I-sense thereafter becomes the permanent central basis of our conceptual consciousness. Whatever arises for you as "experience" or a "world of qualities" is just your own mind that has given rise to an I-self conception, which is happening as a flowing process within the miracle of consciousness whose emergence is in turn dependent upon your anatomical body structure of molecules and energy shaped in a specific pattern. Consciousness arises due to an infinite number of comprehensive, interdependent and interpenetrative cause and effect conditions.

The ego, self-concept or I-thought is a special kind of meta-thought (actually a bundle of thoughts) at the center of all other thoughts. This I-thought gives you the sense that "you" are thinking "your" thoughts when in fact nothing of the kind is happening. Knowledge is just talking to itself without an intrinsic living self being involved. During the process of thinking it is essentially the thought process itself that is doing the thinking, not a separate, stable, eternal "I" that is an independent, inherent *atman*, soul, *jiva* or sentient being. Nevertheless that I-thought of being a self must be there for consciousness to work and an inner subtle body needs to be there also but the thinking process itself, Knowledge, is automatically doing all the thinking and understanding without any real individual, self-entity, soul, *jiva* or *atman* being involved. The processes of consciousness, Knowledge, give rise to an assumed, apparent I-self that thinks it is the doer when that very I-self is just a product of myriad conditions which produce it as a result. Knowledge is the doer, not an I-self. Knowledge, when it talks to itself, is just a process of producing more Knowledge that also includes an illusion of understanding.

So when you are thinking, it is *not you* who is thinking, it is Knowledge (the process of consciousness) that is doing the thinking. Once you die and leave the physical shell as a subtle body, it is still Knowledge that is doing the thinking within your new astral (subtle) body. If you generate the Causal, Supra-Causal and Immanence bodies it is still Knowledge that is doing the thinking and perceiving within those new bodies that are an interconnected, embedded component within Shakti. Never once is there an independent being, soul or doer behind the thinking and perceiving. It is only Shakti undergoing transformations within a part of itself and that body (a collection of processes) is functioning in a special way based on its structural form, attributes and powers.

You know yourself in Knowledge, that knowing is Knowledge and the knower is Knowledge. It is all just Knowledge referencing itself in a circle. Therefore in a grand sense the Knowledge we generate through thoughts and conceptions, despite its usefulness, is all just a relative illusion. It is all conditional on what we already know and nothing is absolute within that circle of Knowledge. There is no such thing as an independent living being or soul within that circle. There is only Knowledge knowing itself in a vehicle that can generate Knowledge that makes knowing possible. When we know something it is actually Knowledge knowing Knowledge, so as the *Diamond Sutra* of Buddhism explains, where is there a person in all this? It is just an automatic process going on.

Is there any true self at all? The true I-self must be the only real witness, and to be real it must be unchanging and ever-present. Therefore the True Self is the unchanging, ever-present, unshakable fundamental substratum. But since the unchanging universal ground state is insentient because It is not a being, there is no witness at all. There is witnessing going on but there is no real sentient being doing the witnessing. *Witnessing by a sentient being* is just an illusion, the miracle of consciousness. To say that the fundamental essence is the Witness is also just a way of speaking. It never changes while everything else is proceeding through complex interactions and transformations, and It is thus like an ultimate Witness even though It really isn't anything at all. What a grand farce!

Ramana Maharshi said, "As all mental activities like remembering, forgetting, desiring, hating, attracting, discarding, etc., are modifications of the mind, they cannot be one's true state. Simple changeless being is one's true nature." The true nature of "changeless being" means that everything superimposed upon It is a farce, a falsity, an illusion ... and so is the fact of consciousness and witnessing. If we take the passing show to be real then we fall into a spell of wrong understanding. But that doesn't mean that we don't witness because we do. It is simply that witnessing is not what we take it to be.

Thus there is an ego principle and cognizing principle within consciousness that generates the self-thought and other thoughts, and both are just the operations of consciousness that enable us to maneuver within the field of life. They are standard operations of Knowledge doing its natural functional activity that arises due to the anatomical structure of the brain. The thinking process is not I, me, or mine but just something that is happening within a human structure (body) that develops a concept of being an embodied organism. It is just another one of the infinite manifestations of things in the universe that are neutral or automatic in character. It is just another operation, process or functioning within Shakti rather than something transcendental to Shakti. It is part of Nature rather than separate from Nature. You are part of Nature rather than different from Nature, and yet your sentience (such as your thinking and imagination skills) makes you think you are perfectly separate from the rest of Nature even though you are equal with everything else in being part of a oneness that admits no multiplicity. We dissociate ourselves from the Ultimate Reality although we are a unity with Shakti/Nature – we are Nature and subject to every aspect within it – and Shakti or Nature is inherently unified with our essential nature. Nature is essentially the pure transcendental foundational One purified of all forms, and therefore you are That.

You are special because of sentience or consciousness whereas most of the universe is indifferent because it lacks this inevitable functional ability (property). But now you can understand that what we call consciousness is not actually consciousness, but nonetheless we conventionally call it consciousness because it delivers to us a measure of facticity. Shakti is actually inanimate, and an insentient evolute of Shakti simply appears to have consciousness without any reality to the process. Everything is just an illusion like a flower that seems to hang motionless in the sky. To be true consciousness sentience would need to arise within an inherently self-so sentient being independent of Shakti, and that consciousness would need to produce an accurate worldview transcending Shakti (be independent of Shakti), but it is entirely part of Shakti as well as fraught with errors and essentially illusionary. It is one of the manifest universe's uncountable attributes or functions, and arises within a "living being" that is also just an inanimate transformational process within Shakti that we designate as a living sentient being.

There is no such true thing as a living being within Shakti, but we identify them as such for communication's sake. All is one. If we consider individuality, there are actually only "neutral" processes going on within Shakti that we cannot say are either good or evil or anything at all because those are characteristics invented by the mind and not inherent within either the cosmos or original substratum. In other words, Heaven and Earth are impartial, good and even are human conceptions. You will find nothing but the universal substance, Brahman, existing in all, good and evil. From the standpoint of the original substance-essence there is nothing really happening that we can call transformations or interactions since everything is Itself – All is one. Being living beings with consciousness, we only call ourselves living beings for identification's sake but now you know the real nature of who and what you are. This is the enlightenment view you have achieved, which is to know who and what you ultimately are, which is not the self you typically identify as or assume yourself to be, and how consciousness operates. This is how to understand reality.

We are ignorant because we think that we are independent when we are really dependently-defined constructions (agglomerations or convergences of processes) within a giant soup of infinite interconnections that ultimately form a unity of oneness, but we fictionally take ourselves to be limited selves separate from this whole. When we empty our minds of limitations this brings us closer to unity with the world and the way things are.

We are conscious agents or entities, the consciousness of Shakti, the Knowledge processes within Shakti. We are units of consciousness, and so because of our existence the whole of Shakti is conscious. Being an intersection of countless conditions *without there being anything that is only intrinsically us*, we are actually nothing at all – a being without form. While we appear to be a limited part of the All separated from the rest of it by the isolation of space we are actually the All, and yet we are nothing at all since we have nothing that is our own-being nature. Our seeming localization is the intersection of infinite conditions within Shakti, which means that you are *all of Shakti* – the entire universe. As Jesus said in the *Gospel of Thomas*, "Lift up a stone and you will find me there." Krishna said in the *Bhagavad Gita*, "I am in one sense everything and present everywhere, but I am independent and not part of cosmic manifestation." Jesus and Krishna are the universe as well as the fundamental substrate, and so are you. You are a beingness without form, you are a beingness with all form.

Localized we can consider ourselves a body, set of processes, region of transformation, a ripple in spacetime or wavefront with the property of consciousness that is always vibrating and connected to all other things in the universe. If you realize your essential oneness with spacetime then you don't have to do anything to unite with Shakti, God or the universal substrate because the perfect union is already there. You just have to live your life well to enjoy well-being, which requires you to master consciousness and your activities (behavior), and work on attaining the transcendental bodies to dissolve the problem of longevity (survival and continuity). During the meantime, or even after that attainment, you must also solve the problem of having a life purpose rising above the mundaneness of life and simple existence that gives you a good reason for being in the world, and the most rewarding paths involve servicing humanity while working towards divinity. Born of the world, you can become a lotus that rises above the mud.

Created things are nothing in themselves but identical to Shakti itself, God Himself, and the foundational substrate Itself. Since your life is God's being (Shakti's being), then God's existence must be your existence and God's beingness must be your beingness, neither more nor less. Should you not help through service the other parts of yourself that are also you, and also ultimately God? Your life belongs to the universe for it is not your own.

From another viewpoint we are an object within Shakti - a seemingly localized phenomenon, field or body with the attributes of livingness and consciousness. From another viewpoint, we are an agglomeration of the simplest particles (called "simples," "pixels," "particles," "quanta," "bits" or "atoms" to denote being the smallest possible indivisible units) and energies that have assumed a certain pattern, but when we look at our pattern/identity from the vast vantage point of Shakti there is no inherent pattern there at all. What pattern? The structure is constantly changing and doesn't build anything real or constant, so there is no fixed pattern. What true inherent, intrinsic pattern is there? Furthermore, what is there as a temporary structure or pattern actually flows into everything else so if there was an actual pattern its size would be infinite – the All. Hence, once again there is no such thing as a pattern, person or individual self.

You are a being without any form. If there were a pattern or body to you it would be constantly changing due to impermanence, so once again there is no definite fixed pattern at all but just a region of transformation that appears to have consciousness. Therefore there is no such thing as an inherent person, being or entity. That is just a way of speaking we made up.

Furthermore, when we deconstruct an aggregated object such as a flower we find that it is entirely made up of separate, fragmented, *non-flower elements*. A flower *is not real because it is not fundamental* since it is made of molecules, and then atoms, and then even smaller units of quantum granularity within a large soup (the universe) of flowing energies or fields and so forth until you get to the final fundamental nature. Perhaps you might even think of it as a complicated happening of quantum events, but is that the most fundamental decomposition? In terms of manifest reality there is a hierarchy of combinations of various evolutes or entities that produce existence at their own level, but we are after the fundamental nature of a flower. It is not composed of flower elements but entirely of things that aren't intrinsically the flower. It is composed of electro-magnetism, gravity, space, time, atoms, energy fields etc. that co-exist and also its (derivative) existence is due to a history (evolutionary process) of sunshine, water, soil, seeds, weather etc. that were needed to manifest the flower. Its existence depends on countless conditions or elements other than and different from the flower. Its entire existence depends on *elements that intrinsically are not the flower* – which are non-flower elements. What then is a flower other than a compendium, a conglomeration, an agglomeration of diverse processes or conditions in a localized region (a ripple in the fabric of Shakti) whose components are themselves not flower-nature elements?

There is no innate flower-nature there within a flower, but all these independent elements connect to create what we call a flower. Since there is no such thing as an inherently existing, intrinsically-so flower essence/nature that produces the flower this conclusion carries forth for humans too. There is no permanent soul or self-nature within you but there are many independent elements that have come together to compose your existence. A flower is itself just a conglomeration of other-than-flower conditions, in fact infinite conditions, and because its existence *is due to these other conditions* without there being anything of itself within its appearance/origination (that is purely the flower-essence) its manifesting pattern is empty of being intrinsically so, empty of an independent existence, empty of a true existence, lacking of a self-so nature. There is nothing within its compositional elements that is a flower at all – the flower is an aggregate phenomenon. It is just a karmic formation – a product of infinite interdependent origination – a pattern of appearance within an infinite Indra's web of simultaneously-so intersecting conditions. *It is a nothingness since it totally lacks attributes and phenomena and yet through interdependence is everything.*

Nonetheless, on the conventional level a flower is there as just a flower, full of flowerness, and conventionally identified/defined as a flower by sentient minds who recognize the flower pattern. But even that flower is just a temporary appearance, a transformation that appears in the nature of a flowing dream since the form of the flower (what makes us call it a flower) is always changing and flowing away. It will first be a bud, then a bloom and then wither and die. Within the immensity of Shakti it is actually an iota of no fixed form that, even though it appears as an iota, is actually seamlessly connected to all of Shakti via energy streams and wavefronts. And, ultimately beyond that appearance is just the undifferentiated, patternless original nature.

Thus, we can break each phenomenon we see in the universe into simples, but the essence of the simples is the final universal substratum. Each of those simples, quanta, particles or atoms unfolds into the whole universe through a field of infinite interdependence, Indra's web, and the whole itself enfolds into a specific region to produce every localized phenomenon. Even though the existence of a phenomenon, such as ourselves, seems localized, its existence is actually the whole macrocosmic universe.

Therefore since every localized phenomenon is nothing but an agglomeration or composite structure there is also nothing unique and personal to any sentient being in the sense of an intrinsic nature that materially exists on its own. All sentient beings are *entirely* composite constructions that exist through infinite interdependence involving the entire cosmos of Shakti. They are never independently existing via own-beingness but inter-be with every other thing. All living beings are just patterns or processes within Shakti, and thus neutral (non-living) patterns or processes because "living" is just an identification we make that lacks any ontological meaning. We use it to identify ourselves whereas we are actually quite mechanistic and automatic, though we don't assume so, because we are actually just attributes, constructions, processes or functionings within neutral Shakti that are defined by certain characteristics and ruled by certain laws of cause and effect. Our conditioning even defines how we behave – our behavior.

Nor is there any such *true thing* as consciousness because consciousness itself is not transcendent to manifest reality; every thought you have is within God, within Shakti. It seems to us that consciousness exits outside of time and space because it doesn't seem to have the properties of matter, and it seems to be something outside of Shakti transcending Nature, which then sets it apart from or above the mundane world. However, it is part of Shakti since you are a drop of Shakti. Everything consciousness creates is an imagined order, an illusion or delusion, a fictional story, a fantasy or dream reality, a superimposed Maya … and those outputs are also components of Shakti rather than something transcending Shakti. They don't transcend Shakti because they are components within it, so they are part of the fabric of Shakti and therefore *inherently insentient neutral processes*. It's not that consciousness isn't really there and therefore is an illusion. Something does appear in our minds, something indeed seems to be happening, and that appearance demonstrates the existence of consciousness just as much as an illusive dream or a direct valid cognition of objective reality. It just isn't what we normally assume it to be because of our own ignorance. We see a Maya (illusion) due to all sorts of (perceptual and mental) inadequacies that veil an accurate perception of the world, and the functioning of our consciousness not only distorts images of the world but projects/superimposes extras onto them that cause us to incorrectly identify with our empirical self as our True Self.

We call what we experience "consciousness" but there is no such true thing as consciousness in the sense of what we take it to be. There is no valid experiential process owned by a true sentient being that knows Shakti while transcending it (thus making it ultimately superior by being free of matter and being apart from what it is observing), and what appears within the mind is often not a correct cognition. There are only transformations or processes going on within Shakti, but we call some of them animate, living or sentient for the sake of differentiating them from other phenomena within Shakti. "Consciousness" falls within this category of transformations. Your consciousness is just another conditional thread woven into everything else within the total fabric of Nature.

In manifest existence there is only (insentient) Shakti – lacking independent *jivas, atmans*, souls or living beings that are not part of it – undergoing transformations within itself and the "consciousness" of these sentient beings is just another functioning process within Shakti (that doesn't reveal anything definitive in an ultimate sense). Nonetheless we call the worldview that consciousness creates "reality" because that way of seeing and experiencing the world "works" for us and for all beings of the same species who produce a worldview in a similar way. As facticity it is relevant to us (our culture and society) and helps us maneuver within Nature, but it is not the absolute reality that appears to us nor is it in honesty a truly accurate version of Nature. However, those false thoughts and conditional imaginations work for us. What a remarkable miracle is this great gift of consciousness within manifest existence! What a marvel, what a gift, what a treasure is this wish-fulfilling gem!

All living beings of similar species share a similar anatomical structure and thus share similar mental processes. They share similar "seeds" of consciousness, meaning that the worldview that appears within their consciousness is extremely similar across the species - a consensus, consensual reality or shared perspective. Humans, as an example, commonly agree on enough of the same neural fabrications (that produce a consensual worldview) that we can socially function together, as is the case for other sentient animal species. We cannot, however, experience the echolocation of a bat, but bats share mental processes that can interpret such sounds and thereby share a common worldview enabling them to live together. Due to their different sensory capabilities (due to their varying anatomy), different species will construct different images of the world. Cats and dogs cannot see in color nor do they possess the higher mental abilities that humans possess, and so it is apparent that their worldview is constrained by physical anatomy and is different from our own. Owing to millions of years of evolution, their bodies and systems and mental functions are organized and ready to function in a specifically species way that we do not enjoy.

There might even be other functional capabilities better than consciousness possessed by other beings (*or something entirely different than living beings that we cannot imagine*), but we can only go so far as our consciousness goes so we can never know we don't possess those higher attributes, qualities or capabilities. We can never even know what they are. The real world is so different than the similitude (mere representation) we experience via consciousness that we cannot call our mental images of it a truly valid cognition, but our consciousness produces what it does and we should be happy for what we have because consciousness is the greatest miracle of manifest existence that we know. Knowingness (awareness or the *chit* of *sat-chit-ananda*), which is the experience of being aware of one's existence and the manifest universe (the *sat* of *sat-chit-ananda*), is the most valuable treasure possible. It is a wish-fulfilling gem that reflects the world within its facets, and it grants wishes because consciousness gives us the power of Knowledge and volition (activity).

The mental constructs within our minds (thoughts, emotions, sensations, images, forms and phenomena) are not our selves, they are transitory conditional fabrications that lack their own self-nature, and there is no inherent "I" to experience them. What you see of the world around you is just an internal mental approximation created due to cognitive algorithms (rather than a direct perception of the way things really are), and therefore an illusive similitude rather than the true reality of Shakti that is in front of you. Why then let phenomena bother you so that you lose your composure? We grasp after them as if they were true entities when they are simply imaginations running through our brains. They are not a true reality but just an energy and neurochemical reaction. We are experiencing neural fluctuations caused by bioelectrical reactions, and unfortunately while doing so we often let our animal impulses rule our behavior leading to unfortunate results.

Although we are bodies we are really just composite phenomena, aggregate processes or a nexus of events made up of the same atoms and energies as everything around us, but within the nexus of our special physical form we just happen to produce thoughts, awareness, consciousness or Knowledge. Brain activity together with subtle energy creates the "I." Because it produces the "I" we can say that our "I" and our neurons, nerves and energy are actually the same thing.

Consciousness can only arise within a receptacle or container and for us that sentient generator is a living body with its special anatomical structure together with vital energy. Experience arises from a physical basis of inanimate atoms and an energy basis of an internal subtle body that is released upon death. Consciousness does not just arise from brain activity but requires an underlying subtle energy as a substratum throughout a living body. Its vital energy, Qi, or inner subtle body is essentially an even more fundamental body than the material body, and is what we normally call the "soul." Together they produce the viewpoint of a being due to an agglomeration that has a functional attribute called consciousness that is essentially a special biochemical, bioelectrical reaction – a neurochemical and neuroenergetic reality.

An individual is a complex, tightly integrated process of extreme intricacy within the one ocean of manifest reality and not some separate, independent existence. Its thoughts are part of that ocean too rather than something that transcends Nature by existing wholly beyond it. You are an iota of the manifest ocean, you are an integral part of Nature rather than an independent existent that stands apart from it. You are an appearance of and within the primordial soup of energies that has generated the universe and all its aspects. No objects of the universe exist absolutely through and by themselves as own-natures, but only appear through relationships. There are no inherent "objects" within the universe and all its apparent changes are just the universe interacting with itself. It is only itself, just itself and what is transcendental is the primordial substrate that is its original nature. You are the manifest reality, therefore you *are* one with everything that is manifest. You can therefore view yourself as the microcosm that is the macrocosm. Your lack of a personal intrinsic essence, your nothingness means you are all things. You are *all of manifest existence*. You are also the One unchangeable substrate in which the universe manifests itself. The True Self is the only substance pervading the universe (in reality nothing else exists) and you are It. You are also its appearance – Shakti. The universe is nothing different than you.

You *are* Nature. You *are* Shakti and the universe is your body. You are the universal Indra's web of infinite fields, energies and phenomena. We are one of the universe's innumerable expressions, a flowing process in continual transformation. We just happen to be a "living" phenomenon, object or process that has consciousness that lets us have *higher* thoughts such as "we are living beings" or "we are separate." Consciousness is not outside of Shakti, it does not transcend Shakti, it is not independent of Shakti but is a fluctuating component of Shakti. Who said consciousness is supreme since consciousness is just an illusion we make up, and that illusion is not above Shakti in any transcendental way but just another (inanimate) process within the matrix of Shakti? And yet, consciousness *is supreme* because it enables us to *know our existence and experience a world of qualities* by providing us with awareness.

Consciousness is not really an independent function free of the world, but we conventionally think of it as such. It is a dependent fabrication caused by laws of cause and effect within the brain and outside of it rather than totally free, and not something transcendental that views the world. It has a status of equality ("of one taste") with all the other multiplicities within Shakti, so it is not higher in any sense than any other of the countless processes within the universe that comprise its fabric. It does not transcend Shakti in any way, shape or form but is just another function within Shakti, so you can say it is a functional attribute of Shakti. Every thought you have is within God too. From the aspect of Shakti, there isn't even any such real thing as consciousness or living beings since to Shakti everything is just primordial Shakti (Saguna Brahman the first evolute, or Brahman with attributes that is also known as Ishvara the Creator/Creation), and whatever has developed within Shakti is just Shakti rather than anything special. Furthermore, the one source of the mind and material things is the original substratum, so how can consciousness be ultimately real?

Shakti itself can be thought of as an always-changing description of the possible attributes of the fundamental substratum of the universe; the underlying fundamental substrate always remains the same but changes are found in any description of the Source's possible manifest attributes. You can think of this as meaning that ever-changing Shakti is God from different perspectives, or the multiplicity of Shakti produces the innumerable descriptions possible of God, or the personification of the Ultimate Reality is Shakti which is therefore the ever-evolving body of God, Shakti is the manifest imminent body of God that reveals His qualities and those qualities are interfused with God, etcetera. Of course the opposite descriptive mechanism that points to Brahman or God is *"neti, neti,"* "not this, not this" because Brahman is attributeless (think of Brahman as having no personality traits). One descriptive scheme describes all the possible manifest attributes of Brahman (and there is an infinite number of such descriptions) while another refers describes Its unchanging essence as empty, meaning that It is free of all attributes such as time and matter and energy.

Consciousness seems that it doesn't possess the properties of matter and exists outside of time and space, thus setting it above Nature and the mundane world, but it is a linked (dependently constructed) component within Shakti and not an independent reality on its own that transcends Nature. But to us, we are independent living beings with mental capabilities that are the great miracle of existence separating us from the darkness of insentient matter/energy, and therefore consciousness is the greatest possible treasure.

With consciousness we can know life and the universe, have families and relationships, can create homes full of love and laughter, can experience beauty and engagement and bliss, and can connect ourselves to virtuous principles and commit our lives to noble purposes with meaning. We can live lives with happiness and find meaning in life. In spiritual cultivation we learn how to use consciousness, our bodies and our conduct so that we can experience many aspects of life, but the core reality is that we have existence (a body) that possesses the attribute of consciousness enabling us to know experiences and perform volitional actions, and even though it is all a farce without an intrinsic I-self we can within the fiction of consciousness experience various wonderful mental states including flourishing, lightness, shine, flow, happiness, engagement, immersion, freshness, meaning and bliss. We can even pursue very long-lived bodies that are nearly immortal, thus solving the problems of survival and continuity.

Consciousness is the producer of our experiences because the lived experience is internal, therefore for enjoyable experiences we must learn how to master both the unwanted fluctuations of our minds and the powers of consciousness. We need to master all the skillful activities it enables us to perform, such as learning the principles of cause and effect, so that we can achieve whatever we want in life including wondrous states of inner being such as comfort, the feeling of active vitality within us, mental satisfaction, peaceful tranquility or the state of flow and bliss.

Consciousness is what we are capable of, and there is no use in complaining about any of its natural faults or limitations. It is essentially what we are, so our job is to correct it, master it and use it to its best. We are a light within the darkness of mere being, that which illuminates the insentient matter of the universe (our greater body). We are designed to produce more and more Knowledge – it is our destiny by our universal construction – so we must harness consciousness, master it, make it more skillful, purify consciousness and ennoble it. We must take it to a level of excellence and use it to guide our behavior to similar heights of nobility as we define them.

Our unique defining feature is that we can produce Knowledge and deliberately direct our own actions and behavior because of our consciousness. We can effectively master and control the changes of universal phenomena. Our consciousness enables us to understand what the world seemingly is and what we ultimately are, which is not "people" in the sense of what we normally take "people" to be. It lets us experience a world of qualities through apprehension, and thoughts connected to willed behavior enable us to accomplish whatever we want according to our intentions and desires. This is why consciousness is referred to as the wish-fulfilling jewel in Buddhism. Our Great Learning in life is to master our bodies as well as consciousness and all its capabilities so that we can achieve happiness, flourishing, well-being and fulfillment. Through consistent and sustained deliberate efforts we can enhance our physical condition, improve our intellectual capacities and cognitive abilities, purify our inner psychological terrain and improve our behavior are activities to gain what we want.

The normal way we think of ourselves is that we are permanent souls and should act a certain way according to religious rules and the social propriety we've been taught, and we should go about living life pursuing our dreams while following social traditions along with those religious rules and regulations. No one thinks "I am a process within Shakti, with the great gift of consciousness, and I need to learn how to master it and use it wisely as well as cultivate the longer lasting transcendental bodies inherent within my energy structure. With consciousness I can engage in all sorts of activities during life, follow my dreams and achieve thriving, flourishing, fulfillment, well-being and long-term bliss rather than just experience short-term splurges of happiness, pleasure or excitement. My physical body will decay, but upon death a subtle vital energy body within me composed of my Qi will be released from my physical shell that then constitutes life as a deva, hence there is survival after death. Since knowingness and vital energy then leave my prior physical shell, it will be as dead. The subtle body (astral body) within me is rather longer lasting, although it too is subject to deterioration, but through periodic energy rejuvenation it continues to exist through rebirth from one life to the next. It is the soul within me, necessary as a substrate for there to be consciousness, and is the basis of reincarnation. Yet higher energetic bodies can be released from within its matrix too if that body also cultivates its own internal energy. Upon its death that subtle body (astral body) will undergo transmigration and this cycle of reincarnation will keep repeating – managed by beings with higher spiritual bodies - unless sufficient karmas have been resolved and purities cultivated in the earthly plane and I finally cultivate a spiritual body out of the subtle body whose elemental composition is so transcendentally high that its longevity is nearly forever (the Supra-Causal body of the "Formless Realm"). At that time I can escape the lower realms of reincarnation permanently since my body will no longer be composed of the most corrupted (impure) levels of energy and matter. Therefore I can make my soul immortal, or as Taoism says I can make myself into an Immortal."

"To do that I need to cultivate spiritual practice, which in turn requires that I cultivate my Qi, my mind (mental processes), my character, behavior and merit. It is a path of self-cultivation of inner energy work yoga and transforming my personality, disposition, thought patterns and behavior/actions so that I merit the requisite help. To attain an immortal body requires that I purify my personality and thought patterns in order to deserve the help required from higher beings to purify and energize my Qi to achieve the higher bodies, otherwise I will continue to undergo a process of recycling." With the knowledge of enlightenment, which means the existence of higher spiritual bodies, this is the more accurate way of viewing life. This is why the spiritual path is essentially that of mastering consciousness, purifying your mind and behavior, and cultivating inner and outer yoga.

There is no separation from Shakti because we only exist by being defined through its totality. We are simply a *functioning process* within this immense Indra's web, a transient operational construction lacking a self-so nature. Even so, we still have life, consciousness and the capability of cultivating a nearly indestructible body if we through spiritual cultivation start cultivating a purification of the energy within our own body and take it to its highest transcendental basis. At a basic metaphysical level we are just a continuous substance or set of processes that has special properties and functions, which we take to be in the shape of a limited packet or body, and one of our attributes is the capability of consciousness that we can use to manipulate our attributes as well as the attributes of Shakti/Nature. There is no real inherent I within us, nonetheless we do possess the attribute of consciousness that assumes an inherent I-self, we do exist as apparent beings, and as beings with consciousness and a non-intrinsic I-self we can still experience states of happiness, mental freshness, flow and the simple bliss of being alive.

We are not the only universal things without intrinsic self-hood. In fact, nothing within the universe has its own inherent selfhood. Phenomena are not themselves (what we take them to be). As Indra's web illustrates, they are composite, conditional creations appearing at the intersection of cause and effect that lack a separate, independent, intrinsic nature because they are composed out of all the other elements of the universal web (which are reflected in them). It seems like there are separate objects or entities in the universe but there are not; the view of separateness arises because we cannot see all the interconnections between objects that creates one continuous whole. Nevertheless, for the sake of convention we always act as if we and objects are *isolated entities separately hanging in space*. Even so, all things have the same Mother and Father, namely Shakti and the fundamental ground state essence, and so they are part of one body, one unity, one whole. Shakti (which includes all forces and phenomena) and the fundamental essence permeate each other and constitute the entire universe – a duality of yin and yang. The whole of the cosmos exists as a single block of one thing: Shakti permeated by Parabrahman, supported by Parabrahman, or composed of Parabrahman that is essentially Parabrahman the unchanging fundamental substrate-substance.

To be "a sentient being with consciousness" really means that Knowledge within a physical body can be generated and reference itself in a self-reflexive arc. Knowledge (a set of thoughts) itself – and not an actual being, soul, entity, *atman* or life – is the ultimate experiencer of everything since it is always referencing itself in a loop in order to produce understanding. It produces the sense of a self, thoughts, interprets them, and produces a world of understanding. There is conceptualization and intellectualization going on, but no one who is doing the thinking. Knowledge is doing the thinking. Doing and thinking exist but there is no real doer or thinker, yet there is still doing, thinking, understanding and experiencing.

Yes, we have an experience of a bodily self, perspectival self, volitional self, narrative self and social self but there is actually no continuous, distinctive, intrinsic I-self within those experiences. These selves are constructed selves and not your true eternal self, and they appear not because they are inherently existing but because they are constructed by conditions. The experience of being a self is just an artificial construction of the brain developed through/by myriad conditions within the entire soup of Shakti whose intersection of agglomerations produce an apparent body-self-spirit. If there were no such thing as consciousness then due to the conservation of mass and energy you would just be some other portion of Shakti, which itself is also ultimately empty of inherent existence since Shakti depends on Parabrahman, the ultimate substrate. You are Shakti that is infinite and never-ending, and you are also the fundamental substrate that is infinite and never-ending. You are everything and you are nothing. Inherent emptiness is your true body, true self, true beingness, true self-nature and even your consciousness. This is the enlightenment view.

Again, there is no real *atman*, self or living entity that is the ultimate doer or experiencer of any thought or action. This is the teaching of the *Diamond Sutra*, and the view of enlightenment. You can even say that since there is no self *that it is the universe doing the experiencing and thinking*, or you can say that it is God doing (responsible for) everything, or that "Parabrahman is the ultimate Witness." It is actually the Knowledge created within a certain body that is doing all the thinking, knowing and understanding, and the process is happening automatically in a mechanistic fashion. Since that is Shakti, the universe, it is the universe that is doing all the thinking and experiencing and understanding. Since that is God it is God doing all the activity. Since it is the fundamental substrate then it is the fundamental ground state that is doing everything, but since It doesn't move we can say It is the causeless cause or Ultimate Witness, but It isn't witnessing anything since It isn't living and because nothing is actually happening. One might say that we are the modes or attributes of God identical with His essence and that the energies of God enable us/Him to experience something of the universe/Himself, but in actuality nothing is going on.

The I-thought of being a personal soul-self is therefore just a delusion or illusion. It is the illusion of a narrated dream, and yet you are indeed experiencing a (fictional) view of the world and a personal (apparent) existence. Within that existence (*sat*) that possesses consciousness (*chit*), you can seek out and experience peaceful states of contentment and bliss (*ananda*) such as when you *feel shine* (a state where you predominantly feel bliss-happiness and effortlessly exude this into the environment around you) or *flow* or the *vivid freshness of clear and sharp mental awareness* together with the feeling of being alive. Bliss states are comfortable mental-emotional-physical states where you are calm and balanced, clean and pure, as well as unperturbed because you are *absorbed* in an experience without mental distractions, dullness, scattering or confusion. This is also referred to as pristine clarity, which is a mind free of disturbances such as in a state of clear concentration that is also called empty mind. Actually, our natural state of mind is to be peaceful and happy until we disturb it and we practice meditation to learn this.

Meditation practice progressively takes you through a sequence of successively more refined mental states of calmness and concentration in which the mind becomes focused in clear concentration on the moment of awareness, which is called pristine clarity or "one-pointed-concentration." The beauty of emptying the mind of the coarse thought-stream while maintaining the state of awareness and presence is that this brings us closer to unity with the world of which we are part. The flow state of bliss is experienced in such a state of concentration.

On the other hand, extreme joy, peak experiences, pleasant sensations and feeling shine are temporary and thus unsatisfactory in the long run although very enjoyable, so as part of the Great Learning we should learn how to forgo attachment to any pleasant sensations arising due to our senses, which is called controlling our senses. What you are truly seeking is a mind-body equilibrium that frequently touches states of bliss (due to health and excellent internal Qi flow suffusing every cell) and always feels comfortable, peaceful, contented, full and satisfied, but where your mind is crystal clear and alert rather than dulled by satiation.

Because you have a body and mind you essentially have only physical and cognitive skills. Although earthly life does not last long, you must cultivate both your body and mind so that you can pursue and enjoy states of great lucidity (bright or luminous awareness), happiness, bliss, mental freshness or clear vivid alertness-awareness, flow, comfort, and fulfillment (that are absent of suffering) during your existence. You must learn to enjoy the immediate experience of presence. You must also cultivate your character so that you can exhibit virtuous, skillful conduct naturally and naturally give rise to states of mental and physical bliss.

Your thinking comes from your character, training and life experiences, which produces your behavior. You should try to maximize your longevity by cultivating healthiness in this life along with the higher transcendental spiritual bodies, and until you achieve the higher spiritual bodies the continuity of your existence will be maintained through the process of reincarnation that is administered by higher beings. When an Arhat's highest spiritual body finally dies, another type of continuity is that it will retain many of its attributes and memories after rebirth. These feats are all accomplished by cultivating the great miracle of Shakti that's yours, which is your consciousness.

People don't normally recognize that their sense of being a self is the result of infinite Shakti conditions coming together in the moment. They think that the certainty of being a self arises from actually having a solid, pure core conscious self or soul entity inside them. However, there is no such homogenous or permanent core self-entity within you. The "I" cannot exist without its various compositional factors so "I" does not refer to a standalone soul but a compositional structure. The "I" used in expression is meant to indicate that its underlying source is a soul or spirit, but that soul or spirit is a composite construction rather than an intrinsically solid entity free of separate parts and dependent arisings. You are a composite construction having consciousness, and the energy and interconnections that have gone into creating you are vast beyond measure and impermanent by nature. *Everyone is this way* because each individual phenomenon is just a woven spot within Shakti even though we look like independent packets moving in empty space.

Some cultivation schools teach that you should stop thinking of yourself as a body or person but as the entire universe, nothingness (empty space) or even universal consciousness to help you break your (limiting) identification with the physical body, which you are not. Sometimes, as taught by Hasidic master Dov Ber of Mezeritch, you are instructed to think that you are nothingness (emptiness), but you must recognize that absolute nothingness and absolutely everything (all things) are the same. Hence you are neither one nor the other, or you can say you are both, or you can say you are just one depending upon what you want to emphasize. The great miracle is that you have this great treasure of consciousness within all things that provides for you a world with qualities and the thought of being an I-self.

Within your consciousness there is indeed the sense of a narrating "you" (a self or observer) experiencing things (objects) that Buddhism calls the "residual conceit 'I am.'" This I-sense arises out of a particular anatomical composition that gives rise to conscious mental processes that are memory dependent, and which color their output with subjective projections of likes and dislikes, learned beliefs, accumulated prejudices and other subjectivities that do not objectively reflect reality. Your mind is not perfect (non-errant) in forming its conceptions about the world or reality, and there is no standalone soul involved within the processes of conception. In other words, our mind contributes subjective features to objects thus making our knowledge polluted/tainted; Knowledge automatically contributes features to objects that they may not have, and there is ultimately no doer or knower doing this other than (polluted, non-perfect) Knowledge itself. A mind sees the world through the filter of its collected passions, and thus wrongly projects impassioned concepts, perspectives and emotions onto situations, objects and people. Meaning is therefore subjective to the thinking mechanism.

In other words, thinking just happens but there is no one there thinking while it happens, and the thinking that arises is often errant or biased rather than objective. This is why we must learn how to correct our thoughts in life, and build up understanding (wisdom) to get better at thinking, decision-making (evaluating the best course of action with reason that is as free as possible form passion, prejudices and bias) and doing things. It is thinking that creates a (conception of a) separate self where there is none. During thinking, Knowledge is experiencing thoughts (knowledge), that's all, and the thoughts are a biased point of view that is often errant. One must always strive to correct these biases. Knowledge simply generates Knowledge in a process of Knowledge generation inherent to the living entity. The no-self-there Knowledge arising within a physical body (that is a component of the fabric of Shakti) is doing all the thinking and understanding and doing based on its accumulated Knowledge, its thinking processes and the influence of new sensory perceptions. Who understands this? No one – not a real (independent) person or being – yet understanding is still there.

Thoughts and perceptions are mental constructions that arise within a mind-body complex without there being a real observer, on-looker, doer, witness, person-agent, soul, *atman, jiva* or cognizer within the process. As Buddhaghosha stated, "There is suffering, but no one who suffers." As the *Diamond Sutra* says, "A Bodhisattva does not receive any rewards of merit because there is no self-concept that a soul, entity or being is there." There is absolutely no inherent being involved in the process of a giver giving a gift to a recipient either. There is just a process going on. And in the ultimate sense there is no process whatsoever.

Why all this emphasis on the creation of thoughts? Because when you achieve the subtle body you can shrink in size due to the *siddhi* power of *anima*, and one of the things you can do (as explained within the *Vimalakirti Sutra* and *Avatamsaka Sutra*) is go into people's brains and observe the processes that form thoughts and conceptions. This is why there is an emphasis on having you understand consciousness and the real nature of a human being. This is the training path of all devas wishing to become Bodhisattvas. Buddhas and Bodhisattvas learn how to influence people's thoughts and alter their internal energy, and so the process of thought-creation is stressed within many spiritual schools.

Various kinds of thoughts arise in response to different kinds of stimuli, but they all arise automatically, mechanically according to the laws of cause and effect ruling consciousness. We don't know those laws or principles that determine the stream of consciousness but they are there. Everything happening within the mind, and in the universe, is mechanical or automatic due to laws of cause and effect that rule all. Everything arises, is sustained, and dies away due to laws of cause and effect, including the contents of your consciousness. The fact that thoughts arise and then die away is liberating because this impermanence allows you the power to stop needless mental suffering whenever it automatically arises within us. You can learn to end it. One of the major tasks of a living being is *learning how to habitually manifest beneficial mental states rather than afflictive states of mind*, and how to end mental suffering and replace negative states with positive ones. *You must in life learn how to engineer the mental states you want and external conditions you want too.*

The universe generates phenomena like a vast, perfectly oiled machine operating according to all sorts of causality laws. Only the unmanifesting original nature without characteristics, which is like pure empty space, transcends the manifest cosmos and is without rules of transformation because it never transforms. It always stays the same as the one absolute reality pervading all of the universe as the ultimate substance-essence and/or support of the cosmos. Like phenomena that arise within it, thoughts are expressed in a particular moment when the laws that govern consciousness cause them to arise, and they are subsequently replaced by other thoughts due to those same laws. What arises within your mind does so because of the mechanical functioning of Knowledge. That is all. You may not know the laws of cause and effect that rule the generation of thoughts within consciousness, but they are operating all the time because consciousness is not random. Since consciousness naturally appears, the key is to therefore learn how to gain control of our consciousness/mind (the thought-stream) so that we can silence unwanted afflictions and suffering, thus taming our mind, and bring about more beneficial states of being.

Within our mind-stream is the I-thought that is at the center of our internal dialogue. Even though all sentient beings say "I" in reference to their body-self, saying "I" actually refers to your core self-nature, and therefore references the fundamental essence of the universe rather than just your body since that substratum is your true unchanging Self. In other words, when Reality has taken form through individuation you refer to It in language using the word "I." The Self must be understood as the true content of the content "I." The I-self we imagine ourselves to be is really the absolute whole looking at things through a particular point of view, which makes us the consciousness of the cosmos or mind of the self-nature.

Saying "I" is actually your True Self (the True Witness) announcing Itself. Or, the I-self can refer to the whole of Shakti the cosmos. Or, it can conventionally refer to your smaller body-mind complex, which is what we normally take it to mean. For all of us, we are just a fraction of the one aggregate consciousness of the universe and our innermost Self or true I-ness is the fundamental substratum of that Creation. The real I is your formless infinite true self-nature and you must transcend the outer forms of identity to arrive at your real Self.

At the deepest level, all men who say "I" are actually referring to this same self-nature ground state, and so we are all brothers and sisters due to this ultimate equality among men. We are indeed social equals – men and women of equal worth because God is equally present in all of us. You can honestly say, "The Self in me is the same Self in all," and must recognize that because of infinite interdependence or co-arising that you are again part of all people and they are part of you. You must recognize the truth of universal brotherhood and social equality because it is a fact, and should strive to bring this recognition to reality in the structure and functioning of society. The recognition of your lack of inherent, intrinsic selfness and your composite nature that arises due to infinite interrelationships should lead to less ego grasping, greed, violence, anger and more compassion if your life.

You can say that our "I" refers to all of Shakti, or you can take the "I" as conventionally referring to the individuation of body-mind that infers the conventional idea of an individual soul or spirit within your physical body. However, in actuality you are the unity that has become multiplicity. You are the fundamental ground, the fundamental substratum that has become Shakti, and your individuation as a composite being is a transient apparent self that lacks inherent status. Only through spiritual practice can you gain any degree of "immortal" standing.

Out of ignorance people see their I-ness as different from the ultimate I-ness or beingness in others. However, their ultimate self-nature *is* the same. Since our Is-ness is not different than the ultimate beingness of other humans – since the Self in oneself is the same Self in another and in everything – are we not then members of a universal brotherhood? Are we not related? Yes. Despite the differences between us as particular persons, all human beings share the unity of the same ultimate identity. All human beings, despite their differences as particular persons with different races, genders and so forth, are part of a grand unity of manifestation that shares in one ultimate nature, one fundamental essence. Zhuangzi therefore said, "Heaven, earth and I are born of one, and I am at one with all that exists."

Because we are therefore siblings do we not have a responsibility to help one another, or to help the body and consciousness of Shakti that we are part of in order to help our Self? Other sentient beings are equal to you in joy and sorrow. They all want happiness and an end to suffering. Although you cannot feel their pain because you do not yet possess a Supra-Causal or Immanence body, as training you should take them for your Self and act accordingly such as by practicing the Golden Rule of behavior. As training their pain should be considered equally yours, and you should try to work out ways to dispel the suffering of others for it is suffering just like your own.

Our very existence is connected to the whole world through the interdependence of interpenetration, and thus our existence is related to all beings and what they know and feel. Our existence is related to groups of greater and greater size such as our family, community, state, country and world, and we need to learn how to master our conduct and relationships within these greater and greater wholes that eventually include the whole of Shakti. Hence we should be careful in what we do and especially take care of others as well as the entire world because we are defined through the relationships.

Harming another is hurting yourself because others are all aspects of Shakti that is you, your body, your manifest self. Shakti is your body and you are its consciousness while other sentient beings are also a portion of Shakti's ultimate consciousness that is therefore *your consciousness*. You are the embodied Self, so why would you hurt others who are also your Self? It makes no sense to take the attitude through selfishness and ignorance that this is okay.

Understanding that you and the multiplicity of things are the same thing is called the *wisdom of equality*. If you understand the wisdom of equality you should now realize that you are perfectly equal to others in also being (part of) Shakti's body and consciousness, and your existence is not more intrinsic than others. Neither is your importance. You have ultimate equality with all men in being the original nature. You simply have different properties, skills, abilities or attributes than others and different functions or destinies. Some people may have more skills or ability than you, but you are perfectly equal to others in ultimate importance. Why would you then harm any of your brothers and sisters, or part of your ultimate body or its consciousness (which includes their sentient nature)? As an ethical rule, you should at the minimum refrain from doing to others what you would regard as an injury to one's self. You should regard "self" as your own small self-entity or your greater self of Shakti.

There isn't any independent nature in phenomena that makes something a separate self. There isn't any such thing as a self-so standalone living entity, being or life. There are only portions of Shakti we point to in space, which aren't permanent phenomena bordered absolutely (though they appear so), and we then conventionally say, "This is such and such." Those designations, configurations or identifications help us sustain our existence and occur within a stream of consciousness that is itself simply a flowing process of continuous transformations. That process is going on within a phenomenon called a living being that is part of Nature/Shakti rather than transcendental to the cosmos, and thus is inseparably linked with everything else in existence like a piece of taffy that is stretched infinitely in all directions. Within Shakti there are simply infinite processes simultaneously going on (where reality is itself neutral), and complex transformations evolving everywhere without any such true things as sentient beings or virtue or justice or a moral order, and as to Shakti itself, from the standpoint of the original nature the universe doesn't even exist. However, from the standpoint of conventional existence there are beings with consciousness, their consciousness gives consciousness to Shakti (makes the universe conscious), and through consciousness they can build moral worlds with meaning and significance.

Our most fundamental essence or truest Self, our core or true self-nature, is not the "little self" or "soul" of the apparent manifest individual we normally refer to as "I." It is the infinite, beginningless, primordial essence that is our self-so, uncaused, uncreated, always existent self-nature. The great power of consciousness ultimately came from this True Self of ours, and religions often teach meditation "without attributes" so that we try to mentally imitate the undifferentiated fundamental peacefulness of our ground state that is unfathomable by thoughts. No concept can capture It, so we must let go of concepts to be like It. This practice, over time, trains our consciousness to develop several desirable characteristics for life. For instance, some religions say that liberation is stabilizing yourself in your Real Self of perfect natural peacefulness while maintaining full conscious awareness. They say that bliss is attained by naturally imitating our original nature that is peaceful, without attachments, unperturbed and without any stains such as desires. Meditation thus becomes a method of calming oneself and developing a "blissful" inner peace free of stress.

This provides some clues on how to properly use our mind. The ordinary mind operates in a certain way, but most of us develop habits of incorrect usage that we must transform through self-cultivation practices. We have consciousness, we are consciousness (which is why the Zen school says "Mind is Buddha"), but society provides too few lessons on how to use the mind properly, such as how to change emotional states, other than a strong focus on causality and logic.[4] Cultivation is not just about learning moral rules and following ritualistic regulations (even though they have their importance in domesticating humans to control their wild animal nature) but involves learning how to use the mind rightly, skillfully, optimally because consciousness is all we have. Learning moral behavior is part of that training, but the actual training is about how to use consciousness in terms of the principles of correct thinking and behavior and virtue is one of the aspects of "correctness." There is no rulebook for how to operate a mind, but spiritual cultivation attempts to teach us how to use our consciousness correctly. Spiritual practices help to purify the mind of afflictions and through training teach you how to concentrate and consider correctly. They help you develop and gain control over the many processes and powers of consciousness and develop beneficial mental states. They help you purify and elevate your inner psychological terrain that is fraught with afflictions, unwanted defilements, prejudices and distortions due to the natural algorithms of consciousness, which can be corrected. This development of the human being is the path of the Great Learning that certainly includes the task of learning how to manage your mind (consciousness) and create peaceful or blissful mental states and environmental or personal conditions absent of suffering.

You are the embodied True Self that has somehow become an emanation within Shakti with the power to shape it. In spiritual cultivation it is common to use meditation practice to try to center in your inherent True

---

[4] See "Thinking Better - Critical Thinking" within *Buddha Yoga*.

Self unencumbered by your manifested body and consciousness, which means your mind is to become peaceful without identifying with your body-mind or distracted by the afflictions of bodily discomfort or mental wandering and suffering. You are to rest your mind in its natural state without thoughts, which is similar to our True Self that is free from attachment and desire and thus tranquil. This means cultivating through meditation practice a state of calm clear awareness that still allows thoughts to arise, rather than blocks them to achieve emptiness, just as the universe is naturally empty but produces phenomena without ever suppressing them. You abide in peacefulness while giving birth to consciousness and the knowing of thoughts since that is your natural function, and you don't rest in a state of thoughtless torpor or dullness as in sleep. As a being with consciousness you are to cultivate pristine awareness in life, which is the most enjoyable, blissful state of alert consciousness and living.

Shakti, the manifest universe, is one with the fundamental substrate, so by maintaining clear awareness of our mental doings we remain the active consciousness of Shakti *that we are meant to be* rather than the darkness of insentience. With clear awareness ("spiritual illumination" rather than "inert existence") we are to let things freely arise in our minds, remain free of fusion and open to correction, adjust what is wrong or improper, and should remain free of unwanted distractions and involuntary perturbations during active engagement so that we do not lose our state of pristine experience. In this way our consciousness can experience peaceful flow and the most enjoyable states of beingness.

The idea that our original nature is pure and formless, without attributes, is posed as the ideal mental state (one of peacefulness) achievable through meditation practice, but this does not mean that you should be thoughtless because then a world of qualities would not appear. It just means that the natural state of the mind should remain active and aware but empty of coarse narration and distractions or afflictions and thus able to alternate between clear concentration and absorption or peaceful bliss, calmness and purity. No-thought at its extreme (where there isn't even any recognition of the world) is wrong because it means a lack of consciousness that is a denial of your structural function, and is equivalent to non-existence as a sentient being. Meditation practice is not to be this way. Its purpose is to create the habit of self-observation so you can correct yourself, and to help you develop skills to eliminate mental afflictions.

The ideal mental state is where the mind is calm (unperturbed), perfectly pristine, clear and lucid, and quiet/empty of distracting afflictions so that it can concentrate (become absorbed) within experiences. The perfect mental state is a state of flow where the mind experiences the present moment with a feeling of fullness and subtle bliss, where there is a merging of action and awareness, where the mind is pristinely clear and knows what it is doing, and where the mind remains unperturbed by challenges and not agitated by distractions because it is blissfully absorbed in the experience and forgets egoistic feelings. In this state of flow there is effortless concentration and the optimal performance of tasks, and you lose yourself in your activities because it is such an enjoyable state of high focus and high performance. It is like being really, really present in the current moment where the world seems to come more alive and the annoying chatter of the inner monkey mind is silenced.

During "flow" or "being in the zone" the I-thought seems silent (there is a loss of reflective self-consciousness and a diminishing of the wandering inner narrative), and you are present so fully that you "are lost in your work" which means that you lose the sense of self in what you are doing. Your effort appears effortless because it seems devoid of a person "doing" it. However, there is a great sense of engagement, absorption, competency or agency (effortlessness) over the task at hand that is experienced with great immersion. There is an intrinsic pleasure – a subtle bliss – in being immersed within your activities and with being in sync with what you are doing where your thoughts don't get in the way of that enjoyment. The world becomes a more enjoyable adventure rather than a problem to be overcome if you can tap into this state as your way of being.

You can cultivate this state during life, *which is spiritual practice*, but it requires that you cultivate both your mind and body, especially your breathing, physical health, concentration and inner Qi flow. Spiritual cultivation therefore requires daily yoga practice and/or martial arts or other exercises so that you stretch all your muscles to improve your body and inner Qi flow; various forms of pranayama work to flood the body with oxygen and Qi; inner *nei-gong* work; and mindfulness, self-observation and awareness practice so that you practice being in the moment and from that absorption can more easily enter into the state of flow.[5] If you stay with the moment of

---

[5] To actually cultivate this achievement one should adjust their spine through chiropractic techniques to make sure all bones are aligned and nerve/disc impingements eliminated; undergo bodywork modalities to fix any muscle problems; daily stretch all muscles (through yoga, martial arts, dance, etc.) so that the Qi flow within them (which is connected on consciousness) becomes smooth and optimal; through pranayama practices increase lung capacity, pump Qi throughout the body using breath, open your Qi channels fully, and change your breathing patterns to the more optimal 5.5 second inhalation and 5.5 second exhalation pattern (which works out to about 5.5 seconds per breath that is the

presence all the time, or live in the "I am" every moment, you can create the state of flow presence that produces a life with quality. This is the mindset of enlightenment people strive for which involves pristine mental clarity and awareness, tranquility, happiness, detachment and bliss.

When you "feel shine," that happy blissful state is also a type of flow state dominated by the emotion of happiness, joy, bliss or glow. Most spiritual practice neglects the body, but to experience the state of flow you must put effort into optimizing your body's health (which requires diet and exercise) and optimizing the internal Qi circulation within your body through *nei-gong* practice, pranayama work and similar exercises.

An idea sometimes posited is that clear, lucid awareness is "pure consciousness" that is entirely empty and free of thoughts, and so we should be cultivating this über-awareness "absence of thoughts" state that is like the Unmanifest ground state of reality that is free of any qualities. Actually, *all consciousness is "pure consciousness"* because all consciousness is purely, solely consciousness (thoughts). Quiet consciousness that is awake but seems empty of thoughts (including the defilements of the passions or negative emotions) – and which some people take as being "pure consciousness" since it seems empty – is still chock full of fine thoughts such as the automatic recognition of objects made possible due to silent mental processing "done in the dark." Our automatic cognitive biases, for instance, flow silently into prejudicing our overt consciousness due to preprogrammed conditioning rules we've developed over time, and this

---

pattern of most prayers and mantras); improve your posture so that you are always sitting or standing erect so that your Qi effortlessly proceeds up your spine directly into your brain, and center your Qi within your body so that you always feel centered and it always reaches the back of your brain, especially the cerebellum; train in *nei-gong* exercises to move the Qi within your body everywhere to wash and keep frictionless its inner circulatory patterns; perfect your diet so that it does not become an impediment to mental clarity, health or life; regularly undergo yearly body detoxification regimes to remove accumulated poisons from the body that would affect its health and functioning; eliminate internal blood clots and circulatory obstructions (and improve blood flow to the brain) such as through the use of supplements like nattokinase, ginkgo biloba, bromelain, Vitalzym, etc.; train in various forms of meditation to clarify the quietness and alertness of the mind; learn mindfulness, improve your ability to concentrate and perfect other mental abilities (so that you can always be peacefully engaged in the moment); train in virtue and consummate conduct while striving to eliminate one's shortcomings; train in detachment and so forth. Nothing can bring lasting happiness in life, but it's already there in the nature of a tranquil mind (the mind's true nature free of disturbances) that when engaged with situations is within a state of flow. Suffering cannot be totally eliminated in our existence but we can pursue well-being in life.

happens below our ordinary level of awareness. In fact, the bulk of our cognition is unconscious (automatic or involuntary). For instance, if the internal dialogue within your mind is quiet but you are still experiencing the image of the world then there is still mental activity going on even if your mental state seems empty of internal dialogue otherwise there cannot be any recognition of objects. The meaning of "pristine clear awareness" or "lucid clarity" (bright mind) is that your internal mental dialogue seems somewhat silent but you know (are aware of) the contents of your mind and the activities of your body clearly. This is the proper use of consciousness – *clarity in knowing its contents!* The Great Learning also requires you to train yourself to properly and optimally use consciousness (for mental and physical behavior) in the ways required for any circumstance.

If you suddenly found yourself without the possibility of thoughts, how would the world appear to you? Would you see a world of qualities? Could you recognize anything at all? You wouldn't be able to cognize any objects to recognize anything, which is the same as being in a coma or deep dreamless sleep. There would be no world of manifestation without an I-self or conceptions or without process of discrimination/differentiation, and without those elements it is as if you have no existence, which is a state of no-thought. Without thoughts, there would be no perception of anything. Is this not the condition of inanimate matter, which is most of the universe? What a treasure is the knowingness of consciousness!

As a living being with consciousness your proper functioning within the universe entails using your mind properly that you are designed to possess as an attribute rather than negating it through suppression or abandonment in some way. You should strive to master it and bring its powers to full glory. In the universe all things have form and function; function follows form, and form gives rise to function. Your structure or form gives rise to consciousness, and the highest use of that function is to use it fully, blissfully, skillfully, properly, virtuously, optimally to fullest measure for marvelous accomplishment. Incorrect spiritual cultivation is when you dull or cut off the functioning of your consciousness to "become empty" unless it is naturally resting as required such as in deep sleep. You should be training your consciousness to use it better and more fully.

Proper cultivation is to tame consciousness, purify consciousness, master consciousness, optimize consciousness's functioning and develop all the possible abilities of consciousness to levels of great skillfulness … for your benefit, the benefit of others and for the benefit of the world and universe at large. This is the genuine spiritual path. What else would it entail? Mastering consciousness includes mastering your mental states which includes the ability to get rid of mental events that afflict consciousness such as bad emotions, recurrent thought afflictions, addictions, irritations and so forth. It includes mastering your behavior since behavior is the expression of your thoughts. Your behavior should not only be skillful, compassionate and kind but guided by wisdom, which is a product of your Knowledge and thinking processes as well. Since thoughts are the root of behavior, mastering behavior involves mastering your thoughts (the operations of consciousness), and changing the patterns of your perspectives and habit energies that give birth to your thoughts, actions and behavior.

What you see as objects in the world are only appearances within your mind. They are a representation only, a similitude, a creation of your consciousness. They are mind-only. The universe (to you) is therefore but a state of consciousness; what you see is only a projection of your mind. A world is outside of you and you can derive causality laws about its nature and make materialist assumptions about its behavior that can be confirmed. However, you only experience what is outside you *within your consciousness as a representation of that outside world* and somehow consciousness inverts the picture so it looks like you are experiencing an external world. Your mind pretends that the objects are "out there" in order that they can be appropriated and you can then go about maintaining the continuity of your existence.

What you experience is just an approximation of the world within your mind where you add subjective qualities to the view that don't exist in the pure picture. We always add emotions on top of stark reality where those emotions are conditioned by our existing concepts we have internalized. In short, *we experience a Maya of our own making*. Funny, isn't it? Consciousness has faults, and yet despite its deficiencies it is the greatest possible treasure – the knowingness of one's experience of existence and the universe – whose worth is beyond all other treasures. Who knows how other species experience their own version of consciousness?

You cannot experience anything outside the theater of your mind. The whole world you experience is a happening inside your mind (but of course the events are outside of you). Knowledge of your self is constructed in your consciousness too just as the world is constructed in your consciousness. To you the world is your mind only and what you experience as objects are actually mere concepts rather than the things in themselves. The images in your consciousness are to you the world but they are not the actual world because they are simplified internal mental representations that you somehow invert so they seem outside of you. In other words, *consciousness is only conceptualization so it never reaches real things.*

The world we each see is thus illusory, a make-believe representation, Maya, a story in our brain generated by millions of neurons, each a tiny biological machine that together with vitality generate the mind of mental states and conscious experiences. We only have so much sensory input, mental processing capability and memory storage space but there is so much more outside of the mind than we can take in and represent as our version of reality. Through consciousness you never experience the real world, you only experience your own mind containing abbreviated simplified pictures. Furthermore, what occurs to you is a very limited product of your own mental tendencies that has additional qualities or judgments you've appended that don't exist in the real world, but do for you because of your prior conditionings (experiences that have formed Knowledge). We add feelings onto the facts of reality but they are not the objective truths of reality.

The map of reality within your consciousness is not the reality. It is only an imperfect representation lacking true fidelity. It is a construction of mental objects that represents the real world, and thus indeed builds a world for you, but the picture is faulty in various ways. All things that appear to you are a transformation of your mind, a construction or fabrication within your consciousness that is composed together with your I-thought, and those thoughts build a conventional world for you. However, there is no sentient being involved in all this building of images or thoughts. There is only Knowledge that is experiencing Knowledge and no self is involved. Without consciousness you could not know thoughts or sensory images of things, and so they only exist for you because you possess the attribute of consciousness. For you things appear one way and for different animal species they appear another way.

When the mind arises (from sleep) then thoughts stir, and the mind then creates fabrications such as phenomenal objects. The mind creates reality, and when the mind stops arising then the universe ceases *for that knower,* who then also consciously ceases to exist because at that point there is no sentience/knowing. When Knowledge disappears - as knower and the process of knowing the known (objects) - then the universe disappears for that Knowledge. Then you have peacefulness or rest that is similar to the original nature.

The absolute nature of Knowledge and the universe of countless things always reside in an absolute state of unmoving suchness, stillness, purity, emptiness or perfection. That is the absolute nature, fundamental substratum or True Reality of the conventional world. Eternal, pure, uncreated, non-moving ... all things appear moving but ultimately reside in this state. Fundamentally speaking, there is nothing that can be known of the fundamental nature because it is absent of attributes just like the stainless emptiness of space. Furthermore, since It is absolute there cannot be a knower of It and thus It cannot be an object of perception. No concept can capture It. Thus it is unfathomable by thought, beyond all conceptions and experience.

If you think about the Unthinkable One you only have recourse to a form of thought. It is only the fabrications within the mind that let you become aware of an apparent world that you make for yourself (to represent objects outside of you). Of course that worldview works for you because its survivalist nature and attributes have developed over the course of evolution, but those thought constructions cannot possibly reflect the full attributes of Shakti there in front of you. An abbreviated similitude or representation is all you ever see/experience that is therefore in reality an illusion. Parabrahman is unfathomable, and what you perceive of Shakti is a falsity saturated with the principles of your own mental organization rather than an absolute true cognition of the world, so you have no power to grasp the world in itself. It too ultimately remains beyond cognition.

Animals which share the same basic anatomical structure create very similar mental representations of the world within their consciousness because of what Buddhism calls "shared karmic seeds," which basically means they share the same physiological structure and sensory apparatus that gives rise to their similar consciousness processes and a shared perspective of reality. Humans create a worldview within their consciousness that is somewhat similarly calibrated from individual to individual even though you might also say that there are as many realities as there are individuals due to each person's unique differences. Basically, humans typically share many agreed upon definitions for interpreting their internal worldview. Other beings see/represent and experience the world differently from us, some in better ways and some in worse. They have different structures to their nature of awareness, to their kind of conscious experience. They experience a different view of reality than ours. Who can say which is best?

Even within the human species there are some who can see more, hear more and differentiate tastes better than others as well as those who think differently in marvelous ways. What we have is not what is optimal or that which creates a truest representation of the world, but what evolution has produced for fitness, which means for the task of survival. We construct within consciousness a Maya of external reality that has consistencies that allow our survival. Hence, we do not perceive nor understand reality perfectly or best. Our task is to therefore use our consciousness *as best as possible*, despite any of its problems or limitations, and train it to function better. That is spiritual cultivation. Spiritual cultivation is not about worshipping gods or deities but about this: mastering the human condition in the highest possible manner.

At any moment of time, when alive and awake you are only experiencing your own mind rather than the world, you are only experiencing the conceptions of your consciousness and nothing more than that. Buddhism calls this Mind-Only, Consciousness-Only, or Mere-Representation. All you can ever experience are your own thoughts, emotions, sensations and representations of Shakti. As to experiencing Shakti, everything you see or experience is really *only in your own mind*. Our experience of life is an appearance within our mind so it is a "functioning of our mind" – an experience produced by mental functions – but of course this doesn't mean that there aren't phenomena and a universe external to us. It is just that our representation of the universe and objects is faulty and incomplete, thus Maya. For each of us, consciousness is all there is. *It is the only thing there is for us* because without it there is no self, no world, nothing at all except the oblivion of insentience. If consciousness did not exist in the universe then for each of us there would be nothing at all because none of us would exist in a fundamental sense. It is this light of illumination (knowing) that separates us from darkness and makes us special in the universe.

Your conscious experiences are shaped at all levels not just by your biology but by your prior experiences that have caused you to develop particular habits of thinking (patterns of operational consciousness, such as special mindsets or perspectives) unique to you. This includes particular patterns in your way of being (your character, personality and disposition) and within your mechanism of mental processing such as special ways of looking at things and specific likes and dislikes or other emotional flavors that you append to phenomena. You can even train your mind-stream to develop a particular perspective or filter through which you view life and your experiences, and thereby create a certain disposition in yourself as your core way of being. Choosing how/what to become and then working to develop those characteristics and that type of being is also a type of spiritual practice. This is the essence of spirituality, as is cultivation of your transcendental bodies, perfection of your mental processes and mental states, and perfection of your behavior (which includes your goals and activities).

Our own specific way of humans being conscious is just one possible way of being conscious out of innumerable possibilities for sentient consciousnesses. The common human way of experiencing consciousness due to "shared karmic seeds," which is based upon our specific human anatomy (with its limitations) and our social training, makes it possible for us to form communities for our survival and prosperity. An individual cannot live alone in isolation, but exists by depending on a community of others. He requires society for his survival, his protection/defense, his flourishing and his happiness and well-being.

The spiritual path and Great Learning therefore not only require personal self-development but learning how to match with others and assist in the functioning of society where it is required that everyone conform to certain standards that promote cultural uniformity, social cohesion and contribute to our overall welfare. *Everyone* must cooperatively collaborate to produce the net flourishing of society within a shared culture, and so social connections with others are a necessity for our survival. This is where the rules of propriety and good conduct come into play, for these are invented standards within a neutral universe where we are the ones who must invent the moral order and proper way of doing things. Living in societies requires adopting similar values, virtues and rules of propriety that are disseminated by law, by society, by culture and by religion. Because we share a consensus reality we can and do achieve this for our survival. Most other living species cannot match with us because they share a type of mental reality different from our own.

In other words, humans have a general common way of experiencing reality different from other species such as insects or fish. Furthermore, each one of us possesses our own individual way of experiencing (consciousness) that is uniquely particular to us within the general schema of human consciousness. Hence there is no "one truth" to experiencing the world or viewing a matter. Each of us sees the world with a different viewpoint, and yet there is a certain enough shared commonality that we can trust one another to live and thrive together peacefully. We must create certain common standards so that we can do this, and they often appear as religious commandments or codes of conduct and propriety used to unite us so that "I" can live with "We." The way forward must be built up out of a collection of different viewpoints in society, which must therefore share a certain minimum similarity of views, and there must also be a certain measure of tolerance for other viewpoints since we all think differently and experience the world a bit differently.

The general schema of human consciousness – our way of processing sensory events and producing mental states – produces a common consensus reality, but we all have our own unique perspectives and some unique processing styles, and sometimes this is even due to small anatomical differences between us. Brain injuries, for instance, are a major cause of psychiatric illness that ruins people's lives, but brain rehabilitation programs can often restore any loss of anatomical function due to troubled brains and stop people from needless suffering or doing bad things that arise from abhorrent dysfunctions in consciousness. Aside from such cases and other exemptions, we typically share many similarities with others in how we think and process sensory phenomena, and this is mostly due to our shared biological mechanisms, common algorithms for producing consciousness (the thought-stream), as well as common social conditionings from culture and education.

Here is an example of human conditioning. Tell me which shape is rounder, "Kiki" or "Bouba"? The question is nonsensical, but because of prior conditionings that associate auditory sounds with visual perceptions (sound-shape associations we have already formed internally), most people would say that "Bouba" is rounder than "Kiki," which many people imagine as being spikey due to sharp inflections in the sound of the word. If you think about it carefully, you will realize that neither sound should be preferred when naming the two shapes, and *it is only due to conditioning* that most of us develop the same preference. Another example of conditioning is the fact that the only thing you hear by virtue of having ears is sound. Only through training, learning or conditioning (the formation of memories or Knowledge) do you give sounds meaning and recognize what sounds are. You can hear a sound, but conditioning enables you to recognize it is a bird, or even that it is a specific type of bird. Otherwise sounds are just noise.

Your mind is your world of reality, and that reality is created based upon your nervous system, memories, perceptions, and thoughts that all work together to generate a world of qualities that appears within your consciousness. We experience the world through the patterns of human consciousness, and so we see the landscapes of the world in the particular way unique to humans. However, beyond the perception of our senses is a hidden world of qualities of which we are unaware. Other beings, such as animals and insects, see and experience the world differently than we do (and are sometimes aware of some hidden qualities), which creates their own species worldview.

For instance, colors are not necessarily properties of things but the way objects appear to us because of (the anatomical limitations of) our eyes and brains; they are a way we perceive objects through a composition that the brain makes so that we can extract meaning from the world. Some animals can perceive colors and others cannot, and of those who can see colors, some are limited in the colors they can perceive and others can see even more than humans. Individuals also see the world somewhat differently from each other due to anatomical eye differences in their rods and cones although we share extremely similar methods of perceptual construction and conceptual fabrication due to our common structure.

Your own five senses certainly don't provide a full picture of the world because they don't provide a picture for you of all the forces that create for you the destiny of a moment. What you see is only an approximation, simplification, similitude or mere-representation due to your sensory and mental limitations. It is a computation your brain makes so that you can make meaning of the world for the purposes of survival and thriving, and not for completeness or bliss and enjoyment. The world you see, which is constructed in your head, provides you with a very abbreviated representation but you think that this is the way the world is when it isn't. Your viewpoint is subjective, limited, an approximation and thus delusional.

You create within your mind a limited reality of images and conceptions that is incomplete (because you don't have infinite knowledge since the finite cannot encapsulate the infinite) and simplified (because the true texture of the world is infinitely complex) and your mental processing even causes that image to be lagged because you must decipher your perceptions of whatever you are experiencing as the present moment. Your brain, which is the organ of intellect, may even be damaged and therefore process information incorrectly. You might also have faulty sense organs, such as cataracts in the eyes or suffer from color blindness, which distort your sensory intake of the world *before* you superimpose extra mental garbage onto your perceptions to further pervert them. Basically, there is so much more outside of the little illusion we take for reality inside our minds. You create and superimpose a Maya upon the world, but the illusion of Maya you create enables you to survive and thrive. Evolution created it for fitness, not for fidelity or truthfulness.

Our past experiences (conditioning) that have been stored in our brain neurons as memories (Knowledge) create preferred patterns in thought processes and mental states, and these influences fashion our experiences to a profound degree. Prior experiences, teachings, environmental influences and other types of conditioning create patterns and paradigms within the brain's neurons that become part of our software of mental analysis and response, namely our thinking. *Our past experiences condition/configure our mind to work in a certain way and that way produces the biased way we experience the world and behave.* We must train our consciousness to analyze using the highest reasoning abilities that transcend the biases and faults of automatic mental processes so that we can use consciousness at its best, and so that our decision-making consequentially produces wiser, more skillful and more effective behavior. For instance, emotions tend to completely color our experiences and we can become those emotions if we are not careful. We must learn to eschew passions, emotional taints, biases and afflictions to reason through the best course of action for every situation, and then execute whatever actions were judged to be best. This is one of the tasks of self-cultivation! Spiritual cultivation is not about worship, it is about self-cultivation of objectives such as this. For instance, viewed in this light we can say that selfless service on behalf of others, with the right feeling and attitude, is a form of worship (to divinity) and spirituality.

In other words, your mind already possesses memory content, which creates patterns for your thinking and behavior that are based on prior experiences and conceptions. You should, through self-cultivation, strive to correct any inappropriate or sub-optimal models of thinking and behavior that you have developed based on prior experiences or training and replace them, through new personal training, with more optimal models. This is the essence of self-cultivation, which you can view as self-improvement. When you perceive something similar to your past experience the perception, via pattern matching, triggers memories associated with the experience so that old patterns you've developed arise to color your experience, give you related thoughts, and guide your behavior. Our past experiences teach us how to act and they condition our mind to experience the world in a certain biased way. This is what we must always strive to correct through refinement and elevation.

Most all our behavior doesn't happen willy-nilly. Our conduct, behavior and activities are determined in reference to our prior conditioning that has patterned our thinking processes and decision-making to operate in a certain way. We learn to think a certain way and do things in a certain way because of the shaping influences of our parents, culture, religion, society, environment, prior experiences, training and so forth. Because of the conditioning of our religion, culture, environment, relationships, etcetera we adopt behavioral rules, regulations and moral principles for our behavior that we absorb from those influences, and then those patterns become part of our psyche. Our internal mental patterns and beliefs can actually hinder our natural Qi/Prana flow because of the connection between our thoughts and our Qi/Prana. They become like a program, wrapping, coating, or layer of limiting beliefs within us that affects our internal Qi/Prana circulation. For instance, natural confidence often becomes covered by learned patterns of tension and fear reactivity, and when those mental limitations (limiting patterns) are removed our natural confidence returns and an individual may feel a surge of energy and vitality. If you eliminate the appropriate wrong beliefs then your life can improve dramatically.

Certain types of experiences and other forms of conditioning can affect our personalities deeply by creating peculiar internal patterns and algorithms for thinking and doing. Conditioning can even create personality constraints within us that stifle the free flow of our internal vital energy. Thus, conditioning affects your thoughts, your inner Qi/Prana flow and your outer behavior which is why you need to improve your character/psyche and work on getting rid of flaws to improve your health, your relationships, your life enjoyment (bliss) and your fortune. This is the science of happiness. One of the needs for society is to create moral educational systems that condition our thinking and behavior in ways that: encourage peaceful coexistence with one another; produce prosperity, stability, contentment and well-being; improve our health and vitality; and free our creativity rather than stifle us through various methods of forced oppression. The rules of propriety are needed to create peace and order within society while also enriching our lives. They should also allow us to express creative individualism and personal freedoms free of excessive constraints and compatible with the freedoms of others in society so we can each pursue and perfect our own unique wisdom, skills and ways outside of social conformity, yet they should also help us to build up society and drive it forward. They should allow the freedom of individual self-actualization and personal growth, help us to accent the good in society, optimize human progress and happiness, and advance society to a brighter future.

Feeling *truly alive in the moment* is to experience a subtle state of energizing bliss with a subtle tinge of joy or alertness whilst enjoying utmost mental clarity in a state of perfect presence. That enlivening state should seem new, fresh and free of any robotic tendencies of dullness, which prevents you from sleepwalking through life. This state of captivating, thrilling aliveness becomes possible when your internal vital energy becomes full and internally free and your mind-stream – due to mindfulness or pristine awareness – becomes engulfed in the present moment of NOW. You want to cultivate a mental realm of presence free of afflictions, fogginess, confusion, scattering, dullness, waywardness or the monkey mind of distractions. Your attention sinks into the present moment and obviates all other concerns.

Our goal in life as beings of consciousness should be to live in a vivid state of clear presence like this – absolute living stainless awareness that is accompanied by a tinge of subtle physical bliss/vitality from the body. A vivid state of presence means that your mind is extremely clear and quiet and abides centered in an undistracted state of flow that seems pristinely focused. Because of that calm, centered mind and the stainless clarity of attention you become free of attachment to or entrainment with lower influences that naturally arise in the mind (such as impulses or desires) because you transcend that thought-stream with meta-awareness that doesn't identify with your thoughts. Therefore you can break any autopilot, robotic entrainment with your thought-stream to do what is more living, creative, skillful, right and appropriate (virtuous) in every moment, and thereby manifest irreproachable consummate conduct with elegance. You don't have to become identified with your thoughts but can transcend them and then give rise to noble, consummate, spiritual behavior.

The highest mode of life is to live in this mode and to return to it immediately whenever you recognize you are out of sync. Meditation trains you how to do this. It teaches you how to be aware of the present moment because *the reality of life is always now*. Consciousness is your existence, your existence is this present moment of awareness, and you should take care that your awareness is fully actively engaged with reality in the present moment. Meditative mindfulness teaches you not to become lost in wayward distractions that cloud the mind or walk around in a fog of dullness or confusion. Since consciousness is the great miracle of existence, the present moment is a good enough reason to be happy; you need not wait for happiness to happen in the future due to some imagined Utopia of perfect conditions. You must learn to enjoy the movements of life in the present moment, which is true spiritual practice and the Great Learning of Life. Unfortunately, too often our attention becomes captured by the wrong things and bound up in petty concerns rather than connected to the present moment where it can find fulfillment.

The feeling of full living, active living or fully feeling alive that we all seek comes from absorption in the moment while obviating all other concerns because to do this requires that your Qi flows in a more perfect way, and that Qi flow will excite your body cells to a state of inner bliss and joy and enter your head more directly. It will especially flow through the occipital lobe and cerebellum. Only meditation work and inner Qi practice can help you achieve this mode of being so that it becomes a natural feature of your character. You only have to practice paying attention to the present moment closely enough so that you're not doing anything to it (by adding extra garbage like judgments onto the experience) and then you are experiencing the bliss of existence. If you connect with the present moment, which involves an optimal circulation of your Qi within your brain and body, you can actually find fulfillment.

Through our senses we experience things imperfectly (things are not perceived absolutely correctly) and incompletely because we lack infinite sensorial capabilities, infinite knowledge, and the mental processing within our brains is faulty in many ways too. We think and act imperfectly because our conceptual processes *and our Qi/Prana circulation* also have faulty biases. In short, what we generally believe to be the raw inarguable aspects (objective facts) of existence are images formed within our minds whose formation is deeply constrained by our biological capabilities and the processing mechanisms of our consciousness. We never see/experience the world but only see an internal mental representation of the world due to a network of neuronal processing unique to humans that is species-specific. *We never see the world as it really is, but only according to how we are.* We only experience Mind-Only, a mere-representation or similitude of the world. *We never see/experience the real world directly; we only experience our mind.* Our thinking processes and intellect are supposed to be rational logical processes but even our conceptual processing is at times faulty, errant, and biased too. What a mess to be enmeshed in false, errant thoughts everywhere! How much is the need for self-cultivation to right what can be righted in the usage of our mind.

It is not that the world/universe is made of consciousness or some such unknowable thing, but that *the world we see/experience* is a mental product within our consciousness. We are never dealing directly with the world or objects but with our mental ideas/images of objects. Externally there are still objects, phenomena, or things-in-themselves that exist whether or not we personally exist to perceive them, but for us they don't exist if we don't personally exist, if we are inanimate objects lacking consciousness, or if we are sentient but lack the required sense organs of perception or requisite conceptual processes. It is not that the base layer of reality is consciousness but that we can only experience consciousness-only, our minds. All we can ever experience through knowing are internal conceptualizations constructed through the algorithms that rule the processes of our consciousness, and most of this is not under our voluntary control.

It isn't that anything doesn't exist in the outside world of the universe, but that we don't know what the full and true properties of things *actually are* because they appear through the filter of limited sense organs and consciousness. Of course what we have, imperfect as it is, is better than insentience, for the illumination of consciousness is the great treasure of the cosmos, the wish-fulfilling gem of the universe that grants you cognizance and the ability to do and experience whatever you want. But what you cognize is an imperfection, an illusion, a representation, a delusion, a Maya superimposition on the real. Yet, one cannot complain for this is the great gift of experiencing life. What will you do with this great gift of experiential conscious life? How can you maximize it? You certainly wish to avoid pain, suffering and unhappiness as well as experience pleasurable sensations, but what will ultimately give your life true meaning and satisfaction?

This is something you must decide for yourself as you must make your own place in the universe. With consciousness you have freedom of thought and action *and through your thoughts, deeds and interactions with other people thereby become the center of your destiny.* Using the capacities of consciousness you can ferret out truth and act more wisely and skillfully. If you take responsibility for your living and behave rightly you can then escape some types of suffering and experience higher and more enjoyable states of existence, but this requires wisdom, skillfulness and personal effort. Although you are just Shakti, using reason and relying on values, virtues and moral ideals you can find your place in the world and a purpose to your existence within relationships involving greater and greater wholes such as your family, friendships, community, state, country, world and universe. You can find your meaning and life purpose in relation to groups, as is the philosophy of *Ubuntu* in Africa, and through utter dedication to noble causes. When you find your life purpose you will remain strong, motivated and unaffected by problems, challenges and suffering or setbacks in life.

While a world of phenomena does indeed exist outside of you, it is an existence whose appearance is only seen/experienced because you have a mind (consciousness) to know it. Your mind has formed various (limited or imperfect) sensory images of it and has thoughts that interpret those objects, marks or signs to give them meaning. Thus, you form the perspective of conventional reality in your mind (a human Maya of the universe that is the human way of perceiving reality) and thereby "experience the/a world" through the great miracle of consciousness. It is not the way the world truly is, but it is the way the human species sees it and that representation, however faulty it might be, is still the great miracle of consciousness that separates you from ultimate darkness! Every human mind will see the world differently because each individual will think differently than the next and color whatever they perceive by their own emotions and past experiences that become entangled with their mind-stream, so the world and universe we see are *conditional* constructions, *dependent* constructions that have no absolute meaning other than what we ascribe to them. Even so, the illumination of consciousness is still the greatest miracle of the cosmos!

Every being experiences life conditionally, which means dependent upon various conditions such as its prior memories of experiences, its quality of sensory apparatus, the thoughts generated at the moment, as well as the emotional construction of the organism. What you experience in the present moment is your past conditioning interpreting the present. Despite everyone's conditioning being different because of unique past experiences, as stated beings of the same species will share enough commonalities in their perceptual sensory apparatus, nervous system structure and thinking processes/systems to create mind-streams in a somewhat similar fashion and will think somewhat similarly due to shared cultural training, otherwise they could not harmoniously communicate with each other and get along well enough to live together in cooperative, collaborative communities that thrive.

Knowledge is generated by knowing and knowing, awareness, cognition, conception, intellect, discrimination or illumination involves the master self-thought "I," sensory perceptions, conceptions (thinking, thoughts or intellectual operations), and the memories of names and forms (a framework of designations) that help differentiate and identify everything. You should think of memories as records of our experiences that are retained within our organism in order to contribute features to objects and differentiate a field of chaos into meaning.

Comprehension is capable of being stored in the body in the form of thoughts or images, that comprehension is called memory, and it serves as a foundation for conceptual meaning and behavior. Memory is essentially a set of names, labels and forms (patterns) built up over time from experience and applied to new appearances within the mind to derive new recognitions and conceptions. It lets us distinguish, differentiate, identify, recognize or make sense of phenomena within consciousness that then provides the fodder for new states of consciousness. It is the foundation of cognition, understanding, comprehension, discrimination, illumination or Knowledge, without which nothing can be recognized or known. Without memories of "forms, names and labels" that we project upon phenomena chaos would be our field of perception, meaning nothing at all. Without the illumination of a consciousness that discriminates there is no world, nor forms or shapes ... nothing at all.

Perception of the world, which produces Knowledge, is basically the result of a process of informed guesswork. To perceive the world the brain works as a prediction engine to combine sensory inputs/signals with memories (prior expectations/beliefs on the way the world is) through pattern matching to make a best guess as to what has caused those signals. Perceptual recognition of an object is a type of best guess pattern matching algorithm. Subjectively perceived bundles of sensations are turned into objects through logical constructions that reference our memories, and that's how we see "objects." That's how we create a world within our mind and it all happens within our brain.

In other words, the brain does not hear, see, smell or feel the outside world but mechanistically constructs perceptions of objects and phenomena in response to external stimuli according to available neural algorithms that have constraints. Processes generate consciousness. The brain is stimulated into creating an image of the world which accords with the limits of its processing powers and the raw information it receives. The final design of that constructed image is constrained by the limitations of the brain. Reality is an internal picture constructed by the activation of neuronal patterns in the brain. Furthermore, neuroscience teaches us that the picture it paints is sometimes wrong (and certainly dimensionally incomplete) for a variety of reasons. For instance, it sometimes shows us things (creates internal images) that are not true because it thinks that is the way we should see them. Nonetheless, even though imperfect our consciousness still gives us the marvelous sense of being.

Whilst awake, constantly being fed into our brain are information streams of moving colored forms, sounds, sensations, emotions and feelings we can call "qualia." When that raw information, meaning those qualia phenomena, are interpreted (digested and structured) in our minds through its categories to produce a landscape image accessible to identification and behavioral adjustment, that is the operation of consciousness in producing a worldview. Sometimes the brain misreads the incoming information, thus creating optical illusions, and sometimes it may generate its own images/conclusions divorced from the external stimuli that it then interprets as coming from outside. In that case there is no way, other than by rational logic and deduction, to determine whether what one is seeing is really in the outside world or only within their own consciousness, and when incorrect you must use logic to correct your conclusions.

Some people see more colors than others, others hear a wider range of sounds, some are sensitive to a wider range of tastes or aromas ... we experience the world both incompletely and imprecisely according to our anatomical sensory capabilities and neural algorithms, but a world with qualities is what each of us experiences. The brain perceives the world by processing the sensory signals of its sense organs and uses its internal algorithms to give a best guess as to their identity and meaning. This produces discrimination, identification, comprehension, or meaning. That best guess is always determined by the equipment and processes of consciousness, meaning that the picture and its meaning are conditional creations rather than objective absolutes.

In a sense it is all an illusion, delusion, dream or Maya, but we call our built-up worldview "reality" because it proceeds according to regular predictable laws (patterns) and humans commonly agree on its facticity (empirical factfulness) since we share similar cognitive equipment, consciousness processing algorithms and definitions. The concept of being a self is also a controlled illusion or delusion of the brain for what we really are is just a part of the single fabric of Shakti that spans the All of Manifestation.

We look like we are limited beings with a hard boundary separated by space but we are interpenetrated and co-defined by unseen universal forces crisscrossing us everywhere in a richly interacting system that gives us our existence. Our existence depends upon the existence of the elements, water, air, sunshine, plant life, parents, the environment, magnetism, the nuclear force, an unbroken string of ancestors, current and previous societies and so on. The net of causation for our individual existence is infinite. Gravity, electromagnetism, the Higgs field and other forces penetrate everything including us, and combine together to create us along with everything else. Even space itself is changing, twisting and curving when it encounters mass, which is itself just a condensation of energy.

Rather than a packet, we are like a borderless process of no fixed form in a giant network of infinitely interconnected processes and forces meshed together with each other, interpenetrating thoroughly, where energy wavefronts are a glue holding everything together including objects, energies and the system in totality. There is a grand interfusion of phenomena due to dependent cross-defining, and we cannot truly say where one phenomenon ends and another begins. Hence, phenomena are neither different nor the same as each other. Events are dynamic and have a constant participation of all other forces, phenomena, and other processes within themselves, and also participate in everything else as well. They have within themselves the entire universal condition. Within us the entire universe is folded.

Similarly, every thought generated within the mind arises via the connections between the brain stem and all the memories stored in the brain's neurons, and supported by the body's subtle energy. When stimulated the brainstem and neurons add an influence to the present state of mind and help to generate the next sequence of thoughts in turn. The sense organs have their raw perceptual data turned into mental entities by the processes of consciousness, and then these mental events are further altered by thinking which then gives rise to further ideas, emotions, and so on. This called a "perfuming" that produces consciousness.

The intellect is constantly bombarded by a stream of sensory reports and the discriminating functions of consciousness automatically adds names and label differentiators (a framework of designations) so that we can immediately identify objects and their attributes. Thinking activities are constantly being performed all the time as well, and in turn perfume these inputs while the inputs perfume the thinking reflexively and help stimulate associated thoughts to arise. All these operations are simultaneously stimulating consciousness and its operations everywhere so as to generate new thoughts in turn. The thought-stream is like an endless running stream and the process producing it is like a shimmering wavering haze that spins everywhere within the brain and thereby connects memories to the present state of consciousness, thus stimulating related responses and producing new thoughts in turn. In the *Avatamsaka Sutra* of Buddhism the activity of neurons and neural connections firing due to interrelationships (when millions of electrochemical reactions/signals are stimulated to evoke a mental state) is referred to in various analogies such as flaming banners, blazes of light and so forth.

The inputs from our senses and thoughts that perfume consciousness, and the state of consciousness that thus arises, live and perish together while engendering subsequent states of consciousness (thoughts) because of the blending; this is the principle of "perfuming" in the production of the thought-stream. By the perfuming stimulation of consciousness the memories that lie within neurons sprout or become expressed in response to the combinational aroma, flavor, blending, illumination or stimulation of the total mixture of present mental activity. Hence the term "perfuming" of consciousness, as what is produced takes on the aroma/flavor of what came previously. This is how mental states and the stream of consciousness are formed.

As soon as the stimulation of memories and perfuming of thoughts produce new thoughts, the consciousness that has been perfumed into existence acts in turn as a cause to perfume and mature other seeds of consciousness to generate new thoughts (states of consciousness) in turn. These three elements – thoughts that are born, the inputs which perfume/electrify them, and the dormant seeds which are stimulated (provoked into stirring) by this perfuming – all revolve in a cycle, simultaneously acting as operational causes and transformational effects. Consciousness flows ever onward through this process like an endless river that is always producing personal experience, and this is what we call our mind, worldview, the present moment of our existence or even karma.

The generation of a mental scenario within the mind is therefore due to a mutual perfuming and interpenetration of thoughts that includes present thoughts, sensations (sensory inputs from sense organs) and the memories stored within the brain. A mental state that is generated out of a background of influences can be compared to a bundle of reeds that has been stacked together where each reed is supported by the aggregate of all the others in the bundle. However, the thought-stream appearing within consciousness is the ripening of a dynamic process that continuously flows onward without stop except for sleep, a coma, and other special conditions. That dynamic flowing of consciousness that creates our experience of the moment is achieved through a marvelous mutual influencing/perfuming of sensory inputs, memories, and conceptualization processes that produce its appearance as well as our knowing of that experience. The performance of a myriad of mental functions thus produces a world of experience.

Knowledge produces Knowledge, and the experiencer of the Knowledge is Knowledge as well. Where is there any true being, soul, spirit, personality, *atman* or *jiva* in all of this? There is none, and yet a worldview and understanding arises in a continuous stream to an apparent Knowledge maker-knower. That process and the body vehicle in which it occurs, which we call "living" as a matter of differentiation, are a tiny bit of Shakti connected to all else within Shakti just like a neuron is connected to its neighbors within a brain.

Where is there a sentient being in all this? There is none. There is only an agglomeration of processes called a "sentient being, soul or spirit" even though it lacks a permanent core. Due to impermanence one of the major problems of our existence is longevity, which means escaping the clutches of death as long as possible. Impermanence rules all, change is incessant within the universe, so only the highest spirit bodies can forestall the eventuality of death. We must therefore cultivate the spiritual path of meditation, mental purity (virtue), good conduct and good works for society (that protect it and help it flourish), along with inner Qi work, to attain the long-lived spiritual bodies and escape the lower realms of birth and death forever.

Whilst living we also seek happiness, especially the relief-happiness of ending pain and suffering (or even happiness in accomplishment), but the experience of feel-good types of happiness based on sensual pursuits, pleasant sensations or excitement (pleasure-happiness or excitement-happiness) do not satisfy the human desire for inner lasting peace, satisfaction, well-being, significance or meaning. Feel-good pleasure-based happiness and excitement-happiness are short-lived and obey the laws of diminishing returns whereby it gets harder to experience thrills as you become accustomed to them since novelty dies away, and a life of excessive pleasure-seeking can lead to hedonism, self-indulgence, superficiality, degeneration, nothingness (accomplishment), and despair. However, those who cultivate a conscious experience of value-based happiness that provides joy and bliss through the pursuit of activities having meaning do not need a steady stream of pleasurable sensations in life. An individual can also experience value-based happiness again and again merely by recollecting (memories) or by using contemplation. While bad fortune may put people at a severe disadvantage in their ability to experience feel-good happiness, everyone can find value-based happiness by contemplating the meaning in their lives and pursuing activities of greater meaning even if they are difficult. By pursuing value-based happiness (activities that make your life meaningful such as family, friendships, achievement, pledges or vows and so forth) you may regain a sense of purpose for life and achieve a real sense of well-being even in the presence of a world of great suffering.

Our consciousness naturally seeks to minimize physical pain and mental suffering but also seeks sensual pleasures as well as longer-lasting states of happiness, peace, bliss-fulfillment, flourishing, well-being, flow and meaning. However, true happiness and sense-enjoyment do not go together, and they don't occur to those of us who become hedonism machines. The spiritual path of cultivation involves freeing ourselves from being slaves to passions and desires, which is the natural characteristic of animals. As a path of higher development, we strive to ennoble ourselves and our consciousness by controlling our minds so that we are free of being slaves to sense objects. We train to become free of desires and sense enthrallment. Otherwise we would always be pursing new pleasures to titillate the nerves for just a short while, and would have to subsequently seek even greater thrills as we became accustomed to the novelty of those sensual pleasures. This is a road of never-peace, never-fulfillment and misery.

Since the pursuit of sensual pleasures and pleasant sensations cannot produce long-lived happiness, joy or bliss we should train ourselves to pursue value-based activities that produce more stable states of happiness, peace, bliss-fulfillment, well-being and flow. Pursuing value-based happiness should be preferred over the pursuit of desires that provide feel-good happiness, such as the pleasure from excitement or sensual delights like alcohol, drugs, sex, gambling, shopping, etcetera. Once you become clear on who you are and what you value, and then live your life in accordance with those values and goals, those decisions and actions should invigorate you and help you achieve value-happiness since these are of much greater worth than sensual pleasure.

In summary, the experience of the present moment is a conceptualization arising through numerous conditions. A ripening of multiple impressions perfuming one another and your thought-stream produces this present moment of experience, which engenders further ripenings as the present consciousness is exhausted and a consequential one is produced. The consequence of mind-moments being born and passing away because of transformation into new ones gives rise to the appearance of an unbroken mind-stream of flowing experience, and these transitory scenes of consciousness are all due to unseen biochemical, bioelectrical reactions supported by the subtle energy of the life force. Basically, irritating nervous tissue in some specific way produces the stream of consciousness, but the manifestation of consciousness requires the support of subtle energy behind the system as well. Even in states of apparent peacefulness, purity, inner calm, the fullness of quiet bliss, and the experience of clear awareness without distraction there is the movement of atoms and energy that are producing "quiet" consciousness. These states of fulfilling bliss are a type of mental rest free from excessive stress, and what you need to be taught how to achieve during life.

The causes of a particular mental state, and the subsequent thought-stream that appears in its wake, are certainly in a dependent relationship of transformation where one state flows into the next. Conceptualization is produced through the mutual influence of memories, sensory inputs, present thoughts and mental processing, the mental state that manifests is contingent on the old in a continuous manner, and in turn this cacophony stimulates new memories, thoughts and mental processing patterns that create the next moment of experience within the neural system. Throughout all of this, it is useful to remember that not only are we an impermanent, composite body-vehicle that gives rise to this stream of consciousness but that everything we see and think is not the truth but just mental projections. The world to us is just an experience in our mind, an approximation we have constructed of a certain form that has allowed the human species to survive without extinction, and it is an illusion rather than the real world because we have simplified the picture and added all sorts of additional mental garbage, such as emotions and personal views, onto whatever is being experienced. What do you know ... this all happens to an apparent I-self that falsely assumes it is a true identity.

The intellect is the "organ of thinking" that must make sense of all that happens within the mind (the biochemical, bioelectrical flickering and irritation of neural cells because of ions traversing through holes in neural membranes). Its discriminative abilities can be compared to a great army general who is interpreting all the scouting reports he's receiving from his sense organ lieutenants and via his mental reasoning/processing creates a comprehensive meaning of the battlefield. He interprets all the streams of perceptions and conceptions that arise and incorporate into a worldview. If we get rid of these physical sensations and sensory input reports then we have no more outside world, and then the only thing left for consciousness to work with is memory and the intellect itself, which is basically Knowledge functioning to produce thoughts that are more Knowledge. Knowledge is always just producing itself; there is no independent being, entity, soul or *atman* producing Knowledge. Knowledge is producing Knowledge all by itself without an inherent soul being involved.

To get any peace or quiet at all in the midst of this incessant activity, the army general has to separate himself from the ceaseless intake of the reports being fed to him. The meditative act of "sense withdrawal" mentioned in Yoga, or "turning away from the senses," "turning within," "cultivating one-pointed concentration to ignore distractions," "detaching from consciousness," or "detaching from thought" is thus a means for eliminating stress and developing greater mental peace and quiet. It is a way to give yourself some mental rest and train yourself not to become attached to your thought-stream, especially desires provoked by memories or the senses, and to let the mind flow seamlessly from state to state without entrainment.

This is a result you can achieve from the practice of meditation. Formless meditation involves quietly imitating the original nature that doesn't cling to anything, during which time the mind remains alertly aware so it simply watches thoughts and observes them without fusion. During meditation practice you do not internally cling to the mind-stream or the contents of your consciousness. You let everything mentally arise, observe it, and remain detached from the thought-stream as it changes into something else, and it often dies away to reveal an empty state of mind. In real life you correct whatever arises whether it be your thoughts or actions but during meditation practice you just observe the contents flowing through your mind.

You can also through meditation practice train your mind to experience a steady state peacefulness of mental calm, patience, acceptance, tolerance, serenity, stability and tranquility. Meditation involves helping you realize the naturally peaceful state of your mind, which is pure and free of elaborations. Your mind in its natural state is calm, balanced, unperturbed. Meditation practice helps people with busy minds realize that the natural state of their mind is tranquil and empty of thoughts rather than busy. It helps people realize that they can learn to control the operations of their mind. It even helps people increase their attention span.

Buddhism, in particular, talks greatly about the workings of our mental processes because all Arhat spiritual masters can shrink their etheric bodies down in size, go into peoples' brains, and watch the neural transformations as thoughts and memories form due to the Qi movements and electro-chemical processes going on. This practice is regularly done by all the Arhats, *jnani* or *jivanmukta* (spiritual masters) within all religions, and is a requisite part of their training process, but Buddhism teaches the most about the mental processes observed during the formation of thoughts.

It is common practice among devas and the spiritual masters of all religions to read the memories that people store in their brain neurons, which is why it is said that no secrets are kept from Heaven. It is also common for spiritual adepts with higher bodies to train in how to change people's thoughts and emotions, *which is one of the primary ways by which spiritual masters, Buddhas and their deva students try to help individuals in the world*, though they are limited by the restrictions of karma that determine what a person is due to experience. As Meher Baba stated in *God Speaks*, it is easy for a higher-bodied being to control the aspect of a human's mind that functions as thoughts but difficult to establish mastery over feelings (emotions and desires), so during the Twelve Year kundalini transformation period various enlightened teachers and their students will practice controlling the thoughts and emotions of the practitioner undergoing the process to affect their Qi. Using their energy, the spiritual teachers will grab the practitioner's mental mood (neural patterns connected to their Qi) in order to evoke anger, fear, pride, guilt and other Yang or Yin Qi emotions, and every now and then you will be visited by a group that will superimpose thoughts and emotions or evoke the same in an abusive way. Forget any assumption that enlightened beings are always ethical. Devas who attain the Buddha body are more abusive than enlightened humans, Causal-bodied beings are more abusive to those of lower bodies than devas, and so on it goes.

Inside the practitioner's brain at a time of training, masters will use their *nirmanakaya* emanations to simultaneously superimpose their Qi and thoughts within *all* the deva students attending the lessons. The Twelve Year kundalini transformation process can be hellish at times with all this training going on inside the practitioner, which is why if you search the literature you will not find any descriptions about it (except in *Meditation Case Studies*). The most you will ever hear about it from someone who went through it to achieve their deva body attainment, otherwise known as the first dhyana or the spiritual body accomplishment of *Homo Deus*, is something akin to "I spent twelve years with my master," and they will leave out all the painful details. Some traditions are better than others in putting you through the process, and others are worse.

In the Buddhist *Vimalakirti Sutra,* the brain is symbolized by Vimalakirti's ten-foot square room where miniaturized Buddhas (practicing the *anima* superpower of shrinkage of their energy bodies) arrive to teach an uncountable number of deva students who have also assembled inside the room/brain. In the *Avatamsaka (Flower Ornament) Sutra* the neurons, memory cells and neural pathways as they fire (when millions of electrochemical reactions/signals are stimulated to evoke a subjective experience) are symbolized by bright banners, wisdom flames, arrays of lights, jeweled lights, shining pores, magical displays, wisdom fragrances, supreme clouds, banner lights, wondrous adornments, flags, flowers, pleasant thunder, or melodious sounds and other wonderful analogies that the Buddhas can observe as a person thinks, feels and creates mental states of mind.

The reason that Buddhism emphasizes the operations of consciousness in its teachings is because deva students and their masters will often gather in an adept's brain and watch how perceptions form, memories form, thoughts form, feelings form and so forth. Spiritual beings watch the formation of sensory perceptions within the brain to understand the formal structure of consciousness in producing a worldview, as well as how conceptions form, and therefore understand what cognitive factors are intrinsic to human conscious experience and how those factors inform all mental experiences with a specific order. All spiritual masters watch the thoughts form inside people's brains in their training, and from direct observation of the processes it becomes readily apparent that our view of the external world is a simplified imagination, an illusory falsity that cannot capture it. It also becomes clear that we are just thinking organisms without any fixed soul or entity being involved, which is the truth of selflessness (no inherent self). These two realizations are part of the view of enlightenment, which is to recognize what we are in terms of our consciousness and existence.

Buddhist Abhidharma teachings are meant to teach how consciousness works – how a knower forms and knowing appears – and how our consciousness structures what we consider objective reality even though it is subjectively constructed. However, most people will not understand its purpose unless they read these teachings. It is not just a fact that our physical composition can be broken down into an agglomeration of simples, and therefore we are not an inherent, intrinsic being but rather a conditional construction of processes in transient form. It is also impossible for the mind's interpretation of the world to be a mirrorlike reflection of the way things actually are because the mind's prior conditioning of names, labels and categories used to structure consciousness are an alienating principle saturated with the contents/principles of a man's own internal mental organization. They are necessary for cognition but prevent an impartially objective true world conception. To understand this is also part of the enlightenment view. Consciousness forms within us and gives us personal existence but it is imperfect, illusory, undependable, incorrect, faulty. Yet it is what we have that gives us *conscious beingness* so we cannot fault this great miracle for its imperfections. Instead we must learn how to masterfully develop it and use it to pursue our dreams and enjoy the great gift of recognizing our existence and a world of qualities.

There is no such thing you can ever cultivate as a mind clear of preconceptions that cognizes reality correctly through some type of conceptually empty visage of direct cognition. Furthermore, man's thinking processes of the active intellect are governed by non-rational factors too, such as biases and prejudices, that man can neither control nor is conscious of and sometimes cannot correct. So it is not just that you are not an intrinsically real "sentient being" but only real in the apparent/conventional sense. The "enlightenment view" is also that perception of the world is illusory and thoughts are faulty as well, and yet cognition works enough to mentally build a universe for us, but not *the* universe. It builds a human personal universe. This type of understanding should help give rise to detachment in life for you can fathom (1) neither the fundamental nature ground state of Shakti (2) nor the ground of the world (things in themselves), (3) within a realm of impermanence, and (4) what you can conceive comes at the price of faulty incorrectness or imperfection. So why hold so tightly to things or let emotions control you?

If you realize that you can *never know* the ground state of your beingness, that you have consciousness but *only know the world as a subjective illusion* so can never know it truly, that you are basically an *impermanent composite mixture* of simples and energy processes formed within the perfectly *interdependent totality of always-changing Shakti* and you *lack an intrinsic solid soul-self,* then you achieve the realization of spiritual liberation. Upon understanding the true nature of your self and your consciousness and your beingness, you can now more easily *detach from the external world and your consciousness,* such as your impulses, desires and emotions, so that nothing controls you … except what you choose to follow. With this spiritually liberating understanding you can attain peace in any situation and cultivate happiness, shine and lightness throughout life. If you understand these truths you now have the the spiritual liberation of self-realization. The detachment one can achieve through understanding your self-nature and the nature of consciousness (which is called attaining *prajna* wisdom) allows you to attain peace and happiness within any situation, even that of suffering, thus winning you freedom, liberation and spiritual salvation. The science of happiness is based on attaining this understanding that produces mental detachment from the world and yourself – the right way of living your life – and the consequence is being able to live freely in happiness or peace in any situation you encounter.

Brain neurons possess countless tendrils that connect with countless networked patterns, and these generate the mind when stimulated. As vital energy runs through these networks, which is symbolized by fragrant wind or light in the *Avatamsaka Sutra*, that transmission of energy produces mental states and emotional moods. Normally we let them control us, but the understanding of self-realization allows us to become released from their control. Since energy is necessary for mental activity, thus a higher subtle body (an underlying soul or subtle body that is composed of this energy) is necessary for consciousness, and this is what untangles itself from the physical body to leave upon death when the body is thrown away like an old dress, which is another type of liberation. The subtle body resides on the earthly plane in etheric form until its own death, and then is reborn either in a heavenly or earthly woman's womb through the process of reincarnation. Thus the subtle body that is essentially trapped energy that stores, is called the "soul" or "spirit" in several spiritual traditions, and the physical body is said not to be your true spiritual self.

Our experience as sentient life is possible because of the great treasure of consciousness that works approximately in the way described. In the universe, rare is the phenomena of life. With life, rare is the existence of consciousness able to form higher thoughts that enable beings to learn who and what they are, which is the view of enlightenment. Rare are the living beings who learn how to master their consciousness, how to unravel the causality behind phenomena so they can use their consciousness and actions to master phenomena, and thereby learn how to bring about better states of experience and existence for themselves and others. Rarer still are the beings who can discern a spiritual path that enables them to generate higher transcendental bodies inherent within the condensed energy matrix of their physical shell, and which can rejoin beings living on higher planes to live more enjoyably for incredible amounts of time. Such teachings are the enlightenment teachings of spiritual ascension, purification or transformation.

This is the spiritual path to *Moksha* or liberation, which is to attain bodies of transcendental purity that are high enough to leave the lower realms of reincarnation, and through their purity and longevity put an end to your birth and death in the lower realms forever. The "soul" (subtle body or deva body) inside your physical shell is not immortal because it must undergo the process of reincarnation until it is pure enough that higher beings help you purify its energies to a stage of transcendence, which also requires spiritual practice on your part, but through the path and practice of spiritual cultivation you can make your subtle body truly immortal.

While working towards that objective, we have the ability to direct our consciousness in various ways, such as toward benevolent intentions to help other beings and society. We can direct our consciousness towards producing more beneficial mental states for ourselves, and towards producing better worldly circumstances that give rise to better mental and physical states for others too. For ourselves we must purify our minds of errants such as emotional bondages, inappropriate beliefs, unhealthy desires or attachments and work to always cultivate clear wisdom and knowing. At the same time, we must also work on cultivating our bodies so that we always experience an ultimate level of health, comfort and natural ease where our vital energy is full and circulates completely and harmoniously, and so that we thereby set the stage for the deva body attainment whilst alive. Naturally this will require exercise and a good diet along with sufficient internal *qi-gong* or *nei-gong* practices.

Through practicing clear awareness, mindfulness, or watchfulness of our mind-stream (that entails focusing our cognitive attention on our mental processes) we also develop the capacity to liberate/detach ourselves from our habituated conditioning, and can then liberate ourselves from fusion with our mind-stream so that openings always exist that allow us to change its course for the better. We can live more fully in the present moment. We can mentally stand aside to realize what we are actually doing in the grand scheme of things, stop any errant behavior in its tracks due to non-entrainment and non-abiding, and thereby control our conduct so that we transcend our inherent animal nature and carnalities through the nobility of character, higher conduct and cultured behavior. This too is the spiritual path.

Chapter 7
MASTERING ONE'S CONSCIOUSNESS
AND PERFECTING CONSUMMATE CONDUCT

The great miracle you possess, the wish-fulfilling jewel that you possess that inanimate matter (inert Nature) does not have, is your consciousness. You have a mind that can think, feel and perceive the world through knowing. Our experience of the external world surrounding us, and the other mental events within our minds, occur because we are a type of object within the universe (Shakti) called a living being that possesses the great attribute of consciousness. Other types of objects, functions and processes do not have it.

Consciousness is the greatest treasure within Shakti. It is the wish-fulfilling gem of existence, the astonishing miracle of existence that gives us self-cognizance (the knowingness or experience of being aware of our existence) and an awareness of objects, and in this way it separates us from insentient matter. In the Bible it says that the Spirit of God moved upon the waters of Creation and God said, "Let there be light (illumination)," and there was light, and the light was good and separated from the darkness. This summarizes in one sentence the evolutionary development of consciousness (light or illumination) out of the surging insentient cosmos – a universe of darkness without consciousness.

One of the principles of life is to become able to master and develop the abilities of our consciousness in order to improve our own internal and external well-being, as well as the happiness and well-being of other sentient beings. You need to master the functional operations (transformations) of your own consciousness in order to pursue prosperity (flourishing), happiness (bliss) and even meaning and significance for your own existence. In particular, to experience peace you need to control your thoughts and purify your mind of unwanted agitations and defilements, which means to balance your mind and elevate its contents to a condition of greater virtue and purity, by cultivating tranquility and clarity.

Internal calmness is the best foundation for managing your thoughts and behavior that in turn produce your positive or negative states in life. Most spiritual schools therefore teach us to cultivate inner mental peace and calm, which also bring the greatest contentment and satisfaction in life. You want to keep your thoughts pure and clean and pacify your mind of agitations and wanderings so that from that state you can make the best decisions that control your mind and behavior.

As sentient living beings we are pursuing peace, presence, joy, bliss, lightness, happiness and well-being in life rather than suffering, but if we use consciousness incorrectly or apply ourselves incorrectly then we are bound to experience difficulties, pains and suffering. Therefore the Great Learning of life involves a lifelong struggle to master our thoughts and behavior, whose roots lie in consciousness, because they ultimately control our well-being. The Great Learning is learning how to *master your body and your consciousness - your physical skills/condition, mental skills, inner psychological terrain (moods, perspective, mental states etc.) and behavior* - so that they create for you a mental and physical experience of well-being, peace and fulfillment.

Since your survival in the world does not depend on your actions alone, you need to extend your concerns outward to others instead of concentrating solely on yourself ("I"). Your concerns need to encompass a larger sphere of relationships ("We") starting with your family and then extending to your friends and colleagues, and then more extensive groups of people. We emotionally long for connections with other people to satisfy feelings of belongingness and inclusion, need large networks of relationships in order to survive, feel happiness due to the praise and friendship of others, and often even find our deepest meanings for life through our relationships. People cannot satisfy their fundamental needs in life by themselves but need to rely on the support of a larger community to achieve them, namely their family, friends, colleagues, neighbors, community, and greater society. In today's world where the impact of our actions spreads far and wide across networks of relationships, the actions of a faraway despot may actually threaten your life and existence, so because the effects of your actions can potentially spread very far we all need to wisely discipline our behavior due to its possible effects on our communities and the world.

You therefore need to know how to harmoniously conduct yourself productively within extensive social groups so that you can live cooperatively and collaboratively within greater and greater wholes of people in a way that profitably contributes to their existence and maintenance. These wholes (larger groups of relationships) provide our lives with significance, and by thinking of our actions in relation to those wholes we can impart meaning to our lives rather than simply remain animals struggling for our existence.

This is how we are to find meaning and significance in the world, which is in relationship to larger communities of individuals such as our family, colleagues, society, state and even our environment. Seeing yourself as part of a community or *having a place (significance) within something greater or larger than oneself* creates emotional support and the potential for happiness, purpose, and meaning for your existence. As a being that is everything there is, or as "beingness without a body," you belong to no one and no one belongs to you. You are everything or nothing at all depending upon the perspective you take. However, despite the lack of being an intrinsically independent soul-self in the universe you can still find meaning for your existence, and find your own life purposes, through your activities in regards to the Indra's web of relationships that strongly connect with you. You can find meaning within those relationships.

The functions, processes, goal or activities that you choose to go after in life have meaning in regards to conditions or relationships. Historically speaking, the greatest joy and fulfillment individuals report finding for themselves is by being of service to others in various ways through life such as by improving their welfare, and/or by friendly participation in activities that serve ("beautify") portions of the whole, or by leading them out of the lower realms to enlightenment. The heart and mind are purified through service.

Through interdependence each of our lives has a place in the cosmic whole, as well as within smaller wholes that are smaller networks and groups of relationships. We gain significance in our lives through our relationship to the whole of Shakti, which is a manifestation of our True Self, and through our relationship to parts of Shakti – whether those parts be environments, activities, conditions or living beings. We find significance in relationships through the interconnections that bind us because they are responsible for our existence (family), help our survival (family and society) or stimulate our thinking, emotions and caring (friends and noble purposes).

Our relationship to greater wholes such as family, friends and society, or our relationship to actions and activities that affect larger and larger groups of individuals, provides us with real meaning and significance in our life.

This is why religions teach us to put our energies and resources behind causes that improve society and the world, such as when Christians emphasize charity, Chinese emphasize helping friends, or the Sikhs of India show their support for greater social justice in society.

For your own happiness and also to better the world, you must therefore take actions on behalf of the welfare of various groups of people and even make sacrifices for their prosperity, welfare and well-being so that they do not deteriorate over time due to vulnerabilities, recognizing that their upkeep, support and sustenance is essential because entropy is the nature of the universe. You need to know how to behave to live cooperatively and collaboratively within a group for its aggregate welfare because we can only face the harshness of the world if we help one another, and you need to perform sacrifices, good deeds and benevolent kind actions for the benefit of others during life (who will one day reciprocate in kind) instead of just focusing on yourself and/or close family of friendship relationships alone. This requires training our mind to know how to behave as well as achieve. For a group to survive it needs internal laws or codes of conduct, social structures that eliminate oppression, and policing that protects its members by ensuring justice and fairness.

A key concern is to prevent abuse within our social groups by those who accumulate great wealth or power (or who attain high status in some other way) and then assume privileges that oppress others or infringe upon their rights. This means limiting the powers of the fortunate elites, who tend to be parasitic or oppressive, through checks and balances. Groups also need to protect their members from antagonistic or malevolent predatory individuals, within or without, who might prey on people, including powerful entities who tend to exploit or steal from others. Our actions come from our thoughts and therefore learning how our groups should function and how we should each individually behave to achieve our desired objectives in life (what Confucianism calls "gain") is basically a matter of using consciousness.

A government is supposed to provide an organizational framework of laws and structure and social contract for a community such that people can harmoniously live together within it and fulfill their common needs for commerce, safety and prosperity. Together with civic, religious and family influences a government can help provide stability, harmony, peace, justice and certainty in the lives of people so that flourishing and prosperity become within reach of all. The justification for a government is that it promotes the mutual interest, protects its citizens, and under its framework prosperity diffuses among the population in a just way where opportunities abound and the structure meets peoples' needs without being oppressive.

The ideal government fosters the maximum happiness and well-being for the maximum number of people. For people to be able to live together peacefully and prosper, they must be allowed to freely take advantage of opportunities that their consciousness chooses while also abiding by social standards that will help with the building up of society in a fair and just way. Religion, by promoting prosocial and moral behavior, helps establish these social standards of behavioral propriety and shared culture that are needed for "a more perfect union" of group harmony, interaction, cooperation, collaboration, protection, survival and prosperous flourishing. We can follow such standards only because our minds are trained to do so due to social conditioning, rational logic, survival needs and other influences.

As humans we depend upon others for survival not just as a necessity but because we also crave a sense of connection and belonging with others beyond the affiliations needed for survival. We can find meaning in life within our relationships with others. For example, one of the worst types of punishment for humans is solitary confinement because it deprives us of social connections with other people. Therefore the Great Learning of life also requires us to learn how to manage our interactions with people or things and relationships in the social sphere, which we must figure out using consciousness.

Unlike a chemical reaction that simply occurs due to the right conditions coming together, you must learn how to interact with others in a friendly fashion to achieve personal prosperity, group social cohesion and welfare, and to satisfy your own longings for companionship, affiliation, connection, friendship, and belongingness as well as well-being. You must master your behavior by mastering your consciousness.

Specifically, you must learn how to act virtuously so that you are able to live with other members of society in a peaceful, harmonious way, and you must develop a civic spirit to support the welfare of the group by giving back rather than only taking from the bounty it produces. Spiritual traditions teach us to express compassion, kindness, love, fairness, honesty and peacekeeping as a method of governing our violent nature and enabling us to live humanely together with others. They also teach that we need to perform good works and make sacrifices for others not just to repay their kindness to us but to benefit society too.

Christianity tells us to "love one another" while Confucianism says that the Great Learning required of life involves learning how to "love (other) people," "renovate people (others)," "teach the people" or "revitalize the people." The underlying idea is that we should help other people in society - serve others in need and deed. We should work towards the happiness and well-being of all people, and that is love. We should be compassionate in responding to human suffering rather than concerned with ourselves alone, otherwise humanity cannot survive and then we cannot survive.

Many people are suffering in life and when we are in better circumstances than others there is the call to help them if possible out of a sense of compassion and brotherhood. In some cases we should predominately worry about our own self-interest - the welfare of our self or "I" - and in other cases we should be more selfless and worry about the welfare of the group or "We." The guiding principle is to protect and help yourself but always do your best for others as well, and to move yourself to where rightness is. Rightness means what is moral, ethical and virtuous in terms of behavior even if it means that you must sacrifice some of your own benefits. It means not being swayed away from what is moral or righteous because of profit, being ready to stand against injustice despite the costs to oneself, and not forgetting your values and the principles of propriety when you are suddenly tested under strained circumstances. Right is right and righteousness is righteousness even if no one is following the road of ethics and morality, and wrong is wrong even if everyone is doing it. A *man of principle* can differentiate between right and wrong, and he sticks to what is proper and correct despite great profits being available from doing what is wrong or expedient.

Our activities should not only work towards achieving an ending of suffering for ourselves and others but also promote "the good life" among the people. We should take positive steps to improve the welfare and well-being of everyone whenever possible by helping them personally (directly) or by improving their group living conditions. However, we must always remember that we cannot build a better world without improving the individuals within it. We should always express the instinct to care for others, since they are part of our Self, and therefore always treat people with good thoughts, benevolence, consideration, care and kindness just as we would want to be treated ... and we should encourage others to act the same way. Some say we should be this way to pay back or express gratitude to the members of contemporary society and their predecessors for all the sacrifices, hard work and kindness they have undergone on our behalf in order to feed us, move society forward and make our lives easier. The life that is in us right now is the manifest result of the presence, meeting and contribution of an uncountable number of ancestors to whom we owe gratitude for their efforts. The idea is that we too should contribute to the fold, make conditions better for everyone and pay back the kindness of others. Others say we should do so because everyone is our brother or sister - they are familial relations by virtue of being humans, by virtue of being part of Shakti, or because we all share the same one Self. Many reasons are proposed for being a good friend even to others whom you don't personally know. The basic principle is stated as "love one another."

To act with consideration, kindness and compassion by choosing to help others and provide them with aid in various ways (resources, money, teachings, encouragement, comfort, protection, etcetera) is one of the cardinal principles of spiritual cultivation, and shows you are transcending your animal nature and the world. This character trait is a fundamental requirement of the spiritual path because it shows you are not entirely self-centered but interested in the welfare of others, and therefore if given power over others because of attaining higher spiritual bodies you will most likely work for the benefit of humanity. Those who are not virtuous, primarily pursue self-centered gains and lack the merit of helping others will not achieve the highest results of the spiritual path.

Because we share the same self-nature we should treat every person, without distinction, as our own-self, and therefore try to help others just as we would want to be helped when in difficulties. We are taught by the Golden Rule that we should treat every person as we would want to be treated - that we should do for them what we would want done for us but should not to do to others what we wouldn't want done to us. We should not treat others in a way we wouldn't want to be treated. This is a principle to guide your behavior that should be imprinted within your mind.

Everyone shares the same self-nature – the presence of God is in everyone and everything – so we are certainly all related to one another. All beings are also members of the one manifest body of the universe that has one fundamental root-nature shared by the multiplicity we see. Since we share the same body of Shakti when helping others we are actually helping ourselves. In fact, *we must take care of the whole world and environment, including other people*, because we are related to everything and through such efforts are helping ourselves. When you consider the fact that through reincarnation you will be reborn into the conditions you created, it also makes sense to improve the circumstances of society along with its degrees of fairness, social justice, opportunity, beauty and prosperity because you will experience them again!

Consider that from the aspect of Shakti when another feels pain it is Shakti feeling pain, so it is actually you who are feeling pain. Whenever someone feels pain or suffering it is natural that through empathy your compassion arises. An enlightened individual with a transcendental body will know this pain (even while located elsewhere) and thinks, "Their pain is equally mine because they are part of my Self, and therefore I should work to dispel this pain. I don't want to let people stay within suffering if there is something I can do about it." In fact, those with the Supra-Causal or Immanence body transcend the lower realms of matter (just as the subtle body transcends bondage to the physical realm) in an all-pervasive way, and because of their more etheric bodies have attained a type of field-consciousness or high degree of perception where they can sense vibrations in the fields of the denser energy realms. Like the Buddha Kuan Yin (Avalokitesvara) they can actually "hear the cries of pain in the world" coming from individuals suffering in the lower realms of materiality. They constantly hear prayers, pleas and the cries of pain in the world and want to make efforts to alleviate it – if people don't suffer as much then they also won't suffer (unless they simply ignore the pains people go through), but suffering should normally stir the resonance of sympathy and empathy as a basic feature of humanity. They can also see the stream of past and future lives of individuals in the lower realms of matter, and perhaps this is because "all time exists all the time" (all time exists simultaneously) and therefore those pathways can be seen as some type of etheric formations that are accessible only when you are out of the Desire Realm and Form Realm completely.

Gurus say that enlightenment is like living in a state of continual awareness because those who possess the most refined transcendental bodies can sense what is happening in lower realms through the vibrations of fields; those with the higher body attainments are sensitive to perturbations in the denser energy realms beneath them and thus can attain "all-pervasive knowledge." Enlightened masters with the highest level bodies know when someone thinks of them, or recites their name or calls upon them, or recites a prayer or mantra or scripture/book they vowed to protect (such as lists of divine names), or performs a particular ritual or ceremony, or looks at a statue, picture, painting, yantra, mandala and so on. Out of compassion, the enlightened will often respond in various ways to help counter the pains and afflictions of human beings who call for help (since they can hear/sense those pleas), which is why many masters over the millennium have invented prayers and mantras whereby you can call upon them for aid, which is why a mantra given by a Guru is considered the power of the Guru with the disciple. Feeling sympathy for humanity, those who become enlightened intervene to alleviate the problems experienced by suffering individuals once they discover their needs.

We really are one whole. We are *united in one single nature* despite our differences as particular persons, and so you should treat everyone with respect and care because we are all in the same boat. We are all part of one another. However, just recognizing this fact doesn't motivate people to love one another and readily extend help and assistance to each other like a Good Samaritan. You can make many arguments to help others from the aspect of self-interest, but ultimately there really is no valid ontological argument for why you should be kind, compassionate, benevolent and loving other than that *you choose to be that way*. You must be taught this lesson.

Fairness, rights or righteousness do not exist in Nature or biology, nor do good and evil or even meaning and purpose. Those designations are all imagined orders. Nature doesn't care about these ideas that we have created in our minds. Nature has no motives, no projects, no agendas. What we take as spiritual values or –isms are all imaginations we create ourselves for our benefit within a neutral, indifferent universe. We are taught to show humaneness but the highest reason to be humane is *because you value being that way, because you want to be that way, because you choose to be that way*, and that is what makes an individual noble, spiritual and even majestic. This is what raises you above your animal nature, which is violent, cruel and carnal by nature. You personally choose to pursue the goal of consummate conduct because that is the way you want to be, and this type of inspiration is what elevates mankind.

Caring for others reveals your character and shows how you have chosen to be. Caring is what makes your virtues and values manifest – caring for others through benevolent kindness and compassionate deeds makes "your virtuous self" manifest. Such activities help us to exercise our virtuous nature and perfect it. They give us a chance to polish our virtues so that they become even more brilliant.

Sacrificing for others and benevolently acting for their welfare represent our standards for the greatness of a soul. Such activities raise us far above our selfish, carnal animal nature to make us spiritually transcendent. Such behavior is called the pursuit or perfection of virtue and benevolence, and this conduct is the actual spiritual path because through it we transcend our lower nature, purify its tendencies and conquer our egoistic impulses and selfish dispositions. Throughout the Great Learning of life we should learn how to control (purify) our desires, impulses and psychological afflictions through higher knowledge, by cultivating the mind of compassionate wisdom, and by practicing a continuous mindfulness that monitors our thoughts and behavior for self-correction.

The virtues of mankind such as compassion, fairness, kindness, patience, truthfulness, charity, discipline, benevolence and so forth are what make us spiritually transcendent. Continually exercising such virtues is a matter of purifying your own behavior, which is what makes an individual worthy to attain the higher spiritual bodies that potentially have great power over other people. Naturally, wisdom is also required for this merit because the Buddhas will not work day and night during the twelve-year kundalini transformation process to make stupid people enlightened (or non-virtuous individuals) when more qualified individuals are available.

As stated, you can only acquire the higher spiritual bodies by going through an emotionally and physically painful twelve-year kundalini transformation period. The *organized labor* of countless spiritual beings who work on your Qi/Prana to purify it are required to help you attain it. They won't extensively work on the grand mission of purifying your Qi/Prana if you are not a good person, or if you are a stupid human being. The attainment of the deva body from cultivating spiritual practices and virtue is related to the idea that if you are good then God will help you.

All our human standards of behavior – of good and bad – are just imagined orders we've invented for ourselves because there are no such real things within Shakti. There is only neutral, indifferent Shakti, and even Shakti isn't real. As to true reality there is only the unchanging fundamental substratum, and in terms of manifestation there is only the one body of Shakti without true divisions, and the changing cosmos is a manifestation of Its unblemished nature. Within Shakti, the universe, there is no such thing other than Shakti, and there is nothing that is inherently good or bad within it because those are labels we make up that don't exist within neutral Shakti. Shakti is just a single body of energy-matter transformations that we call transformations of form (matter) and formlessness (energy and space), and yet through having a mind we partition out (in a human way) individual objects, forms, names and labels within this one soup due to the usefulness of doing this.

Within Shakti you need consciousness to create differentiations or distinctions (such as identifying objects) and to append meaning to anything. For instance, to even know there is Shakti or a "me" requires a mind (consciousness) connected to sense organs and the thoughts of an I-self. However, there is no such *true* thing as an intrinsic I-self or I-self separate and independent of Shakti because your "I-ness" is a component process or function enmeshed within the whole of greater Shakti. Furthermore, there is no such true thing as consciousness either (that is real because it transcends Shakti and therefore sets us aside from, above or apart from the mundane world) because it is also just another functioning of Shakti. It is just an illusion we make up in our heads to order our world so that our type of living object can maintain its continuance of survival.

Consciousness is not an objective, accurate and transcendental function that provides some *true overview* that transcends Shakti. Shakti composes it, it is a component of Shakti, it is just another functioning process happening within Shakti, it is part of Shakti, etcetera. Consciousness is just a flickering mass of energy in our brains that are undergoing ceaseless transformations via complex interactions. However, we call this dependent process "consciousness" as a way to designate its existence and attributes.

Actually, there is only inanimate Nature transforming in endless ways without any true things within it such as sentient own-beings, transcendental consciousness, good and evil, or meaning and purpose. There are no partitions to Shakti at all, but within this one soup we are designated as individual sentient beings because we have consciousness (minds) and can make this designation to individualize ourselves and thereby differentiate us from the rest of the universe. This helps us with our survival. Our existence as limited, independent selves is what we take ourselves to be, but this is merely a designation of a "packet" born of our subjective conceptions and not the truthful reality. It is wrong thinking, errant thinking, unclear thinking, a false assumption. It appears to be true because we don't know enough, so that conclusion is false due to our own conceptual errors.

To put it another way, it is erroneous discrimination that attributes intrinsic existence to things (including us) and borders to objects without borders. Apparent beings we are, true beings we are not ... at least in the sense we normally take ourselves to be. We are not intrinsic or inherent own-beings but apparent beings. We are not individuals but the whole universe in total. Even so, beings we are, so for our own self-interest we should learn to manage our consciousness, body and actions to make the best of our manifest life and existence that we can, and that means pursuing better bodies, mental states and behaviors.

In terms of Shakti there is only the universe or Nature, and within the living aspects of Nature there is only biology. There is no such thing as fairness, justice, or any other imagined order within biological Nature. There are no such orders within Shakti at all. We invent such imagined orders through our own mental concepts to give ourselves meaning and order for life. We create lots of concepts like this in order to live meaningful lives and maintain our existence. If in the past we hadn't developed this ability to derive order out of chaos then we wouldn't be here because our life form would have disappeared rather than survived during the course of evolution. The creation of imagined orders within our mind is a survival mechanism that has enabled us as a species to continue thriving and replicating over a long course of evolution. We are just a process or part of Shakti that was able to do this, and that is all.

Humans are basically biological units that must cooperate with other biological units for survival issues such as food production, security and protection, and health issues. Humans as a species are always threatened with issues of food scarcity, resource availability, health maintenance (longevity), procreation and safety/protection. We create rules for living and standards of behavior to help handle such issues, and then define virtuous behavior in part based on what is necessary for the survival of individuals and the group as well as based on the principles of virtue and righteousness. If we didn't invent such standards we might die in one of a hundred different avoidable ways. For instance, we might prey on one another or give into malevolent antagonistic behavior (the violent nature implicit in the human animal) that would prevent harmonious communities from thriving. Over time we have as a species learned how to perfect our consciousness and behavior to be able to live within large groups of individuals, and have developed ways to sufficiently restrain the leadership elites from the natural tendency of the powerful to oppress or exploit lower status individuals and aggress upon their person or assets.

Refining ourselves through the pursuit of virtue is certainly noble but also thus necessary. Cultivating good virtues not just makes us better people but yields a better community for everyone by increasing our chances for survival, happiness and prosperity. Wisdom and intelligence are part of the package of necessary virtues we need to cultivate because the journey through life only becomes possible (and certainly much easier) when using intelligence. By using our intelligence we can make situations better for others in a way that will also improve conditions for our self, just as a tide that raises all ships also raises our own.

It is said that showing respect, consideration, kindness, goodness, care and compassion to others earns the merit of a karmic reward such as rebirth in heaven. Karmic merit, or positive karma reward, is a return expected due to the principle that if you cause happiness for others (such as by relieving their fears, suffering, misfortunes and distress) then as a natural consequence you will experience happiness in return. Whether fact or fiction, this philosophy establishes a great positive motivation for performing kind and compassionate altruistic deeds that help other people.

It helps cement society within a cocoon of good behavior, helpful good deeds and goodwill.

In truth, the more we care for others and work for their welfare *the more we will actually forget our own concerns and sufferings in life* because we typically find the troubles we undergo for those tasks meaningful and worthwhile according to our own values. Contributing to a benevolent cause greater than ourselves causes us to forget ourselves (the self-importance we have created for ourselves) as well as our own sufferings, pains and troubles, especially when the sacrifice required is worthy of the objective. Our own internal happiness *grows greater when we perform significant deeds of merit or bestow kindness and compassion upon others*, and this is one of the reliable ways to wash away the pains of life.

If we try to ontologically justify kindness and compassion for others, some say we have an obligation to act for the benefit of others out of the spirit of kinship or friendship because "The Self in me is the Self in all," so we truly are all brothers/sisters within Shakti and equally diverse embodiments of the one same Self. This is true. Your True Self is the same as the ultimate Self in others, and so in helping them you are helping your Self. From the aspects of interdependent arising and the *Hua Yen* view we are all connected with one another as well. Even so, these facts rarely inspire most people to help one another.

Now, giving of ourselves or giving our resources (as a type of charity or help to others) places us in line with the most fundamental force of the cosmos, which is the manifestation of Creation itself since its appearance is a type of *giving out* or expression of the fundamental nature. But this interesting way of viewing personal charity, compassion and social helpfulness does not inspire people to virtue either.

Doing good deeds that manifest blessings for the well-being of others actually has no *ontological justification* other than that you believe it is the right thing to do, and so you engage in those activities because you believe that is right, and because you choose to be that way and exert yourself to become that way. That is all. Mankind invented all its values, virtues, and rules of proper/ethical behavior and the reasons for acting in benevolent ways within a truly neutral universe. They are just inventions to help survival and improve happiness for our species because there is no inherent moral order within the cosmos. We created an imagined reality of beliefs about virtues and values but they aren't ontological truths because Shakti has no inherent patterns. We create those beliefs for our own benefit. The universe is just energy and matter involved in ceaseless transformations. Because it is neutral and indifferent, Nature possesses no such modes, attributes or characteristics such as virtues and values, fairness or rights, good or evil, motives or agendas. Altruism isn't even part of your biological nature. For each individual our own self is the most important thing, and we are constantly engaged in ensuring the well-being of this most precious thing due to our self-love. It is hard to go beyond this to worry about and then work for the welfare and well-being of others. We must be taught to do so.

Few people pursue the path of "making their virtues brilliant" purely out of a desire to pursue a model of perfection. Nevertheless there are some special pathways of consummate conduct, such as Confucianism and Christian perfectionism, which greatly espouse this ideal and say it should become the core of your being. Most religions just provide lists of Dos and Don'ts ("obey these rules") you must conform to and don't stress the fundamental principles of good behavior, such as the Golden Rule, or even explain the scientific principles behind the religious rules promoted for health and hygiene.

Some people pursue a pathway of virtue and purity and service without any other justification than that they choose to be that way. These are the most majestic, magnificent or spiritual of individuals. We call this a commitment to nobility, but there is no such real thing as nobility within Shakti, nevertheless we designate this tendency as "nobility" for the sake of human beings. This is the teaching of the *Diamond Sutra* that we make up all our definitions for the running of conventional life, but they don't really exist in any ontological sense of absolute existence. Nonetheless we need them for human civilization, and they beautify and improve our lives by raising us above our coarse animal tendencies.

Once you have decided that consciously building and perfecting your character is the way you want to run your life within your own mental realm of imagined order, then acting this way becomes obligatory in order to validate the path you have chosen. Virtue, high values and good behavior certainly provide benefits but have no ontological standing, yet we ascribe to them high value *as we should* so that we can run societies and our lives. They create the potential for the experience of happiness and bliss while living. The amazing thing is that sacrificing yourself to help others by improving the quality of their lives, working to eradicate their misfortunes through compassionate deeds, and benefiting the world by means of your own personal virtuous qualities is not only in the best interest of all concerned but of benefit to yourself as well. By helping various aspects of Shakti you indeed help your own self.

A Bodhisattva realizes that he or she is empty of an intrinsic self-so nature because he is an agglomeration of conditions that lack an independent and permanent/fixed soul, entity, *atman*, *jiva* or individual inside them. A Bodhisattva realizes that he or she lacks a permanent unchanging core of own-being that they can consider a fixed real self (other than the empty self-nature). They realize that they are like a dream person or apparition, yet decide they want to help people within the dream of Maya and so they create purposes for their long life by establishing great vows, pledges or commitments of noble behavior. They also set for themselves challenges of mastery and perfection to be achieved. Despite being absent of the permanent existence of an unchanging stationary form or core being they still function and will continue to function because of the process of reincarnation by which they will transform from life to life but carry their tendencies, skills and sometimes their memories with them. The game of life is then one of constant personal growth, progress and self-improvement.

People have no permanent core inside them that constitutes a real (intrinsic) self-entity and yet life continues. Since all individuals will carry potentiating tendencies and skill sets into subsequent incarnations (or into the nearly immortal enlightenment bodies if they achieve them), they should strive to purify those characteristics *in this life*, and work at developing various skills, perfections, excellences, beautifications, achievements and merits so that their next transformation is much more skillful and their life much more pleasant because of them.

This is one of the many reasons to strive for self-perfection and self-development, which includes striving to break free from impure habits and tendencies, shoring up one's shortcomings, developing various skills and masteries and excellences, purifying one's thoughts and desires (cutting down your negative thoughts and cleaning up your mentality), and cleansing your soul of unwanted tendencies. Even though you are impermanent there is a continuity, so you need to engage in some self-analysis to sort out your good and bad qualities, decide on what you want to become and how you want to be, and then work to become that way. You must endeavor to eliminate your shortcomings, purify your unwholesome nature, develop splendorous excellences, and make of yourself what you want to ultimately become. Striving towards virtue and excellence makes us aim at the right marks whereas practical wisdom makes us think properly and undertake the right efforts and actions.

It is not to be feared that you have no true, substantial existent nature because *nothing has a real substantive existent nature*. Since this is the way things are you must just accept it, and then use your understanding to your own benefit. You have continuity but are always transforming, and therefore you have an apparent self that seems stable but lacks a fixed or permanent self-core. All formations are unstable and therefore lack any constant core or self. Even so, as an apparent being you can cultivate merits, excellences and perfections and take them with you throughout your transformations, and this is what we should do. The process of reincarnation guarantees the continuance of our existence that can ultimately last forever as long as Shakti lasts, and during our existence we can cultivate peace, satisfaction and bliss.

Everything arises in the universe dependently so that things appear the way they do. Within the one universal arising of Shakti each phenomenon is actually an infinitely interconnected conglomeration of everything else. This is the *Avatamsaka Sutra* (Flower Ornament) view of Buddhism. Every single thing in the universe is a collection of endless causes and conditions, and lacks "own being" as an inherently existing singular phenomenon. In other words, all things lack an intrinsically existing self because other things comprise it – so it is made of parts or component pieces that are not-self. Every thing is a conditional or dependent thing. Nothing has a self-so own-nature but is a dependent construction composed from the existence of everything else.

From yet another aspect, your *apparent self* isn't a fixed entity because it is always changing, so there is nothing inside you as an unchanging constant core that we can define as your (real) self. You are just an agglomeration of changing conditions that hold together for a period of time, slowing changing into something else without having a constant, changeless, unchanging core. Your own real Self is the unchanging universal substrate.

The appearance of an object may be there in front of you, but it is not what you assume it to be. Every thing we designate as a singular object, form or phenomenon is actually a collection of all phenomena (Shakti) embodied in its existence. A singular phenomenon is therefore all things. Our minds, however, simply carve out a piece of the whole of Shakti and call it a particular phenomenon as a way to identify conventional things for our own usefulness. That mental operation of cutting out a representation from a single tapestry is actually a false imagining, a wrong abbreviation, a set of false thoughts since you are assuming borders where there are none. It is useful but incorrect, and occurs because we cannot see how objects bleed into everything else seamlessly to make one united whole.

Separateness is a wrong conclusion, but we make those representations within consciousness in order to survive as a sentient object within Shakti where the continuity of a living species depends upon consciousness doing that. Our sense organs aren't designed for facticity but for survival fitness. An object within our mind is actually just a conscious construction (mental representation) that symbolizes a tiny piece of reality in an inaccurate, and incomplete way (all its attributes are unknowable), and assumes borders that are non-existent. The superimposition of discrete objects on the universe is called "Maya" in Hinduism and "false thinking" in Buddhism. The universe of things that we can consciously see/experience is not just a Maya (illusion) but called *samsara* in Buddhism.

What we designate as "objects," "phenomena," "forms," "marks," "signs," "names," "labels," or "things" in our minds are just (human) conceptual constructs, yet of course something is apparently there behind them. Our mind contributes features to objects that then makes it possible for us to experience objects as objects, otherwise there is simply a mental field of chaos. The mind therefore constructs the reality we experience – an inner subjective world that is an imagined external realm, Maya, a constructed nature, an illusion that we create and comprehend that is based on our own conceptual constructions. Sure, Shakti is there from the aspect of Shakti, but how we experience Shakti surely does not represent it correctly. We don't produce an undistorted mirrorlike knowledge of the objective world because the objects we experience are "objects" structured by our pre-existing internal organization (the contents of our neurons), so we don't know the world-in-itself but the world as rendered by the already conditioned human mind – an order grounded not in the world but in our mind. We only experience a personal construct of the world, a mental projection.

We see the world one way while other forms of life see it another way. What we see within our minds depends upon our sensory apparatus, our memory of identifiers, and our mental processing functions. In other words, objects have a conceptually constructed existence due to our sensory inputs, our storehouse of memories, and due to the operations of our consciousness (thinking and conceptions) that together create the limitedness of object attributes like colors, shapes and borders. We create the facticity of objects and forms out of the infinitely interconnected tableau of a vast soup of oneness. Their facticity isn't arbitrary, but we cannot truly call it "real" either.

We are ourselves a "living" object/process within Shakti that exists because of an unbroken chain of previously existing humans whose chain of sexual activities and their persistence at survival eventually produced us, and what is special about us as opposed to most matter is that we possess the attribute of life and consciousness that is responsible for our "existence survival." We think of ourselves as isolated objects or things in space but *we are actually places of transformation connected to all others* (and especially affecting the immediate world around us). Or you can think of us as *processes* within a great Indra's net of infinite processes all connected together. You can also think of us as *events*, or as *compositions of simples* whose structure is always changing, or view us in countless other ways, each of which has implications for how we should live.

Actually, everything in the world is part of us, and we are part of everything so we must become stewards and guardians of human well-being. We possess the miraculous powers of consciousness and the potential of voluntary activity as our attributes, and we should use them for this purpose. The laws of nature describe us on a fundamental level such as the fact that inanimate atoms work together to produce what we call our "life," but you can view our existence or composition from so many other angles that each have their own implications, such as the fact that our consciousness seeks the bliss of *sat-chit-ananda* for its existence, and we have to find some way to achieve it.

As an object we have no intrinsic self-so nature or soul that we can identify as a permanent core that is truly and solely us, unchanging and everlasting, yet as stated a continuous process keeps going on that transforms from life to life. However, in truth there is no true sentient being within that process of continuity who is actually thinking and experiencing. We say there is a sentient being, but there is just consciousness (Knowledge) within a body automatically spinning and experiencing thoughts that engender the delusion of a separated self, and that Knowledge process is itself just a network of thoughts (Knowledge). Knowledge is just experiencing Knowledge, a Knowledge process is just experiencing Knowledge. There is a body vehicle together with subtle energy performing mental operations called consciousness that is generating thoughts, and this process is automatically operating on its own as long as the body vehicle retains the state of "being alive." Those thoughts contain within their network of conceptual-spinning the delusion of being an inherently existing, separate, independent human being.

Knowledge itself is the ultimate experiencer of everything (rather than a person) as there is no real permanent soul, self, *atman*, *jiva*, personality, or living entity that is the doer or experiencer of any thought or action. An insentient Knowledge is just experiencing Knowledge, and we call this sentience. A "Knowledge generating machine, process or object" is experiencing Knowledge by, in effect, talking to itself. No one is there, and yet there is understanding. At an even higher level, in terms of the fundamental substratum there is nothing except Itself so from this aspect sentient beings are also an apparitional fiction as well.

Knowledge is talking to itself in a delusory fashion because it takes itself as an entity, soul or knower in its self-talk, and furthermore its self-talk (consciousness) commonly contains errors, biases and delusions. All this happens automatically to a living object possessing cognitive processes that we call a "sentient being" (Knowledge maker). It functions dynamically as a complicated process that, unlike static inanimate matter, for its continued existence or maintenance requires inputs and produces outputs. This living object or process, "us," can form Knowledge for its existence while insentient objects cannot, yet we are just as much an object within the universe as any other phenomenon that has developed/evolved out of Shakti. We are a *living* object, and a living object *with consciousness*. Thus, there isn't really a separate, independent, self-so living own-being, soul, or entity in the sense that you usually assume. Yet there is an appearing being, and it has consciousness, and it can know and enjoy and experience majesty and bliss. However, you must work to make that happen.

We also make a mistake when we look at an object and assume it is solid because it is really composed of atoms that are mostly empty space, so "solid objects" are mostly empty space. Furthermore, due to Einstein's work we also know that any matter that we see is ultimately only energy, so our concepts of monotonous solid objects are delusional.

In the same way, in looking at ourselves as sentient beings we assume we are a certain way when higher understanding (wisdom) tells us that we are not that way at all. There is no intrinsic or core permanent entity, soul, or *atman* within a sentient being. Sentient beings have no absolute metaphysical substrate other than the original nature. They are a continuous but dependently constructed process that will die out unless maintained through various processes that are always moving, vibrating, fluctuating or undergoing transformations of complex interactions. Understanding arises within that sentient machine, but there is really no such thing as a real being, ego, or life within it who understands. There is Knowledge that is understanding Knowledge. That being the case, why are we so egotistical, stubborn, proud, greedy or violent in life and let phenomenal circumstances repeatedly upset our emotions when we can choose to experience peace and bliss or even create our own happiness if we view matters in special ways, such as with equanimity, detachment or dispassion?

To understand this is the "view of enlightenment" because this is comprehending the truth of your self-nature. When you realize the nature of your self this is called "self-realization" but *not* "enlightenment" since enlightenment entails the attainment of the higher transcendental bodies (a hierarchy of selves or bodies) that comprise the *sambhogakaya*. When you understand the truth of your beingness, your true reality and true identity as opposed to your apparent identity or false self then this is self-realization, which is realizing what your true self-nature actually is.

Advaita Vedanta says that this knowledge leads to liberation because it frees you from ignorance, leads to less ego grasping, helps you practice detachment that leads to peacefulness, helps you to stop clinging to your thoughts, desires or phenomena so that you maintain better mental states, and helps you attain a more peaceful mental state where your Qi/Prana can more easily be stimulated to push through and purify your subtle body.

Buddhism says that all Buddhas come into the world to give sentient beings the knowledge and understanding of their true self-nature as well as teach the means to enlightenment, which is how to attain the higher spiritual bodies through self-cultivation that free you from the wheel of life that is a sequence of endless rounds of reincarnation in the lower realms. They teach a process of spiritual and physical *ascension*.

Once you understand the nature of reality (the world) you must understand how to live properly or "best" within it. The problem is how to live well to experience excellent states of being, and how to cultivate spiritual bodies in enjoyable transcendental realms that have great capabilities (due to being composed of higher energy) and longevity so they can delay the principle of impermanence (death) for very long periods of time. Or, the problem is how to maintain your best attributes so that when you are finally reborn that *that new individual* (your repackaged old self) can live a more enjoyable and productive life. That also raises the problem of how you can improve living conditions for society (the world) as whole that when that time comes you inherit those better conditions.

If you understand what your True Self is (your ultimate unchanging Self that is your Supreme Identity) as opposed to your apparent self then this is comprehending the truth about your self-nature. We are transient constructions of processes destined to deteriorate, decay and disappear but one thing keeps the impermanent matrix of ourselves intact, which is the systematic process of reincarnation managed by higher spiritual beings who periodically refresh our Qi and help preserve us (including our inner energy structure or subtle body) out of a sense of responsibility and compassion. Managing this process, instead of letting sentient beings disappear forever, is truly a career of compassion, and one of the reasons why Buddhas and Bodhisattvas are called compassionate. It is a process meant to preserve our continuity, or you can say it is meant to maintain our longevity; due to the existence of reincarnation the problem of death is a problem of longevity or continuity rather than annihilation and non-existence. Only if you achieve a purified energy body whose composition will not decay can you say that you have jumped out of the *samsaric* wheel of reincarnation forever.

Just as we constantly transform throughout life such that you'll be entirely different thirty years from now, during the process of reincarnation our physical attributes and personality transform from one life to the next. A portion of the new developments is due to the genetics and anatomical structure of the new incarnation, but there is indeed a carryover of virtues, skills or traits (and sometimes memories) within the subtle body that reincarnates. Until you develop a nearly immortal life at the stage of the Supra-Causal body or higher, you will continue to undergo the process of reincarnation managed by higher beings.

You must spiritually cultivate enough to achieve the Supra-Causal body attainment and then you will jump out of the lower realms of denser existence forever (the Desire Realm of physical and subtle bodied inhabitants and the Form Realm of Causal bodied inhabitants) because your body composition will be free of the lower stages of matter, and then there will be nothing to pull you back into the lower realms. This is why spiritual cultivation is important in life, but no one will help you achieve the highest spiritual body attainments unless you cultivate virtuous personality traits such as mental purity, disciplined control over your conduct and emotions, compassion and kindness, your intellect, and you naturally take pains to help others. You must purify your consciousness and conduct to a certain level so that these become your natural personality characteristics.

Within consciousness we create mental patterns (conceptual thinking) and a world of objects that help us continue our existence (by helping us manage survival and replication issues), but those mental doings are a false world, an imaginary world, a representative similitude or unreality as to how things really are. We mentally falsify how reality truly exists, yet evolution has led us to being able to create abbreviated, simplified mental representations that enable us to survive and procreate. If they didn't conventionally work for us then we couldn't survive, so even though mental fabrications are fraught with error their fitness ensures survival, but not accuracy. The implication of this is that we mentally construct a reality that *doesn't replicate actual reality in its similitude*, and that we have no idea what physical reality actually is because we're missing most of it and inaccurately represent that which we do grasp.

Evolution has enabled us to create our own unique form of internal mental

Maya in order to survive, and not in order to experience reality more accurately or completely. Evolution just happened to produce us, and our senses have evolved for the attribute of *usefulness* rather than to provide the most accurate or fullest representations of the outside world. That usefulness is fraught with simplifications and errors, but our representations of the world (provided to us through our senses and mental processing) have enabled us to survive because they provide a sufficient level of *fitness*. As sentient beings we have even created shared beliefs – such as religions, traditions, codes of conduct and standards of behavior – in order that we could dwell peacefully with one another and increase our chances of survival. By establishing a culture of common information and values, cooperation and collaboration became possible amongst large groups of strangers who lacked intimate connections with one another, and thereby those groups increased their chances for survival. Our imagined realities of shared values, virtues and beliefs make mass cooperative collaboration possible among us, which is necessary for the survival and prosperity (thriving or flourishing) of a group and its individual members.

We have evolved to maximize the fitness for survival, not for the correctness or optimality or perception. Hence we can see only a limited set of colors and wavelengths of light, but not all of them, while some animals can only see black and white. Who knows what else our visual representations are also missing? Some animals have the ability to smell scents miles away through their nose, or can sense odors or heat through the flick of their tongue as do snakes. We can only hear a certain limited range of sound frequencies too whereas some animals can hear more, and many animals can even sense heat, movement or pressure through echolocation, whiskers or pores on their body while we cannot. What type of world are they experiencing, what world representation are they building up in their minds that is totally different from ours since we have access to a totally different sensory space? They experience what their species needs to know of the world in order to survive. We tend to systematically misperceive reality and our sensory view of the world is quite limited yet it helps us. Who says it is the correct one? It certainly doesn't give us a full picture of the universe.

To us, inanimate external objects such as rocks seem to have a real independent existence on their own, but this is also a magical illusion since our minds give objects hypothetical boundaries that fix their shape by falsely dividing up a single manifest reality (unity). They don't really exist on their own but flow into everything else because the energies that flow through them (which create the conditions necessary for their presence) make this the reality of how things are, and yet we think there is a multiplicity in front of us instead of a single oneness. Furthermore, what appears stable on the surface is not internally monotonous but always moving. While objects seem fixed, stable and monotonous with an appearance of continuity they are always changing. In other words, *there is no constant reality to know*, and so the present is virtually unknowable because manifest reality is inconstant. Hence Heisenberg's Uncertainty Principle.

Forms also appear to us as having solid existences but analysis reveals that they don't exist in that way due to being composed by atoms made mostly of space. Hence, our assumptions about the nature of their existence are wrong *just as our assumptions about our own identities are wrong*. What we see as objects are apparent signs, marks, forms, names or labels that are mere designations within our minds that are the patterns of mental projection. They are just designations that we have created within our minds – names, labels, forms or pattern identifiers – for what are continuously changing bits of infinite processes (appearances) we mentally carved out that actually lack fixed borders.

Infinite flickering processes and fluctuating conditions go into creating an apparent object. We cannot see all the interconnections that define objects because, as stated, we have through species evolution only developed an *efficient way* of viewing the world for survival purposes rather than a true, optimal or complete way of viewing the world that shows us everything. This is one of the reasons why we misunderstand the true nature of objects. We cannot even see the internal energy interactions within solid objects or the microscopic world that reveals their composition as mostly space, so how can we truly understand what they really are? We also always ignore the energetic interconnections between phenomena that are necessary for their existence (which are thus part of their composition) and posit that they have separate independent existences instead, thus creating a Maya (internal representation system) of our own making where objects are separate from one another and unconnected in any way whatsoever within space. Objects are not packets hanging there independently in space.

Humans share a similar type of Maya worldview that they have as a species developed in order to survive over the continuum of human evolution. Each animal species creates its own type of Maya or worldview, and because of our anatomical similarities the human species has its own specific way as well that all humans commonly share.

Our species has evolved the ability to create our mental constructions in the way we do so that (as the type of *living object* we are) we can continue to survive and thrive (through eating, protecting ourselves, etcetera). Without abilities that maintained the prior existence of our species we would not be here after a long chain of prior ancestors. Our sentient species (of a certain type of *living object* possessing consciousness) would not have survived without an internal representation system that allowed it to survive, but which by no means reflects reality in the most accurate way or most fully. What we create within our minds is an imaginary representation, a simplification, a delusion of the world or illusion *but it works for us*. Something is out there (a world external to our body and mind), but it doesn't appear to us in the way that it really is. Our human senses and our consciousness have evolved over time for the needs of survival, not for the needs of discerning reality truthfully, and so represents things in a certain limited way. Now you know the truth of what we call reality, and the question is how to live within it. You now know the truth about your self-nature and manifest reality.

When Buddhas teach human beings the truth of what they ultimately are this is called "enlightening beings as to the truth of their self-nature," and now you have these teachings. Buddhas teach beings what their True Self is versus what their apparent self is. They teach them their Supreme Identity as opposed to their apparent identity, and people can then correctly answer, "Who am I? Who or what is this 'me'?" They teach that their body is a collection of simples (atoms, particles or quanta) and energy fields connected to all other things in existence, and that their apparent soul or individuality is a non-homogenous composite (collection of) dependent processes that, through its structural design, gives rise to a process called "consciousness" that is the great miracle of existence within an insentient universe. It is simply amazing that consciousness exists and that sentient beings have arisen in the universe who are able to consciously experience the existence of a world of qualities. Maybe there is something even greater than consciousness, but how would we know?

To understand this knowledge as a conceptual understanding or realization is called *self-realization*. "Self-realization" means you are realizing something about the nature of your self, namely your apparent worldly self and your True Self, and this information explains what your apparent manifest self of individuality really is as opposed to your true self-nature or permanent underlying nature Self.

The word "enlightenment" means full comprehension of a situation, but the spiritual meaning of "enlightenment" is that you attain the Srotapanna deva body attainment whilst alive. This "flight from the body" "rising to divinity" attainment (making you *Homo Deus)* means that you "enter the stream" for the journey to the Buddha-body, Rainbow body or Supra-

Causal body stage of enlightenment that is called a Formless Realm inhabitant because it can completely twist, turn, fold, shrink, expand and so forth in amazing, seemingly impossible ways due to the fact that its composition is totally lacking all material (form) elements and is primarily higher energies. It gives you an incredible flexibility of form and control of your inner energies such as being able to move them or liberate them in varying intensity. When it generates a physical *nirmanakaya* projection body (*yang shen*) that you can see and touch on the earthly plane then its shape does not have to be an exact copy of the saint's original body but can be taller, thinner, have special marks and so forth. Spiritual schools slowly train you for the formless mode of being by promoting various formless meditations that help you dis-identify from being a solid body of fixed form, and others teach various *neijia* methods[6] that have you develop the potential of your internal energies.

To understand the truth about (1) the absolute foundational substrate of the universe that is our True Self or self-nature, (2) the manifest Realm of Emanations, Creation or Shakti that is the *manifest universe* whose ultimate unchanging nature is its primordial, unborn fundamental substratum, (3) the process of interdependent origination (co-dependent existence) that defines the interconnected simultaneous arising of all elements within Shakti that are all joined together into one whole by an "Indra's net" infinite set of cause and effect interrelations (such as energy fields that span everything), (4) that your existence lacks a self-so innate nature but is instead an agglomeration of energy fields, simples and a set of conditional processes that have temporarily come together through cause and effect interdependence to create your apparent body-mind self – you are a dependent note within the universe, (5) that you are not your body but actually *beingness without a body*, and (6) what you think and perceive is an illusion of Knowledge created by Knowledge spinning Knowledge for itself without there being a (real) intrinsic sentient being within the process ... attaining this understanding is called *self-realization* because by understanding this information you realize the nature of your self.

Attaining the realization of enlightenment means becoming able to correctly discriminate between the eternal substance (foundational substrate of Reality) and the substance that is transitory (Shakti). It means being able to differentiate between your true self and false body-self. It means understanding the nature of your real self or the "nature of your self-nature" ... understanding what is your true self-nature. It means that you finally understand that your apparent self is a bundle of fleeting states that

---

[6] See *Neijia Yoga*.

temporarily exist within a body-mind agglomeration (lacking a homogenous permanent core or eternal soul self) whose structure is dependent upon many things while continuously changing. "Realization" is an intellectual understanding whereas enlightenment is not because enlightenment is a higher spiritual body attainment.

Even though this life of yours is temporary because you must one day die, upon death your inherent subtle energy (Qi, Prana, soul or *atman*) that already resides within the matrix of your physical body then arises into a new life so that you are "born by transformation" into the earthly heavenly plane of subtle energy as a Qi-bodied deva. That, too, is the Srotapanna stage of achievement, or first dhyana of Buddhism. In Christianity it is called becoming a spirit or angel. In time that "heavenly" life will end, but instead of annihilation Buddhas will manage the process of reincarnation so that this subtle energy body is reborn either upon the earthly plane again as a human mortal, or in the heavenly plane again only if as a deva (Srotapanna) you cultivated the inner energy of your deva body enough to reach the Sakadagamin level of purity. Thus, your continuity is maintained until you can ultimately cultivate to achieve a nearly immortal state of existence that resides on yet higher (more refined) energy planes. The higher transcendental body attainments constitute enlightenment.

Your apparent self is an appearing combination of physical and higher aggregates, composed of agglomerations of matter and energy undergoing constant flux, that like everything else in manifestation are ruled by the laws of cause and effect. Further, there is nothing permanent, everlasting, unchanging or eternal in this apparent self of ours that we take as our body-mind complex, nor in the whole of existence. Nothing exists by itself, nothing has a self-so independent own-existence, and no thing is permanent, pure or everlasting (except the original nature). The aggregates that compose our body-mind are impermanent, create pain for us, and are not our true stable Self (self-nature) but simply an oscillating process of vibrations that create an apparent being or display of processes within Shakti.

Over time, within that overall process of sentient life you produce Knowledge and thereby experience thoughts, emotions and perceptions that you continuously identify with, which creates the idea and feeling of being an independent self separate from the rest of manifestation, and you take this identification as your true self, which is incorrect. That is a wrong thought, a big false thought, a big mistake. Only by *dis-identifying from that false self-identity* that you are this body-mind of yours can you understand that you are one with all of manifest reality, and through wisdom you can understand what is your genuine true self-nature. There are many meditation practices in spiritual traditions that help you to stabilize within these realizations.

Because we have consciousness yet live fragile impermanent lives, the main problems of our existence are sustenance, protection, maintenance, suffering, continuity-longevity, general well-being and finding meaning for our existence. We have the great advantage that we do not simply exist but can decide what our existence will be, and the most crucial decision each moment is to decide each moment what to do in order to experience what we want, which is to be what we want to be or works towards achieving what we want and becoming what we want.

First, (1) we have *physical material needs* necessary for our survival, namely the maintenance and continuance of our existence. In order that we don't quickly die we need to pursue resources such as food and water, clothing, shelter, medicine, etc. that are the sustenance necessary for our survival. We need to protect ourselves from predation as well, including by other humans, groups of people or even institutions that might try to take advantage of us. Fulfilling our physiological and safety needs allows us to continue living while also reducing our physical pains and discomfort.

Second, (2) we have *psychological needs* that include a longing for connection and affiliation with others. We desire relationship feelings of love, belongingness, and connectedness. Psychologically, people want to feel part of something larger than themselves, and members of a group of "We." People also have individual "I" needs in that each of wants an absence of pain and mental suffering in our life. All people desire positive states and feelings such as happiness, joy, engagement, sunniness, centeredness, peace, flow, lightness, mental freshness (clear vivid alertness-awareness without distractions), blissful inner vitality and mental bliss. During their lives people want to enjoy both physical and mental states of comfort and well-being so they work to fulfill their material wants for prosperity and their psychological needs for peace, comfort, happiness and bliss.

Furthermore, (3) we have *created human cultures and societies that embody a unified wholeness with others in order to support the fulfillment of our needs and create a greater potential for human peace, prosperity, happiness and flourishing*. Culture has the job of "making good people," ensuring their survival, and binding society together in a harmonious way. Culture passes onto society information dear to us such as social virtues, values, and stories of heroes so that people can build a map of internal values to emulate and thereby derive a sense of direction, proper behavior, upliftment and purpose in their lives. Culture and society are our foundational support for survival, prosperity and flourishing, and by fulfilling some of our fundamental needs the presence of society provides us with the opportunity to pursue interests other than survival such as cultivating our greater potential.

We all seek pleasurable lives, positive mental states and moods, fulfilling engagement with apparent reality, flourishing states of existence, and wonderful relationships within the societies where we live. Through societal connections we fulfill our need for human contact, our desire for our identity to be recognized by others, and our desire to receive respect and esteem from people (ego-happiness). However, humans have discovered that this is not enough for deep satisfaction or contentment in life. We also seek a higher meaning or deeper purpose for our lives other than purely existence. This cannot be satisfied just by engagement in the busyness required for survival or from the fulfillment we feel from the experience of pleasure, relationships, deep engagement with enjoyable activities, and the feeling of well-being.

Because we are an impermanent body-mind vehicle, (4) we need to seek *a better and longer-lasting existence*, which means we should be taking care of our fragile, vulnerable bodies during life (staying in good shape through diet, exercise and various health maintenance activities such as medicine etc. to maximize healthy, vigorous longevity) and should be seeking the higher transcendental body attainments (a hierarchy of selves or bodies) that live very long lives and reside in higher heavenly realms. Sages who have already attained them teach us how to go about attaining them. Those spiritual bodies provide access to higher, more enjoyable and longer lasting existences. If we attain those longer life existences through the path and practices of spiritual cultivation, we will then need a sense of purpose for that longevity which Buddhas create by taking upon themselves various vows, pledges or responsibilities to help living beings in the lower realms who have not yet achieved those heights.

Our presence, manifestation or displaying appearance within Shakti is a nexus of processes that constitute *sat, chit, ananda* – a bodily existence having consciousness that is seeking bliss (a peaceful and joyful experience of life). *Sat, chit, ananda* should not just describe a subjective experience of the ultimate unchanging reality but of life itself. We are designed and constructed to enjoy our innate *sat-chit-ananda* and participate in the bliss of existence, so it should not be suppressed or denied. That is our liberation from insentience. Because we have a physical body we have *existence*, our living body possesses the attribute of *consciousness*, and our body-mind vehicle wants to enjoy various states of *bliss* that are mental-physical states absent of suffering such as comfort, happiness, lightness, sunniness, joy, shine, peacefulness, tranquility or flow. We can pursue other positive states as well.

In particular *we want to feel alive* where we feel full of energy and our mind is vivid or fresh and filled with positive mental states; we want to feel a blissful active vitality inside our cells and want to experience a fullness of peace, bliss or happiness that fills our moments. As a mind-body vehicle we essentially have only two skills – physical skills and cognitive skills – and we are seeking physical sensations and cognitive mental states that satiate the body-mind complex with bliss-like comfort. Bliss does not have to be an active state but can be a comfortable peacefulness of tranquility such as an equanimity that in some way represents a non-movement (like our original nature).

In life we seek both physical bliss/comfort and the mental state of flowing concentration that is pristinely pure, perfect in poise, fully and freely engaged with the world yet undisturbed by annoyances, agitations or distractions. During a "flow" state you can find fulfillment in the present moment through deep immersion in your present activity – where you and the activity are essentially one – without distractions throwing you off balance or interrupting you enough to send you out of that state of peaceful lucid concentration. It is a state where you can drop all your problems and *be fully in the present moment*. To some extent, advanced stages of mindfulness that bring you into a stage of alert, attentive presence are actually synonymous with the flow state where you lose your sense of self but find yourself experiencing concentration and bliss (enjoyment) by becoming fully present with maximum focus, freshness and attention in your activities.

Our physical skills provide us with the ability of movement, which includes the capability of speech and the possibility of other actions. Our mental or cognitive skills produce an internal world of qualities and can fabricate thoughts automatically or by will for deliberate purposes, including for the control of our external movements that we call actions, conduct or behavior. Since our behavior (our movements) is our thoughts expressed (actions which service our thoughts), behavior is the expression of our consciousness. In other words, *our conduct, activities and behavior are the exhibition of our consciousness.* The root of our physical sensations and our feelings of comfort, bliss or inner vitality is consciousness as well. The root of our emotional feelings of liking or disliking something is also our consciousness. Consciousness is the root of our perceptions, thoughts, emotions, will, mental states and behavior. It is sentience, so of course it is the root of our beingness as a being rather than inert matter.

To enjoy positive mental states we must cultivate good thoughts, good emotions and good activities that produce good results. We must also purify our consciousness of unwanted impurities or defilements, which is called purifying consciousness, perfecting consciousness or mastering consciousness so that unwanted agitations or perturbations do not arise within it and thus stain it. Both of these objectives are the targets of spiritual cultivation - the human cultivation required for the Great Learning necessary for living. A related task includes improving the health and status of your physical body (its capabilities) since your body gives rise to either blissful, comfortable sensations or uncomfortable sensations that assault and vex the mind. We often experience physical discomfort due to sickness, accidents, deficiencies or aging so our physical body requires constant maintenance. How to protect, heal, rejuvenate, train and develop our body, and how to master its movements, internal energy and autonomic functions are also part of the pathway of spiritual (human) cultivation.

Our mental and spiritual peace is often marred by disturbing desires, emotions and other defilements that produce for us mental pain and suffering. In seeking internal peace, calm or bliss, we must therefore learn not only how to maintain our bodies to produce physical comfort and bliss but should eliminate pollutions and unwanted disturbances from our mental workings as well. We must learn how to overcome negative emotions, silence unwanted afflictions or agitations, and tame our mental processes – basically control or manage our mind – so that we can achieve a steady state experience of equanimity, happiness, lightness, contentment, the joy of life, pristine mental flow (a state of vivid experience of thinking and immersion in the world without distraction), centeredness, presence, freshness, shine, bliss or other positive mental states *rather than suffering*. Such achievements require that we master various expedient remedies to handle our internal and external problems (so that we find release) and that we pursue self-development work that trains us how to free ourselves from bad mental or physical states or external circumstances whenever they arise. *We need to learn how to gradually evolve ourselves over time into beings with better attributes and behaviors that will enable us to conquer life and enjoy it to the fullest.*

For each one of us, our overall happiness and well-being are also affected by our unique personal circumstances including our relationships, environment, career, status, wealth and living conditions. In general, we need to learn how to both master and transform ourselves, and also our circumstances (their possible configurations, trajectories or transformations) so that we can pursue bliss and well-being that are free from unfortunate states. It is by mastering the processes ruling our consciousness that we develop the ability to escape suffering and experience happiness and well-being in its place.

Here is the point. For all activities in life and all states of being, their attainment depends upon consciousness. For the spiritual life you must master your *thinking mind* and your *emotional mind* - your deliberate intellectual processes under your voluntary control and your automatic, reflexive mental processes such as your emotions, mental states and unwanted mental afflictions that naturally arise within your consciousness.

If you attain the knowledge of what you ultimately are, which is called "enlightenment as to your true self-nature," then among these various requirements for creating a satisfactory life - together with the possibility for cultivating higher transcendental bodies - this understanding should affect your behavior. It should be used to guide your life and self-development.

Even if you don't attain the knowledge of your true self-nature as opposed to your apparent beingness, or pursue spiritual enlightenment during life, the problems of humanity still remain those of survival, reducing your suffering, socially living with others in a harmonious, non-antagonistic nature, cultivating your happiness and well-being, and ultimately establishing meaning for your existence. These things don't just happen. These goals can only be achieved if you work for them by managing your thoughts, speech, conduct and activities according to high standards.

All the standards of virtuous behavior in the world are manmade, even those which come to us from famous sages or holy scriptures that we take as our guides for life. Those standards are designed to produce good behavior within the public by restraining our minds, hearts and behavior from wayward paths. Within these standards, we have defined the most noble human conduct as that which raises us above our basest instincts, passions and desires that are our animalistic propensities, and which cultivates our humanity to the highest degree. This requires that we purify our minds and behavior so that our behavior constitutes consummate conduct, and that we take steps to "cultivate a good heart" where we help other human beings through benevolent acts of friendship, kindness, compassion, and acts of service or good works/deeds that help others in need, solve their problems, alleviate their distress, eliminate their suffering and fulfill their wishes. The spiritual path of self-cultivation involves purifying our minds, eliminating our behavioral flaws and polishing our virtues so that we can live peacefully with others in a society aiming for public welfare, individual safety, justice, fairness, prosperity and flourishing. If you are devoted to this then you have the personality merit necessary for attaining the higher spiritual bodies that give you dominion over mankind.

For the problem of maintaining our physical body or life, entropy insures that our bodies will deteriorate over time, but we can greatly manipulate our physical genetic expression and the development of our body though diet, exercise and lifestyle. We can use diet and exercise to maintain our health and employ rejuvenating practices that will regularly repair and renew it. We should take care of our bodies as if we were going to live forever. In fact, the only route for escaping a continual need of upkeep is to cultivate "immortal bodies" of higher transcendental substance that do not decay for a long time. Those higher energy bodies are inherent within the structural matrix of our present physical body, and if we fail in attaining them on the spiritual path then our subtle energy body is recycled through a process of reincarnation managed by those who have already achieved those higher body attainments. By cultivating higher transcendental bodies we can free ourselves from death (for a long while) and separate ourselves from the suffering inherent within the lower realms of impurity and struggle.

Suffering comes from what we experience and do, but the root of suffering lies in consciousness because it is our mind that mentally produces pain, suffering and unhappiness; without the conscious recognition of suffering there is no suffering. All of spiritual cultivation comes down to cultivating our body, mind and behavior, but especially consciousness, which in turn is the root of our sentient existence and our activities. Therefore to pursue happiness, joy, lightness, comfort, peace, presence or bliss, etc. it is essential during life that we cultivate the roots of consciousness.

In consciousness we mentally create objects that are "out there" in the external world (even though their appearance is only in our brain) so that those objects can be appropriated for survival. We cognize objects in a way where we take the images generated inside our brain as external to our body, and assume we are seeing external objects when we are only experiencing our internal consciousness. In other words, we are only experiencing our consciousness rather than external objects because consciousness is the only thing that we can experience; we do not experience objects directly but only experience mental representations of objects. We create the representations of objects inside our minds and deceive ourselves through an inversion in thinking (projection) that they are "out there" in the world whereas all we ever experience are mental forms inside our brains. We only experience, and only *ever* experience, only mind-objects rather than external objects, and both object-objects and mind-objects are components of the universe. Even so, the path of cultivation is termed Consciousness-Only, Mind-Only or Representation-Only due to the fact that it is all based on consciousness.

Truly the path of spiritual development must entail comprehension of the operations of our mind because our consciousness is the basis of what we are, and what we are is what we must "master," "purify" or "perfect" on the road of spirituality and cultivation practice. Spiritual practice should primarily involve mastering the abilities of our consciousness rather than performing devotional or reverential religious ceremonies, although they are also cultivation techniques that can help to purify your Qi and train your mind. That's one of the reasons they are used in religions. The principles of ethical conduct and prosocial behavior are also important, but *mastering the functions of our consciousness and maximizing its potential capabilities* is foundational for survival. Consciousness is the one great treasure that we possess, the miracle of existence and significant distinguishing factor of our beingness that gives us the experience of life and makes us who we are.

We call any effort to master consciousness as "cultivating consciousness" or "perfecting consciousness," and the particular task of learning how to control its contents is called "taming the mind," "conquering the mind," "controlling the mind" or "purifying the mind," etcetera. The path of spiritual development is centered on training our consciousness so that through its abilities we not only survive but might also experience a better life due to mastering its many capabilities including concentration, imagination, memory, pattern-matching, logical reasoning, planning, decision-making (wisdom) and behavioral control. We should work at cultivating its purity so that it is free of afflictions or unwanted agitations, is permeated by virtuous tendencies, and free of animalistic tendencies such as greed, envy, hatred, anger, lust, attachment or violence. Ultimately we must learn to understand the doings of our consciousness - how it works - and then master its processes so that we can get better at life and experience better states of well-being.

Consciousness gives us innate resources such as the following: an observing self that can recognize itself as a unique center of awareness apart from the intellect (thoughts), emotions and past conditioning; memory which enables us to add to our innate knowledge and learn; emotions and instincts that provide us with basic reactive responses and propulsive patterns for behavior; a metaphorical mind that lets us "know" (identify, discriminate or differentiate) and understand the world through metaphorical pattern matching; rational logical abilities of questioning, planning and analysis; imagination that can mentally rehearse possibilities, creatively solve problems by simulating possibilities, empathize with those suffering (because it can imagine their feelings), and focus attention away from mental afflictions, emotions or other thought processes; and the ability to build rapport and connect with others through various means of communication and persuasion. The path of spiritual development involves learning how to master these and many other mental skills so that we can experience a successful, happy, fulfilling and meaningful life. Consciousness basically gives us the powers of thought and imagination so that we can domesticate Nature and ourselves. The goal for society is to create civilization, culture, codes of conduct, cultivation methods and charitable motivation (altruism where you yield a benefit to non-relatives) so that society's development progresses forward and humanity experiences definite elevation over time.

In terms of the human condition, consciousness creates our I-thought (sentient subjectivity, which is the sense of being a conscious being or the "sentient being of the mind") and produces many other thoughts and conceptions. Due to its errant thinking we assume that we are intrinsically independent beings and have an inherently real essence. However, we are just imaginatively divided up designations of Shakti, or Nature, which just happen to possess the attribute of consciousness. Some objects have special attribute such as producing radiation or magnetism, but each of us is a "living" object that has the major attribute of producing mental activity and behavior. We are a transient compositional product that looks monotonous and stable but is always changing, needs constant upkeep through nutrition and repair, and in fact we are always deteriorating unless there is sufficient upkeep.

In terms of the composition of our body and our assumed inner soul, the truth is that neither our aggregates, our simples, our internal processes, the set of conditions that define us, our collection of parts or network of parts, their continuum over time, nor something separate and apart from them, produces a defining characteristic of a private, permanent and independent unchanging own-self or soul inside us to which you could correctly apply the word "I" or "me." The words "I" or "me" assume an unchanging, fixed immortal self but are just mental labels we expediently apply to an impermanent, ever-changing composite aggregate of experience (that can grow and develop in any way it chooses) whose innermost true core is fundamentally empty of any and all attributes.

There is actually no such thing as a real person – possessing intrinsic existence and identity – who is experiencing consciousness. However, there is indeed a functioning of consciousness that is experiencing consciousness within an apparent person. A Knowledge-creating vehicle is experiencing Knowledge, but Knowledge is experiencing Knowledge without there being an intrinsically real person in the process. There is understanding, but there is no one experiencing the understanding. Knowledge is experiencing the understanding, and so understanding is there for that Knowledge.

There is no such thing as an independent, self-existent being experiencing some transcendental mental function (transcendent to Shakti, outside of Shakti) of true knowing called consciousness. There is no such transcendental functioning or process as "sentience" belonging to an inherently existing spiritual being. Consciousness is just another functioning process within Shakti that does not transcend it, and it lacks an ontological being standing behind it.

There is no such true thing as any type of sentience, or even a sentient God, that stands outside of Shakti viewing Shakti because the consciousness of a living entity is just another insentient process within it, but we call it sentience anyway. There is only ever Knowledge experiencing Knowledge within the process called a conscious living being, and that Knowledge is part of Shakti's fabric rather than something transcendentally outside it. The Knowledge is Shakti, the Knowledge making is Shakti and the Knowledge experiencer is Shakti ... it is all Shakti without a living being involved.

Consequently, not only is there just the process of Knowledge experiencing Knowledge (in a composite transient body) but there is no real person receiving any benefit or merit from any knowledge or undertaking either, including receiving/enjoying any merit from helping others. Sure there is a person there receiving the benefits of what they have done. However, while there may be a process going on of giving and receiving there is no real being inside it, no such thing as the giving or receiving, and no such thing as the things being given or received. In terms of Shakti there is only Shakti going through transformations without any fundamental person being involved, and in terms of the universal substratum there does not exist any processes going on anywhere at all since everything is just Itself. Since there is truly no real person there, why are we apparent beings so proud, arrogant, greedy, envious, hateful, angry and violent? Once you know there is no such true thing as your ego, which is an illusory construction of multiple causes and conditions rather than a non-composite homogenous true self, why are you so involved with clinging and attachment to yourself or things that must pass?

All of us fail to recognize the reality of our fundamental selflessness (the lack of inherent true own-existence) and hold onto ideas of being a permanent self-entity or ego. We hold onto the false notion that our small self is an independent fundamental self and *have no concept as to our true absolute self-nature*. What follows from this lapse are tendencies toward pride, possessiveness, greediness (attachment), violence and other non-virtuous qualities that make it difficult to peacefully enjoy life and get along with others in a harmonious fashion (due to anger, ill-will, hate, fear, greed, attachment, etc.). All our greed, fear, envy, lust, hatred, violence, clinging and misery etc. proceed from the conception that the universe is other than our own self ... something independently separate from us. It is hard to enjoy mental peace, happiness or bliss if you harbor such traits, and all sorts of other negative consequences have this false self-notion as their root.

Self-realization involves learning the ultimate truth of what we are, and then the Great Learning of life involves learning how to master the consciousness and body that we possess as our primary attributes even though we are not intrinsic entities. The purpose behind such mastery is *to experience better states of well-being* - states absent of suffering and filled with bliss or meaning - for our ever-changing existence that will proceed through endless transformations (of birth, youth, adulthood, aging, dying, and subsequent incarnations) until we attain the higher, more permanent spiritual bodies. During that time we want to work to perfect our consciousness and behavior so that we become a blessing to others and can improve the environment for all so that everyone gradually attains better states of well-being and happiness (either temporarily or permanently) because we create a new and better world.

Throughout all the continuous transformations of lives, each life is not about continuous hedonism, self-indulgence or a constant pursuit of peak experiences or pleasure since these do not produce any lasting happiness or well-being. Those pursuits don't stop the rounds of birth and death. If we continually run after pleasurable sensations then "hedonic adaptation" causes us to adapt to whatever circumstances or level of experience we achieve so that we always want more. Therefore, running after pleasurable sensations and (temporary) peak experiences never produces lasting satisfaction, fulfillment or contentment because we always desire an ever-increasing level of novelty and intensity to maintain the thrall.

Just as you cannot maintain a peak experience forever - *whereas you can maintain a non-irritating state of tranquility or peaceful flow for a prolonged period of time* (pristine beingness that is clear, attentive focused concentration without agitation) - you cannot maintain a state of near ecstasy for long either. Therefore experiential highs and peak experiences, while exceedingly enjoyable, are not an ultimate target to which you should devote your life.

We should all be pursuing peaceful states of mind or long-lasting states of (more active) shining. We don't understand how our psychological well-being works and must quit trusting our wants and desires as valid indicators of what will genuinely satisfy us and bring us ultimate satisfaction.

Part of the spiritual path, which has been created by and is continually administered by compassionate spiritual adepts who have already achieved higher transcendental bodies, is that we can also cultivate those same higher bodies that are virtually permanent (nearly immortal) if transcendentally pure enough in composition. This is the march toward divinity. If we fail at this cultivation target during life despite making the spiritual effort we are still further along than everyone else after death *because we made that effort*, and can then make greater progress because we already did a lot of prep work for Qi transformation within our bodies. After death most individuals only then start cultivating sufficient exercises to purify their Qi enough so that they merit rebirth in the heavenly plane as devas again rather than again be reborn as a human being. If you work at cultivation during life then this cultivation task is easier, *which is why Buddhism tells people that one cultivation method is simply to do good deeds and cultivate your personality so that you merit rebirth in heaven and can then work from there to attain the rest of the body achievements.* Humans, and the beings on other worlds, simply revolve through endless lives via the process of reincarnation, which is administered by those having higher Buddha bodies, until individuals cultivate the purity of their mind, values, virtue, conduct and internal vital energy to achieve the higher bodies.

Even so, there is no such thing as a true being, entity, *atman* or life undergoing the process of reincarnation and transmigration. Yes, there is the process of reincarnation and a sentient being undergoing the process but there is no *true being* within it, and so in a sense you can say that there is no such thing as reincarnation. Or you can say that there is no such thing as reincarnation since the "person" is always changing and what is reborn is certainly not the same entity but the memories, desires, talents and relationships of a living process kept in continuance through reincarnation. Or you can just say that from the conventional aspect reincarnation is a very real thing. You can say that there is reincarnation because a continuum of a person's personality with its skills, talents, interests, *samskaras* and history of karmas does undergo a recycling into a new living entity.

As the *Diamond Sutra* says, however, "Bodhisattvas do not entertain the idea of being an ego, person, being or soul" and also, "Bodhisattvas do not receive the rewards of merit (because there is no true person inside the apparent person to enjoy them, so no person enjoys them)." There is indeed what we call a transient or apparent person (an experiencing entity, or Knowledge making process), but it is not an independent being with an inherent, intrinsic own-nature. We lack the attribute of an innate existence, and possess no pure (non-composite) or constant fixed core.

Nonetheless we are a created designation within Shakti. Individually, each one of us is just a set of conditions we call a "person" as a manner of designation. A person, being, soul, entity, or life is a set of conditions that possess consciousness, the great miracle of existence, and we can keep the apparent entity alive through the process of periodically reinforcing its energetic structure. That living organism is fated to decay and disintegrate due to the laws of entropy and impermanence, but by causing it to undergo the process of reincarnation you can recycle the main personality attributes of that composite being. Until you achieve the highest spiritual bodies, this is one of the perennial processes of transformation you are subject to that is administered by "the denizens of Heaven."

It is through consciousness that we experience life; it is also because of consciousness that as an entity we can live and survive. With consciousness we can experience not just existence but the joy of existence. We can even enjoy life when encountering bad conditions if we cultivate cheerfulness, sunniness, optimism or other beautiful mental modes as our natural state. We are the only ones in charge of our happiness, and can choose to be happy or not. We can also develop goals and aspirations that have deep meaning for ourselves, and can devote ourselves to those purposes if they provide us with fulfillment. We can engineer our personalities or our circumstances so that we enjoy the immediate experience of life and also more frequently experience positive states of well-being such as happiness, joy, peace, bliss, flow, lightness, shine, engagement, and accomplishment. It is by using consciousness correctly and deliberately controlling our mind and behavior that we can survive and thrive, but consciousness is capable of so much more than just basic survival needs. It offers us incredible potential, but we are not taught how to cultivate many of its manifold potentials unless we start to cultivate various mental aspects of sports, special skills or spiritual practice etc., which involve training the mind for various abilities.

Buddhism says that our life is characterized by selflessness - the absence of an *inherent ego-self* - and that even *dharmas* are devoid of a self-nature (they are "selfless") because they are conditional dependent constructions. Therefore it says that there is no such real thing as *dharmas* (events, forms, objects, thoughts or even teachings). Buddhism says that things and conditions are impermanent; objects and ourselves have no self-nature or own-beingness;

our body is impure (so we must cultivate to purify it); and that all life is afflicted by suffering.

Essentially, life is a problem because existence is not a Utopia. No one remains continuously happy during the journey through life. In particular, consciousness is a problem because it is often preoccupied with various types of mental suffering or physical pain rather than occupied by serenity or bliss all day long. We should add to this list the fact of entropy that tells us that all things are destined to decay into disorder, which raises the question as to the purpose of the universe and our life. As a guide to life in response to these principles, therefore we need to:

- Learn how to *adapt to, alter and manage the changes and transformations* of phenomena, namely the cause and effect principles that rule Nature and mankind, so that we can use them according to our wishes. Change is constant and everywhere, so we need to learn how to deal with it by mastering it ... and we also need to learn mental detachment (non-clinging) to deal with it since we cannot hold anything forever constant. Mentally, we need to become flexible in adapting to changes and be flexible in trying different approaches to solving challenges. We need to be both flexible and resilient in tumultuous situations, and develop a flexibility in mental attitude so that we can adjust ourselves to changes without losing our composure (such as by allowing ourselves to get angry or irritable). You must learn how to control your reactions to circumstances, especially the influences of other people, by exercising your sentient trait of adaptability. In addition to learning how to *mentally handle change* we also want to learn how to control material reality and its circumstances by "managing its transformations into different states." We need to develop rationality, wisdom and rely on the scientific method to learn how to skillfully manage or transform circumstances in our lives as well as conditions that include our bodies, minds, relationships, our fortunes and so on. Change and transformation are inevitabilities in the universe due to the principle of impermanence, namely the continuous vibration, fluctuation or transformation of conditions that we might also call "complex interactions." Everything in the universe is always transforming into a new state via complex interactions ruled by cause and effect that we should learn and skillfully master (rather than just sit in a monastery and cultivate empty mind). To master change we need to first investigate, discover, learn and then proficiently master the laws of cause and effect that govern Nature and its transformations. Then we can produce what we want in life. Unfortunately, many religions have opposed scientific development in the past, just as they opposed adaptability by insisting on strict adherence to ancient scriptural rules rather than changing with the times. In particular, we especially need to acquire wisdom (understanding) of human nature to better manage people and situations - our living affairs. Knowing what changes to expect of people, phenomena or circumstances, and learning how to guide or manage those changes (as taught in the *Yijing*), will enable us to alter circumstances to our favor so that we can more often experience peace, happiness and well-being in the world instead of suffering. Managing change is connected with the ideals of constant development, growth, improvement and progress, which are not emphasized in many ancient schools of thought or religions. They typically focus on mastering mental detachment or non-clinging and dispassion as methods to deal with changes.

- As to the actual reality of human *suffering*, we need to eliminate, prevent, reduce, or transform situations that lead to suffering in the first place. We also need to learn how to control our minds to prevent, transform, reframe or simply manage any types of mental or physical suffering that arise. We want to transform circumstances and conditions that cause suffering so that suffering does not arise and learn how to avoid the situations where suffering is inevitable. We also do not want to create unnecessary burdens on others and hoist suffering upon them. As to our psychological suffering, we must learn how to control our thoughts and regulate our emotional mind that give rise to suffering, and develop stronger personality traits such as endurance, resilience and perseverance that enable us to handle pain and suffering much better. For instance, the attitude of cheerfulness and optimism helps us deal with the vicissitudes of life, reducing desires helps to reduce situations that cause suffering, calmness avoids emotional upsets, hope helps us ignore suffering, and detachment enables us to bear the sufferings of life more gracefully. The basic principle is that we need to learn how to *mentally and physically* stop suffering, reduce suffering, pacify suffering and bear suffering better so that we can experience superior states in its place. Using reason and an understanding of causality we also need to improve our present circumstances and create a better future free of suffering. Suffering will always accompany our lives so while we should strive to reduce suffering in life the real objective is to *cultivate well-being in general* that can admit to a degree of suffering as part of the mix. There are many strategies for dealing with suffering, and emptiness meditation together with detachment are not the "one all cure all." Other strategies must also be mastered for life.

- As to the teachings on no-self that we are *not intrinsic self-entities*, but rather an agglomeration of conditions or processes that have come together to form an ever-transforming *synthesis sentient being* that lacks any own-nature, we should cultivate a set of attitudes and behaviors in life that reflect this fact of no-self yet enable us to experience greater joy, happiness and bliss as well as peace, prosperity, enjoyable engagement and well-being during our existence. A recognition of our composite nature that lacks an inherent self should lead to less ego grasping, less violence in life, greater freedom and happiness as well as more compassion. Since we lack a permanent self core and are plagued by the problem of death and rebirth due to changing conditions, we must also seek for a greater longevity of our existence if it is possible. For instance, the qualities of non-greediness and generosity, respect for others, forgiveness, kindness, and many other virtues can help you experience a better life while cultivation of your internal energy (along with regular detoxification efforts, a better diet, exercise and improved breathing patterns) can increase your longevity while spiritual cultivation of higher spiritual bodies ("enlightenment") can lead to the spiritual "immortality" attainments that achieve the death of death.

- As to the *impurity* of our bodies and of phenomena and life we need to insist on cleanliness in our environment, for our diet, and hygiene for our excretory practices and for other life involvements. We need to insist on purity in our foods and environments (and therefore create rules of hygiene) so that we remain healthy and don't die due to poisoning by various forms of pollution or disease, especially due to our own excretory products. We must remain organically undefiled from birth to death. Principles of purity and cleanliness need to be established for various areas of our life (as religions or societal customs typically stipulate) such as our diet, hygiene, sexual conduct, the treatment of illness and environmental living conditions because these are survival issues for mankind. The attainment of higher spiritual bodies also requires a purification of our karma, which includes our body, and we transform our body's impure vital energy via Qi cultivation efforts as well as a purification of our lower nature of animal propensities. Therefore the body and mind purification practices of spiritual cultivation are actually a methodology of ascension.

Science can add further principles to this list such as Einstein's famous *mass-energy equivalence* principle that everything within Shakti is essentially energy, and therefore nothing is lost in the universe when something decays, deteriorates or is destroyed because everything is simply transformed into some other form of energy and matter. The *conservation of energy* principle tells us that the transformational products of Shakti (its evolutes or manifestations) are simply itself, and inherently they are just the fundamental essence within which there are no transformations happening at all since all things are just It. As stated, inherently Shakti's fundamental substratum never changes so from Its aspect nothing is changing or even exists other than Itself. Nothing is gained, nothing is lost. The fundamental substrate is everlasting and always present so It is our True Self or core beingness because it is the only thing dependable that never changes.

Whether you consider Shakti as the Creator or consider the Creator to be the fundamental substrate, the distance between you and God is therefore zero. You are ultimately God, and God is you. There is no difference between God and man. Whatever is perceived any time is also a manifestation of the Supreme Being, meaning it is God. It is an illusion to think you are separated from God because God is universal both within and without. God is universal both within and without. In the whole universe, in all states of being, in all forms is He, the fundamental substratum. You are God in incarnate form and manifest as a transient process with consciousness – the consciousness of God – and you need to learn how to properly use this consciousness you have. From the level of a materialistic animal you must cultivate it to a level of purity.

You are a functioning appearance within Shakti – one of the manifestations of the fundamental nature that possesses a body and the great attribute of consciousness – and for your survival and well-being you need to learn how to use them well. This is another way to view all these principles, which is the fact that you must work on perfecting your physical skills, mental skills, and their expression through actions and behavior. The goal is a life well lived, with *a sound mind in a sound body*, that experiences happiness, well-being, service to other parts of itself and meaning. This is the principle that you are a mind-body complex, so you must transform both on the cultivation path and you help others because they are other parts of yourself. But in particular, you must especially develop the various capabilities of your mind, master all the capabilities of your consciousness and learn to control your mind. Since your mind has both deliberate and automatic aspects (such as your thinking and emotions) you must learn to control both, especially the internal emotional afflictions that cause suffering. You must also develop all the physical characteristics of your body, such as its health and athletic capabilities, and gain control over it as well including control over its internal energy and even autonomic functions if you like. Thus you have the additional principle of cultivating both your body and mind to develop their capabilities to excellence, which means gaining control over your body and mind.

There is also the *entropic principle* that the disorder of the universe will always increase over time, which is why complex life has been able to arise within Shakti. Entropy isn't just the principle of impermanence. Disorder means complexity, and complex life has been able to arise within the universe only because the universe has become more complex over time, thus giving life the opportunity to arise. Consciousness has only arisen because of entropy as well. To know your past requires that you develop memories, forming memories means increasing information, and this in turn means increasing entropy. Consciousness can only exist because information increases, and can therefore only exist in systems where entropy exists because more information means more entropy.

We are conscious because we live in a universe of increasing entropy; consciousness cannot exist in a universe of decreasing entropy. Entropy requires that we train our consciousness so that it can adaptively deal with inescapable change in a very skillful fashion, and the entropy of deteriorating conditions means that we should master and use causality to improve matters for ourselves, society and posterity that are destined to degrade. Because of entropy we must make continuous efforts to maintain our lives, improve deteriorating situations and develop much better living conditions in society for our subsequent generations, which in Buddhism is called "beautifying a Buddha land."

On our planet the universe produced biology, or life, ages ago. Over time, atoms have formed complex molecules and then life, which has evolved into many forms. Life developed, but there was no intended purpose for its creation. It is just another on-going process that has evolved within Shakti due to prior evolutes and the laws of interaction that produce the appearance of manifestations. Some of that life developed sentience, or cognizance. Some of it developed higher intelligence and cognitive skills, which includes our species. Because of a Cognitive Revolution in the past, human life was eventually able to move from a more animalistic hunter-gatherer stage of existence to a more organized stage of existence involving agricultural communities that produced their own food. This constituted an Agricultural Revolution, and because of this evolutionary development our food supply became much more plentiful over time.

Bartering the food surpluses created by this Agricultural Revolution, human groups began to engage in expansive trade for other goods and services with members outside of their tribal communities. When food supplies became amply available in fixed locations this enabled some members of the population to start devoting more of their time to non-agricultural activities such as the arts and technology. Eventually an increase in human prosperity *and cognizance* produced a Scientific Revolution wherein humankind was able to make even more progress in terms of understanding the laws of nature ruling cause and effect, and man learned how to use these principles for even greater welfare. He eventually developed the fields of science, logic, math, medicine and technology along with other deeper forms of (cause and effect) understanding that are the basis of our modern culture of economic prosperity, higher living standards, technological advancement, higher education, decreased morbidity, increased longevity, human rights and so forth.

All throughout this evolution man has sought a well-being of prosperity and happiness, the absence of suffering in life, and the determination of some meaning or purpose for his existence. All throughout this time mankind has also always had the opportunity to cultivate the higher transcendental bodies of enlightenment. *Spiritual schools typically describe them as mental attainments, such as dhyana or mental emptiness-concentration absorptions, but they are in reality body attainments with concomitant mental states and attendant abilities.* It is by cultivating mental purity and inner Qi work in conjunction with help from higher-bodied spiritual masters that you can attain them.

The mental attainments (samadhi or dhyana) that spiritual schools urge adherents to cultivate are simply the attendant states of consciousness that accompany each type of spiritual body attainment. Also, the path of spirituality is misleadingly taught in terms only of purified mentality for a variety of beneficial reasons. If people otherwise always referenced their internal Qi transformations as a measuring stick they would quickly realize that they were not successfully cultivating the required Qi transformations necessary for the Sakadagamin subtle body attainment during their life, but would have to wait until after death to attain it. Thus they would likely give up on the spiritual path and cease cultivating their mind and behavior. Hence, cultivation teachings misleadingly emphasize "empty mind" or dispassion and mental detachment efforts (which perfectly fits the poverty state that typically characterizes the lives of spiritual adherents) rather than the inner Qi work required of the path that all people practice continuously once they become devas.

As an individual you undergo many struggles in life while trying to maintain your personal existence. During life you interact with your body, external objects, and other living beings. You are part of the environment as well as society with whose members you have filiation relationships that give you meaning. Through reflexivity you have an influence on all these things and they have an influence on you. If you act unwisely or affect them in unwholesome negative ways then the consequences will rebound to influence you because those circumstances surround you. Environmental pollution and war are just two examples of negative circumstances we create ourselves that then surround us and affect us, which is one aspect of the meaning of interdependent arising and karma. Because you are an integral part of Shakti connected to its whole body (you are one body with the universe) the consequences of all your actions follow the laws of interdependence and will rebound to you in some way. Everything is connected and ultimately one, and your behavior will affect the whole. What you do affects the whole and the whole affects you, so refrain from deeds such as pollution or other activities that destroy the environment or stir up troubles within society (such as fracturing the bonds between people within the populace) because they will reflexively affect you, which is a return we call karma. Similarly, a parent's evil deeds will visit his/her children and the evil deeds of children will certainly visit their parents.

You are the *entire universe in an embodied being* because you are identical with the universe that is your greater body in total. Your actions as an individual are also connected to the cosmos as a whole. They produce consequences for yourself and others that can proceed across time and space to affect both living beings and non-living objects. As an embodiment of the whole of Shakti you gain significance in your life through your relationships with the whole or its parts, which are ultimately the source of meaning. Your significance not only derives from your relationships with Shakti (or parts thereof) and with what is happening in the moment, but derives from the past (and is already incorporated into the manifestation of the present) and from the future that is dependent on the present.

Your life, due to interrelationships, has a place in the cosmic whole of Shakti, and you should think and act in recognition of your role in the larger relationship sets of which you are part: your family, friendships, occupational organization, society, environment, country, world and universe. These relationship groups give your life meaning and significance, and by thinking of your actions in relation to larger and larger groups of people you can make your life more meaningful and significant rather than just remain a minor fluctuation within endless scintillating Shakti.

There is an infinity of processes (transformations, interactions, evolutions or formations) simultaneously proceeding within Shakti that are occurring because of infinite interconnections, and because of ignorance some of those processes with consciousness ("sentient living beings") think they are individual, intrinsic, separate own-beings. Of course this is errant (false) thinking just as it is false thinking to assume that the solid objects we see with our eyes are actually solid rather than composed of atoms that are mostly empty space. Nevertheless we live our lives believing in countless misconceptions like this that champion distortions of reality rather than the truth, and we hold to this incorrect thinking (false thoughts) rather than differentiating truth from fiction *until we realize the truth*.

Some sentient beings are experiencing great pain, suffering and unhappiness in their existence not just due to poor situations but due to their own incorrect thinking and bad decisions. The desire to benevolently help beings who are suffering is the expression of compassion, and it is the apex of spiritual nobility and evolution when you *choose* to care, arouse compassion and help others suffering in various ways. Whether or not you help your brothers and sisters is entirely up to you, and yet by the standards we have created any selfless acts of consideration, kindness and compassion for others, and thoughts of sincere charity, are a measure of your spiritual maturity.

This is the spiritual path because we are all brothers and sisters in essence and existence, together seeking to better our lot. We are all socially equal in a great universal brotherhood because all people are your body and your Self. If you are not the type of individual who helps others you are not going to be helped for the twelve years (of organized labor) required for the kundalini transformations necessary to purify your subtle body within your earthly shell so that it can become an independent life free of your physical nature. Spiritual beings aren't going to help you if you are not a helpful individual who cares for others, so being kind, compassionate and helpful to others is the master key to spiritual attainments.

People want to live somewhere where they can be happy and do things that make them happy, and *you must create that world and those circumstances* by performing all sorts of good deeds with a good heart to elevate the human condition, including that you must work to refine your own behavior since this brightens matters for all. You can become a light that you want others to see in the world and a source of positivity that makes things better or moves things forward.

The practice of self-refinement, self-perfection and self-improvement towards the ideal of consummate conduct is an activity that improves not just your own life but the world. The idea is to domesticate our wild nature so that it comes under the control of our mind and is ruled according to the standards of ethical, moral, virtuous conduct. This is the groundwork necessary for spiritually ascending above our coarser animal nature, and so this pathway is the basis of the spiritual ladder.

You can also find purpose and significance in life through how you live and what you do. One way people find meaning is through relationships, another is by devoting themselves to an overarching mission or pledge larger than themselves, yet another is by devoting themselves to certain goals they select, and another way to find purpose for your life is to take on the challenge of trying to master ideal behavior such as emphasized in Christianity. The big task is to transcend your animal nature by purifying your desires (attachments) and inclinations, your mind of negative emotions, and to perfect your conduct. These are the normal instructions of most religions that teach us to improve our characters, purify our mental corruptions and practice kind and loving ways.

This is a road of purifying consciousness, perfecting its abilities, and cultivating virtuous (consummate) conduct. It is a road of self-improvement that has you working on perfecting yourself. The ultimate possibility is to become the best version of yourself possible that is also a source of great positivity to the world - a light you want others to see. By pursuing these goals you can *elevate yourself to exceptional purpose* other than simply just existence because on this path your conduct, behavior and activities start to matter due to their effect on others. The ideal is to live life large with joy and gusto while also making a dent in the world through improvements, however large or slight, which have significance for yourself or the life of the world.

Whether living in this realm or living in a higher realm, because you now know what you really are you should place a different priority on certain areas of life. You will be proceeding throughout endless rounds of incarnations, long or short, until you attain higher spiritual bodies with extremely long lives and incredibly great capabilities. Hence, what are the requirements for being able to attain at least the first of these attainments while alive known as the subtle body, deva body, astral body, impure illusory body, *Homo Deus* or Srotapanna stage of Arhat attainment? What are the ways in which that reality is reached? This achievement requires the cultivation of virtue, merit (good works and good thoughts), meditation and inner energy work as well as the grace of higher spiritual beings who have succeeded before you. If virtuous behavior is not a standard part of your personality then no spiritual beings will help you attain this higher body attainment while you are alive and you will just have to wait until you pass away and then finish cultivating your etheric subtle body within the earthly plane's heavenly realm.

In terms of the conventional world, whether you have an inherent independent and intrinsic existence or not, and whether you have a long-life existence or not, you still have a self-recognized existence because you are a living body with consciousness. The highest and most noble pathway for this existence is the pursuit of self-perfection or rectification of your character and actions that entails continuous betterment and social merit-making (performing good and getting rid of evil). You don't want to inhibit the growth of the good qualities that lie dormant in yourself or in society by not cultivating them. This will lead to a better life for the "I" and "We" (individual and society) that makes their existence possible and the chance of higher spiritual attainments where you can escape the lower realms forever.

With this pursuit as your guiding pathway you can then order your life accordingly towards the cultivation of your consciousness and virtuous ways in thought and deed so that you gradually become *a man or woman of principle*. The practice of self-refinement or self-improvement through mindfulness (the pursuit of mental purity, ethics and virtuous as well as skillful conduct), and the task of improving the well-being of others and the quality of their lives – which is called "beautifying a Buddha land" (that includes purifying a country by promoting ethics, virtues and good deeds among the populace) – is that pathway. In the universe there is actually no *real* person (a permanent core consciousness or innate self) to receive a reward for whatever good an apparent person does, so there is no one to receive any benefit. However, there is a karmic return that occurs to an apparent person who can enjoy, and one takes on the challenge of self-improvement and bettering the world for the benefit of providing positive feelings, meaning, and purpose for our own existence.

The stream of consciousness within us is like an endless flowing river. Just as a river at no point is ever identical to any other version of itself ("you can never step in same river twice"), no state of consciousness can be perfectly repeated because the contents of consciousness are always changing.

Nonetheless, you can train your mind to be acutely aware of your moment-by-moment mental states – your seeing, hearing, smelling, tasting, and touch sensations; your thoughts relating to the past, present or the future; and your feelings, attitudes, outlook, perceptions and intentions/behavior – so that you can police your mind to control your consciousness. By controlling your consciousness you can guide yourself to accomplish any sort of achievement you desire.

All your mental states are influenced by your prior conditioning of past experiences as well as by psychological laws, physical laws, and biological laws that control both the universe and the rules that manifest your thoughts and emotions. However, you can rise above any type of past conditioning to always stand as a new person, and can always chart a new direction for your activities and life that departs from your past conditioning. This is called changing your fate or fortune which you can do through the capabilities achieved through self-cultivation.

Consciousness gives you the ability to acquire Knowledge and understanding, including the self-knowledge of what you ultimately are (the enlightened view of your true self-nature). It gives you the ability to live by the light of reason rather than be guided solely by just animal instincts, which is why we must develop our human minds to their fullest capabilities. A sound mind of sound reasoning also protects us from living according to false or nonsensical notions just as living according to virtuous principles of morality helps us live emotionally unshattered lives. It enables us to develop a proper understanding of the world and avoid mis-living, which is living incorrectly due to a lack of ethics or because we think the world is different from the way it is.

You can use consciousness to seek greater well-being by working on improving your body, your mental patterns, your conduct and environment. You can use consciousness to improve your physical capabilities, for example, not just through exercise but by training as an "adept perceiver" to enhance your abilities of sensory-perception and take them to new levels. You can also train your consciousness to consistently act in certain optimal ways, which is regularly done in sports training, and can become more efficient at accomplishing any types of specific tasks you choose. You can try to act properly in every situation, and Confucianism calls the task of learning how to properly and effectively act in everything the Great Learning. We are all subject to the necessity of mastering our consciousness and behavior, which is the Great Learning of life.

Buddhism calls consciousness the flow of karma. To know karma entails there being consciousness capable of mental perceptions of sensory inputs, mental conceptions (thinking) and emotions. The human subjective experience – whatever appears in our mind – has a structure that appears in a particular way due to our human anatomical design, neurological operating processes, and our memories. Consciousness produces Knowledge, so through consciousness we have the ability to know and learn because this produces Knowledge. As sentient beings we can expose ourselves to experiences that create new memories or neural patterns, and can also reprogram or retrain our mental processes to regularly produce superior results of any desired type in order that we develop special abilities and valuable characteristics that we prize.

Thus, it is important that you train yourself by exposing yourself to the highest and best examples of behavior, performance and outcome to emulate such as models. By impressing our psyches with the best models of conduct and achievement we can then imprint upon our mind (and memories) the highest archetypes of ideal behavior and attainment. This is a great boon for someone's life. By adopting a specific ideal model of behavior as your guide you can specify how you wish to become in life and then mold yourself (work) to become that way by dedicating every single action of your life to (conformity with) that ideal. You can also envision how you wish the world to become and then work to make it that way too.

What is stored within your memories as an ideal vision or model for your personality and your behavior will carry over into your ordinary life, especially if you reinforce the model ideal over time. Those tendencies will also impress themselves upon your subtle body so that a relevant influence (*samskara*) is carried with you into your subsequent incarnation. If you develop certain negative personality characteristics, you will carry those tendencies with you into another incarnation unless you make cultivation efforts to purify yourself of such pollutions.

The choice to act in a certain way or do something depends precisely upon the contents of your consciousness. You must therefore strive to fill your neurons with the highest and best models of ethics, values, virtue, wisdom, perspectives, skills and behavior upon which to draw on for life, which is part of the Great Learning. In addition to the practice of self-correction through the mindful observation of your thoughts and actions in real time, this is one of the ways in which you cultivate consciousness and more virtuous ways of being.

Consciousness has two aspects that are the primary focus of cultivation work (self-improvement) – *automatic* mental processes and *deliberate* processes of cognition that are under voluntary control.

The automatic processes of consciousness are like reflexes that just happen without thinking, which includes the processes by which your mind creates an actual world of experiences. Your mind through neural processes (that activate patterns of neurons in the brain) automatically transforms the sensory inputs of sense organs (upon *contacting* an object) into images within consciousness, and then interprets that field of chaos with pattern matching to create identifiable perceptions (objects). This automatic ability naturally *distinguishes or creates* a worldview of qualities - phenomena, objects or meanings with conventional significance. That pattern recognition arises out of an initially unorganized tableau of sensory mental objects, and the process automatically happens without any need on our part to consciously think about it. We can recognize objects because that is just the way the mind works, a process of conscious recognition developed over the long course of evolution. The mental differentiation of sensory inputs into objects, marks, signs, phenomena, meanings, qualities, names, labels and so on happens automatically within our brains without need of any deliberate powers of discrimination or identification.

The automatic processes of consciousness also include: the mind's ability to naturally generate emotional reactions or *feelings* of pleasure, pain or indifference (likes and dislikes or neutrality) when it contacts such objects; natural reflexes and established habits (habitual responses that are learned tendencies) that automatically determine how you manage your body and react to circumstances; an ability to automatically interpret circumstances with implicit biases (such as stereotypes or certain outlooks) due to the pre-programmed storehouse of memories you have acquired through learning and conditioning; and mental perturbations, annoyances, irritations, agitations and other unwanted guests within consciousness that also spontaneously arise such as negative self-talk or negative emotions. Many of these mental processes, although they are automatic functions of consciousness, can be "purified" or retrained to become better mental mechanisms in the sense that they produce mental states superior to their former output, and training consciousness in this way is a task included within the process of self-cultivation. We can even learn how to control some of our involuntary physiological systems such as our body temperature or blood flow.

Another automatic mental process is the basic and fundamental automatic urge, tendency, or intention that moves the primary mind to become involved with mental objects, meaning the involuntary *volition* or natural power that causes the mental continuum to cognitively "take" or become engaged with an object. This grabbing is a natural function within the process of consciousness. The ability to pay attention – either little or much – to an object with *mental engagement* or attentive focus so that the mind stays on the object (as a form of concentration) and doesn't move elsewhere is another automatic mental process as well.

As to the deliberate processes of consciousness – normally called thinking, rationality, conception, reasoning, understanding, comprehension, discrimination, consciousness, cognition or intellect – they particularly operate in a patterned way that references our storehouse of Knowledge memories. Deliberate active consciousness not only includes our intellect, decision-making and imagination but also includes our factor of will, self-will or willpower that controls our attention, concentration, intent, volition, and perseverance. These mental powers rule our behavior.

Through the training of consciousness our wisdom (understanding of things), intellect and discrimination can be widened and sharpened; our ability to master conditions broadened; our perspectives, outlooks, attitudes and views can be uplifted; our ability to maintain willpower or perseverance strengthened (the ability to concentrate on a single purpose until completion, which is actually *dharana* in Yoga); and our commitment to creating better futures for ourselves and others strengthened.

Ultimately our active processes of deliberate consciousness, which we often call "thinking" or "wisdom" (understanding), can be enhanced or improved and this increase in skillfulness is the role of self-cultivation. You want to learn *how to think better and control yourself (act) better.* We need to work on developing our deliberate processes of consciousness so that we can think better to create a more wholesome interior life along with better external behavior and conditions. Mastering consciousness (the mind) has the purpose of ensuring our survival and improving our well-being through our activities. We want to think and act better to achieve gainful results in the now and for the future that can even affect subsequent generations other than joust ourselves.

Thoughts and feelings are no more than fleeting vibrations in consciousness that cannot stay. They are connected with internal biochemical reactions that are changing every moment, and which are essentially irritations of energy through nervous tissues whose vibrational effects can be broken down even to the atomic level. These fleeting vibrations can affect us substantially in either positive or negative ways. For instance, in addition to physical pain hurting us, we typically become particularly distressed by certain types of mental states that involve emotional suffering, and these are just two examples of how mental states register pain for us.

When we don't stay centered in ourselves and don't manage our thoughts correctly we can lose our internal tranquility, which is the natural state of the mind, and then losing that natural peacefulness we become more open to mental suffering. If not peacefully centered we become subject to excessive pride, conceit, hatred, anger, greediness, envy, malice and many other negative traits. If not empty and peaceful we tend to give rise to harmful thoughts, desires and habits. If we don't consider matters in a state of internal peace and calm it becomes easy to develop incorrect beliefs or make wrong decisions.

If we do not train in wisdom and thoughtfulness it thus becomes easy to fall into errant views or delusions. For instance, many people create unnecessary limitations for themselves by creating a fixed self-image of who they are and then they cling to that false identity with attachment (ex. "I am an accountant") when they are nothing of the kind. They lose themselves in an abstract, artificially constructed self-identity that cuts them off from their own inner vitality, thus imprisoning themselves while depriving themselves of the possible joy of life. They lose themselves in a world of their own abstractions – an artificial construction meant to provide comfort – that imprisons them and cuts off their authentic true self and its natural flow of vibrant vitality. You are actually free to do and become whatever you want in life, and should carefully consider matters in order to select a possible future to become the reality that you want.

Our natural state is not to be restrictively imprisoned within a thought-cocoon or false self-identification or become alienated from our deepest essence that drives our vitality and passions. We must (through meditation practice) train consciousness to be able to regularly reach and settle within its natural mental purity so that we can detach from our thought-stream and thereby free ourselves from robotic fusion with all sorts of self-created habitual ways of thinking that form the psychological patterns of our normal behavior. If we pursue the goal of emotional self-mastery where we can control our own emotional experience then we can reduce suffering as well. In life we want to be able to choose what we become emotional about and when we become emotional, and secondly we want to be able to choose how to act when we are emotional. These abilities will reduce our suffering in life. Unfortunately, Nature didn't give us any tools to be able to do this so we have to learn how and train how to do this ourselves, and it's hard work.

The roots of suffering in life can be addressed in many ways. For instance, just a few strategies include the following:

- By developing continuous mindfulness of our mind-stream we can notice suffering whenever it arises and can then take steps to cut it off or transform it by developing a different thought-stream (or change our external circumstances) before it takes a deeper hold on us. Monitoring our thoughts also enables us to catch errant thinking and correct it in real-time. With enough practice you will become able to instantly identify the thoughts that will cause you to suffer so that you can resist the urge to indulge them, interfere to cut them off or transform them and thereby avoid a trajectory of emotional pain. You can also avoid involving yourself in actions that set off an entire sequence of suffering events. However, mindfulness must be practiced all the time because you don't retain the skill unless you practice it. Through mindfulness you can increase the gap (of time) between impulse and action (such as spotting that you're about to get angry), and then you can respond more properly to situations such as by thinking "I'll let it go" when you are slighted. However, you need meditation mindfulness practice of a minimum of about 20 minutes a day for four days a week, and at last six months before your practice starts to have an effect in increasing your awareness and lengthening that gap between impulse and action, and your heightened attention *will only continue if you continue to do mindfulness practice.*
- By learning how to detach from our mind-stream and the situation at hand we can, due to the lack of mental fusion, reinterpret events with a more positive attitude that discards the negative interpretation automatically supplied by our consciousness. For instance, we can tell ourselves to reinterpret pain and suffering as a challenge or opportunity instead of as a problem, which will then make it much more bearable. Also, even if we are insulted by someone the mind is the only thing that can hurt us. We must believe we are being harmed to be harmed, so being harmed is often just a matter of interpretation, which is something that we can control. We can also correct mistaken reasoning and in that way permanently reprogram the algorithms that produce emotional suffering. We can also rearrange our prejudices, beliefs and attitudes (that repeatedly cause us to suffer) to perceive the world differently so that negative emotions do not arise. By replacing old pathways of reasoning with new and more accurate ones you can become quicker at reappraising situations and thereby bypass the possibility of many negative emotions;

- By mastering mental stability and concentration we can better ignore disruptions and distractions such as suffering, irritation, annoyance, or pain when they appear by sustaining the mind on other thoughts;
- By training ourselves to turn negative emotions into positive ones after they arise, such as by turning the nervousness before an athletic event into excitement, this "emotional regulation" can transform suffering. "Emotional regulation" involves shaping which emotions one has, controlling when one has them, and selecting how one experiences or expresses these emotions. If you can control your emotions you can become emotionally invincible and eliminate suffering;
- By training ourselves through repetitive practice so that positive states arise instead of negative emotions (such as when doctors remain calm during patient seizures or soldiers enter into a state of preparation before battle instead of panicking) we can reduce suffering;
- By engaging in activities that reduce suffering or reverse it, such as by singing or smiling to make yourself happy when you are sad, we can modulate the amount of suffering we might bear or even become able to ignore it or transform it;
- Emotions are reactions to our cognitive interpretation of events. By following Epicurus's advice to reinterpret events to make them more palatable, reduce your expectations so that you are not disappointed, and by engaging in optimistic positive thinking or hope that will bring you forward through difficult situations, these are some various ways to deal with suffering. Emotional suffering begins with an appraisal that something is triggering your emotions based on your previous life experiences, and if an impulse arises that is able to trigger an emotional response then it will show in your face, voice, posture and energy. However, through mindfulness we can spot an emotional impulse within ourselves when it arises and then deflect or reinterpret the situation in order to avoid suffering;
- By going along with the movements of the world rather than fighting the momentum of trends, and by staying flexibly mobile and adaptive instead of fighting reality and resisting change, we can also minimize instances of suffering by going along with the flow;
- One view is that if you suffer you should suffer consciously. By training ourselves to simply bear pain and suffering better while remaining positive and optimistic, as is taught to soldiers, we can

build up our tolerance or endurance for negative states. In other words, by getting stronger emotionally (becoming tougher, more resilient, developing grit, determination, patience, persistence, self-control and mental fortitude) we can better cope with suffering;

- If you have a "Why?" it is always easier to bear the burdens of suffering, especially the discomforts needed to do great things. Therefore by committing ourselves to a higher purpose that has meaning we can touch moments of self-forgetfulness while experiencing suffering or just improve our ability to bear or ignore pain due to recognizing that sacrifice must be made for achievement. When suffering has a purpose to it then it is easier to bear and can contribute positively to our sense of value-based happiness. Specifically, by establishing worthy objectives and aspirations we can bear sufferings and deprivation as the price of achievement and thus ignore many negative feelings and afflictions in life;

- By just allowing afflictive emotions, feelings and other unwanted guests to come and go as they please without holding onto them with a fused attachment they will readily pass through you and depart cleanly due to a lack of clinging engagement or enmeshment on our part. Attachment blinds us because it lends an imaginary attractiveness to an object of desire, but attachment can be lessened because of an impersonal analysis of the situation (wisdom understanding that unravels desire) and willpower. This is called fathoming the Reason Why for something and then using that insightful understanding to dissolve the issue at its core;

- Through training we can lower the volume and frequency of negative feelings and afflictive emotional states by learning various techniques that master mental processes. This includes working over the long run to transform our habits of consciousness (patterns of thinking) so that we regularly generate less negative emotions (and more beautiful mental states) as our natural state of mind. Meditation practice, which leads people to experience the peaceful natural state of their mind, helps in this direction;

- By confining, limiting or reducing our desires, yearnings, cravings and attachments by practicing dispassion and detachment we can reduce our negative states of suffering. Transcendental states are characterized by the extinguishment of craving and desire;

- By changing our behavior, routines (habits), activities and circumstances so that suffering does not normally arise we will then not encounter it. This includes altering the present circumstances to minimize or remove any negative conditions producing suffering such as by improving circumstances so that suffering does not arise in the future. The basic idea, however, is to avoid entering a situation fraught with suffering and then you can avoid it. If you know what triggers afflictive responses then you can avoid that arena, or you can prepare yourself ahead of time. Of course if you transform conditions or circumstances so that they are no longer suffering-prone then you have eliminated the problem;

Countless other strategies for eliminating, minimizing or transforming suffering are available, including strategies to better handle the recurrent vexations that regularly irritate our lives such as hunger, sexual desire, the desire for sleep and so forth. Among these various remedies are strategies that manage what Buddhism calls the omnipresent mental factors of consciousness.

Our consciousness is supposed to operate in a manner similar to a clear mirror that simply reflects images; a mirror never sticks (attaches) to whatever arises within it. In other words, the thoughts and images that arise within our minds are supposed to flow through them like the stick-free reflected images that appear within a clean mirror. We should know our mental products clearly (just as we can clearly see images within a mirror) but shouldn't attach to them with any type of fusion (unless you are practicing concentration etc. for a specific purpose). Therefore you have to learn how to be more detached from wandering thoughts, emotions, sensations, etc. in life. If you cultivate a calm demeanor then you can train not to let your mind-stream affect you by causing excessive emotional turmoil. Its contents are not part of your true self but just passing fancies that appear within your mind. If you are free of desire then you can more easily detach from your thoughts and emotions and thereby minimize states of suffering.

We should certainly experience both negative and positive emotions in life as well as positive or negative physical sensations, but we shouldn't especially cling to them or hold to them with attachment. We should stand back as a witness and let all things pass away after their usefulness is completed rather than cling to them in a bondage of fusion. Only in states of concentration are we to remain centered on mental topics.

Thought-objects are supposed to flow through your mind and then depart naturally because all things are by nature transient and impermanent, so of course mental products should not stay. You should not continually hold onto afflictive thoughts or non-virtuous tendencies with binding force - such as holding onto a grudge, anger or holding onto despair - because detachment is the proper operation of your consciousness just as the fundamental substrate of the universe doesn't attach to anything either. Impermanence means that mental states will alternate from joy to sorrow, boredom to excitement, pleasure to pain, and vice versa. Only for purposes of concentration do you usually remain holding onto a topic strongly, and we demonstrate our necessary mastery of steadiness and *constantia* when we perseveringly hold to a course of action to complete some project or even vow.

While it is proper to experience negative mental states such as sadness, we should not *excessively cling to* negative emotional states when they arise and cause ourselves unnecessary affliction due to a disproportionate attachment. We should just let unwanted negative mental states pass away as they should without retaining them. As an example, when it is proper to feel sadness then we should feel sadness, and we should let go of our sadness and grief after it is no longer proper to remain absorbed within these states.

After pain is gone, for instance, you normally don't continue holding onto that state of suffering but move on and learn from the experience. You adapt to a new normal and don't hold onto the pain forever. The best situation is to achieve a state of flowing consciousness that is clear and bright, unburdened by anything other than its present focus of attention, and you just handle difficulties and suffering that arise whenever they do. This is the practice of using consciousness correctly.

You are not seeking the absolute nonexistence of suffering in life since this is impossible. You are seeking knowledge of how to prevent it, skillfulness in how to handle it and you want your overall life experience to be that of well-being that can admit to suffering in its overall mixture. You just don't want a life predominated by pain, suffering and misery. Furthermore, society desires that you have enough compassion that you act to prevent it in the future not just for yourself but for others as well.

This is what spiritual cultivation is all about, which includes training you to incorporate the tendency of helpfulness into your character and develop various powers, skills or abilities whereby you can help others. It is not just about cultivating the higher spiritual bodies but about transforming your personality and disposition for the better, in effect blunting your sharpness and softening your rigidity. It is about living life more optimally by reducing the causes and forms of suffering that arise, and administering antidotes to those who end up in suffering, pain and need.

We can also use wisdom, insight, intellect and reasoning to determine why negative mental states arise in the first place. From that analysis we can then work to unravel, dissolve or avoid the causes of suffering at their root. With such understanding we can make appropriate adjustments in our lives, our circumstances, our mental processes and in our ways of doing things so that afflictions are resolved at their roots and do not arise again.

Positive feelings, such as happiness and joy, are also mental states that we can actually train to generate at will. Happiness is a choice because we can choose to (alter our emotions and) make ourselves happy if we learn the appropriate techniques and then put in the effort to use them when needed. We can also learn to substitute other positive states for suffering. Despite unfortunate life conditions, we can cultivate a steady cheerful, sunny disposition and happy state of mind.

Aristotle said that we should cultivate happiness over time just as we should cultivate virtues. For instance, we can gradually learn how to cultivate tranquility, peace and serenity independent of our current feelings and then over time that mental state can become a permanent personality attribute. Every time you follow the same pathway a specific pattern is activated in your brain, becomes more defined, and it becomes easier to activate those circuits the next time. In time a bad neuronal pathway can become an unconscious default so that your brain, seeking efficiency, will just use that unwholesome default because it is the easiest, most familiar route. It becomes a *samskara* or personality trait. You have to cultivate positive pathways and use them often enough that they become the defaults to override negative tendencies.

Sow an action and you develop a tendency, reaffirm that tendency and you create a habit, develop a habit and you produce your character, and from your character you form your destiny. Your thinking is derived as a product of your character and life experiences, and your thoughts in turn produce your behavior. You write the story of your life through your character (personality) that gives rise to your thoughts and deeds such as your interactions with objects or other people. Because of your character you perform certain actions and behaviors and are magnetically drawn into groups and relationships in tune with your personality, so by changing your character you will change your fortune and destiny.[7]

Your fate, fortune or destiny ultimately arises from a bundle of personality traits that you develop either consciously or unconsciously which become your character, and in spiritual cultivation we try to *consciously grab hold of the process of character formation* to reshape the personality into what we want by eliminating character flaws, breaking bad habits, cultivating positive virtues, adopting new outlooks and ways of interpreting events (perspectives), and replacing what's suboptimal in consciousness with whatever is better.

Through *mindfulness and self-rectification practice* to correct our faults or inadequacies and move towards adopting particular virtues (such as exemplified by the efforts of Liao Fan and Benjamin Franklin); *bhava-attitude meditations and visualization practice* to impress upon ourselves new character traits (when an idea exclusively occupies the mind then it is transformed into an actual mental or physical state); the *repetition of affirmations* that help you develop the character traits that you want, or *repetition of prayers and/or mantras* requesting heavenly assistance to aid you in developing those traits; repeated real world conduct and action *in harmony with those desired traits* to reinforce their germination and development; introspective examination practice to ferret out the roots of our attitudes and behaviors standing in the way of positive development so that you can change them and dissolve afflictions, errant tendencies or limiting beliefs; a *regular schedule of repetitive disciplined training* to regulate one's behavior and establish new habits (such as experienced through the training program for Marines or the monastic rules within a monastery that regulate the life); principal awareness to *inject our activities with higher ideals*; and by various techniques (such as NLP, ACT or CBT cognitive behavior therapy) to *regularly emulate ideal models of behavior* that provide inspiration for aspiration ... we can work at modifying our personality characteristics and mental processes at their core.

Over time this set of practices, along with others, will change our personal path in life because by applying these techniques we will rewrite our mental programming (change our character, personality and way of doing things), and the way our mind is structured ultimately determines the person we are

---

[7] The only astrological reliable remedies for changing your fate or fortune mentioned by the great astrological sage Parashara are (1) mantra recitation like the Vishnu Sahasranam, Mrityunjaya, Durga Saptasati, ... which would also mean Buddhist mantras, Christian prayers etc. and (2) *dhan* or charity, which the *Bhagavad Gita* describes as giving money or aid to a really needy person through a sattvic, unconditional donation without expecting to get anything in return. In short, you should mantra for help from Buddhas and perform good deeds to help others.

and the life we will live. We want to brighten our personalities because our thinking and emotional habits as well as our outlooks, perspectives and mindsets control our lives and determine our happiness or suffering in life as well as our success or prosperity. We can deliberately reprogram and restructure our standard thought patterns, elevating them to something much, much better.

As an example, all of us are known for our unique emotional tone that has both positive and negative qualities, and despite any great goodness of our character or personality we will all at times become troubled and sometimes unbalanced by bad fortune, negative emotions or emotional turmoil. Happiness in life is temporary and fleeting rather than constant whereas sorrow and afflictions always appear. However, we can eliminate from our character strong tendencies towards negative emotions or negative character traits and work to develop sunniness, cheerfulness and optimism instead. As a general rule, Buddhism advises that we cultivate constructive emotions as antidotes to destructive emotions whenever negative states arise within your mind. You would accordingly try to cure anger, hatred and fear by arousing compassion, love and patience in their place. When you cultivate constructive emotions over a long time you will tend to develop them as personality traits to the degree that you actually practice them. The result of cultivating positive emotions over time is a calmer mind and greater peacefulness.

A key principle in spiritual cultivation is to become able to design our emotions, which means not just dealing with them but learning how to change, modulate and essentially control them. You want to learn how to change your emotions at will rather than let them control you. Emotions can lead us in the opposite direction of our highest goals and ideals so we must take special pains to learn how to manage them, especially when they can cause us to act in ways we will later regret or simply cause us to suffer unnecessarily. You should use reasoning to manage your reactions whenever you encounter destructive emotions. Our emotional system was not designed and did not evolve for consciousness to play much of a role *so we need to use various techniques to gain control of it.*

Mindfulness practice helps you recognize that an unwanted emotion is stirring, but it does not provide a sure-fire remedy for changing an undesired emotion into something better. Other than the general pathway of trying to cultivate a calm, collected and peaceful mind of equanimity, typically there are five basic strategies or common ways by which we can usually control our emotions. We can (1) choose the situations we enter (in order to avoid emotional troubles), (2) change situations once we are in them (to alter our circumstances that produces emotional experiences), or (3) choose to pay attention only to the things that make us feel the way we want to feel during situations. These are called *situation selection, situation modification* and *attentional deployment*. A fourth method is (4) to try to change ourselves - our default emotional response through training techniques like meditation or activities like listening to music, eating special pick-me-up foods, exercising, or getting some sleep – a methodology called *response modulation*. The fifth technique, *cognitive change*, (5) involves learning how to control our emotional experience from within by rewiring our emotions in real time so that we can neutralize or reverse negative emotions quickly. Basically you want to become able to design your emotions so that you feel the way you want to feel *on demand* such as feeling confident prior to a sporting competition or some other activity.

The question of "how do I want to feel" or even "what would (how should) my ideal self feel?" is connected with "how can I train to become that way?" Certainly athletes pursuing peak performances must retrain their emotions to be able to excel at their sport and must gain the ability to change their emotions at will.[8] Because we all have emotional weaknesses that can harm us we should all train for the ability to transform them, which is a task at the heart of self-cultivation practice.

For every negative emotional pattern we have, especially those that blemish our psyche with regularity, you should know that there are various strategies available for deprogramming the proclivity. As just a few instances:

- Anger blocks compassion, and its greatest remedy is delaying our reactions or responses until we can think clearly because anger muddies our decision processes. Patience, tolerance and acceptance are typical cures for the tendency to become angry. The Buddhist antidote for neutralizing it is to generate these qualities in response to its arousal. Our own anger can be addressed by the various strategies of delaying our responses (taking a moment before reacting and responding), maintaining control of our outer expressions, training our inner experience of anger to mirror our outer expression of calm, and analyzing the hot situation including considering things from the other person's point of view. As Marcus Aurelius said, everything depends on how you interpret it. Man is not disturbed by things but by the views he takes of them. Also, when we monitor the sensations within our body as a habit due to meditation practice (mindfulness is paying attention to whatever is happening), and in real time sense any

---

[8] See the techniques within *Sport Visualization* (Bodri).

changes within our body (our respiration, sweating, muscular tension, temperature, etc.) that correspond to anger (or other emotions), then we can realize when we are becoming emotional and can have a choice as to whether we want to become emotional (such as angry) or not.

- Shame is a result of acknowledging other's people's judgments, but you can counter shame by viewing their judgments and opinions as subjective products of their own prejudices, perspectives and issues rather than as objective measures you need to acknowledge or take as your own. Their measuring stick need not be yours. If you are secure in determining that your justifications are superior to the judgments of others and you remain in control of your interpretations then shame will not arise.
- Jealousy and possessiveness can poison relationships, but they can be countered by appreciating the time you spend with other people, which cannot last forever, and by training yourself to never consider them yours.
- Sexual desire is a natural response in life for without it there would be no sexual congress and the continuation of humankind would cease. However, it can easily draw us into temptation and excesses with unfortunate consequences. To be overly controlled by sexual desire is the problem, and spiritual paths offer many remedies for dealing with lust. One of the methods espoused by Buddhism is for men to view the object of their desire as their mother or sister when lust arises. Another remedy, espoused by St. Francis of Assisi, is to consider the consequences of giving into lust in terms of the possibility of pregnancy and the burdens that would then entail. These are just two of the many remedies for lust and sexual desire that also include exercise, breathing practices, keeping busy with something else and more.
- Guilt can plague people their entire lives, but if you reflect on whether you made the best decision you could have made for a particular situation given the information and/or options available to you at the time then you can reduce or eliminate feelings of guilt because you did the best thing possible, and no one could ask for more than that. To avoid guilt you should start to make a habit of thinking of other people first instead of just acting for yourself alone. You can start factoring their feelings into your determinations, and can list out the reasons and consequences for actions you are considering.
- Anxiety as a character trait commonly plagues individuals of a certain temperament, but more often than not the worries we have never

come to fruition and our anxiety usually represents false positives. Shantideva advised us to remember the futility of worry whenever it arises and to instead focus on the best course of action instead of being paralyzed by panic. The Marines teach soldiers to forget anxiety and worry before battle and to throw themselves into the busyness of making preparations instead.

- Grief is an emotion that is proper in many circumstances, such as after the death of a loved one. Buddhism reminds us not to hold onto the emotion of grief forever, and Judaic tradition espouses that we show great grief for a certain period of time and then be done with it. We should remember that all things are impermanent, including life, and inevitable loss characterizes many circumstances including our life, health, beauty, fame, riches, status and so forth. Fate causes our fortunes to bob up and down, so we should not get attached to our prosperity but treat the comings and goings of fate with a wise detachment that tells us to adapt to the new situation. Knowing the impermanence of conditions, one can practice non-clinging and non-grasping to one's good fortune, and also practice gratitude for the time that one has in enjoying blessings.

Success and happiness in life are hastened or delayed by your habitual thought patterns, which are the power behind your recurrent actions that head you in consistent directions. Tendencies in thinking and behaving are like magnets that draw to you good or bad fortune, so you must cultivate your thinking and behavioral habits, which form your personality and create your fortune, so that they dependably lead to elevation. You must consistently think and act in certain ways in order for happiness, cheerfulness, optimism, tranquility, equanimity or even kindness to become a standard feature of your personality, as well as a determining factor of your fortune and destiny. This is why we work on cultivating virtues and purifying our consciousness.

The way to become happy is to cultivate happiness (act happy and think more positively), and the way to become peaceful is to practice internal peacefulness and equanimity. Within all of us there is a sanctuary of stillness that we can reach through meditation, and within that natural tranquility we can be ourselves in peace and harmony. You cultivate mental peacefulness by mimicking the action-free, peaceful nature of our True Self that does not engage with, hold onto or interfere with anything but stays detached from all phenomena and their interactions. It infuses, permeates or supports everything (like an all-pervasive divinity) but doesn't control anything. It is unattached, desireless, and effortless. Being ever inactive it is continuously quiet, calm and serene.

You are also this ultimate substrate so *you* pervade the universe, and the universe also exists in you. Therefore try to be more open-minded and accepting in all you encounter and experience because it really is all just *you*. This doesn't mean you should accept errors or harm in life and fail to engage in self-correction. You just need to learn to more accept people different than yourself and customs different from your own. Furthermore, when corrections are due then you correct matters, and when you hear of others suffering then you should see if you can make some efforts to help them even if you have no direct relationship with them.

Our natural mental state is to be peaceful and calm until we disturb that peacefulness. Meditation helps you retrieve this natural underlying state of tranquility that is empty of disturbances. By practicing meditation where we simply watch our thoughts with detachment by standing back as the witness, we can learn to become more accepting, peaceful and relaxed just like our foundational ground nature, which is free from all forms of misery or attachment, and can allow thoughts to die down so that we access the naturally empty (tranquil) state of our mind. Seek That within which no sorrow is found.

The Self is who we are but through ignorance we identify with our body-mind complex and take it as our true self. Neither our body nor our thoughts are what we are because we are the peaceful fundamental ground state of the universe. If you detach yourself from your body and thought-stream and rest in the empty natural state of your mind you will at once become happy, peaceful and free from worries. We can learn to disconnect from the unlimited desires and scattered thoughts that usually cloud our minds so they die out if we detach from them and pay them no heed. We can gradually decrease our tendency to get lost in wandering thoughts so that we develop clear minds empty and free of many useless things that would normally clutter and distract our consciousness.

Inner peace leads to happiness and contentment, so we must learn how to tame our minds (which includes elevating our psychological health) as part of the Great Learning of life. It is easy to convert a peaceful, clear mind to happiness whenever you want, and this is another reason to cultivate mental calmness since it enables you to have an easier time of accessing positive mental states. A still mind can see reality as it is so a clear mind also leads to better decision-making and positive outcomes, and clarity enables you to concentrate with focus on completing a task without distraction.

In a state of clarity and calmness you can deeply engage in something with great focus and attention. You need a clear and calm mind (which is called a state of concentration, or pristine awareness) if you want to operate with peak performance or experience a state of flow, and so meditation is practiced for so many reasons like these.

For life, and as a teaching of spiritual cultivation, we want to actively transform any physical conditions, mental conditions, social conditions, environmental conditions, and other circumstances that might lead to suffering. We want to transform any of our mental or behavioral tendencies that tend to produce suffering such as physical pain or afflictive emotions. We also want to properly handle any physical or mental sufferings when they arise, and not hold onto them so that they quickly depart rather than remain the focus of our attention. We don't want to keep holding onto negativities so that they stay longer in our minds and psyches than they should. The principle is to learn how to transform the various moods or states of the mind.

Attachment occurs when we overly involve ourselves/play with our mental sufferings - when we cling to, merge with, identify with, unify with or fuse with them. In life, we need to develop sufficient wisdom to *avoid* circumstances that would cause us suffering, *detach* from suffering rather than cling to it, and need to learn how to *transform* afflictive emotions at will. It requires training to develop these abilities, which is done along the road of spiritual cultivation since most spiritual paths provide you with an organized way to become competent at these abilities. We want to more frequently manifest wholesome states that are pleasant to experience - such as happiness, joy, peace, shine, mental freshness, lightness, bliss, flow, and peak experiences - and which lead to a higher level of continual well-being with minimized suffering. However, we don't want to be overly ruled by negative *or positive* mental states when making decisions but want wisdom, peace, balance and rationality (together with compassion) to serve as the overriding principles for guiding our choices and behavior.

To perfect our deliberate mental activities we must learn how to master both our cognitive-mental skills *and* our physical skills since we are a mind-body entity. The mastery of our consciousness will help us fulfill our needs in life to accomplish personal goals and aspirations, experience personal happiness and well-being, and move forward towards higher objectives where we can find meaning and purpose for our existence. We fulfill many of those needs through the actions of our body. As a human we essentially have only two skills – *cognitive and physical abilities*, and we must daily strive to elevate both of these skill sets. This is the crux of spiritual cultivation practice.

Mastering deliberate consciousness entails developing mental skills, vocal skills and physical body skills of thought, word and deed (which includes our conduct and activities) since they are controlled by the mind. Vocal skills include communication, language or linguistic abilities; singing abilities; and special active literacies such as persuasion, negotiation, etcetera. Developing the physical body includes shaping its form, shape, structure and capabilities through diet, manipulation and exercise, while developing physical skills includes improving your general physical preparedness or fitness such as strength and agility. This includes mastering basic mind-body coordination; mastering the physical movements required for manipulating the physical world; perfecting more complex athletic abilities; mastering the ability to bear physical pain and operate under stress; mastering control of your breathing and internal energy; mastering control of your blood flow, blood pressure, temperature, heart rate and other involuntary physiological functions (reachable by biofeedback and mind exercises); and so on. The basic factors of fitness to be mastered include physical flexibility, agility, coordination, strength, endurance and speed. As to mental skills, the cognitive skills to master include all the possible capabilities of the mind.

Intelligence is commonly defined as "the ability to reason, plan, solve problems, think abstractly, comprehend complex ideas, learn quickly, and learn from experience." Mental skills include intelligence and the ability to: develop specifically desired (types of) thoughts (including abstract thinking); know one's mental states and understand one's mental objects; focus your attention and concentration; control mental afflictions; guide the movements of your body; control your behavior (including inhibition control of desires); imagine possibilities (such as anticipating the work you must do to complete a goal, or mentally time travelling into the future); visualize intentions or non-existent realities; anticipate events, plan for unfelt needs and therefore create plans and strategies; remember facts or experiences over the short-term and long-term; make correct assessments, deductions, or inferences for problem solving and decision-making using deductive, inductive, dialectical and hierarchical conceptual reasoning; accumulate wisdom (understanding or comprehension) and knowledge that produce learning; guide the movement of the internal energy within your body; access and control autonomic internal states; transform your emotions through insight and reasoning or via other techniques; and so on.

As stated, basically human beings have only two skills - physical skills and cognitive skills. As to our cognitive skills, we have both the automatic and deliberate aspects of consciousness, namely the unconscious and conscious operations of the mind such as spontaneous emotions and our deliberate intellectual activities of thinking, reasoning and analysis. On the road of spiritual cultivation we work at mastering both of these aspects of consciousness – those that happen automatically and those that we can consciously control. Our body and mind, our physical skills and cognitive skills, are the equipment we have, and the path of spiritual cultivation involves an energetic effort to perfect their operation and enhance their capabilities.

Thus, on the self-cultivation path practitioners make deep efforts aimed at reprogramming their inherent psychological operating system; correcting the inherent flaws of consciousness itself; improving their cognitive, emotional, physical and behavioral skills and functioning (through consistent and sustained efforts); and basically just train how to use their mind and body much better so that they experience better mental and physical states of being. A spiritual practitioner is therefore always engaged in various training mechanisms such as mental introspection, knowledge and wisdom development, visualization, meditation, concentration and so forth. The objectives are to enable themselves to closely examine, rectify and improve their actions (conduct and behavior), beliefs and biases, coping mechanisms, emotional drives, habits, values, and so forth. This is the basis of the cultivation path. It is about learning how to use our body and mind better, our physical and cognitive skills better, how to experience better mental and physical states of being, how to create positive change in the world for the here and future, and how to cultivate the highest immortal spiritual bodies that take us out of the lower realms of *samsara* forever.

One key to mastering the deliberate functions of consciousness is to transform the memory patterns stored in our neurons since these are the patterns for our thinking and behavior. The contents within our storehouse of memories are unconscious, meaning that they are beyond our knowing unless stimulated into arising. We cannot climb in and change what they are or change the automatic anatomical way that consciousness functions in spontaneously accessing them. However, we can easily create new ideal models or standards of thinking and behavior and impress them into our neural memories through repetition so that those patterns become the new operating system. This is regularly done in sports training and other high performance fields where individuals must learn to act in very specific ways, including under conditions of severe stress when normal intellectual processes shut down and the mind automatically defaults to its most basic responses and learned patterns.

For these situations, and so that we can attain higher levels of perfection for normal ways of being, we want to store up as memories various *ideal models of behavior, best algorithms* for thinking processes, and *excellent emotional reward states* so that these optimums become the default operants for the mental processes that generate our thoughts, emotions, words and actions. This means we have to repeatedly practice consummate ways of thinking, doing and emotionally rewarding ourselves so that optimal patterns become the default patterns within our memories, and thus the standard operating patterns of consciousness. Because this also involves purging ourselves of unwholesome patterns that have been running us this is often called *purifying your mind and behavior* or *perfecting your mind and behavior*. We must also work at transforming our attitudes, mental perspectives or ways of looking at things.

If we change our standard templates of behavior, which are stored within our neurons, it becomes easier to conduct ourselves in better ways because by doing this we transform the roots of our behavior. Those roots are the default patterns, stored in our neurons, which consciousness accesses to produce our thinking activity and actual behavior. They are the basis of our character, personality, disposition, demeanor, mindset, outlook and perspectives, and therefore the root of our destiny since character creates destiny. For each individual they are different but as human beings we all share some common similarities.

To master our cognitive skills and behavior we must also cultivate a calm and clear mind that is steady and levelheaded so that from a tranquil and stable state of "pure (clean) and empty" we can produce better deliberations (decision-making) due to less agitations or prejudices and can concentrate on accomplishing things without distractions.

This then is the basis of virtuous living and consummate, noble or even majestic conduct and behavior. Through persistent exposure to high standards of behavior you can start to adopt these patterns as your own, and so you should associate with environments that foster such excellence so that you might absorb those influences. In this way you can work on developing exceptional skillfulness, propriety, wisdom and kindness-compassion as well as concern for others. To achieve mental purity you must also strive to free your mind of excessive desires, emotional bondages, limiting beliefs and various vexing mental afflictions or agitations, but it requires repeated meditation practice and inner work to help purify your mind of these tendencies. You must also learn to eliminate any tendencies for mental scattering, lethargy, confusion and distractions because one of the goals is to master your mind.

Frankly, if you work hard at self-cultivation you can become liberated from many of your prior forms of conditioning and experience tremendous gains in self-improvement and self-perfection. By always being mindfully watchful over the contents of your mind (clearly aware of your own thinking processes) you can steadily police yourself and gradually achieve these goals. A continuous clear mindfulness (self-observation or witnessing) of your thought processes and the regular practice of introspection (self-examination) are necessary skills for the human organism yet this is not taught in our educational systems. These practices help you master the operations of consciousness (thoughts and emotions) that control the mental states and behavior for a sentient being. They are major tools for the Great Learning of life.

This is the second principle, which is to become mindful of the real-time workings of your consciousness that are operating according to patterns you learned through your past conditioning. Mindfulness, watchfulness, self-policing or self-awareness means becoming aware of your thoughts, desires and emotions, assessing them for propriety, and then correcting them when necessary. You shine the light of awareness on your thinking in real-time so that you are always rooted in the present and continuously assessing your thoughts (and your conduct) in a self-corrective feedback loop of self-recertification and recalibration. By watching your thoughts you can cultivate an aware state of presence (real-time present mind), but while so doing clear awareness requires that you should *not suppress* the vitality of life you feel inside you to produce more mental quiet but let your thoughts flow. In time all the Qi channels in your brain will open up if you let go of your thoughts while maintaining astute awareness of them.

Being mindful of our thought-stream and then correcting it is a sure-fire methodology for perfecting, correcting and purifying our consciousness, controlling our conduct and behavior, and managing our activities. We do so by monitoring and correcting our thoughts in real time, and also by diagnosing and subsequently correcting recurrent faults, flaws, inadequacies and weaknesses in our character and behavior once discovered so that we do not continually repeat errors over and over again. This is how we improve ourselves over time. It is a process of self-correction, self-rectification, self-purification or *purgation* and this has to become our passion project. Those people who examine their faults at all times and strive for correction are first-rate individuals destined for a greatness beyond their karmic fortune. To put it another way, to become just a good person with miscellaneous defilements is not the ultimate stage of achievement.

If we can achieve an active mindfulness of our thoughts, emotions and actions we can continually assess ourselves and cut off errant behavior in its tracks to substitute better thoughts, emotions and conduct for the lesser. By becoming more aware of our emotions we can try to self-adjust our feelings when awry to alter our emotional state and restore our mental alignment. Or, we can let those emotions simply occur and pass away without attaching to them, thus allowing painful karma to become exhausted without residue. If we are not consciously aware of our emotions, thoughts, mental afflictions and ways of behaving we are likely to act unwisely in a manner destructive to our well-being or the well-being of others.

We should always be monitoring our emotional state so that we can control our feelings and emotions. This is the pathway to cultivating values and virtues. We also want to be particularly aware of our mental afflictions and annoyances, as well as moments of incorrect thinking, so that we can ignore them or eliminate them rather than mindlessly merge with them. We should always be clear about all our intellectual operations so that we can continuously act with higher wisdom - namely logic, skillful reasoning, intellectual analysis and decision-making that is clear of ignorance, prejudice or bias. And, by always knowing our own thoughts in a detached manner rather than fusing with them - unless it is an aspiration or concentration we wish to hold onto with persistent determination - we can more easily ignore errant impulses and inclinations that are just passing fancies. To attain this ability of detached self-observation is one of the reasons individuals practice mental watching meditation as a primary spiritual practice. Meditation is a practice technique for developing several different abilities of consciousness.

As humans we typically entangle ourselves in recurrent desires, impulses, attitudes and habits of our own making that then exorbitantly bind us as personality traits. We become like a silkworm that imprisons itself in a self-woven cocoon. Detachment and fair evaluation enable you to transcend these self-created bindings to see situations for what they really are and then deal with them in more appropriate ways than how your habit energies would cause you to act. They enable you to step back from being fused with your normal modus operandi and thereby become more alive rather than robotically entranced (as if sleepwalking or operating within a haze) due to automatically deferring to non-thinking defaults. They enable you to live in the "Now!" of the present moment of immediate experience with an awareness of yourself, a bliss of pristine clarity (calmness together with focused absorption in the moment) and superior inner energy circulation.

This is essentially the purpose of the mindfulness practice of self-observation, which is a mental practice you should learn not just for self-correction but as a training vehicle for helping you to live in the present moment rather than losing yourself, as you normally do, by becoming fused with your thought-stream and dulled through that entrainment. Attention to your thought-stream helps to prevent you from deeply fusing with the momentum of your own thought-train and thereby running headlong into mistakes that might have been avoided. On the other hand, you become authentically independent by transcending attachment to your thoughts as well as even to society's standard ways of looking at and doing things. Mindfulness practice is a way to transcend your conditioned nature and become a "true man" who expresses his authentic (rather than robotic) self and lives vibrantly in the present.

Mental detachment is a way to train your mind to operate differently, and enables you to take your mental skills to a much higher level. For instance, you can learn to detach from learned bondage to recurrent desires, impulses and emotional afflictions and thereby gain freedom from that release. Mental observation helps you become free from the control of your negative emotions while other techniques train you how to transform negative mental states into neutral or positive states or manage them in other different ways. These are good skills to have. Mastering detachment means cultivating a mind of alert awareness, and it is through awareness of your mind that you can start conquering yourself such as your emotions.

By retraining our mental operations, such as developing a presence of mind that is not fused with our thought-stream, we can learn to function better and produce better mental states. Buddhism teaches that to become free of the suffering of existence requires awareness and detachment, but this remedy is far from sufficient since forms of suffering (unpleasant experiences) will always arise in the mind. The principle to seek is *well-being rather than the absence of suffering, and to master the ability to transform conditions to relieve suffering.* Well-being, in particular, is a compromise or mixture of many mental states including acceptable degrees of suffering.

As beings with consciousness, the objective in mastering our attribute of consciousness is to produce well-being for our self and others including the absence of pain in the body and trouble in the soul. One principle is not to excessively hold onto suffering, and to develop enough wisdom and skillfulness that through your thoughts and actions you can avoid or manage suffering and create well-being in its place. Suffering will always be here so while we need to reduce the suffering in our lives we should ultimately strive for well-being such as states of inner calm, happiness/joy, peace, lightness, flow and so on.

Yogis, monks, sadhus, sannyasin and other spiritual adherents are commonly taught to realize that they are All, that the dancing universe is not real and they cannot really know it; they should not identify with their (imperfect) mind and senses; they should hold nothing in their mind; they should thereby strive to be one with God without any attachments; and that if they rest in desire-free consciousness without clinging (as they walk around in living life) they will find peace as if nothing exists, but this is an idealism that never really eliminates suffering. It is only meant to encourage detachment from clinging to thoughts for the ultimate purpose of quieting your mind's mental activities and improving your internal Qi flow that produces the spiritual transformations necessary for attaining the transcendental body attainments.

These teachings are just a training technique because enlightened individuals attach to mental objects all the time. The Buddhist teachings to rest in the samadhi of *infinite emptiness*, the samadhi of *infinite consciousness*, the samadhi of *infinite nothingness* or the samadhi that is *neither thought nor no-thought* are also just training techniques rather than honestly attainable mental states. These are all just meditation practice methods to help you practice letting go of your thoughts so that you can separate awareness from your mind-stream or cultivate an "empty mind." There actually is no way to form a thought of infinite nothingness; there is no such stage of thought that is not thinking (mental activity); the idea, image or experience of infinite emptiness is still an image of emptiness and thus not empty; and so on. You can bump into experiences that appear to be these mental states – usually because a Buddha gave them to you through a *nirmanakaya* projection into your brain – but they are not really real. They are just mental practice vehicles. They are mental stations that you practice for emptying your mind of coarse mentation. The Mahavakyas of Hinduism are also not just teachings meant to provide you with insights but affirmations meant to help you silence your thoughts as well.

Yet another meditation technique entails the instructions that you should "go back to the state of pure being where the 'I am' is still in its purity before being contaminated by thinking, such as 'I am this' or 'I am that.'" This too is meant to shut off your thinking mind so that you can taste a bit of mental emptiness. Similarly, "You must transcend the knowingness of existence and reach a point in meditation where you don't even know that you are." Or, "As the absolute, you are none of the qualities of existence so should stabilize in that state since it is your true nature."

Naturally these are all types of emptiness meditation that point you towards reaching an empty mental state via widely different approaches. The world has hundreds of such *shamatha* or cessation techniques. I particularly like the non-denominational instructions that you should "strive to be one with

God without any attachments," which is a method that helps you let go of thoughts or phenomena and flow with life. Christianity also teaches us to "find peace in the contemplation of God" which is another meditative type of emptiness technique.

Yet another technique belongs to Vedanta, which reminds people that the "I" is the perceiver of your perceptions, but the real I (you) is beyond thoughts and words because it is the one fundamental eternal reality. Recognizing this fact, you are taught to inquire who you are and meditate on this fact, which is another type of formless meditation practice.

Vedanta instructs people that their individual sense of I is a false entity that only springs into existence because it rises and associates with something else other than itself, which means that the "self" arises in juxtaposition to thoughts about an "other." In other words, the individual sense of the self or I-thought can only exist as long as it is associating with something. The reasoning then goes that if you can sever the association between the subject "I" and all things then the "I" goes back to the Self and disappears – presto, you attain a state of empty mind. When you try to do this through inquiry or meditation practice then, as in the previous techniques, this is yet another alternative form of emptiness practice meant to help you quiet the thoughts within your mind.

Yet another method is to cultivate detachment so that you can more easily enter formless (empty) meditation states and deal with the vicissitudes of life. One method for doing so is to ponder the sequence of Creation out of our foundational substrate and the fact that each soul or *jiva* has the ultimate aim of returning to the original state of purity and perfection from which the universe (and entity-self) has been born and must therefore realize that all world processes – birth and death, creation and destruction, Yin and Yang, the descent of the soul into matter and its subsequent reascension into the heavenly planes – are the play of the one unchanging Self. Birth after birth the *jiva*, soul, or living entity works out its karmic joys and sorrows, merits and demerits, and comes to eventually realize that all beings are identical in essence to the one Supreme Soul (foundational nature), and therefore there is no reason for attachment to the desires of the world. The realization of one's true nature helps to create dispassion towards the world and free individuals from mental bondage to matter, or to time and space, because there is no other entity apart from one's True Self. Everything is an illusional play while the empty substratum of reality is the one true nature of reality.

These are all methods of emptiness meditation that help you calm your mind, realize its inherently peaceful nature, and by resting within that clear (empty) peacefulness you can reestablish the natural tranquility of a balanced inner Qi flow that is required for cultivating a higher spiritual body.

Detachment is certainly one strategy for dealing with the world and its pain and suffering. It helps you become situated in a transcendence from thoughts where you can subsequently attain peace, freedom or release. Nevertheless some of the other principles for dealing with suffering include tying up mental states of suffering; silencing them or transforming them; retraining the mind to think, view and react differently so that suffering doesn't arise in the first place or its causes are avoided; to become stronger and more resilient for handling suffering; involving yourself in activities that bring happiness and meaning despite the sufferings of life; and working to permanently transform conditions so that suffering is eliminated or reduced in the now or future to everyone's benefit.

Similar to the guidance offered by *The Great Learning* of Confucius, Taoism espouses a principle that we need to always "drop off and change." We need to *drop off* what stands in the way of well-being for ourselves and the group. We need to *change* what isn't working and adopt whatever improves matters. Change is inevitable in the universe so we need to learn how to remain flexible in dropping off old ways and changing to whatever is better so that we smartly adapt to changing conditions. A major problem with many religions is that they espouse unbreakable behavioral rules that ossify society, thus preventing society from evolving into something better such as by making improvements in social progress. The principle to follow should be to "drop off and change."

The general rule for attaining happiness that is touted about by spiritual schools is that we need to reduce our desires, practice ethics, virtue and wisdom in our behavior, learn detachment, refrain from excesses (practice moderation), and transform our negative emotions or living situations in life. We need to relax our minds and throw its burdens down to find peace. We also need to eliminate incorrect behavior that produces unfortunate outcomes, drop bad relationships (ex. untrustworthy friends), etc. and work on perfecting our personality, disposition and perspectives so that we can find contentment. We need to cultivate ways to live better, and the solution for doing so means we must be perfecting the processes of our consciousness.

Essentially we must drop off the unwholesome and adopt the wholesome. You must drop off non-virtuous ways of being and doing and adopt skillful virtuous ways instead. This is the meaning of "drop off and change." We must abandon errant thoughts and behavioral tendencies to experience the inherent cleanliness, purity and virtue of our minds that exists whether or not we know it is there. The universe is characterized by constant change so in order to survive we must always adapt our behavior, and this is the meaning of drop off and change. To transform ourselves toward perfection we must purify our mind and behavior. Certain aspects of our character have to be cleansed out of our psyche, and to diminish errant tendencies and thus purify ourselves is also a meaning for drop off and change.

Suffering will always be here in our lives, but by learning how to more easily drop off and change (behaviors, errant methodologies, aspects of ourselves, etc.) we can readily reduce many of our afflictions, annoyances and sufferings in life. We can pursue well-being by changing ourselves or our behaviors to suit a new reality rather than by insisting on following outdated ways or methods that no longer work for us. For many things in life suffering is just part of the equation (such as childbirth) and you simply have to invent optimal ways to deal with it. However, by "mastering Nature" ("mastering the changes" of phenomena) and by working in tune with the natural trends or transformations of conditions you can decrease your sufferings in life because you will be going along with the flow of reality rather than fighting it with stubborn insistences.

This Taoist teaching is a positive road for humanity's development – to "go with the flow" when appropriate rather than always fight the tide. Becoming a "master of the changes of phenomena" means learning how to expertly change/guide phenomena and circumstances, but also knowing when to stand aside from the momentum of events and go along with the flow in order to preserve or even enrich oneself.

The purpose of self-refinement is to elevate your wisdom, decision-making, emotional realm, personality, skills, attitudes and perspectives, behavior, etc. so that you can handle life better and exhibit a stage of excellence in being. Self-cultivation entails a collection of psychological methods or routines for doing this and involves perfecting how we think and act so that we experience mental peace, comfort and happiness through thinking and conduct that is ethical, compassionate, skillful, and effective. Self-cultivation means subordinating yourself to a noble model of behavior that raises you above ordinary men who are not aware of themselves or interested in self-improvement. It entails the pursuit of noble conduct that produces excellent, exemplary, efficient results including the reduction of suffering in your life and the arising of well-being in its place.

We are diamonds in the rough but through cultivation can become virtuous as well as majestic on a personal and communal level.

You will experience the results of all your actions as karma, so it is best that all your actions in life be as irreproachable, admirable, elevated, noble, spiritual or majestic as possible. The *Upajjhatthana Sutta* states, "I am the owner of my actions, heir of my actions, born of my actions, related through my actions, and have my actions as my arbitrator. Whatever actions I do, for good or for evil, to that will I fall heir." In the *Cula-kammavibhanga Sutta* Shakyamuni Buddha said, "Beings are the owners of karmas, heirs of karmas, they have karmas as their progenitor, karmas as their kin, karmas as their homing-place. It is karmas that differentiate beings according to inferiority and superiority."

Another Buddhist sutra explains that the actions which lead to a short life make people short-lived, the actions that lead to longevity make people long-lived, the actions that lead to sickness make people sick, the way that leads to health makes people healthy, the way that leads to ugliness makes people ugly, the way that leads to beauty makes people beautiful, the way that leads to insignificance makes people insignificant, the way that leads to influence makes people influential, the way that leads to poverty makes people poor, the way that leads to riches makes people rich, the way that leads to low birth makes people low-born, the way that leads to high birth makes people high-born; the way that leads to stupidity makes people stupid, and the way that leads to wisdom makes people wise. These principles are sometimes called the rules for the manifestation of karma, but they simply summarize the laws of cause and effect that if you act in a certain way you will produce a corresponding consequence.

Consequences follow your actions and your actions are controlled by your mind. How good or bad consequences ultimately are depends upon the skillfulness of your decisions in producing proper actions. In life you must work on developing wisdom (knowledge, understanding and skillfulness in managing cause and effect) and perfecting your behavior in line with that wisdom (as well as the positive virtues of kindness, compassion, honesty, fairness, etc.) to make it more effective at attaining/achieving whatever you want. In life you pursue "gain" and wisdom helps you achieve "gain."

Another goal should be to purify your animal nature to make your conduct as elevated, admirable, irreproachable, consummate, majestic or spiritually noble as possible. The principle is to instill a moral compass within yourself and turn away from whatever is unwholesome while cultivating values and virtuous ways in their place so that you become *a man or woman of principle* who resides in righteousness. Cultural training in ethics, virtue and consciousness is what separates us from being just animals.

Your behavior is controlled by your thoughts, which in turn originate in your mind. In other words, your behavior is your thoughts expressed. Behavior is what services your thoughts - it shows you how your mind has responded. It is our behavior that needs to become upgraded to irreproachable, skillful and consummate conduct.

Perfecting your behavior so that you exhibit consummate, skillful conduct of the highest excellence ("brightest virtue") involves purifying the contents of your mind and perfecting its operations because your consciousness produces the thoughts that become your actions. Actions become tendencies, which become habits, which become your character, which generates your destiny. You can transform all these outcomes by attacking this sequence at its roots, which involves purifying your mind by improving its thought-making processes. Your conceptual processes should be rational, effective (skillful or elegant) and replete with virtuousness. To improve your thinking and behavior, you must develop a mental feedback mechanism that monitors your thoughts (and behavior) and that upgrades, corrects or recalibrates them when necessary. This is the lifelong practice of managing consciousness.

According to the Noble Eightfold Path of Buddhism the "correct" use of consciousness should produce proper thoughts, speech and behavior; proper intentions and motivations; proper attitudes, viewpoints, mindsets and perspectives; proper skillful actions and efforts; and a righteous (proper) livelihood, career or occupation. The correct usage of your mind also entails being continually mindful of your own thoughts and behavior through self-observation; regularly self-examining your behavior and its outcomes objectively through introspection in a self-improvement effort to correct your faults or improve your effectiveness; periodically resting consciousness in its peaceful, relaxing natural state that is empty of agitations; and ignoring distractions that cause your mind to wander (concentration) so that you can persevere at activities and accomplish your objectives. In Yoga, *dharana* means holding the mind on some particular object of your focus, and here it applies to holding your intent on accomplishing a purpose until completion.

When we are born we have inherited genes from our parents. Together with this genetic inheritance we also carry over into a new life, from our immediately previous incarnation, some of our character traits, interests and skills or abilities we previously cultivated, especially skills of deep achievement. If one had achieved any stage of Arhat attainment then they will usually retain some memories of their past life that constitutes another type of continuity (immortality) as well. These are reasons why some people are born with exceptional innate skills in fields like music, math or athletics that show at a young age. Another example that proves the carryover of personality traits is that genetic twins develop remarkably different, unique personalities (emotional patterns, behavioral patterns and ways of thinking) and interests despite being raised in the same way in the same environment. As a child we will absorb/acquire certain lessons, attitudes, and traits from our family, environment and culture thus making residential influences very important to our lives and futures. Our parents, culture, society and environment help shape our disposition but some of our attributes definitely come into our lives from our previous incarnation.

Our character traits become incorporated into our subtle body, which is what undergoes reincarnation from the state of being a deva spirit (within the earthly heavenly plane all around us) back to being a human again. Those characteristics, together with the karma of our past deeds and our actions in a new life, become the basis for our destiny. We should in this life strive to build excellent character traits and predispositions, learn new skills and abilities, perform virtuous deeds that create excellent results, and adopt excellent aspirations, pledges or vows to guide our behavior that we might want to help guide our migration from life to life. This is spiritual cultivation, which in addition to the task of cultivating your internal energy to release a transcendental body is all about rectifying your thinking and actions, meaning that it is all a process of self-improvement. It is all about improving yourself until you merit and can one day attain a higher spiritual body with those traits (*samskaras* or tendencies) and then leave lower realms behind forever.

To improve your behavior you can purposefully design and execute a plan (like athletes do in order to build skills) to acquire whatever abilities, knowledge, character traits or merit you want to acquire rather than just randomly do things in life without a specific purpose and then willy-nilly absorb unwanted conditioning influences from your environment subject to the winds of fate that then make you a puppet of existence. This is not a good plan for self-development.

As the proper path of spiritual cultivation, rather than just following the Golden Rule or blindly obeying the standard Do's and Don'ts of religion (such as the Ten Commandments, *Yama* and *Niyama* rules of Yoga, etc.), you must do more to purify your desires, thinking processes, and behavior rather than simply constrain them. The spiritual path is not about simply obeying rules laid out by religion and taking their compliance as mandatory ("obey"). It is about personality transformation, transforming the world to become better, and about transforming your body to attain the Srotapanna deva attainment and beyond that are distinct levels of energy-being existence already inherently within you.

For the road of spirituality you must work on yourself to cultivate:

- *Virtues, Values and Goals within a Path of Heroes:* You should strive to develop within yourself the highest virtues, values, ideals and ethics, and train yourself to act accordingly so that they become the natural expressions of your purified personality. In other words, the goal is to train your personality so that it softens and naturally produces elegant thoughts and behavior that embody both excellence and the highest virtues or ideals. Three of the goals for this cultivation work are to achieve and then reside in wholesome mental states due to cultivating virtues, to also inspire other people to virtue and good deeds, and to perform benevolent deeds that exhibit such virtues. You should surround yourself or associate with people, activities, and environments that will help you grow in the right directions and help you to attain and express the heroic virtues you want. Your association with virtuous people and self-work at cultivating virtuous ways is called polishing your virtues, brightening your inherent virtues, cultivating the brightest virtues, or "making sheer virtue brilliant." Like an actor training to imitate some personage for a role, you can definitely train yourself to become a certain way, such as replete with selected virtues, and develop that persona. You can also train yourself to be able to achieve some goal that would require you to learn new skills and then upgrade your personality, psyche and disposition with special excellences for that achievement. One training technique is to frequently stabilize in an immeasurable concentration (*bhava* or meditation) focused on feeling the amplified Qi of having desirable positive attributes or virtues, and then remembering to manifest those traits or behaviors in real life whenever possible to "lock them in" by actually becoming that way. You fix yourself in a given attitude mentally, energetically and behaviorally and then gradually become that way as part of your personality as you try to regularly manifest your efforts in the real world by applying what you cultivated. You adopt an ideal model of behavior to be a certain way, or select an exemplar personage or model deity for emulation (such as a Jesus, Buddha or Krishna), and mold yourself by trying to always be like that archetypal ideal by dedicating to your ideal every single action of your daily life. Trying to become like some archetypal ideal produces certain arrangements in your consciousness, and certain Qi feelings of your internal energy that will transform your Qi just as soaking meat in a sauce will cause it to absorb that flavor. This is the Path of Heroes, or *Viramarga* method of Kaula Tantra where you rest in a *bhava* absorption by fixing your self in a given attitude – you spend a prolonged period of practice fixed within a given attitude where you feel the Qi energy of that attitude penetrating all throughout your body. You must feel the corresponding Qi energy because the practice *cannot just be mental*. This practice is similar to the mental factor meditation methods of Esoteric Theravada (*boran kammatthana*) and the *yidam* meditation methods of Esoteric Buddhism. In these cultivation techniques you try to hold onto the pure mood/feeling of being a deity or hero (*bhava*) in service to the highest principles that help people, and gradually work at transforming your Qi and personality along these lines by repeatedly revisiting this specific emotional attitude, flavor or mood. Or, you try to hold onto the feeling of possessing a certain personality attribute in vast measure and try to become that way in real life as done through the four immeasurable meditation practice of Buddhism. In the *boran kammatthana* tradition of South East Asian Buddhism you invite certain mental factors or emotions to arise within your body (invoking the mental factors/emotions as if they were gods) and "invite them" to transform your body and mind (especially because sentiments stir your vital energies). You try to transform the physicality of your body using intense emotions that affect-stir-vibrate its Qi, and in this manner try to recreate yourself as an Arhat or Buddha by strongly emulating specific emotions inside you. Because you must go outside of your comfort zone to break your old patterns to become a *new you*, you should remain indifferent to the discomfort of the transformation process to become better, and make your training as playful as possible despite it being uncomfortable. If you don't take yourself so seriously then it becomes easier to change old habits, limiting beliefs or errant personality characteristics and take on new attributes. The most important aspects to being a good person are polishing your personality template (character) and consummately acting in the proper manner that manifests the brightest human virtues. As Confucius said, *the goal is to make illustrious virtue manifest within yourself, and then use it to change the world for the better.* When you correct yourself through mindfulness practice that compares your behavior with a higher ideal, this self-rectification through comparison is how you can cultivate your virtues and values. When you cultivate good virtues and are careful in your thinking, you will yield a better community for everyone.

- *Self-Correction:* Mindfulness is a practice essential to the proper management of your thinking and behavior because it allows you to correct your mind-stream as well as your conduct or performance. You can easily practice the "watch the contents of your mind" methods of Liao Fan, Benjamin Franklin, Frank Bettger, Wang Yang-Ming, Christian monasticism etc. so that your thinking and behavior steadily improve through continuous self-correction. Confucius said that when you meet someone better than yourself you should analyze why and turn your thoughts to becoming his equal; when you meet someone not as good as yourself you should look within yourself and examine whether you can still improve. You can transcend your animalistic passions and impulses through the practice of constant mindfulness, self-observation, self-assessment and efforts at self-rectification to thereby become more spiritual. Under the grip of blind passion or desire, however, a man loses his self-control (internal discipline) as well as his intellect, judgment and power of understanding. You need to place focused attention on your thoughts at all times in order to keep to a correct course of action, especially if you want to cultivate a new fortune, personality or life. Nobility is not the result of your bloodline but of elevating your behavior along the lines of impeccable moral values, ethics and virtue. Nobility is always becoming superior to your former self due to continuous self-improvement. Along these lines of pursuing irreproachable virtuous conduct, which is the actual basis of spirituality called "rectifying yourself" or "refining your person," you want your conduct, actions and behavior to also become wiser, kinder and more compassionate as well as more skillful and effective for the short-term, intermediate-term and long-term. By adhering to an introspective system of self-management you can pursue self-improvement towards such perfection, which certainly involves learning how to cut off bad behaviors when they manifest, preventing them from manifesting in the first place, or transforming them into something better when they arise. The goal is to become closer to any model of ideal perfection you choose. The alternative to self-correction is to have a coach, master, manager or group of individuals who subject you to continual correction through their feedback advice so that through their advice you can also transform your behavior towards the direction of excellence. In the "8M'" method taught within *Quick, Fast, Done* (Bodri) you rely on motivation, a methodology, massive intelligent action, a monitoring feedback system, a master or coach, meditation, mantra practice requesting aid, and the merit of good deeds to help you make changes in yourself or to accomplish objectives in the world.

- *Asking for Help*: To help achieve your goal and maintain your efforts, or to help you change your perspectives to make achievement easier, you should regularly ask higher powers for assistance such as by reciting relevant mantras or prayers that ask for their spiritual assistance, which they will often supply through *nirmanakaya* emanations that put thoughts in your head or energy into your body and efforts. You can also recite affirmations that help you reprogram your mind in order to help with the crystallization of achievement.

- *Train in the Most Skillful or Optimal Ways of Doing Things:* You can study (through reading, listening, apprenticeship, tutelage or direct experience) subjects such as history, psychology, science, business, nutrition, medicine, sports, etc. and learn their most valuable wisdoms/principles or their most skillful and best ways for doing things and then adopt those optimal patterns as your own. In other words, you can expand your wisdom and insight through various avenues of learning with the aspiration to discover the optimal ways of doing things and the "ways of highest good." Then you can adopt these into your normal behavioral patterns whereafter they will become part of your character and method of doing things in an excellent way. You can train to become more skillful at doing things according to those optimal patterns or methods of excellence, and adopt them into your life. Once you learn the optimal ways of behaving for various objectives you can then adopt those "best methods" as your own so as to become better at your activities and conduct. This will certainly help elevate your behavior and activities to a level of excellence. If you learn more knowledge and develop more understanding then you can also *innovate according to principle* and act in better free-form ways too.

- *Installing Improved Default Behaviors and Habit Patterns:* You can train to develop new default behaviors, habits, and personality traits through mental rehearsals, such as visualization practices (see *Visualization Power*), that will help to install new neural patterns in your brain, especially patterns in line with the objective of becoming your highest and best self. Our neurons store our patterns of behavior and send messages to one another within the brain, and when messages are repeated over and over again those particular interconnections are strengthened so that some neural pathways become the preferred pathways for our default behaviors. Neurons fire together and then wire together to store the patterns for certain types of experiences or behaviors. New behaviors that you desire, if strengthened through visualization practice together with actual real world efforts, actually reshape our brains and can become our dominant behaviors. Then you must work to make these patterns your new defaults by trying to repeatedly manifest/express them in real life so that they become the actualized default patterns for your behavior. You can also work to develop new patterns through immeasurable *bhava* (emotional attitude) practice together with mental rehearsals that will deeply impregnate your consciousness with the automatic flavor of the character traits, attitudes and behaviors you want to develop. Then you must reinforce those new behavioral patterns through efforts of deep, deliberate practice that display them in the real world.

- *Adding Special Intent to Your Actions:* Through "principal awareness" you can add a higher intent or elevated emotional content to all your activities and through that positive framing of a higher purpose thereby upraise them to a stage of majesty or nobility. The reinterpretation of your activities through a different type of framing has immense utility for eliminating negative connotations to your life events and purifying or uplifting even mundane activities. Cultivating "principal awareness" involves maintaining a state of presence while deeply identifying your activities with a higher goal or meaning and holding onto elevated emotions connected with those ideals (infinite *bhava* practice) while you perform the activities. You can even focus on feeling the Qi channels within your limbs while doing so. Or, you can focus on feeling the energy of a (related) internal organ while holding onto a special emotional intent if that emotion is related to the standard organ-emotion correspondences noted in Traditional Chinese Medicine, such as the heart being associated with love, the lungs with justice, the kidneys with courage and so forth. You can select the emotions you want to cultivate during an activity, support that effort of instillation through an affirmation that positions what you are doing with that new emotional impetus, and thereby elevate your participation in any activity as you hold onto those attitudes during participation. Principal awareness involves viewing whatever you are doing as having a higher ultimate purpose that is worthy, uplifting and fulfilling – *especially if it represents greater service to society* – and holding those thoughts in your mind so as to affect the Qi of your entire body. Or, you can just overtly hold onto deep but inspiring emotions (including sunniness, happiness or cheerfulness) to impress that energy into your inner Qi body when you perform an activity. You choose your own attitudes in how to make sense of the world, and by reframing your activities with higher meanings and emotional contents you will add higher intentions to those activities that will transform not just your behavior but your personality too. By concentrating your intent during the performance of an activity you can embed your actions with a higher meaning by seeing them as having a more elevated purpose. This is how you can "purify" or "elevate" even ordinary activities, and thus make your behavior more noble and majestic, which is by instilling them with a higher purpose or meaning and strongly feeling this new interpretation emotionally within you (to the extent that it affects the Yin or Yang quality of your Qi) as you engage in those behaviors. This practice is a way to gradually *beautify your personality and behavior*. You must interpret unique activities you engage in with a higher meaning of service, thus spiritualizing them, and when participating in those activities you practice holding onto that interpretation with concentration, including the amplified *positive* emotional feeling of what you are doing. This is similar to the *Viramarga* "Pathway of Heroes" cultivation method of "holding onto a *bhava*" or fixing yourself within an attitude during specific meditations or visualization practices. In this method you also align yourself with a given attitude and hold onto its energetic content and emotional feeling in order to transform your Qi. A simple example is holding onto the feeling and affirmation that "I'm creating a brighter smile (to make others happy)" when you brush your teeth instead of just performing the action mindlessly, or saying to yourself "I'm building a cathedral" when as a bricklayer you are simply building a wall. In this way a mundane activity leaves the realm of mindless roboticism and takes on greater meaning. As stated, you can even turn higher intents into affirmations that you can mentally recite while holding onto a relevant emotion, and should always notice the feeling of the Qi thereby stimulated in your relevant Qi channels that are being activated (such as those in the arms and face in this case) in order to help you maintain that higher idealism. The principal awareness method of adding higher intent to an activity might first involve dissolving beliefs that are holding you back in some way, and then slowly you can reprogram yourself through relevant affirmations.

- *Emotional Motivation:* Prior to some activity that requires a certain level of performance or unique type of behavior, you might try to put yourself into a special frame of mind, such as by repeating affirmations, or put your emotions into a special mood such as by listening to certain music (just as athletes do in preparation for a sports contest). In other words, you can determine-create your own internal emotional experience by choice, and learn how to regulate it to your benefit by using various methods such as NLP neurolinguistic programming. To alter your emotions in real time you can use affirmations, self-talk, mental rehearsal of prior peak states of success, and other types of positivity effort. The purpose of this *emotional priming* is to help you "groove to a certain frequency" or "get into the zone" in preparation for a particular level of performance, and you can carry that preparation into the real world. By remembering your vows, visions, pledges, highest ideals, dreams or aspirations and being committed "no matter what," the recalling of personal commitments or prior accomplishments during your activities may help you maintain a level of excellence in situations where you are severely tested and where optimistic positive thinking is not enough. If you can learn to hold onto positive emotions that help you persevere and persist towards accomplishing a goal then you will accomplish more in life. By learning how to maintain specific emotional attitudes with perseverance, which is a type of concentration training, this will help you sustain the determination and resolve for accomplishing many projects.

- *Maintaining Clarity, Presence and Focused Attention:* You can strengthen your ability *to be pristinely present with clear awareness during all situations* rather than become blinded by or absorbed within a confused, lethargic, robotic or wandering state of mind. Awareness will help you improve your behavior because you won't lose sight of what you are doing at any moment and through the practice of mindfulness and centering yourself in the present moment you will always be able to correct yourself. The ideal is to stay focused with attention in all circumstances and be so "centered" and "present" that you are outside of every situation because you are standing back in the clear awareness that can see what you are actually thinking and doing and can then adaptively correct your behavior in real time. You can recognize a mistake in real time and then quickly adjust yourself until you get it right. Meditation practice can help you gradually achieve a continual state of presence – the vibrant and pristinely clear feeling of freshness when your mind is quiet but fully open and observant in the moment of Now and you simultaneously feel a bliss of aliveness within your body – where your mind is continuously pristinely aware, vivid, wide awake, calm, clear, peaceful and *balanced*. This is like the state of flow where there is a state of flowing clear consciousness without distraction while you are deeply engaged with activities in a type of living concentration. You can learn to cultivate and always maintain a pristinely clear state of crystal lucid awareness free of distractions so that, at decision points, you can *apply reasoning according to principle* (wisdom) and thereby select the best behavior for the situation rather than become entrained or enmeshed in following learned responses such as reactionary emotional solutions. A stable, tranquil mind of ease and presence is also a better ground state for any personal efforts to refine your character. Through calmness you can, together with virtuous intent, select the most appropriate courses of action for your deeds/activities and execute them with the highest levels of skill. Most people engage in thinking with their Qi pushed forwards within their brains rather than letting it remain centered in their head whilst also flowing *fully* through their cerebellum at its rear. If through non-clinging to thoughts they learned to produce mental activity with their Qi remaining centered in their brain rather than pushed forward, and so that it *also* flowed freely and profusely through their occipital lobe, then they would have a much easier time of cultivating inherently natural states of mental calmness, peace and clarity. To practice this, remember that the atomic composition of your skull and brain is mostly empty space, and your brain-head both exudes to and freely receives energy from the surrounding universe through this solid looking but ultimately empty structure. Through training you can achieve a more centered but non-clinging personality that is a more authentic you, and enjoy an always and everywhere state of pristine clear presence because you cultivate to open all of the brain's Qi channels including those located within the back of your head. To achieve this objective, it will help if you seek out chiropractic adjustments so that your spinal bones are perfectly aligned, especially the Atlas and Axis cervical vertebrae that are located at the base of your skull whose positions can be corrected with a "toggle adjustment." Also remember that yogis, sadhus and sannyasin are taught to go about their activities in life with a sense of detachment where they are to constantly remember that they are not the body and should live like someone without a body so that they become detached and attain a serene nature. They're taught that they are "pure consciousness in nature," that the universe is nothing real, that they should hold nothing in their mind and not identify with their mind and senses, that they should strive to be one with God without any attachments, and that if they rest in desire-free consciousness they will find peace as if nothing exists. This type of practice will tend to keep your Qi *centered* within your brain and the letting go of your thought-stream will produce an enjoyable quieting of your mind where your consciousness becomes predominantly clear and quiet. When you combine this non-meditative time practice with meditation and active *nei-gong* work on opening the Qi channels in your brain (according to DTI pictures, etc.) you will then fully open up the Qi channels in your head.

There are many additional methods for cultivating your personality, behavior and Qi other than these methods. These are just some of the available methods for helping you become your highest you, be your best in life, and achieve your best performance in whatever you do.

Behavior comes from the mind, but how does our mind develop its patterns of behavior? We develop certain personality characteristics or behavioral traits (particular ways of thinking and acting) due to our genes and the influences we absorb from our parents, society, religion, culture, education, personal experiences and so forth. These influences are a form of education that helps us form our character or self. What we are exposed to in our environment, and what we learn from education, training and experience, are influences that become incorporated within the neurons of our brain as memories and patterns. These influences *condition* our consciousness with set reactive patterns. When we repeat behaviors over and over again these habitual patterns become the normal reactive patterns of our consciousness. Consciousness functions by referencing our storehouse of memories, and without those memories our mind could not make sense of the world or function in producing control of our body and physical activity. The mental processes that produce thoughts and behaviors depend upon the memory patterns stored in neurons that serve as defaults for mental functioning, and this is how we develop those standard patterns.

We have also developed active bias tendencies too, such as being predisposed through evolution to perform certain behaviors and various social things that help groups cohere in peaceful prosperous ways. If we had not learned had to cooperate and collaborate within groups of shared culture then the human species would have died out through extinction, and therefore certain parenting, behavioral (such as fearing snakes) as well as social tendencies have developed within us due to evolution. But genes are not destiny because genes can only predispose but not predetermine. Genes represent "nature" but "nurture" – such as social indoctrination into behavioral standards – can override their influences.

You can transform yourself and your behavior so that your genes are not your destiny. Every thought and action you take can become a vote for the new type of person you wish to become despite any genetic predispositions. There are many ways to be and perceive in the world, and you can choose the way you want to be regardless of genetic influences, cultural influences, environmental influences and even your own ingrained habits and conditioning that you learned while growing up to become who you are. You can go against all these factors and choose to cultivate elevated thinking, elevated perspectives, an elevated demeanor and pursue consummate conduct regardless of your background or conditioning.

We are sometimes prisoners of the momentum of our actions or external events, and that momentum (a force larger than ourselves) can be another barrier to elevating our conduct and improving our behavior. Because the heat of the moment and a lack of self-control can carry us into negative territory, this is another reason why individuals should continuously observe what they are thinking and doing with a detached über-watchfulness so that they can really comprehend what is going on from a higher perspective free of entanglement. That freedom from fusion with their thought-stream (including any justifications for their behavior or their emotions) can enable them to stop errant activity in its tracks and turn a situation around.

Our personality or character (our habitual dispositions) causes us to think and act in certain regular, repeatable ways. We become wired to think and act in certain regular ways due to our conditioning but can learn to step out of these learned patterns through the efforts of personal cultivation practices, such as detachment and introspection, and own ourselves again. Mindfulness helps us notice flawed thinking and our preconditioned patterns of flawed beliefs when they manifest themselves, especially those that have turned into ingrained habits, and this awareness gives us an opportunity to drop those lines of thought or transform them into something else.

Habits are simply the expression of our previous conditioning. They are things we learned to do, and then we consistently expressed that behavior until it became the natural way to behave. They are patterns that have stuck, but *they are not natural at all because we weren't born with them*. They can be replaced with new patterns if we master awareness of our actions and thought-stream and also use the best methods of behavior modification to transform them into new habits entirely.[9]

Naturally, if mental illness or recurrent mental problems arise due to problems in brain health (such as injury/damage to the brain's anatomical structure like a cyst or tumor) then the issues have to be handled another way. In such cases you are still not stuck because repairing the brain (through surgery, diet, supplements, biofeedback, meditation, etcetera) can improve errant behavioral tendencies. Such interventions can repair a life. You can definitely change your life's trajectory not just by creating new mental patterns but through rejuvenating activities of *physical brain repair*.

Mindfulness helps us with our self-regulation and self-rectification efforts. It spreads the time gap between our actions and (their stimulating) impulse thus giving us time to reappraise our responses and act in a higher fashion. It independences us from conformity with ingrained conditioning so that we can detach from errant thoughts and behaviors in real time, and change them. We do not have to be beast machines that perfectly identify with our thoughts and emotions through fusion (since we are not our thoughts or emotions) but can always rise above them and choose higher ways of thinking and behaving that spiritualize us.

Normally we get caught up in a lot of mental stuff that is just wandering nonsense that makes us prone to suffering (such as negative emotions, self-talk or criticism), but we can shift our conscious relationship to our mental products so that we do not get sucked into our thoughts or emotions. When we become aware of our mind's tendency to wander, or its tendency to become identified with thoughts, we can shift our focus back to the

---

[9] See *The Power of Habit* (Charles Duhigg), *Atomic Habits* (James Clear) and *Tiny Habits* (BJ Fogg).

present moment.

To become "lost in thought" is to be thinking without knowing you are thinking, but through mindfulness we can recognize that we are thinking and that our thinking is separate from our awareness. Thereby through mindfulness we can break our tendency toward being robotic (non-living) by identifying with our thought-stream ("abiding in thoughts") and restore ourselves to a higher status of aliveness and beingness ... all because we can recognize when we are thinking without being aware that we are thinking, and can then drop that dulling blind entrainment.

Basically, mental mindfulness leads to an improvement in awareness and our conduct. It is a method for training ourselves to be *self-correcting*. Refining our character and conduct lies in balancing our mind so they don't go astray, balancing our mind involves preventing our mind from wandering or fusing with our thought-stream so that we lose our state of presence (a clear and present awareness of what we are doing), and these tendencies are conquered through the self-regulation possibilities of mindfulness where we always observe what we are thinking and doing.

Awareness, wisdom and willpower can help us to break free of being joined to fixed ways of thinking or doing things so that we can elevate our behaviors, purify them, transform them, cut them off, eliminate them and so forth. Together with the humility to admit mistakes and constant self-adjustment or self-correction, this is how we should police our conduct and improve our behavior. It comes down to rectifying consciousness (mentally aligning with propriety, righteousness, nobility and correctness), purifying consciousness or mastering consciousness.

It is very important to be exposed to the best models of behavior when we are young and most impressionable. If so, those behavior patterns will become our default operating system until we change those reflexive defaults. If we switch our defaults to something that represents a higher perfection then even better states of well-being will come within reach. The other reliable way to overcome our prior defaults, such as our instinctual reactions, is by cultivating a state of vivid, lucid presence. If your mind is stationed in a clear state of presence this clarity will allow you to rise above adhesion with the grain of the thought-stream and select a better response for the moment. An over-seeing mind that is tranquil, which cultivates good sense, and with perfect clarity knows the moment can override reflex-based responses and the momentum of learned behavior.

A moment of afflictive emotions is something created by your consciousness. However, if you are mindful of the contents of your mind and *recognize* you are experiencing annoyance it is less likely for you to become swept away by it. By becoming mindful of the contents of your mind you can spread the time gap between impulse and action and thus successfully police your behavior such as by resisting an urge to shout when angry or by resisting compulsions that would normally produce activities on your part automatically without you thinking about those processes.

One goal in life is to install excellent mental programming through training, and then to monitor and adjust your thoughts in real time so that your mind produces elegant thoughts and behavior that embody excellence. The ultimate goal is not just wonderful interior states of contentment but that your external behavior also becomes compassionate, skillful and effective. You should also strive for your actions to ultimately exhibit elegance, grace, nobility, and elevation. The key during life is to learn to use your mind in a way that harmful states do not arise, either internally or externally; to cut off harmful states that have already arisen through any of a variety of expedient methods; to cause beneficial states to commonly arise; and to cause those beneficial states that are already existing to keep continuing. You are trying to cultivate magnificence or majesty.

When unwholesome, disturbing, agitating or disruptive thoughts and emotions intrusively arise within your consciousness you should surely try to cut off such afflictions. A wide variety of methods are available for purifying our psychological disturbances, which is the intent of spiritual cultivation in giving us various tools to perfect ourselves. Training for this goal is one of the tasks involved in learning how to master your mind. For instance, by not giving mental disturbances any attention and distracting yourself with something else you can often silence unwanted mental intrusions. This is because focusing your concentration on some other topic and paying unwanted guests no mind by ignoring them will draw energy away from those annoyances.

You can also try to reinterpret a troublesome situation differently by looking at it through a perspective that changes your emotions regarding the circumstances. You might also try replacing/switching bad thoughts with better thoughts using NLP (neurolinguistic programming) practices, CBT (cognitive behavior therapy), ACT (acceptance and commitment therapy) or the methods of psychitecture.[10] There are many possible strategies for conquering your emotional mind, which is a major obstacle producer in life that often takes us in the opposite direction of our goals,

---

[10] See *Designing the Mind* by Ryan Bush.

causes us to take actions we regret, or causes us to suffer unnecessarily. We must learn to use our higher mind to tame our animal brain by using methods that can change, modulate or control our emotions.

By regulating your emotional mind, by eliminating unwanted mental afflictions, by triumphing over craving, desire, anger, greed, envy, fear and excesses, by acting with morality and compassion rather than being purely guided by self-interest, by learning how to remain detached from your thought-stream, and by learning to concentrate without interruption, you slowly begin to conquer your mind and your behavior.

When negative thoughts or afflictions still arise, yet another approach is to reflect on their unpleasant nature or the consequences of responding to them. This is called *dissolving unwholesome thoughts and attitudes through wisdom analysis and contemplation*. It means learning your "reasons why" and then unraveling those root impulses in order to transform your tendencies. Analysis of why certain thoughts arise and pondering their consequences will help you to resist them, gain control of your mind and behavior, and dissolve their reoccurrence potential when you work on unraveling their roots. To help silence them you can ponder their disadvantages such as scrutinizing the dangers and drawbacks of following such conceptions. If you find problematic thoughts that are responsible for your bad moods then you can also work to restructure them for good.

The Great Learning of life for *Homo sapiens* entails that we learn various techniques for managing and controlling this attribute we possess called consciousness, and the attribute that manifests behavior called the body. Humanity has developed many expedient methods to help us change our thoughts, emotions and mental states such as prayer, mantra, mentally calling upon a saint or other religious figure for help, breathing practices and modern techniques such as NLP, CBT or ACT. We can use them as appropriate to help conquer our minds.

For instance, alternate side breathing, kumbhaka pranayama, Wim Hof breathing and other pranayama methods can temporarily alkalinize your blood. This changes the biochemistry of your brain, which then affects the functioning of your neural processes and therefore your thoughts and thinking. The rhythm of your breathing also affects your Qi flow that is connected with your consciousness, and it can also calm or excite your thinking, mood and emotions. In fact, there is an optimal breathing pattern for life where your mind calms and your heart, lungs and blood circulation reach a state of coherence where your body systems become coordinated to peak efficiency, and this is an optimality that helps with producing clear thinking. This *coherence breathing*, which should be practiced in all spiritual traditions or monasteries on its own or through prayer or mantra recitation that have the same frequency, is to inhale softly for 5.5 seconds (expanding the belly as air fills the lungs) and without pausing exhale for 5.5 seconds (bringing in the belly as you exhale to empty the lungs). Each breath is to feel like part of a circle where Qi flows up your spine or descends down the front of your body (or down the center of your body).

Better muscular-skeletal alignments that help your Qi to circulate more smoothly also lead to better steady states of concentration and higher states of clarity, namely quieter mental states free of afflictions. This is why people should undergo regular chiropractic adjustments, strive to maintain straight postures where their Qi proceeds smoothly up their spines into their heads, and why they should center themselves within a feeling of the Qi within their bodies that should *not lean forward* to the frontal cortex of the brain (due to too much usage of the intellect). The feeling of Qi within your brain should be evenly distributed throughout your head and in particular should fully reach back to fill out your brain's occipital region and cerebellum.

Even in the Buddhist sutras the lessons on regulating and watching your breathing entail the fact that you are supposed to *feel the energy of your body (Qi) that moves your breathing* rather than concentrate attention on your breathing itself. You are supposed to be cultivating your Qi, not your attention, yet everyone gets this wrong! In fact, as Yoga master B.K.S. Iyengar once said you can even (and should) feel the energy in all of your fingertips or cells if you cultivate correctly. Hindu *Kriya yoga*, Chinese Taoist *nei-gong* and Vajrayana practices also instruct you to feel your Qi everywhere within your body so that you grab hold of the sense of the energy of your body because this is what arises as the basis of your deva body after death. Most cultivation practices are about feeling the energy of your entire body as that energy pulses and moves everywhere internally because in feeling that energy you are feeling the energy of your subtle body that arises upon attainment of the Srotapanna deva body. At the highest stages of attainment in the Formless Realm your body is entirely energy. In any case, better health, posture and blood/Qi circulation improve your mental states.

As to some of the gradual methods for retraining your thought patterns and behavior over the long run, the possibilities include living in a better environment to absorb more positive influences, monitoring and adjusting your mind and behavior through watchfulness or mindfulness practice, and modeling someone who has ideal characteristics so that the emulation induces positive change in the directions desired.

In spiritual cultivation you should concentrate on cultivating three things: (1) your internal energy, (2) empty mind meditation practice, and (3) perfecting your conduct (with an emphasis on doing good deeds, accumulating merit and cultivating virtuous qualities and traits in yourself). *Meditation* practice helps you cultivate mental and behavioral excellence, and *pursuing a purity of behavior* involves doing good deeds and cultivating virtuous ways. By *cultivating your internal energy* you improve the health of your body, purify your forthcoming deva body, and improve the clarity and calmness of your mind.

The center of all three types of these practices is consciousness because it controls all three efforts. Therefore you need to learn how to manage the operations of your consciousness with excellence because consciousness creates your world, creates either suffering or well-being, and ultimately controls your behavior that produces either pain and suffering or the great welfare of prosperity, success, flourishing, happiness and contentment.

Whether you are ethical, moral and virtuous or not, and whether you perform meritorious deeds or not depends upon the workings of your consciousness. Your conduct and actions are your thoughts expressed. Those activities produce either good or bad deeds and favorable or unfavorable results in the world, and favorable or unfavorable mental states in consequence.

The most favorable mental state is that of inner purity or equanimity that is quiet, empty or calm. When the mind is pure (clean, empty and peaceful) then this mental state is an elevated but sustainable form of subtle joy or bliss. It is a bliss without any irritation of excitation. Happiness and joy are active, stimulating, exciting forms of bliss but you cannot maintain them forever. They are coarse and unrefined as compared to states of sublime purity, but their benefit is that they are a form of shining or shine where you are really feeling alive as compared to states of sublime purity.

The highest form of bliss, however, is where your body's inner vitality flows freely everywhere inside you and that inner energy circulation is so good that your body feels light or non-existent – you feel bodiless – or you can feel a tinge of subtle bliss everywhere (as opposed to strong invigorating and pleasurable physical bliss everywhere, which is a lower stage of attainment). At the same time, during this flow state your mind is pristinely clear and internally quiet without distractions, fully immersed in activities while feeling energized with focus, and the experience feels intrinsically rewarding. Within the flow state you can find a deep fulfillment through engagement in the present moment. It is as if your consciousness is unified and you attain supreme peace during your engagement with activities.

Thoughts produce actions, and some of the principles to more skillful actions (that produce what you want in life) are better understanding and know-how (wisdom), more proper attitudes and accurate perspectives, improved decision-making, patience and more self-control (internal discipline). All of these functions of your working consciousness can be considered attributes of your personality. Furthermore, you can and should learn the best optimality rules from various fields, and from this understanding start thinking and acting in the most skillful ways that man has discovered or created.

Studying the best or optimal principles of action, activity or accomplishment from various fields is another way of developing your wisdom and skillfulness. The rule for life is to *put into practice methods that most reliably produce the highest levels of excellence.*

Another aspect of your existence that you should concentrate on improving is the state of your physical body. This includes your physical health, your athletic capabilities and the fullness of circulation of your internal Qi/Prana energy. Exercise, diet, the environment, detoxification efforts, regular skeletal alignments or other types of physical manipulation, *qi-gong* breath work, and visualization efforts can all help you improve your body and its athletic abilities.

Your body is destined to decline over time, so you must adopt methods that will keep it in good health, and make special efforts to repair, renew and rejuvenate it to fight the inevitable entropy of deterioration – sickness, aging and death. To maintain your body in good health is a duty otherwise we shall become a burden on others, lose the possibility of physical bliss, and not be able to keep our mind strong and clear.

Basically, you should take care of your body *as if you were going to live forever* because with that attitude you will tend towards its proper upkeep and maintenance. To become more physically fit you need to enhance the functioning of your cardiovascular system and work on perfecting your mind-body coordination as well. You also need to especially work on improving your muscular strength, flexibility, agility, endurance, stamina, energy, and so forth since they decline with age. In general, sports and athletics (where you work at becoming proficient at various sports skills such as jumping, kicking, running, throwing, etc.), yoga, martial arts, stretching exercises, dance and so on are all forms of exercise that will help to make you more physically fit, improve your Qi circulation, and *help you with your spiritual cultivation.*

By regularly stretching your body's muscles, tendons, ligaments and fascia through yoga, dance, rebounding, sports, martial arts and other exercises you can gradually re-orient their structure to greater capabilities. The stretching also makes it easier for your Qi to flow within you and seamlessly circulate through all your tissues. This is important for cultivating your inner deva body while alive. You can also learn how to align your body according to its natural inner energy circulatory patterns that can be guided by your will, and this effort will help open up the Qi meridians within your body's tissues. This will not only lay a foundation for better health and greater longevity but for spiritual cultivation as well since the Twelve Year kundalini awakening (twelve-year transformation period that occurs prior to the subtle body attainment that is managed through the grace of higher beings) essentially involves rotating your Qi/Prana continuously day and night throughout all your tissues to purify them.

There is also the aspect of perfecting your physical movements, physical capabilities, and your structural form through actual physical practices rather than internal energy work. Your body of flesh is your "lived distance," so it makes sense to gain as complete a control as possible over this lived space while also making it as excellent as possible in terms of its health, form/shape, internal energy, and capabilities. The ideal optimum is to be able to feel the living energy (bliss) inside every cell of your body, which is the purpose of yoga, the soft martial arts that stress inner energy work, and the *nei-gong* techniques of Taoism and Vajrayana.

Hence the goal is not just to pursue an excellence of health, energy, form, movement and expression. The goal includes attaining a living state of *flow* or "being in the zone" where all your mind-body systems are in sync; your hormones are well balanced; your circulatory flow of blood, breath and Qi are optimal, in coherence and don't run into obstructions; you are present so fully that you lose the sense of self; your mind is quiet, peaceful and pristinely clear; your mental activity seems effortless; your wisdom and decision-making are functioning in a state of excellence; you experience an overall feeling of health, comfort, lightness, alertness and well-being ("bliss") in your body and mind; you perform tasks effortlessly with engagement (attentive concentration that ignores distractions); and you react and move in all circumstances with precision, elegance, grace and ease (which includes "good manners"). Here you can function at the level of peak performance, and at the same time the feeling of your body should be blissful, comfortable, full of energy and that of freedom. It would be an ideal situation if being in the zone was one's ordinary state of mind all the time.

Internally our Qi energy should circulate without encountering knots, restrictions or obstructions, and that smooth flow of vitality will lead to a physical sensation of energized fullness and cellular bliss/comfort. We should also be experiencing a very calm, clear and peaceful state of mind due to that superior Qi flow. We should always be enjoying a lucid state of pristine mental clarity (which seems quiet) accompanied by physical ease. In other words, mentally you should always be experiencing a vivid pristine awakeness that is accompanied by a subtle tinge of physical bliss within that clear peacefulness. We are beings of consciousness that live, and you want to physical feel the active vitality of the life force inside you so that you really feel alive with positivity, or reach a state so excellent that your physical body isn't felt anymore at all, while you definitely experience the blissful joy of life and experience the world and all its qualities.

The body is the producer of your consciousness, and so you must take care of its health and cultivate its internal energy to a higher stage where your Qi can flow freely without obstacles, impediments, blockages or restrictions within you. Otherwise you won't be able to experience these attainments. Your health and the condition of your internal energy should become so excellent and optimal that you forget the feeling of having a body because its Qi-flow is so comfortable, which is the meaning of physical bliss. The goal is to reach a comfortable physical state where you always feel a bit blissful and perfectly at ease.

What are we ultimately trying to experience in life other than internal peace, a wide openness, freshness and clarity of mind that vividly experiences the world while knowing our thoughts perfectly, and feelings of joy and bliss? What are we ultimately trying to express other than skillful consummate, majestic conduct that doesn't hurt others and achieves what we want? We are all dependent constructions – manifestations or aspects of the fundamental substrate and dancing Shakti without an absolute self or permanent consciousness at the core of our being – so *nobody exists on purpose as an intended consequence of Shakti*. Nevertheless through cultivation practices we can make something of ourselves and achieve these goals and more.

We can determine our own life purpose and develop our own trajectory through Shakti where we can always experience a virtuous *joie de vivre* or joy of living as we execute that purpose throughout our transformations, whether those transformations be within a life or between incarnations. This means cultivating a cheerful full experience of life - a zest and gaiety of existence – that has meaning and exalts the spirit. It means filling our consciousness with wondrous delight, an infectious spirit of goodness and appreciation of living that *brings everyone and everything forward.*

Spiritual cultivation should entail cultivating and radiating an inexhaustible *joie de vivre* - a vitalizing energy together with a joy of living - rather than an enforced (passive) equilibrium of suppressed emotions and restricted behavior as you see in many monkhood traditions. You must never lose the ability to simply enjoy being alive, but some spiritual traditions incorrectly try to squeeze this out of people through incorrect notions of discipline, detachment and dispassion. Isn't the invigorating joy of Springtime life energy that makes us feel alive something we want to experience, or a peacefulness conjoined with feelings of subtle bliss rather than a dispassionate stale inertness or dried out lifeless state? Even the desire of wanting to accomplish something exists because we want to feel the bliss of achievement, and so we direct our active inner energy into activities and accomplishments for the bliss they ultimately provide.

The angle of attack for achieving these objectives is to concentrate on mastering our mind, behavior and internal Qi flow, and so we must work to master all the aspects of consciousness that give us control of controllables. This is called cultivation, and it is primarily concerned with how to master our mind, our energy, our bodies and our activities or behavior. We must especially concentrate on mastering our thought processes, emotional moods, mental states and unwanted mental afflictions that naturally arise within us as these can mar the pleasure of the life experience and also lead us into wrong behaviors. Most individuals in life want to feel connected to others in a positive way, remain free and authentic (true to themselves) in their lives, feel competent at what they do, and want to experience joy, bliss and meaning in their activities. All these objectives can also be achieved through the proper application of cultivation practice.

We must train our personality, attitudes, and perspectives so that we can always enjoy life even during misfortunes. How? By cultivating inner optimism, upbeat sunniness, cheerfulness, and natural ease where you don't take yourself so seriously since you and your situation are not intrinsic. It also becomes easier to bear misfortunes and unhappiness if you understand that all situations are destined to change, and you cultivate a stronger, more resilient personality with better coping skills. We must train to always improve ourselves and our living/societal conditions *for the present* and *for the future* so that both present and future states of happiness can always be enjoyed for ourselves and others. Many religions and spiritual schools only address present behavior and do not stress leaving behind a legacy of better living conditions (environmental, social, cultural, economic, etcetera) that you create through good deeds to make a brighter future for subsequent generations of mankind.

We must include "others" in our self-improvement scheme because we live in a community of relationships, such as our family and society, where we are all part of one another and all involved in one another. Because of that interdependence the reflexivity of helping others by our actions (such as by improving the group's welfare or another individual person's well-being) will usually help our self in turn. For instance, if each of us cultivates good virtues and good deeds this will also yield a better community for everyone and thereby improve our living environment. But an extra effort is required in making sacrifices to improve matters for subsequent generations, our posterity, by acting so as to "beautify" conditions for them. Since we are reborn into this world it makes sense to always be improving it rather than raping it through our actions. We always want our children to enjoy a better future than us and we must be the ones to create those conditions for them.

Spiritual cultivation should therefore be growth-oriented and growth-motivated rather than something that just addresses the current situation, and it always involves the effort of cultivating yourself and your circumstances for a better future rather than just accepting or adjusting to current circumstances. It's about making changes in ourselves and in our environment or circumstances. It's not just about "me" but about "we." The emphasis in cultivation is on self-improvement and improving worldly conditions, which is a type of growth or progress in creating a new and better world, and when you work on improving conditions for others we call it kindness and compassion or even Karma Yoga. Spiritual cultivation means not just improving things for yourself but working to achieve the happiness and well-being of all people.

You are part of both a society and the environment (Nature or Shakti). Your life is part of a much bigger picture, and is integrally connected with a larger whole. We comprehend the universe incorrectly because of our inaccurate conceptual constructions and limited perceptions so we fail to see the depth of our relationships with others and how our individual actions can affect the world. Our mind's subjective interpretation of the universe achieves its existence because of earthly conditioning where we are an expression of the earth, so even though human thought does not mirror a ready-made objective truth of the universe the human mind is ultimately the world's (and Shakti's) own process of cognition and self-revelation as well as your own. There is just one fabric of space-time within which we are some of its fluctuating ripples (waves in the ocean of being) but those ripples that are us are connected to everything else by our presence and by our deeds or actions. The apparent multiplicity of the universe is a veil of illusion superimposed upon a more fundamental, single, fluid-like body that extends and vibrates infinitely in all directions so as to be continuously transforming every moment. Your job is to learn how to *skillfully, wisely, compassionately* guide these changes to create a better environmental, social, cultural, economic, etc. future for all.

You are the unity that has appeared as multiplicity, and the multiplicity that has enfolded into a localized ripple. Throughout life you interact with everything surrounding you - society, the environment, external objects, other living beings, your body and even your fortune that are also ripples within cosmic space-time. Through reflexivity you have an influence on all these external things that you contact such as society and the environment, and they have a rebounding influence on you. Hence if you harm external conditions the consequences are likely to eventually affect you in some way because those situations continually surround you. You are part of their fabric and whether it is now or in the future they are bound to return to you in some way.

This is another aspect to the meaning of interdependent origination where in being a part of Shakti you are connected to everything. Thus, what you do affects everything else, and through reflexivity everything else in turn affects you. What you do affects the whole and the whole affects you, so it certainly makes sense to be extra careful in refraining from harmful actions on a mass scale – such as polluting the environment or stirring up troubles within society (rather than serving society) – because the consequences will eventually rebound to hurt *you*.

Everyone and everything exists due to the circumstances of infinite interdependence because everything is part of the one single soup of Shakti and there is nothing else manifest besides it – all formations belong to it as part of the one manifestation. Because of the infinity of interdependence for every part of Shakti you can say that everything is the center of life and every moment is the most important moment. Each part of Shakti exists because of the whole, but that existence has no purpose other than to be. The universe is unconscious, impersonal, mechanistic and purposeless so man is *not* the privileged focus of Creation nor is he master of his own house unless he makes himself so. Therefore we must for ourselves derive purposes for our existence through our functions and relationships. As stated, no one has an intrinsic nature or "exists on purpose" in the universe so you have to make a purpose for yourself that is your very own vision. Life itself has no inherent meaning, but each one of us has meaning and we bring that meaning to our life. You can eventually cultivate nearly immortal bodies that will allow you to be devoted to the meaning(s) you chose and can become devoted to many purposes throughout time.

The joy of living is to experience this moment, this *now*, this present within this one fabric with vitality, bliss, happiness and a freshness of clear awareness of the present moment. That is the opportunity that the great miracle of consciousness has given you. You should want to experience this bliss with the fullness of vitality, and you should wish that your family, close friends and even the world also experience it. But how can we arrange things so that life becomes better for everyone, consciousness become better for everyone, bodies become better for everyone, conditions become better for everyone and we all experience such bliss more of the time? How can we arrange circumstances or conditions so that the welfare of everyone improves through greater prosperity and security and we can all experience health, happiness, great welfare, the bliss of flow and significant meaning within the dream world of consciousness that we are privileged to experience?

One goal of spiritual cultivation is that it should enable us to more cheerfully enjoy life in the *present Now* so that we can fully live the adventure of the life we have been given. Thus, one of its aspects is that we must train our minds to have is the skill of being able to eliminate negative mental states so that we can more often experience states such as internal peace, happiness, clarity and blissful flow. This means learning how to "purify the mind" or even subdue the mind that is the creator of suffering.

Consciousness is the basis of who and what we are so we must learn how to master all its capabilities. In particular, for a better life we should strive to rise above our ignorant instinctual animal tendencies that arise within it and pursue a shining nobility of values, virtues, and elegant conduct that elevate our life and our relationships. We want to eliminate, control, purify or elevate the baser tendencies of human nature so that we can live peacefully and prosperously with mankind *and Nature* for we are part of Nature and should not be destroying the natural world. So that all might better enjoy better lives we should foster an environment that promotes constant progress in personal and societal excellence, its flourishing and well-being, and this must include working to cultivate the higher transcendental bodies inherent within our physical structure because these individuals, upon attainment, can help those who have not yet achieved escape from the lower realms. This is why individuals fund temples, monasteries, convents, etc. and the monks, nuns, yogis, sadhus, etc. in various spiritual traditions.

If suffering is the aspect of life we dislike most, then in addition to improving our worldly circumstances to eliminate its causes, and training our minds to become more cheerful and resilient, we must definitely pursue the more permanent solution of the higher spiritual body attainments that win us rebirth in more pleasant realms with more pleasant lives. Religious worship and devotion only help transform your Qi/Prana so much. You can only attain these spiritual bodies by also engaging in *intensified spiritual practices* that purify and strengthen the circulation of your internal energies so that a new energy body can become liberated/detached from within your present body. This takes the cooperation of countless higher spiritual adepts in twelve-years of organized labor, and if you are not a good person they won't put that time into you. Their grace comes from your merit, which is the musculature you need to go forward.

You want to cultivate through intensified spiritual practices a higher independent energy body that separates from its lower, denser, more impure nature – your physical body. We are trying to generate from within ourselves the release of the independent subtle body (that we normally arise within upon death) while devas in heaven are trying to generate the Causal body from within their energetic bodies made of Qi. These "births by transformation" are like a decomposition of a body into successive component layers where the more transcendental energy aggregate can separate from the matrix of a lower aggregate to enjoy a higher and more enjoyable state of existence that resides in a higher plane. This is enlightenment.

Passing away and "going to Heaven" for ordinary people involves a recycling sequence of reincarnations between being a human and becoming a spirit in the heavenly earthly plane, which is an invisible realm of Qi all around us. The process of alternating between the life of a deva and human continues until one finally cultivates the yet higher spiritual bodies, which is easier to accomplish in a heavenly existence. As an act of service, Buddhas are always working on purifying the Qi within our bodies to help us maintain our health, and they administer the process of reincarnation so that sentient life is not lost through inevitable deterioration.

The highest transcendental bodies reside on higher spiritual planes and their composition does not decay quickly. They live much longer lives, which Taoism refers to as "immortality" (since its adepts become longer-lived "Immortals" or "celestial masters" due to the fact that the composition of their body does not decay quickly), and thus enlightened adepts "put an end to birth and death" by staving it off for a very long time before their next transition. By attaining those higher bodies through cultivation efforts, which are linked together to compose a single *sambhogakaya* as described by Buddhism and illustrated in Tibetan and Taoist pictures, we will attain abilities that enable us to help others by using these bodies and their powers to influence people's thoughts and energy.

Religions have developed methods to help us cultivate the purity of our Qi through reverence, worship, devotion and other spiritual practices, but the real kundalini transformations that gain you the deva attainment require devotion to a schedule of intensified inner energy yogic practices that purify your Yin Qi and Yang Qi. Many people become monks, nuns, yogis, etc. so they can fully devote themselves to spirituality but neither know the proper road of practice or that the actual objective is this outcome.

Society as a whole must also become transformed along the lines of purity and maturation too. For various reasons, over time all societies have set up standards of conduct and behavior to shape human lives and emphasized special virtues and values that have enabled us to survive. Religions, in particular, have set up the practice of *Dharma*, or good behavior, by which a man works at his own welfare and that of society as well. *Dharma* is the basis of peace and happiness for all. Becoming more civilized has gradually progressed mankind over the millennium from the level of animal behavior to human conduct, next noble conduct and then even spiritual conduct that destines people for enlightenment.

When noble consummate conduct and spiritual conduct become your standard way of thinking and doing, then those patterns become *samskaras* (tendencies or impressions) that you will carry with you into subsequent lives just as musical skills or other aptitudes you develop will also follow along with you. In other words, your ways of thinking and behaving become a karmic force *(samskaras)* and are carried with you into future births. Hence, impressing behavioral rules and values upon society through religion, tradition, laws and the social environment gradually helps to evolve society upwards over time since there is a carryover effect of civility throughout subsequent incarnations. In the meantime, we must get on with the task of living life in the present now that includes such events as birth, adolescence, adulthood, marriage, having children, experiencing sorrows and misfortunes as well as happiness and blessings, getting sick, old age and death.

In cultivation we are to train ourselves and make efforts to transform (the conditions of) society so that we can all experience greater human flourishing of not just health and prosperity but a cheerful, healthy, vibrant enjoyment of life – at minimum a pleasant life, but in all cases a life *absent of misery* where we feel happy and genuinely alive. We are to train ourselves so that we can achieve prosperity, pleasure and happiness in the world.

We all seek mental states filled with positive emotions such as peace, purity, contentment, lightness, happiness, joy, cheerfulness, sunniness, optimism, satisfaction, warmth, comfort, confidence, courage, vitality and other feelings of well-being. We are also seeking feelings of self-esteem, social acceptance, connectedness and accomplishment. There are many wonderful things we seek to experience in life, and they are all consciously available to us because we have a mind and a body. The trail of spiritual cultivation is absolutely, essentially focused on having us master the two fundamental attributes we possess - consciousness and a body - as well as our conduct/behavior that is the usage of them both and the accomplishments they enable us to produce.

Most of us want to experience happiness and pleasure in life such as pleasant sensations but Pleasure-Happiness is just a temporary, transient experience compared to the long-lastingness of internal purity and peace. What we are really seeking in our active mindsets are activities requiring a fullness of engagement, a sense of accomplishment, and deeper meaning or life purpose that give us a good reason for being in the world. Thus you should be training yourself to prefer higher forms of satisfaction other than simply pursue an endless stream of transient pleasurable sensations. You should be training yourself along the lines of spiritual growth to "perfect the individual" and find happiness and satisfaction from your progress along these challenging lines. The Bible even speaks about this.

In Ecclesiastes 2 King Solomon said, "I said to myself, 'Come now, I will test you with pleasure to find out what is good.' But that also proved to be meaningless. 'Laughter,' I said, 'is madness. And what does pleasure accomplish?' I tried cheering myself with wine, and embracing folly—my mind still guiding me with wisdom. I wanted to see what was good for people to do under the heavens during the few days of their lives. I undertook great projects: I built houses for myself and planted vineyards. I made gardens and parks and planted all kinds of fruit trees in them. I made reservoirs to water groves of flourishing trees. I bought male and female slaves and had other slaves who were born in my house. I also owned more herds and flocks than anyone in Jerusalem before me. I amassed silver and gold for myself, and the treasure of kings and provinces. I acquired male and female singers, and a harem as well—the delights of a man's heart. I became greater by far than anyone in Jerusalem before me. In all this my wisdom stayed with me. I denied myself nothing my eyes desired; I refused my heart no pleasure. My heart took delight in all my labor, and this was the reward for all my toil. Yet when I surveyed all that my hands had done and what I had toiled to achieve, everything was meaningless, a chasing after the wind; nothing was gained under the sun."

All earthly pleasures and glories are transient joys. They only provide an ephemeral quality of sensory pleasure that cannot even approach spiritual satisfactions. We indulge in sense-pleasures that give temporary enjoyment in the beginning that quickly fades and produces misery afterwards. We indulge in what seems delightful to the senses, pleasurable or attractive on the surface, but which can later generate inner turmoil and disaster. Value-based happiness, on the other hand, is what works best for human beings rather than Pleasure-Happiness although it is natural in life that we refresh ourselves with pleasurable activities from time to time. But in essence, we should be seeking a well-being that entails mastery of our body, mind and behavior; the freedom to express our authentic selves along with our life energies (since this will invigorate us and produce a richer life); healthy relationships with others (such as intimacy, friendship, respect, cooperation or collaboration); and through wisdom and skillfulness we want to improve our welfare through activities that control Nature and arrange conditions to be as we like. For the greatest well-being we need to learn how to control ourselves and our futures and find satisfaction and meaning in whatever we do.

Thus we must train our wisdom, skillfulness and behavior/conduct so that we can accomplish whatever we want in life. This involves learning many things as well as mastering various skills and mindsets. We should be training in discipline, self-control and mindfulness, which are our internal methods of self-rectification, and learn how to control our desires with higher knowledge and self-discipline. Then we can correct our improper tendencies, emotional afflictions or psychological limitations and through the purification process of refinement become able to center ourselves in our higher selves. Through self-control of our behavior, purity of the mind within, wisdom and noble conduct we hope to always be centered in *a state of blissful presence* and thereby change our present and future fortunes into a higher stage of flourishing. Physically, we also want to feel happy, successful, healthy and energetic all the time.

Deep inside, most of us want to have developed good psychological roots so that we always openly display virtues such as kindness, and most of us want to be characterized as having a giving nature. We just want to be that way. You can make efforts to be giving and help others by taking pains to eliminate their sufferings and misfortunes and help those in desperate need; help them to succeed at their dreams and activities; work to eradicate their fears and worries; help them to taste the peaceful tranquility of their natural state of being; cool their excessive desires; cause them to break the barriers of habits, avoid going along with bad things and help them to leave misfortunate paths; inspire them to improve themselves and cultivate the merit of kindness and good deeds (motivate them to perform great good deeds); help them derive the means of eradicating their own misfortunes; and develop public projects for the greater benefit of the people.

We therefore train to develop within ourselves various virtues such as wisdom, patience, skillfulness, kindness, honesty, fairness and compassion so as to not just live our own life better but to also become able to do such things. These qualities enable us to love and cherish all beings. We do this to refine our character and make it replete with fine mental states as well as the capabilities of excellence.

Therefore we train in learning, mastering and perfecting new mental and physical skills of various types. We train in developing mental skills such as concentration, memory, logic, imagination, mind-body coordination, inner energy control, and emotional control. We train in polishing our virtues and virtuous behavior so that we become more noble, rise above our inherent animal propensities, and establish thriving harmonious relationships with other members of society. We train in proper, virtuous, consummate conduct that is perfectly appropriate for every situation. We train in how to change our mind's learned programming (conditioning) by adopting new and better mental habits, outlooks or perspectives, attitudes, dispositions or traits. In other words, we train to develop new types of (wholesome) thought activity and behavior. We train in how to change our conditions through skillfulness and wisdom, including our fortune. We train in setting meaningful beneficial goals, aspirations or vows for mankind and work towards achieving them even endless lives for completion.

Confucius said that we should practice propriety, train to *brighten our inherent virtues* and act to help other people and society (so that we become of service to ourselves and others, which is to beneficially service society by *enriching the world with benevolent activities*). He said that we should continuously pursue these endeavors *until we rest or reside in the highest levels of excellence.* His idea was that human effort can be used for self-betterment, but you can also enrich the world with your efforts by trying to improve social, economic, cultural and other situations, solve problems for mankind and thereby make lasting contributions to society.

However, we should actually strive to do much, much more. For instance, we should be training our minds so that we can achieve sustained states of happiness, lightness, tranquility, cheerfulness, sunniness, peacefulness and flow during life otherwise we are just existing (or even suffering) rather than truly feeling alive. There are all sorts of positive states we should be learning to cultivate. We should be training our minds so that we can also abide in sustained states of mental calmness, tranquility, peace and purity or focus and concentration absent of mental afflictions that cause us to lose the state of being centered in our self.

In life we want to be revolving between the peaceful-blissful states of mind and happiness-blissful states of mind; it is okay for mental calmness to periodically become punctuated by peak experiences of happiness and bliss rather than remain in enforced equanimity. We should also train our bodies so that they become healthier through diet and exercise, and should be training them to attain higher abilities of physical excellence and comfort due to our efforts. Naturally we should be broadening and sharpening our mind's many abilities and develop our own virtues, skills, merits and excellences to a stage of excellence ... and possibly splendor.

In pursuing all of these excellences the inherent aim is a steady state of internal peace and tranquility, satisfaction, comfort, happiness and bliss, but we are really seeking efforts that provide us with meaning in a universe without purpose or aim because meaning allows us to bear suffering if there is a purpose to it. Meaning, as well as enjoyment, makes the journey of life worthwhile.

Life is neither fair nor free of suffering but it is still good. In the fabric of the universe there is no such ontological thing as meaning or purpose. We must therefore create it as a guide for our own lives. Space-time simply exists, and we are just some ripples within it that have developed a property called consciousness, fraught with deficiencies, but which is a miraculous property that gives us the potential to experience ourselves and our surroundings. We should therefore be training our bodies and consciousness for the best experiences and activities/actions possible, and since we are social creatures who need others for our survival we need to be developing our behavior and abilities to help others within our groups (community, society, country, world) as well.

We can develop a pristinely clear, calm and quiet mental realm through meditation practice that reveals the unperturbed natural state of our mind, and we can also experience active mental states such as novelty, excitement, pleasure, happiness, cheerfulness, joy or bliss. We are in charge of our own happiness – being happy is up to you and no one else – but if it is unattainable we should seek meaning and purpose in what we do.

Everything of a manifest nature is transitory, and experience shows that states of unhappiness will eventually pass away and be replaced by fortunate states, which will also transform in turn. However good or bad a situation is it will always change. Prosperity, health, happiness and so forth cannot last but must change, so at times they will disappear and then reappear if conditions warrant. Hence it is a poor strategy, even a defeatist strategy, to continually chase after transient pleasant sensations or exalted body-mind states that only temporarily produce "feel-good happiness" even if they are "peak experiences" because they are impermanent and will pass away. Naturally steady states of peaceful comfort, calm and bliss are much better targets as they are in tune with the natural state of our mind that is peaceful until disturbed.

We can also achieve something that has greater longevity than momentary happiness or satisfaction and that creation, even though it is just a personal imagination, and that objective is "meaning." Inherently we are all seeking a higher purpose or higher meaning for our existence, so for personal fulfillment we should devote our potential to meaningful purposes that produce the peace, satisfaction and comfort we seek. Usually such feelings arise when we perform countless good deeds and selfless service for others rather than for ourselves. Saint Paisios of Mount Athos would often say, "The more one sacrifices for the other the more one feels like family." True happiness comes from making other people happy.

The key problem for the human condition is the presence of suffering and agitation in life and the consequential lack of physical and psychological well-being. We must learn how to use our consciousness to avoid suffering, eliminate suffering, minimize suffering, bear suffering better, or transform it into something more palatable for ourselves and others. Some of the ways by which it becomes easier to bear suffering include developing a stronger, more resilient and more cheerful personality, working to improve conditions so that it does not arise, and establishing greater levels of peace, protection, fairness and prosperity in society. We should conduct ourselves and manage our societies so that life is always improving and suffering is reduced as much as possible or forestalled. We should always work to improve our conditions or circumstances so that suffering does not arise, and then we will experience more positive conditions in life. Instead of remaining complacent we should vigorously work on correcting errant conditions in order to improve our lives for the better.

During life, most human beings seek prosperity (abundance that is a lack of want); financial freedom and independence; a fulfilling and rewarding career where you have the independence to express your authentic self and are competent at what you do; a high level of health and energy; to be surrounded by order and beauty; involvement in challenging but greatly rewarding activities requiring deep engagement and the focusing of our intent; the opportunity to show one's autonomous, free, true, authentic self in the world; peace of mind and internal tranquility; frequent positive states such as peak experiences of mental delight, joy and pleasure; high status and prestige within the social chain and within dominance hierarchies; intimate loving relationships; high-quality friendships and social interactions with others as well as affiliations that fulfill the need for affiliation, belongingness and connectedness with others; self-esteem from appreciation or acknowledgement by others (a deep human urge is to be important, be great and be praised or appreciated); to be virtuous in thought, word and deed and exhibit magnificent, consummate conduct; feelings of personal fulfillment (self-actualization), competence, mastery or achievement from success in one's endeavors, from mastering certain *dharmas* or from overcoming challenges etc.; worthy goals, ideals and worthwhile life purposes that provide you with meaning in life and deep satisfaction. We strive to manifest these conditions through our actions, and their accomplishment requires specific types of thinking, training and doing. To achieve any of these goals we must train our thinking, feeling and ways of behaving. We must strive to master our consciousness to be able to produce these conditions that will help to eliminate states of suffering or conditions that cause us to suffer.

There are no such things as rights, fairness, ethics, justice or proper-improper conduct in biology or Nature. These are imagined natural orders that don't truly exist in the neutral fabric of the universe. There is just Nature, and there is no book of ethics inscribed within it. There is just the fabric of space-time. That is all. We just happen to be ripples or processes embedded within its one fabric that have an imperfect property called consciousness. You can say that Shakti is fluctuating around us (after all, it is a roiling, seething froth), or that the cosmos is just a single field of karmic formations traversing through their various transformations, or that we exist in a dancing cosmos, but in every possible descriptive scheme and explanation for the universe the universe is still just a neutral, *inanimate* Shakti where we call living beings "animate" as a matter of designation. There are no such true things as living beings so the designation as "living" is a fiction used for the purposes of differentiation or designation.

We are the ones who create the definitions for the multiplicities within Shakti. We are the ones who create an ethical, virtuous, moral order within Shakti. We are the ones who create meaning or purpose for our lives and we do so through our interpretations within an existence that requires a social group for its survival and maintenance. How will we structure our lives and our societies within the fabric of this world to produce what we treasure most, but which reflects justice and fairness so that the greater do not exploit or oppress the weaker and lesser have-nots?

Our culture defines for us what is considered proper, virtuous or correct because Shakti has no such natural orders. These qualities are imagined orders that we made up in our minds and established as collective principles. Shakti, in truth, is just the manifest existence of appearances within a single unified field of energy-matter transformations. The plurality is a unity, the whole of the cosmos is just one existence. From that standpoint there is no such absolute or intrinsic thing as a "living own-being" within it, although of course we apparently exist. Furthermore, there is no such absolute, perfect or cosmos-transcending function as consciousness either even though we assume that consciousness transcends the material world. Even more so, the universe is all purely matter-energy transformations, and any implicit orders or patterns we assume there to be within it are our own subjective interpretations. The multiplicity of objects that we see are a falsity because there is only one unity, but we created these mental identities as designations, forms or labels so that we can maintain our lives and survive. We must ourselves, using consciousness, therefore create the concept that something is proper in order for societies to survive and prosper. Thus our societies determine what we take as our standards of proper behavior for our individual benefit and for society's benefit. Survival, happiness and thriving are all at stake.

These conclusions, however noble, are also an imagined order without any ontological validity, but as people we choose to give them meaning and significance. Nonetheless, they are imaginations created by our minds for our shared societies of people peacefully living together where the only thing truly operating is Shakti's cause and effect interactions of fluctuating energy and matter transformations. When you transcend these outer forms of identity you finally get the underlying fundamental essence that is free of all differentiations entirely. That is our fundamental ground state, the ultimate unshakable truth that is a singular property, and the true reality behind the cosmos of vibrations. That is our true self-nature.

Even though we lack an innate existence we have an existence. Each one of us must do what they must to help maintain their own existence (the "I") and support the group that makes their life possible (the "We"). As a social species that lives in groups we must invent culture to enable us to live harmoniously together to achieve a group prosperity that helps everyone, and therefore we invent rules of propriety, virtues and values. All of us accordingly become culturally conditioned and rewarded for behaviors that fall in line with these invented standards because they are needed for our survival and the peaceful flourishing of ourselves as a species. Without them our survival and prosperity are at stake.

As explained within the *Lotus Sutra*, enlightened spiritual masters who achieve transcendental Buddha bodies at the highest levels of sentient existence often behave in ways that appear immoral and unethical to us when measured by such standards. They do not constrain themselves to social conformity but often flout the accepted standards of social propriety to follow higher standards of virtue and righteousness. While externally they might sometimes appear to break laws or traditions they are often acting according to higher principles that are more important than traditional codes of conduct, but ordinary people cannot see this. The point is that Buddhas do not bind themselves according to the ordinary definitions of ethics, virtue and propriety but act from a higher place that is very ethical and virtuous even though their actions might not appear to be so. You must cultivate the spiritual path to get to that level.

Generations of humans across the world have developed specific cultures to help man transcend his animal nature so that we can experience human flourishing and prosperity. They have developed social rules of propriety and established human values such as standards of virtue. Their purpose is to *civilize our behavior* to a state of shared culture so that we can peacefully collaborate and jointly develop group safety and prosperity. We *are* animals, but we have the benefit of higher consciousness and its reasoning abilities that let us improve ourselves enough to transcend our animal tendencies and achieve superior states of being, but our mode of living requires societal cooperation, peace and harmony. If we did not live in communities, some of our shared imagined standards simply would not exist.

The fundamental way of the Great Learning is that we cultivate our minds, bodies and behavior to their highest octaves – thus vastly improving our cognitive and physical skills – and continuously pursue states of highest excellence in living. The goal is that we cultivate steady states of well-being (abundance, prosperity, health, happiness, peace, comfort, joy and bliss, etc.) absent of suffering; that we cultivate virtues and excellences of our body, mind and behavior; and that we not only make our virtues "bright" or magnificent but strongly manifest them in the world for either attaining our own goals or for helping others. The fundamental way of the Great Learning is to always pursue such endeavors in life until we rest and reside in states of highest excellence.

To accomplish or experience any of this, you must take self as the basis. You must take consciousness as the basis, and you must be cultivating your body because without your body your consciousness is not possible. Consciousness as a Knowledge producer depends on a body vehicle so you cannot neglect the cultivation and upkeep of your body, which is the receptacle of consciousness. Consciousness also depends on there being an inner subtle body or "soul" (composed of a specific type of energy) in order to be operative, so you must also cultivate your Qi/Prana energy that is the basis of your soul or deva body. Without society or relationships you have no possibility of survival either. Hence the spiritual path always involves cultivating your body, internal energy, mind and (social) behavior to states of excellence. While cultivating your conduct, activity or behavior to a state of excellence you must also *work for society's overall welfare*.

Hence the spiritual path, the cultivation path, the path of perfection or continuous betterment involves cultivating your mind, body, behavior and activities. There are things you pursue for the "I" or apparent self and those that you pursue because you belong to the "We" or group that are therefore considered acts of merit. If you are truly alone you need only pursue excellence for your own needs of survival, achievement and happiness or well-being. But since we live in a community of relationships, which we must depend upon for survival, and since our happiness and well-being also depends on the happiness and well-being of others within this group, we must definitely cultivate virtues that correspond to accepted standards or duties of proper group behavior. Lobsters (which live solitary lives) don't need virtues, humans do. We must also become civic-minded in working for the success and prosperity of the group and its members as a whole, which is similar to the Greek or democratic ideal of civic responsibility and public duty. One possible target objective is the maximum happiness and well-being for the maximum number of people.

Society stresses character values and virtues not just in order to maintain the social order of the family and state and to lay the foundational conditions for prosperity, but to develop the spirit of humanity. They are needed to guide man into creating a civilized society – a stable, harmonious, peaceful society. Just as we want to cultivate a peaceful mind, we want to develop and sustain a harmonious peaceful society replete with virtuous relationships among its members. We want everyone to be able to dwell peacefully in the present moment, and respond to people and events with authentic kindness, compassion, fairness, and honesty. We want everyone to love and take care of one another. This requires the goals of beautifying our consciousness with virtuous tendencies, perfecting the abilities of consciousness and perfecting our consummate conduct.

Chapter 8
THE PHYSICAL BODY AND THE
FOUR TRANSCENDENTAL BODIES

Religions, and especially spiritual cultivation schools, typically talk about five planes of existence or beingness in addition to the primordial original essence that is our ground state substratum (God, Parabrahman, original nature, etc.). However, there are many more despite the limited revelation. Through various reasons, human beings have discovered the ability to cultivate more etheric spiritual bodies free of the densest matter of the earthly realm and instead comprised of the energies or etheric substances of these higher transcendental planes.

Each higher energy realm "closer" to the original essence, in terms of the layers/levels/sequence of causal evolution, is composed of more subtle, refined, purified, fundamental, primordial, higher, or more transcendental energies than a subsequent evolute, which is considered denser or more impure. A denser evolute *has all the higher energies inherently within it* and must be purified in order to separate out a more transcendental body clone from within it. As with all things, the energies of all these planes interpenetrate, and together comprise a single universal whole – Shakti the Logos, universe or Triple Realm – whose fundamental nature is the ultimate truth of the universal substratum.

Of the five planes or realms there is the (1) material plane or chemical dimension of matter, (2) subtle plane, (3) Causal plane, (4) Supra-Causal plane, and (5) Immanence plane. These planes can be experienced by human beings (and other beings in the universe) who possess the requisite body - a material physical body, subtle body, Causal body, Supra-Causal body or Immanence Body, respectively. These bodies have increasingly refined compositions that represent a gradual ascent back to the Absolute, where each higher body represents a potentiality already within the lower body, and are known by different names in different spiritual schools, but they are the same phenomena. Each is composed of a different energy or etheric substance. The higher or more transcendental that a body and its realm are – meaning the closer it is to the first principle, cause or fundamental substrate – the more perfect or pure is considered the stage of spiritual achievement.

As stated, all the phenomena of these planes exist because of a complex interaction of cause and effect spanning across all realms, energies and phenomena, in effect the result of a great mixing of infinite, co-dependent arising that is infinitely old - beginningless. In other words, there is only one space-time, one fabric of manifest existence, and everything occurs within it as an inescapable part of it. Within its one body everything is connected with everything else.

The formations within Shakti all have interdependent origins within its single fabric, and therefore no a single thing is intrinsic or inherent due to its self alone. Nothing has an own-being existence. In particular, one can consider the phenomena of our material plane a condensation of higher energies since once investigated the decomposition of matter reveals the components of space and an agglomeration of transcendental energies that seem solidified when they manifest matter. The most fundamental basis of all these energies and phenomena is the one primordial original substrate, the original one, the only truly existing one, the most fundamental ground state or unchanging essence that supports All.

By the process of spiritual cultivation you can generate a body, out of your own physical nature, composed of the energies from each of the higher realms. The process entails releasing a higher transcendental body from within the matrix of an "impure" body composed of lower plane energies/materials. You cultivate the animating vital energy within a lower body to "purify" that energy and when it becomes purified and released you have a higher body attainment attached to the lower body. When you die on the earthly plane "the soul is released upon death," which is essentially the arising of your subtle body from within it that has inhabited or interpenetrated your physical shell all your life. This is why most people feel they are passengers within their body during life. Spiritual masters achieve an independent subtle body while alive, and can use the body to do good deeds in the world such as help them with their troubles. If you cultivate your subtle body then you can release a Causal body composed of the higher energy within it, and then so on.

Locked within the matrix of our material plane body is an energetic superstructure of vital energy or Qi (Prana) of similar shape to our body, which cultures commonly call the soul that is released upon death as a more perfected form of the physical body. Through the arduous process of spiritual cultivation you can attain its independence whilst alive and then have use of both it *and* your physical body. This is the meaning of enlightenment whose concomitant, attendant mental state is more joyful and purified than the mind transfixed within the material plane, and the same goes for each new body you achieve. Enlightenment is actually a body attainment, not a mental realization attainment, but it is taught as a mental attainment requiring virtue and purity in order to lead people to purify their consciousness in order to merit it.

All living beings therefore have within themselves etheric superstructures of more transcendental energies that can be released, and spiritual cultivation is the way to release that internal superstructure for human beings. When an individual acquires a higher body attainment composed of more transcendental energies, he/she then expresses himself/herself as being that particular body, identifying it as themselves, although they also retain control over their lower body vehicle(s) that then serve like lower appendages. They then say that the material plane seems like a shadow existence compared to their "truer reality" whose energies are closer in nature to the fundamental substratum. Each new body abides in a higher plane of energetic existence, which seems perceptibly *brighter* to the attendant/concomitant mind of that new body than the previous level of existence, and this is due to the more efficient energy construction and flow of that new body vehicle.

The physical body of the material plane is known as the food body, gross body, coarse human body, impure physical nature or body of flesh and blood. It is also referred to as the form skandha in Buddhism, *annamaya* ("foodstuff") *kosha* in Hinduism and a resident within the *Dharam Khand* Realm of Moral Duty of Sikhism. Although it is a solid phenomenon composed of atoms, space passes through the physical body with ease as our body moves because space is finer than matter, and thus a body moves through space without obstruction. It is not that a body divides space, such as parting air as you move through it, but that a body moves through motionless space that never changes. The body, composed mostly of space, passes through space as it moves, and space passes through it.

Although it looks solid, the matter of the physical body is mostly empty space itself and its atomic solidity is actually condensed or confined energy. Since the body's inherent nature is energy, this is why the process of spiritual cultivation, and death, can free an energy-based copy of the physical body from the confines of its denser shell. There is survival after death. When the end of life arrives for the physical body it is because the subtle body within it, composed of its vital energy, has finally been released into the earthly heavenly plane around us that religions normally refer to as Heaven.

The freed subtle body is also known as the deva body, *yin-shen*, will-born body, Yang spirit, astral body, impure illusory body, man's soul, *suddha deha*, etheric body or body composed of Qi or Prana. Those who die attain it naturally and we then call them angels, fairies, spirits, devas or asuras. It is a body of "impure atoms" because it still has etheric matter (Qi atoms) as its substance. It is referred to as the sensation skandha in Buddhism and *pranamaya* ("energy") *kosha* in Hinduism. It is the initial fruit of the spiritual path to liberation (that gives rise to some minor spiritual powers) and is the purer, more spiritual, more transcendental, truer element of human existence. However, you can say the same for each subsequent higher body attainment.

Once you attain the independent subtle body, which requires a devotion to intensified spiritual practices and then passage through an intense twelve-year process of kundalini transformation, you are considered "twice born." The subtle body attainment is also called the first dhyana achievement in Buddhism and is said to be characterized by the "joy of separating from the body," which is because you finally attain the freedom of a spiritual body independent of your physical body shell. With the achievement of the deva (subtle) body you enter the stages of personal transformation that lead out of *samsara*, namely the series of higher body attainments. Thus this attainment is called "Entering the Stream."

Humans who attain the subtle body attainment reach the Srotapanna Arhat stage ("stream-enterer") of enlightenment, thus becoming *Homo Deus*, while devas who start out at this level (such as those born in Heaven) and cultivate their body to a higher stage of purity reach the Sakadagamin stage of the Arhats. This is just a higher stage of subtle body purification whose attainment means that upon death the deva-attainee will definitely be reborn in the realm of devas (Heaven) rather than the human realm. Both of the subtle body stages correspond to the *Guyan Khand* Realm of Spiritual Knowledge in Sikhism.

For this reason you should cultivate the purification of your inner Qi body within this life through cultivation exercises because even if you don't succeed in attaining enlightenment during life you will be far ahead of everyone else who didn't cultivate because you will have purified your subtle body to some degree. As devas, everyone in the Desire Realm Heaven of our earthly plane is cultivating their body to reach the second dhyana (a more purified state of their body) during their life which then assures for themselves a rebirth in Heaven when that life is over rather than a rebirth in the lower earthly plane as a human once again.

The Causal body is the next higher body and is also known as the Mental body, Wisdom body, Mantra body, body of vibrations, *pranava deha*, man's spirit, Grace body, or purified illusory body. It is composed of a higher energy known as Shen (Taoist nomenclature) that is more transcendental (refined) than the Qi/Prana of the subtle body and capable of greater superpowers than the subtle body. It is free of all lower gross matter and impurities, but it is considered a denizen of the Realm of Form since it still has a solid-like structure. In Sikhism it is the third level of development or sphere of spiritual attainment that corresponds to the *Saram Khand* "Realm of Spiritual Efforts." It is also referred to as the conception skandha in Buddhism and *manomaya* ("mind-stuff") *kosha* in Hinduism, and is the stage of an Anagamin Arhat.

The Supra-Causal body is also known as the Clear Light body, Wisdom Light body, *jnana deha*, Dharma body, Rainbow body, Buddha body, Arhat body, and is composed of what Taoism calls Later Heavenly Qi (energy, Prana or wind). It is "one with the universal life" composed of lower levels of energy, meaning that it can sense the happenings in all the lower energy realms of Nature because its energy realm interpenetrates them at a very high stage of refinement. Hence it can be a witness of the universe able to freely hear and comprehend the minds of lower sentient beings (whose thoughts are composed of lower energies readily accessible to this body's more transcendental level), and able to access their knowledge and wisdom. When someone attains this body we say "their wisdom opens up" (which is why it is called the Wisdom body) because they no longer need to enter into someone and read their neurons to know their thoughts (as is necessary for subtle-bodied devas and Causal-bodied individuals, whose attainment stages are orthodoxly called the second and third dhyana). Rather, they can sense thoughts in the environment, or use *nirmanakaya* emanations to access the brains of many individuals, including animals such as snakes, parrots, dogs, elephants, etcetera. The Supra-Causal or Wisdom body is referred to as the volition skandha in Buddhism, *vijnanamaya* ("wisdom") *kosha* in Hinduism and corresponds to the *Karam Khand* "Realm of Grace" in Sikhism. It is the body that can finally project *nirmanakaya* emanations.

This stage of achievement is also called the fourth dhyana attainment of becoming a full Arhat, which is the classical meaning of "becoming enlightened." This everlasting and imperishable (long-lived) body is the attainment that people normally think of when they hear the word "enlightenment," and the attainment of this transcendental body (which is free of all coarser levels of matter and energy and consequently exhibits a tremendous flexibility of shape) is considered Sivahood, or "*nirvana* with remainder" because it is "formless" yet imperfect since there is one remaining attainment left that is a still higher level of physical purification.

In Hinduism it is said that through spiritual exercises such as meditation, mantra, reverence and devotion you will purify your physical body (dense matter), subtle body and mental body that are the lower three *koshas* in order to attain "the state of final release," or *Kaivalya*. This means the attainment of this body that belongs to the Formless Realm since it is free of all lower forms of matter and energy. This body, free of particulate matter in its construction, can therefore twist and turn in all sorts of shapes without restriction, which enables it to create all sorts of energy movements and effects (such as feelings of hot or cold or vibrations) within any human body it enters such as kundalini energy. The strange currents of hot or cold energy people feel inside themselves during cultivation practices are typically due to a Buddha helping them move their energies with his own. The phenomenon of *shaktipat* (where a guru "sends you his energy") is exactly this – a *nirmanakaya* body emanation sent inside you to move your Qi/Prana by using its Qi/Prana. It is not a stream of energy projection or activation of *your* energy. It is the master's energy moving inside you because of one of his body doubles inside you.

Being free of the lower realms and now understanding himself as belonging to the unity of all things in the one soup of Shakti (an attainee realizes that there is no such thing as a separate independent existence), at this stage one recognize that they are part of the one Ocean of Shakti (fabric of the universe) and becomes free of ignorance, delusions, and misunderstandings as regards the origins and evolution of life. Thus one becomes emancipated from Maya (delusions and ignorance) because he understands. Devoid of ignorance he realizes his eternal existence in the infinite ocean of Shakti as Shakti itself.

This Supra-Causal or Buddha body can generate energy copies of itself, called *nirmanakaya* emanations, which can be projected as independent entities in the world to perform specific deeds. When you finally are able to attain this body through cultivating the internal energies of the Causal body you will exist with a body vehicle whose structure doesn't deteriorate quickly because of the long-lived nature of its compositional elements (referred to as "light"). Therefore it is said you will live practically forever as an "immortal." When it must die, your etheric body is so high that it can carry strong memories of your life with you into a new incarnation, which even happens to some extent when lower level Arhats are reborn, thus *ensuring a type of continuity, unbroken continuum or immortality from a different aspect than deathlessness*. With the attainment of the Supra-Causal body you escape further incarnations in the lower realms because of its transcendental composition that is absent of unpurified matter, and with immortality you insure continuity to escape the cycles of birth and death too.

The next attainment, or Immanence body, is also known as the attainment of Complete and Perfect Enlightenment, or the stage of becoming a Great Golden Arhat. This is akin to the true man of Taoism, and the highest *atman* of Hinduism within the hierarchy of bodily sheaths. It is a body composed of Primordial Heavenly energy – a term for the highest energy level we can reach and still maintain a body. It is referred to as the consciousness skandha in Buddhism, the *anandamaya* ("bliss") *kosha* in Hinduism, the Stage of No More Learning (No More Training or Non-Practice) in Tibetan Buddhism, the stage of God consciousness in Kashmir Saivism, the tenth Bodhisattva *bhumi*, and the stage of "*nirvana* without remainder" because it is said that no higher body vehicles are possible. Once you first attain the stage of Buddhahood, which means attaining the Arhat's Formless Realm body that is equivalent to the *Sach Khand* "Realm of Truth" attainment in Sikhism, there is this yet higher body attainment that is composed of the highest fundamental energies of Shakti where a body formation is still possible because linkages can still exist between some forms of rarified components. At this stage it is said that one does not hear, smell or see but becomes sight, sound and smell simultaneously (because through the all-pervading mind of this level of energy beingness one can instantly know what goes on *within the lower vibratory realms*), which Buddhism calls the interchangeability of the sense consciousnesses.

It is often explained in Buddhist texts that your mind or consciousness is a great wakefulness without center or edge, an immense all-pervasiveness that is primordially empty and free and present within you from the very beginning. This is describing the mental vibratory reach (capabilities) of this stage of beingness as regards perceptions of lower plane happenings. That all-pervasive knowledge is possible due to living as an energy body whose transcendental existence plane (Formless Realm) permeates the cosmos of denser matter like empty space, and your body and your lane of existence being more refined than the denser realms your consciousness ("spiritual light") is "not a companion of material things." The energy plane of one's body reaches everywhere and you can sense vibrations within that plane, which is why a Supra-Causal-bodied Buddha knows when someone is thinking of them even if miles away. "I and everything melt into one. The flower becomes I, the moon becomes I."

Consciousness runs through an energy body instead of matter body so it is always immaculately clear and bright, detached from views and feelings, much quicker than your ordinary mind, and is what the Zen school refers to as, "Mind is Buddha." At this stage of your energy body existence, which is sometimes called the *real man* in some spiritual schools (such as Zen, Taoism and Islam), your mind is described as a penetrating spiritual light or all-pervasiveness that is primordially empty and free in extending through the universe, and this is the stage of attainment that all spiritual schools want you to reach. Since that purified, refined or transcendental energy level is already inherent within your physical body it is also always said that you are already fundamentally enlightened.

In the Buddhist *Heart Sutra* it is said, "Form is the same as Emptiness, Emptiness is the same as Form. The same can be said of the Sensation, Conception, Volition and Consciousness skandhas. All things are characterized by (come from) Emptiness. For Emptiness there is no beginning or ending, increase or decrease, purity or impurity. There is no …"

What this actually means is that, "The physical body is no different than the fundamental substrate (Parabrahman), the primordial foundational substratum is the same as our physical body because it permeates it and is its ultimate composition. The real nature of your physical body is the primordial universal substrate and the same can be said for the subtle body, Causal body, Supra-Causal body and Immanence (Great Golden Buddha) body. They are all characterized by an emptiness of inherent, intrinsic existence; they are all essentially the fundamental universal substratum that is like empty space. This fundamental nature is unproduced and has no beginning or ending, undergoes no increase or decrease, doesn't come from anywhere and isn't going anywhere (isn't transforming into anything else), and is neither defiled nor non-defiled (since apparent configurations arise within it)."

Atisha describes the ultimate saying, "Here, there is no seeing and no seer, No beginning and no end, just peace … It is non-conceptual and non-referential … It is inexpressible, unobservable, unchanging, and unconditioned." Thus, within It there is no seer nor seeing nor objects to be seen, etcetera. It is the state of a single substratum – a peaceful pure Alonehood … It is non-composite, unconditioned, unchanging, indestructible, without attributes like space, unfathomable, unobservable, non-conceptual and non-referential – an unborn self-so eternal like an empty space or void that lacks all matter, energy or other types of phenomena, and so It is often called Emptiness. Within It there is nothing else; from Its aspect there is no such thing as Shakti for there is only Itself, and yet Shakti is not absent from being an appearance within Its nature.

Therefore, ultimately within the foundational substrate there is no such thing as the chain of dependent existence (cause and effect relationships), yet dependent existence (cause and effect) is not absent since phenomena appear and function with apparent facticity. Yet they have no substantial, inherent, self-so intrinsic existence or own-nature where they exist in-and-of themselves. There is no such real thing as life that is intrinsically real because it stands/exists on its own, and yet life and consciousness appear.

We are a creation within the space-time of Shakti that is like a bubble within an ocean or the impermanence of a flickering lightning flash, and what we see and experience of Shakti is a limited mental approximation of manifest reality that is an illusory dream construct we mentally create. That view of purified reality is certainly neither a complete nor accurate representation of Shakti and its similitude is delayed when being resolved into images, yet evolution has given us this ability of consciousness to make mental representations so that the object called a "living human being" could survive and replicate.

There is only one absolute reality - the one fundamental substrate - and everything else is a transient, non-intrinsic, composite (conditionally created through infinite interdependence) existence within the fabric of manifest Shakti that is ultimately, in its absolute nature, the single fundamental substratum. The fundamental ground is intrinsically free from change, beyond birth and death, but can produce all things - Shakti. The space-time existence of Shakti is the foundational substrate in an apparent manifest sense yet empty of any dependable composition, always changing, yet something we can perceive as a momentary existence even though it lacks solidity (but appears solid and continuous). Since our mental images of the phenomena within Shakti are imperfect and incomplete approximations, this makes them falsities or illusions once again.

The unchanging fundamental substrate and its manifestation of Shakti are one and the same. This is the essence of non-duality. *Nirvana* and *samsara* are interdependent. The fundamental substrate is neutral, intrinsically pure and clean, intrinsically free from change, intrinsically complete in Itself, and yet produces (the appearance of) *samsara* which is the result of a wrong point of view.

Chapter 9
GENERATION OF THE HIGHER SPIRITUAL BODIES

The Yoga school says that the purpose of the spiritual path is to resolve the physical material body back into its most primal constituent components, which means cultivating higher transcendental bodies that are "closer" to the original nature in terms of their composition, namely the layers of universal emanation or planes of existence, until the composition of your ultimate body is as high/refined as you can go. The higher the transcendental purity of your body the closer its resolution to our primordial substrate.

The practice of Yoga has the purpose of taking man back to his Source (source-nature) or self-nature, which is his True Self. This means the fundamental substrate of all existence, the self-subsistent being of Nature. You cannot attain a physical body that is the fundamental substrate, but the highest body you can attain involves resolving your physical nature to its highest constituent level, and that's what you work for as the target of Yoga. This is called the Immanence body that is "fused with the universe" or "oned with eternity" because of its compositional (purity) level, and of course you still maintain your own individuality (individual identity) upon that attainment since it is simply a higher body achievement. It is your highest possible evolution since it is closest to perfect reunification with your absolute nature, the self-subsistent substratum of the universe.

As the most primal constituent form of ourselves that we can attain, this is our real true life composed of the highest transcendental substances possible, and is called the "real man," whereas the Form Realm and Desire Realm body aspects of our *sambhogakaya* (subtle and Causal bodies) are second and third level reflections of this life. This is the true body of the real man, the awakened body of the Buddhas, and in some cases you could consider the Immanence body equivalent to the *atman* of Advaita Vedanta that is trying to return to Brahman.[11] This is the real human being "buried in the mountain of form," and when it is buried in (what it considers) the illusory physical body of form then the human mind takes charge.

Taoism says that we must return to our original nature, our primordial essence. "Returning to the Source" does not mean dissolving the mind-ground and all its layers of manifestation into the transcendental all-ground of nature. If you did that then you would become extinct/annihilated as a sentient being, and there is no point to that. As with Yoga, you simply have to cultivate transcendental bodies until the composition of your ultimate body is the very highest possible.

The Confucian school also says to trace all things back to their source, which can only be done by generating these higher transcendental bodies. Like every other spiritual school, it also provides names for these stages of attainment.[12]

Some schools of Hinduism say that the fundamental substratum is consciousness, which is nonsense. However, we can cultivate a very high transcendental body that still possesses life and consciousness and dwells in an extremely refined transcendental plane. Hinduism tells us to cultivate a state of bliss in life, which is only attainable by possessing a higher transcendental body as your major body vehicle since its attendant mental state and realm of existence is considered blissful compared to a material body and the earthly world. Also, the physical sensation of being (living in) that body is more comfortable as well. Hinduism also says that "the *atman* must return to Brahman," meaning that you must achieve a higher body attainment as close to the original nature (Brahman) in composition as possible. The ultimate purpose in Hinduism is to reach the ultimate source of life and consciousness, which is the foundational essence. Once again, other than perfect annihilation the highest you can go – unless teachings for higher bodies have been kept from us – is to achieve the Immanence body attainment.

---

[11] Most Shankaracharya in India usually achieve this stage of enlightenment, which is the actual *Moksha* of Hinduism, and most Sangharaja (Supreme Patriarch) in the Buddhist Hinayana traditions of Southeast Asia typically achieve it (enlightenment) as well but never tell people. The same goes for many Christian monks and nuns (many of whom are declared "blessed" or "saints"), some Grand Rabbis (Rebbe) of Hasidic dynasties and many leaders of Sufi lineages.

[12] See *Color Me Confucius* by William Bodri.

Buddhism says you must prove that all things come from the original nature by cultivating to attain it, but you can only prove that all things arise from the primordial fundamental nature by cultivating transcendental bodies composed of higher and higher essences, each new one composed of a level of energy-substance that is more primordial/transcendental than the previous. Each higher body attainment (the stages of an Arhat in Buddhist terminology or Arihant in Jainism) leaves behind coarser elements from the old and is thus "closer" to the original essence in terms of composition, purity or refinement.

Thus according to Taoism, out of a physical body you can generate a body of Qi, out of a body of Qi (the subtle body or deva body) you can generate a Causal body composed of Shen, out of a Shen body you can generate a Supra-Causal body composed of Later Heavenly energy, out of a body of Later Heavenly energy you can generate an Immanence body composed of Primordial Heavenly energy, and so on. These Taoist bodies are matched with the stages of the Taoist Immortals that were also known as "celestials." In a sense this is saying that the subtle body is the soul of the physical body, the Causal body is the soul of the subtle body, the Supra-Causal body is the soul of the Causal Body, and the Immanence body is the soul of the Supra-Causal body. These bodies are the *koshas* or sheaths of Hinduism, or the skandhas of Buddhism. Also, in Buddhism it is explained that from the human body the Srotapanna stage of Arhatship is attained, from the Srotapanna stage the Sakadagamin stage is reached, from the Sakadagamin stage the Anagamin stage of Arhatship is attained, from the Anagamin stage Buddhahood is achieved, and from Buddhahood as a base one can reach the stage of unexcelled perfect enlightenment.

Islam explains this by saying that spiritual development means passing through various planes or levels of divine manifestation, and at each level we transmute by shedding a skin. This spiritual path in Islam is called "the return," and has the same meaning as developing a new body of higher elements out of a body of coarser elements that belongs to a lower plane. In Islam the planes of existence are said to be like screens that separate us from the highest purity of Allah, the foundation of All, which of course is the fundamental substratum. Islam says the purpose of spiritual cultivation is to engage in an "unveiling" or "tearing off of veils" to see God's face and experience unity with Allah, the original nature or Parabrahman. Kabir said, "Open the folds of your veil and you shall find God." This too means that you must progress through a sequence of higher body attainments that you achieve through the purification practices of spiritual cultivation.

Christianity teaches that God wants us to return back to Him. Furthermore,

Christianity says that we should strive to become partakers in the divine energies of God. We are also to seek communion with the saints who have achieved heavenly bodies, which means they are more near God the Father Supreme because of the process of divinization, deification, beautification, ascension, transcension or *theosis*, which is the glorification of an individual to a divine level.[13] This is achieved through your own spiritual efforts by cultivating an incorruptible, refined, transfigured body of glory and power, which refers to the initial subtle body (*Homo Deus*) and then higher body attainments. Christianity also specifies hierarchical ranks of angelic beings that reside closer or farther away from their Divine Source. Christianity simply fails to disclose that there are many possible bodies rather than just one.

Thus the various religions and spiritual paths of the world phrase the cultivation of our inherent transcendental bodies - which is attaining enlightenment, "attaining the Tao," becoming an immortal, achieving liberation, emancipation of the soul, transcending the earthly plane, the attainment of Arhathood, becoming a *jnani*, becoming a saint, etcetera - in many different ways.

The spiritual cultivation path for attaining the higher bodies entails transformations within your physical body to purify impure elements of its own vital energy, which composes the subtle body that is the first higher spiritual attainment. The result is that you first purify the Qi/Prana of your physical body and gradually generate from within it a body of transcendental elements that can leave your physical body at will – the subtle (deva) body attainment composed of vital Qi energy that Indians call Prana. This "soul body" is already existent within your physical body as the vital energy part of its structure, which is why it is released at death for everyone, but due to spiritual practice you can purify its essence and enable it to be released whilst alive and still retain a tether to the lower physical body so that both bodies can live where the higher body can still use the lower. Then you "live in the world while transcending it."

Spiritual cultivation is essentially a pathway of Yoga to cultivate (purify) your Qi/Prana so that you can produce this independent spiritual body as the *initial fruit* of the spiritual path, thus making you an enlightened Arhat at the lowest stage of spiritual attainments. When ordinary individuals die their internal body of Qi/Prana leaves their physical shell, but it is much weaker and much more impure than any body that is purified through the kundalini

---

[13] See *The Mystical Path of Christian Theosis: Practical Exercises for Experiencing Christian Purification, Illumination and Glorification* by Elijah John.

transformation processes of Yoga and spiritual cultivation. It is this subtle body, called the "soul" in Christianity, which is responsible for the energy of consciousness that works through your anatomical structure. You cannot have consciousness without Qi energy, namely a "soul" of subtle energy composition within your physical body. This is what leaves your body at death. It transmigrates from life to life bringing along with it the accumulated dispositions it has developed (*samskaras*), and which become part of the new personality upon rebirth. Hence you can compare them to hereditary traits but they are actually your own traits that you carry forward from a previous life.

On the cultivation pathway to generate the independent subtle body you must use your will to mobilize and guide your Qi/Prana so that it circulates and spreads in every part of your body, making it go to your four limbs, muscles and ligaments, internal organs, skeletal bones ... all your tissues everywhere. You want it to "wash" or "cleanse" your tissues through a frictional washing. This is called cultivating your Qi/Prana, rotating your Qi/Prana, or revolving the "vital breath" of your body so that this Qi, Prana, vital energy, wind element, life force or kundalini energy penetrates and purifies your underlying energetic matrix everywhere. This is how you purify your physical nature and its inherent inner subtle Qi body.

You accomplish this via various spiritual exercises that stimulate your Qi/Prana, typically by rhythmical mantra sounds, breathing practices or by arousing positive or negative emotions that stimulate your Qi/Prana, and by moving your Qi/Prana with your will or by the physical movements of special exercises. If you purify and strengthen the Qi/Prana of your body (your vital energy) sufficiently and in the right way, then out of your body's physical matrix and vital energy you can eventually generate an independent spiritual body formed of your Qi/Prana that can then leave and return to your physical shell as you want. This subtle body attainment, known as the deva body, is the first stage/fruit of the genuine spiritual path. Attaining the deva body is equivalent to breaking free from your animal form. It makes you an Arhat, Arihant, *jnani* or *jivanmukta*.

This generation process occurs when the physical body is "burnt out" through the continual application of the "fire of yoga," and eventually produces the "divinized body," "purified body" or "perfect body" that is the subtle body. Once again, this accomplishment is just the first stage of the spiritual path, which is called the first dhyana or Srotapanna Arhat accomplishment that is also known as *Homo Deus*. It is the liberation of the human spirit in an independent form, composed of Qi, from the bondage of the physical body.

This subtle body, composed of "pure elements," which means your purified Qi/Prana that is the elixir of life, is called the "house of kundalini" because purifying and transforming the Qi/Prana within your body to cultivate its emergence is sometimes called kundalini yoga or *kriya* yoga (as well as *neigong, neijia, anapana*, inner energy work), and these particular yoga activities correspond to purifying your Qi/Prana. The subtle body (deva body) composed of Qi/Prana has free movement in the world although unseen by men, and its residential realm is called the earthly heavenly planes since it is earth-bound and all around us. This is the level of etheric existence achieved by ordinary human beings, so this is what is known as "Heaven."

The next stage of transformation is that the subtle body can through a similar process generate from within itself a more transcendental Causal body, Mental body, Mantra body, Shen body, or purified illusory body that is entirely free from all gross matter and impurities, including those still remaining in the subtle body composed of Qi. The achievement is equivalent to the fifth and sixth Bodhisattva *bhumis* in Buddhism as well as the third dhyana attainment. It is also known as the stage of the Anagamin Arhat attainment. The Causal body is a transfigured body higher in transcendental energy-matter composition than the subtle body composed of Qi/Prana, so it resides on a yet higher plane (invisible to the subtle body) and has access to other transcendental worlds called Pure Lands ("blessed worlds of the virtuous") that the subtle body cannot access. Naturally the Causal body has dominion over more siddhas or superpowers than the subtle body.

The next transformation is that this Causal body, with more cultivation, can generate from within itself a Supra-Causal body, also known as a Clear light body, Dharma body, Buddha body, Rainbow body, light body or bliss body. With this attainment, called *"nirvana* with remainder" that equates with the seventh and eighth Bodhisattva *bhumi* levels, you can identify with universal life that resides on the lower planes. You can know their thoughts, emotions and pleas or prayers for help. This is why Swami Vivekananda said, "thoughts live, they travel far." Just as light can be divided into the colors of the rainbow, this "light body" can generate countless invisible *nirmanakaya* projections of itself to perform tasks and functions throughout the cosmos.

In attaining this body you become a Para-mukta, meaning you attain Sivahood or what is typically though of as the "enlightenment" or "liberation" that leaves the coarser physical planes behind forever. In Buddhism it is a Formless Realm inhabitant. While attaining the deva body is equivalent to escaping from your animal form, attaining the Supra-Casual, Rainbow or Buddha body is equivalent to breaking free from physical form. This is because its composition is akin to pure energy that is forever free of the lower realms of matter including etheric atoms, which is why its longevity is legendary. The process of attainment is that the energy of your physical body of impure elements is refined through spiritual cultivation practices to produce your subtle body of pure elements (refined Qi/Prana), next the Casual body is produced by refining the energy of your subtle body, and then the Supra-Causal body, Buddha Body or Arhat body is attained by refining the energy of the Causal body. At this stage it is free from all gross matter and impurities, and is imperishable and everlasting.

This is the body level that escapes the cycles of reincarnation in the lower realms forever, thus transcending *samsara*, and is equivalent to achieving the mind of *bodhi* or *bodhi* mind. The concomitant (naturally accompanying) consciousness of the individual who attains the Supra-Causal body is the unexcelled, all-pervading mind of enlightenment that can sense things in the lower (denser) realms of energy-matter, but this Buddha body only achieves *nirvana* with remainder. Nevertheless, since forevermore this body cannot fall into the lower realms because of its transcendental composition that is so refined and purified of lower atoms and energies, and essentially becomes the vehicle of immortality, it is also the level of attainment equivalent to the Bodhisattva vows.

Going further through cultivation, this body can cultivate from within itself a body of Immanence said to be close to God Supreme, meaning that it is the most transcendental body attainment you can reach, and thus is equivalent to Complete and Perfect Enlightenment or the perfect *nirvana* attainment (*nirvana* without remainder) of No More Learning that is final liberation. This is the stage of *anittarasamyaksambodhi* or Perfect and Complete Enlightenment that corresponds to the highest fundamental human being, and thus the most real man or *atman*. It is the attainment that goes along with a Great Golden Arhat's body, which is the Immanence body attainment. Higher bodies might be possible still but earthly teachings are restricted regarding such information, and only pose this body as the final termination target for your cultivation efforts.

This process of spiritual emancipation, liberation, release, *Moksha*, self-realization, *nirvana* or enlightenment starts with your understanding that the ultimate evolutionary source of energy and matter, and thus life and its attendant consciousness, is the original nature or *dharmakaya* that is the primordial substance of the universe. You are essentially an evolute, emanation, or transformation of this ultimate foundational essence, which is thus your Real Self since It is your foundational self, or fundamental substance. That makes it your primordial, primal, original or fundamental self-nature.

One proves this by purifying your body back to its most fundamental elementary forces, thus creating higher and higher transcendental bodies in the process. Each new body stays attached to the lower body from which it was generated, and each resides on a different plane that is invisible to the previous plane of existence. Each is capable of different powers and skills that you can master which can affect the denser plane(s) below its own level of manifestation (plane of composition).

A set of these bodies linked together, or these bodies together with all their *nirmanakaya*, or simply the highest body attainment you reach just by itself, is called the *sambhogakaya*. In Hinduism this is the *Vishvarupa*.

This information on the transcendental spiritual bodies is the key knowledge that most spiritual traditions withhold from practitioners for a number of good reasons that will not be discussed. Your superior understanding is now similar to that of Copernicus whose knowledge of the planets revolving around the sun, even though true, was inconceivable to most Europeans in his lifetime. The prior solution for explaining planetary movements referenced Ptolemy and his successors who all employed increasingly numerous and eventually absurd mathematical devices to maintain earth-centricism just as religious adherents similarly bend over backwards striving to explain miraculous spiritual states and saintly spiritual powers without referencing the higher spiritual bodies of the saints and sages. Yet these higher bodies and their abilities are openly described in the Buddhist *Surangama Sutra*, in Chinese Taoism, in Tibetan Vajrayana, in Hindu Tantric Yoga, in Confucianism, in Islamic Sufism, in Sikhism, by masters such as Meher Baba and the great Tamil siddhar sages like Ramalinga Swamigal (Vallalar) whose explanations of the body attainments are simply wonderful.

If you understand that *this is the spiritual path* of ascension to full enlightenment – that these bodies are the meaning of the Bodhisattva bhumis, dhyana or samadhi attainments, *skandhas*, *koshas* and the like – then it should produce a revolutionary impetus in your spiritual practice. To achieve them you must cultivate meditation, *neijia* inner energy work and merit (goodness as a human being in terms of character and action) in a gradual systematic fashion. Many people practice without knowing what's what but now you should be more sure of the practice.

Chapter 10
THE STAGES OF SPIRITUAL ATTAINMENT[14]

An individual who successively cultivates their subtle body to attain the deva body that can come and go out of their physical body at will is called a Srotapanna, which is the Christian stage of *Homo Deus*. This is the first stage of Arhat enlightenment attainment. It is also called attaining the first dhyana in Buddhism or *vitarka* (coarse mental grasping) samadhi in Hinduism. Its attainment is called a "birth by transformation" since it arises out of the physical body due to meditation work, morality, merit and Qi cultivation efforts. You have to cultivate your inner Qi-body with countless inner energy practices (*nei-gong*) for its birth to become possible After it emerges the Indian yoga schools say you are one of the "twice born." Jesus also explained, "Unless one is born again he cannot see the Kingdom of Heaven," which is referring to the deva body attainment. This deva body attainment is equivalent to becoming *Homo Deus*.

With the subtle deva body an adept attains the famous eight yogic powers, or *siddhi*, of Yoga texts because the subtle body composed of Qi/Prana can change its shape and form to become bigger, smaller, lighter, heavier and so on. This is why a subtle body can shrink itself to enter into someone's physical body and learn to read the memories stored in someone's brain, which is one of the training practices after achievement since this is how spiritual beings help human beings. Using this new body he/she can perform minor miracles (tricks) in the physical world such as converting a dry tree into a green one, stop railway trains or cars, fill a dry well with water and so forth. Of the eight yogic powers, the *ishita siddhi* of "lordship over someone" means possessing an individual with one of your higher

---

[14] See *Nyasa Yoga, Move Forward, Color Me Confucius, God Speaks* (Meher Baba) and the story of Ramalinga Swamigal (Vallalar).

bodies or by using a *nirmanakaya* projection, and causing them to think or do what you want since you can control the thoughts of all lower-bodied beings.

If you use a higher body to enter into someone's lower body you can therefore control them such as suppressing their spiritual powers by blocking them through control of the energy of your body that is possessing someone else's lower body. This is how "higher" masters can block the superpowers of someone with lower attainments. It is not because of higher superpower skills but because they have one higher body, such as an Immanence body entering into a Supra-Causal body.

The individual who cultivates the subtle body to a higher stage of purity is a Sadragamin, or second stage Arhat. This is alternatively called attaining the second dhyana or *vicara* (refined mental grasping) samadhi. Devas start out with a subtle body already whereas humans start out with a physical body and must first cultivate an independent subtle body, which normally is ejected from their physical shell upon death. Thus this higher stage of subtle body purification, where the Qi/Prana of your subtle (deva) body is refined to purify even more of its gross matter, is simply specified for the benefit of devas who already possess a subtle body. Devas are considered to possess the first dhyana, and by cultivating the purity of their Qi to the level of the second dhyana (Sadragamin attainment) they can avoid reincarnation on the earthly plane.

Normally when a deva dies he or she will be reborn in the human earthly plane. However, if devas cultivate their Qi while in Heaven then they can purify it enough that they will be reborn in Heaven again upon that death, which is why all devas are always working hard studying with a spiritual master and cultivating their Qi. Their two major cultivation techniques are kundalini yoga where they focus on concentrating or moving their Qi in various parts of their body,[15] and sexual cultivation where they stimulate their happy, joyous emotions and Qi during sexual congress without losing

---

[15] See *Nyasa Yoga, Buddha Yoga, Neijia Yoga, Bodhisattva Yoga* (forthcoming), *Visualization Power* and *The Mystical Path of Christian Theosis*. If you were aiming to transform the Qi of a country, city, temple, company or other organization of men you should read *Culture, Country, City, Company, Person, Purpose, Passion, World*. Together these books are the true school of Vajrayana that cultivates the form and energy of a structure. If you were interested in mindfulness practice and cultivating inner virtue and purity of mind you should read *Color Me Confucius, The Mystical Path of Christian Theosis*, and *Meditation Case Studies*. In order to help rejuvenate the physical body for Vajrayana practice you should study and apply *Detox Cleanse Your Body Quickly and Completely* and *Look Younger, Live Longer*.

energy. The purpose is to excite their Qi everywhere inside their body, make it circulate better and infuse every cell with bliss. Furthermore, this means that people who cultivated during life, even if they did not attain the Tao (enlightenment), are much further ahead than those who did not cultivate because they purified their Qi to some extent, and will have an easier time in Heaven as a deva in purifying their Qi to the level called the second dhyana.

In other words, the first and second dhyana of Buddhism refer to two different purification/cultivation levels for the same subtle body composed of Qi/Prana. As a human, when you die you attain an impure subtle body as a deva, which is equivalent to the first dhyana or Srotapanna attainment. You will be reborn in the earthly plane again as a human when your heavenly life is over *unless you cultivate its purity to a higher level, which is the second dhyana*. Devas in heaven, meaning the earthly heavenly plane, will be reborn as humans when they die unless they cultivate the second dhyana Sakadagamin attainment whilst alive (the work extensively on cultivating the Qi of their subtle body) so that their rebirth can remain in heaven as a deva. The Sakadagamin attainment is the same body as the Srotapanna except that its Qi energy is more purified or refined. When devas enter human bodies to help spiritual practitioners cultivate their Qi, higher bodied beings help those devas purify their bodies as well, especially when devas enter into humans to help transform their Qi during spiritual practices.

Therefore devas are always helping humans cultivate their Qi during times of religious worship or Qi practice (such as during kundalini yoga activities or certain types of martial arts) because they also receive help at the same time, and especially during meditation practice when their efforts to move your Qi via their own are not thwarted by you strongly clinging to your thoughts or physical body sensations. If you hold onto your thoughts during meditation practice you will bind the movement (circulatory flow) of your Qi, and thus their efforts to move their Qi inside you to help move and purify your own will be obstructed. This is another reason why people are taught to practice "empty mind" or witnessing meditation practice where you detach from internal sensations and your thought-stream. This makes it easier for spiritual beings to enter into you and help transform your Qi for the first dhyana attainment.

The individual who cultivates the Causal body is an Anagamin, or third stage Arhat. This is the third dhyana attainment of Buddhism and the *ananda* (bliss) samadhi of Hinduism. Using this new body composed of Shen (a type of energy higher than Qi/Prana) he/she becomes capable of performing grand miracles such as giving sight to the blind, restoring limbs to the maimed, and sometimes even raising the dead to life (although at this stage the life restoration ability only applies to lower creatures rather than human beings). He can experience yet more of the different planes and worlds of the transcendental spheres, called Pure Lands.

The individual who cultivates the Supra-Causal body is a full Arhat, or "Buddha," which is called attaining the fourth dhyana, "*nirvana* with remainder" achievement or *asmita* (existence) samadhi in Hinduism. With this body he becomes capable of raising the dead and even creating new life such as a *nirmanakaya* that is part of himself. He can also generate many *nirmanakaya* emanation bodies to do simultaneous activities in lower realms, and even project one into a womb to be reborn in the world of men. A reborn *nirmanakaya* is an individual who usually attains the Tao (achieves the subtle body attainment) at a very young age because the *nirmanakaya's* father (or mother) and spiritual friends are typically working on cultivating his or her Qi all the time because of the tether that connects the two.

The individual who cultivates the Immanence body is a Great Golden Arhat, or Complete and Perfectly Enlightened Buddha. This is the Buddhist stage of No More Learning, or "*nirvana* without remainder." Since you (supposedly) reach the highest body attainment that is as close to your original *self-nature* as possible, this is why enlightenment is called perfect "*self*-realization" or the final liberation. The highest spiritual target is reunification with self-subsistent ground state beingness if possible, and the highest possible body transcendental body composition (with attendant consciousness) if not. This fulfills an individual's trajectory in the universe, and then their dilemma comes down to advanced self-mastery of their moods and behavior, mastery of skills and excellences in their personality, the development of healthy relationships, and the selection of functional activities (Buddha vows) in the universe to give their life significant purpose. While the Arhat's Buddha body can generate *nirmanakaya*, the Immanence body can generate *nirmanakaya* emanation bodies that themselves can project *nirmanakaya* bodies and they practice using all these bodies within you during the Twelve Year kundalini transformation process in order to transform your Qi/Prana.

When spiritual masters create body doubles that appear simultaneously in different places they are playing with these various *nirmanakaya* emanations and their capabilities. Some you can touch, some seem transparent, and the highest ones can even carry objects from one location to another. These tangible body doubles are called *yang shen* emanations in Taoism, and you can find stories of these spiritual body doubles in Taoism, Orthodox Christianity, Sufism, Buddhism, Hinduism and many other traditions because the feat is a non-denominational capability for anyone who achieves the higher spiritual body attainments. As stated, the stages (and capabilities) of the spiritual path are non-denominational rungs of the very same ladder.

The higher transcendental spiritual bodies starting with the subtle body are all considered stages of "enlightenment," realization, spiritual attainment, spiritual salvation, divinization, *theosis*, ascension, transcendence, Arhat attainment, deification, beautification, glorification, *Moksha* or liberation. However, most spiritual literature focuses on just the Supra-Causal Buddha body attainment, and most people think of this stage as "Buddha" enlightenment whereas even the subtle body attainment is considered enlightenment.

Devotees of all religions and spiritual traditions can and equally do cultivate to attain all these bodies. They don't achieve anything other than these body attainments, and then practice using the energetic abilities of these bodies that we normally think of as miraculous superpowers or "powers of the four dhyana." Moslem, Jew, Christian, Hindu, Taoist, Buddhist ... everyone achieves the same body attainments. To attain a higher body, which takes you out of the material world, is the ultimate purpose of the spiritual path. The purpose of the spiritual path is to attain these higher bodies and eventually the Supra-Causal body (Buddha or Arhat stage) so that you can jump out of the lower rounds of reincarnation forever.

These bodies are inherent within the condensed energy of your physical matrix and their generation is the natural result of spiritual practice that purifies your Qi and conduct. Their production is not the monopoly of any person, sect, spiritual school, tradition, practice or religion. However, even though everyone attains the same body achievements we find that Buddhism, Hinduism, Jainism, Taoism, Sufism, Confucianism, Yoga and other traditions have very different names for these common stages of attainment.

An individual on the spiritual path might cultivate prayers, mantra recitation, visualization practice, mental introspection, pranayama, concentration practice, stretching *asanas*, bhakti, *anapana*, *nei-gong*, kundalini yoga, sexual cultivation, sexual restraint (*brahmacarya* or celibacy), a special diet, fasting, meditation, charity work, good deeds and all sorts of other cultivation techniques to attain the higher bodies, but if their cultivation of mind, body and behavior are insufficient they will not attain the first subtle body and rise to the spiritual realms during life. You need merit (a good character, good deeds, mental purity and virtue), and must cultivate your Qi and meditation during life for this achievement.

The key is to use techniques to cultivate your Yin and Yang Qi so that your inner Qi body becomes stronger and then independent of your physical form in that your spirit (Qi body) can leave your physical form at will. From this subtle body attainment you can then cultivate to achieve the yet higher transcendental bodies of the spiritual path.

The first stage of cultivation practice is called "laying the foundation" where you work at restoring and replenishing your body, its health and its energy so that it reaches a state of flourishing (optimum health for its age, physical constitution and other conditions). This includes diet, herbal or other medicines, physical manipulation to correct and structural deficiencies, and exercises. After replenishing the basic constituents of the body so that they conform to the requirements of higher spiritual practice, later you can work on cultivating its Qi, which is called harmonization, refining, purification, transformation, improving its circulation or "nourishing life" depending upon what objective or aspect of the path you are targeting in your practices. This is also called the Stage of Virtue Training and Wisdom Accumulation because at this ground stage of cultivation you also work on polishing, perfecting or upgrading your personality, perspectives, habits, skills, ethics and ways of doing things, which is the foundational stage of general religious practice for the public where you work on purifying your personality and conduct. In Patanjali's Yoga the state of *Niyama* refers to physical purification, spiritual observance, self-study (wisdom and knowledge accumulation), and devotion. These factors overlap with the activities of the foundational Stage of Training in Virtue and Accumulating Wisdom that is found in most religions.

Next comes the Stage of Intensified Yoga Practices, Path of Application or "arts of the Way," which is also called the stage of transforming your Jing (your physical body made of semen) to Qi because it entails cultivating the Qi of your body so that through a process of refinement your inner subtle body of Qi becomes purified, strong and finally independent of your physical nature. This is the stage of "refining your Qi," "refining your Jing (essence) and transforming it into breath (Qi)," "harmonizing your breath" or "refining the form" since you have to cultivate both your physical body and the circulation of its internal Qi energy to do this.

This is a stage of actual *doing*, which requires *nei-gong* work in moving your Qi with your will (mind or intent),[16] although this active work also leads to

---

[16] See *Neijia Yoga*, *Nyasa Yoga*, *Buddha Yoga* and *Bodhisattva Yoga* by William Bodri.

a state of mental quiescence. You should strengthen this inner quiet and clarity through the meditation practice called "emptying the mind." If enough preparatory cultivation work is done of meditation and inner Qi *gong-fu*, you will initiate a twelve-year period of *kundalini transformations* were your internal Qi moves by itself because it is then guided by Buddhas who take over the transformation process by using their own energy. Upon success, your inner spirit body composed of Qi can leave your physical body at will through the top of your head.

With attainment of the independent subtle body, called the deva body (since it is a heavenly body that can enter and leave your physical body at will), this is called the Stage of Attaining the Tao. This stage of Srotapanna Arhatship constitutes the achievement of spiritual enlightenment or liberation – also called "crossing the shore," "ascending into Heaven," "the winged transformation," "liberation from the corpse," "becoming twice born" or "entering the stream" – but it only constitutes the initial lowest stage of the ranks of possible attainments. Even so, with the subtle body attainment you enter the stream of personal transformations that lead out of *samsara*, which is why this attainment makes one a "Stream-enterer."

From this point on, you enter the Stage of True Cultivation Practice where you next cultivate the energy of this subtle body, which becomes your new center of life, to attain the Causal body (which is called refining Qi to attain Shen). Then you refine/cultivate the energy of the Causal body after its attainment to achieve the Buddha body, which is called "refining Spirit (Shen) to attain Emptiness (the Supra-Casual body)." The physical emptiness of the Supra-Causal body is that it is now free of all vestiges of coarse matter because the Anagamin (Causal) body still had some impure energy-matter elements even though it is known as the pure illusory body.

Finally, the vital energy of the Supra-Casual Buddha body is cultivated to attain the Immanence body, whose attainment constitutes the Stage of Complete and Perfect Enlightenment, the Stage of No More Learning, or final liberation. It is so difficult to achieve this highest body attainment, just as it is so very difficult to split a photon of light, that Taoism terms this cultivation stage as "breaking Emptiness to return to the Tao." "Emptiness" refers to the Buddha Body, Rainbow light body or Dharma body that is a formless body free of material elements, as is light, and "return to the Tao" refers to achieving the highest body attainment whose composition, due to physics, is (or we are taught) as close to the foundational substrate as we can get.

The entire spiritual path is exactly this. Otherwise it is a path of accumulating merit in this life and improving your personality, mental patterns, habit energy and skills so that you have a better fortune, better conditions and better foundation in this life and in a subsequent life to achieve this task. Thus, people go round and round the cycles of reincarnation endlessly, which is administered by Buddhas so that people's etheric bodies do not disintegrate (they are working on strengthening the integrity of people's bodies throughout people's lives) until individuals finally attain the purified subtle body and can then start working to cultivate the nearly immortal, indestructible Buddha body.

You might not attain the deva body while alive, but you still must cultivate your Qi even after death to attain the second dhyana in heaven so that you merit a heavenly rebirth rather than return to the earthly realm when your heavenly life is over. This is how reincarnation works; if your body's energy does not become elevated, purified or refined there is no way to become reborn in a higher realm because your composition is too dense or impure, so spiritual cultivation is necessary. Since the major spiritual accomplishment people can and should reach requires that they cultivate/refine their Qi through exercises, good thoughts and good behavior, Qi cultivation in various ways and forms has become the predominant but unrecognized practice of the spiritual path.

Many of these methods can lead to health and vigor, the elimination of illness, and extension of your lifespan. By cultivating the circulation of your Qi and opening of your Qi channels you will smoothen your inner Qi flow. Personalitywise this leads to inner calmness and greater mental clarity due to harmonious inner tranquil Qi flow. The better Qi flow throughout your body and brain will help you to develop a mind of greater clarity and peacefulness, thus enabling you to enjoy life more and make better decisions so that you change your fortune for the better. When you start thinking with greater calm and clarity due to self-cultivation practices you can start to overcome your own distortions of judgment and cultivate wisdom so as to make better decisions in your life. Therefore, even if one does not succeed in attaining the deva body, one still gains tremendous advantage from engaging in spiritual cultivation practices. The practices are still beneficial to your mind, body and fortune.

Lacking sufficient cultivation to achieve the subtle body while alive, individuals on the spiritual path who cultivate will from their endeavors still achieve a higher measure of good health, energy, longevity, mental clarity and an improved fortune in this life and the next as a result of their efforts. For instance, cultivation efforts that affect your Qi/Prana can sometimes cure illness, and in the absence of illness (attained through meditation and

Qi practices) one will see health improvements, greater energy and the prolongation of one's life. Thus, you will improve your health and longevity from Qi practices, breathing practices, virtue training and meditation practices. Furthermore, once they die such individuals will have an easier time of cultivating the higher bodies as a deva spirit in the earthly heavenly plane because they already performed a lot of Qi refinement work and self-improvement activities while living.

Few people succeed in spiritual cultivation during life, but everyone dies. If you cultivated your Qi during life you will be much farther ahead than everyone else since their own residual Qi will be less purified than your own due to a lifetime of spiritual cultivation efforts and selfless good deeds on your part that helped to purify your Qi to a great extent. Everyone gets the correct spiritual teachings in the afterlife because they can see all around them the process of reincarnation being managed, masters using multiple spiritual bodies to help people and so forth, and so then they start to cultivate their Qi with ferocity since the spiritual road is finally made clear. All false dogmas they followed in life are revealed for the falsities they are, and the true path of spiritual practice is known everywhere. Qi cultivation then becomes one of the primary occupations of the devas, and their two primary practices are kundalini yoga and sexual cultivation (where they try to excite their positive emotions and simultaneously stimulate their Qi during sexual congress).

One who practices policing their mind and behavior through mental watching/witnessing practice will also be cultivating their character, the refinement of their Qi as well as good fortune for this life and the next life due to their pursuit of virtue, merit and the avoidance of faults and error in life. An energetic vigor for correcting your personal faults and weaknesses and doing good deeds (accumulating merit) will also bear positive karmic fruit not just in personality improvements but in Qi purification. Ashrams in India, for instance, are meant to lead a person by stages through virtuous deeds, enabling an individual to purify his character of flaws, and finally attain an enlightenment that transcends the physical nature.

Human beings who don't succeed in attaining the deva body during life will still improve their life to a major extent because of improving their thinking processes, personality traits, health and energy, Qi purification benefits and due to changing their fortune for the better. They might not succeed in attaining the deva body but they can still improve their lives in all sorts of ways by spiritual cultivation efforts that bring them to a progress point halfway between the spiritual and physical realms, which then puts them at a fantastic advantage after they die and are reborn in Heaven.

Chapter 11
THE THREE REQUIREMENTS FOR CULTIVATION SUCCESS

The way to spiritual enlightenment or *Moksha*, which means to achieve the transcendental spiritual body attainments, is essentially a pathway of Yoga. In the final analysis, spiritual practice and spiritual attainment is all a matter of Yoga in the end. It requires special forms of Yoga to transform your Qi, your body, your mental patterns, your thinking, your conduct and your personality. Most of all it requires inner energy Yoga to purify the matrix of subtle energy within you that flows within all your tissues.

It cannot be overemphasized - the spiritual path is actually a pathway of specific types of Yoga to purify and strengthen your Yin Qi and Yang Qi so that you can generate an independent deva (astral) body, yet people don't know this fact since the structure of the pathway is hidden to the uninitiated. Adepts typically keep silent on the best methods of practice and the actual body attainments as well as the new powers possible with each new body-self achievement.[17]

Spiritual practice is Qi/Prana Yoga and mind Yoga through and through, and the individuals who ultimately achieve success must work hard at specific activities that purify their mind (and thus their behavior) and cultivate their Qi/Prana. By character (personality) they must be ethical, virtuous, kind, compassionate, non-abusive and open-minded people who have a natural tendency to help others.

The spiritual path involves maximizing our virility, vitality or Qi through exercise, celibacy, meditative purification efforts and by improving its internal circulation. However, you cannot just strengthen your Qi but must

---

[17] An admirable exception is *God Speaks* by Meher Baba.

refine it, which means to purify it of defilements and refine its quality. Just as a difference in Qi quality (virility that you can feel exuding from the body) can be easily sensed between a domesticated dog versus a wild wolf, humans have different levels of Qi refinement due to their personal cultivation. You must also purify the tendencies of your character/mind and cultivate the powers of consciousness such as reasoning abilities, wisdom and knowledge, the ability to focus and concentrate (and persevere with your will), imagination and mental rehearsal abilities, the ability to change your mood at will, attentiveness and so on. Furthermore, you should also be cultivating the propriety of social relations (noble behaviors) that spiritually raise you above the animals by developing traits such as kindness, compassion, helpfulness, fairness and the tendency to perform good deeds in general. This means refining your behavior so that you are not coarse and rude which in turn requires emotional control, self-control, development of your intellect and self-rectification.

Spiritual practice entails cultivating the *beast and brain* within you - your body and its Qi energy as well as your emotions, thinking and your behavior. The path of refinement must address your body and its inherent energy as well as your thought processes (consciousness) and conduct. You select a possible future you want to become as your reality - what you personally want to become as an ideal higher stage of excellence - and then you start cultivating your properties/attributes to develop to that state. The highest stage of perfection is to generate the independent deva body whilst alive, but if you don't achieve this attainment during this lifetime you still want to have practiced lots of inner energy work (and breathing practices for all types of different activities) so that you can finish the task in the heavenly plane, or at least purify your Qi to such a degree from those efforts that you don't have to be reborn on earth again.

To attain the deva body (enlightenment) while alive there are three major cultivation requirements.

FIRST, it is necessary for you to *cultivate meditation practice*, which can be either "meditation with attributes" or "meditation without attributes." "Meditation without attributes" or "emptiness meditation" is a mental practice that mentally imitates the emptiness of the universal substratum, which means that you pursue mental quiescence in various ways. In this type of practice emptiness is a *meditative dwelling*, which means that you try to abide in a mental emptiness of some kind (a lessening of thoughts in conjunction with great openness and awareness). You can use various practices, such as the thirty or so emptiness exercises in the Appendix of *Neijia Yoga* or those within the *Vijnana Bhairava* of Kashmir Shaivism, to try to enter into an station of emptiness and calmly abide therein without clinging to that state. Another alternative are the samadhis of infinite space, infinite consciousness, infinite nothingness and neither thought nor no-thought. There are many emptiness stations proposed by various religions as targets/methods of practice.

Mental quiet and calm – mental emptiness - is an enjoyable state of mind during which your Qi becomes a bit purified, but more importantly, during a state of quiescence (emptiness) it is much easier for higher spiritual beings to transform your Qi, and their cooperative help along thee lines is necessary for the spiritual path.

"Meditation with attributes" typically entails concentrating on mental forms such as thoughts, emotions, shapes, colors, etc. to train the abilities of your mind so that they become more powerful. Visualization practice, mental rehearsals and *bindu* practices (where you keep your mind and Qi focused on a particular point within the body without moving) are a type of concentration practice, as is simply sticking with a perplexing math problem (without a break) and becoming absorbed within it until you solve it.

Attribute meditation is often called *concentration practice* because you often hold your mental formations together with a certain emotional quality for an extended period of time. You will not just be developing concentration skill from this effort but reaping the benefit of the fact that this will change the quality of your Qi depending upon what you concentrate upon (and dependent upon whether you hold a large emotional content at that time), so it also becomes a type of Qi purification work. Some of these concentration techniques involve first observing your thoughts so that eventually they die down to produce a quiet state of mind, and then later you are to experience the mind's natural state of non-complexity. Concentration is also required for performing various rituals that require countless simultaneous actions, and afterwards the mind can rest in an emptiness of pleasure-release after the performance is over.

For success on the path you must cultivate an openness of mind that always allows the freedom of new thoughts and emotions to be born. You must also train your awareness and sense of self-presence not to become blindly lost in your thought-stream. You don't want to block consciousness by trying to produce a blank state of mind as what you think is the meaning of emptiness, nor do you want to block the possibility of novelty or self-correction. The essence of consciousness is not a blank state because it potentially contains the whole universe, and therefore you should similarly always be limitlessly open to new thoughts and experiences, and should be encountering life with a type of fearlessness and courage. However, you must correct whatever arises within your mind just as you would clear a fallen tree off a road or swerve to avoid it. Proficiency in the skill of watchfulness and detachment, where you can view your thoughts like an independent observer, requires the meditation practice of observing your own mind without becoming fused with your thought-stream (*vipassana*). This is essentially mindfulness practice. Practiced over time, this produces a calm, quiet but clear and sharp mind. You want to practice in such a way that you open up all the Qi channels in the back of your head so that alertness and clarity become a primary feature of your personality while you also soften its rigidity.

During meditation practices where you watch your thoughts you must cultivate self-awareness, mindfulness, or watchfulness of your mind-stream so that you can always see your thoughts and behavior to correct them, which is a basic requirement of life. Yes, this is a basic requirement of life but we often become lost in our thoughts and fail to do this self-editing function. You must cultivate a state of pristine lucid presence, which means that your awareness is wide open and observant, and remain awake so that you clearly know both your external environment and the thoughts of your mind.

When you detach from your thoughts and emotions then the busyness within your mind will gradually calm down, your mind will become emptier of wandering thoughts or agitations, and within that calmness and indifference your wisdom will then become more accessible during real-life situations. In other words, you must refine your ability to detach from your thoughts and forego fusion or identification with your thought-stream. Then you can cultivate better thoughts, insight, clarity and decision-making. You should also refrain from attaching to states of internal emptiness or quiet that you reach and neither take pleasure in them or indulge in them so that you are free of clinging to imperturbability. Then you can become naturally happy. Most of all you want to become able to leave behind lower-order mentalities.

As a natural tendency, most people become fused with their thinking. You must retrain your normal mental processes to be observant of your mind/conduct, and refrain from thought entanglements where you become lost in, merged or fused with the doings of your mind-stream and/or behavior keep blindly follow their momentum such as when getting angry and then staying with that anger rather than transcending it. You must learn how to transcend your mind-stream through a dispassionate über-knowing that doesn't attach to your thoughts and identify with them. You must cultivate meta-cognition, which means really knowing what you are thinking, feeling and doing, and the habit of instantly correcting them when they go off track. You must learn how to detach from what's going on in your mind (and the external world as well) so you must learn how to detach from bondage to your emotion-prone thought-stream and ego and then you can cultivate a state of calmness and dispassion. This will serve you in times of emergency.

You must cultivate the ability to interrupt mechanical, robotic thought entrainment so that you can change the thoughts you are generating, ascend to a higher perspective than the current one you are following, and so that you can also experience more peaceful mental states absent of afflictions. Thoughts are something your brain produces that may or may not be true and may or may not be useful, so you should not just automatically identify with whatever thoughts arise within your mind but should observe them with meta-awareness to know them but not blindly fuse with them and correct them or transform them when you find them errant. Blindly following old traditions rather than flexibly adapting to a situation or breaking rules when you must is a type of wrong attachment along these lines.

You must also cultivate the ability to concentrate (on objects within your mind) without wavering your attention; you need to learn how to generate and hold a state of stable concentration. This includes learning how to employ the powers of your imagination such as by making mental visualizations or mental rehearsals. The character qualities of perseverance, persistence, determination, steadfastness, tenacity, resilience, endurance, discipline, willpower, backbone, patience, forbearance, commitment, focus, grit and so on are all forms of concentration too because they entail staying with a purpose or activity without cease until there is accomplishment. They all involve the ability to persevere in staying with something, to remain stable and "stick with it," which is the meaning of concentration. In Patanjali's Yoga, *dharana* means holding your mind on some particular object of your focus (since you want to develop concentration and focus as an ability of your mind), but the major point to stress is that you become able to maintain a purpose until completion rather than just hold onto something (abide within it) in your mind. You can cultivate such traits through mental concentration practice such as visualizations that require you to hold stable images within your mind without distraction. At the end of most concentration practices you are usually taught to let go of everything within your mind so that you can enter into a state of empty mind where you are then practicing meditation without mental attributes.

You must also cultivate the mental ability to be able to ignore, reduce or eliminate (cut off) random mental afflictions and defilements that arise within your consciousness, or transform such annoyances whenever they arise. In other words, you must learn how to gain control of your spontaneous automatic mental functions, and you can do this through certain types of meditation practices and other forms of mental training such as NLP neurolinguistic programming, ACT acceptance and commitment therapy or CBT cognitive behavior therapy.

Through meditation practice you can learn how to concentrate, how to monitor your thought-stream without attachment so you can correct it, how to manipulate/transform your thoughts and mental functions into better octaves, how to encourage your internal dialogue to die down peacefully so that you experience a quiet, empty, peaceful, stress-free mental state, and how to keep yourself open to newness whilst in that quiet state of mind. Meditation practice trains you to control your mental functions, find mental peace, improve your behavior, control your body and cultivate your internal energy. With a lot of work you can sometimes touch a state of flowing presence where you are pristinely clear and feel fully alive, are mentally free of distractions while fully engaged in the moment, and you feel (perhaps playful but certainly) vibrant with active inner vitality. During flow your mind is pristinely pure and focused, and you physically feel renewed and rejuvenated every second.

SECOND, through various exercises you must actively strengthen and purify the Qi/Prana (life force, vital energy or wind element) of your physical body to a higher stage of refinement.[18] You must learn how to accumulate, concentrate, protect and nourish your Qi or vital energy which is the basis of your inner subtle body that is termed the deva body (or astral body) once released from its physical shell. In Orthodox Christianity this is accomplished through prayer, singing, and devotional activities such as by worshipping God.

These efforts are sometimes called Qi purification, cultivating life, refining the breath, inner alchemy, kundalini cultivation, cultivating your wind element, *kriya* yoga, laya yoga, Nyasa yoga, Vajrayana practice, Tantra, *neijia*, *neidan*, *anapana* or *nei-gong*. They entail a school of physical culture that involves better breathing patterns and internal energy exercises to get you to a higher stage of inner energy *gong-fu*. If you do not actively cultivate your Qi/Prana (life force that is the substance of your subtle body) in one way or another then the deva body attainment will not be reached during this life.

---

[18] See *Neijia Yoga* and *Nyasa Yoga* by William Bodri.

You can cultivate it directly or just let it happen to you by practicing other techniques that affect it tangentially as a consequence. To cultivate your Qi directly you might use methods that involve your breathing (*qi-gong*, pranayama, mantra, singing, chanting), the stirring of emotions, visualizations, energy absorption techniques, and other relevant cultivation methods that move your Qi as done in Nyasa Yoga.

In ancient times students would segment their body into sections and cultivate their Yin Qi and Yang Qi in these sections as demonstrated by the fact that at the end of their lives many masters would rise into the air and prove their mastery over these energies by making the left or right, top or bottom sections of their body appear as fire or water alternatively. You can segment the body into one section (the entire body), the left-right or top-bottom sections, the head-chest-lower body trio and so forth. The Yin and Yang Qi within each body section can then be cultivated through various intensified exercises such as mantra vibrations, visualizations and so forth. These intensified inner energy yoga practices are called preparatory work since they prepare you for the deva body Srotapanna Arhat achievement.

The Qi cultivation methods leading to the most progress teach you to hold your Qi in certain parts of your body, forcibly push or pull your Qi through certain parts of your body, guide your Qi to circulate/revolve in special pathways throughout your body, or teach you to wash certain parts of your body with many Qi revolutions, bring sounds and lights into certain parts of your body to vibrate their Qi, and so on. Such activities need to be done hundreds to thousands of times per day, and are usually performed under the guidance of an accomplished teacher. If you do so correctly then sometimes the very next day your muscles may seem to lock up but this is not to be feared and quickly passes. Sometimes you just hold your Qi stationary in a special location as taught in Yoga with its locks and bandhas.

Arousing strong emotions is an additional way to stimulate the Yin Qi or Yang Qi throughout your body (to modulate your Qi with a specific Yin or Yang Qi tone quality) because emotions will move your energy into an excited state or theme that will affect/vibrate the Qi throughout your body, as does exercise. An emotion creates a sensation throughout your body, that sensation activates your Yin QI or Yang QI appropriately, and in this way you exercise that type of Qi and actually refresh and purify your subtle body.

If you hold a *bhava* (a given attitude whose energetic content is felt throughout your body) for a long period of time then that emotional mood will also affect your Yin Qi or Yang Qi accordingly, and thus help to purify the Yin or Yang elements of your inner subtle body. This is done in the nearly extinct *boran kammatthana* esoteric Buddhist tradition of South East Asia where you invite certain emotions to arise within your body-mind complex *with the intent that they envelop you*. You invoke the relevant Yin or Yang mental factors/emotions as if they were gods, and suffuse them throughout your body-mind while inviting them to transform your body and mind. Naturally you must try to *strongly feel* the relevant emotion.

In the *Abhyasa* yoga of Hinduism, you regularly and patiently practice a certain attitude over a long period of time just like this where the attitude can be an emotion, feeling, passion or interest. Alternatively, yogis and sadhus often practice a *Vairagya* yoga effort of detachment to be *without* (free of your) emotions, feelings, passions or interests. In this case the yogis want to "go beyond color" by subduing all their passions and desires. Sometimes ascetic sadhus or sannyasin train in mastering disinterest and dispassion in order to break dependencies, become emotionally more robust and bring control to a restless mind, whereas by holding onto emotions and desires etc. they are training in concentration in in purifying their inner Qi/Prana body.

In the *Anapanasati sutra* of Buddhism and related sutras, you are alternatively taught to sit in meditation practice where you breathe in and out while trying to feel the Qi of your entire body, or *feel mental joy while simultaneously feeling the Qi of your entire body*, or you try to smoothen the Qi throughout your body so that you calm your body formation while breathing, or *feel pleasant bliss throughout the cells of your body while breathing*, ... all of which help to purify your Yang Qi. You are also taught to cultivate emptiness ("release the mind," "calm the mental formations," "observe mental cessation," "practice relinquishment," etc.) while feeling the Qi flow within your body that is moved by your breathing. Further, you are taught to arouse and feel negative emotions while mindfully breathing slowly and deeply in order to purify your Yin Qi (emotions such as distaste with the suffering of life, disgust from the remembrance of the sight of decaying corpses, guilt for remembering personal faults and failings, humility and contrition for repenting of misdeeds, sorrow for the sufferings of the world, etc.). If you hold onto negative emotions (that totally envelop your body and flood your consciousness) while slowly cultivating your breathing with intent (which means feeling the Qi of your body everywhere inside you as impregnated with or pulsing with those qualities), those emotions will penetrate and change the quality of the entire Qi of your body and mind, and thus wash the Yin essence of your Qi/Prana. To the uninitiated this type of emotional washing sounds like it is not cultivation at all but it is done to monks and nuns throughout their careers and in particular you must suffer through thousands and thousands of times of this during the twelve-year kundalini transformation period.

The basic purpose of most of these techniques is to arouse Yin and Yang Qi within you due to specific remembrances, arousals, provocations, invitations or meditations; to hold onto the aroused Yin or Yang Qi respectively that should totally suffuse and then subsume your body and mind with absolute permeation; and through a prolonged practice session of this nature you end up toning, purifying or "washing" the relevant Yin Qi or Yang Qi of your subtle body that must emerge in order for you to become enlightened.[19] During the Twelve Years of the kundalini awakening process the Buddhas will put practitioners through countless Yin or Yang emotional experiences to wash their Yin or Yang Qi respectively, such as the emotions of great sadness or pity (Yin); excitedness and boldness (Yang); hopelessness and forlornness (Yin); pride and arrogance (Yang); dread, anxiety and distress (Yin); purity, peace and joy (Yang); intense self-satisfaction and superiority feelings (Yang); infinite lightness and purity (Yang); fear of death or absolute extinction (Yin); boundless love, desire or even lust (Yang) that are all mentioned in the second set of Demon Mara States described in the *Surangama Sutra*. Many other methods and emotions are used on you during this process so this short list is only indicative. When trying to purify a practitioner's Yin Qi, the Buddhas put individuals through very painful emotional experiences (such as some of the negative states within the list of one-hundred Sufi stations) or even use their own *nirmanakaya* energies to cause physical annoyances or pain within their student's bodies to arouse their Yin Qi, especially during the last years of the twelve-year period, all of which is distressing to practitioners and prompts many to consider suicide from excessiveness during the process.

---

[19] Since the ancient Romans found that their soldiers could fight at best for six minutes before they lost their energy and needed to be relieved, and since sexual congress lasts on average about six minutes before exhaustion, it is beneficial to continuously hold an emotional *bhava* for at least six minutes of practice time. According to nadi astrology a new fortune occurs every 24 seconds, which is the minimum amount of time you would want to hold onto an emotion for training purposes. During the time one holds onto a specific emotion, you might also listen to relevant Yin or Yang music to help strengthen and reinforce the selected emotional mood, look at relevant pictures and so forth to help arouse the corresponding Yin or Yang emotions etcetera. At the same time you should also attempt to arouse corresponding Qi sensations within your entire body while pulsing it with breathing. It is important to *feel your Qi being vibrated, excited or moved by your breathing* or some other stimulation method while toning it with a Yin or Yang emotion because this will wash the Qi of your subtle body.

The soft martial arts teach you how to develop and lead your internal energy throughout your body so they also help people cultivate the independent deva body whereas the hard martial arts do not do so. During martial arts practice, adherents are sometimes told to imagine that their Qi is like that of an animal such as a tiger (Yin), Snake (Yin), dragon (Yang) and so forth to purify/stimulate its Yin or Yang Qi qualities. Furthermore, martial artists often employ esoteric methods to practice during certain Yin-strong or Yang-strong periods of the day to absorb a bit of those essences for certain techniques, and learn to match their breathing with their forms in order to move their Qi and gain control of its movements.

Thus, all people should not only learn yoga and sports when young but also a soft martial arts practice such as *Taijiquan, Baguazhang, Tongbeiquan, Yiquan (Da Cheng Quan), Liu He Ba Fa* or *Xingyiquan* so that they begin to learn how to move their Qi and start developing the deva body attainment from an early age, thus hastening their spiritual advancement. All monastics – whether Christian, Buddhist, Hindu, Taoist, Jewish, Sufi and so on – should be learning both yoga and the martial arts (that stress movement, coordinated breathing that affects/pushes your Qi, and internal energy practices) to speed the achievement of the first dhyana, which is the subtle body or deva body attainment of *Homo Deus*, the Srotapanna rank of Arhat attainment which is also known as the first dhyana within Buddhism. It is the astral body of the European mystery schools, impure illusory body of Tibetan Buddhism and Earth Immortal stage in Taoism. If you are interested in developing or exhibiting exceptional physical grace or elegance then you can add dance to the recommendations of yoga and martial arts for it will not only help in cardiovascular development but add an extra training emphasis to opening up the Qi channels in your legs, arms and shoulders due to the required movements. Rebounding is useful in exercising every cell of your body through shaking vibrations and it also stretches most body tissues.

For instance, Zen monks doing walking meditation should not simply "walk with awareness" but while doing so might hold their arms in various *Baguazhang* postures that would stimulate particular Qi channels within their physical body, and should simultaneously send their energy along those limbs and meridians while walking. Then the practice contributes to both health and accomplishing the Qi transformations required of the spiritual path, and it becomes even more effective when practitioners hold onto the relevant emotions of the organ systems being activated by the accented meridian postures.

In order to improve your Qi circulation you must initially force your Qi to move throughout your body in various ways that wash its tissues, and you accomplish this by leading your Qi with your mind/will. Zen practitioners typically only practice meditation but they should be practicing physical exercises along with internal energy circulation techniques that move their Qi throughout their entire body because they are seeking enlightenment, and you cannot attain enlightenment unless you do inner energy work to produce the deva body's emergence. In Buddhism, Ananda awakened after Shakyamuni Buddha because he concentrated on intellectual study while Shakyamuni performed inner energy work. Unfortunately, the Zen school is deficient in the physical culture necessary for the achievement of the *sambhogakaya*, which includes the deva body first stage attainment of the spiritual path, whereas Taoism is not deficient in this aspect. You want to mentally circulate your Qi to wash the Qi of all your simples over and over again in order to prepare for an independent deva body to be released from within the human body, which normally happens only upon death. You want to learn how to match your Qi movements with your physical movements by grabbing the Qi of your body while moving in exercises because you must strengthen your subtle body that is entirely composed of Qi.

The Zen school makes the mistake of not concentrating on cultivating the *sambhogakaya* while Yoga, Tantra, and Vajrayana energy practices do, so the Zen school wants the ultimate attainment but cuts off the pathway for getting there by refusing to cultivate the inner subtle body of Qi. Masters within the Zen school should work on reestablishing the physical culture necessary for the first dhyana attainment of enlightenment. If you are only cultivating emptiness meditation practice then you are depending on higher spiritual beings to do all the Qi movement work for you so it is best to do some inner *neijia* yourself, especially since you will be practicing *neijia* full-time after you attain the Srotapanna deva body made of energy. All Zen and Advaita Vedanta practitioners, in fact *adherents of all spiritual schools*, should be attached to a form of physical culture that involves physical exercise, the proper breathing patterns for every type of activity, and inner energy *gong-fu* that circulates their Qi.

For spiritual cultivation it is best to use multiple Qi-affecting techniques *in conjunction with physical exercises* like stretching, yoga, dance and the martial arts where you can try to move your Qi/Prana within every muscle and organ as taught in *Nyasa Yoga* or *Neijia Yoga*. If you stretch your muscles through yoga, dance, rebounding or exercise this will make it easier for the Qi to flow through them. You should also try to match your internal Qi flow with the physical structures of your body, either in stillness or movement, thus "washing them."

In yoga your body typically remains motionless during stretching postures and at high levels you can try to move your Qi/Prana within those outstretched muscles. Similarly, in dance or the soft martial arts or athletics you try to match your breathing and inner Qi flow with your physical movements and combine the two into one. This cultivates the internal Qi structure within your body so that it can eventually emerge as an independent astral body, which as stated normally happens only upon death. The soft martial arts are the best physical exercises for teaching this type of inner energy work and speed your progress towards attaining the deva body. Some practices related to the martial arts that also emphasize the enhancement of internal Qi circulation include *Yi Jin Jing* (Damo's Muscle/Tendon Changing and Marrow/Brain Washing Method), *Si Er Quang* (Twelve Postures), *Ba Duan Jin* (Eight Pieces of Brocade) and *Wu Qin Xi* (Five Animal Sport).

The goal of outer physical and inner energy training methods are not just higher physical skills and smoother inner energy circulation but an ultimate level of physical comfort, relaxation, grace and ease. Calm Qi leads to a calm mind, so these exercises lead to better mental states. Leading Qi through your organs, muscles and bones as an exercise clears their Qi channels and energizes them so that they function more efficiently. The goal is the harmonious functioning of your body's entire energy in movement or in perfect tranquility. Once again, this is the preparatory work necessary for purifying the Qi of your subtle body.

Excellent Qi training enables you to reach an internal state of natural Qi/Prana flow that makes the body so comfortable that its presence seems as if non-existent, which is called "forgetting the body." To do this you need to learn how to build up your Qi and circulate it through your body by mentally leading it. *Brahmacarya* (celibacy or sexual restraint) is therefore also practiced so that you do not lose the internal energy normally lost through ejaculation that is necessary for strengthening your internal subtle body and performing such washing exercises. For women who cultivate, sexual orgasm is not a detriment because they can regain any energy loss very quickly.

You can often feel the raw energy, power or aura of those who are celibate, which is feeling/sensing their Qi, because their energy exudes from their body due to the retention of *brahmacarya*. Then the problem is to refine that energy. This is the objective of spiritual cultivation practice, namely to retain your Qi from leakage, or absorb/accumulate or augment Qi energies so that you become filled with energy. You want your Qi to be in all your tissues with fullness and then others will see your body shine or feel it exude from your body. Then you must refine it through cultivation exercises that include elevating your mind and behavior because your personality is impressed upon your Qi, and you don't want that influence to constitute a pollution/defilement rather than splendor. In particular you want to cultivate the Yin aspects of humility, forgiveness, compassion, loving kindness, respect and honor. This, along with mental mind yoga that calms your consciousness, is how you successfully cultivate your subtle body to achieve the Srotapanna attainment.

By practice that regulates/cultivates your body, mind and breathing you can calm your consciousness and reach a state of undistracted clarity wherein you can even feel how the Qi is distributed throughout your body and you know how to adjust it by pushing it this way or that way. Inner clarity requires calmness, stability and tranquility. Further, calmness and peace are the basis of a stable, harmonious society which is why individuals should cultivate it again. Individuals must cultivate spiritual practice, and we need methods to tame the wildness of society as well.

Confucius said that when your mind is calm it is steady, and if steady it is at peace. Only when it is at peace (calm and unperturbed) are you able to think properly (without distractions, emotional bondages or excessive prejudice). He then said that "proper thinking" becomes possible within calmness and leads to "gain," which is because it can produce better analysis and decision-making (judgment) and therefore can enable you to attain what you want ("gain"). Calmness is actually a state of concentration, and concentration leads to better performance during activities.

Also, by cultivating a "formless mind," which is a relatively quiet or empty mental state of detached clarity that isn't experiencing clinging to its mental fabrications, through that non-clinging you allow your own Qi/Prana to arise within you and start transforming your Qi channels through a flow that is not affected by mental interference. In other words, your thoughts and Qi are linked, but when you let go of your thoughts then you lessen the mental grip or influence on your Qi, and that's the time it reverts to its most natural inner circulation. This is one of the reasons people look rested after vacations because they didn't just rest their minds. "Emptiness mind" also allows for Buddhas and their junior deva students to enter into you and use their own energy – from their bodies made of Qi, Shen and higher energies – to move your own energy in a type of washing, purgation or purification of your subtle body. This is happening to people all the time unawares.

The moment you cling to your thoughts or inner physical sensations then the free movement of Qi/Prana within your body is altered due to that mental gripping, thus making it difficult for your Qi/Prana to circulate freely without bias. Hence learning meditation to achieve an awareness that is detached from your thought-stream helps you totally transform the entire Qi/Prana of your body because it leads to better, more natural internal Qi flow. While it is often uncomfortable to bear the transformations of Qi going on within you that open up your Qi channels, by letting go of those feelings while maintaining awareness you actually allow your Qi to open up your body's energy meridians everywhere and produce a more perfect subtle body that expresses the honesty and authenticity of your true being.

In short, your personal daily practice schedule for spiritual cultivation aiming at the Arhat enlightenment – the accomplishment of transcendental bodies or dhyana attainments – should include (1) emptiness meditation practice where mental emptiness (no-thought or the silencing of thoughts) is achieved in some way and then becomes a meditative dwelling place (mental station), (2) *vipassana* self-observational awareness practice, (3) some type of concentration practice with or without visualizations where you evoke intense positive and then negative (Yang and then Yin) emotions to wash the Qi/Prana of your inner etheric subtle body, (4) *neijia* or *nei-gong* inner Qi work where you rotate your Qi throughout your body in various ways hundreds to thousands of times per session, (5) some type of *Vairagya* detachment effort (where you are not grasping at concepts of self or phenomena) during hours of regular life when you are not sitting in meditation practice, (6) mindfulness practice during regular life to police and correct your faults and behavior, followed by a daily introspective review, (7) yoga, martial arts or some other athletic practice that stretches your muscles where the exercise also requires you to learn to combine your breathing and inner energy (Qi/Prana) with your movements, (8) and mantra, reverential singing or prayer recitation practice that itself moves your Qi and calls for aid and assistance from various families of enlightened adepts who have vowed to respond to those mantras, songs or prayers.

You can add pranayama and many other cultivation practices to this list as well, which might total 5-6 hours per day for an adept within a monastic tradition, and the point of this short list is to illustrate what you are actually doing in terms of basic principles. Since the target is an immortal transcendental body that makes one a Buddha, it makes sense to also start developing the skills, mindset and merit needed to become an enlightened Buddha of a certain type as outlined in *Buddha Yoga*. Whenever possible you should perform act of merit throughout life, but if you choose to become a particular type of Buddha you should particularly strive to learn the appropriate skills and execute acts of merit in line with your ambitions.

THIRD, you must also cultivate spiritual virtues, values and compassionate helpful behavior as well as wisdom and knowledge. This is the self-refinement, self-improvement or *Samskara*-kaya (Perfection-kaya) aspect of the spiritual path. Personally you need to be an ethical person in life who adheres to virtuous ways. After all, we need society to function according to virtuous principles of ethics and morality otherwise people will not be able to live together peacefully. You also need to perform good deeds or meritorious acts to accumulate merit for the path and to start expressing the behavior of an enlightened Buddha.

If you are not a kind, caring, compassionate, virtuous, ethical individual then the Buddhas and Bodhisattvas will not agree to devote themselves to you for the twelve years of daily organized labor required that is necessary to sufficiently transform your Qi for the deva body emergence. If you are not that type of individual then you must start cultivating ethics and virtuous behavior in this life so that it becomes your natural personality trait, and so that those *samskaras* will then be carried over to a subsequent incarnation where you finally become qualified for the higher body attainments that help you escape the lower realms forever. There is no fixed soul or self that experiences rebirth, but there is a continuation of the process of life for a non-intrinsic being having certain qualities, and the rebirth of an apparent being is conditioned by various factors and their relations such as your personality, wisdom and mental capabilities), mental perspectives, skills, habit energies, vows and the merit you accumulated in life from doing good deeds. The takeaway lesson is that you must work on improving yourself *now* so that the improved you has enough merit for enlightenment.

You should therefore think of religion and spiritual practice as a pathway for character development (that includes developing your personality traits, wisdom, skills, relationships and merit), and this is an absolute necessity for spiritual attainment. You cannot just study religious texts but must work on refining your personality too, which is more important since people who know nothing at all often attain the Tao because of their wonderful set of personality traits. You especially want to cultivate the Yin aspects of humility, forgiveness, loving kindness, compassion, care, concern, respect and honor. You want to purify your mind and behavior in a permanent manner and work towards noble, consummate conduct as well as compassionate efforts on behalf of others.

No one will help you attain the deva body with power over others unless you merit the attainment. Spiritual practice is therefore a pathway that requires unrelenting good deeds, personality development and efforts at self-perfection on our part. Perfection-kaya also includes perfecting yourself physically as well as pursing more ethical, virtuous behavior. You must work on polishing your personality, attitudes and conduct to eliminate personal faults and imperfections. You must also take care of your health as well because your physical body is the template of your deva body so you need to keep in good shape.

Taking care of your physical body and physical health means healing or repairing your body (such as annual chiropractic adjustments or herbal medicine interventions), which in spiritual traditions is called "nourishing your body" or "physical rejuvenation." Although neglected in most spiritual traditions, cultivating your physical body is an important and essential part of the spiritual path that is absolutely necessary, which is why yoga and the martial arts are highly recommended. A healthy diet is important too. With this in mind, note that the path of extreme asceticism may hurt you and your chances at spiritual attainment rather than help you.

Even so, people primarily think of Perfection-kaya as just perfecting our minds and behaviors because spiritual cultivation is the road of self-development that includes cultivating your personality, ethics, virtues, values, wisdom, skillfulness and conduct. Christianity, Judaism, Islam, Buddhism, Hinduism, Sikhism, etcetera all stress this. You work at cultivating your virtues to a state of brilliance, walking the path of the highest good, performing good deeds to help people, and pursuing such endeavors until you rest and reside in the highest states of excellence. Actually, you must also perform good deeds for society as well to help it attain a higher degree of perfection because it is part of your larger body.

Most people think they are "good" people, but that's because most have never been tested in situations where they could "break the rules" and behave unethically without anyone finding out. They have usually never been anywhere where they could be criminal, evil or just bad and get away without being caught. In such situations some people will indulge themselves and others refrain, and that's when you discover what people are really made of. Most people think they wouldn't do unethical, immoral or criminal deeds but many give into the temptation when conditions permit if they think they won't get caught. When you give people power they also tend to become corrupt by using it to exploit others, and this is a temptation for sages as well as ordinary people.

This is why we must be devoted to spiritual values and virtuous ways as our guides to life despite any temptations, and choose good over evil. When the temptation to be "bad" wins then the brain gets a little dopamine kick, the neurological circuits for that behavior improve and the tendency grows stronger because it was rewarded by a burst of pleasurable hormones. The danger of a single wrong act ("I'll just do it once") is that it turns into a habit (like a drug addiction), the habit becomes your character, and then your character becomes your destiny.

This is why you should never introduce people to any vice, no matter how minor, for you never know if it will kick off a string of recurring visits that amplify over time. Habits get reinforced over time, which means that habits contribute a large share to your personality, life and identity. On the other hand, virtuous tendencies gain strength with exercise and if you hold onto inner strength to remain virtuous under circumstances of temptation then unwholesome tendencies will shrink and their effect on your life will decline. Nevertheless, the original neurological circuits for doing bad (if you performed such deeds previously) will always be available if you created them, such as with addictions, so you need to develop methods for dealing with nearly irresistible urges, temptations and inclinations.

Stress can weaken one's willpower and allow learned pleasure-seeking circuits to manifest, but there is a pathway to purification. The paramount principle is not to practice what you don't want to become in the first place because you will build those neurological circuits from indulgence, and then you will have to build another mechanism to inhibit them. Once established in the brain, neurological circuits can decay over time but they can still have an effect on your actions if you are not careful with self-discipline and self-control.

Here is the fundamental method for cultivating virtuous, compassionate behavior. First, you must be taught the standard models or ideal principles of ethical, virtuous behavior. Afterwards you must monitor what you think, say and do in order to fall in line with these standards because you build yourself in the way that you think, speak and do. All human beings should be taught the basics of ethics, virtue, morality and good deeds when they are young in order to create the right type of brain patterns and behavioral tendencies. Society needs to be populated with good people and good citizens in order to function and this is the method for insuring the outcome. Usually religion teaches us the principles of ethics, morality and virtue but the training must also come from our parents and society.

From the start as children, we need to be taught to avoid doing evil things and do what is right, proper and wholesome and to stick to these standards.

Unfortunately, students are fed a thin gruel for ethics education in contemporary culture. We need to be indoctrinated into human culture that stresses a civil society and group welfare revolving around stronger families, social coherence, civic responsibility, justice, fairness and law, ... and which steers us away from bad paths toward good ways of behaving and doing. This involves adopting social values of honesty, fairness, justice and all the other virtues that humans prize as supreme.

Unfortunately, we often fall away from such standards because of temptation, lack of internal discipline and a deficiency of self-control. Nevertheless, you need to be taught what is wrong and avoid it just as much as you need to be encouraged on the path of righteousness and proper conduct. Children enter adulthood with the idea of adding more and more Knowledge to their brain, but are never taught how to monitor and change the software of their mental paradigms and behavior. Your entire life runs on the software in your head and yet you are never taught how to optimize it. Children need to be taught how to find inner peace, how to control their emotions and behavior, that they should monitor their thoughts and behavior in order to apply adjustments when necessary, and how to change the patterns or mindsets that generate them. They need to be taught that you are in charge of and responsible for your own future and should be encouraged to create it.

Thus you need to be taught how to develop mental clarity, which can monitor your inner thoughts and outer behavior with detachment, and you need to develop the virtues of discipline, self-control and self-correction. If you develop faults and errant tendencies over time – and we all do – then when you enter the spiritual path you need to create mechanisms to keep them in check and you certainly need to develop a presence of mind to spot them in real time and correct them whenever they appear. Certain unwholesome aspects of your character have to be cleansed out of your psyche. You cultivate virtue by correcting your faults and flaws, eliminating the roots of your errant ways, living according to a code of ethics, and basically by becoming a good human being. It is a matter of remedying the defects of your character in various ways. You can start to manage your behavior by mastering your consciousness, and you can pursue this through mindfulness practice and self-discipline.

This effort is called purification of your mind and behavior, or self-perfection, and in Christianity the (sometimes painful) process of working on yourself to purge your behavior of flaws and faults is also known as catharsis or purgation. This involves turning away from everything unwholesome, not becoming totally taken over by sensual indulgences or passions, not losing control in the face of anger, fears or other negative emotions, and becoming "pure of heart" in thought and deed. It is the pathway of "perfecting the soul," "growing in grace" and "making illustrious virtue manifest" that is expressed through noble, consummate conduct.

The highest ideal, however, is to not just to work at becoming free of faults or "non-sick," which is becoming normal, but to cultivate the exceptional so that you can reach the stage of a saint. This can only happen through the cultivation road of self-improvement that uses mindfulness, *vipassana* and introspection. You want to follow the Hindu practice of *sadhuta*, or correctness/rectitude that results from deeply conforming to moral and ethical principles and having virtuous ways become your character traits. The goal is to become noble, good, virtuous or even saintly by *living* the virtues described in the holy texts you study rather than just memorizing the texts. You want to incorporate, assimilate, or basically just deeply absorb positive virtues into your very life so that they become part of yourself.

Self-perfection efforts – the work of *sadhuta* - are not just a pathway of inculcating rectitude and goodness in yourself to become more virtuous. They also constitute a pathway of expressing compassionate activity to help others, especially those in dire need, and *sadhuta* is a pathway that works to revitalize society. Therefore it entails selfless acts of charity and offerings to help others whether they be individuals or groups. This sacrificing of oneself for the behalf of others, and taking the entire world as one's family, is the meaning of saintliness and spirituality.

This effort of pursuing mental and behavioral purity, unrelentingly performing good deeds to help others, and engaging in irreproachable, immaculate conduct not only cultivates your personality but also transforms your Qi through those refinement efforts. You can, for instance, distinguish a wild animal from a tame animal, or an educated individual from an uneducated one because the differences in coarseness and refinement become obvious. In some cases you can feel the difference in energy refinement by sensing the Qi of those bodies. Spiritual cultivation should be a training process of elevation that puts you into the upper categories. Its pathway of self-improvement makes you fit for enlightenment, namely the transcendental body attainments that are only achieved through the help of higher spiritual beings, and a strict training regimen along these lines – a gradual and systematic process – is often laid out in monastic environments so people can achieve this. Monastic systems offer a regularity in training, along with a system of checks and balances for efforts at behavioral modification, where cultivating the path becomes an integral part of your whole life and the training helps you transform your personality as well as inner Qi body, but it is a process that takes time and deliberate practice just like the effort needed to master a musical instrument. Thus it is said of Yoga, "It is only when the correct practice is followed for a long time without interruptions and with a quality of a positive attitude and eagerness, that it can succeed." Most monastics do not know that this gradual purification process is going on but it is happening nonetheless.

When you consider *what you carry with you into subsequent lives* (incarnations) it includes the basics of your personality (character traits), certain predispositions or tendencies, interests in or proficiencies at special skills, good or bad relationships, the tendency or not to perform good deeds and acts of merit by helping others, and your long-term vows, goals or pledges of things you wish to accomplish along with the type of person you want to become. On the spiritual path you should be cultivating every one of these aspects so that you get better each and every life in all these ways and more. This is how you earn the merit to attain enlightenment.

Perfection-kaya is the necessary pathway of self-perfection that moves you in this direction. It also involves cultivating wisdom and skillfulness, but the root basis is to cultivate splendid virtuous ways and to continuously pursue this endeavor until you reside in the highest levels of excellence (excellent states). "Wisdom" is the knowledge or understanding of cause and effect that, together with a tranquil mind of calm stability, helps you make smart decisions in life. It helps you determine the proper behavior for different circumstances or form wise expectations of possible outcomes. Thus wisdom, knowledge and study as a unit become a necessity for compassionate activity and consummate conduct.

Wisdom training entails studying widely to increase your knowledge, understanding and skillfulness in various areas of life. The more you read and the more skills you acquire the more you will excel in worldly life, and the more you will be able to contribute your brilliance to the world. The goal or aspiration is to become able to create excellent states for yourself and for larger and larger groups of relationships, and eventually the world.

This is indeed the road of self-cultivation, self-improvement or *Samskara-kaya* (Perfection-kaya) that involves cultivating your personality, ethics, virtues, values, wisdom, knowledge, skillfulness and conduct. You are to *cultivate your virtues to brilliance, to walk the way of the highest good, in all activities manifest the highest virtues of excellence, to make your cultivated virtues manifest in helping people, and to pursue such endeavors until you rest and reside in the highest states of excellence.*

Naturally, Perfection-kaya involves improving your body as well including its form, health and fitness potential. It basically includes improving your general physical health, preparedness and fitness. During the spiritual path you should not neglect exercise, which is an unfortunate deficit in most religious traditions, and should perform muscle stretches, strength training and cardio-vascular activities that improve your health and fitness. For instance, Shakyamuni Buddha was a martial artist before getting married and Zen master Bodhidharma taught stretching exercises to Chinese Buddhist monks at Shaolin Temple since they were neglecting their bodies during their cultivation. Zen masters within the Zen school should work to reestablish this emphasis on physical culture that includes inner energy work in additional to physical exercise. It should also include the proper breathing for every type of activity, which is addressed nowhere. For instance, while Hatha Yoga teaches you certain rhythmical forms of breathing, it does not teach that you should breathe in such and such a way while running, when concentrating, when meditating, when you are experiencing anxiety, when freediving, when performing physical work and so on.

You don't want to just exercise your body and improve your health but also want to improve your mind-body coordination and your *sovereignty over your inner energy*. Personal exercises for controlling your breathing and internal energy will not only calm your personality and mind but will increase your internal Qi circulation for the benefit of purifying your inner subtle body. The basic factors of fitness to improve include your body's flexibility, agility, coordination, strength, endurance and speed.

In addition to practicing personal virtues such as filial piety, honesty, trustworthiness, fairness, justice, righteousness, humanity, peacefulness, compassion and kindness, spiritual teachings emphasize that you must engage in altruistic behavior that focuses on helping others. You must accumulate merit for the path by performing good deeds, which becomes your major occupation after achievement.

All people are connected together. All people are your brothers and sisters regardless of the racial, gender, national, religious or other differentiations we make using our mind. Hence Guru Nanak's injunction, "Accept all humans as your equal and let them be your only sect." Therefore we should treat all people with loving kindness, concern and have compassion to help them with care whenever possible. We are all members of a universal brotherhood due to each one of us being a non-intrinsic component of

Shakti with equal worth to everything else. Furthermore, we are all within each other due to infinite interdependence. Most important of all, we all share the same True Self - the one fundamental self-nature that is our singular ground state of being. There is only one fundamental Self in all of us. We are all equally manifestations of this unchanging True Self. Therefore, the ability to openly accept all others and act towards them with thoughtfulness and benevolence is how you merit the heavenly body attainments that constitute enlightenment, which is by eschewing your own self-centeredness and taking the welfare of others, who are another part of your body, as an overriding concern. That is essentially the career path of a Buddha, which is centered around helping others.

Doing good deeds to help others is called different things in different spiritual traditions: loving others, teaching the people, renovating the people, performing good works, being a good neighbor, helping the poor, altruism, philanthropy, charitable works, being a Good Samaritan, helping orphans, widows and the poor or oppressed, doing good deeds, or accumulating merit. This is an essential portion of the requirements for spiritual attainments, and absolutely essential for the spiritual path because otherwise you would not be worthy of the blessings. The way that you "manifest your virtues and excellences" is by making the effort to help others.

You should promote, create and applaud any positive changes people experience within their lives, including changes that will help the subsequent generations after you are gone, and this tendency must become part of your natural character as well as the trait of fairness, justice or righteousness to do what is right, protect what is right, push to create or advance what is right and basically make things better for others. Sikhism provides many admirable examples of these principles. You must conduct yourself so that you become increasingly noble in character and conduct, so that you constrain your natural malicious animal temperament, and cultivate higher virtues that purify your animal nature so that your life improves (or at least suffering is forestalled), and so that you improve the lives of others. One is rewarded with the spiritual body attainments not just because you are virtuous/pure but because you become devoted to helping others.

Taoism in general says that you need to accumulate 3,000 great good deeds (saving a single life is considered one great good deed) and 800 minor good deeds in order to deserve enlightenment, which it calls "Immortality" since the transcendental bodies live for a long time and can escape reincarnation in the lower realms. In Taoism the stages of attainment are not called Arhats but Immortals. The Taoist adept Ge Hong said that you need to accumulate 300 good deeds to become an earth immortal (Srotapanna or Sakadagamin) and 1,200 to become a celestial immortal (Anagamin). The Earth Immortal and Spirit Immortal stages correspond to the deva body attainment and then the Causal body attainment respectively. Ge Hong's numbers simply symbolize the fact that you need to perform acts of merit to be worthy of the stages of enlightenment. Taoism also states that the key to immortality, namely enlightenment, is that "you cannot exist for yourself," which means you must develop the mind and behavior of compassionately aiding others.

Mencius said you needed to nourish your vital force (Qi) with righteous deeds to attain enlightenment. Confucius said you have to make your virtue brilliant, serve people (in need and deed), and walk the path of highest good so that you reside in the highest level of behavioral excellence. Confucius said that you need to manifest your virtue in deeds that help the people, which he called teaching the people, loving the people or renovating/revitalizing the people. Western culture would add to this list the behavioral golden mean of moderation, which is the rule of living according to temperance and *avoiding hubris* so that your actions appropriately stay within reasonable bounds.

The basic principle is that only those who work at polishing themselves to become more virtuous[20] and work on purifying their thoughts, personality and behavior, and those who unselfishly work at benefitting others can achieve the Tao. In other words, you must work on assimilating moral ethics as well as noble values and virtues into your personality, and must also perform many good deeds in order to merit the subtle body attainment. This is related to the idea that if you are good then God will help you. Only an ethical, virtuous individual who behaves responsibly and looks beyond their own interests, who focuses on people's dignity, happiness and welfare, and who actively works to help society, is worthy of a body with powers above others. How do you become this way? You must devote yourself to a system of regular practice that leads to such goals. You need a system that emphasizes certain traits, behaviors and training exercises with regularity. This is why many people enter the holy life.

The spiritual path is not divorced from active engagement with society, in particular to help reduce people's sufferings and bring about better conditions for their existence. Four important keywords are loving-

---

[20] See the self-improvement stories of Liao Fan, Benjamin Franklin, and Wang Yang-Ming in *Move Forward: Powerful Strategies for Creating Better Outcomes in Life* by Bill Bodri and Christian mindfulness practice in *The Mystical Path of Christian Theosis*.

kindness, caring, compassion and effort. The idea of loving one's neighbor is that we should want everyone to experience peace, joy, health and prosperity in their life, and so we should intervene in people's lives and world affairs to make this happen wherever possible. While Confucianism calls making these efforts "loving the people" or "instructing (teaching) the people," which also includes leading the people by becoming an exemplary model of behavior, the idea is to actively create positive change in people's lives. You "love people" by *doing good deeds* to help those in need, and by working to solve problems that plague society at large. Love is not to be considered simply an emotion but a demonstration through loving activity. The idea is to spread happiness and blessings to many people and to remove their woes through your deeds, and by bringing happiness and benefit to others you will contribute to the welfare of people. If this becomes a feature of your personality, this is how you attain the merit required for enlightenment.

For your own life, you need to become more active and create the beneficial conditions necessary for experiencing greater happiness, health, peace and prosperity in your own life. You must *do* in order to *improve*. You must work at creating better life conditions for the now and for your future, which not only includes the health of your body but your living conditions. You must learn more knowledge and master more skills, and then apply them.

As regards your mind, you need to learn how to generate positive emotional states as your natural outlook such as upbeat optimism, cheerfulness or sunniness and even glow or shine. You must learn how to control your mind so that it becomes predominantly occupied by positive states rather than negatives ones. You need to learn how to control dissonant mental states, how to banish afflictive emotions, and must always conduct yourself properly in irreproachable conduct. You have to become a better person in what you think, say and do.

To appear in the world as a source of benevolence for others (who offers kindness, compassion, empathy and altruistic help/assistance) you need to cultivate wisdom, skillfulness, discipline, patience and virtuous behavior. Then you can (1) offer teachings, instructions and training to others; (2) protection, safety, security, refuge, defense, courage, bravery, guardianship, emotional comfort, emotional support and fearlessness to others; and (3) can actually help them in terms of giving charitable resources, your time, money, energy, and efforts to help solve their problems, reduce their sufferings or produce a better future for them. The ideal is to do all you can do to help others in all the ways you can whenever you can.

Animals have two incessant worries in nature – to obtain food and prevent themselves from becoming food for others. They seek things to eat but don't want to be eaten. They are either predator or prey, and the fear of scarcity haunts the predator as it hunts for food while the fear of predation haunts the prey as it tries to avoid being hunted and killed. This is why human attention naturally veers toward either the highest opportunity or highest threat, which is because the evolutionary root of this duo is the search for food or predators. These two concerns are like the human needs for resources (wealth) and protection (safety or security), and we organize ourselves in cooperative, collaborative, peaceful societies united by social cohesion precisely so that we can obtain food and resources, and become protected from threats such as warlike outsiders, exploitation/oppression by the powerful, injustice or the worst behaviors of each other.

Hence, two basic forms of charity are that (1) you can give to others resources (of nourishment or sustenance) such as jobs and money, or (2) you can establish forms of protection (justice, fairness, security, safety, self-defense skills, policing, protective relationships, laws within society, military force, etc.) that give people a sense of security, safety and encouragement in their lives that creates comfort by removing their fears. We have quite a few opportunities in life to affect the well-being of others, and these are the major ways in which we can and should do so. All individuals are seeking prosperity and protection (including protection from being oppressed by those in power) just as animals seek food to eat and seek to protect themselves so as not to be eaten. The two major forms of charity are to help others in these directions.

A third form of charitable giving is that (3) you can also give people various teachings (*dharma*) so that they can raise their state of existence. For instance, there is a famous saying, "Give a man a fish and you feed him for a day, but teach a man to fish and you feed him for his life." Naturally giving people *dharma* (teachings) includes teachings about the road of spiritual cultivation and enlightenment that takes them out of the lower realms of cyclic existence and suffering forever.

When you provide these things we say that you are loving one another, instructing the people, caring for others, helping society, rectifying the people, or one of a thousand different phrases that indicate you are showing kindness, love and compassion to other people. Providing these three forms of charity to others is what makes you a superior human being rather than just an animal.

If you do not cultivate good behavior and virtuous ways in your character and if helping others is not one of your natural tendencies (characteristics) then no spiritual beings with transcendental bodies will help you achieve the higher spiritual bodies in life because you wouldn't merit them. Without such a personality you might even harm people with the powers they provide. Therefore as a spiritual adherent, such as a layman, monk or nun, at the very minimum you should work very hard to transform your Qi and personality so that you get a chance to complete the task in Heaven if you don't complete it during life. The assistance of spiritual beings for your spiritual transformation is absolutely essential for stimulating, purifying and transforming the Qi/Prana of your body and its Qi channels so that your Qi flow within your subtle body strengthens – which makes you stronger, calmer and healthier – and you can eventually eject a subtle body out of your physical shell. They must use their own energies inside you to move your Qi to help this process of transformation, which is a process of Qi purification of your Yin Qi and Yang Qi, otherwise you cannot succeed on your own. Who will do that for you if you are not a virtuous individual? This necessity is why aspirants usually train under a qualified spiritual master.

If you do not cultivate your body's Qi/Prana, namely your vital energy or life force, then you will not be able to feel internally light or become able to generate and liberate an independent spiritual body, composed of your Qi/Prana, from the sheath of your physical body whilst alive. You won't be able to achieve a stable micro-flow mental state either without being optimally healthy in terms of your Qi circulation, breathing and health.

In other words, enlightenment is impossible without improving your internal Qi cultivation. You must engage in many spiritual practices to cultivate and purify the Qi/Prana of your physical nature and make its circulation flow much better so that your internal subtle body made of Qi can finally attain liberation while you are alive and you can escape the material plane of form. This is a feat of internal Qi Yoga.[21] Once again, in addition to your personal *tapas* or *sadhana* (work at spiritual cultivation) external spiritual help is also needed for emancipation or liberation.

On the spiritual path, discipline is especially needed for sticking to a plan of regular cultivation effort and restraint from sexual activities that reduce your inner Qi treasury. If you are a man you must cultivate sexual restraint/discipline so as not to carelessly dissipate your Jing (semen) and Qi while on this pathway. If you are a man and let the "elixir" (Jing or

---

[21] See *Neijia Yoga* in particular.

semen) leak through ejaculation then your Qi/Prana will be lost along with your semen, and then the force of that energy will not be available for opening up and purifying your body's Qi channels, especially the upwards reaching channels within your spine. That internal energy must not be lost because it is necessary for strengthening the integrity of the subtle body that is intrinsically inside your physical body, and as your etheric double is what people normally consider your soul.

"Without water in the boiler there will be no steam in the pipes. Without gas in the tank there will be no power in the car." If you lose your Jing you will lose your Qi/Prana, which is why men typically feel weak after ejaculation (or physical excesses of various sorts). Without this Qi/Prana you will not be able to purify your inner subtle body incorporated within the matrix of your physical body. Shakyamuni Buddha said you cannot attain enlightenment if you endlessly succumb to lust, which is very hard to completely eradicate, and hence he restated this same principle in a different way. This is one of the many reasons why men practice celibacy on the spiritual path, which is for the conservation of their inner Qi that is necessary for physical transformation. The continence of celibacy (sex sublimation) is hard to maintain, however, unless you also follow the auxiliaries that include diet, being selective about the company you keep, and being careful what you expose yourself to as influences since they may lead to impure thoughts that produce sexual activity.

If you do not cultivate meditation practice (and in particular mindfulness witnessing practice) then you will always have the tendency to become fused with your thoughts, habits, perspectives and attitudes, and solidify the control that neural templates have over your life. This will cut off your possibilities for greater growth, evolution and spiritual progress. You will not be able to fully transcend your animal tendencies nor ennoble your character to its highest potential if you don't learn how to free yourself from recurrent improper thought patterns or impulses. Ingrained mental perspectives and limiting beliefs, such as thinking that your self-identity must be a certain way, will also hold you back if you maintain them. Mental watchfulness can help you catch yourself making errors like this so that you can detach from these lines of thinking and conduct.

Furthermore, if you do not practice meditation then your mental state will always cling to your Qi/Prana and thereby inhibit its free circulation within you. If you continue to tightly hold/cling to thoughts as a habit this will prevent the vital energy within your body from arising and moving in the ways that will naturally purify your inner Qi force, so people practice meditation to learn mental detachment for this benefit among many others.

Meditation practice also teaches you how to focus and concentrate your ordinary mind that typically jumps from subject to subject like a monkey. It teaches you how to enter a quiet zone within your mind. Gradually, over time, it enables you to quiet the afflictions that constantly bombard your mental states and if you use introspective wisdom, you can often unravel the source of those afflictions at their root so that they are gone forever. Introspection allows you to reassess yourself objectively, take efforts to reboot and get better.

Mindfulness is a common meditation practice. It entails becoming aware of everything that flows through your mind. It means to know any desires, greed, hatred, or even good things that automatically arise within your mind, but not to necessarily follow those trains of thought. Mindfulness teaches you the skill of watching them come and go without becoming enmeshed, merged, fused or identified with them.

Mindfulness does not have the goal of eliminating or suppressing thoughts but of noticing them as they arise, but through that detachment your mind tends to clarify and brighten. Through the detachment of refusing to be bound to your thought-stream and the momentum of where it would take you, you can start transcending your animal nature and then your human nature to cultivate a spiritual nature. An engrossed identification or fusion with your thoughts might have you continue doing something wrong regardless of wisdom to the otherwise. However, by being a detached observer of your thoughts you can pay attention to what is happening and realize what you are doing due to that distancing, and so through a detached watchfulness you can correct wrong activities in your life. This will improve your life tremendously.

A detached but clear knowing of our thought-stream becomes a habit due to meditation practice, although this only happens after months of practice to develop this tendency. Nonetheless it will free us from remaining hostage to our emotional mind and our physical desires. It will enable us to transcend our personality patterns, assumed limitations and other sticky patterns and conditionings we have built up over time that create a false identify, suppress our Qi/Prana, and inhibit our full vitality because we try to conform to something that isn't us. It allows us to reclaim who we really are and focus on being ourselves rather than trying to be someone we're not. It allows us to rise above cultural customs, traditions or laws to be more authentic, follow our conscience and do what is right. Detachment frees us from our preconditioning, our prior programming and our limitations that may have been running us for years so that our authentic self can shine in life. You don't have to earn your promotion within the system, so if each of us *holds to our authentic self* against whatever may try to move it we will then live a richer life and become noble men and women of principle.

If you do not learn to cultivate an open (empty) mind that can accept everything then you will not be able to bear what you see with your subtle body when you become a deva, including all the hidden bad thoughts and evil actions of ordinary human beings that are going on all around you every day. It will then be difficult to practice kindness, love and compassion that are the prerequisites for success on the spiritual path. You must respect others despite their faults and failings, but you must also insist on righteousness and accountability. You must place a great emphasis on self-correction too, otherwise you will become haughty and arrogant and tend toward hubris when you have power. No one can become a Buddha if they do not love people and righteousness, practice self-correction, and cultivate a mind of kindness, humility, tolerance and acceptance as regards others.

Without always cultivating a self-corrective watchfulness of your mind that inspects its own contents – which itself frequently contains bad thoughts and negative emotions that require correction – you will tend to become more arrogant, proud, contemptuous and critical of others, and thus unwilling to help those in need who have failings while you refuse to examine your own deficiencies that need correction.

If you don't recognize that everyone is ultimately spiritually equal to one another *and also imperfect* then you will tend towards arrogance and pride rather than humility, and develop the tendency to hubris and abuse using your spiritual powers over others. This is why learning to serve others is important, including your community, because by selflessly serving others you become more humble and overcome your ego. Watchfulness enables you to cultivate virtue and ethics through the attendant practice of self-correction. The traits of repentance and contrition are therefore emphasized in many religions because they lead to self-correction, better human beings, and a better society accordingly.

You also will not be able to ever find mental peace if you do not practice meditation and rest your mind's tendency to relentlessly produce thoughts and desires. Only when mental afflictions, annoyances, and the flames of craving-desire are extinguished can your mind touch true peace, rest, repose, contentment or tranquility. Of course there is naturally a limit to this because *without desire or craving you would never give rise to any actions*, which would of course result in death because there would be no impetus to eat, drink, defecate, or even live. The point is that you should cultivate *a free mind centered on the pure self* so that you attain the ability to remain impassive to (detached from) emotions or impure impulses when necessary, and remain temperate (restrained, disciplined and levelheaded) in the face of the passions, pleasures and sensual indulgence. *One needs to cultivate the golden mean in one's own behavior and a solid approach is to pursue the meditation practice of detachment and introspection.*

If you do not practice witnessing meditation where you always watch your thoughts to polish your behavior then you will never be able to cultivate the virtue, propriety and the consummate conduct required of the spiritual ladder. Without self-observation (self-witnessing) and introspection – which require mindfulness meditation practice – you will never become able to fully transform your habits of prior conditioning so that you continually manifest more beneficial states of mind and can abide in mental purity. Accordingly, you will never refine your Qi/Prana to a higher level of purity, refinement and excellence either just as Confucius advised.

If you do not cultivate concentration skills to develop mental stability, you will always flit from thought to thought without ever being able to settle mentally and find mental peace. A wandering mind is usually a scattered, distracted, unhappy mind whereas a mind that can focus and concentrate is usually a happy mind free of confusion that can accomplish great things. This is another reason for concentration practice.

Without concentration skills you will not be able to remain focused long enough to perform great deeds since most great achievements require longsuffering in persistence and perseverance. You can consider this "sustained concentration practice" that is devoted to a goal. You need to learn this because you are in charge of your own self-determination. You are the one who is in control of your life, your mindset and your efforts. Concentration and commitment to a course of action (which is also a form of concentration or "staying with-itness") are key skills necessary for success in many life ventures *including spiritual cultivation*. These are virtues you must cultivate because to achieve success you must stay on the path.

If you cultivate witnessing meditation practice then learning and self-correction as well as peace and blissful mental micro-flow will come easy. You will become able to abandon language and experience a lucid mental state of clear presence that is quiet (because the self-narrative is quiet due to words being absent) yet there is still clear knowing – a clarity of knowingness. It is a state where you feel even more alive. Knowledge can know Knowledge without need of an overtly loud I-presence, and it can experience the bliss of life even though its true state is selflessness.

Spiritual cultivation does not just mean to practice meditation and an oversight of your thought-processes so that you don't just robotically follow whatever arises within your mind. It means to cultivate character virtues within your personality that include mental strength and toughness so you can resist failure (giving up) when you are faced with overwhelming odds or strong emotions such as fear or hopelessness. Persistence and perseverance demand this.

Cultivation is meant to help you develop the skills you need to *survive and thrive in life,* and not just be able to live the simple sinless life of a monk, nun or ascetic shut off from the world because they live a protected life in a monastery, cloister, ashram, cave, etcetera. The emptiness/selflessness of the self and world does not mean we should withdraw from life or avoid its problems. It gives us the potential for self-development, greater creative powers and greater enjoyment of our existence.

Since your struggles for living will always resume in a new life you must work at self-perfection and developing the skills for life in this one. If you don't achieve enlightenment you still want to leave this life having accumulated merit from developing your skills, your way of thinking, improving your personality and from helping others. You want to have developed shining character traits to take with you into Heaven, as well as specific skills, knowledge and wisdom you desire and therefore cultivation is never divorced from developing your character and personality.

Basically, meditation practice and self-review are necessary exercises for cultivating your personality, thoughts, conduct and actions towards purity, virtue and merit. This is *sadhuta,* or the pursuit of purity, rectitude, goodness, nobility and even saintliness. Meditation and introspective self-review also help you cultivate mental peace and purity, purify your Qi/Prana, and progress you towards attaining the subtle body that is the first stage of genuine enlightenment that is never just some mental breakthrough or realization.

Chapter 12
MEDITATION PRACTICE[22]

Many spiritual paths insinuate that there is some way that you can mentally "realize your fundamental nature" – whether though meditation states of thought or thoughtlessness or it just spontaneously happens after lots of cultivation practice – and that this will somehow produce *nirvana*, *Moksha*, liberation, or spiritual salvation. However, the very best experiences that can ever happen to you through consciousness is that you undergo peak experiences, experience beautific mental states, develop some special mental skills, or periodically develop some type of amazing understanding (thought realizations) that may or may not permanently change your character or behavior.

You cannot mentally cultivate a mental scenario of "enlightenment" that is some type of omnipotent, omnipresent magic mindset or mind. There is no such liberation or salvation. However, you can cultivate *higher transcendental physical bodies* that become the new center of your life. Even so, a life on a different plane of existence will have just an ordinary mind as we find here. Nonetheless, during that cultivation process you might start clinging a little less to your ego, cleanse your mind of wandering thoughts and impurities, phenomena, you might reduce your negative propensities and character traits, and you might gain all sorts of other benefits that clean up your conduct and character. You might bump into many unusual mental states on the cultivation trail, but after they are gone you are the same person you were previously. However, you should work to permanently change your body, your personality/character, your way of thinking and dong things and you should try to make the world a better place too.

---

[22] See *Meditation Case Studies*, *Visualization Power*, and *The Little Book of Meditation*.

The primal substratum of the universe – our true self-nature – is empty of attributes such as phenomena or energy, which is why it is sometimes called "Emptiness" (an unbounded absolute vacuum of all things), so because It lacks any phenomenal content you can never think about It and realize this Beingness through thought. No concepts can capture It. You can only learn about It such as the fact that you are this unmanifest fundamental essence-entity, this ground state essence of manifest reality, and Shakti the universe is its manifestation.

The terms "Emptiness," "Void," *dharmakaya* or *sunyata* are used to represent our fundamental substrate/nature and thereby encourage an analogous meditation practice of emptying your mind of wandering thoughts and afflictions so that you can experience a naturally quieter mental state that is free of fabrications just as It is. Sometimes when the mind is extremely quiet and it seems as if there are not thoughts at all, or you somehow bump into a peak experience of no-thought, people take this for enlightenment when it is just a temporary state that can (at most) encourage your practice. It is definitely desirable to experience (what seems to be) a thoughtless state of non-ego that seems open, pristine, empty, clear and universal, but it is not enlightenment. Actually, such experiences are usually blessings/grace given to you by someone with an Immanence body or higher to encourage your practice. The Fifth Patriarch of Zen said to the Sixth Patriarch that if you do not see the fundamental true nature of your mind then cultivating will bring you no benefit. In other words, if you don't touch quiet mental states like this now and then you won't know how to practice correctly.

The natural state of the mind is a peaceful clear state just like the solitude of the fundamental substratum (our self-nature) yet it is replete with the capability of awareness. You are mentally imitating your True Self (intrinsic nature) when you achieve a tranquil mind of awareness that know thoughts but doesn't attach to thoughts, and where your inner narrative is quiet but your mind seems brilliant with illumination/knowing, but practicing to achieve this ability through *vipassana* or other exercises doesn't mean that you should suppress your thoughts or become like a babbling idiot who does not think because they're sunk in oblivion.

The idea espoused is that when not engaged in concentration, decision-making, analyzing etc. then your consciousness should be naturally calm and peaceful without elaborations just like the primordial universal substratum, your True Self, and then your personality will then enjoy a natural bliss of being stress-free, calm, serene and tranquil. Your Qi flow within that state, if you cultivated well, can help you achieve a state of brilliant open awareness or illumination. The state of inner peace and calm, with or without brilliant awareness or even flow, is much more enjoyable than the perennial excitedness of mental wandering. Your mind is in its best state for analyzing and making deliberations or decisions when it is peaceful and at ease, and since inner peacefulness is also one of the most enjoyable mental states it is targeted as an objective in spiritual practice. Studies show that a mind enters into one of its happiest states when it becomes centered in the present moment like this.

To become more peaceful and clear, your mind should not attach to the thoughts that flow through it unless you are performing special mental concentrations, and from that dispassion as regards restless thoughts, emotions, afflictions and desires the background chatter you normally suffer will tend to empty out to produce tranquility. This is just one of the principles of consciousness, namely that if you let go of your thoughts and simply watch them with detachment then they will die down in volume and produce a mental realm that we term "empty" or clear. Furthermore, our natural state is peaceful and happy until we disturb it and the practice of meditation helps you retrieve that natural underlying state of peace and calm that lacks formations so is blissful.

If you learn how to rest your mind (*shamatha*) you can directly cultivate a state of peaceful emptiness where the mind seems to empty of internal dialogue and overt me-ness, and you can achieve this by engaging in thought-free meditation or by just watching your thoughts (*vipassana*) until they die down. This is called reaching cessation. To achieve a mental clarity where your mind is not inundated with chattering annoyances, but is only engaged with the object of interest, you can practice various meditation styles to free yourself of these unwanted distractions. The desire to refine your character to a higher stage of purity and perfection, and the ability to make good decisions, depends on cultivating a clear and balanced mind so spiritual schools give you a variety of techniques to arrive at these results.

The fundamental substratum of the universe always allows things to appear within It, and so you should also always allow thoughts to naturally arise in your mind rather than try to suppress consciousness to arrive at cessation. However, you should correct whatever arises that is errant in your mind. You must correct your thoughts but not forget your state of presence and become overly identified with your thinking. Since the fundamental substrate does not interfere with any emanation by clinging to it, you should never overly attach to your thought-stream such as by letting anger or jealousy consume you via fusion, refusing to be corrected by facts due to egoity, and not leaving behind the past of suffering or pain so that you can grow past those experiences.

Religions advance various analogies to the original nature – such as Aquinas's description of divine simplicity where God is a oneness without divisibility or attributes in any sense whatsoever – in order to promote meditation practices that let us touch the inner purity of our empty awareness that is free of thoughts, which in turn produces a blissful inner peace that is like the unmoving original nature. Spiritual masters say things like "the Pure Beingness is the same as awareness," "pure witnessing is one's true nature," "cognize the Self as one's true nature," "the fundamental nature is consciousness without consciousness," "the Self is pure consciousness," "you need to recede to the state before the body," "Parabrahman is the origin of all knowledge," "Brahman is the only witness," and so forth in order to encourage thought-free meditation practice. Hinduism, for instance, says that liberation is the stabilization of the soul in its Real Self (the fundamental substratum) where there is a cessation of all pain, attachments and true fulfillment due to mental purity. Patanjali says, "Nothing in all Creation is so like God as silence." These are all just statements meant to encourage meditation practice.

The universal foundational nature is not consciousness at all nor does it possess consciousness as an attribute since it is purely an inanimate attributeless substratum like empty space, but these ideas are promoted to encourage people to cultivate a pure mind. For instance, if you attain the Immanence (Great Golden Arhat) body then that body would be your *atman* or highest purified self (unless there was a yet higher body possible). You can affect lower energies with this body, of course, but that doesn't mean that your realm of energy-matter that composes your body is consciousness.

Many religions declare that you are the embodied Self. In other words, you are a manifestation, attribute or function of the uniform original essence that Itself lacks consciousness and all other attributes, such as a soul-ego of personality - and it would be most natural if your mind was as detached from existence as your real essence is so that you could closely mimic the nature of your true nature. This is just a skillful method of encouraging meditation practice rather than truth, and is designed to encourage meditation because of its many benefits for consciousness.

Religions often make analogies about the original nature being like pure consciousness, empty mind or being the ultimate "Witness" or true knower and so forth because they want to encourage meditation practices where your thoughts die down and a realm of crystal pure perception remains, which is like the perceptive capabilities of the higher spiritual beings since their bodies are only energy. Even so, the mind of someone who is enlightened is exactly the same as yours is now, so these are only practice instructions in order to achieve certain cultivation benefits. One practice is to continuously watch your mind-stream so that your mental clarity brightens, but to be detached from your thoughts and whatever else runs through your mind so that its extraneous activity outside of your focus/attention eventually subsides or "empties." The mindfulness practice of inner watching is also a method of desire modification because it allows you to see that your cravings, desires and impulses are just thoughts *rather than you*, and this realization helps you learn detachment as a natural quality of yourself.

Basically, religions want people to start becoming more aware of their mental contents because this self-awareness will enable them to control their behavior better as well as learn from mistakes and leave behind the past. By observing their thoughts they can adjust for emotional biases and overcome distortions in judgment. Consequently they will make better decisions for their actions without holding onto a legacy of prior emotions. Mindfulness teaches you to break through the spell of becoming lost in thought so that you can notice that *a thought is just a thought rather than you*. Because of this realization you can more easily transcend poor thoughts or negative emotions and resist their pull so that your behavior is always more proper.

As stated, becoming aware of the contents of your mind can help you calm your mind because if you remain separate from your thoughts and don't feed them energy they, and other mental agitations, will gradual calm down and leave a quiet realm in their place. As another instance, if we cultivate a non-attached awareness of our feelings associated with our desires, we can decrease our desires by lessening their hold on us. Not only can we better resist them, but we will thereby reduce the pain and suffering they cause us whenever they go unsatisfied.

These are all very positive life results, and just a few of the purposes behind meditation practice. They are good results for individuals and good for society as well. The lesson from these results is that we need to detach from clinging to our thoughts and stop identifying with them so that we can clearly see them as independent from us, realize when they are wrong rather get blinded within them due to entrainment, and then change them when we find them to be errant. This practice enables us to rise above our habitual tendencies, focus our attention on the experience at hand, and in general just be more open to better thinking and behaving. If we detach from our cravings, passions, sensual desires and errant mental tendencies (because we can watch our minds in a detached manner), and if we can learn to let go of playing with our thoughts, our wandering thought-streams will die down to reveal a naturally peaceful state of mind that is *pristinely clear, comfortable, stress-free, relaxing and blissful*. This is a plus because it will bring us peace and rejuvenate us – all due to meditation practice. With great practice we can even reach and experience a state of internal peace that is akin to the contented pre-linguistic state of the mind before thoughts are born.

This empty state of mind - where you are still present and fully aware - is called pristine awareness or mental clarity. It is not supposed to be a dry stale clarity like dead tree Zen, but a blissful clarity where your vital energy is flowing inside you because you are healthy and you don't suppress that inner circulation to quiet your thoughts. Your vitality flows so well, in fact, that you can often forget the feeling of your body completely, or feel a subtle bliss in every body cell that is extremely comfortable. Your mind through meditation can reach a state that is quiet, tranquil and free of your inner narrative so that it becomes peaceful and yet you can know everything with extreme clarity through a lucid, wakeful aliveness that is accompanied by a subtle physical bliss. Thus it is sometimes called a "bright mind" or stage of illumination. However, this is the state of your ordinary mind when you are really healthy, and this is the "ordinary mind" stage that masters want you to reach in Zen.

The Zen school does not want you to suppress your inner flow of vitality in order to produce a suppressed, quieter state of mind nor does it want you to suppress yourself in order to become a "good boy" who can follow the rules with the result that you abandon the fullness of vibrant life and become like a eunuch with castrated vitality. Many enlightened spiritual masters (not the charlatans), you will discover, are really vibrant characters who live life to the fullest because that's what you are supposed to achieve. Zen master Nan Huai-chin used to point out that a true Buddha was the combination of a saint, hero, thief and Mafiaso. Therefore the path to enlightenment is not one of becoming an ostentatiously well-behaved but emasculated goody two shoes or well-trained show-pony conformist who always follows the rules. Those individuals would hardly be qualified to save their nation in a time of trouble or distress.

As stated, religions want people to be examining their minds constantly so that individuals learn how to control their thoughts and emotions, especially mental afflictions, and you can learn how to do this through meditation practice. *If you can control your mind then you can control your behavior, change your character, and thus ultimately control your fate.* You can transform yourself into someone worthy of enlightenment. The spiritual path involves gaining as much control as possible over your mental processes, as well as developing your mind's cognitive abilities and other mental and physical skills to their fullest. That's what you need to do as a living being who has a body and consciousness. All these benefits will make your life better.

Meditation traditions commonly make the analogy that a relatively empty clear mind, pure consciousness, or pristine clear awareness is akin to the foundational substrate of the universe devoid of transformations (since it is like attribute-less empty space). In this analogy, our thoughts are like Shakti the Logos, which somehow *spontaneously* arises within the fundamental nature. They are like energy (what cultivation schools call the "wind element") that somehow arises within an empty fundamental substrate and which then goes about its business producing uncountable transformations that evolve endlessly.

These are the "karmic formations" or "constructed fabrications" of Buddhism that are the second link in the twelve-step chain of interdependent origination. Buddhism says we don't know how the primordial empty substrate that is perfectly pure (stainless) and free of influences gives birth to any type of manifestation that is Itself but different in appearance, and yet it happens. It calls our understanding "ignorance," which is the first of the twelve steps in the chain of dependent origination. Ignorance means that we don't know how manifestation happened, which is the second step in the chain of dependent origination. Hence you don't know how, but the universe/Creation somehow does manifest out of a void of nothingness.

Religions also often say that the natural state of the mind is empty of thoughts, the fundamental state of the mind is empty, the fundamental nature of the mind is unborn/unmanifest, the nature of the mind is free of defilements and so on. Once again, these are just various ways to encourage people to practice meditation where you detach from fusing with your thought-stream and let thoughts subside into quietude. In particular, they want you to practice emptiness meditation where you try to experience a mental scenario empty of thoughts. They want you to practice being free of thoughts but disguise the intent with unusual practices or vocabulary.

For instance, Elder Aimilianos of Simonopetra said, "The meaning of 'pure prayer' has the same sense that is given to it by all the (Christian Church) Fathers. Pure prayer means prayer that is free of thoughts, prayer that does not introduce any outside elements; it contains no mental forms, shapes or images. Pure prayer is not the personal property of monks or a small group of individuals. It is for everyone; it is the one activity that is the most fitting to the human person."

Thus, even Christianity espouses the practice of emptiness meditation but calls it "pure prayer" or "centering prayer" or "sacred quietude." Different religions use different terms to refer to the same practice of training the mind to remain clear and aware and detached from thoughts and Qi-clinging while your attention remains undistracted by the mind's inner movements. They use different terms for same practice that is essentially meditation.

Thus, the world's religions commonly extol you to "cultivate tranquility," "be at peace," "separate yourself from your passions and desires," "transcend your thoughts and rise above your passions," "don't become attached to your thought-stream," "don't get entangled with your thoughts and lose your state of presence," "let go of your thoughts and surrender everything over to God," "be still and know the Lord," "center your thoughts on Him," "keep your mind always poised in Him," "think of He who cannot be lost," "let go of your past conditioning to become alive in the moment," "be here now" and so on. There are a thousand ways to instruct individuals to meditate without mentioning the word "meditation."

A common lesson is to maintain an awareness of your thought-stream, which is a separation from thoughts that ultimately gives you greater control of your thinking and behavior and puts you in a state of presence rather than foggy, dulling entrainment. You are not to become enmeshed within your thought-stream and identify with your thoughts unless it is for a special activity like concentration. Another lesson is to use various tricks that directly place you in an empty state of mind.

The practice of religious worship where you cultivate deep reverence for a deity is another practice that will quiet your mind because you reduce your mental chatter during acts of worship and obeisance. When performed in the correct way, religious worshipping practice can become another form of emptiness practice because the required humility of reverence is a way to silence your ego and pacify your thoughts. You must let go of your ego and thoughts when cultivating worship or reverence, which require humbleness and humility.

Selfless service on behalf of others, with the right feeling and attitude such as by forgetting your ego, can in this light be viewed as a form of worship as well. The act of creating a better world for others can be similarly viewed this way too. The more you can let go of your thoughts and ego and thereby release those ties on your thinking and vital energy (since thoughts and Qi are linked because thoughts can affect your Qi), the easier it is for your Qi/Prana to assume its most natural internal circulation.

That's the important part of such practices – the quieting of your mind and inner Qi transformation rather than the worship itself. Furthermore, during a time when you are letting go of your mind (your thinking's hold on your Qi) the easier it will be for spiritual beings to use their own Qi/Prana to help temper your Qi/Prana for the health of your body and purification of your subtle energy. On the other hand, if you strongly attach to your thoughts it will pervert the natural circulation of your inner Qi/Prana, and make it harder for heavenly beings to help you.

Advaita Vedanta says that in the motionless fundamental substrate (Parabrahman) of Absolute Aloneness, the One Without A Second, there somehow arose movement in the form of a manifestation of energy (wind) just as wind seems to mysteriously arise from nowhere within a vast empty sky. No one knows how this occurred in the formless, empty universal substrate that never undergoes any modifications. The intrinsic nature of that arising energy must still be the singular substratum Itself, from which all other phenomena also somehow developed based on that original evolute. The existence of the fundamental substrate does not depend upon the energy that arises within It, but the original fabrication of energy depends upon the fundamental essence as its support and substance - its foundational essence. As John 1:3 states, "All things came into being through Him, and without Him not one thing came into being."

In the same way, thoughts somehow arise within an empty mind of clear awareness, which some confusingly call a substrate of pure consciousness. Actually, everything that appears in the mind is "pure consciousness" or "purely consciousness." Our thoughts arise via a neural process we don't fully understand – laws of nature control our cortical functions and brain activity to determine how neurons interact with sensory inputs and with one another and our subtle energy to produce our conceptualizations – and however it's done thoughts indeed arise within our minds to produce a conventional world of phenomena and an inner narrative. They mentally produce for us a conditionally derived world of appearances that we then take as reality even though we know consciousness has faults that have produced errors in that picture. The world image that appears within us is only a similitude of the outside reality that cannot possibly capture the way that external reality actually is so Buddhism calls it an illusion or delusion. We simply create a limited *mind-only representation* replete with errors but this is what consciousness and our organs of perception provide. This is what has evolved for our species in order that we can adapt to the world to survive and replicate. We think we are always seeing the world but we are always just experiencing an image of the world within our consciousness – we experience our consciousness only. The base layer of reality (Shakti) is not consciousness, but the world we see inside ourselves is mind-only – a construction of consciousness-only.

The picture of reality that our thoughts and senses create is a quite limited, simplified picture of the world that is fraught with incompleteness, error and even time delay due to the period required for mental processing to build that picture. It is also filled with various misleading subjective biases that we add to it because of our past experiences and prejudices. We always superimpose biases (such as subconscious attitudes, opinions and emotions) upon situations, thus orienting ourselves improperly because these influences don't reflect the most actual state of affairs before us. Unconscious mental processing is always influencing our thoughts and experiences and therefore adding prejudicial biases to our mental state, which is why we must always watch our thoughts to correct them.

There are many different ways of experiencing and explaining the world and we cannot say which one is the best. Animals have senses that produce mental perceptions we cannot even imagine unless we describe them in terms of the five senses we already possess. For instance, some fish in the ocean do not use eyes but sense their surroundings due to pressure sensations throughout their body, and even though we explain it this way is this really the way they would explain this? Some people with synesthesia perceptually couple sounds with colors or tastes when those perceptions appear in their mind, and therefore experience the same world differently than others. Who knows the correct way to experience the world? There is none. There is just a conventionality we share among ourselves.

Furthermore, the thoughts and images we internally generate are a continuous stream of impermanent flickerings (chunks followed by chunks) that traverse our minds like a flowing dream. How can that be a reflection of true reality? They present a picture of a stable, monotonous world of solid objects that are actually always changing because they cannot stay the same for even an instant, yet our mind-stream ignores the instability of micro-changes and creates a smooth view of stability, refreshing it after milliseconds. Hence even our consciousness is discontinuous although it appears continuously flowing. Our consciousness is not continuous but occurs as a series of discrete chunks of perceptual moments that are refreshed every few tens to hundreds of milliseconds. So (1) external phenomena look monotonous throughout this view but never remain the same thing for even an instant because they are always transforming into something else (a new state) even though they falsely appear to be stable monotonous things, and (2) consciousness looks continuous too but is actually a series of separate quanta time slices that are linked together in a way that they appear unbroken in sequence.

Meditation helps you realize that thoughts follow one another in sequence, are not a dependable reality, but behind those thoughts and in-between those thoughts is a natural substratum of empty pure awareness that you can learn to access.

Most spiritual schools only promote meditation and other non-Qi spiritual practices since most practitioners will not succeed at generating the deva body during life. Meditation practice, however, will still help the faithful improve their lives in many ways by providing them with periods of stress-free mental peace, and by improving their mental clarity, health, longevity, conduct and fortune. *It is basically a tool for helping us develop various powers of consciousness and improve the usage of our consciousness because it* helps us gain the ability to correct the errors of consciousness. *Neijia* Qi/Prana work accomplishes some similar objectives as meditation, but unfortunately *nei-gong* will attract the involvement of devas who will often cause troubles for practitioners when they start playing with your thoughts or the Qi/Prana of your body on their own without supervision. Therefore most spiritual masters encourage meditation practice instead of *nei-gong* inner energy/breath work. For countless reasons, meditation is promoted as the foremost spiritual practice.

Although it is a form of mental training, meditation practice always leads to some measure of Qi/Prana purification, and *virtuous behavior will also refine the quality of your Qi/Prana as well.* Your Qi/Prana will automatically start to move more optimally when you let go of your mind-stream since it tends to affect your Qi since your Qi and thoughts are linked. When released from this linkage (because you are in an empty or detached state of mind where you don't attach to your thoughts) your Qi will then begin to undergo a purification process due to better circulatory movements. When your Qi moves through your Qi channels it clears them of obstructions through friction, and multiple revolutions through the channels will purify your Qi/Prana just as milk undergoes transformations through the churning that produces butter and other milk products.

If you refrain from holding onto your thoughts and your Qi/Prana it becomes easier for higher spiritual beings to assist you in these purifying transformations because they can enter into you and use their own energy to move and thus transform your energy. When meditating you will therefore start to purify your Qi/Prana because of such influences, but remember that this happens during prayer practice, mantra recitation and other spiritual practices too which is why Christian monks, Sufi Moslems, Jewish rabbis and others also achieve the Tao. Just as letting milk sit will let the heavy cream separate from the lighter liquid, the same principle applied to the mental realm means that meditation practice will enable your coarse thoughts to settle and then you can taste a bit of mental purity that you can then bring back with you into your regular life.

One of the natural results of purifying your Qi and improving its internal circulation is that you will live longer in this life and increase your longevity in Heaven as well. Virtuous conduct and positive emotions start purifying your Qi/Prana of its coarse animalistic nature, but for an ordinary individual are not as powerful at purifying your Qi as meditation practice, which in turn is not as powerful as *nei-gong* Qi practice. However, virtuous conduct, wholesome attitudes and positive emotions are also extremely important because they will color the quality of your subtle energy body with *samskaras* (behavioral predispositions, inclinations, tendencies) and this will affect your Qi enough that it will change your personality and help determine your character in a subsequent rebirth. Well all have a set point or baseline of characteristics hardwired into our personality due to our natal influences and conditioning, but we can change them if we work hard at self-perfection efforts and cultivation practices.

Transforming your character traits will affect your inner vitality and Qi flow, and during the Twelve Year kundalini transformation period countless spiritual masters will mentally activate your character traits connected with your body's Qi time and again, and will even be tested by their own teachers as to whether they can do this, in order to show students the connection between our personality patterns embedded within our neurons (*samskaras*) and our Qi/Prana. For long-term benefits, it is paramount for human beings to pursue virtuous conduct and high spiritual values. It is advantageous for everyone that each of us elevates our behavior so that positive patterns become predominant and produce not only happiness but irreproachable, noble, majestic conduct. Everyone should be working on bettering themselves as well as creating a better life for themselves and their family and for society too.

Meditation trains people to do this because it teaches us to focus our awareness on our mental doings and conduct so that individuals can start policing their thoughts, words and deeds (behavior) to become better human beings. This active policing for self-improvement and emendation (self-rectification) will better the current and future well-being of everyone, namely people's fates and fortunes. This inner attention will improve our mental skills for this life and also for our next incarnation within cyclic existence.

Meditation is the basis of all sorts of mindfulness, witnessing, watchfulness, awareness, self-observation, introspection, self-policing, self-assessment, self-correction, repentance, self-rectification or self-regulation practices that train your focus, attention and awareness so that you can bring your thoughts and actions *under greater volitional control*, thereby improving your life and fortune.

Meditation helps you cultivate a peaceful mind, and if your mind is calm and peaceful it becomes easier for you to act according to higher considerations rather than to become distracted by or entrained with passions and emotional impetus. Confucianism says, "refining one's person lies in balancing one's mind." In other words, cultivating oneself – your mind and behavior – lies in achieving inner balance. This doesn't just mean that you should only cultivate a calm, relaxed frame of mind because you should also cultivate a healthy body whose Qi flow is optimum as well, and you should always be open to experiences of joy and peak experiences.

When your mind becomes tranquil and clear (calm and balanced) you can make better deliberations, and thus much better decisions that will produce much happier outcomes in life. A balanced mind is a much more pleasant mental state as well because it is free of unstable irritations, agitations and other unwanted pollutions. A balanced mind has an easier time of acting from higher considerations (such as nobility) due to its greater perfection of purity, and by acting from a higher perspective you will not only make better decisions but become better able at resisting negative tendencies because you don't identify with them but see them for what they are – simply thoughts that need not impel you. This independence will improve your agility at changing situations for the better.

The inner calmness produced from meditation practice is a state of concentration that can lead to better performance, and the highest state of concentration is "flow" where you are catapulted to an extremely high level of performance in your active worldly engagements that you normally don't enter. It is a peak state – an optimal state of consciousness of focused intent and seeming effortlessness – where we feel our best and perform our best, and it starts from the experience of inner calmness and concentration where extraneous thought complexity does not get in the way of our engagement with experience. The state of flow is intrinsically rewarding and once touched people seek it for the rest of their lives. Those who have the most flow in their lives because they often enter "into the zone" are the happiest and most contented people on earth. Flow is one of the most enjoyable states of human existence, and we can prepare for it and access some of its characteristics through cultivation practices such as meditation.

Hence, one of the important reasons for regular meditation practice is that it trains you to be able to concentrate; it trains you to develop a tranquil mind from which you can make better judgments, deliberations or decisions for your actions and reactions; it enables you to detach from wrong courses of action because you are separate from those decisions and don't identify with them; and it also prepares you for the ability to naturally enter into states of micro-flow or macro-flow. "Macro-flow" is another name for the flow state of mind recognized by super athletes or craftsmen who lose all sense of themselves during their activities, while "micro-flow" is a mental flow state where only a few of the requirements for flow are fulfilled. In this book all flowlike states of mind are called "flow" even though they differ from the "effortless mind" flow states of research literature.

You want to do everything possible in life to make flow your natural state of existence, the default mental state for your ordinary mind. Therefore you should cultivate meditation practice to train at achieving some of the known characteristics of flow such as a quiet mind and concentration. This will add to your performance abilities and your enjoyment of life.

In a state of flow your concentration is nearly total because your mind is focused, your attention is heightened within its field of focus, and you put aside any distractions that might interrupt the task at hand. It seems as if there are no thoughts in a state of flow – it's just pure. You are and it is, and within that state you feel complete, alive, and everything falls into place just as during an internally quiet but blazing *Now state* of unfettered pristine consciousness. There is a merging of action and awareness and you might even lose your sense of time during a flow experience. This is because your awareness is narrowed down to the activity itself, which becomes your entire field of absorption, and within that space you can lose your sense of self and time.

Flow is a state of profound mental clarity that flows ... and meditation trains us to attain a similar state of flowing pristine clear awareness. A Yoga saying runs, "In deep meditation the flow of concentration is continuous like the flow of oil." Flow is a state that involves a high degree of concentration ... and the meditation practice of watching thoughts *is* prolonged flowing concentration practice. Within the state of flow there is emotional detachment that accompanies the high degree of clarity ... and meditation specifically trains us to achieve this detachment conjoined with clarity so that we can view things from a removed/distanced standpoint of dispassion. During flow there is a loss in our feeling of self-consciousness due to a merging of action and awareness ... meditation practice teach us to abandon the *loud* sense of the I-self that strongly appears when we attach to thoughts in order that we experience a special state of empty presence that lacks mental complexity. Of course you cannot actually get rid of the I-self, nor should you try, because then consciousness would not function and you would become as mindless as the natural world that just runs naturally without any self involved in the process. Actually you are like that but don't know it.

Research studies reveal that when people lose themselves in a task, such as when they are engaged within flow, portions of the superior frontal gyrus portion of the brain (which produces our sense of self and introspective self-awareness) start to deactivate and upon that deactivation of neuronal structures we experience profound mental alertness, attention and awareness while our mental chatter and complexity decreases. In flow your actions seem effortless and automatic where one right decision leads to the next right decision because the mind is operating so clearly, logically, fluidly, adaptively ... and the mindfulness meditation practice of watching our thoughts and behavior in order to correct them in real-time has the same purpose. During flow you mentally have immediate feedback on all your efforts where successes and failures are apparent, so your behavior can be instantly adjusted as needed and there is a sense of personal control over the situation ... meditation teaches us to watch our thoughts and behavior and adjust them immediately as required so that we are in control of ourselves. However, accessing the flow state during intense activities is *the most efficient and effective decision-making strategy*. If you can enter into micro-flow or macro-flow you will achieve a balanced, clear state of mind that will be the best there is for making decisions.

Physically speaking, during flow your mental absorption for the task at hand is so perfect and your Qi flow so excellent that you will sometimes forget the existence of your body and its needs ... the highest levels of spiritual cultivation require us to fix any of our spinal bone misalignments so that there are no structural obstacles or impediments to our internal energy circulation, require that we practice muscle stretching exercises on a regular basis, advise that we perform pranayama breathing exercises on a daily basis that will open up the body's Qi channels and improve our respiratory breathing, require us to eat proper diets, restore our body to health by curing any illnesses, and directly work on improving our inner Qi flow through *nei-gong* exercises so that its circulation becomes so good that we can feel energy in every cell (bliss) or forget the feeling of the body everywhere entirely.

Meditation efforts can help you cultivate some of the conditions necessary for flow (in "micro-flow" only a few of the requirements for full flow or macro-full are fulfilled such as concentration, good inner Qi flow, excellent breathing patterns, mental absorption, and so forth). For instance, we normally associate meditation practice with "the pristine mental clarity of a Zen master." Well, this is one of the aspects of mental flow. We also normally associate meditation practice with concentration and states of absorption, which are also the characteristics of mental flow. Some individuals can achieve a taste of "being in the zone" through yoga practice, and some can achieve runner's high (a low grade flow state) due to great athletic conditioning and rhythmical breathing during running that synchronizes perfectly with their inner Qi flow. As stated, being in shape healthwise, Qi-wise and breathingwise can help you attain the state of flow or simply attain states of mental clarity. These are all cultivation concerns for purifying your inner subtle body.

Being "in the zone" (experiencing flow) is to find yourself in a state of heightened performance and enhanced decision-making capability where you can use your mind and physical abilities to full potential while completely immersed in some activity and the state of presence. To achieve this mental stabilization, spiritual schools emphasize *vipassana* practice and continual mindfulness, which is to stop being lost in thought where you are thinking without knowing you are thinking. Instead you should be mindful through clear awareness of what you are thinking and doing every moment because the whole purpose of cultivation is to teach us how to use consciousness better and master our mind-body duo.

Mindfulness means heightened focused attention and awareness of your mental state just as in flow. This enables a heightened level of self-governance and self-rectification. Mindfulness means to maintain observant focus, concentration and alertness over what you are thinking and doing without becoming distracted or slipping out of focus. It means paying real alert attention to what you are doing rather than lapsing in attentiveness by becoming diverted, and yet that attention is effortless. Mindfulness, which is a mental ability easily developed through *vipassana* practice, means to be focused on the present, *being here now*, and being wide open to the experience of the moment rather than lost in thinking about the past, future or lost in wandering distractions. It means remaining focused on the primary topic of the mind-stream rather than becoming sidetracked by wandering thoughts, annoyances or emotional afflictions that take you away from the primary concern. Mindfulness practice creates many of the positive mental tendencies that point you in the direction of experiencing flow.

By continually practicing mindfulness you gradually learn how to quiet your mental agitations, control your emotional mind and its impulses, and manage the unwanted defilements that often spontaneously arise within consciousness. The practice of continual mindfulness of our thought-stream leads to internal quiet because mental complexity gradually dies down as a result of the attention without clinging. Then, within that clearer calmness you will be better at decision-making and adjusting your actions as necessary to gain whatever you want. With mindfulness you can make decisions with more care and within the state of flow your decision-making seems super-efficient and natural because there is a conjunction of clarity and calmness and absence of any unnecessary mental complexity. It's a state that seems absent of thinking because it seems emptier yet more intensely alive, which is the sign of a state of concentration, and we want to touch this state through meditation practice.

Learning the skills that move you in these directions – because of all these benefits and certainly also because this is one of the most enjoyable and pleasant of human mental states – is important for "mastering the mind" and "managing consciousness" where you gain control of yourself. This is part of the Great Learning of life that we are all involved in, and so religions commonly teach these skills through meditation exercises.

Mindfulness is therefore taught as a meditation practice because it teaches you how to clearly know with presence, self-correct your thoughts and behavior, use your mind correctly by not getting lost in wandering byways that separate you from being present in the moment, and basically pushes your mental state towards calmness, clarity and happiness. This is how we want to experience consciousness. The moment is what is alive, the moment is what is now, the moment of experience is our life. *All living is in the moment* and yet we normally become so entangled in mental fabrications that we lose the sense of presence. We want to be fully alive with clear awareness rather than so identified/occupied with our thoughts that we live enmeshed within a foggy entrained haziness. Although the present mind has no duration, this is where life is so this is where we want to situate ourselves rather than lost in distracting dullness. When an individual attains the deva body then everything in that heavenly life seems more perceptibly vibrant and alive, and we want to start training toward this in our spiritual practice.

Meditation practice teaches you how to experience each moment of life cleanly, openly and directly without extraneous biases, attitudes or preconceptions. It teaches you to recognize that the thoughts you have are just thoughts, not yourself, and you don't have to identify with them or follow them even if they seem impelling. Meditation practice also trains your abilities of focus and concentration and lengthens your attention span so that you more easily persist within activities to accomplish whatever you want.

Of course, thoughts should always be allowed to freely arise within your mind; you should not block your thought processes to produce inner quiet but just let them die down because of detachment (the refusal to attach to them). By watching your thoughts you will become better able to recognize errant influences, cut them off, transform them or simply refrain from acting on them, and because of always being mindful of your thoughts your mind will tend to quiet over time because in not giving them extra energy your thought-stream will die down. When your mind becomes empty but clear, this will allow you to experience the moment directly for what it is without adding extra superimpositions.

When your awareness is made wide open because you don't cling to thoughts it is like viewing everything freshly for the first time. It is like a "beginner's mind" or "mind of a child" where everything seems vivid, clear, new, fresh and open. Perhaps you can remember times in your life when you experienced such a state of wonder, awe and tinkling bliss. By continually focusing on just the moment of experience you can learn to develop a pristine *bright mind* that allows a world of experience to arise in living fashion, which is the state of flowing bliss. Flow is about the purity of the experience when focusing on something. This is the natural human being in his most enjoyable state, which is a target of mental cultivation.

The absolute substratum of the universe is often emphasized as transcending phenomena - being empty of any attributes, marks or signs - and so It is stainless and pure, changeless, endless, infinite, imperceptible, unknowable or unfathomable. This is the reason that Christian Apophatic theologies developed which maintain that we cannot say anything about God's divine essence because God is so totally beyond material being, and therefore beyond all possibility of knowing – we can only know what God is not. As just one example, John Scotus Erigena commented, "God Himself does not know what He is because He is not anything … He transcends being." This leads to mental negation practices where you try to abandon things in your mind (anything conceivable or imaginable) to become closer to God since God is where the mind does not reach. Look, these are just tricks to have you progress to emptiness meditation practice where you abandon thoughts.

Alternatively, spiritual schools stress the emptiness, infinite, pure, transcendental to form etc. qualities of God in order that you try to think about (meditate on) these formless characteristics as a way of pushing you to abandon thoughts about anything, which is again a type of "emptiness meditation" practice that can move you towards *bright mind flow* as a natural potential of your life.

The substratum of our utmost nature is therefore to become an object of meditation practice (even though you cannot make an accurate image of It). The purpose is to have you give up your thoughts and rest your mind in an emptiness like endless spotless space, which is basically just the union of clarity and awareness. There are lots of things flowing through empty space or the Zen school's "10,000 miles of endless open sky," so empty space meditation doesn't mean that you try to eliminate/suppress the thoughts in your mind. It means you put your awareness into a mode that is unattached and vast like empty space where it just knows, observes or is aware of whatever passes through the mind with freedom and non-attachment. This is clarity, awareness and presence.

The fundamental substratum is sometimes described in Hindu texts as an undisturbed state of consciousness although It is an insentient, inanimate substratum lacking attributes just like vast, infinite, stainless empty space. Basically, the emphasis of the empty fundamental substratum of the universe is used to promote the practice of "meditation without attributes" that is also known as "emptiness meditation." In these practices emptiness is a mental station or dwelling of calm abiding where you abide without abiding (without clinging to) in states as close to "emptiness" as you can develop in your mental continuum. Thus there is Patanjali's statement, "Yoga is the cessation of the mind and then there is abiding in the seer's own form." Because things arise within fundamental substance that does not interfere with them in any way, which is why it is said that "God is unified and one with the world but unaffected by its corruptions," this alludes to the way we should manage our consciousness to always be stationed within awareness and mentally detached from our thoughts and passions (non-clinging, non-fusion) since this imitates our primordial nature.

By taking steps in life to reduce our cravings and desires we can also more easily achieve the calmness, peace and tranquility emphasized by meditation teachings. By reducing them or transcending our cravings and desires by recognizing that *they are just thoughts we need not follow* we can make for ourselves an opportunity gap to act in the highest ways that distance us from our animal nature. An additional benefit is that by practicing mindfulness of your thinking and conduct while striving for nobleness your Qi/Prana will also start to change in quality because you will start purifying your subtle body.

These are some of the many benefits of meditation. It is a practice that can help us attain the subtle body achievement because it leads to a purification of our Qi and Qi channels (Prana and *nadis*), and it also helps us master various abilities of consciousness (such as concentration, focus, attention span, etc.) that will then improve our lives.

The Indian siddha sage Thayumanavar instructed, "Ever-permanent, without any blemish, without any ignorance, without support, ever-full, undecayingly pure, far as well as near, like the Light beyond the three luminaries (Sun, Moon and Fire), the One Charm that includes all, overflowing with Bliss, undiscernible to mind or speech, standing as the Colossus of Consciousness—on that vastness of the beginning of Infinite Bliss, let us meditate." This is telling us to practice meditation on the emptiness of our foundational nature. Enlightened Yoga master Tirumalai Krishnamacharya also said, "Knowing all objects to be impermanent, let not their contact blind you. Resolve again and again to be aware of the self that is permanent." This is a different way of instructing you in emptiness meditation again because the only permanent element, of which he speaks, is the empty fundamental substratum.

Some spiritual schools say that to "recognize God" (the fundamental substratum) is the ultimate aim in life. They say that the crown jewel in spiritual studies is to stabilize in the One Without Qualities that is similar to infinite empty space. The ultimate God is That from which everything is born, the ultimate Father of manifestation that is Itself unborn, everlasting, and pure in the sense that It is primordially absent of everything that isn't Its singleness beyond matter and energy. It is also pure in the sense of being free of attributes such as the phenomena that have arisen within It (since those phenomena are exactly It and nothing else). Try to think about this emptiness during meditation practice.

There are many forms of meditation practice that are images of emptiness in some way, and thus are called "emptiness" or "empty mind" meditations.[23] A related idea is that the closer we get to our fundamental nature (God) via emptiness meditation practice the less mental perturbations or disturbances there will be for us. Everything in this world is in a state of flux so the whole universe is an incessant sea of change except for the fundamental substratum that never changes. Meditation is thus championed as a way to become closer to the only thing constant and dependable in our lives - our ultimate substratum, or God.

An alternative spiritual cultivation technique similar to meditation is to engage in life without being attached to your body and while holding nothing in your mind, and not identifying with the relative aspects of your being but to live like someone without a body so that you gradually attain a serene nature. This is *Vairagya* detachment practice. You try to perceive everything as nothing but the supreme original substrate and try to become empty (detached) by always imagining or remembering that you are as boundless as space like the fundamental substance. Not only this, but you try to make everything you do replete with perfect virtue and morality as if you were standing in the presence of God every moment all day long.

These are all didactic devices with an ulterior motive. No one can possess consciousness without a body because the anatomical structure of the brain and nervous system, along with subtle energy, are required to produce thoughts. Thoughts are needed for there to be Knowledge (consciousness), and all we can ever know or experience are our thoughts. Therefore, emptiness or empty mind does not mean having no thoughts at all, which is a state of insentience that would equate with personal non-existence (an annihilation of consciousness). Even if your mind seems quiet and empty, as long as you are awake and identifying (recognizing) the objects of your environment this means that your thought processes are operating in the background even if the sense of I-ness or me-ness seems silenced. During "empty mind" there is a lot of information processing going on "in the dark" free of any inner feel that it is happening.

"Emptiness" actually means that your awareness is very clear rather than clouded, and that you allow thoughts to arise and depart within your mind without trying to stick to them or obliterate them into non-existence. You use consciousness in a way that mimics the original nature that allows things to freely arise within It and transform into something else without clinging to any of the transformations, but you know the contents of your mind clearly because that is the purpose of consciousness. That's what you

---

[23] See the appendix within *Neijia Yoga* for an extensive list of formless (emptiness) meditations you can cycle through.

essentially are – consciousness – so you never try to dull it or obliterate it. You're trying to free its potential through no-attachment while knowing, and then it will become "bright" or blazing. This is what the mind within the higher transcendental bodies approximates because those bodies are closer and closer to pure energy so even consciousness functions better with less friction. The mind seems brighter and more vivid, which is the ordinary mind for each new level of spiritual beingness, because the body composition and its vital energy, which affects the efficacy of consciousness, is better.

If you need fusion or entrainment with your thoughts for a special function then so be it but normally you should not identify with them but remain the clear awareness that knows your thoughts clearly. Just as we should learn from our mistakes after the fact, in real time we must always observe our thoughts from a higher vantage point so that they are subject to the immediate feedback process of self-rectification. We have been given the great miracle of consciousness, and all spirituality does is teach us how to use it properly with instructions like this: watch your thoughts so that you correct your thoughts and behaviors, and develop wisdom and self-control so that you make less errors in the first place.

We need to master our consciousness as part of the Great Learning required of life, such as the need to learn how to concentrate so that our thoughts don't just wander here and there willy-nilly but deliver what we want. There are all sorts of things we need to learn for life, but foremost of all is that we need to learn how to master our consciousness. We need to master all sorts of mental factors and abilities such as emotional control, concentration, logical reasoning, an understanding of cause and effect, imagination and mental rehearsal and so forth. We must develop positive character traits that enable us to cooperatively get along with others in society, but foremost of all we need to learn how to master our mental processes and mental states because those processes control our behavior. If we don't learn to manage our mental processes and behaviors then we are nothing more than animals.

During meditation we should allow our thoughts to be born and disappear without becoming involved with (entangled in) them because immersion leads to a forgetfulness (dulling) of the present moment. It will cause us to lose our sense of clear awareness and presence. Buddhism also says that if you cling to objects this will lead to suffering, but as a matter of fact you cannot become totally passionless. You cannot totally eliminate pain or suffering in life because they are natural spontaneous reactions meant to occur.

However, you can use your mind in a way that *avoids unnecessary suffering*. What you can do is let go of the past and refrain from clinging to negative emotions and carrying them around, such as holding grudges or not moving past broken relationships. Naturally if we need to hold thoughts for concentration purposes then we should do so, and if ethically improper thoughts arise within us we should not follow them, should cut them off or transform them if possible. So what we are actually talking about is how human beings should use their minds correctly, and meditation is one of the training vehicles for learning how to master our minds, bodies and behavior. As an animal with consciousness, we're talking about some very basic principles that are at the heart of the issues of survival and prosperity (flourishing).

As human beings trying to use consciousness to elevate ourselves above our animal nature, we should abide by the principle of always being mindful of our thoughts rather than blindly fusing with them and our conditioning, such as a false self-persona we create for ourselves over time. If we continually cling to some image of who we are then we will inhibit change headed towards becoming a better self. We must train our consciousness in various ways to rise above our animal passions, and so we also practice meditation in order to develop the tendency to stop getting locked into our thought-stream thus allowing for novelty and self-correction. This training in mental detachment, which helps our Qi flow, is accomplished by emptiness meditation practice.

No concept can accurately image something pure, infinite and empty of attributes, and since the fundamental substratum is Utterly Empty It cannot be represented by any mental image. It is thus unfathomable or unknowable; you can create thoughts of It but can only know its immanence (state of being inherently existing) since you are consciously existent rather than Its attributes of formlessness. We can only mentally know images of things rather than know an ultimate purity because any mental image of It is already a pollution of true purity. Phenomena have attributes or qualities so are the only things that the brain can register. We can never consciously fathom the empty original essence using thoughts, and therefore there is no such thing as "realizing your fundamental nature" through some mental experience! You can understand something about It, but that's all. You can only experience "realizations" about its nature that are thoughts and therefore manifest things rather than directly experience its unmanifest substance via a thought construct.

None of us can ever directly know through consciousness the nature of the fundamental substratum although we can talk about it, and people confuse the understanding of these facts with "self-realization." You can realize things *about* your True Self or ultimate substratum that is your self-nature just like you can realize things about baseball or cooking, and that's all. You can never realize It in terms of creating a perceptual experience in your mind, but you can think about It and Its qualities of formlessness, infinity, eternality, beginninglessness, etcetera. People get confused about this after reading too many Zen stories where someone "awakened to enlightenment," and get mislead about stories of Hindu masters who realized this or that fact to achieve liberation, and so on.

Our fundamental nature cannot be reached through thoughts and is perceptually veiled from us because an apparent reality is superimposed upon It – Shakti – and thus It is inaccessible to perception. Within the ancient Egyptian religion, the imperceptibility of the foundational substrate was called the "Veil of Isis" to denote the fact of superimposition veiling It. Similarly, according to Sufi theology you must engage in an "unveiling" or "tearing off of veils" to see God's face and experience unity with Allah, which refers to casting off lower body shells/sheaths to attain the most primal form of man (the *atman*, Immanence body, or an even higher body if one is possible). Basically, our thoughts of It restrict our knowledge to something second-rate. Then again, we *are* the foundational substrate in manifest form so we directly know, realize or experience It all the time in everything around us because everything is It. It is both manifestly known and transcendentally unknown. Knowing is actually knowing some aspect of It ... some of Its attributes or functions. Knowing is knowing It. Consciousness is It. Thus consciousness is Brahman ... and so is everything else.

To perfect ourselves as aspects of the original nature we must perfect our powers and abilities of consciousness since *they are the core of our special beingness* and necessary for our survival or existence. Consciousness is the great treasure of existence that separates us from being the darkness of insentient matter. The light of illumination (knowing) is priceless, the great miracle and prize of the cosmos that is wondrous that it even exists! It is the essence of our livingness, and it therefore it becomes imperative for people to learn how to manage their consciousness in the best possible way. That's one of the purposes of meditation practice. You should be learning how to master all the abilities of consciousness other than those just needed for ordinary life.

Spiritual schools therefore give us exercises for developing various mental powers and they ask us to meditate in order to teach us how to concentrate, learn how to become more mindful of our thought-stream, learn how to manage/change our thoughts and emotions and behavior, learn how to improve the quality of our Qi/Prana and its circulation through quietude, and learn how to find the quiet natural peace of our minds. However, individuals should not cultivate an enforced thoughtlessness in order to reach the mental quietude normally associated with meditation practice because the fundamental nature does not suppress anything. Through meditation practice, such as *vipassana*, we must allow our busy mind of thoughts to die down naturally to reveal the naturally calm state of consciousness that is already there beneath the busyness – pure empty awareness.

We need to practice enough that we start opening up all the energy channels within our brains for this to happen, and then the processes of consciousness will become more efficient just as they are for devas who have subtle energy bodies. We need to cultivate a lucid and vivid presence of mind that is accompanied by a physical body bliss that originates in superior Qi flow, and this will be a very pristine state of awareness that is accompanied by feeling very alive. The spiritual path involves developing all the powers and abilities of our consciousness, learning how to use our mind in the best possible ways, and mastering all possible *dharmas*.

To review, the images of emptiness formed by the mind are not real emptiness but just conceptions (thought images) of emptiness that cannot capture it because the only thing consciousness can give you is thought, and emptiness is without thought. Whatever we conceive of in our minds as emptiness or purity is a mind-object – Knowledge – and therefore is not real emptiness or purity but a semblance meant to look like an emptiness of some sort. True emptiness is not a mental entity but a complete absence of mental complexity, and therefore during meditation practice you always keep letting go of whatever arises within your mind. Therefore, "Nothing can be said about the condition of the absolute nature using thoughts." It is inscrutable, unreachable, unfathomable by thoughts. Thus the Apophatic spiritual approaches advise silence, the abandonment of all intellectual inquiry, the abandonment of "images in the soul," formless mind (emptiness) meditation and so on. In Christianity this practice of *theoria* will lead to *theosis*, which is a process of becoming divine called "divinization" which means the attainment of the subtle body. Every religion targets the same objective but uses different theological terms to get you to practice virtue and good deeds, inner energy work, and emptiness meditation (and other contemplative practices) in order that you attain the deva body.

Teachings about the fundamental ground state of reality give rise to the meditation practice of naturally empty mind whereby you try to put your mind in tune with our formless original nature that lacks a body. You do so by letting thoughts arise without clinging to them, and you *recognize (know) them* with an awareness that seems to transcend them without clinging to them. The knowing, interpreting, deciphering or understanding of thoughts is also just a thought process too – Knowledge operating or knowing – but it is part of a much finer mind-stream in the background that is interpreting thoughts with thought activity. Knowledge is just knowing Knowledge, and there is no doer within the process. There is just Knowledge doing everything. There is just Knowledge operating on its own without any inherent self being involved. There is an apparent self involved, a manifest self involved, a false self involved but no intrinsic permanent process of knowing involved – there is just a conditional process of knowing. Knowledge is knowing Knowledge without an intrinsic independent living being involved, and yet understanding is there.

Knowledge is always proliferating more Knowledge and understanding that Knowledge, and no such thing as actual emptiness (no-thought) can be experientially realized as Knowledge since thoughts are the antithesis of emptiness. Nevertheless, we can use the practice of making an image of emptiness as a training vehicle to reach an empty, detached state of mind and *we should constantly train to be more aware, more detached, more open and mentally flexible*. In Christian religious instruction it is colloquially said we can "become one with the Father" or "find Union with the Supreme" in order to encourage meditation practices that involve emptiness in one way or another.

Spiritual practitioners in some schools are sometimes taught to envision the fundamental substratum as something so grand and vast that their mental structures cannot accommodate the required imaging and thus shut down to become silent. The hope is that their cognitive stream is shut down by the attempt to fathom grand awesomeness, and then they might experience the peace of mental stopping in this way. All sorts of tricks like this are used as spiritual training practices such as statements that the attributes of God are incredibly sublime or transcendentally enormous; when you then think about those attributes it silences your mental functioning that can similarly lead people to enter, if but for an instant, a more peaceful state of mind. Another technique is to put all your concentration into visualizing an image with utmost stability and when you can no longer hold the visualization you give up the effort and rest in mental emptiness. These are all forms of emptiness meditation practice. For monastic environments, I prefer that adherents cycle through various "images" of emptiness every week, or regularly pass through various methods of pointing you towards experiences of empty mind just as explained.

Mental silencing is also the natural outcome of great awe or reverence, which is why reverence is practiced within many religions. When you humble yourself this tends to dampen the intensity of your internal thought-stream. Spiritual reverence helps you touch the quietness of your natural mind and therefore worship can be an excellent spiritual practice. For those whose planet Jupiter aspects their 1st house ruler in their astrological natal chart or whose Jupiter occupies their 1st house, they will find that the religious pathway of devotion and prayer is very beneficial for their cultivation practice.

The original nature needs no worship, for It is an insentient inanimate ground state without thoughts or ego. How we developed out of it no one knows, but human beings have appeared within it with consciousness and we try to mange our affairs to rise to greater states of being. The ground substratum – whether you call It God, Brahman or Parabrahman, etc. – is not a being with consciousness, but as the underlying real, unchanging ground state of existence It is our beingness. *It is you* so there is no need to worship or even show gratitude to yourself, especially since you just happened without a plan or purpose. However, you should respect your manifest self and others. There is a need for improving/bettering your life, a need for eliminating or forestalling suffering, a need for self-responsibility for your actions in the world, and a need for finding a personal purpose or meaning for your own existence.

Many things require your consideration in life, but worship of the highest and most transcendental substrate is not a necessity, nor can it even be recognized (appreciated) by our inanimate substrate that is our self-nature. To It, nothing is happening at all. The fundamental elements of the manifest universe should not be worshipped either. We are a transient process within Shakti that need not worship Shakti nor our unchanging essence, but to set up a deity and then worship Him or Her is a useful type of cultivation practice. Even though delusional, spiritual worship has many benefits so it is commonly promoted to society. Reverence for any sort of higher power is a cultivation activity that can quiet your mind and produce many other benefits essential to life.

Consciousness is sometimes described as a duality of (empty) pristine awareness conjoined with active mental fabrications. A background of empty mind is considered to be empty pristine awareness that is empty, pre-linguistic consciousness absent of thoughts (though it is just composed of hidden finer thoughts), and this is matched against overt thought activity.

Compare this to the fact that there is an empty fundamental substrate (original nature) of the universe and the manifestation of ever-changing Shakti arises within It whose infinite evolutes are also Shakti *and* ultimately Itself.

The thoughts of our consciousness are actually the same thing as empty pristine awareness (which is not really empty at all since there are always thought processes going on). In other words, everything in consciousness is one type of consciousness or another; you always are experiencing purely consciousness, pure consciousness or consciousness only. This is why there is a school of Buddhism called Consciousness-Only or Mere-Consciousness to denote the fact that our experience of the world and ourselves is only an appearance within our individual consciousness, and thus to some extent often mistake-prone or delusional.

Supremely quiet consciousness, seemingly empty consciousness, or thought-filled consciousness ... they are all just active consciousness filled with thoughts even if the mind seems empty. The only thing you are ever experiencing in life is not the world but your mind – your consciousness! The task of life is to learn how to use this consciousness correctly despite its faults and expand its powers and capabilities. Therefore in life we must learn how to master its automatic functions, deliberate functions, its ability to produce mental states and behavior, and so forth.

There are a variety of mental states lacking thoughts such as a coma, anesthetic lull, or deep sleep, but of what benefit are they other than for rest? Only if you are physically or mentally annihilated, extinguished or exterminated are there no thoughts at all, and non-existence is certainly not the highest state of spiritual existence nor something we should be targeting for our existence. It is not what you want to cultivate. Non-existence means your life is gone because you have transformed into some other set of insentient components of Shakti so you have become exterminated, annihilated.

Conscious existence is what we always want to maintain and maximize, so in life we must strive to improve our cognitive abilities and make our consciousness suffering-free, blissful, capable, skillful, and filled with meaning. In any case, it needs to be pointed out that pristine clear awareness seems like it is absent of thoughts and empty but it is still a mental state filled with very fine thoughts otherwise there is no such thing as awareness or knowing. We just say that it is pristine and empty or pure consciousness without elaborations/formations. It is just that the mental activity within this state of clear awareness is missing the loud voice of the coarse inner narrative, and when your Qi flows strongly throughout your body at this time to produce a feeling of bliss because of coursing through all your Qi channels then your awareness seems to brighten and you feel very alive. That's when you feel as if you are in the moment of presence, and even if your mind seems very quiet there is still a lot of very fine thought activity going on. Nevertheless we want you to station yourself in that state and the state of flow as much as possible. In short, the thoughts within the visage of "empty mind," such as those that automatically identify phenomena for you, are "finer" than the coarse thoughts of inner narrative consciousness but they are still there in states of inner silence and pristine presence.

From the standpoint of the foundational substrate there is no difference between you being an insentient portion of Shakti or a sentient living being. From the standpoint of manifestation, Shakti is a body of vibrating energy-matter fields and doesn't care either. In fact, although you are sentient there is no such true thing as genuine sentience within Shakti. Why? Because consciousness (sentience) has no ontological primacy and is not a function that transcends Shakti as we assume consciousness does. A true sentience would transcend Shakti, but that is impossible since it is a conditional construction embedded within it. It is not independent and free of the soup of interdependent origination that creates it. You assume that you and your consciousness are intrinsically independent of Shakti and transcend it, but you are just another part of Shakti and so are your thoughts. They are part of the structure of the universe integrated with all its other pieces. While it seems to be something that lacks matter and transcends phenomena, it is not something that surmounts the universe, and actually requires a physical body and energy for its production.

The universe is naturalistic, and there is no such *intrinsic thing* as a living being or sentience within it in the sense that we take them to be inherent and independent. All living beings are a conditional creation, an agglomeration of all sorts of non-self elements. Where is there a singular unified self-person or soul in all this? You are just a ripple within its one fabric, an always changing composite construction that has a functional ability of apparent consciousness. Also, your seemingly independent sentience is just another function within Shakti rather than a consciousness that transcends it.

Even so, consciousness is the great prize or treasure of existence because most of manifestation is dark (insentient). It brings order to where there is no order and meaning, and yet its order is no order at all. Order is a conventional illusion we establish, and thus just an imaginary way of viewing things where there are no ontological patterns or orders.

The reason that meditation practice is promoted in all this is because it helps you gain mastery over various aspects of your consciousness and your activity in the world. As sentient beings, consciousness is our main tool of beingness and knowing. Of course, it doesn't exist if we don't have a body with vital energy, so they are important too, but consciousness is our knowingness without which we are just another insentient clump of something or other within Shakti. Consciousness is part of your beingness so why wouldn't you aim to gain as complete control over it as possible, especially since by mastering it you can reduce it flaws and bouts of suffering?

As a living sentient object produced by the evolving transformations within the universe, we should develop our powers of consciousness as much as possible. Meditation practice also leads to the purification of your Qi/Prana, the purification or transformation of your Qi/Prana in turn leads to the attainment of your deva body, and your deva body is the first heavenly spiritual attainment that leads to yet higher body attainments with greater longevity that can escape the lower realms of reincarnation (cyclic existence) forever. Its attainment serves as the foundation for higher body attainments that are essentially the true spiritual ladder of transcendence that gives you very long lives (termed "immortality" in some traditions) in enjoyable realms that are free of lower existences. Even when you die in an upper realm you can retain many of your talents, *samskaras* and memories in a subsequent incarnation, and so some continuity is retained to counter the problem of impermanence.

The spiritual pathway of mind, body, behavior and Qi purification leads to better lives with less suffering, and consummate union with your highest spiritual self and Self. As you progress upwards along this spiritual hierarchy of being, your more transcendental bodies live in more pleasant realms with more pleasant circumstances for longer periods of time than an ordinary human life span and they are, in a sense, closer to our fundamental nature in terms of their level of composition. If you attain the Buddha body or Rainbow Body of the Formless Realm that is often compared to light, which is the stage of a full Arhat, you can leave the lower levels of reincarnation forever because those realms are all based on more condensed or etheric forms of matter. To enable you to attain this body vehicle is why the spiritual path has been established, and this result is called liberation. Religions call enlightenment a mind attainment so that you practice, but it is actually a body attainment with a concomitant mental attainment that is just the ordinary mind of your new body in that realm.

In other words, achieving "enlightenment" is attaining the first independent spiritual body - the deva body that puts you in reach of jumping out of the lower realms forever with highly refined bodies made of energy. The subsequent body attainments afterwards mean that you are climbing the ranks of enlightenment (spiritual achievement). When you finally attain the Arhat body that is also known as the Buddha body, Dharma body, Rainbow body or Clear Light body, we call this attaining the "mind of *bodhi."* This is how people normally identify enlightenment, which is through a mental attainment rather than the body attainments whose consciousness is the accompanying mental attainment. This Arhat body receives a special designation because of its capabilities and composition that is finally free of all lower forms of dense matter. This is why it belongs to the "Formless Realm" rather than the Realm of Form. "Formless" does *not mean* that there is no body, but that the "formless" body can change its shape dramatically at will in what we would think of as miraculous ways because of an even more transcendental stage of etheric atoms.

Basically, a short synopsis of the road of spiritual cultivation practice and its rationale is as follows. Somehow the universe (Shakti) was created and thereafter, through an evolution of complex interactions finally life developed within it. Some forms of life eventually developed consciousness, and gradually higher consciousness appeared within many types of beings throughout the universe - including humans. You can talk about how all phenomena within the universe are linked to one another through the interpenetration of cause and effect to make one seamless whole of energy-matter fields, that all things are impermanent because they are ever-changing, that they are each selfless entities that lack an innate intrinsic nature that isn't defined through interdependent conditioning, and you can discuss many other aspects of the universe and the phenomena within it but that is irrelevant for our main story of spiritual cultivation. You can emphasize that there is only One Supreme Being or fundamental foundation/substratum that manifests Itself in countless forms in numberless modes of life. The main story is that within the universe many forms of life have developed, each of which has a body-mind complex since consciousness requires a body.

The problems of sentient life are that living entities need to perform actions for their survival (such as eating and avoiding being eaten), life needs to replicate in order that its species does not become extinct, and suffering unfortunately pollutes the mental states of consciousness and afflicts its well-being. Unlike inanimate matter and energy, sentient life is a composite construct possessing a feature/attribute called consciousness that forms an imperfect picture of the world (perceptions). It has many flaws in its various processes that produce thinking, emotions, will and behaviors, but it is still the great treasure of existence despite its faults and failings because no matter the mechanism for how it occurs it provides knowledge of self-existence and the world through awareness though imperfect. We are a form of animal life in the universe capable of higher consciousness, and we can and must master the capabilities of our bodies and our consciousness – our perceptions, emotions, thinking, will and mental states – to solve many of our survival and replication issues. We can even use consciousness to create well-being and enjoyable mental states free of suffering, and through our capabilities of thought can find meaning and purpose to our lives.

Because we are a body-mind complex we have two main skills – cognitive skills and physical skills. Our job as humans is to survive as individual entities that require familial and community relationships since friendly cooperative living is necessary for our individual and group survival. Survival and flourishing (prosperity) requires that we develop the wisdom, knowledge and skillfulness capabilities so that we can master the changes of worldly phenomena for our benefit. Survival requires that we master our bodies and minds, our physical and cognitive skills. These are mundane concerns because they are issues of survival and flourishing.

Mastering our minds means mastering our *deliberate* activities of consciousness that we can consciously control, such as decision-making and willpower and behavioral control, and our *automatic* processes of consciousness such as our emotional mind and mental afflictions or agitations that spontaneously arise within us to blemish our mental state. If we master these two aspects of our mind we can experience more wholesome mental states such as happiness, shine, peace, tranquility, presence, centeredness, flow, bliss, calmness, clarity, freshness/bliss etc. that can replace mental states predominated by suffering.

Spiritual practice ("cultivation") is all about mastering and perfecting our bodies, minds and behaviors for the purposes of survival and well-being within Nature, which therefore requires cooperative, collaborative behavior with society since we must depend upon others to survive and thrive. To peacefully live together with others requires that we develop spiritual values and the virtues of good conduct. Spiritual practice is also about refining our behavior so that we become noble beings rather than just animals ruled by coarse thoughts, instincts, desires and passions. Spiritual practice, and the effort of mastering our consciousness, enables us to create flourishing states of harmonious peace, welfare, prosperity, abundance, happiness, and well-being for ourselves, our families and our greater living groups such as communities so that they are absent of emotional turmoil, suffering, injustice and deprivation. It enables us to achieve personal *arête* (excellence or virtue), *phronesis* (practical and moral wisdom) and *eudaimonia* (human flourishing and prosperity) and therefore live a wise and good life.

Within the context of personal cultivation, meditation is a type of mental training and spiritual practice that has several benefits. It is one of the training technologies that helps us understand how our minds work, and helps us master our various capabilities of consciousness just as *nei-gong* practices, physical exercises, medicine, and diet are modalities that help us master the health and physical capabilities of our body. It is just a fact of the universe that our physical body is a condensed form of energy and that through spiritual cultivation methods we can purify the energetic components of this solidified matter so that either upon death, or during life, our body can split into a constituent physical part and transcendental subtle energy part called the "soul" or deva body that is composed of Qi/Prana. This transcendental body part, which is an etheric duplicate of our physical body, is the first higher step of the spiritual trail of progressively higher transcendental body attainments, whose stages are the various ranks of enlightenment.

The process of cultivating the deva body whilst alive requires many intensified yoga practices that are commonly transmitted through religion or spiritual schools, and this achievement also requires the assistance of many higher bodied (spiritual) beings who will only help you achieve this liberating attainment by purifying your Qi/Prana via their efforts if you are a virtuous individual. Since meditation helps you calm and purify your mind (where you can leave behind lower-order mentalities) and behavior, which means perfecting your character and virtues that then merits you for this heavenly attainment while alive, for this and many other reasons it is a major part of every spiritual path.

This essentially summarizes the spiritual path, which is designed to lead you to mind-body-behavioral purification and the higher spiritual body attainments ("enlightenment") of liberation so that you can escape the lower realms of suffering forever. The pathway requires that you work on self-development, namely character development, self-control, and intensified yoga practices that are essentially inner Qi work. If you fail at the deva body attainment during life you still want to have put major efforts into improving the capabilities of your consciousness and your character so that virtuous or just excellent character traits are carried over as attributes for a subsequent incarnation. Furthermore, you want to have improved your life for yourself and for others through acts of merit, including for the benefit of your subsequent incarnations. In terms of self-improvement you must learn how to master your consciousness, which is what you essentially are since your life is as your consciousness (experience) is each moment. This means learning how to optimally develop the deliberate trainable capabilities of consciousness, and how to control the automatic functions of consciousness such as emotions and afflictions. You ultimately want to be able to control your thoughts, your mindset, your body, your internal energy, your will, your actions (behavior, conduct) and your fortune. Meditation practice is one of the key training methods for these objectives of the spiritual trail.

Spiritual saints, gurus and masters constantly tell us to observe our minds to understand them, and that we can through the meditation practice of mindfulness learn to understand the mechanics of our mental self and then master our mind so that we cease to suffer unnecessarily. Naturally they also want us to police our thoughts so that we exhibit better conduct and control of our behavior. *Spiritual teachings are ultimately about consciousness* because your life is as your consciousness is each moment; all you have is your (conscious) experience. Everything we have and all that we experience is because of our consciousness. Of course you need a body and living energy (life force or Qi) in order to have consciousness, but in a way you are ultimately just consciousness. Consciousness is also about behavior because your conduct/activities are your thoughts expressed.

Therefore you should be working on improving all the various aspects, qualities and powers of your consciousness throughout life. Spiritual saints and masters emphasize that we should work at improving our minds and behavior because from their higher bodies they are seeing people's mental activities all the time, and since they see how the quality of our thoughts leads to good or bad behavior they admonish people about the need to practice virtue and work on practices of perfection. Don't ever think you can hide whatever you are thinking or doing *or did* from Heaven. Everything is stored in your neurons, which means it is open access to spiritual beings at all times, and upon death you truly go through a life review where all your activities are judged by the Buddhas of your country. When you go through the twelve-year kundalini transformation process those memories will be rehashed over and over again, so there is nothing that will ever be missed or that you can explain away and escape since your true intentions of the time you do something wrong will be incorporated within your neural memories as well.

Once you attain the subtle body and master the *anima siddhi* you can shrink down in size to enter someone's brain and start watching the thought processes formed within the brainstem and brain's neurons, which is why Buddhism makes a big deal teaching how thoughts form and consciousness works. This is because deva students are studying the workings of consciousness within people's heads all the time since it is a way for them to learn how to intervene in people's thoughts (for the better) and emotions and thereby earn the merit required for enlightenment. Only the most virtuous people are accorded this honor, which requires years of organized labor to wash the Qi of your subtle body until it can emerge from its physical shell, and only virtuous people who won't use their thought-giving powers to harm people can even earn such a blessing.

The teachings Shakyamuni Buddha gave on how consciousness works were not derived from meditation practices per se but from having achieved the higher body attainments that allow you to see how thoughts are formed in the brain. Everyone in Heaven already knew and knows these principles but he was he first to explain them to the human level of beingness. He just taught what everyone in the upper realms already knew since spiritual beings are messing with people's thoughts and emotions all the time.

The whole point is that you are a non-intrinsic being with consciousness, consciousness works in such and such a way, it produces a worldview with qualities as well as thoughts and emotions, and you can improve all its mental activities to lead a better life with less unnecessary suffering. The focus within religions is usually on improving your behavior and thoughts, and meditation practice starts you on the road of observing your ordinary thoughts so that you can purify them, uplift them and achieve humane, then noble, then consummate and then spiritual conduct.

On a daily level, meditation practice also leads to a more open mind that doesn't blindly cling to its conditioned mental processes that we develop over time due to genetic, educational, cultural, environmental, and other influences. Through the meditation practice of constantly witnessing your thoughts – seeing them as if you were a distanced third party observer who is emotionally detached from the thought-stream (dispassionate) being observed – you can train in developing flexibility and adaptability of your mental processes. In particular, you want to cultivate a flexibility of mental attitude so that you easily adapt yourself to all new circumstances without losing your composure by becoming irritable or angry. With mindfulness you will gradually perceive more *objectively* if you don't attach to the *subjective* interests, desires, judgments or preconceptions that sometimes arise within you that you normally incorporate into your thoughts. These biases are misleading, warp your decision-making and displace you away from a more direct cognition of naked reality that more perfectly captures knowledge of things as they are.

Of course an "unbiased" mind of presence must still operate according to our standard mental algorithms that produce perceptions and thoughts, and which definitely contain incorrect, misleading and prejudicial biases, but being able to examine our thoughts in real time means that we do not have to cling to (strictly or robotically follow) the habitual processing algorithms that automatically generate our interpretations, decisions and so forth. We must cultivate an independent, detached mind of clear presence that is always open to new things and is able to change whatever arises within consciousness. Within a "mind of presence" your sensing, feeling and judgment should become more objective and accurate because you don't identify with your thoughts through fusion and thereby become more emotionally balanced and mentally clear.

If you practice cultivating a quiet open mind of awareness akin to a lucid, pre-lingual state of presence, you can eventually achieve a state of vivid, alive awareness that is fully awake, immersed in the field of experience and yet open to newness like the psychological state of flow described in self-actualization literature. This lucid, blissful "Now" experience makes every moment seem fresh, new, interesting, and even exciting or thrilling. It is as if you are being renewed and rejuvenated every moment. In such a state your body may feel blissful in a subtle way, full of energy or just comfortable.

The path of spiritual cultivation entails renewing yourself each day so that this is the center of your experience. Your mental substratum should be free of afflictions and a noisome self-narrative, and thus empty, but your focus and awareness should be sharp and clear. If you cultivate very well, your body might even seem almost non-existent or you won't notice it due to the lack of any internal discomfort because your excellent internal Qi flow circulates so well and produces physical ease. Your mind will be clear and centered, perfect in poise, void of unwanted distractions or annoyances, and your body will be relaxed and free of internal obstructions so that its Qi energy flows harmoniously everywhere using its most natural patterns with perfect balance. There is an immense purity of the experience when you achieve this state.

This is the *sat-chit-ananda* of Hinduism, the state of "presence" in western nomenclature, the "being centered" in western culture, "*Shen Xin Ping Heng*" in Chinese culture ("body and mind balanced"), and the "no mind no body" or "body and mind both forgotten" of Zen. In this state your body experiences ease and lacks all internal tension because its inner Qi flow becomes extremely natural, harmonious, balanced and free of all obstructions. Only excellent forms of exercise together with *neijia* can achieve the peak possibilities to this. Thus it feels like there are *no partitions* to your body; "nothing" or "emptiness" has the same meaning as "no partitions." Your body experiences a comfortable feeling of health and energy where your Qi/Prana circulates so smoothly and comfortably everywhere that the sense of being or having a body is forgotten, as if it is non-existent.

If as a practice technique you throughout the day hold onto the mentality that "you are a being without any form" and according let go of your body-mind complex, which is a detachment method that follows from the teachings of Advaita Vedanta and Buddhism (such as the principle of interdependent origination and the *Avatamsaka Sutra "Hua Yen"* view of interpenetration) you will gradually free up some of the Qi obstructions within your body so that your Qi flows more freely/optimally over time to approach this physical perfection. When the feeling of the body is forgotten because of better Qi flow (which you can also attain through regular stretching exercises together with *nei-gong* practices) then this is the meaning of the physical body "being empty" (experiencing emptiness) due to optimal Qi flow. This feeling of bodilessness is also the physical aspect of *ananda* "bliss" as regards body sensations, or "bliss" can mean that the energy flow is so blissful that you feel alive and full of active vitality. The mental aspect of *ananda* bliss is to be peaceful, calm and quiet. The active mental aspect of *ananda* bliss means bubbling states such as happiness, joy, optimism and excitement-pleasure or radiating sunny mental states such as glow and shine.

The *sat, chit, ananda* state of "body and mind balanced" or "no mind no body" where your mind and body together reach a state of balance, calm and equilibrium is also "mind and body become one (are unified)" since to experience this state your Qi throughout all your body tissues, units or segments has to become threaded into one whole that is experienced as a single unit without parts. Your thoughts can then affect the entire Qi throughout your body instantly. How? At this stage of Qi cultivation your mind is peaceful and calm (quiet) because of smooth internal Qi flow and so it is free of disturbances/agitations because it has achieved your natural mental state. Experiences (including thoughts) still flow through your mind but without overt afflictions while your body feels extremely comfortable or blissful because of the health-related cultivation work you've done with exercise, diet, breathing and *nei-gong*. Hence you experience "body and mind balanced," "no mind, no body" or "body and mind now one" or "a state of living presence." You're just there doing whatever you want to be doing, and experiencing with focused attention just what you want to be experiencing with absorption, and there are no internal distractions to your focus nor an inner critic or loud internal monologue rambling about within your mind. There is just the experience and any thought activity necessary for the moment. The absorption in the experience is unaffected by distractions; it is unperturbed as it enjoys whatever is the experience. Physically you are feeling absolutely great or forgetful of your body (or time) entirely, and are "in the zone" or "in the groove." The experience is just the experience and nothing more.

This is just beingness – beingness with consciousness that is the great miracle of the universe and the greatest treasure of existence. This is *sat-chit-ananda* ... beingness-existence, consciousness-awareness and bliss, peace or comfort.

This is the apex of sentience because in this state of flowing clarity you experience the "beautiful foolishness of things" without any defilements infringing upon the experience. Consciousness knows the beauty of the universe through the workings of the mind in the most blissful, vivid, and suffering-free manner possible. Thus the mental realm is vivid, clean and pure and you experience life and the world of qualities with the fullest interest and engagement.

How do you train for this? Through meditation work and other spiritual practices.

Experiencing the tapestry of the universe without any unwanted pollutions defiling your consciousness means your experiences will appear with heightened clarity when the distracting aspects of your consciousness are silenced. Open and free, fresh newness is then experienced every moment. You truly feel fresh, alive and awakened. Attention becomes wide open to whatever your experience is.

This high state of lucidity, brightness, illumination, clarity, calmness and newness without excessive mental chatter is your *natural mind*, and should become your *ordinary mind* or natural mental state. To achieve this state of presence so that you experience it every moment is the highest blessing. It lays bare the precious treasure, the astonishing miracle of consciousness that can experience bliss (quiescence, presence and clarity) every moment if you cultivate well enough. You achieve this through the practice of spiritual cultivation, specifically through meditation and inner Qi practices. This is meant to be the mind of enlightenment, which is your ordinary mind free of afflictions ... and of course your ordinary mind full of afflictions is your enlightenment mind as well.

In this centered state of being fully present in the moment and enjoying the experience vividly, your emotional mind enters a calm, peaceful and harmonious state while your logical mind remains steady, sharp, able to access its wisdom and free of confusion. The mind is quiet of self-talk and extraneous agitations but you are still always flowing with new thoughts, emotions and experiences. Your mental realm, replete with the glory of experience, seems settled, quiet or silent because extraneous chatter and other complexities do not accompany the thought-stream, and your consciousness is always balanced but vivid and alert. You can connect with life in a beautiful deep way. Consciousness experiences the external world of boundless qualities together with your thoughts and emotions, within that immersion your focus and attentiveness are heightened, your mental realm seems pure with the engagement, and your mind is free of unnecessary burdens.

The mind is calm and balanced (free of urgency, hesitations, fears, afflictions and emotional biases) in this state of flow thus making it possible for wisdom to orient you properly and for you to make accurate judgments and correctly respond to the situations at hand so that you act properly and adapt masterfully to gain what you want. When you are calm and clear you can see things clearly (accurately), which is why you should practice meditation since it strengthens your ability to be present in the moment and not be mentally wandering. With a stable, calm, peaceful mind you will be able to experience a peaceful levelheadedness of undisturbed concentration that can become absorbed in the Now of the present moment of experience with complete attention and awareness of yourself. When your concentration seems effortless, attention is bright and your mind is quiet this is the state of quiescence and presence.

Quiescence or internal peace is the highest state of mental bliss, which we normally call emptiness, and you can also call the sensation of very comfortable body feelings a blissful state as well. Both mental bliss and physical bliss are the target of spiritual cultivation practice that is a mind-body science, and they help you renew yourself every day.

This achievement of mental peace, and quiet mind with full awareness is the "consciousness" (*sat*) of Hinduism as well as the "open, empty, clean and pure" of Buddhism. Buddhists call our fundamental nature the "highest, purest, clearest" but this mental state can be called the highest, purest, clearest as well. This empty clarity is the state of "balance" or "harmony" in Chinese philosophy. It is the Zen state of "clean and pure" where the mind becomes free of defilements, and where the pristine mind-stream becomes the greatest experience of the moment. The experience is clean, or you can say it is pure. What would sully it? Afflictions, irritations, distractions, worries, agitations, annoyances, frustrations, fears and worries, negative self-talk, negative emotions, desires, passions, cravings and other defilements. However, these are now absent just as in a state of flow or pure presence. The experience is just the experience and nothing more – it is absent of these defilements. Without defilements you have the state of blissful consciousness, clean and pure, empty and open, fresh and present.

This is the *state of vivid presence* where the mind operates in a state of flow that is undisturbed, absent of distractions. Thus, we also call this the empty visage *clear consciousness*, concentration, absorption or immersion. It is also the attainment of "emptiness," so emptiness doesn't mean that your mind is empty of contents (emotions and thoughts and thinking) because then you would be asleep. It means that your mind is free of complexities (complex formations) and *unnecessary* inner chatter or agitation while enjoying/experiencing its mental realm. But the experience is not just in your head for you should always be feeling the blissful vitality of your whole body that helps you feel you are alive. For this reason, all spiritual adherents must truly cultivate their body and the best circulation of its internal energy.

This, then, is also the state of flow and being centered if there is vivid presence of mind, or "immersion in concentration without distraction." It also entails the body feeling truly blissful, comfortable or even non-existent not because it is ignored but because it is optimally healthy and its inner Qi circulation is so good. It takes much cultivation work to reach this as your natural state. It is your highest state of beingness where your mind is bright and you feel comfortable and fully alive due to the Qi pulsing all throughout you.

You are truly beingness without a body, boundless as infinite empty space, or you can say that your body is the entire whole of the frothing cosmos (Shakti) full of virility, movement and vitality, or you can say you are just your solitary physical body. However you take yourself will influence your mentality, behavior and cultivation. You can physically cultivate the smoothness of your inner Qi circulation to an apex of excellence where the flow seems non-existent because it is so good, or can cultivate the active inner vitality felt in every cell that makes one feel the bliss of living and joy of life when you feel truly alive. How can you cultivate these states during your regular practice?

Perhaps you remember experiencing a similar state of clarity with full vitality when you were a child, or perhaps some peak experience due to sports activity - a state of feeling fully alive. The axis of spiritual cultivation entails reaching this state and then renewing it on a daily basis until it becomes continuous. You are not looking for a peak experience but to cultivate your body and its internal energy to excellence, and to train your mind so that you can experience the most stable aspects of flow (presence, concentration, heightened clear awareness, being empty of mental complexity and chatter, physical bliss, ultra-performance, etc.) as your natural state, which is how you should be living your entire life. This requires some physical practice, which is why yoga, the soft martial arts and dance, rebounding or athletics are recommended along with *neijia*. The Zen school and Hindu sadhu traditions would greatly improve with this added emphasis as would the Christian, Jewish, Moslem and other paths of training for spiritual aspirants.

The fact that you can stop clinging to your thought-stream and experience a vivid, lucid peacefulness from being *in presence* rather than being transfixed within your mind-stream gives you an opportunity gap to become more alive, more real and more spontaneously active rather than turned off and tuned out due to entrainment. Cultivating the ability to detach from your thought-stream so that you are not simply a robot following programming but a real individual who can take a distanced step back to see what's actually occurring allows for new ideas, opinions and facts to come into your mind and influence you. It allows you to escape from the clutches of being a slave to a programmed mind. It allows you to break the link between thoughts and unnecessary psychological suffering.

By becoming more open to new ideas and influences you can change the trajectory of your life, or at least in many instances the momentum of the situation at hand. When your mind becomes calm, clear and balanced you can also make more accurate judgments due to your wisdom fully operating, and therefore can overrule your emotions and correct your actions to alter your fate and destiny. Confucianism accordingly says, "refining your self lies in balancing your mind." Only a calm, clear and levelheaded mind can vividly reflect the reality at hand – reality as it is – and experience it in a pristine, lucid (bright) way that reveals its utmost glory. Thus Patanjali said, "When the mind is clear, empty of memories and knowledge, things are seen exactly as they are."

If you also act with deliberate wisdom to override the automatic programming you've developed through your prior conditioning, this is *living in the moment* rather than following thought-entrainment. This can change your situation and fortune for the better too. Even a spiritual master has embedded conditioning that affects his mental processes – we all do – but by always cultivating a mind that does not fuse to everything that arises within it he opens himself up to the opportunity to experience the world more fully with immersion. He becomes more alive. He gives himself the opportunity to solve problems and make decisions outside of the preconditioned pathways of normal response patterns that are conditioned within his neurons, and which therefore determine ordinary mental routines. Circumstances normally determine how we think and act because they automatically trigger our prior conditioning, and only the effort to be detached and non-robotic prevents this automatic conditioning from taking over. Meditation, and striving to maintain the state of presence that meditation teaches, enable this.

The nature of our consciousness is that thoughts are born and perish from moment to moment, ever streaming through the mind like a violent torrent of water flowing onward without rest. Sometimes the volume of thoughts is loud and sometimes quiet, nevertheless the thought-stream is continuous until we sleep and even then some brain processes continue operating although unnoticed due to unconsciousness. The sequence of thoughts that arise in the mind flows onward without interruption, never giving rise to mental peace, and this endless dynamic continuum produces an ever-present field of experience with qualities. Thus we can say that the mind is a *field of becoming*, and as non-intrinsic beings this is how we experience our existence. We need to learn how to master the experiences and functions of this consciousness.

Meditation practice can produce a reduction to the complexity and volume of the ceaseless flow of thoughts in your mind by somewhat temporarily silencing the torrent of the thought-stream. Then you can taste the naturally pure, peaceful, stress-free nature of your mind to find peace and contentment for a while. It is a way for you to calm down your mentation and find internal peace. When that happens your Qi/Prana will start to transform. It will become free of attachments to the thought-stream that normally biases its movements here and there, and then it will circulate much better. Better circulation of Qi flow will, in turn, lead to clearer, calmer and more comfortable mental states too.

Basically, consciousness is always receiving inputs from the visual, auditory and other senses, and because of these impulses it is continually being stirred. This continuous stirring helps it maintain its onward flux. Consciousness is continually perfumed by new impressions that affect the thought-stream, which is always transforming by activating the seeds for new thoughts to be born. Every thought eventually perishes but before doing so serves as a cause for new thoughts to arise. Thus, a thought (in the mind) never remains continuously single, never stops leading to further thoughts, and a thought cannot remain in your active consciousness even when you concentrate on holding it with stability to retain it. Your mental realm is always changing but you can learn to affect many aspects of it.

Concentration, which is being able to stay with an activity for a long time such as when you maintain your hold on a thought with stability, is the basis for mundane accomplishments. Its importance as a mental ability has given rise to various forms of spiritual practice such as visualization exercises for concentration training. By practicing concentration you can learn to extend your attention span and hence maintain your determination and perseverance because it requires that you ignore distractions that would normally interrupt your focus. Furthermore, a focused mind tends to be a happy state of consciousness whereas a wandering mind tends to be an unhappy mind. All these points prompt the practice of meditation with attributes, namely concentration exercises that train your mental stability because they require you to sustain your focus and attention.

There is *meditation with attributes* (such as concentration practice or vipassana where you silently observe your mental formations) and *meditation without attributes* (such as emptiness, equanimity, *shamatha*, calm-abiding, formlessness or thought-free practice). The ever-moving, ever-changeful, ever-vibrating dancing Shakti can be paired with "meditation with attributes" while the all-pervading fundamental substrate that is spotlessly empty like space can be paired with "emptiness meditation." Note the analogies with energy and empty space, and the thoughts that arise within consciousness versus quiet thought-free awareness (said to be the natural state of your mind). The primary spiritual training technique in most traditions is *vipassana* meditation, which heightens the mind's focus, clarity and attention to its inner world through a single-pointed and non-attached awareness of one's ever-changing field of consciousness. This training uses your powers of attention to more appropriately, objectively and effectively examine the world and through its usage you become not just more clear-headed but develop an enhanced awareness of the whole.

It is also often explained that in the empty, motionless original nature (Parabrahman) that is continuous without attributes, somehow there arose movement in the form of a manifestation of energy (the wind element). As to *how* Shakti (fundamental energy) originated, Buddhism labels this process with the word "Ignorance" (the first step in the chain of interdependent origination) since no one knows how this was possible just as no one understands how consciousness first developed or how thoughts arise in our minds. No one knows how the universe was born out of an empty state because it cannot possibly occur within/to a pure fundamental substratum of Aloneness that never undergoes any modification. Yet Shakti the phenomenal universe was born, and Buddhism calls the cosmos "karmic formations." It uses other names as well such as Triple Realm, *samsara*, the universe, cosmos and so on.

Analogously, the natural state of our mind is like the pristine peace of the original nature since both are free from emotions, desires, passions and other constructions. The infinite essence is free from all forms of misery and we can become that way by seeing that suffering is just a bundle of thoughts and emotions, by refusing to identify with those mental formations, and then letting misery leave us rather than prolonging unnecessary suffering by clinging to it. Mental events like suffering spontaneously arise within our consciousness all the time and we should let them naturally come and go without clinging to them, just as somehow energy arises within the fundamental substrate that doesn't cling to it but lets it transform without interference. It is this naturally pure, pristine state of mental awareness, which can consciously know while being very quiet and clear, that we want to cultivate in spiritual practice as the analogy to the fundamental substratum. Doing so has benefit for our life and our Qi flow that is necessary for the attainment of the subtle body achievement.

It is also sometimes said that the natural state of your mind is like a clear light that illuminates phenomena. To "illuminate" means that your mind gives you the power to know, to be aware, to understand, to have insight or realize something. Therefore in some spiritual schools human consciousness or awareness is sometimes called "light" or "illumination" to refer to knowingness. The meditation practice of watching your own thoughts (*vipassana*) is also meant to help you realize what you are thinking and doing, which is "illuminating consciousness." You are simply cultivating awareness and insight, and from awareness (the knowing of your thinking) you open up the potential for change, and thus improvement.

Merely being able to observe the contents of your mind enables you to change course without becoming lost (enmeshed) in a thought pattern and then get carried away by it. We all have wholesome and unwholesome thoughts, skillful and unskillful thoughts, happiness-producing and sorrow-producing thoughts. Once you start observing the character of your thoughts from moment-to-moment you can see their nature and then make wiser choices that avoid suffering, unskillful actions and unwholesome outcomes. From those better decisions you can start to experience more happiness or at least *cease to suffer unnecessarily*. If through introspection we see that our thoughts are unhealthy for us because they might produce suffering – such as greed, anger, jealously, etc. – we can let go of them and live happier because of a decision to let them go and change direction.

Our natural state of mind is often called luminous mind, bright mind, pure consciousness, illumination, or pristine awareness, which of course are misleading terms because thoughts are still there despite these analogies to an empty mind. With awakeness the mind is always replete with thoughts "finer" than coarse cognition or the loudness of the inner narration. We also sometimes use the phrase "pure consciousness" to denote an empty mind but thoughts are consciousness too. All types of mental doings are just consciousness – *pure* consciousness or *purely* consciousness. The point is that you can, through meditation, reach a stage where your mind's inner narrative of self-talk (that you usually hear in your head) becomes quieter, and this produces a cleaner state of clarity. To realize that the natural state of your mind is empty/quiet like this without extra complexity is one of the purposes of meditation as a spiritual practice.

Thus we have three forms of mental training often used in spiritual schools: concentration practice to help you develop stability of your mind; witnessing practice where you watch your thoughts and behavior so that you can develop your clarity and correct your mind-stream and conduct or activities (deeds); and emptiness meditation which brings you mental peace by imitating the natural inactivity of our ground state nature.

Naturally there are other forms of meditation practice and mind training as well, such as various forms of contemplation, and various forms of vital energy training too. The Great Learning of Life demands many different types of training so that we can master the many abilities of our consciousness and our bodies. For instance, contemplation practice exercises your mental powers of logic and analysis, which you can use for analyzing your mental patterns or investigating the roots of your mental afflictions. The intent is to know them and understand them so that you can dissolve them. Contemplation helps you derive insights that can improve how you manage your mind and behavior.

When we start training our minds to develop new abilities so that more of its capabilities unfold we are attempting to more fully employ our great gift of consciousness that is the crux of our beingness and the core focus of development on the spiritual trail. The spiritual path includes learning how to use all the powers of our consciousness and how to use our ordinary consciousness correctly with minimum errors or bias. True spirituality involves making use of all your mental processes and cognitive capabilities so that you develop your mental skills to their fullest and then develop better characteristics in your personality and behavior. When you do this it is called mastering *dharmas*, whose meaning also includes mastering various skills and bodies of knowledge.

What is the highest *dharma*? Consciousness itself, which means awareness of your self and the world. This understanding is called wisdom, which has many branches. *Bodhi*, the enlightenment mind, is just the ordinary mind we have. The most natural state of consciousness is a quiet, peaceful, carefree, enjoyable mind of equanimity replete with perceptions of the world. This is called bliss or equanimity (peacefulness/tranquility) or *nirvana* or liberation. It is nothing special other than to consciously exist with a clarity of sentient awareness but without mental pain, suffering, irritation or affliction. It is not a state of perfect no-thought or thoughtlessness but entails *beingness accompanied by consciousness*, so it involves non-irritating (blissful), clear thought activity of active or passive modes.

Hence the emphasis on cultivating peaceful states of mind (moods) though meditation practice, which is one way to help achieve this as a natural mode of your character or manifest beingness. As stated, we can also experience enjoyable or "blissful" active mental states such as peak experiences and moods of joy, happiness, sunniness, lightness, centeredness and flow, etcetera. We can cultivate towards these states through a variety of means including better health (ex. blood sugar affects consciousness), meditation practice, physical exercises that stretch our muscles so that we attain better internal energy (Qi) flow upon which consciousness rides, *neijia* inner energy work as an alternative method of improving that Qi flow and the peacefully clear quality of attendant consciousness, as well as through pure, virtuous behavior that leads to a happy life free of negativities that would produce afflictive, disruptive mental states. If you follow the *dharma* of good behavior you can develop a more peaceful life and state of mind. The practices of mental witnessing, introspection, concentration, visualization and even inner energy work are considered cultivation or meditation practices, and are the primary building blocks for spiritual attainments since they help you cultivate your character, behavior and attain the higher spiritual bodies. Meditation helps you cultivate *clarity in knowing your consciousness* so you can better develop your mental abilities and control your consciousness and its deeds, and hence is supreme. All sorts of mental practices can be used to train the deliberate and automatic processes of our consciousness (such as our moods), and we should try to develop greater mental capabilities and instill the best neural patterns of consciousness possible through these various techniques available to us. Meditation helps us achieve this and therefore is considered the core of spiritual practices.

Chapter 13
SELF-IMPROVEMENT, SPIRITUAL VALUES AND VIRTUOUS CONDUCT[24]

One of the ways to summarize the foundational stage of the spiritual path is, "Be good, turn away from evil and do good deeds." Basically, the ground stage of spiritual practice is to work on elevating your thinking and behavior. You cut down on errant conduct and negative thoughts and clean up your mentality. You are taught to give up evil or incorrect ways, work on cleaning the faults and weaknesses of your lower nature, and start purifying your mind. You work on correcting its errant tendencies in your thinking and conduct as well as waywardness of your emotional mind. You work not just at becoming free of faults or "non-sick" (normal) but at cultivating the exceptional within yourself through personal practice.

You basically work at self-mastery - gaining control of your thinking and emotional animal mind to free yourself from bondage to the impulses and desires of your lower nature. You also work on freeing yourself from limiting beliefs that thwart you from working hard because they place a barrier between you and the possibility of higher attainments, being bound by the incorrect thoughts of other people or society, being bound by the self-image or self-identification you've constructed of yourself, and being bound by planetary influences. You start working on elevating your behavior with the ideal being consummate conduct in all you do – you want to manifest the brightest virtue and excellence in all your efforts. In Christianity this self-development work is called "Christian perfectionism."

---

[24] See *Color Me Confucius*, especially Chapters 6, 8, 9, 10 and 11, *Liao Fan's Four Lessons*, *The Autobiography of Benjamin Franklin*, and *How I Raised Myself From Failure to Success in Selling* (Frank Bettger).

You should actually be engaged in this self-development work all the time. You should always be working at purifying your unwholesome tendencies of thought, word and deed in order to become a better person, which is the task of ennoblement or self-perfection. Confucianism calls this refining oneself, working to make your virtue brilliant and pursuing consummate conduct. The great masterpiece of life is for you to live appropriately and become the self of your highest vision who is aligned with your highest ideals despite forces that would lead you away from this objective. Self-development work has this as its purpose.

You shouldn't just be doing this at the foundational stage of cultivation, but throughout the entire process of cultivation because there is no final stage of "No More Learning" or "No More Self-Improvement" even when you attain the Immanence body. You are always learning and engaged in perfecting your behavior because power tends to corrupt those who attain a degree of control of others. As you progress in stages you gradually attain more degrees of power over others, and power tends to corrupt people since we all have imperfections. Therefore you must really devote yourself to a continuous path of self-correction and self-perfection on the spiritual trail.

Remembering that power corrupts people (because everyone has imperfections) and powerful people oppress or exploit the weak, when you attain each new higher body you must become even stricter with your own behavior due to attaining more and more powers that enable you to control people for your own benefit. The tendency to intervene in people's lives for fun or training purposes (such as giving them strange thoughts or experiences during drug trips) becomes a problem. Therefore on the spiritual path you must always be working on elevating your mind and behavior so that they become virtuous and pure through and through from moment to moment. Self-observation, mindfulness and introspection practices help you to accomplish this. They help you to reassess, reboot and get better. To truly become a more virtuous individual you must always be watching your mind and behavior and correcting it whenever you spot errant tendencies. It is better to stop bad habits from becoming established than trying to get rid of habits already embedded within your psyche.

We are all trained when young as to what is right and wrong (proper) and taught socially acceptable behaviors to help shape our characters towards virtuous behavior and harmonious cooperation with others. In life we must forever continue this process of self-improvement, and must continually work at eliminating our vices and faults while polishing our virtues and trying to become more skillful and effective at whatever we do. We must constantly work at becoming kinder, more caring and accepting, more ethical, more respectful, wiser, more skillful and more compassionate.

This is the Great Learning required in life. We must always be retraining ourselves to remove errant conditioning we have already adopted, including animalistic impulses or responses, and replacing those influences with something better. The neuroplasticity of the brain, and our ability to change the algorithms of consciousness, enable us to terraform our mind and transform its algorithms that don't serve us into better ones that do. To accomplish this you need to devote yourself to deliberate improvement practices in a gradual training regime, which is the road of spirituality or self-cultivation. People enter the religious life to do this. For example, among many things the asceticism of monkhood weakens desire's hold on us and helps us break many addictive tendencies for bad habits, and in this way it serves as a useful vehicle of transformation for helping us purify our mind and behavior. You don't just become "spiritual" by performing religious ceremonies or by meditating. Rather, you start upon the road of spiritual practice by first giving up your bad ways of living and being and replacing them with better ways instead, and then gradually learn step-by-step how to gain control over your mind, its emotions and desires so that you transform your personality and way of living. Then you must continue doing this throughout your life so as to be improving all the time, which is how you cultivate *shining virtue and irreproachable conduct*. Slowly, slowly you can work to become a better self, and then ultimately your ideal self.

Our first instinct in a situation might be to lie, steal, boast or hurt others, but at the foundational stage of spiritual practice you train to have your intellect control your emotional mind and animal impulses, and try to transcend such baser ways of behaving. This gets easier as you pass age twenty-four and become an adult, and yet harder if you fall into sensual, materialistic or evil tendencies. You must therefore always practice having your intelligent brain, which has been taught right versus wrong, control your instinctive or emotional brain that might want to lie, steal, get angry, be selfish, get drunk, take drugs and so forth, and you must detach from becoming ruled by transient material desires. Be residing in purity your mind can always live in purity.

The discipline of self-control and self-improvement, and the cultivation of virtues such as patience, kindness, honesty and generosity are what evolve us towards higher purity in thought, word and deed, and they also produce a better world. All religions have a foundational stage of this type of training to civilize people in order to yield a better community for everyone. In short, the foundational ground state of every religion includes principles and rules for proper individual and group behavior.

Ethical teachings and rules of social propriety enable everyone to cooperatively live together in a harmonious way, and this enables people within society to live peacefully with one another so that society can thrive and attain prosperity. Even a pride of lions has rules for the behavior of the group but animals that live individually do not. This foundational training effort of ethics, morality, values and virtue is therefore beneficial for ourselves and for society. When countless people work at cultivating their moral behavior then our societies achieve civil harmony and become permeated by humanity and social justice rather than lawlessness, selfishness, immorality, violence and chaos. If everyone works on improving their behavior then society runs better, and so behavioral rules of dos and don'ts are emphasized at the foundational stage of religion that teaches proper conduct.

Pursuing virtue means applying wisdom and clear thinking as well as ethical and moral principles to your way of being in the world, which requires you to always correct ways that don't fall in line with higher moral standards. You work at transforming any unwholesome patterns of thinking and behaving that have become ingrained within your psyche and which have wrongly conditioned your personality and ways of doing things. In Confucianism this is called "refining one's person" and "making your virtue brilliant." The ultimate goal is to cultivate perfect goodness, to make your virtues brilliant, and then *walk the way of the highest good in the world*. You want to polish your virtues to shining excellence, and then make your bright virtues manifest by doing good deeds that help people and the world.

Basically, you look at how you think and act with true honesty, having created your own patterns, and then become responsible for improving those patterns. You want those patterns to manifest the highest good, to reveal the brightest virtues, and you want them to reflect your authentic self – the heart core of who you are and want to be. In other words, you want to make your intentions perfectly genuine, reflect your most authentic inner self, and express them in the most magnificent fashion.

You should always be reworking "your patterns" into something not just better but magnificent when possible. This is the meaning of Confucius's term "illustrious virtue." You must elevate these as much as possible and transform them into something true to yourself but also spiritually transcendent. The goal is to emulate the various Buddhas, sages and saints who are all devoted to different pledges, visions, vows or commitments that reflect their own individual aspirations and missions of compassionate activity or becoming excellent at something.

This cultivation work is a struggle because you must try to act in the highest possible manner free of the negative influences surrounding you. It is a struggle because you have to catch your thinking and behavioral errors in real time that are due to errant tendencies you somehow adopted and incorporated into your way of being. It involves building new patterns that are free of wrong patterns and thereby manifest brighter excellence and virtue instead.

You are also looking to cultivate for yourself a clear and peaceful state of mind that, within the calmness and stable levelheadedness you cultivate, can pick the best behavior for the moment rather than default rash actions. This too is spiritual cultivation, which is to cultivate mental clarity and stability. The key to consummate, noble conduct is reaching a steady state balancing of one's mind, which in turn requires meditation practice. Only through mental training can you reach a level of concentration that is free of perturbation and thereby tastes calmness, rest, tranquility and even flow.

The spiritual path is that you work on the self-improvement task of incorporating higher standards and ideals into your personality, your psychology, your psyche, your thinking, your attitudes, your relationships, your habits, your physical skills and your behavior. This is the foundational stage of the cultivation path but *this is also the heart of the cultivation path*. This is the Great Learning of Confucius, which entails not just learning *how to control yourself* but how to raise yourself up to majestic consummate conduct in thought, word and deed and thus experience a better inner and outer life.

This is the spiritual path. This is the path of religion. This prepares you for the privilege of the higher spiritual body attainments. This requires not just self-control, but study to learn new knowledge, skills and ways of thinking and behaving that will change your life, such as learning to exercise and eat better for better health that rejuvenates your body. In fact, the activity of rejuvenating and renewing your body by curing your illnesses, healing any damage you've developed over the years, and revitalizing yourself is a major part of the foundational stage of spiritual practice for every religion. In the *Niyama* stage of Yoga these health restoration/maintenance activities are referred to as physical purification. Such mundane concerns are an essential part of the spiritual path and especially emphasize in Taoism. You are a living object with consciousness, and the spiritual path involves learning how to live your life well. Your consciousness and behavior depend on your body so you must work to keep it in excellent shape. There is no escaping this requirement on the spiritual path. Ascetic extremes that harm your body are wrong.

You want to nobly walk the way of the highest good in life even if it means you are poor or despised by others due to circumstances. Therefore you must always be committed to cultivating higher virtues, values and ways of living, being and doing that transcend your fears and desires for social approval. Externally you must strive for strength, elegance and purity in word and deed while internally you must strive to develop peace and harmony instead of turbulence, agitation and confusion. You must work on purifying your thoughts, words and conduct, and practice watchful mindfulness and correction of your inner and outer behaviors so that they become more admirable, noble, and efficacious. It is not that you should suppress your errant tendencies, and thereby wrap yourself with a tight layer of binding constraints. Rather, you should actually *unravel and retrain your inherent errant tendencies* rather than simply suppress them, and spiritual work means dissolving them, re-channeling them or transforming them into something higher.

You must also work on improving your life so that it runs better. The goal is to cultivate stronger moral, ethical and virtuous inner and outer behavior. You want to cultivate yourself to be able to frequently experience a more pristine, lucid, flowing state of beingness where you feel internal happiness and a contagious joy for life. Calm, peacefulness or equanimity and happiness – a sunny, cheerful and optimistic disposition – are what the road of spiritual practice wants you to achieve as your natural state. It does not target a perfect lack of suffering but peaceful states of tranquility or active states of happiness, bliss or other states of well-being such as shine. You should be cultivating positive stable mental states that are tied into living a peaceful life of purity that has maximum vitality, but also experience bliss and well-being. One should definitely be pursuing happiness as well as meaning, which are to be found in following one's life purpose.

Because we live in societies of relationships, another tendency we need to develop is to perform good deeds that improve public situations for the better, such as by making altruistic or philanthropic efforts on behalf of friends and strangers. This produces happiness for others (especially the downtrodden and unfortunate) by reducing their suffering and increasing their well-being. Christianity calls this "good works" while Buddhism calls the performance of good deeds "accumulating merit." The feeling that we should help others rather than just ourselves by making charitable, philanthropic or even social justice efforts should become part of our personality, and is one of the necessary components of virtuous behavior.

The individuals who become this way eventually become Buddhas. Without becoming a good person with an admirable personality, and without developing the natural tendency to compassionately help others to alleviate their suffering and concerns, no Buddhas as a group will work on you for the full twelve years required to perform the kundalini transformations that purify your subtle body for the Srotapanna (first dhyana) attainment. Hence, spiritual liberation or the enlightenment body attainments are only achievable through grace – the grace of others that religions call the "grace of God" instead. Virtue, ethics and morality are the fundamental mode for spiritual progress, and determine what role you play in life and the world. Without being a virtuous person you are not qualified for the Srotapanna attainment.

The foundational phase of spiritual practice is also a stage of study and wisdom accumulation where you first start to study spiritual cultivation teachings so that you understand the principles of the cultivation path and how to engage with others in society. Without this it is difficult to pursue virtue and self-perfection. You must study with an aspiration to increase your worldly wisdom in fields such as psychology, history, economics, persuasion, human relationships, medicine, hygiene, exercise, diet, science, technology, and so forth in order to live wiser. You must study the cultivation path so that you know what to expect and how to guide yourself.

Basically, the wisdom required of this stage necessitates that you learn how to live a healthy and more prosperous, happier life. You must study with such aspirations in mind in order to transform in those directions. This stage therefore includes practicing yoga, the martial arts, dance or athletics since they are fundamental methods for developing your human fitness potential, as well as pathways for cultivating the higher spiritual bodies too.

Such body wisdom requires you to know what not to eat or drink, how to dress, rules of hygiene, how much to work or rest, and how to manage your sex life to protect your health. Basically you must learn the principles for the well-being of living such as by putting yourself in harmony with the transformations/course of Nature, and thus bring yourself in accord with the functioning of the universe. You have an innate connection with the universe that allows you to harmonize with the world in your activities and behavior. You also exist through an interdependence with others within which you can find greater meaning for your life.

A "life of virtue" requires such wise behavior. Since people's own self-destructive behaviors are often detrimental to their health and well-being, individuals must take responsibility for their health by taking steps to restore it. They must learn to take appropriate precautions in order to avoid any harmful effects from their environments that might damage them. They must also learn how to restore their injured bodies and deteriorating vitality, both of which are essential for the spiritual path. *Your natural vitality must not be injured because it is necessary for the spiritual path.*

This is "becoming virtuous as regards your physical nature." It is only by nourishing your life and bolstering your health through proper exercise, diet and meditation that you can lay down and maintain a good foundation for the spiritual path since it includes generating higher bodies out of your body's inherent Qi energy (Prana). This type of knowledge and effort is included at the fundamental spiritual stage of virtue training and wisdom accumulation, which is why many religions promote dietary rules and prohibitions, although people normally only concentrate on virtue and ethics training.

Christianity and Judaism use the Ten Commandments for ethical guidance, Buddhism speaks of the Ten Wholesome Actions and Eightfold Path, Moslems look to the Koran and Sharia for ethical guidance, Confucianism has the Five Virtues and Five Relationships, and Hindu ethics are to be found in the Vedas and Upanishads while Yoga distinctly points to the codes of *Yama* and *Niyama*, etcetera. All spiritual schools and religions champion certain character values, ethical standards and codes of conduct and they all have various instructions on ethics as part of their foundational teachings. Those teachings are applied to the individual but benefit society so that everyone within it can live together and flourish.

Basically, ethics involves incorporating concepts of right and wrong behavior (propriety) into your life, meaning that there are things you should do and things you should not do, things to refrain from and things to strive for in terms of the twelve relationships. The twelve basic relationships of life are your relationships with: others (the "six relationships" of you and your parents, siblings, spouse, children and authorities); your physical body; society (your community, city, state, country and culture); the environment (including your living conditions); other life (living phenomena) and insentient phenomena (objects); *your personal attributes* - your personality, psyche, character, attitudes (mentality and emotional behavior), ethics, conduct/behavior, wisdom, spirituality, skills and fortune (fate); and *attributes you cultivate* - your life (activities), goals and vows (noble directions and purposes). Ethics are connected with the principles of propriety in conduct and behavior, fairness and justice, moral integrity, proper living, spirituality and the way things should be done (which all require that you rectify yourself when you go astray), and involve the principles of humaneness, kindness, respect and consideration for others.

The primary rules of ethical restraint and ethics/morality in general involve doing no harm and holding people accountable; not aggressing against another person, their property and liberty (their autonomy), being honest (straightforward, dependable and non-tricky) in your dealings with people, keeping your promises and providing them whatever they deserve or are owed; being nice and promoting mutual interest; *being provocable (returning cooperation with cooperation and defection with defection [ex. instituting punishment, shame, shunning, abandonment when people deviate from the expected norms of virtue] in order to establish accountability that insures the continuance of a system based on virtue*; being respectful of others and their self-rule; not doing to (imposing upon) others what you would not want done to you (this includes not harming others or increasing the risk of harm to others, and when harm cannot be avoided we are obligated to minimize the harm); doing for others what you would appreciate them doing for yourself (treat them in the same way you would want to be treated); treating all people equally, fairly, impartially, and working for the benefit of those unfairly treated; doing good and preserving the good whenever found while cutting off any evil after encountering it while preventing potential evil from being born (arising) but encouraging potential good to arise (these principles encapsulate the idea that we have an obligation to bring about good in all our actions, cut off evil whenever we find it, and to take steps to prevent harm); and basically being unremitting in the doing of good deeds by doing them with all your might and by every possible means so as to be doing all the good you can, by all the means you can, in all the ways you can, in all the places you can, to all the people you can, as long as you can.

Within these principles are the basic ideas to respect other people, do them no harm, hold everyone accountable and that we have an obligation to bring about good in all our actions, cut off evil whenever we find it, we should take steps to prevent harm and correct harm or injustice that has been done.

Basically, the idea is to show caring concern and a *love for others* through helpful, kind, compassionate efforts and behavior that includes charity and other forms of aid. The primary ethical principles include more than just this short list but this is the gist that can be found in most basic religious teachings.

For instance, in the *Mahabharata* of Hinduism we find, "This is the sum of duty. Do naught to others which if done to thee would cause thee pain." In

Judaism the *Talmud* says, "What is hateful to you, do not to your fellow men. That is the entire law; all the rest is commentary." In Buddhism the *Udanavarga* states, "Hurt not others with that which pains yourself." In Christianity the *Gospel of Matthew* says, "So in everything, do to others what you would have them do to you, for this sums up the law and the Prophets." In Zoroastrianism it is said, "That nature only is good when it shall not do unto another whatever is not good for its own self." In Islam a Hadith runs, "No one of you is a believer until he desires for his brother that which he desires for himself."

The list of basic disciplinary rules or proper behavior also includes self-control restraints such as injunctions not to steal, lie, kill, commit violence (non-injury), be cruel to others or abuse others, indulge in sexual excess or improper sexual relations, overindulge in sensual pleasures and so on. Because people commonly destroy themselves from addictions or excessive behavior in regards to drugs, alcohol, smoking, gambling and speculation, fighting, sadistically abusing others (using power/control over others), dangerous sports, overeating, sexual relations, pornography, gossiping, shopping and debt, etc. most religions warn against these and other such activities too.

The active principles of virtuous behavior we must practice include treating others as you would want to be treated yourself, offering charity, your knowledge and kindness in a compassionate way that takes care of other people's welfare, acting with honesty and integrity, instituting and enforcing justice among people rather than letting evil thrive or allowing the powerful to hold sway in unfairly exploiting people, doing what you know is right rather than wrong, etcetera.

Cultivating ethics is the act of cultivating admirable values and virtues that ennoble your character because they raise you above your inherent animal tendencies, which is an effort that consequentially purifies your conduct, your Qi, and your fortune. Different religions have proposed diverse lists of "virtues" or "values" as ideals for the consummate conduct of self-perfection. Basically, they raise you above your animal nature by requiring you to gain control over your passions and desires so that these impulses don't control you. They entail elevating your thoughts, words and behavior, which is also called purifying or spiritualizing them, and this also nourishes and refines your vital force (Qi/Prana). People who simply cultivate good deeds and virtuous behavior progress a long way in purifying their Qi/Prana just from such daily natural activity.

Wisdom demands that ethics be applied according to common sense that considers circumstances, and not according to inviolable rules from ancient religious texts or traditions such as you find in Hasidism. The rules-should-never-change approach locks society into ancient social attitudes that might no longer be appropriate, thus imprisoning society at a lower stage of development and preventing it from advancing. This happened in Confucianism, Islam and Judaism which all failed to update themselves and adapt to the new economic, social and psychological evolutions within society.

Jesus became a role model of correct behavior (even though it went against religious rules or traditions) when he spoke of a man rescuing a mule on the Sabbath even though Jewish religious law forbid work on that day – an artificial injunction invented by mankind and not by God. As another instance, while the rule is never to lie you should certainly misdirect an intended murderer if he were stalking someone to kill. As yet another example, it is immoral to refuse an unapproved drug to a dying patient who has no other options. The well-being of others is central to ethical decision-making rather than whether or not you break some code of conduct.

Rules of proper behavior naturally develop within societies or are imposed on the people by their governments and religions. They perfume the people in a certain way over time – *imparting a coloring to the soul for certain tendencies* – that gradually changes social traits and the ideas of acceptable behavior. In reality, ethics must become deeply ingrained as a personality trait so that they become part of you. Ethics, virtuous ways and higher values must become fundamental mental patterns within your personality that permeate your psyche.

You develop those traits through the osmosis of watching role models, absorbing those influences from your culture and society, giving other forms of pure food to your mind, by directly being taught the dos and don'ts of proper behavior, and also because you personally ponder the proper way to act in situations on your own. Wisdom and compassion are to be guides to true ethical behavior and altruism. One of the best guiding principles for an ethical life is to simply refrain from harming others, namely "don't do to others what you wouldn't want done to yourself."

To cultivate the road of self-improvement required of the spiritual path, which means perfecting your thoughts and behavior that are in turn due to ingrained habits you developed due to prior experiences, you must always be watching your mind and policing your actions. You must try to eliminate your bad habits and form excellent new habits in their place. You want to eliminate internal mental and emotional afflictions that interfere with the determination of, and execution of, wise and skillful behavior. You want your attention to always be monitoring your mind-stream in order to bring them under voluntary control and in line with higher ways. Only if you control your mind do you control your life.

This is why you need to learn meditative introspection, witnessing, mindfulness or watching practice, and try to bring these habits with you into regular daily life. In a certain way they help to make you the most alive by freeing you from robotic, automatic or blind, insentient entrainment with your thoughts. Additionally, introspection and self-reflection lead to self-improvement and without these practices you can never hope to practice self-perfection.

The main way of transforming errant behavioral habits is through the method of inner watching, introspection, or mental witnessing wherein you continuously watch yourself to police your thoughts and behavior through heightened awareness. Self-watching is a way to establish mental and behavioral propriety because by doing so, where you center yourself in awareness rather than your thinking, you can disentangle yourself from the momentum of your thoughts and actions and open yourself to the opportunity for self-correction. You develop this ability through sustained meditation practice where you stand back and watch your thoughts to become aware of your own thinking processes. In this way you develop the ability to "know your own mind." This teaches you to assess yourself and pay attention to what is happening. When bad attributes are noticed in yourself you strive to fix them. When bad thoughts or actions are noticed/witnessed you should immediately cut them off and replace them with something better. When the right thoughts arrive to do a good deed then instead of remaining complacent you should also rouse yourself to perform those good efforts *if that is wise and proper*. The activity of being virtuous through vigorous effort is what cements virtue in one's character.

Another way of developing higher virtues is through the immeasurable *bhava* meditations, such as those found within Buddhism, that involve perfuming your mind, body, and Qi/Prana with gigantic positive emotions that you envelop yourself within during a session of meditative absorption. By permeating your consciousness, and thus your Qi/Prana, with tremendously large emotional perfuming influences (by imagining that you possess a virtuous character trait while feeling it inside you and all around you boundlessly), these character traits are bound to influence your Qi/Prana and start bearing more fruit in this life and the next. Cultivating a sunny disposition, more joy in the moment, and various virtuous qualities can be developed in this way.

Yet another method, called principal awareness, is a type of mental reframing that alters the way you view any of your activities by embedding them with strong positive intentions that position them in your mind as undertakings of a nobler, higher mission. While performing some activity, this means framing (reinterpreting) it differently in your mind rather than holding onto a mundane meaning, and *injecting it with higher virtuous intent*. Whenever possible you can use this technique to ennoble your activities with a higher idealism. The famous example that comes to mind is of a stone mason who was building a brick wall for a cathedral while holding onto the higher thought "I am building a cathedral" or "I am building a place where people can communally gather to experience God" rather than simply "I am building a brick wall." Similarly, when making breakfast for your children you can think "I *get* to make breakfast for my kids" instead of "I *have* to make breakfast for my children." This is viewing the activity as an opportunity rather than as a burden.

The principle of cultivating a clear mental presence of pristine awakeness is that there are no "ordinary moments" in life that should be permitted the temptation to lethargically slip into a non-alert mind that sleepily operates on auto-pilot. Every moment in the universe is the most important moment. Your sensory channels should at all times be fully open, your inner vitality should always fully circulate smoothly within you and thus give you a feeling you are saturated by a healthy bliss of vitality, and your mind should always be fully alive, awake and aware – essentially brimming with pristine fresh awareness as you perform all your activities. You should view your activities as playful joyous adventures rather than as problems to be overcome, and instill them with a higher meaning whenever possible in order to reduce the impact of any pain, monotony or other negative qualities they might entail.

Just as when performing religious rituals or ceremonies, you should give rise to deep emotions in order to stimulate your Qi/Prana (which is the purpose of religious practices), you should perform the actions in life that need to be performed with a sense of vivid aliveness and wakefulness – the "alertness of a Zen master" – while your inner vitality flows without circulatory obstructions within you. By also elevating all your actions to a higher state of purpose, instead of acting mindlessly and robotically, and embedding them with a measure of elevated humaneness, you can change your attitudes and outlook on life, your character and even your fortune. By living in the moment where you allow yourself to experience all the vibrant qualities of the world, while you may not be able to change any unfortunate circumstances affecting you, you can still experience the active joy of living.

There are many methods that can help you live life better, improve your awareness of your mind and phenomena, transform your character towards virtue where you cut off the tendency toward bad thoughts and deeds and create better thoughts and deeds in their place, and increase your inner Qi flow and vitality. The methods for becoming more alert and alive and vibrant, which require better internal Qi flow, require meditation work and *neijia* inner energy practices (see *Neijia Yoga*). You start laying the groundwork for this accomplishment during this foundational stage of the spiritual path where you are working at transforming yourself toward the direction of excellence in mind, body and virtue.

You must learn how to think and act with greater wisdom and skillfulness in life according to higher values, but also improvise your technique according to principle. This means that you need to develop greater wisdom and understanding so that you can surmise the likely outcome of events if you act in a certain way, and then you should act in the best way possible after evaluating all your alternatives. Whatever you are doing should always be rectified in the moment when lapses are noted. You want to adopt best practices wherever possible, improve situations for the better by cutting off errant events and replacing them with what is better, and act in a way that is not just expedient for the moment but best for the short-term, intermediate-term and long-term whenever possible.

What are the virtues and values we need to cultivate in life? Every religion has its preferred list, but it comes down to two factors: values and virtues for the "I" that are necessary for an individual's survival or achievement, and the values or virtues necessary for being able to peacefully live in a group ("We") that also help the group to both survive and flourish.

For instance, some of the particular character traits you need in order to survive if you were living on your own by yourself include self-sufficiency and self-reliance; critical thinking; discipline, self-control, self-regulation, self-restraint and responsibility; goal-directed adaptive behavior and resilience (toughness, the ability to recover quickly from difficulties); a high tolerance for pain and suffering; prudence (cautiousness) and temperance (moderation); resourcefulness, creativity and inventiveness (high agency behavior); being resolute, firmness, persistence, perseverance, will power; simplicity; diligence, commitment, forbearance, patience and grit; dispassionate reasoning and analysis; industriousness, effort, and conscientiousness (doing work well); confidence, courage and fortitude; alertness; wisdom and knowledge; ambition; confidence, bravery and courage.

There are a variety of virtues and values that are necessary for the maintenance of public welfare because they enable and promote peaceful, cooperative, collaborative living within society, thus ensuring its survival. Because of their great importance, we should be actively teaching these virtues and values in our communities, school systems and religions because they are the glue which hold both families and society together and enable us to thrive and flourish with peaceful prosperity: familial responsibility; filial piety and the Confucian six relationships; honesty (truthfulness), sincerity, straightforwardness (non-crookedness), integrity, reliability and trustworthiness; fairness and justice; friendliness (friendship), hospitality and humanity; kindness, compassion, empathy, love and caring (consideration for others); respect, tolerance, acceptance, non-hatred and open-mindedness; good manners; generosity, sharing, non-stinginess, selflessness, helpfulness, gratitude and reciprocity, benevolence, charity, altruism or the giving of oneself; collaboration, cooperation, group participation and teamwork, civic responsibility; propriety and social intelligence; mercy and forgiveness; humility; and the ability to learn socially. For living in society, the Golden Rule of *don't do to others what you don't want them to do to you* leads to principles such as non-harmfulness, non-hatred, non-stealing, non-adultery, non-lying (don't bear false witness), etc. while *do for others what you wish others would do for you* leads to principles of charity, support, service, friendliness, helpfulness, care, compassion, concern, etcetera.

Self-cultivation involves mind-body purification. You must work to cultivate the Qi/Prana of your body to attain the deva body and higher, or at the minimum to become healthier, extend your longevity and feel great during life. In the Zen school this is called *attuning the four elements of your physical body (physical nature)*, but few work at it since Zen students rarely even perform yoga or martial arts exercises and certainly don't work at cultivating their Qi/Prana. On the pathway of spiritual transformation there must be physical health, mental health, intellectual health, ethical health, spiritual health, social health and aspirational health as your foundations. You have to be cultivating your internal energy, your mind, your behavior, your activities and aspirations, and ultimately your behavior involves accomplishing deeds and getting along with others. This in turn means that you need to cultivate the social values and virtues of proper, ethical, moral, virtuous behavior.

The ultimate success of the task of developing the deva body whilst alive does not just require the right methods of cultivation and a commitment to practice but self-corrective work, good deeds and the pursuit of virtuous being otherwise higher spiritual beings will not help you with the necessary kundalini transformations. Hence it is a pathway of becoming a good person, cultivating virtuous character traits while getting rid of errant ones, doing good deeds and becoming involved in worthwhile activities, and maintaining a commitment to the right ways of living and gradual positive elevation.

You have to consider what it means to be enlightened. Upon full, complete and perfect enlightenment you have attained the *sambhogakaya* of a linked set of bodies – the physical, subtle, Causal, Supra-Causal and Immanence bodies (the human eye, deva eye, wisdom eye, dharma eye and Buddha eye of the *Diamond Sutra*) where the Supra-Causal and Immanence bodies can use their energies and also create *nirmanakaya* projections of themselves, and of other similar shapes and forms (after training), to perform deeds of compassionate activity in the world. Those bodies will have very long life existences.

What will you do with those long lives? What responsibilities, pledges, commitments or aspirations will you undertake? You will not just be engaged in cultivating your mind and body in each realm of existence to higher stages of capability and excellence, and not just be cultivating states of passive or active bliss (such as equanimity/peace or flow and sunniness or joy), but with so much time and in search of purpose you will be cultivating your relationships, skills, virtues and *Buddha vow activities*.

What is the seed of these aspirations and accomplishments? The answer is the pursuit of virtue, purity, noble behavior and service. The seed of virtue is to be taught virtuous ways by your parents and society - ideal models of behavior - and methods of self-development and self-correction that reliably instill them within your character. These methods include mindfulness practice (meditation), contemplative introspection of our behavior and self-review, "principal awareness" to inject our activities with higher ideals of virtue, the emulation of individuals who ideally model the virtues or activities we admire, intense *bhava* emotional attitude meditations and associated visualization practices to help develop virtuous character traits, the repetition of affirmations and prayers asking for spiritual aid to help us develop those traits, real world merit-making (acts of service) in line with the virtues we desire (especially those in line with the Buddha vow activities we would want to perform in the universe), and broadening ourselves with culture to elevate us by expanding our learning and horizons. Even if you don't attain enlightenment in this lifetime, this is how to cleanse your faults, "sins," flaws, imperfections or corruptions to finally merit enlightenment so this is the way to enlightenment.

Chapter 14
GENERAL PRINCIPLES FOR QI/PRANA INTERNAL ENERGY PRACTICE[25]

In spiritual cultivation you proceed from study to practice, and from practice to study. You need to mix study and practice together (theory together with meditation and inner energy work) to achieve the final result just as you must mix flour and water together to make bread. Unfortunately, in many traditions the adherents only study spiritual books and perform neither meditation nor meritorious deeds nor inner energy work. Some traditions don't even emphasize good behavior. In some schools they perform physical exercises but no energy work or self-corrective work that polishes the character and improves behavior.

You need to engage in inner energy practices, meditation practice and behavioral training to attain the higher transcendental bodies of enlightenment that correspond to *Moksha* or liberation. In Visishtadvaita Vedanta adherents try to accomplish the inner energy work through devotion (*bhakti* practices of mantra, chanting, worship, cultivating intimacy with God, cultivating the attitude of being a servant of God, etc.) and merit accumulation as well as behavioral excellence through the path of action (Karma Yoga) since the intellectual path of Advaita Vedanta without practice is not enough. In various monastic orders within Hinduism the practice requirements require meditation practice, spiritual study, devotional activities (prayer, chanting, ritualistic puja) and service activities too, which is an admirable and effective mixture just as we find with the Christian Capuchin monastics. To achieve enlightenment you must perform meditation practice either directly or indirectly without knowing it, directly perform inner energy work or activate *neijia* Qi work through your

---

[25] See *Nyasa Yoga, The Yoga of Siddha Tirumular, Yoga Yajnavalkya*, etcetera.

devotional/spiritual activities, and must start performing acts of merit that help other people. Acts of service performed for others must become part of your character along with the traits of kindness, caring and acceptance of others including all their faults.

You attain the goal of the spiritual path from perfection in study and practice together because study alone will not strengthen, purify and then liberate the inner subtle body from your physical nature, which normally happens only upon death. Practice without a guide will lead you nowhere also. In other words, study alone will not get you to the first dhyana attainment, which is the Srotapanna deva body achievement, because it is only achieved through cultivation practice, and haphazard cultivation practice without adherence to principles will produce no substantial progress either.

For the generation of an independent subtle body during life you need meditation work to stop holding onto your thoughts (which thus frees your Qi to circulate better since Qi and thoughts are linked), and to sharpen your mental clarity so that you can spot and then correct errant thinking and behavioral tendencies. As a living being you need to cultivate and perfect the various abilities and activities of your consciousness and meditation practice enables you to achieve mastery of more capabilities than we can mention.

You also need to perform energy work on your inner Qi/Prana so that you become energy-rich and energy-pure. The deva body (Srotapanna Arhat or *Homo Deus* attainment) is your inner subtle body but it is locked inside your human frame until death, or until you release it through spiritual cultivation. Cultivating its freedom through inner Qi exercises is sometimes called "growing the embryo," which is terrible terminology because the word "embryo," "baby" or "womb" makes people incorrectly think that there is a small body like a baby developing inside you. Actually, you are simply purifying and strengthening the Qi inherent within your full form physical body, and the subtle body when ejected is an exact duplicate of this adult structure. Once it is freed from the physical body, which is the "mind-born" body achievement of enlightenment described in the Buddhist *Surangama Sutra*, you have the beginnings of the *sambhogakaya* attainment because it will still be attached to your physical body, and you will have then two bodies that you can use. This is the first stage of enlightenment equivalent to the first dhyana.

This type of purification-ejection process of a new and higher transcendental body out of an old (lower) one is the spiritual path, and sometimes it is called "building a

Buddha within you." Because you can keep generating bodies in this fashion you can gain access to the abilities of higher spiritual bodies with greater capabilities than the physical body, and by using these higher bodies spiritual "masters" are able to perform miracles in the world. The miracles don't "come from God" but from spiritual beings using their bodies to perform certain deeds in the world. To release the subtle body while alive you must perform lots of intensified yoga practices that purify its Yin and Yang qualities, and greatly increase the freedom of its internal energy circulation. You can pursue this path by becoming healthy, energy-rich (through celibacy and better Qi circulation) and by engaging in intensified yoga practices or martial arts forms that stress the mastery of breathing and inner energy as do *taijiquan*, *baguazhuang* and *xingyiquan*.

Furthermore, if you are not a virtuous person, spiritual beings will not help you in this process and their help is absolutely essential for purifying your Qi, as is the assistance of a qualified master to oversee the process. Therefore, it is impossible to succeed unless you have a good teacher and are also a virtuous human being deserving of higher bodies because you are intent on helping others and devoted to self-improvement of your own character and behavior.

The principles of effective practice differ for each type of spiritual cultivation technique. The principles of practice always take into account the welfare of your mind and body – you are never to hurt your mind or body through spiritual practice! You are always to preserve and improve your health and well-being otherwise it will be difficult to proceed onwards and succeed. Remember that the deva body is a duplicate of your physical body, so you shouldn't harm your body in any way. In particular, you should not undertake extreme ascetic practices that tax or risk your physical body, you should never ignore taking care of medical conditions, should cut off habits harmful to your health and welfare (ex. smoking, drugs, drinking, etc.) and should not devote yourself to harmful physical sports that produce frequent physical injuries.

The main objectives of spiritual practices are to calm your mind and stimulate the Qi/Prana of your body into moving so that this change of state purifies your Qi/Prana. A greater circulation of your inner Qi, or the act of washing it over and over again, will gradually strengthen your inner subtle body composed of Qi/Prana until through purity it can weaken the chains to the physical body and finally leave your physical shell while you are alive. Then it becomes your main body of being, the center of your life, although still attached to your physical body that then becomes like an appendage that you learn how to control using that new body. The higher body can reside within its lower shell or somewhere else, and when traveling somewhere else we say "the master is in samadhi" because he seems non-responsive (as if in a thoughtless trance) because his spirit is absent due to traveling elsewhere in the higher realms. When a master repeats a long discourse/lesson to his students (and the students wonder why he repeats the same lesson over and over again) it is often because he is absent for a prolonged period of time and asks another spiritual master to possess his body during that interval and deliver a lesson that draws from his memories. Inner energy practices to mature the independent subtle body attainment (Tibetan Buddhism calls it the "impure illusory body") are sometimes called "attaining control over the life process within your self" because Qi/Prana is the body's vital energy or life force.

You should practice as many different types of spiritual exercise as possible, each of which works according to different principles for transforming your Qi/Prana. Through *simultaneous* practice of *many different cultivation exercises* at the same time, each which affects your Qi/Prana via *different principles*, you will maximize your chances for real Qi/Prana transformations that will purify its nature and produce the independent subtle body quickest. Since you don't know which techniques will work best for transforming your Qi/Prana, the use of multiple techniques simultaneously, each of which works on affecting your Yin or Yang Qi/Prana according to different principles, is highly recommended.

For instance, one might during a single day practice meditation, Mantrayana recitation, pranayama, yoga stretching with visualization on your muscles, and inner *nei-gong* work (*"anapana"*) to move your Qi. This is an example of practicing multiple techniques simultaneously rather than just a single cultivation method. Using multiple methods will mean that each of them will have an effect on transforming (purifying) your Qi/Prana via different principles. The harder you work – the more types of methods you practice and the longer and more consistently you practice – the higher your chances for success, and the quicker your success if success is to come. Success is the result of consistent effort applied across time. The longer and deeper you practice the more profound will be your results.

Some of the major principles of practice for different spiritual exercises are as follows:

Mantra and Prayer Recitation: Reciting mantras or prayers while listening to the sounds/words quiets and calms your mind to help you attain a state of quiescence. A mantra also invites into your body the energies of a particular family of saints or Buddhas who have vowed to help practitioners who recite their lineage's mantra, thus helping to purify your Qi and hasten your spiritual development. Mantra recitation also transforms your Qi/Prana directly because the resonance of the sounds vibrate the Qi/Prana within your body and the rhythmical breathing used during recitation *pushes* your Qi/Prana in a regular, smooth, rhythmic circulatory pattern. This produces Qi/Prana purification just as the churning of milk produces butter. When prayers are continuously recited in tune with your breathing this will help to regularly circulate your Qi with a push and purify it as well. As stated, different mantras, prayers, and spiritual songs (as well as books, passages, and spiritual texts) when recited, sung or read are "answered by," "protected by," "attended to" or receive response from different enlightened masters who through their vows assume responsibility for them. Naturally these are masters who have achieved the long-lived transcendental body attainments and fill their time with this as one of their compassionate activities attended to by *nirmanakaya* projections. In response to hearing within their Supra-Causal or Immanence body the recitation of a mantra, prayer or text they have chosen to protect, they arrive via *nirmanakaya* emanations to work on the Qi/Prana of the practitioners who recite them. Therefore a good mantra/prayer is one that you feel moves the Qi/Prana within your body. In other words, higher spiritual beings will respond to mantras, prayers, spiritual texts and rituals due to their personal vows to protect/help those who recite the chosen mantra or prayer or perform the ritual or read the scripture they have vowed to "protect" or respond to. However, even without this help there are certain mantra *bija* sounds that often *naturally resonate* or stimulate the Qi/Prana within particular parts or segments of your body, and therefore also help to strongly purify your Qi/Prana through the power of sound vibrations alone. To make mantra or prayer practice even more effective, you can (1) generate strong emotions at the same time you practice recitations to better arouse your Qi/Prana, (2) think of being the ideal model of a particular personality trait and hold that core *bhava* emotional experience in your mind-stream and as a body feeling, (3) combine mantra/prayer recitation with visualization efforts that also move your Qi/Prana inside you or concentrate it at a selected location, or (4) using your willpower try to stimulate/vibrate the Qi in different areas of your body according to the sounds. Then mantra or prayer recitation becomes the more effective method of Mantrayana practice.[26] Basically, whenever you recite a prayer or mantra *you should try to move the Qi within your body*, and it's even better if you impregnate the Qi of your entire body with a specific Yin or Yang feeling/emotion (via various methods as explained) to help activate that internal Qi for purification purposes. By moving your Qi through

---

[26] See *Nyasa Yoga* and *The Mystical Path of Christian Theosis* (Elijah John).

rhythmical breathing, rhythmical recitation of sounds that vibrate it, by actively trying to move it internally, and by impregnating it with various qualities you help cleanse your subtle body's Qi, which is an absolutely necessary preparation for ejection as an independent deva body. Countless individuals throughout history have used prayer recitation or mantra recitation as a means to calm their mind and transform their Qi as part of the intensified preparatory yoga work necessary for attaining the deva body enlightenment attainment. A continuous recitation of the Jesus Prayer, as practiced in the Eastern Orthodox Christian tradition, is one such technique while various sacred mantra recitations are a standard practice in countless eastern religions.

Mantrayana: Certain mantra sounds are incredibly effective at naturally vibrating (stimulating) the Qi/Prana in certain sections of your body through resonance, such as the three consecutive sounds of "Om Ah Hung," "Om So Hum" or "Ah Rah Ham" affecting the Qi/Prana in your (1) head and arms; (2) chest region; and (3) abdomen together with legs, respectively. Many people know "Om Ah Hum" due to its association with the Buddha Samantabhadra, but the mantra "Ah Rah Ham" is just as effective in vibrating the three sections of your body consecutively when you focus each sound on a different body section. Actually, when reciting the syllables of this mantra they should be felt in all parts of your body equally, as is the preferred case for all three-syllable mantras unless you are specifically reciting each syllable within a partition, and the sounds of "Ah Rah Ham" can also be used to *pulse* the entire Qi of your body in rhythmical fashion when recited. "Om So Hum," "Om So Ha" or just "So Ha(m)" is usually associated with breathing methods. "Aim Hreem Shreem" (where "Aim" is pronounced "I'm") can also be used to move your Qi/Prana for exciting/vibrating the Qi of your entire body or for stimulating it in your three body sections consecutively. As stated, usually you try to feel each syllable in your *entire whole body* with each syllable's voicing. Or, for instance, when reciting "Ah" you might feel the energy start in your head and move towards your feet as you hold the syllable, or start from your feet and move upwards, or start within your stomach area and move outwards everywhere, and so forth for each syllable respectively. You can recite one, two, three, four or five syllable mantras in order to cultivate the Qi/Prana of that many different physical body sections respectively, and if you simultaneously hold onto an emotion at the same time, or simultaneously hold onto the idea of being one with/like some spiritual great, the practice will impress your Qi/Prana with the influence of those extras. You can also recite mantras on certain *bindus*, *marma* points, acupuncture or acupressure points too in order to stimulate the Qi around those points. Another alternative is to try to feel the effect of the sounds along certain acupuncture meridians or within certain body parts and pathways. In esoteric Theravada (*boran kammatthana*) the Pali phonemes ("sacred syllables" that are basically mantra sounds or *bijas*) are brought into certain body parts while Japanese syllables are used in Shingon, Hebrew letters in kabbalah work, Sanskrit sounds in Hinduism and certain mantra sounds within Buddhism. If you recite mantras while trying to feel, move, excite or stimulate the Qi/Prana in different areas of the body, this effort can be helped by also simultaneously using emotional excitement or other vitalizing and invigorating techniques such as visualizations and rhythmical breathing. And, if you also put your mind/will on those areas to move your Qi/Prana in conjunction with reciting and feeling those sound syllables within you, you will quickly stimulate your Qi into moving throughout your subtle body and thus purify and strengthen its structural integrity. Adding visualization efforts to the relevant body sections at the same time - such as by using your imagination to mentally flood an area with bright light or change its color - will also help to transform its Qi/Prana because those actions will bring Qi/Prana into the region and the color adds emotional content that changes the temperament/flavor of the Qi. The best mantras have sounds that actually move/vibrate your Yin Qi or Yang Qi – and thus change the body's Qi temperament in that way – because those energies resonate in particular sections of your body just as "Om" seems to vibrate most in the head and "Ah" resonates in the chest. "Ram" (Rang, Rahlam, Rah) and "Vam" (Vah, Vang, Lam, Lang, Lah, Nam, Hum, Hung) are also very useful sounds for vibrating the Qi/Prana within particular body sections such as the top/bottom or left/right sides of the body. "Om-Ah-Nu-Ta-Rah" is a famous Tibetan Esoteric School mantra to help in "*tummo* generation," which is just the arousal of Yang Qi that we always classify as Qi/Prana transformation. Its usage (especially within Tsongkhapa's teachings or the Six Yogas of Naropa tradition) is not higher or better than any other mantra technique nor does it produce more secretive or superior results as compared to other methods. For instance, several famous Indian yoga mantras for activating or transforming the Qi/Prana/kundalini of your body or chakras include "Aim Hreem Kleem Shreem Yam Ram Lam Sham Dam Van Tam" and "Om Lam Hah Hreem Rah Aim Hum Souah Rah." Some mantras call for Qi/Prana help from higher spiritual beings, some work on purifying just your Yang Qi/Prana or just your Yin Qi/Prana through direct sound resonance, and some work on transforming both the Yang and Yin Qi/Prana of your body. Therefore, mantras can particularly vibrate the Qi/Prana in certain sections of your body or "raise your kundalini." This is how you quickly transform and purify the Qi/Prana of your inner subtle body, which is by energizing your body with certain types of Qi that are tuned by the attendant emotional tones you generate. A Shingon saying runs, "A mantra is a mystery. Reciting or singing it brings merit." That's because its sound can alter (help purify) your body's Qi, and because certain Buddhas and Bodhisattvas have vowed to respond to certain mantras by emanating a *nirmanakaya* projection body to envelop your body and help transform your Qi as you recite it. Different Buddhas from different traditions (along with their students) respond to different mantras according to their vows. Thus it is said, "A person who becomes an expert in sound yoga can attain the supreme reality."

Meditation: Meditation practice, where you achieve a degree of mental quiescence by watching your thoughts while refusing entanglement with your thinking, enables you to achieve a dispassionate oversight of the workings of your mind. From being free of fusion with your thought-stream you can correct your thoughts or let them calm down (because of not injecting your thought-stream with more energy) so that you arrive at a peaceful mental state, which is necessary for spiritual cultivation in every school and tradition. A variety of meditation practices are available to achieve this goal, especially formless meditation practices as recommended by Kashmir Shaivism, or mindfulness and formless mind practices as recommended by Zen, *Dzogchen*, *Mahamudra*, Great Perfection and other spiritual traditions. The world's religions promote many different types of meditation practice but the most frequent commonality is "watchfulness" (mindfulness) where you observe your thoughts, and "emptiness meditation" where you try to calm your thoughts and experience inner stillness. With watchfulness you stand apart from your thoughts by observing them with dispassionate detachment until they calm down, your mind grows tranquil and your mental clarity (awareness) increases (the "mind grows bright" or "illumination brightens"). Because you monitor them you develop a mind of clarity where you can see them clearly and thus move to correct them. Several "emptiness" or "formless mind" meditation approaches that abandon thoughts include mentally imitating empty space; imitating what you believe it is mentally like to be dead or non-existent; or concentrating on a mental image until wandering thoughts disappear and then letting go of even that quiet state in order to rest in real mental emptiness. Your thoughts can be calmed through these and many other meditation practices so that your Qi/Prana proceeds more readily through your brain's innumerable energy channels, which become cleared, and your awareness (mental illumination) sharpens because your mental realm accordingly becomes quieter over time and thus "empty" of unwanted agitations. Your thoughts and Qi are connected in that your thoughts can move your Qi. When you attain mental silence in this way, which is a state relatively free of thoughts, you free your internal Qi circulation from its corresponding attachment to thoughts and then it begins to circulate more smoothly so that it works through the many Qi/Prana obstructions within the natural circulatory routes of your inner Qi body. Meditation practice can (1) result in mental tranquility that is a restful state of peace and relaxation, and because of the calmness and tranquility you can *make better deliberations and decisions*, (2) result in greater clarity or awareness of what you are thinking, which will *improve your powers of self-correction or self-rectification*, (3) *strengthen your various mental skills* such as concentration, focus and the ability to ignore distractions, (4) through the achieved inner clarity enable you to attain *better self-understanding or insight into your reasons for doing things* when through that clarity you watch your thought processes and determine why certain thoughts and behaviors arise, and (5) enable spiritual beings to become *more efficient at transforming your Qi* with their own energies because during thought-free meditation practice your thoughts do not hold tightly to your internal energy at that time, and thus it can be more easily moved by spiritual masters trying to help you. Many meditation techniques are available such as those found within *Nyasa Yoga*, *Meditation Case Studies*, *Easy Meditation Lessons*, *The Little Book of Meditation*, *Color Me Confucius*, *Twenty-five Doors to Meditation*, *Buddha Yoga*, *Neijia Yoga*, *Meditation Techniques of the Buddhist and Taoist Masters* as well as the *Vijnana Bhairava* and Swami Adiswarananda's *Meditation and Its Practices*.

Yoga Asanas: Correct posture is an indispensable requirement for successfully practicing sitting meditation, pranayama exercises, martial arts, athletics and yoga *asanas*. Only a correct body alignment allows for the proper Qi flow or internal Qi circulation throughout your body. The better that your Qi flows properly throughout your body without bottlenecks, obstructions, or impediments to its circulation the greater will become your ability to feel the entire Qi/Prana of your body as a single whole or forget the feeling of your body entirely because its Qi/Prana flow becomes so smooth and perfect. Also, the easier it is for your Qi/Prana to flow smoothly, the more you strengthen your inner subtle body and prepare it for "birth by transformation." Any posture held for spiritual practice is an *asana* and sometimes unusual or uncomfortable positions are held in order to cultivate the Qi/Prana in hard-to-effect body regions. While one of the highest objectives of Yoga is to gain complete control over your limbs, organs and other parts of the body, some of the best poses are those which promote the frictionless circulation of the Qi/Prana within your subtle body, will then helps to purify and strengthen it, and which helps you to tame your thoughts and emotions because an internal fullness of Qi and better internal Qi circulation engenders calmness and clarity. Stretching your muscles by holding an *asana* posture (or martial arts pose) not only increases physical dexterity and flexibility, which is what ordinary people usually think is the ultimate purpose of Yoga, but has the purpose of activating and stimulating the Qi/Prana throughout your muscles, organs and tissues by improving their Qi circulation. Some postures, such as the sitting lotus posture used for meditation practice or the standing horse posture of martial arts, are uncomfortable at first, which means that your body must force its own Qi/Prana through the muscle energy channels in order that you can master the position. However, previously uncomfortable postures once mastered allow you to engage in prolonged Qi/Prana cultivation efforts for a long period of time. The standing *san ti shi* trinity posture of *Xingyiquan* is an *asana* that you hold for a prolonged period of time, thus allowing Buddhas, Bodhisattvas and enlightened martial arts masters to possess your Qi/Prana during that time and use their own energy to help improve your Qi circulation, which is why it is so effective. Yoga has this same real purpose of purifying your inner subtle body by washing it with Qi/Prana because *correct yoga postures will stretch your muscles to eliminate circulatory impediments to your internal energy flow and they will bolster specific Qi circulation pathways that will help to improve Qi circulation in selected muscle groups and regions.* This is why Yoga becomes a spiritual practice, for otherwise it is just exercise. For true Yoga (1) you can mentally focus on body regions for prolonged periods of time to draw Qi/Prana within them to wash them with energy, such as by concentrating on "chakra regions." This means holding your focus and intent on your Qi/Prana in a certain area of your body. Concentrating on a region will pull the Qi/Prana to that area due to the mind-body connection between thoughts and Qi, and that subsequent collection or concentration of Qi/Prana will "wash" or purify the underlying subtle body. *Bandhas* or locks, for instance, are used for concentrating and holding the Qi/Prana in certain body locations for this purpose of washing your subtle body, which is called "opening the *nadis*." (2) You can also *use force to pump your Qi/Prana* through specific body locations, as in pumping exercises like *mula bandha*. Pranayama is another method used to forcibly push Qi/Prana through body regions to open their circulatory obstructions so that the improved Qi flow through them will help to strengthen and purify those Qi flow routes. (3) You can *wash* a body region with Qi/Prana by using your will to circulate your Qi/Prana in various revolutions within that area (leading it via your mind). You can also use special circulatory or vibrational techniques for specific anatomical parts that you repeat over and over again to improve your Qi/Prana circulation within those parts. Two examples: (a) humming "mmm" when trying to feel or push Qi/Prana through your upper palate; (b) using the sounds "Cha" and "Chr" to push or pull the Qi/Prana through your teeth and gums; (c) or pushing the tongue up against the palate to exercise the muscles of the thyroid and throat since this moves them (while simultaneously reciting "Jha" since this sound stirs the Qi in the throat and thyroid region). Touching the palate with your tongue curled backwards (some incorrectly call this the "tip of the tongue") also provides a bridge so that you can push-circulate your Qi through your tongue to your palate, nasal cavity, cerebellum, back of throat and so forth in various rotational patterns that you guide via your will. (4) When your body is held motionless in *asana* or *mudra* positions that stretch muscles, you can practice stimulating, exciting, energizing, invigorating, moving, circulating, pushing or pulling your Qi/Prana through the muscles being stretched by combining the stretching with other energy techniques. This includes mentally focusing on the feeling of the muscles to sense the shape of the muscles, using visualization efforts on the muscles being stretched, reciting resonating mantra sounds on or as if from within those same muscles in order to stimulate their Qi/Prana (the best sounds vibrate the Qi/Prana within the part being cultivated), and giving rise to Yin Qi or Yang Qi emotional tones to overall stimulate your Yin or Yang Qi into moving. This is Nyasa Yoga. Wherever you put your focused concentration within your body your Qi/Prana will automatically follow to that spot because Qi and consciousness are linked. By adding emotional content during your practice session so as to stimulate your overall Qi/Prana into a certain mood, you will greatly enhance your efforts. (5) You can guide your Qi/Prana through various *pratyahara* circuits in your body, moving it from point to point and location to location. You concentrate your Qi/Prana at various locations within the body, circulate it within that region and then move it to a subsequent region. This will wash selected body sections in sequence, and then you must link the Qi/Prana of these regions as a unified pathway. Various pathways are revealed in *Yoga Yajnavalkya*, *Nyasa Yoga* and *Neijia Yoga*. For instance, in the *boran kammatthana* Esoteric Theravada School of Buddhism you are taught to concentrate "spheres of light" (which actually means Qi) at the tip of the nose and then move it to the back of the nose between the eyes, between the eyebrows, top of the head, back of the head, epiglottis, heart, navel, and then around the navel. You progressively draw your Qi/Prana from the intranasal cavity inside the nostril down to the *dantian*. With other methods you place the Qi/Prana (light) spherical-concentrations in different arrangements within the body both horizontally and vertically at points such as the navel, at points on the level of the navel surrounding the navel, at the heart and so on. (6) Eventually after using all these techniques you can eventually build to the point where you can feel the entire Qi of your body as a single unit or unified whole – which is the ultimate target – because the Qi of all individual parts becomes connected. There are various exercises available that lead you to being able to feel the entire Qi/Prana of your body as a single unit. The point of all these techniques is to try to first move your Qi/Prana through your muscles by pulling them with stretching exercises, mentally focusing (concentrating) on them, or by guiding it along special pathways, and in this way "wash" those pathways with Qi/Prana that purifies your underlying subtle body. This is called inner energy Yoga, inner alchemy, Tantra, Vajrayana, *anapana, kriya yoga, kundalini yoga, laya yoga, nei-gong, neijiaquan, nei-dan, boran kammatthana* etc. Eventually from these forms of inner energy work you will be able to feel the entire Qi of your body as a single unit, and its internal circulation will become orderly and free without obstructions or dysfunctions. *When practicing such techniques, always try to feel the Qi/Prana within the body location being emphasized rather than just imagining inside your mind that you are moving it, otherwise often you will think you are moving your Qi but not actually producing any actual physical sensations or circulations.* You could spend years in wasted efforts if your mental thoughts do not move the Qi/Prana throughout your body because you are just visualizing events in your mind without connecting with, touching, grabbing or feeling the actual Qi/Prana sensations in your muscles and organs. Thinking about moving your Qi/Prana is different than actually doing it, which is the point of such practices, so *always make sure that whatever you visualize or imagine is felt within your body* because you are supposed to connect your will and intent with your Qi/Prana in those regions to actually stimulate them. After all body areas are stretched you should try to feel the Qi energy of your body parts threaded together as a single unit. The Qi everywhere within your body should be naturally connected because then you are cultivating your subtle body and preparing it for emergence. The entire purpose of Yoga is to produce greater health and *purify your subtle body so that it can emerge from the physical shell*, but people don't know this highest of objectives. Once all your Qi/Prana is transformed and linked so that it feels as if it is just one single unit, the birth of the spiritual body can occur. Since that stage is one of frictionless inner Qi circulation then at that stage of cultivation your body will feel blissful, almost as non-existent. Furthermore, the smooth internal Qi flow will produce a calmer temperament of peace and quiescence that you might also term blissful. This is the *sat, chit, ananda* of Hinduism where the mind (consciousness) becomes open, clear and empty (blissful) while the body is so comfortable it feels is as if non-existent. To transform a body into the healthiest state possible you will find that diet, medical/nutritional remedies, exercise, detoxification and physical manipulation are also important. For optimizing your body's structural alignment, first undergo chiropractic treatments to align your bones, next undergo AMIT therapy to reactivate all your muscles, and then engage in either passive stretching exercises (Yoga, Pilates, etc.) or active exercises (dance, rebounding, martial arts, Ginastica Natural, sports, athletics etc.) in conjunction with inner Qi/Prana exercises and mental work. The best physical development work would include yoga practice, the soft martial arts and dance since dancing would help you develop exceptional physical grace and elegance. Dancing is also a form of beneficial cardiovascular exercise, but it especially produces elegance of physical movement in your legs, arms, shoulders and other areas because it forces you to open the Qi channels in all your body parts through movement. The best yoga teacher is not the one with the best expertise of personal attainment, or the one who is the best teacher/instructor, but the one who is enlightened and uses his own energy to push open the Qi channels of your body when you are doing stretching routines, for this is what frees the independent subtle body whilst alive, thus giving you the Srotapanna deva body attainment that makes you a *jiva*. Yoga master Yogeshwana Ramamohana Brahmachari and Tirumalai Krishnamacharya attained the subtle body attainment of enlightenment through the pathway of Yoga practice that must always include internal energy exercises in additional to stretching poses and meditation work. See *Neijia Yoga: Nei Gong for Yoga and the Martial Arts* for this missing half of yoga exercises. *Nyasa Yoga* will also help.

Martial Arts: You can either practice stimulating, moving, pushing or pulling your Qi/Prana through your muscles when you hold your body motionless in Yoga postures that are stretching your muscles, or do so when your body is moving as in dance, sports, athletics, gymnastics, or martial arts. Martial arts, when practiced correctly, also opens the Qi meridians within your body and harmonizes your Qi flow. This cultivates your Qi, improves your health, and calms your mind. In particular, the soft martial arts are a foundational training method for cultivating your inner Qi body which is why they are greatly recommended. Wherever you put your intent within your body due to martial arts inner energy exercises, your Qi/Prana will follow because your Qi and consciousness are linked. Practicing to have your body follow your mind through physical movements is called uniting mind and body. The pursuit of then combining your Qi with your movements is in martial arts called "unifying" your Qi and movements, "uniting your movement with breathing," or "combining your breath with your practice." However, "breath" actually means your internal energy or Qi/Prana rather than just your respiratory breathing although your breathing patterns should also be matched with your movements. By washing your body's Qi/Prana via martial arts inner energy practices, you will prepare your subtle body for emergence as is done through inner energy Yoga. The practice technique is to try to feel your Qi flow through your muscles, and to also *guide* it through your muscles when they are exercised/stretched, which is called *anapana*. There are three levels of Qi – there is superficial skin Qi that guards the body, deep Qi that penetrates even the center of your bones, and Qi that penetrates the body's matrix between these two – skin, muscles and bones. All these levels of Qi are cultivated via the inner energy methods of the soft martial arts such as *Taijiquan, Baguazhang, Xingyiquan, Tongbeiquan, Yiquan*, and *Liu He Ba Fa*, which therefore help you *directly cultivate your deva spiritual body*. In the inner martial arts you practice accessing and then moving your Qi throughout your entire body so that the Qi of every appendage becomes linked together as one unit, thus cultivating the essence of your entire subtle body. You also concentrate on bringing the Qi to, or projecting it from, your lower abdomen (*dantian*). When you practice the soft martial arts and combine your efforts with breathwork or *qi-gong*, each posture helps to open a different Qi meridian or group of meridians. The opening of meridians is a foundational stage of practice that stabilizes, harmonizes and thus transforms consciousness by improving your body and cranial Qi circulation so that your mind and personality become calmer and more stable. Hence, martial arts practice will transform your personality too. In martial arts you are often instructed through teachings like "feel as if you are a tiger hunting," "feel like a river flowing," "feel like snake slithering," "feel as strong as a mountain" and so on when doing certain movements in order to stimulate or arouse your Yin or Yang Qi/Prana respectively (as is done in Nyasa Yoga). With these instructions you are not just trying to master special physical movements but also trying to arouse unique types of Qi feelings via different imaginations or emotions. Done correctly, this will activate and help purify Yin or Yang Qi within your subtle body, and thus the martial arts teaching is true that "you can become enlightened through the proper practice of *tai jitsu*." Thus, you should always practice combining your feelings of Qi/Prana with your physical martial arts practice in order to more quickly cultivate your inner subtle body. You can use various types of emotions or visualizations/imaginations to assist in stimulating different types of Yin or Yang Qi inside your body so that you can directly access the cultivation of your subtle body and not just your physical nature; both Yin and Yang Qi must be separately cultivated. Or, you can practice absorbing the essence of the sun or moon to more directly cultivate Yin Qi or Yang Qi rather than having to rely on arousing emotions to do so. Step-by-step, martial arts teach you to align your joints with the natural flow of internal Qi energy, feel that energy, and with intention guide that vitality to even your extremities and tips of your body so that you can eventually feel the energy of your entire body, which is then sensed as a single unit. Many prior martial artists through constant practice of such techniques achieved the enlightened Srotapanna deva body attainment, which in Taoism is termed becoming an Immortal. They were all practitioners of *nei-gong* and spiritual practices. Yang Lu-Shan (founder of Yang style *taijiquan*), Liu Hung Chieh (taught by enlightened Buddhist master Tanxu), Wang Ziping (a Naqshbandi Sufi), Taoist Lu Zijian (who also practiced Esoteric Buddhism) as well as Wang Shujin (a leader in the Taoist sect Yi Guan Dao), Sun Lu-Tang (who practiced inner *nei-gong* alchemy), Wu Jian-Quan (*taijiquan*), Liu Li Hang (Wudang Taoism and martial arts), Wang Ji Wu and Wang Fu Yuan who attained immortal arts skills (*xingyiquan* masters), are just a few of those who achieved the subtle body and then higher spiritual attainments by practicing inner martial arts. They practiced *kung-fu* and spiritual practices together, which is why they succeeded. The creator of *taiqiquan*, Zhang San Feng, is considered the founder of all inner martial arts and is therefore considered a Taoist Immortal and Buddha worthy of veneration as are some of the founders of other traditions if enlightened. Martial artists with the deva body Srotapanna attainment never tell anybody about their achievement because people wouldn't believe them and it would also invite too many challenges to fight, but this explains why some can demonstrate amazing superpowers. With the martial arts that practice inner *nei-gong* you not only cultivate your inner Qi body but also directly train to develop some of the eight supernatural *siddhi* skills available only to the Srotapanna Arhats, Immortals or devas (whose bodies are composed of Qi) such as lightness, heaviness, and swiftness in movement and walking. Hence, the soft martial arts directly cultivate the Tao and prepare you for the deva life even if you are not successful in achieving the Srotapanna attainment while alive.

Pranayama: Pranayama breathing exercises, which are especially promoted in the Yoga schools, Tientai school of Buddhism, and *qi-gong* methods of Taoism, can stabilize your mind and have a therapeutic effect on your body. They can expand your lung capacity, increase your blood flow, oxygenate your blood and temporarily alkalinize your body. Changing your pH will affect your internal chemistry and therefore your mental states by altering your consciousness. The first important step in learning breathing exercises is to master the *asana* of a stable posture and then afterwards pranayama, or regulating your breath. In the Buddhist *Anapanasatti sutra* you are taught to "breathe in and experience (feel) your entire body, breathe out and experience (feel) your entire body; breathe in and calm your entire body formation, breathe out and calm your entire body formation; breathe in while internally arousing the emotion of joy, breathe out while internally arousing the emotion of joy; breathe in while arousing the sensation of pleasurable bliss within you, breathe out while arousing the sensation of pleasurable bliss within you; breathe in and calm your mind, breathe out and calm your mind ..." while in other sutras you are taught to notice the "hotness" and "coldness" of your breath that refers to the Yang and Yin Qi of your body since they are considered hot/warm and cold whereas breath has no temperature at all. Pranayama initially teaches you to control your breathing but ultimately aims at purifying your Qi/Prana through the vehicle of your breathing that moves it and enable you to control it. When breathing you should feel the entire Qi/Prana of your body, and then wash it by holding different Yin or Yang emotions (such as the *Anapanasatti sutra's* "sensation of pleasurable bliss") during extensive sets of inhalation-exhalation cycles. Pranayama expertise begins with the regulation of your respiratory breath(ing) and then gradually proceeds to the stage of washing/purifying and then gaining control over the life-currents or inner vital force of your entire body, namely your Qi/Prana. In other words, pranayama aims to help you start gaining control of the life-currents of Qi/Prana within your body through mastery of your breathing and breath, and gradually with expertise you can direct your internal energy to go to any area of your body you desire to "wash" those tissues and thus purify your inherent subtle body. It is especially important to open up the lower regions of your body from the pelvis to the feet, your genitalia, ears, nose and the hands and fingers. You can also learn how to expand your Qi to your skin through breathing exercises. By learning to move your breath in certain specific ways you can end up stimulating/moving your Qi/Prana, which will end up purifying it. Eventually you can simply grab and move this Qi/Prana by your will, which then becomes *anapana* practice, *nei-dan* exercises, inner alchemy, kundalini yoga, *kriya* yoga, *neijiaquan* or *nei-gong* work etcetera. When pranayama is attended by the mental recitation of any mantra, it is one hundred times more powerful than when practiced without mantra recitation because mantra recitation requests help from spiritual beings and tends to rhythmically move your Qi/Prana on its own as well. If during pranayama practice you simultaneously visualize Qi/Prana currents moving or held stationary at locations within your body and try to feel these energies, or feel certain emotions or sensations, this will also increase its power. Certain breathing patterns can be used to affect your emotions that will transform your Qi as a kind of cultivation as well. You can even visualize that the pranayama efforts are purifying you by forcing poisons to leave your physical body through your feet. You might also visualize your body becoming non-solid and as transparent as crystal during practice. Pranayama attainments depend upon the intensity of the practitioner's efforts. It is recommended to practice them two to four times per day when you have an empty stomach and are not tired or worried. Wim Hof breathing practices, freediving breathwork practices, and other forms of breathwork (such as methods like Buteyko breathing, coherent breathing, hypoventilation, holotropic breathwork, embryonic breathing, tummo breathing, sudarshin kriya, etc.)[27] can improve your pranayama results. They are especially good at lengthening the amount of time you can remain in *kumbhaka* pranayama retention states that are one of the most important types of pranayama exercise. Various forms of breathwork can open up your Qi channels or excite the Qi everywhere throughout your body, which is why they are practiced since this is the basic transformational method of purifying your Qi-body for the emergence of the deva body. There are many breathing methods, pranayama techniques, and breathwork for

---

[27] See *Breath: The New Science of a Lost Art* by James Nestor.

"harmonizing the breath" (such as harmonious 5.5 second coherence breathing), but their common goal is to wash your body with stimulated Qi, produce better Qi/Prana and blood circulation everywhere, and either lead you to a state of energetic stimulation (where you feel full of energy and alive) or to a state of quiescent mental calmness. There are also methods such as *kumbhaka* pranayama that expand your lung capacity (VO2 max), which has a large positive effect on your longevity. The Chinese Buddhist Tientai master Tanxu (Wan Futing) is one of the many individuals who attained enlightenment through a practice pathway that included mastery of breathing practices.

Kumbhaka Pranayama: The *Yoga-sutras of Patanjali* states, "Regulation of breath or the control of Prana is the stoppage of inhalation and exhalation, which follows after securing that steadiness of posture or seat." This is *kumbhaka* pranayama, which forces your Qi/Prana to move throughout your body due to the fact that you stop breathing, just as the lack of food during fasting forces your physical body to rely on its Qi energy for survival. Additionally, holding your breath through *kumbhaka* practices also dilates your capillaries throughout your body, and that stretching is a way of exercising those tissue tubes. It helps to transform the suitability of your tissues for better Qi/Prana circulation. Some breathing exercises are a form of breathwork that moves the Qi/Prana within your body to wash your tissues, as in *qi-gong* and martial arts "guiding your Qi" practices, but *kumbhaka* breath retention exercises force the body to dilate tissues and open up all its internal energy pathways. Yoga texts contain many *kumbhaka* breath retention exercises, which can be learnt therefrom, and even have advanced yoga exercises that involve moving your body while holding your breath. This is similar to methods such as *baguazhang* that teach you to hold your body and its appendages in certain positions while you mentally guide, pull or lead your Qi along acupuncture meridians to open those channels. There are many different *kumbhaka* techniques. If a breath retention technique is not practiced according to rhythmical ratios of exhalation, inhalation and retention, and instead for the purpose of just holding the breath for as long as possible, the general principles are to: hold your breath as deep within your body as possible, for as long as possible, using as little force with as few muscles as possible, and then forcibly expel it as quickly as possible. Or, *use whatever classical instructions are provided within the instructional text you are using*. It is not so much your breath that you want to feel within your body while inhaling, holding, moving and exhaling. You want to circulate your Qi within you. You should combine your techniques with freediving or Wim Hof breathing exercises if you want to hold your breath longer, and periodically measure and record on a graph the length of your retention period so that you can track your progress and try to improve upon best efforts. Shri Samarth Muppin Kaadsiddheswar Maharaj is one of the many individuals who attained the Tao through a pathway that included mastery of *kumbhaka* breathing practices, which can extend an individual's life span when performed regularly.

Kundalini Yoga, Kriya Yoga, Anapana, Nei-gong, Neijia: Kundalini Yoga, *kriya* yoga, and *anapana* practice involve moving the Qi/Prana of your body in various ways via your will (thoughts), which is also basically *nei-gong*, *neijiaquan* or *nei-dan* work. You train to pull or push your Qi/Prana with your mind such as by rotating/revolving it hundreds to thousands of times in specific patterns within your body. You might focus on a body region to bring Qi/Prana into that area, or use your will to circulate it in various patterns elsewhere and especially in particular areas you select for a work session, which might be cultivated according to a schedule you set up. The entire purpose of incessant Qi/Prana stimulation is to gradually eliminate impediments to the flow of Qi within the Qi channels (*nadis* or circulatory routes) that penetrate all your tissues, and to circulate your Qi/Prana over the molecules and their atomic bonds again and again to purify them. Hundreds of masters and their students will take shifts doing this to your body continuously during the Twelve Year kundalini transformation process if you have the merit, which can only happen after years of devotion to intensified inner energy yoga, and this is absolutely necessary for the Srotapanna deva body attainment. Another method concerns mentally fixing your Qi/Prana through focused concentration in various body locations and then taking/moving it slowly, step-by-step and stage-by-stage, to other sections of your body. For instance, Yogi Boganathar suggests leading your Qi/Prana from the big toes to your ankle, knee, thigh, genitals, navel, heart, neck, uvula, nose, space between the eyebrows, forehead and crown of the head; the *Yoga Yajnavalkya* has a different sequence for how to sequentially move your Qi to open up all the sections of your body. Taoism has a Small Circulation and Great Circulation where you revolve your Qi along certain large meridian pathways within your body, guiding it along these routes, and this practice is also used in the martial arts. For instance, you can lead your Qi up into your brain through the nerves in your spine or lead it up via spinal nerves and skin/muscles surrounding the spine. After leading Qi to your brain you should then *wash* the brain's anatomical structure with Qi revolutions of countless different patterns. You should use anatomical and DTI (diffusion tensor imaging) brain images as maps to guide your efforts to revolve your Qi along the brain's various nerve pathways. Normally when the brain is filled with Qi it becomes energized and functions more fully, reaching a state of quiescence and clarity, which is the basis behind meditation and this work. The *Nitya-natha-paddhati* reveals "sixteen containers" where you can lead and concentrate your Qi/Prana: big toes, anus, rectum/sphincter, male genital organ, lower abdomen/entrails, navel area, heart, throat, uvula, nasopharynx, root of the tongue, base of the upper teeth, tip of the nose, base of the nose, point between the eyebrows, and eyes. You can also *hold* your Qi/Prana at these or other vital points. A common introductory practice is to especially work on moving your Qi/Prana up and then down your spine into your brain hundreds of times per day, or to circulate it in circular orbits (loops) up your spine into the brain and then down the front of the body *and* through your alimentary canal, or to hold it at various places. Practicing Qi/Prana revolutions or holding patterns in various parts of your body will bring different results/delights to a practitioner in accordance with their ability to move their Qi/Prana to these spots and rest it there. Just as in martial arts you should practice moving your Qi/Prana hundreds to thousands of times per day for the quickest results. To become enlightened (attain the higher transcendental bodies) is not a matter of study, worship, meditation, mantra, introspection, yoga, improved behavior or other similar efforts. These practices are helpful but *it is primarily accomplished through inner energy work*. As the famous Zen text *Transmission of Light* said, "In the distant past, Ananda had awakened the aspiration for complete perfect enlightenment in the presence of the Buddha called King of Emptiness, at the same time as did the present Buddha Shakyamuni. Ananda was fond of intellectual learning (rather than meditation and Qi practice), and that is why he had not yet truly realized enlightenment. Shakyamuni, on the other hand, cultivated energy, whereby he attained true enlightenment."[28] You absolutely must cultivate inner *nei-gong* or *neijia* energy work for the attainment of enlightenment. Thus, while you need to practice meditation to cultivate mental stillness and clarity of mind (i.e. King of Emptiness), the practice of formless mind meditation where you let go of your thoughts and vital energy allows higher beings to more easily move your Qi/Prana with their own (because they don't have to fight your thoughts and their grip on your Qi circulation) when they enter into you to help move and subsequently purify your body. The general key to success is *inner energy work* that involves moving the Qi/Prana within your body and gaining control over its properties and movements. Many practices for doing this are revealed in *Nyasa Yoga* and especially *Neijia Yoga* that essentially reveal the basics of Tantra and Buddhist Vajrayana methods. Paramahansa Yogananda and Swami Muktananda are just two of the many individuals who attained their deva body through the pathway of kundalini/kriya yoga. See *Neijia Yoga*, *Nyasa Yoga* and *Buddha Yoga* for practice details. In Orthodox Christianity many Hesychasts ignite the kundalini transformation process by

---

[28] *Transmission of Light*, trans. by Thomas Cleary, (Shambhala Publications, Boston, 2002), p. 9.

continually reciting the Jesus Prayer until they eventually start hearing the prayer automatically being recited on its own within their heart, the energy within their body starts rotating and they see signs such as flames within their body. This is similar to the process of using continuous mantra recitation to ignite/initiate the process. As Saint Ekaterina (Malkov-Panina) said, "When you are in contact with the Holy Spirit the Holy Spirit prays for you! You pray with your heart at that time. Just like a mill; once you put the belt on, it keeps running by itself without you." In other words, after continually reciting the Jesus prayer, when you are ready (after a sufficient amount of practice) a Buddha will enter your body and start moving your Qi/Prana and reciting the prayer as if on its own, which is a sign of an undergoing kundalini transformation process disguised as the prayer being self-operational. Many Orthodox Christian monks and nuns attained the higher bodies through the method of continuous prayer recitation.

Kundalini Yoga Clarified: In the *Gospel of Ramakrishna* (Vol. I, p. 499) Sri Ramakrishna Paramahamsa said, "The mind of a worldly man generally moves among the three lower centres: those at the navel, at the sexual organ, and at the organ of evacuation. After great effort and spiritual practice the Kundalini is awakened. According to the yogis there are three nerves (Nadis) in the spinal column: Ida, Pingala, and Sushumna. Along the Sushumna are six lotuses, or centres, the lowest being known as the Muladhara. Then comes successively Svadhisthana, Manipura, Anahata, Visuddhi, and Ajna. These are the six centres. The Kundalini, when awakened, passes through the lower centres and comes to the Anahata, which is at the heart level. It stays there. At that time the mind of the aspirant is withdrawn from the three lower centres. He feels the awakening of the Divine Consciousness and sees Light. In mute wonder he sees that radiance and cries out: 'What is this? What is this?' After passing through the six centres, the Kundalini reaches the Thousand-petalled lotus known as the Sahasrara, and the aspirant goes into Samadhi. According to the Vedas these centres are called 'bhumis' or 'planes.' There are seven such planes. The centre at the heart corresponds to the fourth plane of the Vedas. According to the Tantra there is in this centre a lotus called Anahata, with twelve petals [In the Six Yogas of Naropa the heart has a Dharma chakra with eight petals for concentration practice]. The centre known as Visuddha is the fifth plane. This centre is at the throat and has a lotus with sixteen petals. When the Kundalini reaches this plane, the devotee longs to talk and hear only about God. Conversation on worldly subjects, on 'woman and gold,' causes him great pain. He leaves a place where people talk of these matters. Then comes the sixth plane, corresponding to the centre known as Ajna. This centre is located between the eyebrows and it has a lotus with two petals. When the Kundalini reaches it, the aspirant sees the form of

God. But still there remains a slight barrier between the devotee and God. It is like a light inside a lantern. You may thin you have touched the light, but in reality you cannot because of a barrier like glass. And last of all is the seventh plane, which, according to Tantra is the centre of the Thousand-petalled lotus (Sahasrara). When the Kundalini arrives there, the individual goes into Samadhi. In that lotus dwells Satchidananda Shiva, the Absolute. There the Kundalini, the Awakened Power (Shakti), unites with Shiva. This is known as the union of Shiva and Shakti." Thus, this is a standard explanation of kundalini, and like most others is incorrect and meant to mislead you because masters and their spiritual traditions for a variety of reasons *do not want you to know* the truth - that enlightenment is a transcendental body attainment that allows you to escape from a lower realm, and with that new body comes an attendant clarity of consciousness that you would have due to that body being composed of a higher form of energy that circulates in your brain without as many obstructions or impediments. To put it another way, the universe has many layers or planes of existence, the transcendental bodies are the inhabitants of these different planes, and the mind you have for each body at each plane is considered a different level of consciousness even though it is just the same old ordinary normal mind you have now but for a new body on a new plane, and thus replete with some higher capabilities. At each level of existence there is no magical mind, just an ordinary mind – just an ordinary mind like you have now but for that body, yet its sensory capabilities expand because that body penetrates through lower planes of matter/existence. There are also no "chakras" within the body or on heavenly planes. The only "heavenly plane" is a new plane you reach with a new spiritual body. The chakras refer to sections of your body – horizontal sections – delineated by the standard partitionings of the spine according to vertebrae, and many traditions have you do Qi-work on the body by addressing it in sections under the guidance of a master, hence the idea of chakras was invented.[29] Actually, the sacral chakra of six petals refers to the sacrum since two sets of six nerves protrude from it, while the heart chakra has twelve petals because there are twelve thoracic vertebrae in that region of the spine. The two-petalled Ajna chakra refers to the two sections of the brain stem while the ten thousand-petalled crown chakra refers to all the nerves and neurons in the brain. The kundalini energy is basically *your Qi that resides in all your body cells* since your subtle body interpenetrates your physical body, so "unawakened kundalini energy" does not primarily reside in any chakra such as being coiled up inside the Muladhara. It is everywhere within you and comprises an

---

[29] See *Neijia Yoga* and *Nyasa Yoga*, which clearly describes the "true" chakras and various other partitioning schemes of the body into different numbers of sections with appropriate cultivation techniques that will move the Qi within each section.

energetic duplicate of your physical body that is released as your "soul" (subtle body or deva body) upon death. *Through intensified yoga practices* you use a variety of techniques to work on purifying (vibrating, moving, awakening, washing, etc.) this Qi throughout your body, and then due to their grace (commitment to massive organized labor) a series of spiritual masters will use the energy of their bodies or *nirmanakaya* emanations to move your own energy within you, which you will mistake for your own kundalini when it is actually their energy. You will have many "spiritual" experiences whenever this happens – mental experiences and physical sensations inside your body. It takes many years of organized labor to purify your Qi and produce the deva body attainment, which is the Srotapanna stage of enlightenment. When an aspirant's thoughts stop it is also because such a being intervenes to make them stop rather than that you attain some mysterious exalted state of consciousness, and when you cannot cognize your body or don't seem present it is because they have projected this experiential state into you or you have attained a deva body and are travelling off visiting some other place in the world, but they call this "samadhi" and falsely describe the kundalini process (including descriptions of its final twelfth year of incredible pain) to hide these actualities from individuals. A similar somewhat misleading report can be found in *The Truth Is* (p. 447) by Sri H.W.L. Poonja who wrote, "Kundalini is lying dormant in everybody in the muladhara chakra of the astral body which is in the heart of the physical body. This energy is sleeping and you give rise to it by concentrating on different chakras one after the other. If you are interested in it I don't advise it because it takes special guidance and it can be dangerous. Focusing in the chakras will cause the energy to start traveling upward through all the chakras. Finally it reaches the top and then you will feel that you are not the body, but that you are out of the body. This is a difficult process and takes at least twelve years in a quiet place with a good teacher." Once again, your Qi energy is in all your body cells, not just the muladhara chakra, and you must perform exercises to rotate it in your body sections to purify your inherent subtle/astral body, including pushing/pulling Qi up your spine and then down the front of your body and down your alimentary canal in the center of your body. Poonja says that your Qi ascends because at the earliest stages of purification you spend a lot of time moving your Qi up your spine through mind-led visualizations and other *nei-gong* efforts. If you have enough merit for the Twelve Year kundalini transformation process, at the end of twelve years of spiritual masters doing this for you (with countless revolutions of their own energy everywhere within your body) then your subtle body (astral body) will finally be able to leave your physical body through the top of your head and you become an Immortal (Srotapanna). If you start doing many *nei-gong* or kundalini exercises then lots of local spiritual residents will start working on you as their own training vehicle and cause all sorts of mischief, which is why masters don't normally teach kundalini yoga (or they require you to take an "empowerment" so that you are under someone's supervision and thereby somewhat protected), but you have to do these things if you want to attain true enlightenment rather than just some intellectual realization that you think is enlightenment but is just a bunch of thoughtful insights.

Visualization Practice: Visualization practice is way to develop the mental skill of concentration, and also a way to train to hold your Qi at one place in your body in order to open up all the *nadis* in that region due to the Qi concentration you then bring to that area. You practice holding images steady in your mind for as long as possible to build your powers of concentration, or you can practice mentally rehearsing moving scenarios. The ability to hold a stable concentration leads to a stronger mind and the mental powers of focus that can ignore afflictions, annoyances and distractions – "mental defilements." One should especially practice holding bright images of Qi/Prana – such as flames, fires, lights, the sun, etcetera - in your abdomen, heart, brain, and other areas of your body as is done in Jainism (flames in the abdomen), Orthodox Christianity (flames in the heart), Buddhism, Taoism, Yoga, Vajrayana, etcetera because this will cultivate both your Qi *and exercise your mental powers of focus and attention.* If appropriate, add stimulating emotions to such mental images in order to help vibrate your Qi/Prana by changing its Yin or Yang qualities. The enlightened Theravada Buddhist Bhadantacariya Buddhaghosa in his *Visuddhimagga* (Path of Perfection) introduced the practice of visualizing certain colors and shapes as a way to cultivate a stable mind of concentration. Jesuit monastics would visualize scenes in the life of Christ in order to develop stable mental concentration skills and to evoke certain Yin or Yang purifying emotions, such as the Yin Qi aroused when compassionately crying due to visualizing his pain on the cross. The great Tibetan lama Tsong Khapa performed millions of offerings of mandala visualizations where he would envision a particular mandala and offer it away while holding onto positive *bhava* emotions such as charitable giving, or blessing, thus making mental concentration practice into a method for repeatedly training not just his concentration but his emotions. Sports figures use internal visualization, or mental rehearsal, to train their body to perform athletic activities with excellence, as explained in *Sport Visualization for the Elite Athlete* and *Visualization Power*. Visualization or concentration practice is also used to visualize deities via stable mental imagery, such as the Tibetan *yidam practice* where you visualize and feel the Qi of the *yidam* inside yourself by imagining that you become one with the deity (and then masters who previously succeeded with that technique will come to lend you their Qi to help purify and transform your subtle body). Another yogic practice is to visualize your Qi/Prana at certain points within your body and then take/move/lead it step-by-step and stage-by-stage to other locations.[30] This will move your Qi to those areas and thus help remove various disorders in those regions by opening up the Qi channels (*nadis*) in those localities. Visualization together with willpower can lead your internal energy to any area within your body because "where your intent is your Qi will condense." Supreme martial artists therefore practice leading their Qi into their *dantian*, and then from their *dantian* to different areas of their body. Qi/Prana flooding a region will "wash" the region, warming and softening it, and thus purify and strengthen your inner subtle body in that region. Hence, you can imagine absorbing the essences of the sun and moon to flood your body with Yang Qi and Yin Qi respectively. You can also practice visualizing light and/or colors at certain points within your body, and special shapes or pathways inside your body in order to stimulate your Qi. Another Yang Qi practice is to inhale to fill your entire body with breath, hold that state for as long as possible while feeling your Qi everywhere within you in order to open up the flow of Qi within blocked meridians. At the same time you must visualize that all your flesh is red in color, your body is flaming on fire, you hold onto the *bhava* of intense stimulating joy, and you visualize that your bones are shining with a bright white light as you exhale (and you feel or move the Qi energy inside them). After exhalation, you hold your lungs empty while maintaining the visualization of your bones giving off a shining light. At the final stage of this visualization you abandon all such images and rest your mind in emptiness, as if you were just empty space that supports all things within it without holding onto anything, which is referred to in Hinduism as becoming established in the Self.

Sexual Cultivation: Since sex is a standard biological function you can use it as part of spiritual practice on the cultivation path. This is done in several cultivation schools since sexual intercourse can greatly vitalize your inner Qi movements, stir joyous-happiness emotions that rouse your Yang Qi, and can move your Qi/Prana due to the breathing and yoga-like exercises. The method is to use the emotional excitation and happiness-joy-bliss that comes from the passion of sexual activity (excitation-pleasure), which stirs your Qi/Prana, together with physical sexual congress to move the Qi/Prana in various regions within your body. Hence this is not a method of sexual super-sublimation but of simply using sexual activity to move your Qi/Prana to wash the tissues of your inner physical and etheric body while feeling the bliss of sexual activity that changes the Qi-tone to that of a Yang

---

[30] See *Yoga Yajnavalkya*, trans. by A. G. Mohan (Svastha Yoga Pte Ltd., 2013), and *Neijia Yoga* by William Bodri.

nature, as does love. Sexual relations can be a powerful force for moving your internal Qi/Prana through emotional excitation, which is why many masters encourage their students to marry because then sex can become readily available as a method to transform their body for the spiritual path. It is one of the fastest ways to transform the Qi/Prana of your body because it excites all your Qi everywhere while arousing the Yang Qi emotions of joy, elation, thrills, delight, bliss and happiness, or more gentle Yang Qi emotions like tenderness, softness, gentleness, love, kindness, and warmth during restful pleasure. These emotional feelings *are felt throughout your entire body* and thus they affect the entire Qi of your body, which is the basis of using sex as a cultivation technique. Sexual intercourse can become a very stimulating full-body workout of your Qi. This activizing, energizing, invigorating or vitalizing of Qi can readily open up your Qi channels (*nadis*) because the energy stimulation is greater than for most other cultivation methods, but pursuing sex (without marriage) usually leads to all sorts of problems so it is not allowed in most cultivations traditions. There are dangers such as pregnancy, disease, violence, abuse, emotional harm, and damaged social relations. The alternative is celibacy, which is the standard default that requires extra efforts of restraint together with ardent pranayama practice, inner *tummo* heat cultivation exercises and other techniques to help move your Qi. Celibates can reduce their sexual desires by practicing yoga, pranayama, martial arts or other exercises (ex. prostrations) while frequently fasting or eating a vegetarian diet because it reduces desires due to the lack of stimulating food. The need for pranayama exercises and emptiness meditation for celibate cultivators is emphasized in the story of celibate meditating Shiva who kept all his energies within himself (preventing them from leaking). When he opened his eyes while meditating after being bothered by Kamadeva, the god of lust, Shiva burned him into ashes just by looking at him; as a supreme yogi his body produced hot kundalini energy inside that produced spiritual transformations because he did not lose his Qi energy through sexual leakage. Similarly, in the *Surangama Sutra* Ucchusmma was given the name "Fire Head" because when a man restrains from ejaculation for a long time but does not circulate the Qi within himself then his face often reddens from just cultivating Yang Qi without its Yin Qi companion. Ucchusmma cultivated sexual restraint while envisioning that his body became a mass of raging fire (along with joyous emotions at the same time), a technique through which he cultivated the Qi/Prana (kundalini) of his body and succeeded in the path, but his face became red from too much Yang stimulation. To help reduce such instances of redness you must receive chiropractic treatments for your spine so that your Qi energy rising into the brain flows in a smoother and more natural circulation. When you make efforts to open more Qi channels through mantra practice, yoga, pranayama, exercise and diet you lessen the likelihood of such results as well since this will help to balance your Yin and Yang Qi throughout your body, which is an achievement that Yoga calls the union of Shiva and Shakti in the body. These stories show that you need to cultivate your Yin Qi along with your Yang Qi and not just Yang Qi alone. For instance, the story of the Hindu ascetic Rishyashringa concerned a country experiencing a drought said to be caused by his ascetic Yang Qi cultivation, which would be similar to the case of Ucchusmma. In the story a courtesan had sex with this celibate yogi and this finally ended the drought by making the rains fall, which does not refer to ejaculation of semen but to the activation of descending Yin Qi circulations within the body due to the harmonizing effects of sexual relations. During sex – which involves the Yang Qi stimulating emotions of happiness, excitement, thrills and joy – you not only activate ascending Yang Qi flows within the human body but descending Yin Qi circulations as well to achieve a complete circuit of Qi flow harmonization. Ascetic practices that force your Yang Qi upwards (the fire road of cultivation) are incomplete because your Qi must revolve within your body in a descending circuit too, hence falling rain represents Yin Qi. Your Qi must circulate to return to your perineum by descending down the front of your body along the water Qi channel (the *ren mai* conception channel acupuncture meridian) *and also through the center of your body (alimentary canal)* via your esophagus, stomach and intestines to your anus (since the body is essentially a worm, or long digestive tube, in terms of its structural evolution). For non-celibate cultivators, men should try to prevent ejaculation during sex so that they don't lose their Qi/Prana necessary for opening their Qi channels whereas women experience no detriment in losing energy through orgasm, but in both cases they must still have their Qi circulate freely throughout their bodies and strive to create such vibrant circulations. In Tibetan Buddhism the nuns do not take a vow of celibacy because their school allows them to use sex in the spiritual path as an effective way of cultivating their Qi, and sexual activity as a means of inner Qi cultivation is also taught in Taoism and the Kaula yogic schools of India. However, it is difficult to find the right partner for sexual cultivation due to the necessity for karmic compatibility, sexual compatibility and the requirement that practitioners must first have sufficient merit to be qualified. The cultivation prerequisites for this type of practice mean that the practitioners should have first practiced lots of pranayama, mantrayana, *nei-gong*, and other inner energy work such as the methods within *Nyasa Yoga* and *Neijia Yoga* including the white skeleton visualization technique (where you push bright Qi or bright light to wash the hundreds of bones within the body as well as your organs, muscles and viscera and then at the end of each meditation session their energies are threaded together as a whole). In other words, you need to have done lots of inner energy work (and breathing practices) that already started moving and transforming your

Qi/Prana before you can start engaging in sexual cultivation. A typical sexual cultivation effort with a partner should last two to three hours continuously with minimum male ejaculation, otherwise the man will lose his energy, namely his Qi that he needs for purifying his Qi channels. Women, on the other hand, are free to experience orgasm as many times as happens. However, care must be taken that a woman does not become involuntarily pregnant. The Tibetan female adept Yeshe Tsogyel, who practiced with several partners, has left teachings on this topic of sexual cultivation and you can find *karmamudra* (sexual union for cultivation purposes) teachings within the Six Yogas of Naropa. You are basically doing a form of happy, thrilling physical exercise to excite and mobilize all your Qi inside you, which refreshes the inner energy matrix of your subtle body. You cannot spiritualize lust, but you can use sexual intercourse, combined with greater emotions during that time, to move the Qi within your body. If done correctly, sexual yoga turns into Yoga directly because it invigorates and energizes the Qi/Prana of your body everywhere, while you simultaneously enjoy positive Yang Qi emotions (such as joy, enthrallment, happiness, fun, excitedness, thrills, elation, delight and bliss), and you also engage in various postures, positions and movement activities like yoga enabling you to move your Qi to wash your body's tissues. When it is said that Krishna had thousands of wives this refers to the neurons of his brain washed by a continuous circulatory refreshment of Qi, and the brain's neurons are also represented by the countless petals of the *Sahasrara* chakra or the Gopis themselves. Ultimately you are trying to wash or energize the tiniest simples that compose your body because that is how you can ultimately achieve the separation from your physical body of an additional independent subtle energy component while alive. It takes a lot of energy to move your Qi, but by trying to do so while you are *already* energizing yourself with the powerful (Qi-exciting) emotions and movements of sexual congress makes it easier for Buddhas to enter into your body at that time to move your Qi/Prana and that of any other heavenly students within you since the energies of their own subtle, Causal and Supra-Causal bodies can be stacked like a Russian Matryoshka doll within you and multiple individuals can then be helped at the same time. This is the normal way that Buddhas transform your Qi because it is tiring for them to move their energies and therefore they don't want to waste their efforts on just one person at a time but want to do many people simultaneously, which can happen when they stack individuals with different body achievements inside one another or when they use multiple *nirmanakaya* emanations to help a large group at one time such as during an empowerment ceremony.

Bhakti Yoga, Devotion, Reverence or Spiritual Worship: As practiced in Hinduism (focusing on Krishna, Rama, Kali and other deities), Christianity (by focusing on Jesus or the Virgin Mary), and other religions, the purpose is to self-generate ardent devotion to such a deep extent that your intense positive and negative emotions end up creating internal sensations that stimulate and move the Qi/Prana throughout your body, thus washing your internal subtle body. Thus Krishna instructs, "Immerse your mind only in me, be devoted to me, worship me, bow in obeisance before me. I am pledging that you will attain me because you are my beloved." Sexual intercourse and pranayama practices accomplish your Qi transformations in an entirely different way. Feelings or emotions are internal responses to events conditioned by our existing concepts, and we can use them to generate sensations within our body that move our Qi so that the internal Qi stimulation, when prolonged, can wash either our Yin Qi or Yang Qi. This principle is commonly used in many forms of spiritual cultivation without practitioners knowing about it. For instance, the emotion of tremendous admiration and awe (during worship) can move your Yang Qi while religiously motivated crying or humbling yourself through worship can move your Yin Qi by energizing the body with Yin-type emotions. Sometimes Buddhas will give practitioners spiritual visions with the intent of having them abide within a Yin Qi or Yang Qi state for awhile. Many religions also cause their most ardent practitioners to undergo unpleasant experiences such as intense fear, shaking and trembling (or cold within the body) in order to arouse/purify their Yin Qi. "Fools for Christ" and "Krishna consciousness" disciples, when taught properly, are put through many deep emotional experiences of Yin and Yang to purify their Qi in a similar manner. When going through the kundalini process they will behave in unusual or unpredictable ways such as by sometimes praying, weeping, making unique movements, shouting or urging people to do something, all of which may make onlookers afraid. Religious practice also follows this pattern of purifying your Yin and Yang Qi in more orthodox ways such as when monks and nuns are led to meditate on topics such as glorious Heavenly rewards (which raises their Yang Qi), the fear of Hell (which stimulates your Yin Qi) or the necessity for humility, obedience or repentance for sins (that also stirs their Yin Qi). Cultivating ardent emotional states like this is also a derivative of the "immeasurable emotion" practice taught within Buddhism, which is also similar to the Path of Heroes that instructs you to hold an emotional mood, essence or flavor during an activity or for a prolonged period of time in order to help transform your Qi and thinking patterns. *Boran kammatthana* methods instruct you to invite mental factors into your body in order to tune your Qi/Prana to different qualities and help with the purification transformations necessary to wash your subtle energy (Qi/Prana) and eventually produce a Buddha body. *Yidam* meditation practice similarly instructs you to associate with the energies and personality characteristics of a deity (disposition) to cultivate your Qi in that manner. The practice of envisioning that you become one with a deity, spiritual great, or individual of admirable qualities such as an ideal spiritual savior will not only move your emotions but can also be used for personal development to move you in the direction of obtaining character traits you desire that they possess. Basically, however, *bhakti* practice is meant to deeply stimulate certain devotional emotions and internal sensations in order to move your Qi/Prana. States of deep crying are connected with Yin Qi purification, while joyous states of rapture and ecstasy are connected with your Yang Qi cultivation. True *bhakti* adherents absolutely must experience sorrowful states of mind, such as feeling cut off from God and subsequently crying in despair since this generates anguish that will stimulate your Yin Qi. Your Yin Qi must be purified within your subtle body through this or other techniques that are typically uncomfortable. Songs or hymns of worship that move your Qi internally (because the sounds are projected from different areas of your body) - such as the Christian refrain "Gloria in excelsis Deo," the "Hallelujah Chorus" from Handel's *Messiah*, Gregorian chants and Islamic *dhikr* practices – are also *bhakti* or reverence cultivation practices since they strongly move your Qi through songs, hymns and the attendant breathing that moves your emotions. When singing religious hymns you should always make the sounds resonate within your body while feeling deep emotions, and then this becomes true spiritual worship instead of simple singing. Mantra recitations, or *japa* practice, should always be performed in the same manner with the intention of vibrating the Qi of your entire body, or just certain body sections, and should be combined with feeling strong emotions and internal sensations at the same time. The practice of chanting hymns, mantras and other religious sounds should *never be monotonous* but should vibrate the Qi in different areas of your body, or your whole body at once, and then the practice becomes effective at spiritual transformation. Then it becomes true spiritual practice whereas otherwise it is just voicing sounds. To feel Yin or Yang Qi emotions when singing strengthens the effect of inner Qi stimulation and purification. Religious reverence, as practiced in spiritual ceremonies and rituals, is also a form of cultivation exercise for quieting and purifying your mind that also affects your Qi/Prana. During occasions of religious reverence and worship you should engender a feeling of deep reverence because that deep feeling felt throughout your mind and body is what cultivates your Qi rather than the mechanics of the activity. Or, you might cultivate a state of humility by "surrounding your thoughts to God" during that time, which is a type of mental emptiness cultivation that also cleanses your Qi/Prana. The monkey god Hanuman, hero of the Indian Ramayana epic *who always keeps Rama and Sita within his heart* and who continuously recites "Ram" as a devotional mantra since this sound successfully vibrates the Qi of the entire body (like

"OM"), represents the power of devotion that enables animal man, who is an ape, to reach the higher spiritual stages. Yet another aspect to the practice of complicated religious rituals used by some traditions is that they purify your mind of wandering thoughts when the ceremony requires a high level of concentration by the celebrant in order to perform many actions at the same time, thus quieting his/her thoughts due to the overtaxing concentration, and afterwards the devotee can abandon that challenging state of focus and rest in great mental emptiness as a relief (which sometimes is then called the transcendent experience). Prayer is also a form of worship and comes in many forms for cultivation purposes. In reciting prayers you should focus your mind on the repetition, and feel the meaning of the prayer inside you so that it affects your Qi. Repetitious prayer should eventually lead to an abandonment of thoughts and an experience of mental quiet that is *theoria*, a type of internal illumination where your self is quiet but you fill with Qi. Another type of prayer teaches us to abandon our thoughts and enter into tranquility by instructing us to let go of our ego and "give all our mental concerns over to God." Religions explain that prayer therefore helps us reach a state of supreme solitude centered entirely "on the presence of God" that is a "union with God," hence, prayer is how we can reach the experience of God called *theoria*. Naturally this is just the silencing of your inner mental dialogue/narrative while your body fills with Qi and consequently feels blissful, but it is worded in a more attractive religious fashion. Nevertheless this is considered a deeper connection to God through silence - a silent time of internal sacred quietude that is transformative (due to internal Qi flow during a quiet state of mind). This achievement of being free of coarse thoughts is actually a meditation attainment, which is practicing an internal quietude of the mind rather than engaging in reflective thoughts. That's when the Yang Qi of your body can arise and start washing your tissues and organs. Thousands of men and women over the centuries have achieved the independent subtle body attainment through the religious practice pathway of prayer, worship and reverence, especially within the Christian, Jewish and Moslem traditions. This includes the more recent Eastern Orthodox monks and nuns Gerontissa Makrina, Gerontissa Taxiarchia, Elder Paisios of Mount Athos, Arsenios the Cappadocian, Porphyrios (Bairaktaris) of Kafsokalivia, Elder Joseph the Hesychast, Elder Ephraim of Arizona, Saint Gabriel (Urgebadze) of Georgia, Saint Nektarios (of Aegina) the Wonderworker, Saint John the Wonderworker (John of Shanghai and San Francisco), Saint Iakovos Tsalikis of Evia; Christian saints such as Padre Pio of Pietrelcina and St. Francis of Assisi; Rabbi Menachem Mendel Schneerson; Sufi Sheikh Nazim al-Haqqani, Shaykh Sharafuddin ad-Daghestani, Sheikh Abdullah Fa'izi ad-Daghestani, Shaykh Ahma al-Alawi and Sheikh Muhammed Hisham Kabbani; as well as the Krishna *bhakti* exemplar Chaitanya

Mahaprabhu and Kali *bhakti* adherent Ramakrishna, who all attained the initial enlightenment stage of the Srotapanna deva body via the cultivation route of religious practices that included prayer, worship and reverence. After their initial Srotapanna *Homo Deus* attainment they went further to accomplish the entire path. The Roman Catholic popes St. John XXIII (Angelo Giuseppe Roncalli), Pope Pius IX (Giovanni Maria Mastai-Ferretti) and St. Pius X (Giuseppe Melchiorre Sarto) primarily practiced religious reverence and prayer (*bhakti*) as their spiritual path and each exhibited incorruptible (non-rotting, non-decaying) bodies after death, which is a sign that they too had succeeded in attaining the higher spiritual body achievements (such as did the Buddhist Lama Dashi-Dorzho Itigelov) since incorruptibility is a common result after the extensive Qi/Prana purification one's physical body goes through during the kundalini transformation process necessary to generate the higher bodies. As a result of the higher body attainments - which makes one the equivalent of a saint, sage, prophet, Arhat, guru, *jnani*, spiritual master, etc. - they each became worthy of prayers (mantras) for intercession by supplicants requesting their heavenly aid just as you would normally do for saints in the Catholic or Orthodox tradition, especially the newer ones who have recently deceased. No one ever thinks of praying to a Pope (or one of the other newer Christian saints) for aid, but their incorrupt bodies attest to spiritual attainments and prove they are worthy of such requests *because they truly succeeded through the pathway of prayer, worship, spiritual devotion and reverence.* Those who succeed can usually display miraculous abilities or superpowers such as being able to read people's minds, heal the sick, foretell the future, know what is happening at a distance, project physical *nirmanakaya* emanations (body doubles) in multiple locations that you can see and touch, etcetera. Vedic astrologer James Braha states that when Jupiter occupies the 1st house in an individual's natal chart or aspects the 1st house ruler then the person tends to spiritually cultivate using the *bhakti* pathway of devotion and prayer (like Krishna devotees), and the same if Jupiter aspects the individual's Sun (which represents the soul) or Moon (which represents the person). People who follow austere spiritual cultivation paths that involve practicing meditation, introspection, fasting, detachment of the senses, non-attachment to the world and monkhood will usually have Saturn occupying or aspecting the 1st house or Saturn aspecting the 1st house ruler or Sun or Moon. People who use Advaita (non-duality), Zen, astrology, the Bible, intellectual inquiry, spiritual seminars and any mental path tend to have Mercury occupying or aspecting the 1st house, or Mercury aspecting the 1st house ruler, or Sun or Moon. These three cultivation pathways are symbolized by Krishna (a Jupitarian bhakti type path), Shiva (a Saturnian austerity type path) and Vishnu (a Mercurian mental type path).

Diet, Herbs and Remedies: Eating the right foods, minerals, herbs, and supplements to nourish the body and help to bring about a state of optimal health is necessary for spiritual cultivation. The beginning stage of "laying the foundation" on the spiritual path is also a stage of "rejuvenating the body" and includes eating vitamins, specific herbs, minerals, and special foods that will help to rebuild your Qi and restore you to maximum health. This is necessary for the spiritual path.[31] The most nutrient-dense foods you can eat include red and green vegetable-fruit powders, nucleotide-rich foods, and organ meats.[32] All of these foods are wonderful for your biological substrate because they are easy to digest, absorb and be used to create or repair cells. You should always (1) prefer organic foods, (2) avoid sugar, (3) avoid processed vegetable fats in your diet and (4) reduce wheat flour and grain consumption to lose weight. Some remedial herbs may help your hormone levels, or your Qi/Prana, and others may serve as adaptogens that help bring your biochemistry into balance while yet others may simply help to heal you. Mineral deficiencies must also be addressed. The foundational stage of the spiritual path also includes detoxification of the body's tissues such as muscles, organs, bones and the channels of elimination (intestines) as necessary.[33] Those who can regularly clean their intestines of the filth impacting its walls to keep the channels of elimination open tend to live longer, as is the case for those whose Qi circulatory system runs continuously smooth without blockages[34] (nattokinase and bromelain supplements help eliminate blood clots). Brain scans reveal that using ginkgo biloba, which improves blood flow throughout the body, definitely helps the brain because it produces the healthiest or "prettiest" brain pictures. Chinese culture has created a deep philosophy on the right type of foods to eat in order to help the body adjust to the climate, seasons and health conditions and the western natural foods movement has created its own set of food principles. Ayurveda also offers some principles for this topic but they are not as developed as those of Chinese culture with its Taoist influences. Some foods can certainly be used to adjust your Qi. For instance, hot spices will stimulate your Yang Qi while other special foods may cause a cooling reaction within your body, thus supporting your Yin Qi. Therefore you can ingest certain foods, herbs, minerals, herbal medicines, etc. to adjust the Qi/Prana of your body as necessary rather than just eat for health and growth. Food is better than medicine for improving health, and as stated this is a special knowledge within Chinese cuisine

---

[31] See *Blood Chemistry and CBC Analysis* by Dick Weatherby and Scott Ferguson.
[32] See *Look Younger, Live Longer* by Bill Bodri.
[33] See *Detox Cleanse Your Body Quickly and Completely* by Bill Bodri.
[34] See *Prevent and Reverse Atherosclerosis: Proven Natural Alternatives that Eliminate Cholesterol Plaque Without Surgery* by Stanton Reed.

although remedial measures are also found in Ayurveda and many other herbal medical traditions. Examples of adjusting your Qi include drinking warming teas during winter and cooling teas during Summer (such as Pu'er and Jasmine tea respectively) to help adjust your body. Some schools use fasting as a spiritual cultivation method because the lack of food forces you to depend upon your inner Qi body for sustenance. The desire for food and sex are two fundamental desires suffered by animals that can be used to move their Qi, and so fasting is a time when you can use the force of that discomfort to push the Qi within your body. The internal energies aroused during sex are also used in some spiritual conditions.

Yin Qi Cultivation: The emotions of fear, fright, shock, hurt, anxiety, sadness, worry, disappointment, loneliness, isolation, hopelessness, helplessness, resignation, vulnerability, rejection, unimportance, insignificance, feeling unwanted, feeling let down, feeling confused and lost, feeling on guard and uncomfortable, inner turmoil and travail, physical pain, intimidation, humility, yearning, hunger (fasting), depression, suicide, guilt, embarrassment, shame, humiliation, grief, apathy, disgust, revulsion, jealousy, treachery, sneakiness, greed, and chills all stimulate, vibrate, or raise your Yin Qi. Individuals who cultivate are often provoked by spiritual masters into situations that stimulate their Yin Qi (such as fear, embarrassment, guilt, anxiety and worry, bad dreams, pain etc.) in order to purify their Yin Qi and its channels of circulation. For instance, they might be taught to daily observe the ugly sight of a decaying corpse, which gives rise to revulsion, disgust and sadness thus stimulating Yin Qi. Typically they are put into a prolonged *bhava* state of emotional feelings (strong emotions are evoked) that produces strong sensations inside their body that stimulate their Yin Qi. This is done for hours, days, weeks and even months in order to raise the student's Yin Qi in order to help purify this aspect of their inner subtle body. The principle is that mental states can directly affect the Qi of your body, and so you are put through different mental states to raise your Yin Qi or Yang Qi during specific energy rotations in order to wash the relevant Yin or Yang energies of your body. When you are doing something wrong - such as stealing, lying or spying on others - your Yin Qi also normally arises because you recognize the impropriety of your behavior. The regular daily practice of introspection to find personal faults, errors and bad conduct, to feel *ashamed or guilty* about these imperfections, to learn from those errors, and then engaging in a small ceremony of confession and *repentance* so that you don't repeat them is a wonderful way to periodically refresh your Yin Qi, establish rectitude in your mind and correct your behavior. Imagining that you absorb lunar energy from the moon (cool moonlight); water visualizations; meditating or conducting sadhanas in cemeteries; charnal ground practices; corpse practices; performing ghost,

Hell, purgatory (*preta*) or death sadhanas; seeing sorcery or witchcraft practices; experiencing pain or torture; doing evil deeds; cultivating within a room of mirrors that makes you feel cool or coldish; visiting a cool cave; visualizing or imagining that you undergo age regression; fantasizing that you transform into a young girl (femininity practices), etcetera are all methods of Yin Qi cultivation. Times of sickness; darkness; thoughts of suicide; attending funerals or cremations; sitting in cool caves; working in a monastery's ossuary; engaging in thievery or other criminal activities, visiting a hospital; working in or visiting a mental asylum; eating cold minerals such as calcium; physical pain; visiting limestone or other "cold" mineral formations; standing within a cold waterfall; eating Yin foods, cooling herbs or Yin medicines (such as antibiotics); "seeing ghosts" or having scary visions or "bad" drug trips; sitting or walking naked like a Jain monk; having people learn your embarrassing secrets or just being embarrassed, etcetera are all situations that arouse the Yin Qi/Prana of your body because at those times your Yin Qi is stimulated into moving and temporarily dominates your physique. During cultivation you must undergo sustained Yin Qi cultivation that generates different types of inner sensations that stimulate your Yin Qi to arise for prolonged periods of time. Usually this is done to aspirants by causing them to suffer various degrees of (uncomfortable) Yin emotions to wash their Qi. You must cultivate *both* your Yang Qi and your Yin Qi along the cultivation path; you cannot cultivate Yang Qi alone. It is most common to cultivate your Yin Qi by reciting the mantras/prayers (or performing the sadhanas) of female Buddhas, the Hell Buddha Ksitigarbha (who deals with sickness, death, purgatory and the hells), performing cooling water visualizations that "wash" your body's Qi (Yin Qi is cool, not warm), visualizing that you are the color blue or black or white, performing lunar energy absorption sadhanas, or reciting certain mantras at midnight during a new moon (no light) in a Yin location, etcetera. During the course of spiritual cultivation to transform your inner subtle body for the Srotapanna attainment you absolutely *cannot cultivate just your Yang Qi alone* but must also stimulate your Yin Qi. This is why the Medicine Buddha Bhaisajyaguru is attended by to bodhisattvas symbolizing the light of the sun and moon, namely Yang Qi and Yin Qi since both energies must be balanced within your body for healing. Suryapraba Sun Light Bodhisattva and Chandrapraba Moon Light Bodhisattva (also known as Nikko Sunlight Bosatsu and Gakko Moonlight Bosatsu in Shingon) are the two Bodhisattvas that represent the Yin Qi and Yang Qi of your body. For instance, martial artist Sun Lu-Tang[35] would face the moon and practice absorbing its Yin Qi through every pore of his

---

[35] See *The Internal Practices of Sun Lu-T'ang*, compiled and translated by Bradford Tyrey, (Neijia Books & Publications, 2012).

body. Sun Lu-Tang would also inhale Yin Qi for martial arts practice during the hours of 11:00 pm to 1:00 am when Yin Qi is strong and collects around the physical body, and upon exhalation he would direct the moon's Yin Qi into his lower abdomen and imagine it shining with lunar power. To acquire "heaviness" skills (the opposite of the *laghima siddhi*) he would absorb two hours of the moon's Yin Qi and mix it with one hour's practice of absorbing the sun's Yang Qi (this time ratio is not exact but would be adjusted as appropriate). When sadhus in India sit under the hot sun surrounded by burning coals or burning cow dung, they are using special methods to cultivate their cooling Yin Qi so that they can withstand the heat (while Tibetan yogis cultivate warm Yang Qi in the snow through *tummo* kundalini exercises so they can withstand the cold). When you are naked in public and thus become ashamed or embarrassed this causes your Yin Qi to be stimulated (until you get used to it), and this method is used in the Aghori and Jain traditions to help purify someone's Yin Qi. When individuals are told to spend nights in scary places such as graveyards, deserted forests, wild mountains, cemeteries or haunted locales where apparitions appear, at those times their Yin Qi is stimulated into arising, which also happens when they are told to conduct frightening sadhanas involving dead bodies and (fake) ghosts, demons, Yakshas, and the like. Many Aghori masters have cultivated their Yin Qi in this way. The initial phase of the white skeleton visualization when you visualize that your corpse decomposes in a disgusting manner, is supposed to arouse your Yin Qi and is imagined prior to visualizing your skeletal bones shining brightly, which stimulates your Yang Qi. The female Mahavidyas of India (Kali, Tara, Tripura Sundari, Bhuvaneshvari, Bhairavi, Chinnamasta, Dhumavati, Bagalamukhi, Matangi and Kamala) as well as the nine manifestations of the goddess Durgha and ten forms of Kali also represent different tones of Yin Qi cultivation. In Christianity, adoration of the Mary the Mother of Jesus is a form of Yin cultivation; a female figure is so helpful for Yin cultivation that had Mary not existed then some other female or goddess ideal would have to have been created for the Christian tradition. The phases of the moon represent different types or stages of Yin Qi cultivation too and are used in *Yijing* study and astrology, which takes note of a planet's occultation to judge its power on events or individuals. Prominent female Buddhas within Buddhism include Tara, Kuan Yin, and Zhunti who are matched with appropriate (Yin cultivation) mantras and practices as well. In ancient times the cults of female goddesses (ex. Isis, Demeter, Diana, etc.) provided society with Yin Qi cultivation methods too. Many countries even have Yin holidays – such as Halloween, Mexico's Day of the Dead (*Dia de los Muertos*) or China's Tomb Sweeping Day – which are used by Buddhas at those times to help transform the Qi of large communities of people on a vast scale. When people suffer scary nightmares or "see ghosts" this is sometimes due to spiritual beings trying to frighten them to provoke their Yin Qi in order to open their channels just as eating spicy food temporarily opens up your Yang Qi channels, and when Zen masters report irrational strong fears of death or the hells this is due to the influence of Buddhas as well who try to stimulate their Yin Qi while working to purify their Qi channels. Christian Hesychasts often end up deeply crying during their prayer recitations; their deep emotional response of weeping is a type of Yin Qi cultivation but if done frequently they must protect their lungs and kidneys with proper diets and supplements, otherwise the organs will weaken from the excessive depletion. When you are sick with a cold or flu it is easier to cultivate your Yin Qi since your Yang Qi is depleted at that time. Any adept going through the Twelve Year kundalini process will pass through many Yin Qi experiences, such as half-hour periods of shaking uncontrollably with chills that is a Yin Qi purification blessing by spiritual beings, or being scared deeply by some contrived incident. Men undergoing the Twelve Year process will also sometimes experience Shariputra's goddess flower lesson that he experienced within Vimalakirti's ten-foot square room (that symbolized his brain). The Buddhist *Vimalakirti Sutra* reveals a special gender transformation imagination sometimes imposed on aspirants passing through this stage of Yin Qi transformation. This method explains why Ramakrishna, Arjuna and Hercules ended up wearing women's clothing for a brief period of mental feminization practice (it is only imagined during specific meditation practices for brief periods of time), and why the Greek legend of Tiresias said he experienced a (mental) sex-change into a woman for seven years. The methodology can be further understood by reading *Shikhandi and Other Tales They Don't Tell You* (Devadutt Pattanaik), *Nyasa Yoga* and *Meditation Case Studies*.

Yang Qi Cultivation: Feelings of anger, pride, courage, triumph, heroics, confidence, euphoria, exhilaration, enthusiasm, joy, cheerfulness, awe, optimism, sexual excitement, love, strength, willpower, mirth, brightness, aliveness, attending weddings or other happy ceremonies or festivals, active exercise, fighting, masculinity practices, positive *bhava* meditation-visualization practice, sunshine visualizations, pranayama cultivation, positive planetary aspects (in the sky or happening to your natal planet locations as shown in a birth chart) etcetera are all situations used to cultivate the Yang Qi/Prana of your body. To cultivate the Yang Qi of our body, one method is to enter into a *bhava* emotional state that accordingly arouses sensations inside your body that will, in turn, stimulate or arouse your Yang Qi. An example is to whip up one's devotional emotions to enter into an ecstatic state of bhakti yoga. In Esoteric Theravada the practitioner *pervades their entire body with positive mental states* they select as specific objects of consciousness they focus upon during meditation; the practitioners do not realize that the purpose of such exercises is to stimulate the movement of their internal Yang Qi and have those resultant Qi energies affect their entire subtle body. The Buddhist "Four Immeasurables" meditations on infinite joy, loving-kindness, compassion and equanimity are another form of this technique, and proper instructions for the "four infinite minds" practice are that you should strongly stimulate all the Qi inside your body when concentrating on the corresponding emotion so that the energy infuses you and the practice is then not just a mental phenomenon but a physical phenomenon too; you are supposed to arouse the feeling of those mental-emotional states within your body in order to stimulate and thus activate/purify its Yang Qi. Of the basic human drives and emotions – hunger, submission to others/authority, sexual desire, and the fight or flight reactions necessary for survival – three are used in Yin Qi cultivation methods (fasting causing hunger, submission-obedience-humility in the face of authority, and fear causing flight) and two are used for Yang Qi cultivation, namely sexual desire/enjoyment and the spirit of fighting that requires courage. Other Yang Qi emotions such as pride, arrogance, anger, etc. are also used in Yang Qi cultivation techniques, especially those espoused in Tibetan Buddhism that cultivates "divine pride," "divine anger," etcetera. Some foods cause a heating/warming reaction within your body that is also a form of Yang Qi stimulation. Fire visualizations, pranayama practices and kundalini Yoga exercises are typical Yang Qi cultivation methods but there are many others. Sun Lu-Tang would practice absorbing the sun's energies through his back, while facing away from the sun, at 3:00 am to 7:00 am in the morning to cultivate his Yang Qi. Both India and China have sun and moon (Yin Qi and Yang Qi) energy absorption techniques which typically assume that the moon's essence is felt strongest around the full moon, and the sun's Qi is fresh and gentle during the morning hours and around the beginning of the month (either the lunar month or when the sun changes astrological signs). Sword masters practice absorbing Yang Qi while inhaling, and when exhaling move the Yang energy through their sword to its tip. When Tibetan monks sit in icy cold weather and try to melt the snow around them, they are using special methods to cultivate/activate their warming Yang Qi, which is called *tummo* meditation practice. The capability is based on performing special breathing exercises in conjunction with special concentration and visualization practices. Because of their high altitude evolutionary genetic adaptations over time, Tibetans have twice the rate of blood flow through their capillaries than ordinary people (due to broader capillaries and higher levels of nitric oxide), hence they tend to be better at warm kundalini (Yang Qi) cultivation but not Yin Qi cultivation (note the fierce nature of the Tibetan-Mongolian gene stock), which is why compassion must then be emphasized as a remedy for this genetic stock of people. Indians and Africans, because of their hot weather genetics, can regulate their cooling abilities easier than others, which (in addition to culture) is why they tend to excel at Yin Qi cultivation. This is often exhibited through a cultural tendency towards gentleness and non-violence, which explains why there is a preponderance of Yin cultivation techniques in India that include female deity *yidams*, scary midnight or ghost Aghori sadhanas in charnal grounds, and so forth. Incidentally, even "non-violent" philosophies still require rectification methods that institute punishment when people deviate from expected virtue norms in order to establish accountability and continuance of the system based on virtue. Elder Joseph the Hesychast would every night lead his close Christian monks (destined to get the Tao) through wonderful inspiring tales of saints and then reflections on death, the Crucifixion, their personal sins and then life in Heaven in order to daily progress his students through states of both Yin Qi (reflections on guilt, personal sin, worry, repentance and contrition, death, the Crucifixion, etc.) and Yang Qi (reflections on victory, happiness, Heaven, rewards, etc.) arousal to purify their Yin and Yang Qi and their channels. Solar deities in world religions always represent Yang Qi, such as the Chinese sun god Taiyang Xingjun or Hindu solar deity Surya.

Five Elements Qi Cultivation: While it is said that there are two basic types of Qi/Prana – Yin and Yang (which are often symbolized by two intertwined snakes, male and female) – one can also think of the body as being composed of the Qi/energy of five elements, or the different Qi energies of the nine planets, or the Qi energies of other diverse component factors that each have unique tones or signatures. Thus, methods have been developed to help you cultivate all these different energy flavors or Qi tones. You can cultivate the Earth element Qi of your body through muscular exercise and diet, both of which affect the composition of your physical body, or the white skeleton visualization that focuses specific attention on your dense bones. The Water element of your body can be cultivated by relevant emotional exercises (immeasurable meditations), lunar absorption techniques, water visualizations and *nei-gong* Qi practices on your endocrine glands since they secrete hormones (which are the watery elements within you responsible for health, cellular communications and aspects of consciousness). The Fire or Warmth element of your body can be cultivated by breathing methods, kundalini practices and internal sun or fire visualizations, and there are various ways to cultivate various states of fire samadhi. The Wind element of your body can be cultivated by various pranayama, Mantrayana, inner alchemy, kundalini, *kriya* yoga, *anapana*, *qi-gong*, *neijiaquan*, *nei-dan* and *nei-gong* exercises that move/mobilize your inner Qi/Prana. The Space element can be cultivated by emptiness meditation practice and by imagining that your body becomes an empty sack or formless, boundless, bodiless light. Ramana Maharshi achieved his first enlightenment body (Srotapanna stage) through emptiness meditation and *jnana* (wisdom) inquiry. Wisdom can be cultivated by studying spiritual texts, such as in Vedanta, and by studying psychology and other cause and effect findings in various fields such as economics, medicine, human relations, science and so forth. In astrology the planets represent specific types of Qi-Prana energy, and you can construct relevant exercises to try to stimulate a *planetary characteristic Qi/Prana* within you as yet another means to cultivate/purify the Qi of your subtle body. Vedic astrology has mantras for planetary deities that request their purifying influences on your Qi. Taoists stand in certain postures (such as the *san ti shi* trinity posture of *Xingyiquan*) at specific times of the day, without moving, in order to absorb the specific Qi essences of those hours to "feed" their subtle bodies. In the martial arts there are also *animal form* cultivation practices where you focus on duplicating the energy of a certain animal when performing special movement practices because you want to stimulate your Yin or Yang Qi/Prana through those powerful envisioned characteristics. This is similar to *bhava* practice. After trying to evoke the energy (Qi) characteristics of the animal, you try to link that type of Yin or Yang Qi/Prana with your limbs during movement. You do this over and over again to synchronize the limbs of your physical body's Qi/Prana with energies of a certain Qi-tone, and thus use this as a way to cultivate your etheric subtle body of Qi. Thus martial arts can help you purify your inner subtle body, which is why it is said that you can become enlightened through the proper practice of the martial arts.

Cultivation of Infinitely Large Immeasurable Emotions: The four Buddhist immeasurable meditation practices on infinite joy, kindness, compassion and equanimity are meant to help you cultivate different tones of your Yang Qi/Prana. They symbolize the four dhyana (higher bodies), and by dwelling in them (regularly cultivating them fully) you will slowly change your personality over time to develop in the direction of those personality characteristics. Those emotions will not only change the quality of your Qi/Prana but will also impregnate your cells and internal organs with those emotional energies if you consistently try to feel them within your physical body during practice. Such a result is proven by the fact that organ transplant recipients start taking on some of the personality traits of their donors after a transplant (because the Qi of their new organ became impressed within the donor's characteristics). As a beneficial practice you can also cultivate emotions such as tremendous (immeasurable) courage, valor, vigor, passion, generosity, authority, positive energy, stamina, mirth, etcetera to help you influence your Qi/Prana and change your personality and fortune as you gradually develop those characteristics. Long-term practice will not just stimulate your Qi but also start to permanently flavor your Qi/Prana because you start to transform your personality. If you hold onto a specific pure mood or emotional essence (a prevailing stable emotion or *bhava*) this is *Viramarga* practice (the Path of Heroes) in Kaula Tantra. It involves holding onto a pure dominant emotion or feeling (*Rasa*) but always in service to the highest principles. Such exercises will help to permanently change the *samskaras* or predispositions within your subtle body that reincarnates. By engendering large, intense heroic emotions (and cross-feelings ancillary to the mood), and holding those emotional states in mind and body like meat soaking in a sauce that then becomes saturated with the flavor, through the force of permeation over a long period of time you will slowly affect the Qi/Prana of your body, your thoughts and finally your behavior. Eventually you will transform your mental barriers, limits and prior conditioning ("your heart will break through") and your virility and vitality will become permeated by the pure quality you have cultivated, which should be invoked in service to people. Esoteric Theravada Buddhism uses a similar technique that cultivates mental factors and emotions that are *invited into your consciousness and body* as a form of meditation practice, whose ultimate purpose is to also help transform your personality and the Qi/Prana of the body. It helps *immensely* if you watch your behavior and then act in the same particular ways that express those character traits when opportunities arise because a character trait only takes hold when you practice it rather than just think about it. This is why sports training mental visualization (rehearsal) practice is followed by the actual physical efforts, and yet the visualization practice improves results immensely just by itself.[36] Therefore you must be vigilant for opportunities to manifest the *bhava* (prevailing stable emotion) in regular life. *This is spiritual cultivation*, which is cultivating the spiritual discipline of the hero. It takes vigorous effort to put the full-body emotional training into effect in your real life until those characteristics become an essential part of yourself. The results of successfully transforming your character should start to appear in this life, and as character traits in subsequent incarnations. To make greatest use of this technique, during practice sessions (or during daily idle moments such as waiting in line somewhere) imagine suffusing, permeating, perfuming or saturating yourself with the Qi/Prana/aura of the character trait you strongly wish to cultivate, imagine also projecting it into your outer environment, and simultaneously try to *feel the Qi of that characteristic within yourself and projecting from yourself everywhere*. You can recite amplifying affirmations as well. The Qi and emotional feeling must be large, intense and held with stability. When appropriate opportunities arise then retrieve those feelings and act that way because there must always be a regular

---

[36] See *Sports Visualization for the Elite Athlete* by Bill Bodri.

consistency of actions (*praxis*) to solidify your learning and intent. Consistently visualizing and feeling that you are a wrathful deity, like Yamantaka for instance, is another type of immeasurable practice designed to raise your Yang Qi/Prana, but it will also increase your pride and aggressive tendencies if you are not careful of the *yidam* you select and how you practice. When choosing a *yidam* or deity for "Buddha mindfulness" meditation practice, such as a Jesus or Krishna or Dattatreya, you must be very selective as to the types of emotions and thoughts you practice generating and holding onto during your practice sadhana since they will influence your Qi/Prana because you are actually cultivating those same characteristics. For instance, many Hesychasts recite the Jesus Prayer, "Lord Jesus Christ, son of God, have mercy on me a sinner," that produces a feeling of remorse and humility, which are designed to provoke your Yin Qi. Note the difference between this and the feelings generated from reciting alternatives such as "I give myself to you, Jesus Christ the Lord" or "Come to me, Jesus Christ my Savior." One must carefully select the *bhava* emotional mood they must cultivate to serve as an aid to Qi cultivation and as an antidote to one's deficiencies. Performing activities while holding onto a "principal awareness" reframing of their importance, and elevating your emotions regarding the activity, is also another way to change your Qi, mindset, perspective and personality. This cultivation method is based on the principle that anytime you change your thoughts, attitudes, mentality, and conduct your Qi will immediately alter and transform in those directions, which is another reason you are taught to cultivate virtuous actions, speech and thinking. Therefore if you change the mental frame that you use to view something, such as embedding them with very significant emotional content, your activities can change your Qi. Reappraising your activities with a new frame also allows you to replace old pathways of reasoning with new and more powerful ones and allows you to impart tremendous compassion, kindness and so forth into your behavior. By correcting mistaken reasoning you can permanently reprogram your mental algorithms that lead to undesired emotions and develop a healthier, more accurate and more successful mindset or outlook in their place.

Breaking Barriers and Limitations to Unleash Your Inner Vitality, Feel Truly Alive and Touch Your Higher Bodies: When yogis who have practiced lots of cultivation work practice fasting they are forced to live off (depend upon) their subtle body to maintain their vitality, thus strengthening their inner subtle body by drawing upon its Qi energy to survive (since this helps to open all its channels). When you practice *kumbhaka* pranayama and hold your breath longer than your normal limits, subsequently passing through a state of difficulty that then opens up into a visage of greater mental clarity and lightness, through lack of air you force yourself to open internal Qi channels and rely on your inner Prana/Qi as well. When you encounter layers of resistance in athletic activities like running where you are up against a performance barrier, but through heroic persistence surpass that resistance and push through your pain threshold when you "hit the wall," you force yourself to depend more on your inner Qi body to move forward, and then you are living within the Qi of your subtle body. When you get so good at athletics that tap into your real Qi and begin to move with effortless grace and ease, you can sometimes experience a flowing sublime state of inner peace and joy that is pristinely alert, blissful and the purpose of cultivation. When as an athletic professional you play sports and go beyond your normal capabilities to hit a state of "flow" (where your mind enters a state of concentration that seems focused and quiet without distractions while your body grooves itself to an optimality that uses less effort), you are synchronizing your physical body with your inner subtle body. Athletic flow is expressed during optimum health, optimal blood circulation, optimal respiration and optimal Qi flow that is so excellent because your body is running at peak performance, which then quiets the mind and produces mental clarity. It also involves a strong sense/feeling of being fully alive, which means feeling blissful in all your body's cells due to that optimal inner harmony of respiration, blood circulation and Qi circulation. In ordinary life you may sometimes break through strong beliefs you once had that were inhibiting your virility and vitality, and when no longer being locked up by false beliefs your Qi/Prana will often start to immediately flow much better. By freeing yourself of limiting mental restrictions you will unleash your inner Qi/Prana flow and begin to feel more alive and able to experience "flow" in a different form. When you stop trying to conform to an identity that others have created for you that feels like a burden (because it isn't your true self), you will free your inner Qi flow as well and experience tremendous relief-pleasure. Your authentic self can come out when you let go of a false you self-image and then your virility, vitality and Qi will accordingly respond because you no longer repress them through restrictions; you must always strive to be your authentic self. When an Aghori flaunts societal traditions by breaking behavioral norms, the resultant freedom leads to a special type of unrestricted internal Qi flow too. When you break any psychological limitations you assumed for your potential abilities, and try to push past them to reach a higher level of excellence, you will break the barriers that constrain your life, life force and fortune. Once again, *this* is spiritual cultivation. You can also try to directly cultivate the higher energy bodies by practicing the formless samadhis of Buddhism, each of which corresponds to a higher stage of finer thoughts we call "emptiness cultivation" that is matched with an attendant stage of more refined Qi/Prana. When you practice centering within the four formless samadhi absorptions – such as the samadhi of infinite space, infinite consciousness, infinite emptiness and neither thought nor no-thought – which each require more subtle levels of thoughts and refined Qi, it is like centering your living presence in your subtle body, Causal body, Supra-Causal body or Immanence body respectively, which strengthens the circulatory flows of the energy within your body's energy substrates. Therefore, by trying to center yourself within a clear lucidity of extremely fine thoughts (which is achievable due to meditation practice) you are cultivating the energy of the higher body vehicles inherently within your physical matrix. At the stage of pristine awareness we call "clear mind" where the inner narrative that normally speaks within your mind quiets, you are basically cultivating the higher energy elements of your physical nature. Basically, there are various ways involving your mind, body and breathing to force yourself into relying on your higher spiritual energies (or you could say higher bodies) that are inherently embedded within the matrix of your physical shell but not yet differentiated out into separate entities. They are as yet condensed (undifferentiated but existing as components) within the composite energy we call Qi/Prana that comprises your subtle body that is the densest of your potential spiritual bodies. You can, through various means, force yourself to survive on your inner subtle Qi body (by fasting, pranayama, etc.) in order to strengthen it. You can force yourself to tap into your Qi body through physical exertion that takes you past your limits ("hitting the wall"). There are many methods of breaking through your physical and mental barriers to access your higher energies (such as your inner Qi body), many methods for strengthening your inner energy bodies, and many techniques for synchronizing your breathing, thoughts, and physical movements with the energy of your higher bodies. Many of these techniques are very apropos for sports professionals during challenging events because they involve going past one's physical limitations and transcending one's physical nature by tapping into your Qi energy and yet higher forces of formation. The mundane method of breaking barriers or coverings is actually *detachment* or *non-clinging* and wisdom because it involves freeing yourself from conditioned programming such as limitations you incorrectly assume you have. This enables you to break through false barriers you had assumed for yourself, thus freeing your vital energy to improve its internal circulation. By eliminating layers of automatic patterning you've developed over time, including identification with a false persona, you transcend old learned behavioral traits and past conditioning patterns that certainly bias (crimp) your natural inner Qi/Prana flow and your behavior. Afterwards your Qi can flow more freely because it is no longer a prisoner of artificial restrictions, and you can live at a higher state of vibrant being. Thus, detachment means letting go of any artificial patterning you have developed over time and freeing your virility and vitality to flow as it naturally would without the artificial conditioning that has constrained you. *Thus you become more alive*, but you still require refinement of your character, virtues and Qi otherwise this is just similar to releasing the vitality of an animal. For instance, confidence is something people already have but it is covered over by ingrained habits and learned patterns of tension. If you can free yourself from identification with those patterns, such as breaking your patterns of fear reactivity, you will automatically have more confidence since confidence and its Qi-tone is naturally inside you and just being blocked. That self-development work will equate with a greater degree of vitality, and thus better Qi flow. The ability to detach from what's going on and look at things from an outsider's perspective, to step back from fusion with your thought-stream and the situation at hand, is the purpose of learning detachment through meditation practice. This is the meaning of, "when thoughts arise, (be aware of them but) do not pursue them." It means not becoming merged with your thought-stream but stepping aside and seeing things more clearly, with pristine clarity, as if you were an independent observer who wasn't fused with your mind-stream or the situation. You center yourself in being awareness. Yes you still have thoughts but you don't get entangled with them because you practice meta-cognition that oversees them. Cultivation means "letting go of" or "becoming detached from" subtle mental patterns and reactive behaviors that you have learned/adopted over time which function as suppressive coverings over your psyche. They bias your inner Qi body with unnatural leanings. Such barriers define you because they become incorporated into your personality, and thus help to create your fate by binding your thoughts, actions and energies to constraining patterns that robotically restrict and impede your greater freedom. Whenever you break away from such false coverings your Qi/Prana begins to flow more freely, your vitality rises extraordinarily, and you feel more vital and alive as a result of breaking free of prior conditioning. This, then, is a way of cultivating your Qi. However, just having strong vitality is akin to being like a strong animal. You must refine that Qi through culture. Confucius said that when your native substance (Qi or vitality and personality) wins out over cultural refinement you have the coarseness of a peasant, and when cultural refinement wins out over natural substance you get the pedantry (clarity of minor details) of a clerk. Only when your natural substance and your cultural refinement are in balance do you get a leader, a real human being. Confucius said he *refined himself* by basing himself on virtue and taking recreation in the arts that in his day included archery, charioteering, writing, ritual and music. Today that would include yoga, martial arts and athletics that cultivate/refine your Qi; the active literacies that cultivate your intellect and give you the power of elegant and effective expression; and the arts that pacify your emotions and refine-elevate your tastes and character. Hence, you must not just cultivate your virility, vitality or strength of Qi (animals do this when females breed with the strongest males) but must refine your consciousness and personality with training and culture. Cultural refinement focuses on our animal nature and brain to make noble the beast within us. Refinement or elevation of our intellect and behavior (propriety, wisdom, kindness and compassion) are what make us ascend instead of remaining just animals.

These short summaries reveal some of the common ways to purify the Yin and Yang Qi of your body during the processes of spiritual cultivation. These methods of Qi purification, and the overall process of your Qi gradually becoming purified through the use of these and other various cultivation techniques, is the basis of the methodology to develop the independent deva body attainment.

When you achieve the deva body attainment you become enlightened and thereafter known as a Buddhist Srotapanna Arhat, Hindu *jnani*, Taoist Immortal, *Homo Deus* or 'twice born," and so forth. This attainment is the very first rung of the true spiritual ladder that is kept hidden from people since most would not attain it, and therefore would be dejected about their spiritual efforts and stop cultivating altogether. This is why the path is positioned in orthodox schools as devotion to a long sequence of reverential acts during which your Qi gradually become transformed, and in personal cultivation schools as some type of emptiness attainment or mental realization because in cultivating emptiness meditation people think they are making progress but cannot actually measure whether this is true. Hence they still progress towards the attainment of the deva body (first dhyana) even though they won't achieve it in this life, but they successfully lay the foundation of achievement necessary for success in the afterlife.

Nearly one-hundred percent of spiritual practitioners do not know how to cultivate correctly even if they are monks or nuns because they do not realize they are performing exercises meant to transformationally purify their Yin Qi and Yang Qi. One of the purposes of spiritual practice is to purify and strengthen your subtle body composed of Qi so that you can achieve the independent deva body attainment whilst alive, or (failing at that) lay the foundation for the Sakadagamin stage and then Causal body Anagamin achievement (third dhyana) after death. Now that you know the many ways to go about purifying your Qi and the principles behind these techniques, you should be able to make your spiritual practices, whatever they are, much more effective.

The road of spiritual practice involves cultivating, purifying or refining (1) your Qi, (2) your consciousness (thinking and mental states), and (3) your character, which gives rise to your (4) actions, activities and behavior. Hence we say you must purify your character, thinking and behavior on the spiritual trail. Even if you don't succeed in enlightenment, you still want to achieve a refined state of psychology (mental well-being) and behavior. You want to develop special virtues and abilities such as learning how to focus and concentrate, have patience, have discipline, become compassionate and to put yourself into other people's shoes. However, you also want to make progress in purifying the internal energy of your body since that is the basis of your spiritual attainments and the body of your next life. If you don't succeed at the subtle body attainment in this lifetime you can continue cultivating the purity of your body's Qi after death and achieve the requisite purification of your subtle body from there to attain the Sakadagamin stage of achievement. You get a head start on this objective if you start cultivating sincere Qi/Prana practice during life.

The level of attainment you want to ultimately achieve is the Supra-Causal body achievement that corresponds to a "formless plane" of existence, meaning a level of existence (Formless Realm) where your body is free of all the vestiges of coarse matter including etheric atoms, which is why that body can twist, fold, vibrate and perform all sorts of shape changes and energy pulsations that are used during the purification processes of your kundalini transformations. For these achievements you can cultivate your Qi directly through *nei-gong* purification practices or go about trying to purify it by purifying your consciousness.

How do you purify your Qi by purifying your mind (consciousness)? By cultivating internal values and bright virtues rather than evil deeds and unwholesome tendencies since bad behavior pollutes the quality of your Qi and creates unfortunate tendencies or *samskaras* within its basis. Movies sometimes employ caricatures of countryside yokels versus college-educated hucksters. You can immediately tell the difference between these two types of individuals due to the refinement of their Qi, and you can similarly sense the level of people's educational or character cultivation in real life too. Certain types of wild animals also have an instantly noticeable raw, earthly smell about them as well due to the lack of refinement of their Qi. Those humans who cultivate themselves refine their Qi, and if they truly followed a deep path of virtuous behavior during life some might even exhibit *sariras* in body's ashes after death. Hence, virtuous behavior does change your Qi in preparation for the deva body or Srotapanna attainment.

On the other hand, humans stay animals if they don't cultivate their consciousness. They smell like animals if they don't cultivate their Qi. You must perform both of these tasks on the spiritual path. These are tasks of mental and behavioral purification and elevation.

Whenever you cultivate virtuous, friendly, kind and compassionate ways in thinking and doing; practice regularly scheduled times of introspection where you review your past behavior or thinking and vow to self-rectify errors; strive to break free from animal instincts and impulses; break free from (detach from) the social cocoon of groupthink; free yourself from errant past conditioning such as self-imposed limiting beliefs; or like an outside observer start exercising meta-cognitive awareness (witnessing) that stands aside from entrainment with your mind-stream so that you realize what you are actually thinking and doing in real time and can then pivot to act differently when you see you are errant, you then ascend.

In so making efforts like this, you can create a new life and new future destiny. You can alter the very things that were causing you to have a certain type of fated destiny. You can improve your present state of being and then reside at a higher level of excellence. Because of mental detachment or "distancing" from your thought-stream you can separate yourself from prior conditioning and fusion with your thought-stream to live a new life free of old thinking and behaviors that hold you back. Then you can create a better life than the one they would have produced had you retained those influences as your standard attributes. In the place of the old you can create a new life as you choose.

You aren't just breaking away from your thought-stream or the quality and circulatory habits of the Qi/Prana within you. You are breaking away from the mechanistic programming you've developed within your attribute of consciousness that is another inanimate process embedded within Shakti, for Shakti is *entirely inanimate*. We only call certain things within Shakti "living" for the convenience sake of differentiation (identification). However, you are just a process (we call you a "life") within Shakti that has consciousness, and your consciousness and life are neutral processes within Shakti that we term "animate," but there is no such innately independent own-thing as a "living being with consciousness." Consciousness seems like it is free of matter and apart from Shakti, thus transcending it, but is a process entirely within Shakti that is ruled by cause and effect principles and is composed of Shakti rather than transcendental. However, the beauty of consciousness is that it allows you to be creative within Shakti and proactively change your attributes, activities and trajectories. No matter where you are, you can change everything for the better.

You are a borderless ripple within the fabric of Shakti so you are Shakti rather than an independent life, and ultimately beyond being just matter-energy you are the fundamental substrate of the universe that lacks consciousness, attributes or even movement. That is basically what you are. You are just a different agglomerated type of form, aspect, process, event or functioning within Shakti that is both Shakti and the original nature – both real and non-real, neither having form nor without form, neither living nor non-living. You are part of the cosmos and an individual in your own right, and the realization of self-realization is to know your true relationship with the cosmos (Shakti) and the foundational substrate of the cosmos. You look like a sentient being but there really is no such thing as a sentient being *in the way we assume there is*. There is no such true thing as an innate, inherent, independent, essential, core or absolute soul-self because what we call the "self" is just a dependent construction whose composition spans the entire universe. You are essentially a being without any form.

Everything gets into the act of making or defining you. And yet, of course, a sentient being is there but there is no innate person as the knower. There is just a process going on, a collection of events or simples and energy waves creating Knowledge for that Knowledge and doing whatever Knowledge does. Even so, you think you are a sentient being with special characteristics and do enjoy consciousness, so make use of it as best you can. For instance, the more you become free of your robot-like programming - rather than entangled with your thought-stream and any imagined restrictions you've assumed for yourself - the better your inner Qi vitality will flow. You will thus *feel more truly alive* and better able to experience peace, happiness and bliss, which is what we all want. We all want to feel an active inner vitality and taste the joy or bliss of life rather than just exist. Illumination (consciousness) is liberation from matter and is to be an enjoyment of the innate *sat-chit-ananda* where we participate in the bliss of living. We don't want to suppress this or turn aside from this *joie de vivre*. You want to embrace life. Life should be about more than just existence, and it certainly isn't about thought suppression (a deviant pursuit of empty mind or "emptiness") so that you become mindless like Nature. Once you get in touch with yourself by knowing your true self, you can orient yourself to actualizing and perfecting all the abilities of your mind-body matrix to do great things and taste the enjoyable bliss of the life experience.

To some extent you will always be a slave to your genetic conditioning, cultural conditioning, social conditioning, educational conditioning and what you learn from your experiences etc. since cause and effect rules all, including the fact that all your thoughts, emotions and deeds are influenced by such conditioning (that includes mental structures common to all that have been instilled by society), but you can create different programming to follow in order to accomplish or experience whatever you want.

This should not include adopting behavior that causes you to adopt vices, evil ways or abandon your humanity because a person is not an animal or some other less virtuous conscious agent; humanity is a quality we create in each other to uplift ourselves and it must not be destroyed. It is only to be raised higher. We cultivate humanity by purifying our minds and behavior and by refining our Qi through spiritual techniques. Our existence as humans and even the greater Srotapanna level of *Homo Deus* (first dhyana) is due to the higher qualities we pass onto each other about proper conduct, which is what separates us from lower species. Nevertheless, the point is that most people born within the same period, for instance, tend to adopt the same programmed values as their peers, but you can choose to develop higher values that are totally different from those group values. You can upgrade or even ennoble your adopted values just as you can work to purify the Yin Qi and Yang Qi of your body, and this is a necessity for the spiritual path. You can develop a psyche (your total personality encompassing all your thoughts, moods, behaviors and emotions) containing elements foreign to that of everyone else and hopefully more noble or majestic. Specifically, a personality can be transformed to become more noble, pure, compassionate, wise, patient, disciplined and spiritual than everyone else. This is the spiritual path.

You are a slave to the conditioning of your culture and environment (that produce an energetic impact on your subconscious thought processes even if you are not aware of it), but you can choose to change your thinking apparatus and fill your mind with contents different than everyone else. You can make yourself be the way you want to be and become whatever you want to become as long as you have an ideal for inspiration, aspiration and emulation, which is the road of cultivation practice. You can also choose the future you want to enjoy and then create it.

By viewing yourself and your thoughts, actions and situations from a detached higher standpoint that lets you see them for what they are, you always give yourself the chance to break free of blindly following thoughts that would produce a particular worldly outcome you do not want, and can choose a higher outcome instead. You can self-rectify yourself through mental observation; unlike the flow of a river that must follow a set course you can learn how to self-correct yourself according to ideals and change your direction of movement/activity. Thus, your fate can always be changed by better thinking and behavior. Through better thinking and behavior you can change both your personal attributes as well as life events that determine your fate and fortune.

This capability is one of the purposes of meditation exercises that emphasize awareness, presence, watchfulness, being centered, introspection, self-observation or mindfulness. While you must certainly cultivate the Qi energy of your body through refinement practices, their purpose is to develop the natural tendency to always be fully awake, alive, aware and free from entrainment with your mind-stream so that you can always upgrade your thinking and actions to excellence. Meditation practice enables you to calm your mind and settle in a living state of presence (an awareness of being here and now in some activity) rather than continue going through life in a robot-like condition where your thoughts are compulsive. To be robot-like is to be trapped by entrainment with your thoughts where there is no way to change their trajectory and spiritualize your behavior. On the other hand, we want to live our lives in a state of fully present awareness with elevated behavior. This is the fullest human potential rather than to live in a robot-like, hypnotic "waking sleep."

The meditation practice of continuously watching yourself has as one of its purposes the objective of helping you cultivate a state of presence where you are not enmeshed or caught up in your thought-streams and always blindly following thoughts while losing your state of presence. Presence is the experiential feeling of *living in the Now* where there is a freshness of the living experience. There is a complete awareness of the present moment that fully appreciates the greatness of the experience, and a subtle bliss felt throughout the body. This is why Japanese Zen master Dogen said, "All activities of everyday life are practices." The *samu* mindful work practice ethic of Zen gives you the opportunity to practice full awareness and the beingness of presence.

"Presence" is like being centered so that your Qi runs directly into your brain, your I-thought quiets, the Qi even circulates through your cerebellum and back of the head since you are not pushing it forward, and you experience life and all its glory in that state of alert, quiet, focused, vivid, centered presence. This is to experience the joy of life, or the bliss of life (even if it might not seem blissful), especially when your Qi flow is so excellent that it energizes all your body cells. The "pristine" of "pristine awareness" refers to a type of clarity and freshness to your knowing that is accompanied by a subtle tinge of enlivening bliss within that mental experience. Meditation practice therefore strengthens your ability to be present, achieve the state of flow, and not develop a fluctuating, wandering mind *if you practice correctly*.

Detachment practice actually means "presence," "pristine awareness," "ultimate clarity" or even "wisdom" practice. Through detachment, awareness or mindfulness practice you can cultivate a state of powerful energetic presence, rather than a state of dullness and suppressed vitality, where you see your doings clearly and can *take back control of your life by transcending any prior conditioning that has seeped into creating your thoughts and behavior.* Such practices enable you to always assert your values into whatever you are doing.

By not mechanistically clinging to (following, going along with, getting entangled within or becoming merged with) your deterministically-created thought-stream but always rising above it like a separate individual who independently views it by standing outside of it, you can realize what you are actually doing in all situations and where you are actually going. Through this transcension of "being clear" you can break away from your thought-stream and the fortune that it destines to create a new one in its place. *This is essentially spiritual cultivation.* You cannot just emphasize body (Qi) cultivation on the path but must emphasize this aspect of spirituality, which is the cultivation of *how you run your m*ind that includes your thoughts, emotions, behavior and your overall psychology and character.

This is the crux and core of spiritual cultivation, which is to cultivate yourself (mind, body and actions-conduct) so that you personally move to a better/higher state of being, and to use your powers to also create better states for others since they are your brothers and sisters within Shakti who can also experience unfortunate living conditions. A spiritual cultivator works to decrease personal suffering for the "I" as well as suffering for the "We," and does many things for the sake of the community. He or she works to create more positive states of joy, loving-kindness, warmth, friendship, compassion, etc. in both themselves and others in the present and by solving problems they create a positive legacy for the future.

You cannot escape having a fortune since Shakti is ruled by cause and effect, which means that a line of thoughts and actions will always produce consequential results (fortune) once initiated. You cannot control the outcome of your actions but only your efforts, but still you must make the efforts required to attain whatever you want. Your actions will always have a consequential outcome along a road of effort. You can and should always try to create the special fortune, fate or future you want for your life even though you cannot guarantee that outcome. Once your wisdom realizes any mistakes in your efforts through introspective review, you can change an ongoing course of actions headed for an unfortunate outcome, but only if you are wise enough, skillful enough, and put in the requisite effort.

This is the uncertainty of life, which is that we cannot guarantee results for our actions, and the inherent creativity of consciousness gives us the opportunity to adapt our efforts and correct them in response to conditions as well as select worthy goals in the first place. Your Qi must be cultivated, your mind must be cultivated and your actions must be cultivated through self-correction and refinement, which overall is a process you can call a type of "purification." Insentient objects have fixed attributes and cannot do this. They cannot be proactive, create or plan but can only respond to conditions according to their properties. Conscious beings, on the other hand, have voluntary volition and can monitor and alter their actions and behavior.

Most of the time your thought-stream mechanically (automatically) arises in response to situations. You don't know why certain thoughts arise but they automatically surface due to cause and effect algorithms. You become *more truly alive* by *not fusing* with your thought-stream that is dominated by processes inherent to the machinery of your brain, and thus are mechanistic in nature and sometimes errant. You become deadened by fusion rather than enlivened or vitalized, so a key to a better life is to become aware of what naturally, automatically, mechanistically arises within your mind and then correct those thought products and alter them according to your higher goals and purposes.

We say you need to purify your Yin and Yang Qi and you also need to purify your mind like this for it gives rise to evil, bad and unwholesome Yin thoughts as well as the positive Yang thoughts or emotions. You want to strive to become more noble, consummate, and majestic (as well as realistic) in altering whatever arises naturally in your mind. If anger arises or you immediately think someone is ugly as a natural reaction you should not criticize yourself for what has mechanically, automatically arisen. You simply must stay aware of your natural thought-stream and then *correct whatever arises*, guiding your thoughts to a more noble stage of elevation and refusing to act upon errant impulses that may have naturally arisen. Learning how to do this is the Great Learning of life.

You can pursue greater happiness and bliss by training your thinking apparatus to produce excellence and this pursuit is also spiritual cultivation, which entails doing the very best you can with what you have despite any inherent deficiencies but improving what you can. Your job is to correct your thoughts that naturally arise so that they are mentally aligned with goodness, rightness and your highest, best ideal. Your job is to recognize mistakes in what you are thinking and doing in real time and then correct yourself until you get things right. Your job is to optimally manage all your capabilities of consciousness, and gradually take yourself to a state of excellence that is a potential spiritual nobility and magnificence beyond your current state. To do so you must progressively *discard the negative programs presently running your persona* that pollute its illustrious nature, retrain your perspectives and ways of thinking, develop your wisdom and skillfulness in terms of decision-making and active behavior, and develop the willpower to transcend unwholesome urges, habits (that cause you to do certain things in a certain way), mindsets (that cause you to see things in a certain way) and predispositions to create a new life and new fortune.

Thus, emptiness (a mind that is somewhat quiet of self-talk, wandering thoughts, impelling desires, distracting emotional irritations and inclinations, etcetera) is often considered the highest state since it is the barest state, the most natural state, the unconstructed state, the calmest clearest state, the most enjoyable state. However, if the mind's conceptual processes always reference a substratum of values due to prior trainings in ethics and virtue, and if those noble values and virtues then fully permeate all its outputs (thoughts), we might say that the expression of such thoughts is truly majestic, noble, pure and beautifies reality. In that case, how can emptiness be termed the highest state as compared to the spirituality of a living presence that beautifies or transcends the world?

Thoughts (and actions) to help others in compassionate ways are the highest, most noble and most beautiful states of consciousness. *The mind expressed in elegant, consummate conduct is the most beautiful and highest activity rather than passive emptiness that is pure but does nothing.* When you do good deeds and you feel the joy of giving, is this vibrancy of vitality not a blissful flow state too?

The universe is neutral but we create its moral order. We create nobility and morality or evil and cruelty. In terms of universal structure, however, phenomena co-exist with inherent emptiness just as energies permeate the emptiness of space, so the mental practice of being neither totally empty nor attached to our thought-stream corresponds to the natural state of the universe and this is the way we should be. We should neither attach to emptiness nor to thoughts, which is the Middle Way.

Many spiritual traditions say this is how our minds should operate but we harbor too many mental attachments, including attachments to desires and impulses that impel us improperly. Basically, you should not attach to illusory consciousness with fusion unless you are fixating on a mental topic with concentration for a specific purpose. In that case you are trying to hold your mind on a point with stability for a specific purpose. When you are letting your mind flow, your vitality should become full because of the health you've cultivated for your body where you can feel an inner physical bliss connected to the Qi in all your cells. Thus you can experience *sat, chit, ananda* or existence, consciousness and bliss. *Sat-chit-ananda* should not just subjectively describe the ultimate unchanging reality but your experience of life itself, and it can if you cultivate *chit* and *ananda*. We are existent as beings of consciousness and our nature is constructed to enjoy the innate *sat-chit-ananda* of the universe's existence where we also actively participate in that universal bliss.

The state of "living in presence with (detached) pristine awareness, perfect poise and ease" allows a world of qualities to be experienced in a state of flowing clarity. The flowing clarity of knowing a reality like a dream is another meaning of "neither real nor non-real." In that state of flow the I-self identity you take yourself to be still exists (otherwise consciousness does not transpire) but *does not become overly fused with its mental constructs since they flow through consciousness in a background state of quiet*. With training that (affects your consciousness and Qi channels and) takes you back to the state of a child life can be experienced vividly, vibrantly, with your full awareness and your vitality operating in the most natural and correct manner.

Essentially, through the cultivation practice of meditation where you cultivate emptiness as a meditative dwelling and as a type of awareness-release from binding to your thought-stream (mindfulness) and dwelling/abiding within it, (1) you want to cultivate a clear mind of awareness that is very quiet because it is empty of self-talk and agitations (which requires your Qi to circulate fully within your head and body) and (2) you don't want to be overly binding to thoughts so that you can enjoyably experience the flow of life. That non-binding, non-fusion with your thought-stream due to meta-awareness witnessing provides you with the opportunity to change, correct, alter, rectify, etc. your thoughts more optimally as you deem fit.

Achieving that state means that your Qi – due to prior stretching exercises and inner Qi work – is flowing naturally throughout your body so that you exhibit strength in virility and vitality. Furthermore, your Qi should directly enter your head and stream everywhere cranially with fullness (that tends to produce calmness and clarity) including even in the cerebellum, which then makes one exceptional. This creates a state of centered *presence*, and sometimes it is called "clarity" or "pristine awareness" or even "emptiness" even though the thought-stream (such as mental recognition of objects and awareness of the mind-stream) is still functioning.

In the *state of presence* there is no excessive identification with your body or mind and you execute your conscious functioning in a smooth and effortless manner. There is predominantly the state of presence since self-talk has diminished and you can approach life with a pure and clean mind fully connected with the reality about you. Your mind is quiet but wide-awake, fully open and aware so the experience is like a feast of lucidity. It is not a nihility of thought since thought processes are always producing the world of qualities you experience within your mind. However, there is a pristine lucidity of clear, centered awareness without unwanted agitations, and in that state your body feels blissful/comfortable. Why? Because it is healthy and its energy flows smoothly in proper balance due to a proper diet and all your prior physical exercises and spiritual inner energy cultivation work. That is why you work to cultivate the Yin Qi and Yang Qi of your body. In the state of presence you can concentrate on whatever you are doing with absorption and truly enjoy the bliss of life and the joy of simply living. In a state of presence or flow your absorption in a world of thoughts and qualities remains unaffected by distractions and continues to fully enjoy whatever is the experience.

This feast of lucidity is an optimal way to exist in life as you go about doing whatever you need to do. Thus it is called aliveness or "flow state." It is existence, consciousness and bliss. At times it might seem as if there are no thoughts during this state of *vivid presence* but there are always very fine (almost quiet) thinking processes going on within the mind whenever you are conscious no matter how pure, empty clear or quiet your mind may seem.

The key to "experiencing silence," "pristine clarity" or "one-pointed concentration" is whether or not there are too many wandering thoughts, afflictive emotions, or cravings and desires or other distracting impulses in the mind. The mind always has forms of unconscious processing going on including perceptions without awareness of what is perceived, therefore many mental operations don't openly appear as existing but are always present in fully awake consciousness. Your mind processes many types of "very subtle thinking" even though consciousness may seem pristinely quiet and empty. A mind can process stimuli and act on them without any awareness of it doing so. Thus there is no such thing as truly empty mind when you are awake.

You must choose your future – the future you want to have in terms of how you want your mind to be, where you want to live, what you want to experience or do, who or what you want to associate with, what you want to accomplish, how you want to be, the well-being you wish to create, and so on. You can manifest a desired fate or fortune by creating better thoughts in line with your goals and by also not clinging to errant thought-streams that would lead you astray. Then you must select whatever thoughts or actions appropriate the highest objective, ideal or aspiration after due consideration. Since you are not an intrinsically real "sentient being" but only so in the apparent/conventional sense, the highest viewpoint is to recognize the nature of consciousness, what you really are (the "enlightenment view") and your potential to become whatever you want. Knowing that you are like a dream person in a dream world you should be not cling to painful events that obstruct you but should correct the errant mental tendencies of your mind, and should learn how to actively manipulate Shakti in the best fashion as a living being normally does to accomplish whatever you want while enjoying all that Shakti, your greater body, has to offer.

Nature is ruled by laws of cause and effect, so all things in the cosmos are controlled via cause and effect because and therefore follow definite rules of transformations. However, you can manage these transformations to create or accomplish whatever you want even though, technically speaking, your decisions are also really inanimate events/processes embedded within Shakti and somewhat deterministic because they are produced according to your past conditioning and your machinery of mental processing. There is no escaping Shakti or the fact that you are not an innate, self-so, independently existing living being, personality or entity that transcends it. There is no such thing in Shakti, there is only Shakti – a neutral, indifferent scintillating Shakti that has some conscious components that think they are independent beings separate from Shakti when everything about them, even their consciousness, is Shakti. You are simply a continuous process within Shakti that is more or less uniform, monotonous and stable, but you have the gift of being able to continuously generate mental experiences as well as perform deliberate actions with intent. What will you do with it? That is the big question.

There are many actions you can take to free yourself from the suffering inherent to existence within Shakti, including self-improvement or improving your environment and circumstances, yet the most special set of actions involve conquering your mind and cultivating higher spiritual bodies by purifying the Yin and Yang Qi of your inner physical nature. This is what is done on the path of spirituality, but people don't know it and masters don't speak about this clearly because most people would fail at it during life, and would thus be discouraged if they knew the full truth as just revealed. The spiritual path is therefore worded in a way that does not emphasize body cultivation but mind and conduct purification instead since by so doing you will make progress during life and can finish the efforts of purification in the afterlife to attain the higher bodies.

You are not an innate process with an inherent unchanging I-self, but are a somewhat stable process that is always transforming into something else. You can guide those transformations. You have the power that you can take charge of some of those transformations. You know many of the methods used to cultivate mental purity, freedom from emotional afflictions, ethical values and virtues, the proper way to operate consciousness, and so on. You know about concentration, mindfulness, visualization practice and many other methods used to correct and elevate your behavior or make your actions more skillful and effective. And you also know about the many methods for purifying your Yin and Yang Qi, as just taught, which must be done for the spiritual path.

Essentially you are constructed out of the interconnections with All of Shakti itself and are simply an event made of other events that combine with each other. But so what? You still have the creative freedom of self-expression and can enjoy the life you have because you have the prize of consciousness, so you can give your life significance and meaning through your mind and behavior. The second great luck is that you have the ability to cultivate and attain a nearly immortal spiritual body that can escape the lower realms of continuous reincarnation. The problem for you within the universe is not birth and death but *longevity and continuity* that are attributes maximized through the practice of spiritual cultivation. Reincarnation is managed by higher spiritual beings because our inner Qi body eventually deteriorates, but through their efforts is always being refreshed. This is why higher spiritual beings constantly intervene in our Qi/Prana during our lifetime. Reincarnation prevents physical, subtle and Causal bodies from decomposing and deteriorating into annihilation, and the rounds of reincarnations in the Desire and Form Realms can finally be escaped forever when you achieve the Supra-Causal body and higher that are free of the lower forms of etheric matter.

So in truth, there really isn't any such true transcendental thing as the consciousness of a living being. Thoughts are just another type of inanimate neutral event or process going on within Shakti and are not apart from it nor transcend it even though they seem free of matter. From the aspect of living beings thoughts create a limited approximation of Shakti in our minds – a similitude or illusory reality – but that imperfection is okay because it still provides us with life, and we can correct some of its errant perceptions and conclusions through wisdom and logic. Even so, thoughts can never capture Shakti properly through mental representation. We truly don't know what reality looks like so what we see in our similitude is referred to as an illusion. There *is* a Shakti reality that has qualities, but we can never know the universe directly, fully, perfectly and thus correctly. Yet who cares about such deficiencies since we don't know any better and what we have is still the great miracle and treasure of existence. You just have to cultivate to make consciousness better!

Thoughts are simply part of Shakti, not something that transcends Shakti because of an independence of non-membership. Thoughts are things. They are neutral or inanimate activities or processes within Shakti without a separate, independent, innate living being behind them. They do not provide you with "truth," but with your own personal version of truth that is relevant for yourself and for your class of sentient beings. Your individuality is actually a collected assembly of simples (particles, atoms or quanta) in a particular ever-changing pattern (meaning that there is no absolute pattern at all), or an agglomeration of interdependent conditions and processes within a field – a process stretching through time – without anything *inherently you* being there. This is the truth of the way things are. You therefore have no substantial reality as an innate being although your apparent existence is more or less uniform, monotonous and seemingly stable for awhile. There is no intrinsic, inherent, unchanging permanent self-core inside those intertwining conditions of infinite interdependence that cause your apparent self to manifest - the processes or conditions you call your body or mind - or inside any collection of simples and processes or events no matter what the pattern of the agglomeration. Yet, you can still enjoy the bliss of life through the great miracle of consciousness that we should be taming and mastering on the road of spirituality.

Your consciousness *does* exist within Shakti as an appearance, faulty or incomplete that it is, so you can enjoy it. The great miracle of existence, and greatest treasure, is the I-thought of being a sentient subject that can experience a world of qualities through consciousness. You are just an object or process within Shakti that has the property of consciousness, which is the grandest miracle and treasure of the cosmos no matter what the faults or limitations within its construction. The point is that you are a living object, with a body, that enjoys awareness that can experience a little of what you are and what the world is. Consciousness is simply one of your properties and your Knowledge is your identity for as long as it lasts.

Our challenge, aside from maintenance and survival of our living system, is that suffering often afflicts our consciousness so you should learn how to make things better in your mind-body package and its life (by mastering the transformations of Shakti) in order to reduce or eliminate suffering and produce well-being in its place. Well-being is more palatable/enjoyable and can admit to certain degrees of pain and suffering that cannot be eliminated. You need to learn how to think and act differently so that suffering does not bother you so much when you cannot reduce it or avoid it, and learn how to cultivate a happier, sunnier, more cheerful and optimistic mentality so that you can enjoy Shakti to a higher degree. We are creatures of interdependence so the great goal is that everyone else becomes happier too because conditions become better due to our aggregate efforts at improving ourselves and making the world a better place.

This is why spiritual masters stress that we should work to improve conditions for the sake of others, which is why we work so hard to give our children better lives and better futures than we had. You can eliminate the suffering of others by improving their conditions, and you can train your mind to perform most of the activities that do so. By improving your understanding of affairs (increasing your knowledge and wisdom) you will better understand patterns and regularities and thus know how to better act, and by developing wisdom, knowledge and skills you will become able to improve conditions for yourself and others (achievement).

Unfortunately, consciousness usually gets caught up within its own mind-stream whereby you lose perspective/comprehension of what you are truly doing because of that fusion. You lose your perspective and get lost because you get caught up in things, and therefore make bad decisions or act poorly. When you get distracted or caught up in some agenda while losing presence it becomes harder to attain your objectives. This is why you should, through meditation practice, cultivate a mindfulness of your thought-stream and actions that produces a meta-perspective knowing of them. Otherwise, by becoming entangled within them and blind to what you are doing you will often make bad decisions and perform actions that lead to inferior outcomes. By also cultivating the ability to concentrate through meditation practice you will learn how to deal with distractions, annoyances and afflictions that typically pollute your mind and blemish the state of presence.

You actually become "more insentient" by forgetting yourself and getting blindly entangled with following your thought-stream like a robot under command. This is what is meant by becoming more "mechanical" or "robotic" through the fusion of blind entrainment, and the perfect example of this is succumbing to (automatically acting upon or becoming engrossed in) your most animalistic urges, desires or habits that appear within your consciousness. Spiritual cultivation teaches you not to become imprisoned by your desires and senses, or by your past conditioning but to treat everything fresh and new. It teaches that we should not unite ourselves to carnal impulses, evil tendencies or lower desires that so occupy our heart and mind that our minds become clouded or we feel we cannot live without them.

You can learn how to transcend such pollution, which is the path of cultivation practice that ennobles you as a spiritual being. Attachment means that you identify yourself with whatever fills your mind such as the senses or emotions. In religion this idolatry is "occupying your heart by another God" because your whole being becomes subservient to something other than spiritual ways. Cultivating emptiness and detachment, on the other hand, allows you to counteract many negative traits such as craving and desire.

The remedy for becoming more sentient, more alive, and more transcendent or independent of the forces normally controlling you in life is to reside in your highest spiritual status. That state is detached from conditions. Your highest spiritual status allows you to entertain a wiser, kinder, more transcendental perspective. Actions proceeding from that perspective reflect a higher, better way than what would normally just naturally occur. To attain a higher spiritual status requires the ennoblement of consummate conduct, which is the Great Learning pathway of Confucius in how to most properly use our mind, body and behavior.

You were taught through conditioning to act a certain way but can learn to step out of this learnedness. You can cultivate change in yourself in order to ascend to something better. You can become more independent of your prior conditioning and become more "alive" by reversing the tendency of entrainment where you become merged with your conditioning. You can ennoble yourself to a higher state and transcend the pulls of automatic reactivity by cultivating mindfulness, detachment and the mental distancing of meta-observation that makes you more independent of your thought-stream. By regularly cultivating meditation you can train yourself to become an observer more "outside of" your thought processes and therefore more detached from the heat of the moment, namely the stream of events within your mind-stream and the real world. This lack of fusion allows you the opportunity to improve yourself rather than simply act like an automaton on automatic that is acting like a mechanical process. From a higher perspective that observes/knows your mind clearly due to pristine awareness and non-fusion, you become the master of your thinking and behavior and can get on track and stay on track to achieve whatever you truly want, which is called "gain" in Confucianism.

By always residing within clear awareness and watching your thoughts, and therefore standing apart from fusion with them because you are viewing everything from a distanced perspective of dispassionate detachment, you become more and more *truly alive* because of a lesser amount of robotic entrainment. Without entrained attachment you get closer and closer to the ideal of free will. This is because you free yourself from ingrained conditioning, and you can therefore become less robotic instead of succumbing to the stored patterns automatically delivered by your consciousness as defaults.

This is the spiritual liberation offered by cultivating higher transcendental bodies that are progressively closer in composition to the foundational nature – doing so allows you to conquer your lower physical natures. For instance, the more you can detach from your physical body the less you are prone to coarse animalistic desires and urges that may sometimes impel you. The more you detach from your inner subtle body Qi the less prone you are to getting carried away by your passions, desires, prejudices, aggressive tendencies and emotions. The more you can detach from your thought-stream the more you can transcend ordinary thinking and practice higher behavior. Basically, the less you are controlled by your automatic thoughts and emotions the higher your stage of spiritual attainment. This is yet another reason for the importance of meditation practice.

Normally individuals become entrained with their physical sensations along with coarse materialistic thoughts, desires and urges, but when you stand apart from them, stop identifying with them and transcend your physical nature (through an "awareness that sets you apart") it is as if you are centering yourself in your next higher body, your subtle body, or just consciousness. You thereby train to become a *heavenly being* through such practice. If you can let go of your emotions, desires and passions entangled with your vital energy so that you transcend their pulls, we then say that you center yourself in your body of conceptions/mentation that is higher than the realm of emotions, and you thereby become a more *spiritual being*. If you can rise above thought entrainment and totally leave your lower nature behind, you can eventually become an *enlightened being*, a *sage*.

The greatest degree of freedom and abilities for a sentient being is to attain a body composed of the highest etheric energies of Shakti possible, and one might say that the absolute highest stage of existence is to be just the Unmanifest, formless, inanimate fundamental substrate itself. In that case you have personal non-existence and there is no *sat, chit, ananda* – existence, consciousness and bliss. At that stage there is only nothingness. You can say It is pure beingness, but without consciousness that non-composite existence is as nothingness! It is worth nothing without the cognizance of self-existence, and thus you need a body and consciousness to both know your self and the world. Total peacefulness is a type of nothingness but without the perturbation of existence it has no value.

You *want to have* consciousness, want to experience happiness and bliss within that consciousness, and due to consciousness you want to develop meaning and significance for your existence in spite of all the imperfections of life such as pain and suffering. It is certainly proper to seek pleasure and joy from time to time because without them one finds not the energy to continue to go ahead, but they should not be your sole life pursuit. Humans have invented many ways to pursue joy and happiness in their lives, such as by running after pleasant sensations, but most of these pathways are deficient because they do not produce lasting bliss, comfort, ease or well-being that includes meaning and significance, which is what humans really seek. Humans seek connection, significance and meaning in life and they typically find it by performing good deeds (despite the burdens) rather than by predominantly seeking fleeting states of happiness and sensory pleasure.

Right now you seem to be a separate individual entity but you are part of Shakti, *in fact all of Shakti*, but you cannot see all the interconnections of your body linking your apparent being with all of Shakti. Even though you are all of Shakti you imagine yourself to be innately separate from Shakti or Nature due to ignorance about your embeddedness. However, you are indeed Shakti, and in fact you are part of the aggregate life and *consciousness of Shakti*. All of Shakti is one organism, and you are a portion of the voice and consciousness of Shakti. Your life belongs to Shakti so your life is Shakti's life just as your consciousness is Shakti's consciousness. However, humans have a tendency to identify with a limited sense of existence.

You are also the foundational substance of the cosmos - its absolute essence. Being both, you are neither just the void of the absolute nature nor the non-void of manifestation. You are neither just the empty, peaceful unchanging true reality nor a transient manifestation. Being Shakti you are always changing, but being the original nature you are the permanent Self that is not subject to change or alteration.

The fundamental substratum that is your True Self is the only real substantive nature, and existence (beingness) is Its very nature because It is permanent, eternal. It is always there changeless, dependable and true, so It is the sole Reality you can rely upon, your true nature, your true soul, your true unchanging beingness or core self-nature. Your true reality is That. It is an insentient core because It is inanimate, changeless, pure or non-composite but you just happen to be a sentient creation within It, whatever sentience means.

However, being the pure fundamental essence that is the True Reality you are actually a beingness that is not a manifest existence, and therefore a non-existence (or unmanifesting reality) that is nevertheless true beingness and true existence. Your real body is formless and cannot be grasped, and this is your true self-nature. How can you imitate this fact within your life of manifest nature to experience more creativity, connectedness with others, meaning, happiness and bliss?

The more you detach from clinging to your thoughts the more your mind is like your inherently real nature that, like space, is empty but supports everything while offering no frictional impediments to the transformations within it. Hence, the more you detach from entrainment with your experiences (of your body and mind) and transcend the conceptual doings of your consciousness by stationing yourself within the purity of awareness, the more you become alive, awake, aware, *real* – the highest state of conscious existence that incorporates existence or beingness, consciousness or (the recognition of self) presence, and happiness or bliss that straddles both the state of existence and non-existence, the void and non-void (Shakti). The more you don't cling to thoughts, the better your Qi will flow within you so that you can achieve physical bliss within every body cell and start to feel more fully alive as a sentient being.

This is the highest state of manifest beingness in manifestation. It is using your primary property, consciousness, in the right way such as for the cognition of yourself and reality, and for improving yourself and your environment so that it becomes more comfortable for your existence and for subsequent generations ... including *your own subsequent incarnations!* Proper, correct consciousness creates and follows rules of morality and ethics, as well as standards of virtue and values, so that an individual can live in harmony with others and Nature and experience happy mental states from your animate and inanimate relationships.

One might state that the highest and purest state is being wholly the empty, unmanifest, pure original nature, but It has given birth to the cosmos that is just Itself, so the manifest universe is also pure. You are both so must be both, but you should cling to identification with neither. Within the fundamental substratum there is only purity – no good or evil exists because any differentiated phenomena, such as dualities, are a pollution.

Within the manifestation there is no good or evil because it is perfectly clean and pure so it is only our minds that make something virtuous or not. Good and evil are human constructions – human interpretations in a neutral universe. We create such values in life because we need them in order to live more prosperously even though they do not ontologically exist in the universe. From the point of view of Reality there is nothing good or evil.

Despite appearances, Shakti *is therefore ultimately pure* just as you are ultimately pure, and there is no such thing as the characteristics of evil or virtue *inherent* in the universe or pollution because it is simply itself, and these are principles created by our minds and our understanding of fairness, justice, suffering, relationships and so on. *We are the ones who create the moral order for the universe.* We create the code of culture and then culturally indoctrinate ourselves as to right and wrong. We create it because *we need to create it* for flourishing, happiness and bliss to exist for ourselves. It is a fictional reality, an imagined order, but we create these values for our protection, survival, flourishing and well-being or ease just as our senses and mental apparatus create an imagined view of the outside world that is also not truly accurate but fit for our survival.

In the existence of the universe you are an object – a *living* object – lucky enough to have higher consciousness and can therefore choose to express yourself and perform any actions, aspirations, deeds or vows you desire that might give your own life happiness, connection and meaning. However, your existence and the rules of transformations within Shakti are subject to cause and effect so you might not always get what you work towards. This is why Krishna advised people to work without expectations since you have no control over the fruit of your work, nor should you expect anything in return for what you do. Therefore you need to develop great wisdom for how to proceed to accomplish whatever you want, you need to develop skillfulness to achieve those goals, and you must remember the *Diamond Sutra* injunction that there is no such true thing as a sentient being to enjoy the results of merit. Then you must still perform whatever is necessary anyway and continue with perseverance until you achieve your goals.

You should learn to master the highest and best methods for whatever you have as your body, mind and behavior. You should also learn to master the highest and best methods of performance for every aspect of your life. The apex of perfection is not to be a naked sadhu who silently sits alone without possessions and simply survives, accepting all that comes his way with indifference and calling this poverty detachment or "spirituality." This is not the testing required to develop ethics, morality and virtuousness inside ourselves. The apex of perfection is to master both yourself and phenomena so that you become master of the laws of nature (changes of phenomena) and yourself and then use those skills to create a new and better you and world.

The apex of perfection is not to become an ascetic sadhu or sannyasin or fall into dry tree Zen. It involves a fuller mastery of yourself and worldly activity, and active engagement with the world for your own purposes as well as for activities that help others by promoting whatever is good and cutting off whatever is wrong or evil. The apex of perfection is a consciousness that enjoys mental states of peace, calmness, lightness, natural ease, centeredness, egolessness, pristine clarity-awareness, vivid presence (that accesses a feast of undistracted lucidity), compassion and kindness, wisdom, sunniness, lightness, shine, brightness, flow, happiness, joy, vitality, bliss and so on. One can never subdue all passions and desires to become "colorless," but must purify or elevate their passions and desires to beautification since many are necessary for survival (such as the desire to eat, protect one's life, etcetera).

You can arrive at all this through the road of self-perfection called cultivation, spiritual practice or spiritual cultivation.

The practice of detachment helps you move towards these excellences. Detachment means that you know your thoughts and analyze your situation from a higher perspective of meta-cognition like an independent third person observer. It means to always cultivate a meta-perspective that is separate from your coarse thought-stream thus readily enabling self-correction and engendering better behavior for social activities or achieving any of your objectives.

Mindfulness of your thought-stream weakens the link between self-identification with your thoughts. It is a form of detachment that provides an opportunity for you to intervene and restructure (correct) your thinking and behavior rather than simply be blindly subject to your thoughts as robotic instructions, which is also akin to being inanimate. Through mindfulness of your thoughts you can achieve the meta-cognition that gives rise to better, wiser, more skillful and effective behavior. It also allows you to give rise to kinder, warmer, friendlier and more loving, compassionate behavior.

If you think of yourself as a third-person character it becomes easier to observe yourself and the world to see what you are really doing in real time without your ego getting in the way, and then through this distancing you can more effectively work on a self-improvement path that seeks success and happiness in life. For instance, when you attain the subtle body and through it view your lower physical body, it becomes easier to manage your earthly behavior for the very same reason that you have attained independence from that life and therefore dispassion in regards to it. With each higher body attainment the impressions and experiences of the lower realms seem as if vacant dreams. It is then easy to preach virtue in the lower realms, but have you attained it in the higher realms? Don't put a nonsensical halo above yourself or assume it of others because of their spiritual title since everyone is struggling.

The highest ideal is to learn how to master the changes of phenomena, act with loving-kindness and compassion amongst animate phenomena and life, and then to take the necessary best steps to improve phenomenal states for yourself and others who are *also the consciousness of Shakti* subject to the same pains and sufferings as you.

This is just ordinary life. This is just *being ordinary* in growing and trying to move things forward but not being overly attached to whatever happens, and yet adapting to whatever happens and reacting in ordinary ways - wise, lovingly kind, warm, friendly, compassionate and skillfully effective but benevolent ways. You don't try to silence your existence or cut anything off other than afflictions, suffering and unwholesome states of being. You live a regular life but permeated with effectiveness and compassion, and you pursue what you want to pursue. If you need money for your objectives then you pursue money. If you need status in society so that your words are heard then you pursue status. If you need fame then you pursue fame. If you need power to affect changes then you pursue power.

This is all ordinary life. It is the natural way of things. The highest material path involves attaining mastery over money, power, status, appearance, etcetera – basically "all *dharmas*" – in order to accomplish the highest virtuous ideals and objectives, such as Buddha vows, rather than simply to pursue transitory selfish, base, materialistic pleasures and enjoyments.

The road of spiritual cultivation is that of self-rectification, personal growth and self-improvement, and to push society forwards along these lines is an act of great merit. Your highest, most perfect state is to be a perfection that straddles both existence and non-existence but does not cling to either side. Knowing what you are, you should choose to live life for specific purposes that you decide. You might also say that from the manifest aspect of reality your highest state is a creative existence embedded within Shakti that uses your powers of consciousness and activity to affect conditions for the better so that you and everyone else become happier, more prosperous, etcetera but where you always remain happily detached from those results. If you cultivate the highest spiritual bodies possible you will always be more detached from any results achieved within the lower realms just as you will always enjoy a higher perspective that can guide your behavior. You will reside within a more enjoyable realm due to your transcendental status and have access to greater powers of achievement.

Remember that your body and mind have no substantial reality because there is only the one fluctuating universe in manifestation rather than actual discrete phenomena within it, although of course our minds create the multiplicity of individual phenomena and their facticity when they are part of the one seamless everything. You are a transforming process within Shakti's infinite sea of fluctuating interconnected processes, but your localized embodiment gives you a body and the gift of consciousness that can know qualities of experience and perform creative actions. How then should you live your life? You must learn to use your gift of consciousness in the highest, best ways possible.

For this goal learning is necessary, namely the Great Learning. You should learn how to maximize and optimize the many capabilities of your consciousness and learn how to control it, such as learning how to ignore mental annoyances and subdue emotional disturbances or unwanted involuntary activities. You will always be subject to the processes of consciousness that produce your mental experiences since your mental apparatus produces your existential experience. It is a dependent construction and thus always conditionally mechanical, robotic or automatic to some degree beyond your control. Whatever arises within consciousness is never your fault, but *what you do with the mind-stream that arises is your responsibility*. Therefore you should choose to learn the highest and best ways of controlling your thinking, feeling, experiencing and behaving so that your consciousness is virtuously effective and predominantly filled with positive enjoyable states rather than negative moods or experiences. You should choose to master the highest and best ways of altering or improving mental states and your mind-stream of thoughts so you can actualize optimum states of excellence.

Furthermore, you can also cultivate higher spiritual (transcendental) bodies that live in more pleasant realms in more pleasant ways and thus experience more pleasant lives. Is this not also the purpose of spiritual cultivation, which is to free yourself from suffering and the lower realms of incarnation forever? You must therefore follow a pathway of cultivation practice to maximize your physical and conscious capabilities.

Consciousness is produced only because you have a body, so self-cultivation involves taking care of your body and its internalized vital energy that is the basis of the higher spiritual bodies. Self-cultivation definitely involves perfecting your body and its vital energy, which is why all monks and nuns should pursue a beneficial diet as well as stretching and athletic exercises such as yoga, the martial arts, or dance and other sports. They should also pursue various *nei-gong* exercises that purify their Yin Qi and Yang Qi, and which improve their internal Qi circulation. They should pursue a learning of the skills they would like to have should they succeed in becoming a Buddha of the type they want. The vital energy of every body is actually the next higher body attainment – the subtle body of Qi within you becomes the deva body or Srotapanna attainment – so we work on religious paths and in spiritual cultivation at purifying and strengthening its integrity. We must, during the course of our spiritual practices, pay attention to purifying and strengthening the Qi within the matrix of our physical shell.

As you have seen in this chapter, there are many forms of Qi/Prana work that can be practiced in conjunction with meditation to help you transform your Qi/Prana by quickly purifying and strengthening your inherent inner subtle body. Religious practice strengthens it but not so much as the various pathways of *neijia* yoga previously explained.[37]

Thoughts can move your Qi, but emotions are usually more powerful at creating internal sensations that can influence your entire Qi body. Visualizations and willpower can move your Qi, but sound vibrations are more effective. What is better than reciting sounds to move your Qi is reciting *rhythmical sounds* that can produce a resonance of vibrating Qi energy within you. Reciting rhythmical sounds + arousing relevant full body emotions (that stimulate your Qi) + visualization efforts is even more powerful as a package than any single cultivation method alone. There are many ways to stack various spiritual practice methods together to produce very powerful processes of Qi/Prana purification and transformation.

Many cultivation methods across the world have been developed based on these principles such as the practice of reciting prayers or mantras while imagining that you become one/unified with a deity (since this provides an emotional tone to your Qi while you stimulate that energy through rhythmical sound pressure). If you simultaneously stimulate Yin Qi or Yang Qi emotional states corresponding to character traits when training your Qi

---

[37] See *Neijia Yoga* and *Nyasa Yoga*.

this will help to impregnate them with certain qualities, which we call "purification" since you are usually trying to cultivate auspicious positive qualities through such practices. You must also exercise/stimulate your Yin Qi as well although this typically involves uncomfortable or emotionally painful situations or methods.

You can analyze all sorts of cultivation methods using a decomposition approach to see how many cultivation principles are stacked together to affect your Yin Qi or Yang Qi at the same time because multiple influences makes a method more effective. Bhakti yoga, sexual cultivation, kundalini chakra visualization methods, inner martial arts practice, special mantrayana techniques, and so forth all have multiple methods layered together for affecting your Qi, and some methods are geared to stimulate and purify your Yin Qi while others are geared towards purifying your Yang Qi. Everyone thinks that you just need to raise your Yang Qi during cultivation but you need to arouse and purify the Yin Qi of your body as well, which is why many tantric spiritual paths force you to suffer through prolonged periods of being afraid, depressed, sorrowful, hungry, destitute and so forth. Ordinary people cannot understand this. The process must be carefully supervised or people may end up being hurt severely.

The key to achieving the subtle body is a firm resolution to consistently maintain a cultivation of deliberate methods according to a regular practice schedule of meditation work and Yin/Yang Qi *nei-gong* work. In order to inject some variety into your cultivation routines that will help you maintain a continual practice schedule you might key certain activities to different days of the week, a specific period of time, or various astronomical phenomena (that affect the Qi atmosphere of the earth). These might include the phases of the moon; planets traveling through nakshatras or astrological signs or planets making aspects with other planets or their nodes; the maximum or minimum declination of the planets; equinoxes and solstices; lunar apogee and perigee; eclipses; and so on. You can use astronomical phenomena to bolster the purification of your Yin Qi or Yang Qi efforts by scheduling certain Qi exercises for when the planetary phenomena will have the strongest effect on your Qi or personality.

The ultimate target objective is not just transformation of your physical body, but purification of your Qi energy (which is strongly affected by planetary influences) *and your ability to start controlling your Qi/Prana by your mind/will.* Successful practice also requires that you understand the principles underlying the effectiveness of the practice, as explained.

Chapter 15
MENTAL AND PHYSICAL PHENOMENA
ARISING DUE TO SPIRITUAL PRACTICE[38]

With spiritual progress it is common to see visions, hear unusual sounds such as voices and heavenly music, smell beautiful odors, or feel sensations of heat and cold or energy movements within your body. Most of the visions and sounds are illusions projected into your brain by devas and spiritual masters who are practicing their powers, and you can learn more about this by reading about the "50 Mara States of Delusion" within the *Surangama Sutra*. They do not appear because you are in any way psychic, otherwise you would be able to experience them at will all the time.

The inner vibrational sensations of energy movement, or feelings of hot and cold etc., are due to Qi/Prana transformations within your physical and subtle bodies. Some of these reactions are due to your own efforts at cultivating your Qi/Prana, and others are due to spiritual beings moving their own Qi/Prana inside you to help you purify your subtle Qi body for the spiritual path. A virtuous spiritual practitioner who works hard may sometimes experience a Yin Qi or Yang Qi blessing of cold Qi/Prana or warm Qi/Prana due to ardent efforts. Even if you are just performing religious acts of reverence this often happens.

Some people may seem to become psychic, but their "psychic talents" are usually due to devas who happen to be working on their body from within to help purify their Qi/Prana. A psychic phenomenon happens because devas and their teachers are giving you thoughts or images inside your brain. This can be due to a *nirmanakaya* projection of an individual with a Buddha (Rainbow) or Immanence body, or due to a deva or Causal-bodied

---

[38] See *Meditation Case Studies*, Chapter 4 & 6 and *The Little Book of Hercules*.

being possessing you.

After a genuine kundalini awakening initiates, the first 100 days will entail continuous and powerful Qi/Prana movements throughout your body twenty-four hours a day. The Jewish mystic Abraham Abulafia, founder of Ecstatic Kabbalah, described some of these Qi feelings by saying, "And you shall feel another spirit awakening within yourself and strengthening you and passing over your entire body and giving you pleasure, and it will seem to you that balm has been poured over you from the crown of your of your head to your feet, once or many times, and you shall rejoice and feel from it a great pleasure, with gladness and trembling" (*Ozar 'Eden Ganuz*). The vibrational energies will be strong like waves of water, will be warm and hot, and proceed continuously with fury for many days when the true kundalini transformation *leading to the deva body attainment* starts. This is the transformation series that leads you into becoming a saint, sage or master. To attain the independent deva body whilst alive, you must suffer through twelve years of this process that involves many stages.

If you do not experience these intense sensations around-the-clock for several months then it is not the true kundalini experience. Whenever there is a temporary stirring of your Qi/Prana this will help purify your Qi channels and your Qi. If you undergo a lot of Qi purification effects from continuous spiritual practice during your life then when you pass away you will be much further along than everyone else who died. Because of the prior Qi work you undertook, you will be able to easily achieve the Sakadagamin attainment in Heaven upon your deva body's demise that will lead to rebirth in Heaven rather than reincarnation at the lower human stage again. In other words, all human beings are having their Qi/Prana worked on all the time by higher spiritual beings. Those who devote themselves to the religious or spiritual life obtain more inner Qi/Prana purification work on their subtle body than regular people, so when they die they require less purification work for their deva body in order to maintain a heavenly rebirth. If they sufficiently cultivate their Qi/Prana in heaven they will not be reborn in a human birth upon their decease.

During a true kundalini transformation that only very few people experience in the world (those destined to become "enlightened" in this life rather than in Heaven), the initial intense round-the-clock energy vibrations will last for months, and there will be intense sensations of heat at this time. During the total twelve years of transformations the rotations of Qi energy will continue, but they won't concentrate on transforming the Qi within the fingers, toes, bottom of the feet, sexual organs, eyes, ears, nose, and teeth until near the end of the process. Those endless Qi rotations performed by spiritual masters within your body, which sometimes change their temperament in various ways, gradually purify *in depth* the Qi of the subtle body within your physical shell that is normally only released upon death. As stated, this takes twelve years in total *or more* (sometimes thirteen).

The Indian sage Valmiki who wrote the *Ramayana* was called "anthill" to describe the fact that during the kundalini purification process all the Qi channels of your body are opened up like the pathways ants make within an anthill, and you can feel the Qi coursing everywhere through your tissues just as ants go up and down through their tunnels. Some describe the movement as being like a river, current, or the flow of wind within you and the temperature will be both hot and cold alternatively, but mostly warm during the initial years of the process. Not all circulations which masters perform within you using their bodies will be smooth because some will vibrate violently in different ways in order to shake and purify the Qi in difficult to reach body places, and sometimes you will be struck painfully inside you (or simply subjected to prolonged pain and agony) in order to stimulate your Yin Qi for certain body parts.

Spiritual schools describe the rotations in many ways such as by comparing them to energy (watery or wind-like) rotations circulating everywhere within you that wash your body. You will often feel as if your body is on fire or it becomes as cold as ice in certain locations. Also, you will pass through many Yin or Yang emotions when a spiritual master provokes such emotions within you to change the tone or quality of your Qi so that they can purify either your Yin or Yang Qi respectively. This is why they put spiritual adherents through intense periods of anguish, fear, worry, crying, suffering, depression, fasting and so on when stimulating the Yin Qi of someone's body in order to purify that Qi. Those emotions will arouse your Yin Qi, and if you are feeling intense Yin Qi emotions while strong internal Qi vibrations are occurring then Qi circulations will "wash" your Yin Qi accordingly.

At death all people experience what is called a "birth by transformation" in that the human subtle body, once free of its physical casing, arises as an independent deva body ("soul") that is equivalent to the stage of the Srotapanna Arhat or first dhyana attainment. Devas are the individuals who are doing most of the work in helping you purify your body during life under the guidance of higher masters. Everyone dies, learns the truth about reincarnation and the falsities of their religion, and then starts working on purifying their Qi/Prana so that they are reborn in Heaven rather than in the world again. Therefore devas on this path possess your body to rotate your Qi, and at those times higher masters use *nirmanakaya* energy projections to possess *their* bodies and simultaneously move their Qi in order that *they and you both make progress.* This is why devas are willing to work on you.

Since a subtle body resides within the matrix of your physical body, and a Shen (Causal) body resides within the matrix of a subtle body, and Supra-Causal body resides within the matrix of a Causal body, ... Taoism calls this the process of purifying your Qi/Prana the "refinement" of your Qi. The revolutions of energy that you feel within your body due to masters possessing you with their energy and revolving it is like the churning of milk that produces precious butter, and should remind you of the Hindu story of devas churning the ocean milk to produce amrita, the elixir of immortality (rotating the Qi within your physical body to generate/purify your subtle body). However, heavenly beings will only do this for you if you have earned the merit for a heavenly life whilst alive.

Devas therefore help you in order that they too might themselves receive aid to attain the Sakadagamin body purification achievement, and within their bodies while they are working on you they sometimes receive help from Causal-bodied individuals. A Causal body individual will often simultaneously possess a deva working upon a human so that they might also get their body purified as they progress towards the Buddha body (Supra-Causal body) attainment. In other words, the process of helping people undergo *profound* Qi/Prana transformations is like a set of Russian dolls where multiple beings are within each other so that the Supra-Causal and Immanence-bodied individuals can use *nirmanakaya* to work on several lower-bodied individuals at the same time. They rarely waste their energies by working on only one individual at a time. As to minor Qi transformations, they usually only involve possession by solitary devas trying to help you who may or may not receive energy from their master.

The kundalini purification process can only happen if you are a virtuous, moral person who merits the consideration of such continuous profound energy work,[39] and even then you must also do lots of preparatory

---

[39] *Tai Shang's Treatise on Action and Recompense* from Taoism states that if you want to become worthy of becoming a Heavenly Immortal (gain the Causal body) you need to accumulate 1,300 good deeds, while those who wish to attain the independent subtle body to become an Earthly Immortal need to accumulate 300 good deeds. The spirits of Heaven, namely Buddhas and Bodhisattvas, will not work on you to purify your subtle body's energies to refine them to a more permanent nature unless you are a virtuous personality who is naturally kind-hearted and compassionate enough to help others. This is why you must work on rectifying your behavior.

cultivation work (which is called the "Stage of Intensified Inner Yoga Energy Practices" in Buddhism) before any of this can begin. You will likely hear many inner sounds/voices and see many illusions or visions during the long period of kundalini transformation. The genuine process will continue for twelve years, and will involve the organized labor of countless masters and their deva students who will visit your body to help transform your Qi/Prana for the generation of your deva (subtle) body attainment. Upon its emergence you achieve the lowest of the ranks of the Buddhas, saints and sages.

This process happens to qualified individuals in absolutely every genuine religion that produces spiritual masters, but no one wants to explain the process because it is so emotionally painful and physically painful at times. The students going through the process are usually tricked into believing they are periodically fighting with ghosts, devils or demons at times when the masters are trying to arouse their Yin Qi, or given thoughts that they are being visited by angels, saints, gods or deities at times when the masters are trying to arouse their Yang Qi. In addition to the constant flow of energy rotations inside them, students going through this process will pass through many worrisome, fearful, anxiety-ridden, agonizing mental states to stimulate their Yin Qi and many states of sublime bliss to stimulate their Yang Qi during this multi-year process. These positive and negative states are equivalent to the one-hundred fields or stations of Sufism described by Shaikh Abdullah al-Ansari such as the Yin states of grief, fear, solicitude, humility, renunciation, piety, etcetera and Yang states such as rectitude, betterment, honesty, caring and so on.

Unfortunately, the spiritual masters managing your case (which are usually the individuals within your tradition who already succeeded in attaining higher spiritual bodies) will also use you during this long period to teach their own deva students how to find memories inside your brain and how to alter your thoughts and emotions. The devas are taught these skills so that they can do this for other human beings and in this way perform "good deeds." This is the training for "angels" or "guardian spirits" that teaches them how to help human beings. This is occurring inside everyone all the time, but especially so within the individuals going through the twelve-year kundalini transformation process.

Since devas predominantly desire fun and entertainment, and since many haven't purified their behavior (*asuras*) since they are mostly deceased humans who are now enjoying a heavenly life until their next incarnation, the twelve-year period will be filled with intense suffering as they train and play using you. The final years of the process will be particularly painful because they involve tremendous physical torture as work is done on your sexual organs, ears, eyes, and teeth that were neglected during the previous years. To evoke Yin Qi in these body parts they will give you torturous pain in your asshole, inner ear or right side of your body using their various bodies and will afflict you with harassing "fairy brushing" on the face. People become assholes when giving you pain to "arouse your Yin Qi" and thus prove their skills to their teachers (see the Milgram and Sanford Prison experiment). Devas don't care about you at all but are happy to show off their skills that generate physical and emotional suffering in you to "stimulate your Yin Qi," and higher teachers are also just people who will forget their bounds and cause excessive pain and irritation within different parts of your body and those of their audience (especially in the asshole and ears) *for their fun* ("I'm greater than you") claiming the intensity is necessary for Yin Qi stimulation. Devas will often pretend they are devils to poke, hit or scrape you with their Qi (to stimulate your Yin Qi) but methods vary by tradition and some spiritual schools are more compassionate than others.

This is why no masters describe this twelve-year period or the many happenings during this kundalini transformation process since they don't want to dissuade people from the spiritual path. They usually say, if anything at all, that they "studied with their master for twelve years" and leave out all the painful details. While spiritual masters are transforming you (in wave after wave of *organized labor* to rotate their Qi throughout the energy of your subtle body) they are training their students and often letting them run wild in giving you painful thoughts and emotions in order to provoke reactions that stimulate your Yin Qi during that time. The trials of Gautama Shakyamuni with Mara and Jesus with Satan symbolize this painful process that actually lasts for years. A popular test for devas is to have them find an embarrassing memory in your neurons, stimulate the memory and your feelings of embarrassment (Yin), and then have them use new thoughts to explain away the situation or changing the subject. The Yin Qi purification part of the kundalini process is the most painful aspect of it, especially during the very last years of the process, which is why one should try to do as much (mental and physical) Yin Qi purification exercises as possible during their regular cultivation practice.

At the end of the process one achieve the deva body attainment and thereby becomes a Srotapanna stage Arhat, which is called "realizing the Tao" or "attaining the Tao." To attain the subtle body *is* enlightenment, but only the lowest stage of attainment. Since there are more bodies to cultivate this attainment commences the "Stage of True Cultivation Practice" that ultimately ends with the Immanence body attainment, which is called the stage of No More Learning, or Complete and Perfect Enlightenment.

Chapter 16
ARHATS, BODHISATTVAS AND BUDDHAS[40]

Arhats and Immortals: The Arhat or Immortal is an individual who attains one or more spiritual bodies (*dhyana* achievements), and through them primarily works on his own salvation and on satisfying his own personal interests and pursuits in the universe. "Arhat" is the name of a non-denominational stage of spiritual achievement, and individuals in every religion or spiritual tradition, male and female, cultivate to become Arhats but then they are called by the names particular to their school or religion such as an "Immortal" in Taoism, "saint" in Christianity or "prophet" in Judaism. In modern parlance the Arhat is like a self-reliant, autonomous "sigma male" who has alpha traits but who is highly independent (and does his own thing without following the crowd or necessarily collaborating with others) while an "alpha male" usually becomes strongly connected with leadership roles in groups or organizations. The Arhat or Immortal knows who they are and what they stand for and is more focused on the desires and goals of the "I" rather than the welfare of the "We," so his life path follows his own inclinations and interests which certainly includes acts of selflessly helping others when they seem fit. Having attained the initial fruit of a subtle deva body, or even more bodies, like everyone else he primarily resides in his highest body while his lower bodies act as appendages that enable him to see what each lower realm looks like from the aspect of that realm (since a lower body can only create impressions of the sights, scents and sounds of the world it belongs to), and he can use them to perform deeds in those realms according to his wishes. An Arhat is not especially enticed by any sensual attractions or delights in the lower realms (life there holds no attractions), including money and power, since his truest body resides in a higher realm, but you cannot say he is free of those inclinations

---

[40] See *Culture, Country, City, Company, Product, Person, Passion, World.*

in that higher realm. The desires for sex, superpowers, *gravitas* (money, status, power, dominance) and fun afflict everyone but if you have bodies in the lower realms you can preach about "purity" there while not yet perfecting yourself in your highest physical residence. Having achieved the higher realms, however, to an Arhat each lower realm is inferior, filled with suffering and disposable. This is why the Buddhas are so anxious to free people from the lower realms of being and liberate them from the reincarnation cycle within those realms. The lowest realm of an Arhat's beingness are bodies he can easily discard since his existence is centered in his highest body, which is why Jesus' body can be destroyed on the cross while never touching the health and welfare of his higher body attainments at all. An Arhat identifies with his highest body as his self, and his lower bodies are like appendages that can be thrown off. He or she does whatever they want (subject to the laws of each realm), and so having achieved liberation they follow their own interests and inclinations without any special commitment to other human beings although of course they will at times use their bodies and superpowers to perform good deeds to help humanity. Thus they are sometimes labeled as a *pratyekabuddha*, which is someone who is enlightened but goes their own way just like a sigma male. They're not especially associated with or committed to any of the groups of enlightened individuals (Buddhas and Bodhisattvas) who take on a common vow such as the protection of a spiritual tradition or organization. At times they'll help such groups in their efforts, but they basically concentrate on following their own interests. Specifically, Buddhas and Bodhisattvas have special vows they are committed to, band together in groups of common interest, and are always working on purifying ordinary people's Qi so that human lives do not deteriorate too readily. They work together in groups to progress a worthy candidate through the Twelve Year kundalini transformation period so that they can attain the higher bodies leading to full enlightenment. Arhats develop skills and talents according to their own personal interests, whereas the Bodhisattvas and Buddhas cultivate virtues, skills and excellences with the objective of accumulating abilities that can help others and accomplish goodness on a vast scale.

Bodhisattvas: The Bodhisattva, having attained one or more higher spiritual bodies, is an enlightened Arhat who chooses to spend a great deal of time trying to help others in various ways. They are a person who makes being of benefit to others the guiding principle of their life. They recognize that life is filled with suffering; humans need to pursue well-being and ethical enjoyments to counter the inevitabilities of their suffering; humans are searching for reconnection with others and something greater than themselves in life; they are searching for meaning, significance and fulfillment in their lives; they want to develop self-mastery (and climb dominance hierarchies); and they want to create a better future for their family and the world. Therefore Bodhisattvas try to help them in these and other pursuits. They are always assisting humanity by responding to the needs of people (addressing problems of prosperity, sickness, hunger, career, money, marriage, children, justice, fairness, war, oppression, exploitation etc.) and intervening in their lives, either visibly or invisibly, to help improve individual, familial, social, economic, environmental and other conditions. They believe their life and efforts should enrich the world in some way, and therefore set out to "save the world" through a personal commitment of targeted efforts called "vows," which are utter dedications to noble causes that improve the conditions of humanity.[41] These are their deepest aspirations to make the world a better place, so you can think of vows as committed initiatives, missions or pledges of compassionate activity or personal excellence/attainment in special skills and behaviors. A vow is a pledge to take upon yourself the responsibility to care for people in a special way, or help the world in some special way. Bodhisattvas realize they are *like a dream person in a dream world*, that within this dream all conditions are impermanent so they can be improved, the bag of troubles and burdens that they hoist upon their own shoulders due to their vowed undertakings is light because it is ultimately empty, and any sufferings they assume will end in the long run. Therefore they tirelessly work at fulfilling various personal vows, pledges, or responsibilities they voluntarily chose, and those aims become the drive and ambition by which their life is organized. It gives them power, meaning, happiness, purpose and significance. Vows include such objectives as supporting various special causes, missions, protections, or contributions. Their work at achieving these Noble Aims is *the road of Bodhisattva Yoga*, and is a type of Karma Yoga aimed at helping others. Whether or not you achieve the extra transcendental bodies you can follow the road of Bodhisattva Yoga. This Karma Yoga goal to improve the quality of people's lives and *bring brightness to society* through your personal efforts is what Confucius called "instructing (teaching) the people" or "loving the people," and is what Christianity calls "loving others." Each Bodhisattva adopts a personal set of vows - which set up an entire framework of attributes, virtues, skills, actions, goals, perspectives, mindsets, and behaviors they must consequently adopt or cultivate - and by committing themselves to their vows they try to become a special force in the world that makes a difference in humanity's progress and advancement along those lines. Vows are usually aimed at reducing the suffering, chaos, deprivation, lack and injustices in society while bringing peace, prosperity, protection, happiness and other positive solutions to mankind instead. While free to leave projects at any time because their

---

[41] See the extensive discussion of vows, and how to set your own, in *Buddha Yoga*.

participation is entirely voluntary, the Bodhisattvas don't abandon people but like the infinite interdependence of the universe involve themselves in all sorts of positive relationships and compassionate activities (some of which just constitute "hit and run" efforts) to help the world, and therefore live lives full of excellent deeds. They are always working to master various *dharmas* or bodies of knowledge (such as medicine, wealth making, agriculture, astrology, warfare, persuasion, best practices, optimal management methods, etcetera); skills or abilities (such as yoga, martial arts, dance, sports, cooking, diplomacy, counseling, animal training, the active literacies, etcetera); positive virtues, personality traits or characteristics; and special powers or excellences. They are always working to create new friends and develop beneficial relationships everywhere they go, and making adventitious contributions whenever and wherever possible. In addition to gaining knowledge and understanding of various fields, even with the Immanence body attainment they don't feel they are at a completion stage of "No More Learning" that essentially means "no more work to do for personal progress" and "no more work necessary for self-improvement." Rather, they always work at learning new things/skills and improving their skillfulness in *how to proceed wisely according to skillful, effective, compassionate principle* in all their activities – how to act with wisdom and skillful effectiveness, kindness and compassion, and justice–fairness–righteousness to achieve the results they want. This is Wisdom-kaya, which is the science of positive, effective action that is also kind, fair and compassionate activity. They continuously work at expanding, upgrading and perfecting their knowledge, understanding, and wisdom (especially that of cause and effect) as well as honing their skillfulness and effectiveness in various fields so that they can participate immaculately in activities aimed at even ever greater deeds to liberate beings from suffering. They try to address problems at their roots so that those issues can be eliminated or prevented, and if not they help to manage them or transform them into better circumstances and conditions. They devote themselves to creating flourishing states of harmonious peace, welfare, prosperity, abundance, happiness, and well-being for others that are absent of pain, suffering, emotional turmoil and deprivation. Thus they pursue mastery of what the Greeks call *arête* (excellence or virtue), *phronesis* (practical and moral wisdom) and *eudaimonia* (human flourishing and prosperity). In personal training they obligate themselves to the road of Perfection-kaya in order to master the skills necessary for their chosen vows and strive always to take that mastery to peak excellence. They devote themselves to Perfection-kaya to also master their personality or character traits (qualities), their skills and other *dharmas*. Perfection-kaya is a road of self-discipline for self-improvement and self-perfection that involves embracing the highest human values, ethics, virtues and morality. It involves striving to always exhibit noble, consummate conduct and master excellence in one's skill base. Thus they work at always improving or elevating their character and personality, views and perspectives, knowledge and understanding, intentions, skills and efforts (actions, behavior and conduct) and relationships with others. Bodhisattvas are always focused on self-correction and continuously work at refining (lifting to new heights) their thinking, moods and behavior through study, practice and mindfulness watching efforts to police their thought-stream and conduct. They are dedicated to self-rectification and active learning of whatever they must cultivate in themselves to move forward in self-refinement, personal growth and effectiveness, trying always to elevate and spiritualize their basic animal nature. Our animal behavior can be refined to become human behavior, then noble behavior (consummate conduct), next magnificent or majestic behavior and then spiritual behavior (where you take the burdens and sufferings of others unto yourself in order to relieve the people), which is the path they follow. They devote themselves to skillfulness in thought, word and deed as well as to a great perfection in their appearance, mental state and demeanor, thus attempting to master both their own presence *and* their functioning in the world. They try to offer helpful influences and intercessions by deed or presence of some type, which includes active *nirmanakaya* projections that travel to sources of human difficulty and lend aid to alleviate the problems, which is Compassion-kaya. As part of their devotion to Perfection-kaya they try to transform any of their bad habits and errant conditioning such as by transcending prejudicial thoughts geared to narrow divisions of caste, race, religion, nationality, gender, sexual orientation or creed (or any other distinguishing characteristic) so that with a more open and accepting mind they can help all beings without discrimination. They strive to detach from fixed concepts of morality, outdated or inapplicable traditions or codes of conduct, and rigid dogmas of purity in order to universally contribute to the spirit and well-being of mankind. They see all errant situations as diseases that should be cured, and because diseases are not the same they recognize that remedies must vary skillfully according to the situation. They vow to master all the possible remedies, but most of all they vow to delve in and apply various remedies to the ills of mankind rather than to just recognize them. They try to avoid one-sidedness and transcend all their current patterns of feeling and thinking to employ better ones, not being wed to any one way except what is best for the situation at hand as well as good for the intermediate-term and long-term too. They understand that as an embodied manifestation of the original essence that possesses consciousness they are basically a dream body-mind complex, a cosmic functioning, a living aspect or even fluctuating process of the source essence and universe that can choose its own activities, and thus they devote themselves to mastering skillful intercession in various directions where they've decided to act as saviors to improve lives and liberate beings from suffering. They pledge themselves to the fundamental principles of ethical behavior such as the cardinal ethical principles not to kill, lie, steal, engage in sexual misconduct, etcetera; to respect people's autonomy, not aggress upon their person or property and to be honest in their dealings with others; to respect the obligations within the traditional relationships of parent-child, brother-sister, myself-friends, student-teacher, employee-boss, citizen-society, man-environment, etcetera; the Golden rule to treat (help or do for) others as you would like to be treated and never do to others what you would consider harmful to yourself; to guide one's actions according to the principles of moderation and the golden mean in behavior rather than flying off to behavioral extremes with hubris; to bring about good in all your actions and support goodness whenever you find it while cutting off evil whenever you encounter it, to always encourage unborn good to arise and always prevent unborn evil from arising (such as by taking positive steps to *prevent* harm from occurring); to do all the good you can, by all the means you can, in all the ways you can, in all the places you can, at all the times you can, to all the people you can, as long as you ever can (be unremitting in the doing of good deeds by doing them with all your might and by every possible means); as to the principle of non-violence take no actions that will harm life nor by inaction allow life to be harmed, never cause harm as a general rule, but if harm must be done then minimize the harm you do, your actions must produce more good than harm, never increase the risk of harm to others by your actions, and never waste resources that could be used for good; to treat all people fairly, work for the benefit of those unfairly treated, stand up for their rights and protect them when they need support and protection, impose no unfair burdens on others, and always provide others with whatever they are owed or deserve. Unlike the solitary Arhats who go their own way upon their enlightenment (which is a general description that pertains to most of the residents of the upper heavenly realms who live their lives without any goals or commitments), Bodhisattvas find fulfillment not only in executing their vows but in associating with like-minded others committed to similar pledges or missions.

Buddhas: A Buddha is an individual who has attained the Immanence body with the capability of myriad *nirmanakaya* projection bodies, and builds upon the foundational vows of the Bodhisattva but goes farther. Having attained the higher transcendental bodies and therefore being gifted with a very long lives for each one along with the many powers that those bodies make available, a Buddha starts thinking about what purposes, relationships or activities would now give his (or her) life meaning during that great longevity. Like a Bodhisattva, they then take upon themself compassionate vows (commitments of noble involvement) of service to accomplish very long-term aims, initiatives or missions but *weds themself to those vows*. A Buddha thereby creates an identity for himself through personal self-determination such as his commitment to the permanent vows he creates. Each one becomes devoted to several activities or fields of effort and then specializes in helping within those areas. Through utter dedication to vows of selfless service that help people flourish, reduce their problems and sufferings, offer them protection, comfort and teachings, and in general accent goodness in the world they obligate themselves to vigorous efforts of great benevolent activity and work in groups and communities to achieve those goals. Through their vows they lose self-centeredness because they devote themselves to accomplishing something beneficial for others that is greater than themselves. That constancy of purpose (in various fields) due to their vowed commitments creates happiness, connection, significance and meaning for their very long life. In other words, by taking on very deep, permanent responsibilities of service to humanity their life thereby acquires greater meaning and significance. They devote themselves (perform *bhakti*) to whatever aims, aspirations or missions they vow and catalyze an identity by sacrificing themselves to these undertakings that are so high in value that they are willing to pay a personal price of suffering to achieve them. Buddhas therefore set themselves up to become a fixed feature in society because of their vows. Like a strong tree that grows roots and branches everywhere, they assume a permanent presence in a body of undertaking in order to spread their influence, and with that rootedness of purpose strive to establish peace, prosperity, assistance and direction for all humanity. They voluntarily take the suffering of other beings upon themselves - swallowing poison like Shiva, as well as insult and persecution like Jesus and Maitreya - in order to relieve the conditions of suffering in the world. Like a peacock that eats poisonous insects but manifests glorious feathers in turn, they take the troubles of the world upon themselves so that they can produce beauty and flourishing in their place. Thus they will tread roads fraught with difficulty in order to improve human conditions for the better and even help to create laws, traditions or other systems that automatically solve problems without the necessity of their involvement. Each of their personalities/bodies in each of the various realms (planes of existence) demonstrates a fearless courage and determination to work on problems, and acts without delay. Committed, they don't frighten of troublesome responsibilities but are willing to suffer to accomplish the tasks they chose because the goals are so noble, worthwhile and meaningful. They try to model themselves on the ceaseless vitality of cosmic processes so that they can continue to maintain their compassionate activities despite intermittent waves of weariness and fatigue during the ups and downs of existence. By dedicating their lives to vows they have the potential to become like a permanent cosmic function and so they strive to become an unstoppable field of blessings that is like a force of nature. They inspire people to diligently take up the road of cultivation that leads to spiritual liberation and the ability to also make cosmic vows. Spiritual cultivation involves constant efforts at self-improvement, mastery of one's physical body, breathing and internal energy, the deepening of one's wisdom and knowledge, benevolent cooperation and collaboration with others, endless charitable activities, the purification of one's thinking and behavior, and the promotion of culture and civilization. They teach individuals and societies all sorts of *dharmas* on how to behave and what to cultivate, help to establish conditions favorable to those efforts at self-improvement, encourage people along the paths of virtue and achievement, support all sorts of philanthropic/charitable projects to improve the basic human condition, try to make every situation they encounter better than how they found it, and try to realize all aspects of the Tao. Basically, they try to improve culture, society and civilization to upgrade people's lifestyles and the quality of their lives so as to create the best possible life and living state for others. Although settled in the original nature, they never settle in one phenomenal state too long but make sure conditions always evolve forward and move ahead with positive development so that everyone grows and progresses. Those at these upper stages have developed unbelievable transcendental skills due to incredible practice efforts at cultivating their mental abilities and internal energies, and due to superior inner Qi flow they enjoy exceedingly excellent states of sublimity.

Every higher spiritual body lives longer than the average human lifespan, and each higher body also lives longer than its previous denser parent composite, so upon achieving the higher body attainments you must choose appropriate tasks, goals, aims, vows, pledges, responsibilities, commitments, or offerings in order to give that longer life relevant purpose, connection and meaning, which will be a reflection of your Compassion-kaya, Wisdom-kaya, and Perfection-kaya.

If you develop an indestructible, practically immortal Buddha body through your cultivation, you must determine purposes for your existence that can be summarized as vows, commitments, pledges, or undertakings. Otherwise what will you do to keep busy? Everyone needs significant purpose for their life. Arhats and *pratyekabuddhas* stay busy with their own affairs and enjoyments, but Buddhas and Bodhisattvas commit themselves to improving the happiness and welfare of others through noble activity that helps people. Action-kaya, which is how you behave and what you do in the world/universe, involves perfecting your personality, conduct, behavior, skills, and worldly activity. It requires that you cultivate the "wisdom of accomplishment," namely the knowledge, understanding, skills and actions necessary for being able to accomplish what you want in the world.

A portion of Action-kaya is the Karma Yoga pathway of selfless service and behavior – devoting yourself to benevolent purposes, causes, initiatives or vows of service to others – that we call Bodhisattva or Buddha vows. They are personally meaningful vows of behavior (which take responsibility for always relieving certain forms of suffering in the world or helping to manage certain affairs to go well) that touch upon your innermost spiritual core – your authentic self concerns and your innermost aspirations for what you would like to do for the world. They are guiding purposes for your life.

Action-kaya is an exhibition of your own inner reason for existence, what's important to you in terms of compassion, and what you want to help do to create a new and better tomorrow. As stated, Buddhism calls these pledged responsibilities or accomplishments your Bodhisattva or Buddha vows, which are guiding purposes for your life. These vows make the long lives of Bodhisattvas and Buddhas meaningful because they embody the idea of worthy grand objectives, the development of excellences and mastery of skills, selfless service in helping people, and that service helps to negate the pains, trials and sufferings everyone feels due to existence. You can even find great joy and happiness in service because as a famous saying runs, "They alone live who live for others." You will find that true happiness comes from making other people happy.

Because of the commitment to their vows and all the related activity that this engenders, their life truly becomes a heroic venture. People become invigorated and feel vibrantly alive (feel inner aliveness and bliss) when they are true to their deepest beliefs and follow their passions for helping others. This is when they can connect the direction of their life with their inner vitality and establish a sense of purpose that produces fulfillment, satisfaction and meaning.

While it is idealistic to assume that you can master all *dharmas* equally along the roads of Buddha and Bodhisattva Yoga, in practice people will always be better at some things more than others. Therefore it is best to work at *specializing in some specific fields* of interest that help others rather than try to become a jack of all trades who is master of none. You must start learning those skills now as you cultivate. You must work at developing personality characteristics that will also help you fulfill your vows.

In the human world, large conglomerates that try to do everything eventually break up because they lose their purpose and become inefficient and unprofitable as their size grows. Most any talents can be learned but the key to learning skills is deep, deliberate practice and specialization. Learning always requires a committed effort to mastering both theory and practice.

The primary objective of spiritual practice is to attain enlightenment, i.e. attain the higher transcendental spiritual bodies. Once enlightened, we have to decide upon *life purposes* for our very long lives, which are called Buddha vows or pledges of responsibility, support, protection and promotion of specific activities or conditions within the lower stages of sentient beingness. This includes activities for the earthly, deva, Causal, Supra-Causal (and Immanence) planes of existence. To attain enlightenment we need consistent gradual practice effort over time and during that developmental period we should be cultivating the various virtues, skills, talents, moods and mindsets that we would need in order to enjoy life *and* fulfill the vows of undertaking certain activities connected with being a certain type of Buddha or Bodhisattva of our choosing.

Monastics should think about this deeply and start working on this objective of becoming a special type of Buddha or Bodhisattva. They should start working on developing the requisite skills *now* for those goals as well as start performing acts of merit in line with their pledges or vows. The selection of vows or Buddha aspirations is an extremely important personal affair to your life path – nay, your path of existence!

To simply cultivate our various relationships with others for happiness and meaning, our positive moods of either equanimity or joy (the active or passive modes of bliss), and better control over our minds and bodies along with higher skills is not the pathway of the Buddha and Bodhisattva. Their lives are in some way primarily involved in helping others and that service gives them meaning, significance and contentment with happiness. You can achieve that mode of beingness by starting to emulate people who already perform the functions you want to perform in the world, or who exhibit the personality traits and virtues you want to have.

Arhats work at cultivating the many physical abilities of their higher energy bodies, and they develop various capabilities of consciousness to high levels of skillfulness like Buddhas and Bodhisattvas, but they devote their time primarily to their own selfish interests like a rich man who pursues profit rather than the upliftment of mankind. There is nothing wrong in pursuing the Arhat achievement of enlightenment for your own sake, but you should consider what functions would truly give your life deeper meaning if you achieved the very long lifespans of the Supra-Causal and Immanence bodies.

Chapter 17
COMPREHENDING *THE HEART SUTRA*
AND *BHAGAVAD GITA*[42]

One needs to understand that your physical, subtle, Causal, Supra-Causal and Immanence bodies are all essentially the pure fundamental substratum, and this pure primordial substrate is not different from these bodies. It supports them, It permeates them, It is their inherent absolute composition. Thus the Mahavakyas of Hinduism: "All this is Brahman," "I am Brahman," "The Self is Brahman." It is not something you attain because you are already It.

The true self-nature of your transcendental bodies is essentially the fundamental substratum (which is essentially all things), and thus the manifest forms of phenomena are just one of its many functions, processes, attributes, characteristics or appearances. Everything is essentially the primordial substratum. All things constitute the body of the bodiless. Therefore there is no such thing as a *dharma* or teaching for attaining unexcelled, perfect enlightenment, nor is there such an accomplishment because there is no such *dharma* anywhere that can be attained nor sentient being in true existence who can attain one. No things truly exist since there is only the fundamental substratum, and so such ranks of achievement or teachings do not truly exist either, and yet within the sphere of manifestation all sorts of things conventionally exist including people and this attainment. Understanding this is called the "perfection (realization) of wisdom."

---

[42] See the *Heart Sutra* of Buddhism, *Avadhuta Gita of Dattreya Avadhuta* (translated by Swami Chetanananda), *The Ribhu Gita* (translated by Dr. H. Ramamoorthy), and *Astavakra Samhita* (translated by Swami Nityaswarupananda) which all contain approximately the same message.

In Buddhism it is said that the form, sensation conception, volition and consciousness skandhas are the fundamental nature, and the fundamental essence is the compositional substance of these skandhas. This is the exact same principle. The skandhas are our spiritual bodies, namely the bodies of the human eye, deva eye, wisdom eye, dharma eye and Buddha eye mentioned in Chapter 18 of the *Diamond Sutra* that correspond to the human, deva, Causal, Supra-Causal and Immanence bodies respectively. Essentially they are all the fundamental nature (universal substratum), and the emanation of the fundamental substratum into Shakti includes these bodies of ours. The skandhas are ultimately empty of an innate self-so nature since they are essentially the ultimate substratum, and the absolute substratum is their most primordial absolute nature.

The skandhas and the primal substance are not different from one another. You are composed of these sheaths (internal transcendental energy bodies), without which you cannot exist as an entity, but in the absolute sense you are essentially the primordial substance-essence of the universe, its fundamental substratum. It is you, you are It, and when you say "I" this actually refers to the fundamental substrate. In a sense, by saying "I" this is actually the primal essence pointing at Itself. The true "I" refers to the foundational substrate, your absolute self-essence.

Thus, in one sense you cannot be termed as any of the five transcendental spiritual bodies, five *skandhas*, five bodies (*koshas*) or coverings, nor convergence of the five elements in a particular pattern, nor energy, nor any type of material essence, nor an assembly/collection of simples, nor the intersection of endless interdependent causes and conditions, nor set of processes, nor the condensation/enfoldment of a rippling appearance within the field of space-time, nor a being with consciousness. Your body-mind has no substantial reality, which is the truth of self-realization. You are ultimately just the fundamental substance, and It is you. However, we tend to identify with all sorts of false identities instead of recognizing this fact.

In another sense that captures the apparent realm of manifestation, you are essentially an agglomeration of the five skandhas (spiritual bodies), a mass of energy, or a collection of simples and energy processes within Shakti that due to conditions has temporarily formed a somewhat stable pattern that supports consciousness, but which lacks an innate (independent) own-nature and is always transforming into something else.

In another sense you are *nothing yourself* because you are an infinite interdependence of conditions, processes or events without anything being there that is inherently you or yours. You are beingness without a body because your real body is bodiless. From that sense you are empty of manifest existence, or you can be considered all of Shakti (and have an infinite manifest body) just as an iota of the ocean is the ocean, or you can be considered just that iota. You are empty of an independent inherent existence yet are all of manifest existence, and that manifest existence is essentially the primal absolute substance of unmanifest beingness (or non-existence) that is the substratum of manifest existence, so you are nothing at all. You are all or nothing, or both, or an individual apparent being within a sea of multiplicity. To the average person walking on the street, this talk is all nonsense because they just go about their life assuming they are an independent sovereign sentient being, and everything works out just fine.

Because you are sentient you are part of the manifestation of consciousness within Shakti's body. Since Shakti, the cosmos, is your entire body you are therefore part of the universal consciousness as well as being an individual consciousness. What you think is your fixed form actually blends into the one fabric of Shakti through embeddedness and is an inseparable part of the body of the cosmos even though you falsely think of yourself as some independent entity hanging in space that is disconnected from everything else.[43] This fundamental perception of separation can even produce a false human perception of being fundamentally separated from the universe, of whose substance one is derived. What about all the other separate individual appearances you see? They too are Shakti, so they are you. They are the original substance-essence, as are you, so they are you.

Whether it be Shakti in total, or portions thereof, the objects/phenomena of the universe, including you, have different forms (appearances) and functions yet every one of the multiplicities is not essentially different from being Shakti and the one primordial substratum. Essentially there is no duality. You have been forged into an autonomous individual but must recognize that you and the universe are one for you are derived from the substance of its being, and you are also united with the ground of its being – your being.

The manifestation of All (the universe) is a unity of oneness. The components, phenomena or energies of the All melt into a single whole, and there are no genuine divisions in the totality of manifest reality. What is the oneness of manifestation? Phenomena are all defined by infinite

---

[43] Fields of energy, invisible to your eyes, connect you with everything else.

interpenetration, an infinite crisscrossing of simultaneous cause and effect relations that originate (produce) all phenomena via infinite co-dependent arisings. Due to this interdependence you cannot truly tell where one phenomenon ends and another begins. Objects are all defined by dependent origination – by a conditionedness on all else within Creation – and are therefore characterized by inherent emptiness or selflessness, which means each lacks a self-so independent nature that stands on its own. Infinite interdependence means that essentially you are the full body of the manifest universe – the All. Or, since the All of Manifestation is essentially the one primordial substratum, it means that you are ultimately bodiless, birthless and imperishable since you are essentially the primal substrate.

You now know what you are, always have been and always will be. This is an understanding of your self-nature. There is no way to make yourself an independent, self-so, real phenomena. As the *Diamond Sutra* states, there is no such thing as a sentient being, life or soul because in actuality there is only the original nature, the fundamental substratum of manifestation that is only Itself. Therefore there is no such thing as an object or person who possesses attributes. In terms of impermanent manifestation you are just an ever-changing aspect of Shakti with a very limited longevity unless you take steps to cultivate spirituality to transcend the lowest transient realms of matter and energy. As a human body, subtle-bodied or Causal-bodied entity etc. you will always be a construction of events and processes and always be transforming. You will always be existing as a continuous instantaniation that is always transforming from one form to the next. However, within your existence you have the freedom to move, grow and develop in any direction you want to live the life you want (for as long as it lasts) because no one ultimately binds you. Conditions bind you, but you can use your intelligence to transform them or transcend them. The only major obstacles in life are circumstances, namely cause and effect relationships that might provide you with obstructions. You must use your wisdom and efforts to surpass them. Obstacles also have the potential of being overcome through wisdom, skillfulness, willpower and perseverance.

The laws of cause and effect that define Shakti can present obstacles to the gratification of your desires, which is why spirituality teaches you to be detached from desires yet still perform your duties in the world or pursue your personal goals and objectives, but not to attach to the results of your actions. Therefore celebrate your life with joy and make use of it in whatever way you wish, to go in whatever direction you want, to accomplish or experience whatever you desire, and stick at it until you achieve those goals. You are the fundamental substance, you are Shakti, you have nothing permanent with which to identify yourself so become of yourself whatever you want to be. You are unique, designed to sing your own special song in the world. Make a connection with your innermost potential and work towards your aspirations of a highest best self until it becomes a reality for you. Most barriers that block your aspirations can usually be overcome through wisdom and perseverance so aim high, continually exert yourself with diligence, and work to attain whatever you want because no one ultimately bars you. There are only conditions that need to be overcome.

At the very heart of all things is the primal essence, the true substance of everything that has never turned into anything else. It is the fundamental substrate, the ultimate substratum, the core inherent nature and thus our True Self. Some call It God. Thus it is said, "The universe appears as manifold but there is a single intuition as its soul." Similarly, "There are many bodies but their governor is one." The governor is the ultimate absolute substratum but It doesn't govern anything at all; It is simply the ultimate support that doesn't become involved in any of Its attributes.

All beings and bodies are equally the one single True Self, *your* True Self, your self-nature, the primal substance, the foundational substratum, the original nature. All bodies, phenomena, energies, forces, fields, processes and events are its appearance and functioning as Shakti, which is Its one manifestation. Furthermore, as a drop of the ocean of Shakti you *are also Shakti* since Shakti is the only apparently existing thing. It is not a multiplicity of separate independencies but a oneness, and individual entities (within it) are dependently arisen entities that have merely conceptually constructed existences as independencies. Shakti is a single soup. Therefore all things, including living beings, are an aspect of *you* because you are the universal manifest Self, Shakti, and they are the body of Shakti as well. And, because of being conscious (having sentience) you are part of the aggregate consciousness of Shakti too. You are a component of Shakti's mind/consciousness.

In a sense you can consequently say that the universe is truly alive as a single being with consciousness. Most of Shakti's nature is insentient matter and energy, but some parts of this body have consciousness that in aggregate are its one consciousness. Thus, you are part of Shakti's mind that can move portions of your Shakti-body as you like by performing actions just as you can move your own physical body. Similar to the ecological concept of Gaia that the Earth is one living organism (and we are its consciousness), Shakti can be considered as one single body that has a consciousness that is the aggregate consciousness of all sentient beings.

As with other sentient beings, who are therefore your brothers and sisters, you have the special miracle of consciousness that allows you to guide phenomena within Shakti's body – your body. You are Shakti's consciousness and body so you are responsible for it. You can transform your body of Shakti to produce anything you desire and can learn to control many of its transformations but must always take care of it. Hence, you can more frequently experience joy, happiness, bliss, flow, presence, centeredness, peace and lucidity etc. if you choose to cultivate the conditions necessary to experience those states of mind or produce them through the environment you create. You can also work to bring those enjoyments to others who are essentially just other parts of yourself.

Insentient phenomena, which Christianity calls "darkness," are incapable of conscious experience or comprehension but you have the illumination of consciousness/awareness and reason. Thus you can experiences states of comprehension as well as happiness, sunshine ("shine"), lightness, contentment and bliss – states of enjoyable being absent of suffering.

Since other beings are part of your body, do you not have an obligation to help make situations better for your brothers and sisters by improving their circumstances to relieve them of difficulties when you can? They share the same inner self-nature as you – your Supreme Nature is God (the foundational substrate that is the eternal unchangeable state) – so of course you should make efforts to help yourself. Or, you can think about it in terms of helping your brothers and sisters, or the golden rule of doing for others and helping them in ways that you would appreciate yourself.

Within the realm of Shakti you own absolutely nothing, can hold on to absolutely nothing, and can guarantee absolutely nothing. You can undertake actions but cannot guarantee the results you want yet still must take actions such as those necessary for your livelihood and survival. You yourself are ultimately nothing, a conglomeration of events, processes and conditions that produce *a ripple in the one fabric of Shakti, an apparent being empty of real concrete existence* since there is nothing permanently you there within these conditions except the primal substrate. The primal substrate is your only unchanging core, the only unchanging part of your beingness. However, you can extend the longevity of your existence significantly, as well as its happiness and capabilities, through the cultivation of higher spiritual bodies. You can also learn to create, control and improve the conditions of your own life and future even though you are actually nothing but a small configuration within Nature, which has no favorites. Remember, you are a minor ripple or collection of functioning processes within Shakti and you have an apparent enfolded existence within the universe only because of Shakti's totality.

Lacking a self-so nature, namely a real inherent "I" that is established independently apart from Shakti, in lacking any separation from being Shakti you are therefore just one of its transforming processes that has originated because of its totality. Being produced because of the totality of Shakti, therefore you are playing a role within it. *Your role is that you are a process that masters the changes of phenomena to produce new states that you want and this is possible because you possess something we call consciousness.* You become defined by the purposes you serve so what then is it that you want to personally experience or want to see in the world through your consciousness? What is the light you want others to see? What do you want to bring about or become? How do you want Shakti that is your environment, your body and your self to evolve? Those aspirations can become your own Bodhisattva vows. What meaning do you want to derive for your life or create for others due to your activities?

Although you yourself are a phenomenon having equality with all other occurrences in the universe, you possess two special characteristics called *life* and *consciousness* that come along with your existence. Your consciousness can produce a flowing experience of a world of qualities within a mind-stream that is essentially just a subtle energy stream and bunch of bioelectrical flickerings in the brain undergoing the condition of excitation. Those bioelectrical flickerings of subtle vibrations manifest as conscious thoughts, speech and then actions that change conditions in the universe, which is your great macrocosmic body. They produce your personal experience since they compose the thoughts and images within your consciousness that exists in your microcosmic body. Because of your anatomical pattern of physical construction – which is an agglomeration of energy, forces, simples and processes interpenetrated by infinite intermixing conditions – you experience a mind-stream of error-prone mental processes that includes similitude representations of the external world, but there is so much more outside of your simplified mental images.

It is unfortunate that we easily get distracted by our mental bioelectrical flickerings and don't understand our true self-nature. Unfortunately, we too easily become entangled with insignificant whims and desires and predominantly seek (usually mind dulling) pleasurable sensations rather than remain centered in our witnessing awareness that is the very beingness of our conscious existence. To get entangled or become embedded within the stream of consciousness is a poor strategy for your existence since it never allows you to transcend those ephemeral thought flickerings that can blind you from the living bliss of life.

Entanglement with the products of your consciousness keeps you bound to your thought-stream even when it is unwholesome. When this occurs you become like a mechanical robot or insentient process within Shakti that abides within thoughts and automatically follows karma without trying to change it because you do not transcend your attributes or conditioning (software) because of following them like clockwork. A robot cannot elevate itself above its programming through detachment and über-awareness to see what it is really doing and thereby allow for course corrections to be made. Only by transcending your thoughts do you become the most alive. This is *the real Zen school* rather than the commitment to mental stillness practices that you normally see today.

Further, the ordinary human strategy of forever running after desires and pleasant sensations in life in order to experience feel-good happiness can never produce real satisfaction, contentment, fulfillment, connection with others or peace in life. Instead, you should pursue more substantial types of happiness connected with meaning such as service to others (family, friends, the community or society) and a commitment to higher vows and pledges that have a deep importance to you because they fill you with purpose. If you are going to pursue joy and happiness, why not do so by working to transform conditions for the better that will improve the mental states for your larger self-being, Shakti, that has countless aspects of consciousness within it? In other words, why not try to make others happy too instead of just yourself?

All manifest things are transformations of Shakti, which is essentially the original nature, so these are what you ultimately are. The ultimate foundational ground state is your absolute substance, your inner core being, your unchanging true existence. You are conditionally defined within it, an intersection of infinite conditions coming together spanning the past and present as well as all things. There is nothing that is only *you* in yourself, there is only a conjunction of conditions that have produced your appearance (body-mind complex) that you take as *your self* because of ignorant thinking in connection with a somewhat stable monotonous configuration that is essentially impermanent and selfless.

In being the foundational nature, however, the truth is that you were never born and will never die. You will always exist in some form or another. Shakti will never die either, so you will always be some energetic form of Shakti that is transforming too. You are pure existence itself in a temporal form and as an apparent being are free to chart any course you want in the universe because consciousness gives you that functional ability. That ability comes with consciousness so *use it*. It takes work to change into something else or to achieve some objective, especially if it means losing your comfort zone, but you can do so. What will you then do with your abilities of consciousness? What direction is worthy of your life force and existence?

You can work at accomplishing any vows, missions, purposes, objectives, aspirations, goals, aims, responsibilities or offerings you choose, and there will always be consequences to your actions in the field of Shakti that is the realm of manifestations. You are in a great game that never ends, the *divine play of Lila*, and can choose to make your participation as worthwhile or grand as you want. Why not take the chance to be worthy of life? Why not become a blessing and light to the universe that you want all to see?

It is inevitable that you must therefore adopt a mindset of never-ending continuous self-improvement and develop an intrinsic motivation of personal vows or purposes for your existence other than just fun. Everyone should be trying to put some good into the world, which is ultimately your larger body. Everyone should come to believe that their life, their work, their existence is enriching the world in some way so that they personally derive some measure of satisfaction. You need only point your mind in a direction of positive development and then start working to create that goodness so that you leave golden footprints of transformation everywhere. You need to work on what is of value that you consider most important in life.

So what are you going to give in this life? What will you leave for the world that they would put it on your tombstone? How can you make the sound of who you are? Would you rather try to do something, even if it might fail, or waste your life away due to having made no efforts at all?

Because you are just a fluctuating agglomeration of simples, processes, events and conditions that is always transforming, you must define your own purposes for your existence that will shape those transformations as you like, as well as provide your consciousness with happiness, meaning and contentment. Then your existence will move from a state of suffering to being palatable, and then to being worthwhile and rewarding. This involves performing deeds that put sunrise in your heart.

You are a living object with consciousness, and thus have volitional control over your behavior. You can even change your properties through learning and cultivation. You can change your personality, properties, characteristics, or traits that include your physical body, internal energy, habits, skills, attitudes and beliefs, mental perspectives and outlooks, and your activities or behaviors. Unlike inanimate objects you are lucky enough to be able to guide your own development and evolution, but the downfall is that you are subject to errors and suffering which means that you need to become devoted to learning, self-improvement and self-correction. This type of training falls under self-cultivation efforts but insentient objects cannot do this, and living beings with less developed levels of consciousness (where they cannot learn) cannot change their attributes or functions (behavior) either.

You are a person – actually just an animal with consciousness - who can use your higher-than-ordinary animal consciousness to master the changes of phenomena and control nature. With that ability you can change both yourself and your environment and bring about better states of being for yourself and others. You can change your attributes, adapt to the circumstances or consequences around you, and continually alter your fate or fortune. Although conditioned to think and behave in certain ways, consciousness gives you the ability to amass new knowledge (learning) and change the perspectives, mental modes, ways of thinking, and behavior you've already developed. It enables you to not only change your personality/psyche (attributes) but develop new skills that let you accomplish goals of your own personal choosing. Consciousness lets you pursue whatever you want to pursue in the universe, including significance and happiness.

Your "lived space" is a physical material body composed of condensed energy that has the potential to release from within itself the sheaths, *skandhas* or *koshas* of four higher transcendental bodies through the process of spiritual cultivation. These are actually the *dhyana* attainments of Buddhism and the Hindu yoga sages Vyasa and Vacaspati Misra. Your lived flesh is thus an embodied organism that has the potential within it of four higher transcendental bodies that can be generated out of its matrix. Once liberated, these higher bodies (that are nearer in essence to the foundational substrate) will each reside in higher planes of energy corresponding to their composition and possess various energetic powers over lower denser realms, including the ability to help people in various ways if those individuals choose to exercise kindness and compassion to do so. They have more powers and abilities than the physical body, and live for longer periods of time. Once you achieve a higher body it becomes the new center of your life whereas the lower body out of which it arose becomes like a tethered appendage. Through any of your lower bodies you can view the lower realms in which they reside in the way that their denizens see them.

In other words, beings living in higher planes of energy see a lower realm differently than its residents do, but you can see it and experience it the way the denser-bodied residents do by using a lower spiritual body that is appropriate to that realm. This is why Buddhism says that water appears as water to us, as pus to hungry ghosts (who live in a lower realm), and as *amrita* to devas (who live in a higher realm). This description is not accurate, but the idea transmitted is that materials appear differently to the beings of different realms.

All these higher planes are still Shakti, the Triple Realm. Within all these planes, you are actually a mereological collection of simples (atoms, muons, form elements, seeds of form, etcetera) in composition, lacking in anything that is inherently a separate self-so distinctive you, and your pattern just happens to produce the great miracle of consciousness. That pattern comes about through an agglomeration of conditions, forces, processes or events that lack an own-being "you" within them. However, that pattern produces consciousness or Knowledge. With the great gift of consciousness (awareness), imperfect as it is, you can experience a world of qualities in a mental mind-stream and you can learn to master the world for advantages such as altering conditions so that you can experience happiness, well-being, and a life of meaning and significance. This is what we're after.

You can use the sentience of your ever-changing pattern to experience or accomplish whatever gain, goals, objectives, conditions, initiatives or missions you wish in the universe, and need only decide what is meaningful and worthwhile before applying your will in that direction. Because you have consciousness you can choose to pursue personal mental happiness and physical bliss through various types of cultivation, and thus achieve the triumvirate of existence-consciousness-bliss (*sat-chit-ananda*) in your existence. If wise, you might choose to pursue a higher sense of connection with others along with greater meaning and purpose in order to give your life a significance that outlasts the pursuit of sensation-based pleasures. What you ultimately choose to do is up to you.

You are essentially a patterned agglomeration or ripple in the fabric of Shakti that has appeared as a localized (nodal) intersection of infinite cause and effect conditions that are simultaneously co-defining one another. In being only an intersection of infinite interdependent conditions *without anything within you that is inherently you*, you essentially are actually nothing yourself at all, and thus are inherently empty of self-so existence. This is the meaning of selflessness, no-self or *sunyata* (emptiness of intrinsic existence) that is the message of the *Diamond Sutra*. Of course you are an appearing self or soul, but it is not what you take it to be. You lack true existence or own-being but exist as a selfless embodiment manifesting through dependent origination in the present moment that itself has no extension, no substance and no permanence. However, this moment of Now is where abundance is for your empty self because this conscious moment of yours is the most precious thing in the universe.

You are not this body of yours, nor do you have a body. You are not your thinking, feeling, will, I-sense or experiences. Your appearance is just the intersection of conditions, so you are nothing that is your own independent existence, nothing at all. You are essentially a being without form. Being empty of any pattern of inherent existence, thus you are actually free to work to become whatever you like, experience whatever you want or accomplish whatever you wish and you will transform according to the influence of your self-development efforts.

You are actually all of Shakti instead of the small body you take yourself to be, but you cannot see your embedded interconnections with all other phenomena such as the wavefronts of energy crisscrossing you (which you are also part of) that make this so. Since you have consciousness you are also part of the consciousness of Shakti with the ability to manipulate your greater body of Shakti in endless transformations via mastery of your "individual body" that can creatively participate by producing thoughts, words and deeds. More specifically, you are part of the consciousness of the Earth – you are Gaia's consciousness – because the human mind doesn't just produce concepts or "impose" its order on the world. The world realizes itself within and through human minds and the mind of all consciousness beings within its purview or domain. Human thought does not mirror a ready-made objective truth of the world but achieves its perceptions by coming to birth in a human mind whose conditioned/learned labels, names, forms, etc. come from the Earth domain itself. You are Earth's consciousness as well as Earth's body. You are Shakti's consciousness and body too.

Whether you are considered all of Shakti or just a part of Shakti, your real nature transcends the patterned collection of simples and interlinked conditions that compose your construction. You are inherently the absolute fundamental substrate of the universe, immortal, free of birth and death and ultimately free of karmic formations yet able to give birth to all energies and transformations. As an attribute, function or expression of this Ultimate Nature you are free to grow, develop and evolve in whatever ways you wish; you are free to become whatever you wish; you are free to act in whatever way you wish; you are free to work at achieving whatever you wish. The only constraints are that everything is subject to cause and effect conditions, but the road of self-development allows you to evolve yourself into whatever highest manifest self you wish to become.

Being at your foundational level just the empty, pure, undifferentiated primordial essence-substance of the universe, at that absolute ultimate level there is the extinction of personhood, entityness, selfhood, manifestation or individual beingness. There is only peace. At the ultimate level there is just your true-I, your absolute self-nature, the primal substance that is your True Self. It is just empty unchanging substratum that makes up everything in the universe and is lacking in consciousness. This inherent Emptiness is what you ultimately are, and yet you are an appearance that has somehow arisen/developed out of exactly That, and you have consciousness of your apparent existence as well as of the universe. Even so, you are always and everywhere the formless foundational substratum, and however and wherever It expresses Itself that is you. The small-you that you are is It, and you (a microcosm that enfolds the cosmos) are also the macrocosm of all manifestation - Shakti. Being the foundational substance always and everywhere, there isn't really any such thing for you as ultimate annihilation or extinction – there is just manifest transformation. On the apparent level of Shakti you are undergoing constant transformation into something else every moment.

You are therefore neither existent as a real being nor non-existent. Thus you are "neither real nor non-real." You certainly are not non-manifesting or non-appearing since you are here, but your reality lacks an own-nature. You are not formlessness since you have an apparent existence, but your appearing existence (produced because of intersecting conditions) is not a *real intrinsic existence*. There is no truth, reality, non-conditionality or intrinsic nature to your manifest beingness as an apparent existent. You exist because of this and that. You simply don't have selfhood (I-ness) and borders in the way you imagined yourself to be, in the way you were conditioned to believe. You are like an empty fist used to fool a child.

You don't have any intrinsic reality, immutable essence, or absolute beingness that gives you the quality of independence. You lack an own-nature or dependable core self. You exist in a conditional way … "when this exists that exists, when these conditions arise then that arises." You are therefore empty of a dependable, unchanging core self or anything pertaining to a permanent self because you don't exist in some fundamental way. You must cultivate to a stage that makes you closer to permanence.

You have apparent existence with consciousness. You also have an inherently infinite, eternal, blissful unchanging existence due to being the original nature that is motionless like empty space.

So essentially you are neither entirely formless (void) nor a stable, real independent (non-conditional) form. You are neither real nor non-real, neither have consciousness nor don't have consciousness, neither have a definite form nor are lacking (an instantaneous) form. You are beingness without ultimate form, or an emanation/form that encapsulates true being. You are all of manifest existence and yet there is no such true thing as manifest existence, but you are that appearance as well as its transcendental substrate. The Ultimate Reality is an absolute totality of the manifest and unmanifest natures (*samsara* and *nirvana* are one) where the manifest reality – a single body Shakti - is an interfusion or interpenetration of all things, and thus particular things within it are neither entirely the same as nor different from each other. The parts or particulars or multiplicity of objects with Shakti all arise dependent upon something, so there is nothing that is not empty of having an own-self or anything pertaining to an independent self-nature.

The separate appearances you see within your mind are you since they are part of Shakti and you are Shakti. They are part of your infinite material body that you can influence in various ways (Nature) because you have a mind that can control your actions. Other phenomena that you see in the cosmos are not the same as you in conditions (appearances and functions) yet are not different from you in ultimate entity. The underlying fabric of existence is your true self, the Self of all existence, an unborn primordial substratum that is the fundamental essence of dream-like manifest reality that scintillates or flows in sequences of instantaniations (existents that arise and then perish) that constitute manifest reality. We cannot see/experience that reality directly because we are only conscious of mere concepts or similitudes of its nature that are fraught with error.

To realize this and center yourself in this realization is one of the highest spiritual achievements for it is realizing the way things are. This is Truth. This is understanding your self-nature. This is the view that Buddhas, saints and sages come to teach people. It is the understanding of self-realization, which is only possible to achieve because we have consciousness. Now you know what you are.

This understanding of an immortal nature but transient existence (that is kept alive through the regenerative process of reincarnation managed by spiritual beings) should give you the courage to start making of yourself whatever you want in existence. Don't just sit there in motionless meditation practice hoping to realize something! You are there to master aspects of your consciousness. Conditions and circumstances may seem to thwart your potential at present, but you can lay the foundation for the changes you want to make in your life and way you want to be. If you want to be a certain type of Buddha who finally achieved the higher spiritual bodies then you should start training to be that particular way by collecting or practicing those skills and attributes now. Don't just sit silent in meditation practice. Find your own voice and then start singing loudly because it is your life to live.

Now you understand the reality of your true existence and the cosmic existence. Everything is known through your consciousness so the question is how to use your consciousness best (in terms of utility) or most properly (in terms of operating for highest facticity). Utility means you pursue what you want or must in life, and that creates a thought-stream that controls your behavior. Facticity means that you correct your views of reality according to wisdom and understanding as to the real nature of things, and adjust your character and behavior accordingly. Also, you always maximize the opportunity for your thought-stream to become corrected or edited because you don't bind with it through enmeshment or fusion and thereby lose your sense of presence and an aware knowledge of what you are doing. Becoming more robotic like this dampens your sense of aliveness.

People on the road of spiritual practice often go to the extreme of trying to suppress, block or annihilate their thoughts to create some type of "emptiness" or mental quiet. They incorrectly think that this is the right way to find peace, relaxation or the absence of stress in their life. On the other hand, some people become so fused, entrained or enmeshed with their thoughts (such as in the indulgence of sense-pleasures or emotions) that they lose their sense of presence and their capability at editing and self-correcting their thoughts. In a way, both cases can be considered situations where people lose the autonomy of their I-sense and then, becoming more robotic, start to mimic the inanimate nature of the universe. Think clearly on this: if you lose your autonomous sense of presence and drop into blindly following the thought processes in your head such as emotions or pleasurable desires (while having dulled your sense of being alive due to that abiding) you become the same as an inanimate process doing its thing in the universe. You actually are, so these words are only a manner of teaching you.

You must always remain vibrantly alive, which means ablaze with awareness and the fullness of Qi health or life force. As a witness you must mentally stand apart from falling into either an empty annihilation of thought (suppression of consciousness to imitate the universal substrate) or deep abiding/dwelling within your thought-stream where you lose yourself, such as when overly indulging in sense-pleasures or letting the momentum of emotions like anger control you. The middle way where *you are most alive* - where your I-ness is not dulled and your thinking along with perceptual reality are not thwarted - is to center yourself within a state of clear presence (pristine awareness) that is detached from both emptiness (no-thought or *shamatha* cessation) and deep entrainment with your thoughts. This produces the most conscious flexibility and the most optimal perspective. You can achieve that mode by practicing mindfulness, meditation, and other methods and with enough practice it can become your normal mode of being.

That being so, be courageous in life to take the active steps necessary to become what you want to become and achieve what you want to achieve in life since nothing binds you. Your True Self is limitless, fearless and offers no resistance so be courageous. Nothing stops you, prevents you or stands in your way of trying to create something new. You don't have to remain a slave to prior conditioning. You need to teach yourself how to reside in pure awareness and always clearly know what you are doing.

This requires personal efforts at self-cultivation, especially training practice at self-observation (mindfulness). Nevertheless, become fearless and get started at moving ahead towards what really matters for you. Work towards achieving a personal ideal that includes some type of self-achievement and personal excellence that delivers well-being to you within Shakti. Live happily, and make efforts to help others as well for they are your brothers and sisters within Shakti who desire exactly what you desire, which is happiness and freedom from lower states of existence.

This is the enlightenment view – you are a sentient being (animal), a living object with consciousness, a set of transcendental energy bodies encased within each other, a collection of simples and energy with the property that you can thrive and replicate, a ripple in the one fabric of space-time, an enfoldment or enfolding of the entire universe of processes into a localized appearance, a dependent note within the universe, the intersection of conditions with no (fixed core) immutable self inside them, a continuous event having consciousness that for a while seems stable and monotonous but always changes, a collection of processes that intersect in producing a temporary appearance, a small portion of Shakti defined by its whole, the entirety of Shakti, part of the consciousness of Shakti, an expression of Nature's essential being, and so on. Basically, your existence is devoid of a mystical immutable self because it is constituted by (constructed through) a current of interlacing phenomena, yet you continue existing from birth to birth as long as the causes that sustain you remain effective. Furthermore, consciousness is in some sense illusory.

You are also the primal foundational substance, and altogether neither pure beingness nor non-beingness because you do have a dream-like apparent existence that cognizes an apparent but always transforming reality of facticity, and an essential core nature that remains Unmanifest because It never evolves into anything other than its phenomenal-less self. *This analysis of what you ultimately are is the understanding of your self-nature, and is called self-realization.* Realizing these facts is considered self-realization, meaning you realize what your self ultimately is. Understanding this is realizing the nature of your true self-nature, and now you can adjust your mindset, outlooks, perspectives and behaviors based on this understanding.

When you ask yourself, "Who is this 'me'?" the answer is (1) an ever-changing conditional construction composed by uncountable conditions that simultaneously affect one another and arise within an Indra's net of interdependent, interpenetrative causation (everything is dependently originated) that (2) exists as a single oneness, fabric or unified field of space-time called Shakti (the universe) that does not ultimately exist in some fundamental way, because (3) ultimately It is the one changeless, empty (phenomena-less), foundational substrate of the cosmos. To understand these facts is to understand your self-nature - *what is your ultimate true self* - and this is the "view of enlightenment," the "enlightenment view," or the "understanding (*prajna*) of self-realization" or just plain "self-realization." When you understand this you realize what your apparent self is, namely, what the "me" is within you. You realize your true relationship with Shakti where you are part of Shakti and an individual in your own right that has an imperfect property called consciousness, yet through that you exist with sentience. You are you and you are "God" - the underlying fundamental nature of reality. Your life is your own and your life is not your own since it belongs to your galaxy, it belongs to Shakti, it belongs to the fundamental substratum. Your life belongs to the universe so it is not your life but the universe's life. However, we must also say that it is your life although ultimately composed of and therefore controlled by the universe.

The "enlightenment mind" is something different – it is just our ordinary mind. Our ordinary mind is the same as "enlightenment" because it gives us awareness, it provides illumination of your self and the world, it is knowledge of your self-existence (self-realization) and phenomena as opposed to the darkness of insentience.

Enlightenment is not a mystical state. Just the fact that you have consciousness should be considered enlightenment because *consciousness is illumination*. The ordinary mind is the mind of enlightenment; nothing changes at all in your psychology when you attain a higher spiritual body except that you just attain more capabilities due to that body. Your personality stays the same and your mental habits stay the same unless there are new skills, ideas and perspectives you learn for activity in that realm. On the spiritual path, we want to cultivate special qualities (of virtues, values and purity) in our ordinary mind whether or not we achieve the enlightenment of attaining the higher transcendental spiritual bodies that escape existence within the lower realms. During the course of self-cultivation we want to correct the mental software that produces our personality and thoughts so that we have a more enjoyable life of flourishing and become the best version of our self possible, but we should also train ourselves for a further goal, which is to manifest a noble vision in ourselves to become the type of Buddha we would want to become.[44]

We want to develop the skills, mindsets and behaviors to become like an ideal model of some Buddha that we admire whether it be a Medicine Buddha, Compassionate Activity Buddha, Wisdom Buddha, Wealth Buddha, Agricultural Crop Buddha, Forest Protector Buddha, Musical Performance Buddha, Temple Protector Buddha, City or Country Protector Buddha, and so on. This is a path of progressive realization that requires us to first decide on an inspiration for aspiration, and then we can start getting to work at emulation. By modeling yourself on and acting under the influence of an admirable ideal we select, which then guides your actions via your dedication to its actualization/embodiment within yourself, you gradually become that way.

It is said that a deity enters the world as a dance, as a play to accent the good and pour it into the field of time. They have a happy alchemy that transmits gloom into sunshine. You can become that way, but must choose to become that way and then act under the influence of the ideal that you select in order to guide your growth and development. We have existence (*sat*), we have consciousness (*chit*), but we have to be a certain way and act a certain way to achieve bliss (*ananda*) that includes having a life purpose for our activities that creates meaning and significance for our lives.

As to our ordinary mind, which is the same as the mind of enlightenment, in daily life we ordinarily want to experience positive mental states such as

---

[44] See *Buddha Yoga* by Bill Bodri.

mental peace and calm rather than agitation. Mental calmness is often called attaining a tranquil mind that is free of excessive chatter, negative self-talk, emotional afflictions, mental defilements or agitations and the tendency to mentally wander. Tranquility and calmness, free of attachments to wandering thoughts and desires, are not just mentally enjoyable but enable us to make better decisions in life so that we can masterfully maneuver in the right directions as we encounter circumstances. For these and many other reasons we therefore want to cultivate inner calmness.

Without training our emotions, impulses, cravings and desires can easily become uncontrollable and cause us unnecessary suffering. They can undermine our efforts in life and lead us in the opposite direction of our goals, or cause us to act in incorrect ways we later regret. Tranquility, on the other hand, helps us transcend our emotions and desires and avoid suffering. We tend to be violent animals that pursue our own interests and should cultivate tranquility as a basic psychological trait to curb our aggressions.

Meditation practice is therefore used to train for the "mind of enlightenment," which is just a more perfected form of our ordinary mentality where we have corrected as many of our psychological traits as possible, quieted our mind, enhanced our awareness and optimized our conscious states to be as close as possible to the clarity and enjoyment of flow. If you attain the deva body then you have the mind of enlightenment of a Srotapanna Arhat. You attain the Dharma body or Rainbow light Buddha body and you attain the mind of a Supra-Causal fourth dhyana Arhat. The enlightenment mind is just the ordinary consciousness/mind of whatever body you have, but you want to free it of its fetters and wrong thinking mechanisms. What you should be targeting, through meditation practice, is to develop a different way of using your consciousness as well as mastery of some of its capabilities. In particular, you should work to attain greater mental equanimity along with presence, which is a state of undisturbed tranquility and psychological stability along with pristine clarity-awareness that approximates some of the qualities of a mental flow state.

If one were a monk or sadhu etc. practicing meditation on a daily basis they should split up their daily practice session into several parts. Professional athletes and musicians practice no more than 5-6 hours per day, and one cannot expect others to maintain *quality* practice schedules longer than this even in the spiritual field. (1) One part would be the normal *vipassana* sitting practice of watching your mind without using energy, but when doing so trying to keep your Qi within your brain centered rather than leaning forward but also flowing through its occipital region and cerebellum. You want to thereby train in developing clear awareness while being personally centered without having to hold onto your energy to be centered – being effortless with a full pristine awareness that penetrates all the Qi channels of your brain and skull. (2) The next part of practice would be to try to cultivate emptiness as a mental station or meditative dwelling of calm abiding, perhaps by using one of the twenty to thirty emptiness themes/methods found in *Neijia Yoga* or *Vijnana Bhaivara* and stationing oneself in the consequential "emptiness" state. The Buddhist absorptions of infinite space, infinite consciousness, infinite nothingness and "neither thought nor not-thought" are also emptiness meditation techniques. You want to regularly try different emptiness meditative methods and rotate between them because you never want to get used to some version of emptiness you design in your mind otherwise you will cling to it and thereby make it into a formal image of emptiness or openness. During practice you should never cling to any type of emptiness scenario that you create/enter as an emptiness station. (3) The third part of practice would be infinite *bhava* absorptions where you would combine the methods of the Buddhist four immeasurables (infinite joy, loving-kindness, compassion and equanimity) with Kaula Tantra's *Viramarga* infinite *bhava* methods (where you fix your self in a given infinite attitude/emotion "relevant to a hero" to feel the Qi energy of that attitude penetrating all throughout your body), the *yidam* methods of Esoteric Buddhism (where you hold onto the pure mood/feeling of being a deity or hero who has a certain type of Qi that completely suffuses your body and mind) and other similar techniques such as the methods of *boran kammatthana* that combine *bija* sounds, light visualizations, and enveloping certain flooding emotions within your mind-body complex. In all these techniques you basically invoke Yin or Yang mental factors/emotions within you, amplify the feeling of these factors on a massive scale so that they start affecting your Qi, and suffuse that feeling throughout your body-mind everywhere in order to wash/transform your Qi and also change some neural pathways (your personality). You hold onto an infinitely large emotion, or emptiness station tinged with a positive emotion (which is the true *anapana* practice within Buddhism), to transform your Qi and personality when you subsequently try to be a little more like that in daily life. Most people only do this for Yang Qi but you should do this for Yin Qi as well, and you can also move your Qi about inside you (rotate or circulate it) while doing so or try to match inner energy waves with your breathing and so on while cultivating an infinite, immeasurable emotional tone. The highest ideal is to select a type of Buddha or Bodhisattva you want to become, or just personality characteristics you desire, and then work towards that development by cultivating the requisite traits within yourself and actualizing them whenever possible in the real world. (4) The fourth part of practice would be to strongly rotate your Qi in various directions hundreds to thousands of times per day for each of your body sections or specific body parts such as your spine, head, genitals, internal organs, arms, legs, trunk of the body and so forth. This is *nei-gong* or *neijia* practice. Basically it is inner energy work and you can break your efforts into doing different body sections per day. Because the bottleneck areas for Qi flow within your body are your feet, hands, genitals or breasts, and head (ears, nose, etc.), one should put extra emphasis on rotating your Qi throughout these regions. It is easy to rotate your Qi within your arms, legs, spine and your trunk so by putting extra emphasis on these bottlenecks areas you will enable your Qi to finally flow freely-fully inside you after the easy work is done in opening the Qi channels in your major body sections due to faithful, diligent commitment to such circulation techniques. (5) The last part would be daily life practice. This would be a *Vairagya* detachment effort during hours of regular life, which usually applies to detachment from objects, thoughts/emotions or grasping at the concept of being a self. You work at freeing yourself from grasping at or attaching to phenomena. You can consider *Vairagya* practice as an attitude-perspective-detachment-awareness-mindfulness practice where you take a particular mindset or awareness practice into every aspect of your daily life including all of your movements, physical activities and behaviors (such as eating, washing, walking about, working, etc.). For instance, in Japanese Soto Zen you practice "merely sitting single-mindedly," which is a practice that emphasizes awareness, concentration and mindfulness. Therefore you would practice continuous mindfulness of your thoughts/doings in daily life outside of sitting practice, and sometimes you would extensively abide in one of the mental perspectives of emptiness commonly taught sadhus and other spiritual adherents such as "surrender everything over to God," "all this is Brahman," "detach from your mind and desires," etcetera. A collection of these techniques will be covered later in this chapter. (6) Lastly, while during the day you should practice *mindfulness of your thoughts and behavior*, at the end of each day you should practice a daily introspective review to see your faults and unwholesome qualities, express remorse and contrition, determine the root causes (reasons) for why those faults arose, and make a plan (and vow or commitment) to change yourself or the offending situation. (7) Other inner energy work practices can be added in, as well as mantra, pranayama and *yoga exercises or the martial arts where you supplement* the *exercise routines with attendant energy practices* as described in *Neijia Yoga* and *Nyasa Yoga*. For instance, during Zen walking exercise you can try to open up the Qi meridians in your limbs that are connected with certain organ-emotion correspondences. You would also add in mantra/prayer practices to help transform your Qi/Prana since they vibrate your energy and call for aid from Buddhas to help do so, and should try to change your normal daily breathing patterns. A final addition would be to start special learning skills and performing merit along the lines of aspirations to become a Buddha of a certain type as outlined in *Buddha Yoga*. In any case, these are the basics of a daily "meditation" or "cultivation" schedule that is at best 5-6 hours per day since that's the maximum amount of time that professionals can practice in other fields and maintain a quality effort.

Whether we are experiencing pain/suffering or pleasure or equanimity, we always want to know the present moment of existence via a pristine clarity of awareness that embodies the fullness of consciousness. This is the natural capability of the mind, but usually we dull our awareness by clogging it up in some way. You can achieve the fullness of clarity – a very clear experience of your life – by opening up all the Qi channels in your head, optimizing its inner Qi flow, and by training to be mindful or present by always residing in the state of a clear witness of your mental constructs. This requires cultivation practice to become so present. Then you have to learn how to use your awareness and thinking processes properly so that during regular life, when not specifically cultivating special states such as concentration, you are always in a state of presence that is focused on the here and now and present with what you are doing. You don't want to become a thinking machine lost in some automaton activity.

You want to achieve a duality of pristine lucidity (clear awareness) and subtle bliss in your experience of beinghood. When your mind becomes observant of its activities we want it to remain calm, stable, free of agitations and focused so it can ignore distractions. We want it to become balanced and free of unwanted pollutions such as emotional defilements or recurrent negative mental tendencies. We also want the general theme or mood of our mind, personality and outlook to be positive rather than negative such as by being filled with happiness, optimism and cheerfulness or shine and glow rather than suffering. We always want to be experiencing a great natural ease, we always want to be comfortable in our bodies and situations, and we want to be what we call aware, detached, empty or alive in that our vibrancy through fullness, non-interference (detachment) and refinement is as if we reach a perfection of livingness, clarity and vitality where we are being reborn every moment. We want to experience a subtle comforting bliss (perfect equanimity) in both our mind and body, which is physically possible when you are healthy and full of vitality, when all your muscles are in great shape so that there are no internal impediments to your internal Qi flow (thus making your body very comfortable), and when your inner Qi flow is therefore smooth and natural. These factors also produce mental calmness. Through calmness we tame the chaos inside us and can find peace, refinement, balance and even elegance or majesty. Cultivation can even bring out magnificence.

Spiritual cultivation is meant to produce "happy people" who attain such characteristics. We should become able to experience "shine" in life, which is a type of alert happiness where our body is blissful, our mental realm is happy (a subtle form of joy), energetic and tending toward optimism, and we seem to exude a shining energy of brightness or joy without being overly overt or losing energy. Instead of mental waywardness, dullness or robotic entrainment with our thoughts, we always want to be in a fully present state of shine or glow, which is recognizing our beingness or presence within reality while living within a liberated state of inner happiness or cheerfulness from within.

You are not training for "enlightenment" because the present moment *is* already enlightenment. It is illumination as opposed to insentience so consciousness is enlightenment. Your ordinary mind is it – the greatest miracle of existence, consciousness. The illumination of your ordinary mind is "enlightenment" because consciousness is the great miracle of existence, so the ordinary mind *is* the Tao. The ordinary mind is it, it's what you want rather than some supernatural state.

Even though the present moment has no duration, no substance and no permanence to the consciousness of our empty, selfless nature this is where abundance is for it is the most precious thing in the universe. Each moment of our existence is precious and irreplaceable – something we must value right here, right now – so we must watch/know our minds and take each and every action with care. We miraculously have knowledge of our existence and the world due to our property of consciousness, and this is the Tao. Go along with reality rather than fight it ... unless fighting is necessary. Learn to use the flow of phenomena and your consciousness wisely. Hence, the ordinary moment of knowing your being and the world is enlightenment. It is illumination. Whether you have a physical body, subtle body, Causal body, Supra-Causal body or Immanence body this very moment of time in the place where you are at is enlightenment. Your ordinary mind is enlightenment. The problem is that your mind just isn't clear; you use consciousness wrongly and have cluttered it up with all sorts of imperfections that you can get rid of but haven't tried to remove or retrain.

We have the capability to experience this moment of instantaniation, and the flow of instantaniations, through our consciousness and can even train the consciousness we've been given in various ways so that we experience our beingness and life better. This is the meaning of reducing suffering. Who doesn't want less internal and external afflictions? We should be experiencing "flow" where our mind is absent of inner distractions and unwanted afflictions, enjoyably engages in its activities with absorption, and it skillfully, rewardingly, enjoyably handles every situation at hand. Our mind can know the bliss or enjoyment of life with fewer afflictions if we train our consciousness. This is the purpose of spiritual practice.

We can deliberately reprogram and restructure the algorithms of our consciousness to experience more positive modes of being on a steady state basis, which is the purpose of cultivation since many of our algorithms have learned flaws as well as systematic biases and errors. For instance, if you see monks or nuns who have become rigid or sullen because of their cultivation work then it has been incorrect and their algorithms have been damaged. The pathway they have walked has cut off the joyful embrace of many aspects of life/existence that are inherent to the divine play of *Lila*. They have intentionally pushed aside the natural vibrancy of sentient beingness for an artificial, fictionalized, sterilized ideal of refinement as to how they should behave in order to become free of suffering or more perfect in some other way.

We always want to be enjoying natural states of calmness, clarity, presence, comfort, lightness, and bliss but we always want the potential for active states of happiness, joy, pleasure, laughter, cheerfulness, glow, shine and flow as well. There are both passive and active positive states of consciousness, but most spiritual streams focus on the passive states in order to get you to cultivate meditation practice. However, your activities should always be fully imbued with the breath of life, which means that your vital energy has become so well-circulating and refined that your body-mind has become peaceful, calm and comfortable, or your vital energy has become so full, active and vibrant in your cells that you exhibit the bliss, happiness and Spring-like joy that is inherent to life. This type of active bliss, rather than a peaceful bliss, is fine too.

Life is naturally vibrant, and that is the way you should be rather than working on locking down your inner vitality. You should never suppress your vitality to find peacefulness but do as Confucius advised and work to *refine it*, which he did through immersion in music, the arts, ritual (where your behavior must be a certain way) and culture. After all, we must all rise above our animal nature or lower nature of non-virtuous qualities, which is a task of refinement.

As a Taoist saying runs, "without vitality it is difficult to cultivate the Tao, but with vitality one cannot return to the Truth." Your vital energies of all types must be refined, which is the process of cultivation. In so doing, however, you must not cut off or suppress your inner vitality that is your life force by a forced conformity with artificial formalities and rigidities to "hold still" as you might see in Japanese Zen. Your virility or vital energy must not be thwarted so that you "attain imperturbability" through this or other means but instead must be trained, sublimated, transformed into a higher grade or quality ... basically refined. Life must flow naturally, as you find stressed in Taoism, therefore we must refine, elevate or upgrade our life force and its expression rather than suppress it. That is how we attain the higher energy bodies of enlightenment. If your cultivation school is too austere and sullen and does not lead to happy results then it is truly in error. Shakti is animated and full of life, and so should you be, but there is a great deal of difference between coarseness and refinement such as between an oaf, lout or barbarian and a gentleman. Life does not have to be about *Kama* (pleasure or enjoyment) or its repression but it should be about bliss (*ananda*).

We are a mind-body complex. Therefore, basically we have cognitive skills and physical skills. To develop our cognitive skills we need to cultivate our *intellect, rationality, knowledge, wisdom (understanding) and introspective or analysis capabilities*. This helps to raise us above other animals. Our emotions are automatic reflexes responses that are part of the cognitive palette and they can often be mastered through various methods such as *mindfulness, modulating our desires,* by *cognitively restructuring* our interpretations of events and through many other means. Emotions were not developed through evolution to promote happiness, wisdom or moral values but to help in the propagation of our species along. They also have other purposes helping with survival, such as the fight or flight syndrome, and therefore we must gain control over them and the behavior they provoke by doing what is best for ourselves even if it does not feel good at the time. When we can gain control of our emotions and our lower impulses this is another step upwards towards refining our attributes and behavior.

If we just slapped strict rules on ourselves to suppress inner tendencies or just policed them rather than work to transform our wild forces then when we found ourselves in environments free of those constraints we might go berserk and celebrate in a frenzy of those very behaviors. Hence, the stories of Arabs who drink wine and eat pork in revelry when outside of Arabia. Many individuals who suppress themselves during life due to strict religious rules are found to be extremists who flaunt such injunctions in subsequent incarnations as a sort of catching up, satisfaction of those desires or rebellion, like the minister's daughter who through her behavior wildly rebels against the excessive strictures of her life. Only an elevation that is a transformation to purity will solve many of our problems.

The human mind is also riddled with all sorts of cognitive lapses and automatic biases such as emotional predispositions and prejudicial beliefs or contaminated mindsets, and this affects not only our reasoning and wisdom but our actions and emotional well-being. As stated, our mind not only makes wrong conclusions on a frequent basis but is subject to systematic biases and errors. On the spiritual trail we are to always inspect our consciousness to discover these biases *or other faults* such as unwholesome qualities, and correct them whenever found.

Furthermore, a large degree of our psychological suffering is a matter of becoming lost in thought rather than recognizing that we are *thinking without knowing we are thinking*, and that what we are experiencing are just thoughts that are separate from our I-self. If we become lost in negative emotions through lack of mindfulness we can easily become those thoughts and then suffer needlessly rather than just let them pass away. If we fall into negative indulgences we can harm ourselves as well.

The algorithms of our emotions and belief systems are heavily biased due to our previous conditioning/experiences, and they produce greatly prejudiced worldviews. This is one of the things we work on during the course of the spiritual cultivation trail for attaining the higher transcendental bodies of enlightenment. A spiritual body attainment does not automatically change our personality/character or wipe our mind free of its habitual problems, so during the course of self-cultivation we work on gaining control of our mental and emotional factors and start training them to become more pure and more optimal. You can never totally eliminate the problem of suffering, for instance, so the task is developing mental characteristics that will reduce suffering and produce the aggregate of well-being. You will be able to sense all sorts of minds upon the achievement of higher body attainments so you must learn to be more open, less prejudiced, less judgmental, more accepting, more mentally flexible, more empathic or sympathetic, more understanding such as able to hold differing and even conflicting perspectives, and much more patient and compassionate.

All Buddhas come into the world in order to help sentient beings understand the fundamental nature of their reality, which includes understanding what we essentially are. They teach where we come from and what we are, and that because of our non-fixed nature we have an infinite capacity to become whatever we want and do or experience whatever we want if we learn how to use our consciousness and will/efforts skillfully. They teach the importance of cultivating our characters (personalities) and minds and how to do so. They teach us how to cultivate both the automatic and deliberate mental factors of our attribute of consciousness. They teach that we can detach from bondage to our mental phenomena to let them flow through us and thereby achieve calmness, contentment, forbearance and self-control. They teach how to access states of peace, repose, tranquility, clarity, comfort, bliss, centeredness, presence, freshness, shine, glow, flow and so on. Many natural mental states of well-being like this are intrinsic to the nature of consciousness rather than predicated on the contents of consciousness being one way or another. To achieve them is a matter of discovering the natural state of consciousness and learning how to use consciousness correctly, such as quieting our inner narrative to enjoy life more fully in the present. We must also learn how to use various state-shifting methodologies for consciousness like the techniques of NLP.

A quiet enjoyment of the moment is a form of bliss. It is possible through spiritual practice to learn how to dampen our noisy inner narrative (quiet our thinking mind) so that you can appreciate the experience of aliveness that is a present moment yet without disturbing the moment. This is called presence, clear consciousness, pristine clarity, one-pointedness, aliveness, being centered, flow and many other names that represent the *true, natural ordinary mind of man*. These are the states or modes of mind you should be cultivating on the spiritual path, as well as positive modes such as optimism, sunniness, cheerfulness, happiness, shine and so on that represent the active vitality of life rather than the naturally quiet nature of a mind that isn't experiencing other mental modes or formations. To cultivate such beautiful states you must not just cultivate your mind but also cultivate the energy flow within your body. Meditation and methods of self-correction or self-perfection that purify your mind and character are methods for advancing in this direction.

However, we still have the problem of survival in the realm of Nature that is hectic, brutal and frightening because Nature is a continuous tragedy of conflict, pain and suffering where we get sick, age and eventually die. Within our own life struggles it is hard to hold to a code of ethics, and it takes courage to maintain your own ideals so that you always do what you think is right and never violate your conscience. Within Nature the strong are always trying to overpower the weak, and in seeking food living beings are always stalking and killing one another for nourishment. Humans are always seeking advantages over one another and ways to exploit others for advantage. Life is a tragedy within a reality that is not a Utopia. How to navigate the landmines of life ethically and still experience happiness, peace and bliss is an incredible challenge that requires support from others. We must not just work to handle our own situation but try to make things better for others in the now and for the future so that they inherit even better states of living.

Because of widespread poverty, to flourish with great happiness and prosperity is beyond the capability of many people. Hence, Buddhas come into the world to help people deal with suffering and they express noble behavior that improves conditions to lessen the sufferings of existence. However, many people in today's modern world have led lives that have been monotonously good, so teachings on suffering do not motivate them and different teachings must be used. Self-improvement is one possible pathway. For both the poor and well-off, when you make yourself a better person and establish a legacy of your behavior that continues to improve things for the better even after you are gone then you have really performed incredible great merit.

Without the spiritual teachings of Buddhas we would, due to the fact that we are aggressive/antagonistic animals, become corrupted by the pains of existence and continuously fall prey to negative emotions and behaviors such as anger, hatred, greed, envy, lying, stealing, killing and so forth. Buddhas teach us how to calm our minds, control our thought processes and uplift our conduct *and the world* so that we can spiritualize our natures and thereby move closer to the Buddha-body attainments. Then we can experience states of peace, happiness, contentment, flow and bliss in both the world as it is and in higher realms of existence. Their teachings and guidance help us find a higher purpose and meaning to life.

We need to maintain ourselves to live, but we can only accomplish this through the help of others in cooperative, collaborative arrangements where we band together to overcome Nature and ourselves, and thus Buddhas encourage us to develop our societies and culture and the codes of values and virtues that enable us to thrive. They give us with teachings on human relations, how society should progress, and on methods of self-improvement so that we can change our characters and plant the seeds for even better subsequent incarnations.

Humans remain animals unless they fall under the civilizing influences of spirituality, civics, rationality and science. The hope is that our animal nature becomes cleansed and uplifted enough through the influences of spiritual teachings to become human nature, our human nature rises through self-cultivation to become a noble nature, and then is further purified and perfected to become spiritualized nature. The ideal is to become something significant and magnificent. The hope is also that we use our willpower and consciousness in life to not only develop ourselves, but to create a better future for ourselves and others that removes the pains of our souls and moves humanity forwards.

Buddhas teach people to fully comprehend their personhood, which is a fabricated ever-changing construction of many processes combining through dependent origination, but whose innermost core is the unchanging true self that is the true reality of existence. They help people understand the true nature of manifest reality, that a multitude of conditions agglomerate together to compose their body and create their consciousness, that they have no intrinsic nature of their own, and that their ultimate self-nature or True Self is their permanent core as well as the universal substratum from whence all originates. They come to teach people that their true identity is the universal substratum and that there is a unity between themselves and that substratum. These two are one, *samsara* and *nirvana* are the same thing, you are God and God is in you, etcetera. He is your reality and substance. Some would say you are in God and dependent on Him for your existence. The individual personal self, being Its manifestation, is one with the spotless fundamental essence.

When one realizes the oneness of his personal self with the Universal Self or Supreme Reality (and the truth about the composition of one's physical nature and consciousness), which is your "true relationship with God" (the foundational substratum), this realization is often called self-realization, liberation or emancipation. However, such knowledge does not solve the problems of birth and death or suffering which can only be handled by, among other things, learning how to manipulate the conditions of the universe so as to produce desired conditions, learning how to cultivate material and mental well-being, learning how to manage the operations of your body and mind and bring them to states of excellence, and learning how to cultivate higher transcendental bodies that live extremely long lives in higher planes of existence.

All Buddhas teach the unified oneness of our personal self with Shakti and ultimately the Universal Self, the Supreme Reality, the universal substratum, our fundamental nature. All Buddhas come into the world to enable sentient beings to realize the nature of their self-essence, which is to understand their true self-nature just as you have been told, and in addition to these revelations that lead to the perception of Truth, they also provide for us various pathways of cultivation. They teach us how to manage our consciousness – our awareness, contemplation skills, thinking processes, imagination, etc. – and master the rules of causality (cause and effect) that rule phenomena so that we can learn to control ourselves and our environment to produce better states of well-being. Because we are social animals interconnected with other group members, they teach us how to behave with one another in cooperative, collaborative societies that satisfy our needs for happiness, prosperity and protection, safety, security and fairness, etcetera. A key principle is that of self-regulation since it allows both individuals and the larger culture to thrive because it promotes moral, disciplined and virtuous behaviors.

They teach that although we are transient beings, there is a process of reincarnation that provides a degree of continuity to our existence, and locked within the energy matrix of our body there is the potential of higher transcendental body achievements that can win us an existence of extreme longevity where, even if one eventually passes away at that level, allow a continuity of many memories and attributes to be passed onto a subsequent incarnation. They teach that we should mentally stabilize in our Real Self, cultivate proper behavior and the inner vital Qi energy inside us.

Additionally, we should make efforts that progress mankind forward in order to (1) promote transformations that lead to a better society (which we can thereby enjoy in the present and possibly in subsequent incarnations) and (2) produce personal merit for our subsequent incarnations or the higher transcendental body achievements that free us from lower unfortunate realms of existence. They teach us to improve our own lives *and the state of society* so that we can obtain all sorts of other various benefits such as being able to experience what we want, being able to change our fortunes for the better, and become the people we want to become in life. If we work on ourselves, our conditions and society we can more readily *feel states of shine and other active states of bliss* in our lives and experience the true vitality of beingness.

After receiving such teachings, we must arouse the courage and discipline to start cultivating ourselves – our bodies, personalities (because we are living objects these are attributes or characteristics), spiritual values, knowledge and wisdom, thinking processes, skills, conduct, projects and so on – by purifying, elevating and mastering all the abilities of our consciousness.

They then encourage us to use our powers to improve society and move it forward in positive ways so that it does not succumb to ossification, calcification or stasis due to suppressing changes required by progress, and also encourage us to dial back our errant tendencies. They want us to be self-correcting in personally cultivating ourselves to become better people and more skillful in our activities so that we can also more effectively accomplish whatever ethical, virtuous goals we desire for life.

Buddhas come into the world in order to enable sentient beings to create pathways of higher culture, civilization, cultivation, conduct, charity, cooperation and *dharma* that improve circumstances and lead to better existences for human lives. When humans die their inner subtle Qi-body separates from their physical shell and lives in an earthly etheric plane around us until reincarnation, administered by higher beings, sends deva souls down again into the material plane when that life ends ... unless during that time they cultivate the next higher stage of existence. On and on it goes in cyclical fashion until through spiritual cultivation practice your energy body and your personality/habits are purified to the extent that you can attain a Supra-Causal body that is practically immortal, free of the impurity of all lower realms of matter and energy, and therefore forever transcendental to the cycles of birth and death in the lower planes of existence.

Hence, Buddhas come into the world to teach us how to improve our lives and the structures of society; how to develop our wisdom, skills and abilities of consciousness to the fullest; and how to transform our characters and ethical roots of behavior to higher stages that carryover for subsequent incarnations. They come into the world to teach us how to live with one another peacefully, cooperatively and prosperously. They come into the world to teach us how to attain the higher spiritual bodies that leave the lower realms of suffering behind forever. They come on account that they want us to awaken to the view of the Buddhas, achieve the perfected ordinary mind of enlightenment,[45] and take upon themselves similar Buddha purposes, vows and commitments to join them in helping humanity in various ways.[46] They want to enable sentient beings to engage in the task of self-perfection, perfect their current physical body and ways

---

[45] A mind that has achieved a natural, steady state mode of inner peace and calm (tranquility or "emptiness"), centeredness, pristine clarity, is "present" in the moment (rather than wandering), and experiences a physical comfort of body bliss due to its health and vitality. Mental states of flow, sunniness (a quiet inner optimism, happiness and energy) and shine are also optimum states of the ordinary mind. These are just the qualities of the mental realm you hope to achieve in your ordinary mind through the processes of cultivation. You can cultivate peaceful, calm states of egolessness and desirelessness that are accompanied by brilliant mental clarity and more active blissful states of positivity (happiness, shine, optimism, vigor, etc.) that are vibrantly engaging and fill you with much energy during the life experience. Whether you cultivate a passive or active mental state, it is to become elevated and highly refined.

[46] See *Buddha Yoga* for a wide variety of such vows.

of living,[47] and attain the higher transcendental bodies of enlightenment, and produce a better world for themselves and others, and so they come into the world.

Specifically, they want human beings to spiritually cultivate to attain the Supra-Causal body, also known as the Buddha body, Rainbow body or Clear Light body attainment that is the fourth dhyana, and experience its attendant level of clear consciousness (the mirror mind) and other capabilities. And they want them to devote themselves to Buddha vows that that involve self-improvement efforts (such as skill development) and helping other sentient beings in the universe. After someone achieves this fourth dhyana Arhat transcendental body attainment, its composition is so refined in terms of being free from lower energies and coarse matter that they no longer have to reincarnate in the lower physical realm, subtle realm, or Causal realm that correspond to the human, Srotapanna and Sadragamin, and Anagamin levels of attainment. They can escape the lower realms of reincarnation forever.

From the standpoint of the original nature there is nothing else in existence other than just Itself just as ornaments of gold are nothing but gold, a jar of clay is only clay, and the substances of cheese, butter, ghee or curd are all milk that has evolved into different forms. From the perspective of gold there is no such thing as a (gold) necklace because there is only gold (there). Similarly, objects within the universe are the fundamental substrate and their delineation as objects is simply a mental construct. Thus, there is no such *true* thing as manifoldness (manifestations of phenomena) in the cosmos because there is only the fundamental essence. Those superimpositions are just false attributions upon Parabrahman the fundamental substratum. They are a way to misidentify the world as something else other than what it truly is, but we cannot yet see the true nature of their beingness. As a result, they *do* exist as multiplicities (connected into a oneness) and there *is* an empirical realm of manifest existence. The created world is essentially real. However, we build up our idea of the world that exists only though the mental realm of name and form. Hence to us the world we experience is only our consciousness. It is consciousness-only, mere-consciousness or merely-consciousness. We can never have a valid perception of it but can only experience a similitude approximation.

---

[47] As just one example, for every activity of life there is an optimal way of breathing, and you need to learn the proper breathing method for each different activity such as a specific sport, skill, type of concentration, meditation practice, etcetera.

From the standpoint of the primordial substratum there are no such things as production or destruction, cause and effect, laws of physics, dependent arising, living beings, consciousness and thoughts, holy teachings, stages of life, birth and death, a path to enlightenment, beings that achieve enlightenment, wisdom, karma, suffering, attainments, codes of conduct and so forth in existence as these are all forms of Itself. There is only the fundamental foundational substratum present that is absent of all these appearances that are essentially matter-energy agglomerations or mental constructs that are in turn the fundamental substrate.

Within Shakti there is no definite thing; there is only neutral scintillating matter-energy formations without good or bad, virtue or evil, and within it there are no stable patterns. There are also no genuine souls, *atmans* or entities who cultivate, no one who transmigrates through reincarnation, and no intrinsic selves, souls or spirits that attain the higher spiritual bodies and become released from bondage to ignorance and lower realms … there is only Shakti transforming in various ways without any intrinsic patterns, and Shakti itself is the primordial formless (empty) substrate. Shakti itself is only Shakti *without multiplicities*, and yet multiplicities exist otherwise we wouldn't be here. Yet we are here, but we don't exist in the way we imagine ourselves to be so Buddhas teach us the truth about our self-nature. Buddhas arise to correct our notions on these matters. Next, they point out the implications for how to live our lives, escape the suffering inherent in existence, attain bliss or well-being and help others as well.

Everything in the world is part of you and you are part of everything. You must also say that the apparent living beings of Shakti are not just Shakti but are the primal substratum of the universe in various manifested forms that illusionally seem bound, released or transmigrating through a cycle or incarnations but are essentially free. In the realm of Shakti, cause and effect has produced a manifoldness of phenomena that are actually all seamlessly interconnected as one soup, but you have the gift of consciousness that enables you to define separate multiplicities, realize your true nature, and make a better life for your existence due to your knowledge and knowing. You are not bound but are free to transform in any way you choose and pursue any direction you want. With the amazing miracle of consciousness you can apply self-efforts to become however you want within Shakti in terms of your skills, personality traits, body characteristics, etcetera and can work to develop, achieve or experience whatever you want as well.

Nonetheless, there is only the fundamental substrate here all the time and no such real things as sentient beings. A stable existence or permanent dependability cannot be attributed to any of its manifestations (evolutes or entities) since they are always changing. They are not inherent entities so they are always transforming into some type of new state or beingness every moment. For us that means we must learn how to adapt to the changes of the universe, which requires being mentally flexible, and those who learn faster are the ones with the advantage for surviving and thriving.

Shakti doesn't ultimately exist (if you decompose Shakti into the highest forms of energy then energy or fields of force wave fronts are all you have, and ultimately all this energy was somehow born from the nothingness of the fundamental substratum), and there are no stable patterns within Shakti. Furthermore, the patterns within Shakti can only be discovered through consciousness. From the ultimate standpoint of the Empty foundational substrate there are no things in existence. There is only Itself. Hence there are no masters nor students, no teachings nor *dharma* such as self-realization. There is only Itself, and you need not work to attain It because you already have It since you are It. There is no one who achieves enlightenment, nor is there such a true thing as enlightenment or even higher bodies. There is no such thing as attainment to what you already have or inherently are. There is no such thing as attainment at all!

Ultimately there is no state of virtue and no state of vice, no good or evil, no stage of bondage or ignorance, no stage of liberation, no such things as change or transformation. There are absolutely no modifications within the fundamental substance that is empty of all things (just like space), and which thus is absolutely transcendent without attributes or qualities. The realm of Shakti, whether you say it is perfectly chaotic or replete with patterns, is neither ultimately patterned nor chaotic since Shakti is just inherent emptiness.

Then again, within the world of Shakti all these things exist on a conventional level for it is a manifest realm of cause and effect. However, the essential nature of the universe is temporary agglomeration, the appearance of a form or phenomenon, and then instant change. Our mind names and labels (classifies as patterns) the things we perceive within Shakti for identification purposes so that we can deal with the world that appears within our minds, which are the constructs of Shakti, but they are always transforming into something else. So we say *there are* living sentient beings, reincarnation, ignorance and liberation but they are not inherent, intrinsic existences or realities. They do exist, they are empirical facts, they follow causal laws of manifestation and are predictable.

However, they exist only for as long as they exist and constitute instantaneous, temporary, momentary appearances (the "instantaniations" of Ibn Arabi) or "apparent" actualities rather than unchanging "true" or "real" existences. To say that we are living beings, for instance, is only a conventional (but false) way of speaking because there are no intrinsic beings here since everything is conditionally defined through an agglomeration (we are non-intrinsic entities composed of all sorts of other conditions rather than possessing an independent self-so nature) and always transforming. Thus, you can say that sentient beings are neither truly existent as inherent beings, yet neither are they non-existent because we do apparently exist and have the attribute of consciousness that lets us know of ourselves and appearances (qualities) of the world and thoughts from within our own composition.

From the aspect of the foundational substratum you can say Its oneness or purity means It has no cause or effect, is free from cause and effect, transcends cause and effect, is beyond the relationships of cause and effect, cause and effect do not affect It, cause and effect do not truly exist, cause and effect are ultimately empty, the nature of cause and effect is emptiness, and so on. Imagine if the entire universe was just empty space alone with nothing inside it. In that case, where would there be cause and effect? There would just be an endless void of nothingness – nothing at all. This is said to be comparable to the nature of the original foundational substrate.

Through meditation practice religions teach people to abide their mind in an emptiness like this as a meditative dwelling, but hey are taught to maintain full awareness during that state of "empty mind" rather than fall into some state similar to no-thought (non-thinking) like deep sleep. It's not about developing an internal meditative dwelling on emptiness (*shamatha* or cessation), abiding or dwelling within it, and then somehow seeing through it to awakening (self-realization) because enlightenment is a body attainment. The first dhyana attainment means the subtle body attainment, the third dhyana means the Causal body attainment, the fourth dhyana means the Dharma body attainment, and the stage of *nirvana* without remainder is the Great Golden Arhat body or Immanence body attainment of complete and perfect enlightenment.

There is no such thing as a mental state of awareness/beingness released from all mental fermentation/formations (except for the state of a coma, deep sleep, anesthesia, extinction, etc.) because during awareness of the world or your thoughts, even when your internal narrative seems perfectly silent, the I-sense is still active since it is necessary for the perception of your surroundings and mental states. If you are awaken then mental formations are always going on.

Most spiritual schools, as a means of training, want you to cultivate a pristine mental awareness that is a relatively quiet mind empty of coarse thoughts where you know your consciousness as "the master" who stands apart from the thought-stream because he knows it but doesn't cling to it. Zen talk about host and guest relationships pertains to this sort of relationship between awareness and thinking. The proper procedure is to train in watching your thoughts ("brightening your awareness") instead of blocking them to "experience emptiness." The lack of fusion with your thoughts while maintaining clear awareness of them helps to open up all the Qi channels in your brain so that you are mentally clear, and affords you the opportunity to correct your thoughts whenever required which thereby enables you to rectify your behavior to the level of nobility (impeccable consummate conduct) and then spirituality (selflessness in being of service to others). You're not trying to get to a stage of non-error that is deemed normal or sufficient (because that is as good as you can get) but to cultivate yourself to a stage of exceptional.

In the conventional realm of manifestation there is indeed cause and effect even though perceptually we don't know what the world *really* looks like so don't experience the truth of worldly reality as it truly is. Within Shakti cause and effect certainly do exist and create all its configurations. Even before consciousness arose within Shakti those configurations existed, otherwise there would not have been a history of evolution to produce the conscious life that has eventually arisen within it - us. Without a mind the undifferentiated mass of Shakti cannot be segmented into differences or distinctions, so no multiplicities of any type would be recognized by anyone even though those events, processes, objects and so forth would still exist.

All the various manifestations, phenomena or fabrications of energy and matter in the universe arise out of the complex interaction of cause and effect. Since the best understanding of cause and effect incorporates energy wavefronts and the infinite interdependence of forces and phenomena that underlies all of materiality, you can definitely say that manifest reality is created through an infinite Indra's net of simultaneous co-arising, co-penetrating conditions. Buddhism summarizes these cause and effect relationships as, "When this exists that exists, when this arises that arises."

Conventionally, within Shakti there are sentient beings and better apparent states of existence that you can bring into existence for yourself and others, so why not do so? Why remain attached to inferior states of being rather than make efforts to move ahead in life to make things better for yourself and others? Why not create states absent of suffering but full of joy, bliss and well-being for all? Are you who and what you want to be? If not, then you should make arrangements to change yourself in the directions you want.

Our lives have both attributes and a trajectory or destiny related to our character and actions. We can change these through the cultivation effort of self-improvement, which requires consistent work on improving our personality, thinking and behavior. This in turn requires us to concentrate on perfecting the state of our consciousness and its usage since it gives birth to most of our volitional attributes. To achieve this type of self-improvement we need *a system of regularities that continually point us toward this goal and gradually take our mind, body and behavior through the difficult transformation process of retraining or reshaping.* That is why some people enter into temples, ashrams, abbeys, monasteries and convents and take up the religious life that offers a structured system of gradual training.

We are connected to all things in existence, but are especially influenced by our prior experiences since they have strongly shaped us. To change ourselves to become better (and often in order to create a better future for ourselves) we must find and fix our psychological issues and surpass our mental limitations that cause us to remain how we are. When we encounter resistance to change, we have to dissolve any obstructions through wisdom. We must find our bad patterns and replace them with better patterns or frameworks. We must permanently alter any suboptimal patterns within our psychology, which is the same as transforming our natal chart in astrology, for whatever is better. We must especially transform ourselves by striving to elevate our minds and behaviors above our animal natures. First become human, then proceed to elegance.

Our task of maintaining our lives (i.e. handling survival, nourishment and protection issues) and achieving prosperity entails mastering the conventional states of living. You travel through life using your intellect, so you must master the abilities of your conceptual consciousness and use your mind to master yourself and your circumstances such as by engineering new activities to bring about what you need or desire.

For us, appearances of a world (forms and phenomena, including life and consciousness) certainly *do exist.* You cannot say they *ultimately exist* as inherent truths, but only conventionally exist as subjective apparent truths within our consciousness. We experience the objective world subjectively. The appearances of the world are not non-existent since they represent empirical facts that exist conventionally. However, they are only temporarily true and not "really real" in the sense of having permanent inherent natures, yet they do formally exist with facticity. They are all composite constructions produced from a myriad of contributing causes (cooperating forces). From the aspect of the entirely pure foundational substance they do not exist at all for within It there is only Itself. However, phenomena do appear in the unreal, non-self-so, transitory apparent realm of causality that lacks inherent existence – for we perceive them – and you know of this because you have consciousness. Without a mind you would be an insentient phenomenon for which nothing exists, and yet as an insentient phenomenon you would still factually exist but without conscious illumination.

With a mind you can create an ordered human world within Shakti, create culture and civilization, and live your life prosperously even though the universe/world is ultimately only a realm of disorder where the life within it must constantly experience entropy, pain and suffering. How to improve our lives and our selves in this Triple Realm (the multidimensional universe of space-time) is what the Buddhas come into this world to teach.

Even though we have a mind, within our consciousness phenomena never really appear to us in all their dimensions because the picture we internally create of the outside world is limited by the constraints of our sense organs and the limited framework of our mental processing capacities. Due to the limitations of our imperfect sense organs and lack of additional sensory vehicles, you always experience the world incompletely and incorrectly. As stated, there is incompleteness along with systematic errors and biases. You experience the world conditionally according to the limitations of both your sense organs and your mental processing capabilities that create a very abbreviated picture of the world. These produce a simplified (and somewhat illusory) map of the outside world, which you build inside your brain, and your mental processing also unconsciously adds subjective factors to the picture thus contaminating it with biases and partialities. Many contaminating, biasing factors automatically arise due to your past experiences (conditioning) and are not under your voluntary control when you build a reflective picture of reality within your mind, which is why you must practice mindfulness to spot these insertions and correct them.

What you experience as the world with qualities is only an illusion within your mind. It is only an abbreviated, imperfect approximation of something out there; it is a *mere representation* limited in scope and qualities. It is a type of false imagining that you create through pattern recognition and this is often referred to as delusion, illusion or fantasy even though it is a similitude of something externally out there. In other words, there is indeed an objective reality outside of (surrounding) you but you can only experience it subjectively. Your approximation of reality is therefore inaccurate and hence illusional because it lacks critical details, assumes details that aren't there, and also because it arises within your mind that embellishes it with biases and prejudices since you automatically add likes and dislikes, desires, interests and preferences onto the simplified images.

Nonetheless, this is the nature of consciousness so you cannot criticize what you have but only correct it once you discover its natural deficiencies. Consciousness is what it is, as faulty as it might be, so there is no use complaining about it. There is just the task of mastering what you've got, sentience, which is a miraculous ability. Consciousness is our life, it is what we are, it is our knowledge of our self-existence and the world. It is that by which all things are realized. What an invaluable treasure!

The Great Learning is *to make the best use of your conscious thinking apparatus and cognitive processes* for the health of your psychological realm and goal-seeking behavior. You must work with what you have without complaint because nature has evolved this capability in you that, although precious beyond measure and of inestimable value, has natural limitations. There's no use fretting about the limitations and inaccuracies of consciousness because that's how consciousness is. That is what we have for our minds. Therefore you can only correct its errors, train to improve your usage of consciousness, expand its abilities wherever possible, and basically just work to master it. This is what spiritual cultivation is all about.

Through consciousness you know the world via constructed mental images, and thus you *never directly perceive reality*. You only experience an image of the outer world within your mind that through a trick of inversion makes you think you are experiencing something outside of the brain. Even so, you only ever experience your mind of mental thoughts and images. You only experience a symbolic representation of something "out there." Your consciousness is the only thing you can know; you cannot know the world, you can only know your consciousness and the picture it builds of the world, whether true or false. Nevertheless, this light of illumination (knowing) is a treasure compared to insentience. It builds a reality, but what it builds is a similitude representation (parallel resemblance) of the world. It never perceives nor represents reality perfectly.

Everything you experience happens in the space between your ears because absolutely everything you know is only an experience constructed within your consciousness. The world picture you create from using your eyes, ears, nose, tongue, body etc. is just mere-consciousness inside your mind. The worldview of qualities you create isn't totally real but just an *approximate illusion* that works for you, and it becomes the conventional truth for other humans as well because we all share a similar anatomical structure that produces a similar mechanism (internal operating system) for human consciousness, and therefore we all create a very similar type of world picture.

Phenomena are actually wavering energy vibrations in space, constantly changing and ultimately ungraspable as immutable essences. Not being changeless, phenomena are inherently unreal and intrinsically undependable as "solid objects" but we take them as solid dependabilities. We don't even realize that they are made of atoms or even smaller simples that are mostly empty space, so their apparent solidity is also a fiction since they are mostly emptiness. Stationary objects look like they are just sitting there motionless but because of their composition they are doing many different things at the same time and undergoing all sorts of transformations. Therefore they don't exist in the way they appear to be. The universe is that way as well, and human beings are also not what we assume ourselves to be. They are like an empty fist used to fool a child. This is the truth of the way things are.

All things appear due to conditions, meaning they appear only because there are cooperating conditions and processes that produce them (they conditionally arise), and so in being dependent on conditions they do not ultimately exist in some fundamentally inherent or innate way. They are *dependencies* – impermanent dependent constructions that need various strategies to stay together. Their existence depends upon other things including an entire history of past conditions on top of present conditions. In other words, they have no self-so natures (intrinsic natures) that are *independent existences*. What seems like an independent body flows into everything else due to interdependent arising that basically dissolves any of its discrete boundaries. However, objects do exist non-transcendentally (conventionally or classically) for as long as they do exist, which is always momentary since they are changing into another state/thing every moment. They are actually perceived so they are not non-existent, but we falsely attribute some characteristics to them that are not so. They are all apparently real for just a moment, but our minds make them appear to be continuous on a moment-by-moment basis. Nonetheless, what we think is monotonous is always changing, and hence never the same constant thing. So there is a reality we see, but not the true reality that we are seeing … just a representation of mere-consciousness. Also, what we perceive doesn't exist as we assume it does because we make mistakes due to the way we perceive things. We don't even understand the behavior of things on a very small scale, which is wondrously different than the way things behave on a large scale. We always perceive the world with the imperfections of incompleteness and improperness in various ways, which is why what we internally perceive is only a similarity, resemblance or likeness of the external world missing many details and far from a true approximation.

Even if ultimately unreal because it is a changing dependent existent, what we take for reality and experience as reality is to us reality, so why not master the changes of the reality we experience? Now that you know the truth of the conventional (classical) world, why not learn to become a master of changing phenomena where you can skillfully guide their possible changes to more auspicious states of being? In fact, this is what we must do for both the world and ourselves, namely of lives and especially our consciousness. After all, classical conventionality is the only thing that ultimately matters, not the original nature, because conventionality is our *conscious existence*. We change from state to state all the time ... so what, master the changes! Take charge and guide the transformation of your being into something great. Learnt he principles of self-transformation and then use them, which is why some people become yogis, monks, nuns and so froth.

Without consciousness we are just some type of insentient existent in some form or another, which is ultimately the same as personal extinction or annihilation, so conscious existence is what matters to us! We must therefore learn to master our consciousness and its capabilities. Cultivation practice is therefore all about conquering our minds *and our bodies* that are both the basis of our beingness. The bliss of Advaita Vedanta or Buddhist *nirvana* - a bliss of unperturbed peacefulness - is meaningless without a mind and refers to a conscious bodily existence experiencing bliss, namely *sat-chit-ananda*. We have to master and then perfect the functions of our mind through cultivation efforts to experience the bliss of *ananda* and *make it the natural state of our life*, otherwise we will remain simple animals.

The *sat-chit-ananda* of Hinduism stipulates a bliss experienced by consciousness that *only occurs because you have existence* – a formal or form-based existence. Therefore this is not a blissful peacefulness of no-thinking (no-thought) due to the absence of sentience, or due to the blocking of thoughts that creates a dulled mind of thoughtlessness, or due to the non-existence of physical form. It is not the stale emptiness mind of "dead tree Zen" either where your thinking and inner vitality are suppressed to become unnaturally quieted and subdued. Many meditation practitioners think they should sit without letting their mind move, or without letting thoughts arise in order to attain an imperturbable "samadhi of oneness," but this is a false/wrong emptiness. It is an unnatural deviation to the proper flow of consciousness and life and can never lead to a functional or operational (flowing) *ananda* of true peacefulness, tranquility or bliss within the flow of consciousness.

Consider that the essence of consciousness is not a blank space but contains the entire universe, so consciousness is not to be suppressed into thoughtlessness. It should always be open to new experiences and change. Meditation is just a training practice to produce a fuller undistracted awareness within a consciousness that allows all thoughts, and when bad thoughts arise you transform them. Want proof? Every enlightened sage you meet is vibrantly alive, has a fully active mind and is always correcting their behavior. Just as your perceptions naturally evoke the universe, your thinking must always remain active and ready to sprout rather than suppressed to create an empty theme within, so the type of lethargic peacefulness that some strive to cultivate through meditation practice is not the true peacefulness, empty mind nor bliss of the Tao. It is an obstruction, an abomination. If your thoughts are wrong or errant then you cut them off or transform the impulses into something else, but you don't suppress consciousness into non-thinkingness.

A blissful experience is certainly absent of suffering, but is better described as a state of physical and mental well-being (since we can never entirely rid ourselves of pain and suffering in life) infused with a degree of physical comfort and a subtle happiness that is there in the background as an enjoyment you can savor, but which does not overwhelm your being to the extent of clouding your conscious experience in any way. While we want to be happy and joyous in life, and while excitement-happiness is a positive experience, vibrant states of elation are like a passing brightness that is an exciting or thrilling irritant polluting the peacefulness of a clear mind of inner tranquility. The most enjoyable mental states are sustainable over many moments, which includes the peaceful modes of calmness, tranquility and equanimity that spiritual schools usually term "emptiness." Therefore so that people can learn how to settle and calm their minds, so that they can clarify and pacify their minds, so that they can achieve a fuller awareness of their cognitive happenings and the world, so that they can make better decisions in life, for those reasons and others what we call emptiness (empty mind) is a common target of meditation practice.

Emptiness, peacefulness, or tranquility do not mean (absolute) no-thought but that your mind is clear and relatively quiet of complexity or overt fermentation - *you have sharp mental clarity, acuity and cleanness without internal afflictions and irritations* and you enjoy that blissful, comfortable, calm, peaceful state of mind. This is the natural state of your mind before you disturb it. This peacefulness is its true nature, although an active mindstream is the nature of consciousness as well. The importance of a tranquil mind, however, appears through a comparison with water. When the mind becomes still its natural transparency and reflectivity are the highest like water, which loses those qualities when it becomes disturbed with ripples and turbulence. People cultivate meditation practice to gain that quality of mental brightness and clarity.

During the mental calmness of empty pristine awareness, you experience your existence within an attendant (accompanying) degree of mental brightness, sharpness, peace and calm rather than constantly experience some thrilling degree of rapture, ecstasy or even bubbling joy that cannot give you rest. Bliss is something subtle but pleasant and pervasive, and this is what you should experience if you cultivate your mind, health, and vital energy well enough. The states of flow and shine are some of the many possible blissful states of mind and life.

These are just as few of the bliss states of *sat-chit-ananda*, some of which are more passive and some of which can be more active. Among others, they include inner peace and calm, tranquility, having pristine clarity, mental one-pointedness, being present in the moment of *now* ("presence"), being centered and mentally quiet, feeling fully alive with physical comfort/bliss and lightness but without mental complexities, mental freshness with full lucidity, sunniness (a quiet inner optimism, happiness and energy), flow state, brightness, shine and glow etcetera. These are all forms of *ananda* which includes inner happiness or cheerfulness from within. They are some of the preferred steady state modes of beingness that you would *prefer* to be experiencing all the time and can *remain experiencing for long periods* of time without getting bored or irritated or fatigued by them. They are sustainable and non-irritating beautific states of mind.

Through spiritual practice you want your ordinary mind, which is the same mind as the mind of enlightenment, to attain a degree of inner luminosity, sharpness (clarity), calm and enjoyment as its steady state nature. This is what you want to cultivate towards because you want to enjoy these states even if you don't attain the higher spiritual bodies in this life. The more you can cultivate them, the more they can become a natural part of your character and personality in subsequent incarnations. Isn't that wonderful?

In particular, the state of flow is a form of bliss since it is a clear mind of concentration that can become immersed in life yet is free of mental annoyances, agitations and distractions. During flow you use your mind and abilities to their full potential while immersed in some activity, your actions might require effort but seem intelligently spontaneous and effortless, and you relish the moment. You are clear but immersed in the moment, and this is the proper way to be. The state of shine or brightness is a steady state type of subliminal joy or happiness that naturally exudes from you without effort so that there is no loss of energy, and which easily affects your environment. Sunniness is a more vibrant and hence excited state of constant bliss like optimism, and is a natural personality trait that almost reaches the unsustainable stage of overt happiness, cheerfulness or joy. These are states that combine a joy of life with a state of clear illumination and a body that is comfortable due to its health and vitality.

Many spiritual schools promote meditation so that you master certain mental skills such as concentration or mindfulness, and so that you can achieve an enjoyable quieting of your mind's inner narrative. However, they really want you to experience these states of mind as your accomplishment. Our natural mental state is to be peaceful and happy until we disturb it, and many spiritual schools want you to be able to regain this underlying state that lacks all forms of extraneous pollution. You also want to transform your personality so that you can enjoy more active states of bliss on a regular basis rather than some theoretically empty mental state that is tranquil but absent of all forms of mentation. To regularly experience more mental states of compassion and kindness, sunniness, shine or micro-flow, etcetera as personality traits requires cultivation practice such as changing your outlooks of the world.

You are certainly not trying to cultivate perfect no-thought or thoughtlessness through meditation practices because this is equivalent to being in deep sleep or being insentient. The fact that you can experience bliss (*nirvana*) means that you are aware of your beingness and existence, so it means that when you are happy you fully know you are happy and when sorrowful you are keenly aware of your suffering. The I-sense is still existent in all your states of consciousness. Nothing should be blocked to produce a state of thoughtlessness for then you are an inanimate operative (operating process) within Shakti. Perfect thoughtlessness (no-thought) is a mistaken interpretation about the inner quiet (emptiness) one should be mentally cultivating by mastering concentration and focus, but you often see this mistake in Zen and Advaita Vedanta practitioners who are seeking to achieve some form of egoless pure consciousness that lacks mentation. Yes, your mind should quiet (of wandering thoughts and unwanted irritations) but it should not be eliminated nor disappear. Thoughts will die down naturally the more that you cultivate meditative non-clinging because this will open up more the Qi channels within your brain, and this will produce more internal quiet due to the efficiencies achieved.

What compounds this issue are descriptions of masters sitting motionless "in samadhi" or a "dhyana absorption," and individuals mistakenly think the masters are experiencing thoughtless mental states when they are actually just traveling around elsewhere in the world in their higher spirit bodies. Their spirit is absent so they therefore sit motionless, and people mistakenly think this is some type of mental samadhi (of thoughtlessness or concentration) when it is simply that their spirit isn't present. This holds across all traditions. For instance, Sufi Sheikh Muhammed Hisham Kabbani stated clearly in *The Hierarchy of Saints* that the enlightened often travel from their locations, leaving behind their bodies, to help people who need help and their bodies remain motionless during their absence so you should not disturb them. When the Indian saint Ramakrishna would sit motionless "in trance" some students thought his mind was in some beatific samadhi but he was just absent from his physical shell and traveling about in his higher spiritual bodies. Sometimes masters go on three year retreats in order to (avoid bad fortune or) work on attaining their next higher spiritual body, and they usually do so at locations far removed from civilized society and cities where lots of devas would readily visit them and disturb/bother them by employing their bodies and minds for training purposes, but people don't know this fact either. So much is hidden from the public about the transcendental body attainments as well as the attainment mechanism or their abilities that people are easily lead astray by various stories.

The unperturbed peacefulness of absolute no-thought is equivalent to the insentience of nothingness and non-existence rather than liberation, and so an *ananda* that is a peacefulness-bliss of no-thought or deep sleep is not what we're after. We are interested in the *ananda* bliss of a quiet mind, such as in the flow state, where there still are mental operations going on such as the recognition of one's existence, recognition of objects, a feeling of deep engagement with life, and of course whatever thinking operations (thoughts) that are necessary. We want to experience mental calmness and tranquility within a tableau of lucid clear concentration that is fluid and sharp/clear but absent of agitations and distractions. When the mind is still it is not just enjoyable (blissful) but we can get closer to seeing reality as it really is (given the limitations of our sense perceptions and consciousness) just as you can see better through disturbed water rather than agitated water. At the same time we'd like our physical body to be very comfortable, very blissful, or so comfortable that we can even forget the feeling that it is there. There are many types of physical bliss we can cultivate but it requires exercise, diet and lots of inner energy work.

While we all want to be happy and experience cheerfulness and joy, these excited mental states are considered disturbances or agitations compared to the flow state or the refined peacefulness of calm tranquility, so while they are enjoyable mental-emotional states we should seek higher bliss states that more refined for our naturally tranquil temperament rather than these lower states of joyous excitation. From the vantage point of the higher stages of refined bliss, the lower states of joyousness are a disquieting irritation or disturbance. Yes, we should regularly experience them and pursue them, but for the basis of our personality we should also seek to cultivate higher stages of equanimity, bliss and shine.

A state of peacefulness (emptiness), comfortable (physical) lightness or peaceful, glowing shine are getting closer to a maintainable bliss you might always wish to dwell within, especially when you remember that the self is simply a bundle of fleeting states, a combination of physical and mental aggregates working together interdependently in a flux of momentary change ruled by the laws of cause and effect. The idea of cultivating unmoved tranquility or mental oneness is to achieve pristine illumination - a clear mental state that can experience the moment of beingness without negative internal complexities. Through calm tranquility you will not just enjoy the experience of life but can also make better deliberations with greater care so that you can more reliably attain your personal goals and develop the highest excellences.

You cannot say that the worldly phenomena you see within your mind don't exist, but you cannot say that they exist as "inherent realities" or exist in the way in which they appear to us. You cannot say that Shakti doesn't exist, but it doesn't exist in the way we assume that it does either, yet there *is* an apparent (objective, factual) existence there in front of us that we experience/know through our consciousness. The phenomena of Shakti (the universe) are empty of intrinsic existence and only exist as temporary appearances (instantaniations) that dependently arise with borders that turn out to be the entirety of Shakti. Phenomena are conditionally defined so they arise through an infinite number of interconnections with physical laws, energy, other objects and so forth. Thus there is nothing inherently there as a singular, independently pure phenomenon. In fact, the truth and reality of the universe together *with even your consciousness* are a unity of oneness. Your consciousness is part of Shakti, but you can grab hold of it and make of yourself whatever you want.

Objects, events, entities, forces or processes always have *an infinite composite nature.* However, their inherent changeability due to their intrinsic impermanence gives you a freedom – the potential to change their nature and thus any conditions you encounter in life, as well as your own attributes through self-cultivation. The continuous frothing changefulness of phenomena means that humans must learn how to quickly adapt to the ever-changing conditions of the world to ensure their survival, and to survive they also need to rely on one another in this world of continuous changes. These are some of the keys to eliminating your personal suffering in life, improving your living conditions and circumstantial environments, and ensuring your survival. Because you can change conditions, you should think about the following question: "Why not pursue positive purposes in life that improve conditions for as many people as possible?"

Remember, although you perceive a universe of formal objects what you are actually perceiving is the primordial essence alone. As to this pure, unpolluted foundational substrate, It never changes into anything else so nothing but Itself pervades It. Objects are simply empty appearances that we can consider as an ever-changing description of its infinite potential attributes. The name "universe" or "cosmos" is superimposed on It, but what we call the "universe," "Shakti," "Logos," "Manifestation," "The Triple Realm," or "All" is really nothing but the fundamental essence. On one level we see discrete phenomena, on another level they are one single interconnected soup, and at the ultimate level they are all the one primordial unchanging essence-substance. Individual objects, Shakti and the fundamental substrate are one just as the Holy Trinity of the Son, Holy Spirit and Father within Christianity is said to be one.

Thus you can say that the original nature or foundational substrate neither has attributes nor lacks attributes. It is not "without attributes" since the world of manifestation appears, and yet It does not inherently possess any attributes because It is empty of all marks, signs or phenomena just like empty space. Thus, you cannot say It is pure (without phenomena) because manifestation certainly appears within It, which is what we see and experience. You also cannot say It is impure since those phenomenal appearances of manifestation are actually just It and only It. Although stationary, non-transforming, and unmoving without activity you cannot say It is inert because phenomena have somehow arisen as a realm of continuously changing appearances within It. You can't say It is active (non-inert) because It never moves or changes Its clear substance.

This is all summarized in the *Heart Sutra* and *Diamond Sutra* of Buddhism, and in the conversation between Krishna and Arjuna in the *Bhagavad Gita*. Unfortunately, few people understand that this is the meaning of these texts and that these are some of the teachings they are trying to transmit. The basic idea is that *phenomena don't inherently exist but only apparently exist, temporarily, in a conditional way due to interdependent origination. This includes human beings and their property of consciousness. Phenomena are only known because our consciousness reflects them internally in the nature of a flowing dream of representations.* Further, the fabrication of conceptions within our consciousness to represent the worldly reality we experience only produces an "imaginary" or "constructed" reality/world that is a sentient picture that does not transcend Shakti either. *Lastly, regardless of any higher knowledge like this, we must still perform our duties in the world but cultivate to achieve enlightenment.*

Shakti lacks intrinsic sentient beings having an innate own-nature but contains apparent sentient beings while the foundational nature contains no phenomena at all. Hence the Advaita Vedanta sage Nisargadatta said, "The real never dies – the unreal never lived." Shakti lacks any true things called "living beings" so they are the "unreal who never lived." Shakti is actually a neutral, insentient, inanimate, purely material-energetic realm while living beings and consciousness are just processes within Shakti that we have segmented out through consciousness. At the highest level of viewing them as fundamental energies and field they don't even have solidity anymore. We only call living beings "living beings" and say they have consciousness as a means of identification but this isn't the way things really are on an absolute level. Living beings are essentially just portions of Shakti that we delineate with our minds; there are no such things as independent living beings in reality.

There is no such inherent, intrinsic, innate, or independent thing as a sentient being. There are only *conventional designations of us as living beings* for we are processes, events or living objects having consciousness that each assume he is an inherently existent entity independent of the universe rather than interpenetratively defined and joined with all else in existence. Our consciousness does not "transcend the material universe" either since the thinker, thinking and thoughts are all matter-energy processes within the one matter-energy field fabric of insentient Shakti. Thus consciousness is just another material, phenomenal process within scintillating Shakti although we consider consciousness something that transcends Shakti. Since there is no such true thing as a "sentient being" since this is merely a designation for an apparent portion of Shakti, there is no such true/real thing as sentience either. Insentient Shakti through all its evolutions cannot produce anything other than more processes within itself that are just itself rather than something independent that transcends it. We are all within the Triple Realm and there is no escaping to a Fourth Realm of existence, hence we must learn how to make the best of it and ourselves. We can, should and must cultivate to make ourselves better and our conditions better.

We cannot escape Shakti, which is why we must learn how to control its changes. We cannot escape ourselves, unless we become annihilated, hence we must learn how to control and transform ourselves. The problem with monks and nuns who spiritually cultivate is that they work primarily to cultivate states of quiet mind without actually knowing what they are doing or why. In terms of the capabilities of the mind, they spend years cultivating just one or two aspects since they don't have the proper perspective. How unfortunate! If they actually know enough to start directly cultivating the higher transcendental bodies possible because of our material structure, they typically don't work at mastering significant skills that manipulate and control the changes of phenomena as is emphasized by science and in Taoism. You have to work at cultivating your consciousness and its capabilities, your personality/character, your behavior and activities, and your physical body and its energies.

The original nature is the one true reality and permanent existence – single, infinite, all-pervading, omnipresent, uninterrupted, immaculate, indivisible, unchanging, imperishable, beginningless, eternal and without phenomenal stain. Yet appearances/manifestation somehow arise within It, but from the standpoint of this fundamental substratum of manifest reality there is nothing else at all except Itself so there is no such separate or real thing as manifestation. The road of spirituality teaches that your mind, which gives birth to phenomena, should rest in its natural state that is empty of thoughts, and therefore abide in a state akin to your foundational self-nature that is fundamentally peaceful and free yet somehow able to produce conventional reality just as our natural empty mind somehow spontaneously gives rise to thoughts and other content.

Can your mind be like the original nature that lets phenomena/appearances arise within It without interfering with the process? Can you be pure and clear within your awareness while your thoughts arise and you know them as the master of your consciousness? That freedom and bliss along with the highest clarity in being able to see reality as it truly is (given our limitations) in a pristine mental state is the state we want to experience due to meditation practice. Thus people on spiritual paths train in meditation.

In fact, the only reason Buddhas stress that the fundamental substrate is empty is so that there is some extra motivation, because of the parallels to a tranquil mind of clarity, for imitating that emptiness *and its detached free state of beingness*. You accomplish this through meditation practice that achieves a host of benefits. One such benefit is that you become mindful of the flow of your thoughts through the meta-cognition of knowing them but not fusing with them, which only happens if you cultivate a base of mental clarity as the center of your I-sense. Staying aware of our thought-stream gradually produces an enjoyable quieting of the mind-stream so "emptiness meditation" is promoted as a practice for this benefit of attaining mental calmness and clarity and thereby a blissful experience of existence.

There are other attendant benefits as well. Meditation practice also helps decrease the tendency for mental wandering because it trains your concentration muscles, so your mental illumination should never be turned off in an attempt to produce a scenario without thoughts. You are trying to cultivate mental freedom along with focus, sharpness and clarity. Consequently, through meditation practice we can eventually experience a state of clear awareness while ignoring mental agitations that might cause our minds to wander and during this time we can stay aware of the pure clarity within us. Meditation is simply a training mechanism. *To attain the deva body of enlightenment, you must cultivate meditation practice and you must also perform inner energy work.*

Nonetheless, mental quiescence is a peaceful state achievable through meditation where consciousness still shines because objects are still recognized, and thoughts still come and go but your mind seems quieter than usual because the inner narrative is silenced, its habitual afflictions have been emptied away, your awareness doesn't cling to thoughts, and you develop a natural state of concentrated focus as in flow.

Another reason we train in letting go of our thought-stream is because we make it far easier for higher spiritual beings to use their Qi during that time to help purify and stabilize our own subtle bodies, which need periodic communion with higher energies in order to maintain their health and integrity unless you do a lot of internal energy work on your own through the right *nei-gong* practices. The intercession of enlightened beings within our bodies is regularly going on all the time, but humans do not know it. This is how Buddhas, who have attained the higher bodies that live extremely long lives, try to maintain the life of lower sentient beings and preserve them from disintegration (until they too attain those very long existences) since they are ultimately just patterns of nature.

Those on spiritual roads are taught to engage in spiritual practices that train them to let go of their minds so that their Qi can flow more freely, which then washes and strengthens the structure of their inner subtle body. They are taught to detach from their thought-stream during spiritual practices so that their Qi can also more easily be rotated by junior devas, and then by higher spiritual masters whose time is more valuable so they don't normally do this coarse purification work.

By detaching from thoughts you detach from your body's inner Qi circulation since your life force Qi and your thoughts are connected. This detachment makes it easier for your Qi to circulate within the etheric Qi channels of your subtle body (since it isn't then attached to thoughts that might inhibit or bias its circulation). This better Qi flow then rejuvenates or strengthens the underlying structure of your subtle body. Also, letting go of our thought-stream gradually produces an enjoyable quieting of our mind-stream so the meditative pursuit of quiescence is emphasized in many traditions, such as Zen, where your mind is predominantly clear and quiet.

Many Hindu sadhus, yogis and monks are taught *Vairagya* detachment practice instructions to "detach from desires and sense objects to achieve liberation." They're taught that they are empty of a self or anything pertaining to self, and that objects are free of an intrinsic self-nature too, so that they achieve a type of mental awareness-release (of clinging) from mentally stationing themselves in this theme. Similarly, in the *Diamond Sutra* it is said that "fearless bodhisattvas do not create the perception of a self. Nor do they create the perception of a being, a life or soul." It also teaches us to give without being attached to sights, sounds, smells, tastes, touch or *dharma* ... to not be ruled by objects (seen by our illusion generating consciousness) and give without being attached to anything at all.

Hindu sadhus, yogis and monks taught to disconnect their mind from the concept of being the doer of actions and unite their minds with God (which is a form of emptiness meditation too). They're taught that God is the cause of everything and is the real (ultimate) doer in their life so they should surrender completely to God and offer Him everything they have, including their thoughts and behavior. Through detachment they can live in peace.

They're taught that they are "pure consciousness in nature," and that the fundamental universal substrate – the basis of the manifest cosmos – is pure consciousness, which is nonsense but an effective way to spur meditation practice and peacefulness. There is no permanent consciousness that exists as a substratum for beingness because consciousness arises as a process that requires a body and internal energy. There is no such thing as an infinite field of undifferentiated energy that is consciousness. However, the absolute nature of consciousness is the unchanging fundamental substratum just as is the case for everything else.

They are taught that if they give up their ego and remain absorbed in God then they will experience bliss, which happens because they consequently start quieting their mind and gradually touch inner peacefulness (since this type of absorption is a form of emptiness/formlessness meditation). Thus their Qi will also start to invigorate their physical body during that time. Of course you cannot "give up your ego" or you will become mindless like the natural world, so there is no benefit in getting rid of the I-self. The idea is to let go of attachments and connections in order to rest in an abode of mental emptiness, and it doesn't matter how you get there. Christian monks and priests are told to "find peace in the contemplation of God" in order to receive the same benefits of mental stilling and Qi transformation.

Yogis and sadhus are commonly taught that they are not the body, and to live like someone without a body so that they become detached and attain a serene nature. Some are taught to disassociate from all mental objects that the mind connects with and to focus continuous attention on the sense of "I," which is the center of your thoughts and perceiver of your perceptions. If you focus on the I-sense and stop consciousness from connecting with all exterior phenomena then the individuality of the I can no longer exist, so it will have to withdraw and disappear ... and you can then realize its inherent unreality.

Thus they are taught not to identify with their ego (I-ness) or their thoughts (emotions, desires, drives, attachments, sufferings, will, etcetera) or perceptions or the relative aspects of their being. They are not to identify with their body, mind, thinking (discrimination), emotions, will, the perceptions of their senses or the manifest universe. They are taught to practice giving up the I-concept and achieve an unattached state of formlessness because we are all the thoughtless Supreme Nature. They are taught that they should in their spiritual practice detach from thoughts, desires and emotions to find an internal peace as if nothing exists.

These are all just various types of meditation practice, which is championed because of some common objectives. You might develop certain beneficial mental skills and personality characteristics from such practices, but the most important principle is that these practices enable your internal subtle body of Qi/Prana to be more easily purified so that it can independently emerge from the physical body. Spiritual practitioners across the world search for text-compatible cultivation practices (exercises sanctioned by the orthodox spiritual texts of their religion) that are essentially (1) inner energy practices and (2) empty mind meditation practices like this that can help produce higher mental skills, mental moods and the Srotapanna (first stage) body of enlightenment. Religions try to hide from adherents the truth about the deva body attainment, and in this hiding thereby pacify practitioners who do not achieve it in this life (if they knew it was the *true objective* of spiritual practice) by posing all sorts of other mental realizations as enlightenment instead, which particularly misleads people in Buddhism and Hinduism.

Many Hindu sadhus, yogis and monks are taught to hold nothing in their minds, become empty and always imagine they are boundless as space like the fundamental essence. They're taught to only be conscious of the (empty) Self and perceive everything as nothing but our formless Self, which resultantly gives rise to detachment (awareness-release). They're taught to consider everything as their Self so as to become desireless and happy. They're taught that nothing can bring lasting happiness in life but you already have it within the naturally peaceful nature of your mind, and so they should stop running after excitement or the pleasures of the senses and cultivate dispassion and detachment towards their thoughts and emotions to find relief. You don't get happiness outside of yourself but already have it inside you except that you disturb it through mental attachments, desires, and agitations or other turbulence like the passions. Some are taught to continually think "I am the Supreme nature" and others are taught to think "I shall become the Supreme being" (by offering themselves entirely to God) all as a means of cultivating their mind and Qi/Prana.

Hence people are taught awareness, detachment, mindfulness, non-clinging, dispassion or emptiness practice in various forms and don't realize the underlying principle that is being taught. Such practices calm the mind and improve your Qi flow as is necessary for the purification and strengthening of your subtle body that is normally released only upon death, but which can attain an independent life *during life* if you engage in spiritual practice. This is what all the genuine saints, sages or yogis attain, and higher bodies still although those achievements are typically called dhyana attainments in order that people do not realize that they are actually physical body attainments. By improving your inner Qi flow you can achieve an inner comfort of your physical body and a sense of physical lightness.

Better Qi circulation will not only calm your mind but also sharpen your mental clarity and acuity (achieving what Zen calls "pristine clarity" while others call it sharpness, focus and awareness) due to better Qi flow circulation directly into and throughout the brain. This makes it possible to achieve higher beautiful mental states such as presence, being centered, pristine beingness, freshness and flow. The enlightenment mind is nothing but more peaceful, aware, blissful, uncluttered mental states *for your ordinary mind*. Of course, even a cluttered, confused, lethargic or mistaken mind is enlightenment or illumination. If you cultivate your personality and remind yourself of how you want to be, you can cultivate other mental states too such as a continuous quiet happiness state of refinement that projects out of you called "shine."

When you realize that you are like a dream person in a dream world because you understand the truth of your self-nature, and that what is perceived in this world is in the nature of a dream (similar to what one sees in dreams) then it becomes easier to start attaining some of these beautiful mental states. Why? Because you achieve awareness-release and can then let go of other things since they don't matter so much anymore. This knowledge makes it easier to detach from objects and desires to find relief and pursue meaningful significance instead. For instance, if you take a rope for snake then you'll react with fear, but if your perception is accurate then you'll react differently. Hence realization not only helps you become free of ignorance but free of desires (and other unsettling emotional reactions) too. Detachment arises from knowing what the reality is, and with this knowledge someone who is practicing control of their mind will find that their mentation gradually becomes more and more silent, like water calming down, and within that calmness their mind becomes capable of greater clarity and discernment. "Me" and "mine" also progressively silence and one begins to get a glimpse of that reality.

A whole level of suffering will depart when trivial bondages and clinging habits melt away due to detachment-release and this sort of realization-awakening. Then you will live much more authentically with a sense of inner freedom, independence and liberation, and much more vibrantly because your inner Qi flow should become more robust as well. But suffering cannot be eliminated entirely in life, so everyone needs to work towards well-being as well where the goal of reducing suffering is a subset within that greater objective. Well-bring is not just a mental state but something you must create through your own vigorous activity, but unfortunately many monks and nuns never learn how to do this. They never even learn skills that they'd like to have if they attained a Buddha body, which is an unfortunate lapse due to improper training paths.

Within the ideal of well-being is the need to create a brighter future for yourself and others rather than just dispassionately accepting everything. In working to create a brighter future for yourself, because we are a community of creatures connected to one another it is essential that you should also work towards creating a brighter future for society by fostering brotherhood among men and helping to improve all their conditions. An enlightened person who can "hear the cries of the world" wants to help end the sufferings of all people and relieve their pains. He wants to enrich their lives and protect them and their interests. An enlightened person wants order and justice established within society, wants to encourage people to improve themselves by nurturing excellence, and doesn't want to let society stay at the same stage of development for too long and become subject to ossification. Life involves growth and progress produces happiness, so people usually don't feel fulfilled when they stop growing.

If an individual only focuses on non-clinging as their spiritual practice they will neglect the importance of performing acts of charity and making improvements in the world to help move society forward. One should work not just on improving oneself and one's own conditions but at seeding the world to make it healthier, and working to improve general human happiness. Accenting the good wherever possible includes leaving behind a legacy of improved conditions for others. We should all be working towards establishing better social justice, social equality, human welfare, prosperity and progress.

Actually, many cultivation teachings neglect the ideal of progress because they were especially designed for poor people in poor countries where there was little chance of gains that would help them escape their poverty. Therefore teachings help generally people mentally bear their poverty and sufferings in life (hence the emphasis on detachment) while people work to cultivate the higher transcendental bodies that will free them from the material realm of poverty and suffering forever. By letting go of their thoughts, impulses and desires (via detachment) people naturally reduce their desires, mental suffering, and any internal disturbances to their peace of mind. They also free up their Qi circulation so that it can be more easily transformed, which is another one of the ultimate objectives. But if you are not a virtuous person then no deva or Buddha will work on your Qi to help purify it in preparation for the higher body attainments, so virtuous behavior and mental purity are also strongly stressed on the spiritual trail.

What people don't recognize is that many cultivation techniques are just disguised methods for helping you cultivate mental emptiness, and non-clinging is just one of them. For instance, the Buddhist meditation teachings to cultivate the samadhi of infinite emptiness, the samadhi of infinite consciousness, the samadhi of infinite nothingness and the samadhi that is neither thought nor no-thought are also "emptiness meditations" designed to help you practice letting go of your thoughts so that your Qi can more easily be rotated and thus purified through that refining process.

Gorakhnath's descriptions of *Anama* (the nameless origin, which is the empty fundamental substrate)[48] also serve as alternative meditations on emptiness that are similar to the four formless absorptions of Buddhism: *nija-shakti* is described as eternally present, absolutely pure, motionless (without any pulsation), imperceptible (differenceless), and an undisturbed state of consciousness while *para-sakti* is immeasurable existence, undifferentiated, infinite and unmanifest. Meher Baba in *God Speaks* also provides descriptions of the gradual solidification/condensation of subtle energy into matter (which correspond to the emergence and evolution of Creation out of nothingness) that also serve as a form of formlessness meditation practice. Since the universe is composed of many etheric layers or planes of existence, in some schools this is symbolized by the space, air, fire, water and then earth element that represents our own solid-most plane of existence. Thus they develop visualization practices based on different elements transforming into one another in a type of condensation process, or espouse visualizations involving an increasing or decreasing intensity of light (such as in Sufi master Ibn Habash Suhrawardi's Illuminationism), but these visualization practices are meant to develop concentration skills rather than are emptiness practices.

The practice of "supremely surrendering to God" espoused in Christianity, Hinduism, Islam, etc. is yet another alternative form of formless meditation practice, as are the Advaita Vedanta instructions to "Take refuge in the eternal peace of your True Self." There are countless forms of "emptiness" meditation that involve detaching from your thought-stream to achieve a quieter mental state more pure (absent of desires and attachments), and people usually don't even recognize that their spiritual practice is aimed at this pursuit even though, as you can see from reviewing these various methods, this is the shared commonality within many, many techniques. *A major difference among traditions is the various forms by which this principal practice is transmitted.*

In truth, no one attains absolute desirelessness or true detachment. Why? Because attention is an *omnipresent factor of consciousness* so attention is a mental factor always operating within the mind, and attachment to an object of consciousness is always there for as long as focus and attention lasts. If a spiritual master truly seems to be detached and have no desires it is usually because he has attained the higher transcendental bodies where his spirit is living in upper realms, but he uses this earthly body as an appendage or empty shell to teach people. Hence it is easy to preach of desirelessness and detachment to people on the earthly plane (and act that

---

[48] See *The Natha Philosophy and Ashtanga-Yoga* (V. S. Bhatnagar) or *Siddhasiddhantapaddhatih* (Dr. M. L. Garote and Dr. G. K. Pai).

way) since the suffering experienced within it is to him like a dream to his higher bodies. He's not there! However, within the highest plane he is still subject to desires so don't cheat yourself about a supposed perfection of their character – since you are predominantly residing in a higher planed body your desires focus on that plane instead of the lower ones.

In Vajrayana and Tantra (tantric yoga) the practice of inner energy work is stressed along with meditation practice. In Taoism inner *nei-gong* practice and going along with the flow are emphasized. Emptiness meditation and clear awareness are championed in Zen. Monitoring and correcting your thoughts along with proper behavior are emphasized in Confucianism, and in Christianity you are taught to do good deeds and to extend the spirit of service to sacrifice yourself for others while working at self-improvement. Confucianism, in particular, says that "refining your self lies in balancing your mind" and stresses that you should work to make your virtues brighter while pursuing consummate conduct and also cultivating calmness and clarity.

Different principles are stressed in different religions but genuine religions all share the same stages of spiritual body attainments that are gained through inner energy transformations that purify your Qi/Prana. Why? Because they are non-denominational results, so everyone goes through them. While learning how to calmly observe your thought-stream and detach from desires, cravings, carnal-materialistic impulses, etc. is a common feature in most paths, detachment from the outer world and one's inner world is particularly emphasized in poor countries where the adepts will have to experience poverty while cultivating.

Detachment from our thought-stream by abiding as the "master of awareness" allows us to transcend our conditioned behaviors and actually cultivate self-improvement. Self-rectification and self-perfection become possible whenever we don't fuse with our prior conditioning but through pristine awareness remain transcendent and able in real time to change our thoughts and behavior that are the product of our prior programming. On the spiritual road we need to practice mindfulness so that we rest in our clear awareness and become independent of our thoughts and thinking. We want to have such a presence of mind that we realize what we are actually doing in the moment so that we can correct ourselves whenever we see we are errant. This is called "being the (inner) master." Such recognition only becomes possible when we become independent of our thought-stream and look at what we are currently thinking and doing with a sense of oversight that is apart from a clinging fusion with thought activity.

Zen practice is aimed at teaching this mental flexibility and freedom. It also stresses the moment of presence as well as clear concentration or one-pointedness that is a clear mind of awareness achieved through the consistent meditation practice of inner witnessing. Further, by not rigidly clinging to our mind-stream (which produces a kind of restraint or bias on our inner Qi circulation) this openness provides more opportunity for the creativity of new thoughts to spontaneously arise within us.

By also recognizing that material things are not inherently existing phenomena but are simply transient (conditional) designations that always change their form within the ocean of our manifest Self, and recognizing that we too are selfless beings due to our own non-intrinsic natures, we can attain a measure of release from the tendency to become intoxicated with phenomena. With mental awareness-release due to our wisdom it becomes easier to give up covetousness, attachments or the grasping after phenomena. The mental release resulting from awareness of both our true nature and the true nature of reality (objects) should lighten our greed, covetousness, insistence, grasping and attachment or even hostility towards objects and people. This is why it is stressed in spiritual cultivation.

If we focus on performing our actions in life but being detached from desire then we also plant the seeds of worldly results without desiring those fruits. This can socially translate into activities such as working to help other people in life. In *the Bhagavad Gita* it is said that ignorant people perform actions by being attached to actions whereas wise people perform actions unattached, which helps the welfare and preservation of the worlds. Those who give up attachments to actions and their fruits are always content due to their non-abiding or non-dwelling. After such renunciation, tranquility is attained.

By realizing that phenomena are transient and changeable and that we are not inherent identities either, with such themes in our minds the fires of attachment naturally lessen. There is no reason to grasp at phenomena when all things are recognized as impermanent and our selves are realized as not inherent, fixed things. Desires are realized as transient mental flickerings that will quickly disappear if we don't hold onto them or play with them. Why then should I run after things so greedily?

Our personality/character is derived from a large series of experiences that have given us Knowledge and colored our consciousness through the perfuming of our mental patterns, and it affects all that we do. What we do creates our fortunes but what we do depends upon our personality, character, psyche, disposition and perspectives so our personality creates our fate because it causes our fate. A large part of the spiritual trail concerns transforming our personality or character, in effect polishing and purifying it. Otherwise we cannot merit the attainment of enlightenment.

Desires and cravings are due to your sense organs and your mind. If you can give up all mental craving through detachment and just let them flow through you as if you were the stainless original nature then you can become more peaceful, free and content because you won't identify with or hold onto mental modifications that cause dissatisfaction and pain in life. Through detachment you won't become controlled by your emotions. If you learn how to stay detached from painful emotions then they will just flow through you and you'll be done with them rather quickly. You'll experience pain and suffering and then be done with it.

Our True Reality is blissful, peaceful, tranquil, non-attached and devoid of sufferings caused by any agency. It is untouched by the grief and misery of the world, free from passion, jealousy, greed, pride, frustration, rage, hatred and the rest. Within It no sorrow is found. Can you practice so that your mind is like this? Whatever arises within your mind is not destined to stay but to flow away. How can you train your mind to deal with unavoidable but transient suffering?

You are a being without any form, so you can adapt your apparent form and *train its functions (skills) to be anything you like*. This is because in the highest sense there is no fixed individual that suffers, commits karmic deeds, attains *nirvana* or brings things to perfection. There is an apparent being but no *real* doer of deeds – Knowledge is the doer of deeds – so your attributes are not fixed and you have no reason to cling to any forms of suffering. This is the principle taught within the *Diamond Sutra*.

There is no intrinsic permanent core being in us (except for the immortal substrate) and yet conventionally we exist because we are an agglomeration or collection of molecules, energy and conditions in flux that together produce what we call a "being with consciousness." Amazing! We have the freedom to become of ourselves whatever we want and develop whatever abilities we set our minds on. It just so happens that because matter is a condensed from of energy we can decompose the energy of our physical body into a higher transcendental body clone, and keep doing this through cultivation until we reach the highest transcendental body possible after which decomposition is no longer feasible thereafter.

The primordial essence, the ultimate universal ground state, the primal substrate of reality is by nature equanimous, peaceful, stationary, blissful and free. So should be your clear awareness as it encounters events including suffering, so your witnessing should not fuse with mental states just as the original nature never fuses with the wonders of Shakti. Joy and suffering are both to be experienced within the wonder of consciousness, and naturally you should try to reduce any suffering states of mind through as many legitimate, proper ways as possible. Spiritual adherents know they should cultivate empathic, flexible, open, "empty" minds but take the instructions for spiritual practice incorrectly. The dulling blunt-my-thoughts pathways of no-thought, nothingness, or an emptiness/absence of thought are not the correct path for eliminating suffering since they are the same as insentience, non-existence or annihilation whereas the Great Perfection is existence-consciousness-bliss.

The release from all mental fermentation simply means mental detachment, which is to let things arise and then pass away without holding onto them unnecessarily. Suffering arises, suffering is experienced, suffering passes and this is the proper way of being as well as the bliss of life. The knowing of existence is a type of suffering, and it is also our bliss of experience. We certainly must learn methods to eliminate pain and suffering, avoid it or manage it but we also need to take pains to accept it as well as restructure conditions that would eliminate its possibility in the first place so that we are all always experiencing improving conditions with less suffering for all.

Because the mind should remain free, one of the principles for operating it properly is that we should not try to fuse with desires since when unfulfilled they produce suffering. If we fuse with sense indulgences we will lose our sense of self as well and experience suffering when they end. We should not overly attach to any type of emotion or mental state or sensual perception. When you are just doing ordinary things in life you should not let any negative mental states take possession of you to the extent of fusion.

As to the worldly phenomena we see around us, they are a mass of interlocking conditions/inter-relationships following one another in an unbroken succession until they sufficiently change enough to *noticeably* transform into something else (though they are transforming all the time). "Emptiness" (the lack of an own-nature) is therefore an attribute of objects. The only dependable thing that is real, and which therefore does not change otherwise it wouldn't be a dependable "always truth," is the original nature that is empty of phenomena like boundless space. Consciousness too is unreal, but while we have it we should enjoy it.

You can say that phenomena are one and the same as the primordial substance-essence, or that they are the primordial substance-essence, or that they are essentially the primordial substance-essence, they are inherently the primordial substance-essence, permeated by the primordial substance-essence, are supported by the primordial substance-essence, their absolute nature is the primordial substance-essence, they are ultimately empty or they temporarily exist as appearances before instantaneously transforming into something else, or don't inherently exist in some fundamental self-so way, or only apparently exist, and so on.

Some spiritual schools state this in a religious way by saying that the attributes or operations of God are identical with His essence. The Hindu qualified non-dualist Ramanuja would say that this makes us "the body of God" and that we are creations/attributes of His immortal essence, and because of consciousness we are able to experience manifestations of the Divine. Some religions say that God is both transcendent and immanent, which means that God transcends all attributes or phenomena (as is the case with the fundamental substratum that is empty of phenomena like space) and yet is always immanent or present as the support and substance of everything; God permeates all things as their ultimate substance and support including pervading all forms, teachings, sects, creeds and religions.

Whether you say it is because men have consciousness or because they are godly, men have the freedom to arrange phenomena as they deem fit within the universe but in so doing the consequences of their actions will always be bound to its rules of causality and rebound to them. Causality means cause and effect, stimulus and response, interdependent origination and Indra's net. Causality is karma, karma is causality. Your bondage in the universe is to the net of causality, yet you are free to try or develop into anything you want according to the transformations possible within the realm of causality. All things are bound to the net of causation, meaning the laws of cause and effect (such as the laws of chemistry, physics, etc.) that order phenomena in the cosmos, thus ruling them. Causality structures the infinite network of apparent existence, Nature or the universe (Shakti), which is why manifest reality is called "origination through dependence (causality)." Dependence means that the origination of any object depends on the existence of everything else in a cause-and-effect relationship. If we can learn those interrelationships we can learn how to transform manifest reality for our benefit, which is the Great Learning necessary for our existence and prosperity.

The realm of causality rules the field of emanations, Shakti, but not the original nature, so the Great Learning for a sentient being includes learning how to master, manage or control the patterns and laws of causality within the field of manifestations (Shakti, Nature, the universe or Triple Realm) to gain any results desired – whether they be *Artha, Kama, Moksha* (the higher spiritual bodies), status within dominance hierarchies, relationships, health, peace of mind, wealth, success, prosperity, happiness, spiritual liberation and so forth. This requires the pursuit of wisdom and skillfulness; you must train in acquiring knowledge and understanding and then you will know what to do in circumstances and how to do it. Thereafter, because of your awareness and an intellect of understanding, you can apply yourself to make efforts to engineer the results you wish. You train in understanding and active skillfulness, and then you work to do what needs to be done to achieve your goals and objectives.

This is what you should be pursuing in life, and in particular you should be learning how to cultivate the transcendental spiritual bodies that provide you with a better, longer-lived existence in more pleasant realms. Those bodies give you more power to help people on lower planes of existence, which is another reason to pursue them. You need to achieve them in order to fulfill vows of compassion to help others or to achieve an even greater meaning or significance to your existence. To successfully cultivate this outcome requires virtue and merit, learning and wisdom, and then much cultivation effort.

Since phenomena appear *for us* (because we have minds) we must learn how to master them if we wish to live better lives with less suffering and greater well-being. The transitory nature of conventional reality, rather than the ultimate reality that is unchangeable, means that there is always a chance to make situations better because they must by nature ultimately change, and our job as conscious beings is to learn how to guide those changes. Since we need to master phenomena to improve our circumstances by producing more fortuitous states for ourselves, others and future generations this means that we should not restrict our studies to just spiritual texts but must pursue expertise in the sciences (such as medicine, agriculture, etc.), social studies (psychology, human relations, diplomacy, persuasion, etc.) and even esoteric arts such as astrology (so that we might learn how to intervene to change fate). Because phenomena are open to change this gives us the opportunity to alter phenomena, and our fates, for the better such as the condition of our bodies that can be favorably altered through diet and exercise or the quality of our Qi/Prana that can be improved through *neijia* exercises. If phenomena were not transitory but had fixed natures then no conditions could ever change and we could not improve ourselves or advance our fortunes.

Without doing anything, the primordial substrate of Parabrahman sustains the whole universe. As the basis of the cosmos or Its universal soul, It is essentially the ultimate Doer of all things that acts without acting and does without doing. It is the "causeless cause" because It is the ultimate unchanging support of all existence. Armed with all this understanding and the facts of your innate selflessness and ability to change/transform, which constitutes a *prajna* transcendental wisdom awakening or realization, recognize that you need to orient yourself correctly in the world and become a more active doer who creates your fate. It is up to you to make matters better. It is up to you to seek liberation by cultivating a better personality that merits ascension through the higher spiritual bodies, and then the meditation and inner energy work that is required. Now is the time for you to decide how to direct your life and what you should work towards achieving.

In summary, the fundamental substratum or essence of Creation is neither pure nor impure; It is empty of everything (it is pure) and yet contains infinite emanations, manifestations or appearances (it is impure). Even so, those imperfections or differentiations are essentially the pure Self and the multiplicity we perceive is ultimately an illusion of its characteristics. Therefore It is not nothingness and yet is not anything. Being self-so, It did not come into being, and being permanent It is not going anywhere because It doesn't change into anything else. It does not come from anywhere or anything and is not going anywhere or transforming into anything different. It was never born and will never die; It always was, always is and always will be. It is devoid of a before and after, increase or decrease, an above and below, and an interior and exterior. There is nothing else beside It, which is why some people refer to It as God, Alonehood or the One Without a Second. It is eternal and everlasting, immutable, dependable, reliable and true. It is thus real because It stays. It is the substrate of All so everything is ultimately It. As Advaita Vedanta states, "All is Brahman, there is nothing that is not Brahman, Brahman is the only thing that truly exists." "Brahman" is another word for This our ultimate nature.

Somehow the appearance of Shakti, or *samsara*, has arisen within It. We don't know how this happened since the primal substrate cannot change, so Buddhism labels that process of generation "Ignorance" to denote that we don't know anything about the process of Creation or Emanation since we don't understand this. The act of Creation is therefore a mystery. The emergent entities, manifestations, emanations or "karmic formations" within Shakti compose themselves within Shakti's all-encompassing field of manifestation while still retaining their nature as being the primal substrate in absolute essence – a formless pure substratum like empty space. Hence, "Brahman is everything and everything is Brahman." Everything is fundamentally the primal substratum even though things appear solid to us from their surface aspect.

If you say that "Maya, *samsara* or Shakti does not exist," its appearance and *your life* is right there in front of you, so this isn't true. You cannot doubt your own existence or the appearance of the world in front of you. External realities are actually perceived so they are not non-existent! Your consciousness definitely recognizes objects and the world. Aside from sensory imperfections it is the interpretation of what you see that is the issue. Even so, the world is said to be existent because it appears in our consciousness and has an empirical facticity of cause and effect that produces predictability.

Of course if you say, "Maya, *samsara* or Shakti *inherently* exists" then how can that be so? Phenomena conditionally exist so do not have intrinsic natures. What appears to exist only has a brief momentary existence (so brief you might argue that it doesn't exist at all since every state is but a flash appearance) and then changes into something else. A series of instantaniations refreshed just a tiny bit differently one after another in series is like a dream rather than a true reality that you can touch or grasp.

What appears to exist only has a conditional existence rather than an innate, intrinsic, inherent existence that doesn't change. Furthermore, objects seem to exist as solid entities but are mostly empty space conjoined with vibrating energy, and do not exist on their own because all things must participate together in producing one – no object stands on its own. Every iota of manifestation exists not through own-beingness or through independent intrinsic-ness but through the conditionality of interdependent defining. No objects or phenomena are intrinsically established and what conventionally exists does so as an apparition that appears for but a moment before transforming into something else. No thing can be frozen to produce a dependable unchanging reality of what it currently is in the moment. All things are therefore forever ungraspable like a dream or flash of lightning or fragile bubble waiting to pop. The existence of the world is of the nature of a dream ... but we can be a conscious dreamer and enjoy it.

All things lack an inherent self-so nature, so *are not intrinsically so* but as appearances are apparently so. Their lack of an intrinsic existence is called the emptiness of phenomena. They are not independent existences that exist/stand on their own but composite constructions that exist within a single realm of infinite interconnections that looks like an innumerable set of independent objects or multiplicities. They exist due to fields of vibrating interdependencies that together produce a scintillating whole where nothing within it ever stays constant. Not being solid and stable, the world we see appears in the nature of a simplified illusion where we see it (with mental time delay and pictorial simplifications) as solid and stable. That's an illusion. Our consciousness creates the world like a dream or mirage.

Shakti and the original nature together constitute the entire universe. But everything within the cosmos is ultimately empty, meaning that all phenomena lack their own isolated, independent, inherent own-nature. Everything is produced through a dependency on other things, through an infinite Indra's web of interpenetrating multiplicities. In this interfusion, the whole is in every part and every part is also in every other particular. Whatever you experience of phenomena is like a dream or illusion within consciousness that approximates an outer world while excluding many features and dimensions. Despite deceptive appearances, the only thing ever really present is the permanent original nature that is the transcendental, metaphysical, spiritual truth while Shakti is the apparent truth that changes every moment and therefore cannot be fundamentally true or real at all.

The fundamental substratum or primal substrate is your True Self, your true self-nature, your primordial self-essence, your fundamental beingness and It is the primordial universal ground. Shakti is your body and mind but not your true self. In Buddhism the foundational substratum that is our True Self is often called "Emptiness" to denote a substrate that lacks phenomenal attributes for It is purely Itself – nameless Alonehood, the One Without a Second, the sole Reality that is empty of everything else but Itself just like empty space. You are taught to cultivate mental states of emptiness so that you stop grasping after phenomena and attain mental peace and bliss from the release brought about through this awareness.

Starting from nothing in terms of circumstances (emptiness), we can use our consciousness to pursue or create whatever we want to experience in the universe because it is open to change and we are free to chart our own destiny within it. The Great Learning for our lives is to assume full control over our bodies and minds, cultivate our bodies and consciousness to their utmost excellence, chart and pursue and achieve goals and achievements we want, and to celebrate life with full awareness and mental-physical bliss. You want to cultivate to the point where your psychological realm has been conquered and you are always in a state of peace, clarity, brightness, lucidity, presence, compassion and kindness, wisdom, flow, lightness, sunniness or shine, etcetera and always pursuing a vibrant engagement with changeable life. You want to always be feeling the comfortableness of your active inner vitality and be experiencing the joy of life in fulfilling self-expression.

So do great things in life! Turn away from mediocrity and start defining your own life. Put fear aside and grab the reigns of courageousness to develop more fully in your own style. Design a life that is fulfilling to you rather than follow a track laid out by others while hoping it will lead to somewhere good. Plan your escape and then make the leap out of your comfort zone to start moving in that direction.

You are the Supreme Self, so have courage and abide in your own glory! You are limitless so create as you wish and go after whatever you desire. Fulfill your personal calling for which you have come into the world. Consequences will occur for whatever you do, but put fear aside, be bold and be creative to take great risks, but temper your courage with prudence and wisdom in crafting your plans so that you act skillfully since actions create consequences. Create wonder for the world and find yourself in creative self-expression and happiness! Become the Buddha that you want to be. Everything you see is nothing but your Self.

Everything you see and experience is your Self in manifestation, so be courageous and withdraw from nothing because you are always facing just yourself. Become fearless and free like our primordial self-nature, but only pursue what is ethical, moral and virtuous. The universe by being existent is actually playing a game with itself, a *Divine Lila*, so do something that gives you a good enough reason for being in the world within this divine play.

Choose whatever you want to accomplish in the universe and then start working towards it. Live life without regrets by avoiding what you know is wrong, but pursue what is virtuous that you want to pursue. Go after what you want and don't hold yourself back due to some barriers in your head or ceiling of limitations you've artificially created in your mind. Don't create the regret of not trying, and don't refuse to evolve yourself because change is inherent to your nature so you might as well guide yourself through changes to a state of more magnificence.

Our fundamental nature is without fear. It is fearless, limitless and without resistance. In freedom and boldness It has given birth to all things that will continue transforming in endless ways throughout eternity. Can you not imitate the courageous outpouring of your fundamental essence? Of course you can, for that is what you are! You put yourself in line with It not just through mental peacefulness but through positive activity that masters transformations.

You need to determine in your life a personal Dream or direction that has ultimate value to you in terms of meaning, satisfaction, significance and fulfillment so that it can guide your life. That aspiration or set of aspirations must exteriorize your highest inner values and your sense of life purpose. Through commitment to a code of conduct and an inner vow or personal mission, only then does life attain meaning and become worthwhile. The idea is to *do good rather than seek happiness*, and then you will not only attain a sense of meaning, purpose and significance in life but *happiness will naturally come from your efforts and their results*. Of course you need to periodically refresh yourself with enjoyments and pleasures too – the *Kama* of Hinduism that makes life bearable. Nonetheless the people who seem the most content in the world are those who help others and especially those who live lives of service. *You become happy by making others happy*. If you can get your attention off yourself and onto others then the roughness and suffering of life become much easier to bear, and you will discover a life of meaning within that service.

Hence, don't hold back on being true to the inner calling of your highest self and any inner mission you may have inside you to do something for people or the world. Don't hold back on being true to yourself, on being your authentic self, and on always trying to live up to your highest best self. Unleash your inner vitality in pursuit of your highest calling. Be courageous. Start from now.

You determine what you will ultimately make of yourself in life. You are beingness without a body, so you are the one who determines how you will develop, what you will develop into, and what you will ultimately create and experience in the conditionally built realm of twinkling, sparkling Shakti. Life runs on the principle of causality and can go in any direction you push causes when you put in the required energy and effort. Your choices and actions will therefore determine the direction and outcome of your life (and the world) according to your efforts and the rules of causality where results are produced by efforts. So apprentice yourself to a system that will get you there - get you to where you want to go and to being what you want to be.

Since you are essentially *The One*, what then is a high enough overarching aspiration worthy of being pursued by you? What mission is worthy of your vitality and life, your thoughts, speech, efforts and time? What inspires you the most? Is your life force worthy of what you are doing? The answer is to help create or become the light you passionately want to see in the world, to fulfill the personal calling for which you have come into the world, train to become the Buddha you want to be. If you are a monk or nun or yogi or sadhu and so on you should start doing that. You should start learning the appropriate skills and partake in charitable activities of that direction.

Imagine who and how you could be and then aim single-mindedly in becoming that. Start thinking like that person, talking like that person, dressing like that person, and behaving like that person, and basically, just practice being that *person until you become that person and are doing what that person should ideally be doing*. Become that person that is the more perfected, cultivated and spiritualized you! Our fundamental nature is in enduring bliss and we can become that way *with special attributes or capabilities* if we tap into our innermost calling and start bringing it out into the world.

You might begin by emulating someone you admire and then work on imitating and thus developing their characteristics, including their breathing patterns connected with their virtues. Personal cultivation is hard because it means changing your character, and often your breathing style and inner energy dynamics, so make your training playful when you leave your comfort zone in attempts to surpass your self-imposed limitations and create something new. This type of self-development is equivalent to dedicating your life to a particular vision, pledge, vow or calling.

From the aspect of emanations there are uncountable phenomena in the cosmos including other living beings with minds who, because of their own possession of consciousness can generate thoughts, perceptions, feelings, and Knowledge within Shakti just like you. They can know aspirations, joy, achievement, bliss, and fulfillment. Without a mind you are just another insentient portion of Shakti, but because of the astounding, miraculous phenomenon of a mind you can know your identity as the ripple in space-time that you are and experience a universe of qualities. You can also cultivate higher bodies of transcendental composition and longevity that possess higher abilities to accomplish whatever you want in the universe. What goals are worthy of you when you can essentially live forever in some form or another? You are essentially the undying original nature and can cultivate excellences in any direction you want.

Your thoughts and actions interact with many other living beings, so start learning how to bring the best to all situations – which is the rest of your manifest body – and start acting in this manner. Grab hold of the process of causality and start working on manifesting something wondrous inside and outside of yourself for both yourself and others while evolving towards transcendence. Be your best, be the light you want others to see, the Dream within yourself that reconnects you to your greatest self, and the joy and aliveness you want to see in the world everywhere.

Meaning doesn't just fall on your doorstep so start living your life like it's your second chance and become the source of positivity you want to be or see. Life is too short to be little. Be the most evolved form of yourself you can be. Take authorship of your life by finding your own voice instead of following someone else's script that you might have adopted as an identity you don't really want. Shed some of the artificial layers that you have taken upon yourself within so that you can get in sync with your truest authentic self. Take direction of your life story as much as possible to not only create peace, bliss, happiness, flow state and well-being for yourself but also for others. Don't just smile more, laugh more, dance more and create more but *live for something bigger than yourself*. Do something that will benefit your community rather than just make yourself the "be all and end all" of your existence since this never provides anyone with any sort of deep meaning or life satisfaction.

People usually find meaning through some form of service, and become important in life through commitment to some higher mission or purpose that is of service to charitable objectives or people since we are all one family. Through service missions they witness happiness and receive positive emotions for a commitment that makes the world more beautiful. So what is it that can be your most significant imprint in life? What will make a difference in people's lives? What beneficial impact do you want to have on others? Where can you accent the good in the world? What profound part of yourself can you bring to the world to alleviate its suffering, or create new types of goodness and betterment for others?

Rather than waste your life away, how can you seed the world to improve it and make it healthier? How can you extend your spirit of generosity and cause the world to lean more toward the good? What deeds can you do for others that will produce sunshine in your heart? In what ways can you become a rainbow in somebody's clouds or leave golden footprints everywhere in life? What energy in sync with your own sincerity can you pour into the field of time? Is there some great crusade, something you want to help with or participate in even if just a little, that will give your life some higher meaning?

We can build a better future beyond even our highest expectations if we refuse to accept self-limitations (limiting patterns) and start working to manifest that which is currently beyond ourselves. Select a possible future to become a reality and then start working to make it so. Define yourself, your life and your future through your own guiding purposes instead of blindly conforming to the prescriptions of your culture or letting life sweep you along where circumstances define you because you lack self-direction. Define and then pursue the authentic goals of your native self rather than those sold to you by the larger culture or by other people who are trying to make you into something they want but you don't want. Connect with your highest inner calling.

For your psychological well-being, your decisions should be directed toward your inner ideals, not the ideals of someone else. You should set a course for an intrinsically fulfilling, satisfying and rewarding life by aligning your actions, activities and goals with the vision of your ideal self.

Therefore, make the vow to become a certain type of Buddha or Bodhisattva *because you want to become that way* and are inspired when imagining that you are that way. Make the vow to become a certain type of Buddha or Bodhisattva because you want to express a certain type of effort, activity or effect in the world. Then, start walking the requisite pathway of impeccable character development, cultivation Yoga, and the unrelenting performance of good deeds to make that possible future become a reality. Instead of being a passive monk, nun, sadhu and so on you have to engage in self-authoring and *start training to be that way*. Start learning the requisite skills to become a certain type of Buddha or Bodhisattva, start changing your personality in that direction, start working on refining your behavior, and start engaging in charitable activities which express that Buddha/Bodhisattva type. The further you go up the pyramid of practice the fewer people make it to the next stage, but this is what you need to do to succeed.

This is the stance you need to take for life, which is to take the body-mind complex that you are and cultivate with consistent and sustained effort to *become your highest and best ideal self*. How can you achieve the most meaningful growth by nurturing what is best in yourself and cultivating the exceptional? With enough deliberate practice you can overcome your current self and move closer and closer to your highest self and whatever it is that you want to master or become as an ideal self. Pick a possible future and then start working to manifest it.

Chapter 18
SUMMARY

In the *Nirvana Sutra*, Shakyamuni Buddha said spoke about *True Self, permanence, purity and bliss* thus revealing that the foundational substrate of the universe (Shakti), which is also our fundamental self-nature (True Self), is eternal and everlasting (permanent); perfectly pure (absent of phenomena like empty space); and thus changeless which also means still, peaceful or blissful.

In other sutras he said It is *unborn, unbecome, non-made, non-constructed*. In other words, the universal substrate or fundamental substance-essence did not come into being because It is self-so - something not produced/created but intrinsic because It has always been. Being changeless It is eternal.

In the *Nirvana Sutra*, he also said that his many teachings on impermanence, no-self, emptiness and suffering were just expedient means meant to help lead us to enlightenment. Other religions have different expedient means to help lead people to enlightenment, or just specify the lower objective of helping us attain better lives and experiences within existence.

At various times Shakyamuni Buddha also spoke of *paticcasamuppada*, commonly known as dependent origination or dependent arising. This teaching states that change in a phenomenon within the manifest universe is not due to one factor of causation but due to many factors yet the change is defined by cause and effect. All phenomena actually exist through a mechanism of infinite inter-causality or co-dependence that produces the interdependent arising of our continuously vibrating, fluctuating universe.

In particular, Shakyamuni Buddha spoke of twelve *nidanas*, or the twelve simplified direct links of dependent arising that lead to our sentient species and individual existence. These links follow one another as if in a chain: Ignorance, karmic formations, consciousness, name and form, the senses, contact, sensation, craving or desire, clinging or grasping, becoming, birth and death.

The **first link** in this chain of dependent arising, Ignorance, means we don't know how the changeless fundamental substrate produced the manifestation of Shakti, the universe, which is the **second link** in this chain. We don't know how an unmoving pure primordial substrate, free of manifestations, produced "karmic formations," which is another name for Shakti since all its components or phenomena are dependently defined formations created through cause and effect (karmic) relationships. We don't know how Creation – a realm of matter and energy phenomena – appeared from a perfectly pure ground state absent of anything other than the Aloneness of its pure Self, so we call our understanding "Ignorance." Typically Buddhists take the first link of fundamental ignorance as grasping at the self-existence of the person, but actually the first link of Ignorance means that we don't know how Creation happened.

With the manifest realm of karmic formations that comprise the universe of vibrating Shakti, all phenomena arise from other pre-existing phenomena or existent factors. Furthermore, within ever-dancing Shakti there are no permanent, self-so (intrinsic) or stable phenomena having an own-nature. Nothing has an independent, intrinsic self or essence, and hence all phenomena lack a self-so, independent identity. They are all dependently defined whereby each phenomenon is caused by all others, and therefore all phenomena flow into one another in complex but regular, ordered, set patterns of causality.

This principle of conditionality is at play in all phenomena, and the fact that all phenomena are linked to one another because they share in each other's manifestation makes the realm of Shakti a single whole, a single soup. The underlying true nature of the universe (Shakti), however, is the pure fundamental substratum that is free of conditioned co-rising or cause and effect. Within It there is no such thing as manifestation so It is called pure beingness (as the unchanging substance of the cosmos) and alternatively Emptiness (to denote the lack of phenomenal differentiation within It).

It is important to note that because we have a mind/consciousness we can discover, understand and then use the principles of causal regularity (cause and effect) that produce and regulate the universe. This is an important point to discuss later.

As to the **third link** in the chain of dependent origination, within the always transforming universe of complex interactions a thing called life eventually appeared, and some forms of life eventually evolved a property called consciousness. Thus, sentient life eventually evolved.

What does consciousness produce? It produces the *discernment* of names and forms, namely the appearance and discernment (understanding) of mental fabrications (objects), which is the **fourth link** in the chain of dependent arising. In other words, Knowledge arises within consciousness and is known by consciousness; consciousness produces Knowledge (names and forms) and understands/knows this Knowledge. This is a circle of illusion without objectivity, and yet this is what the process of consciousness produces – a subjective world of observed qualities, internal mental conceptions and the knowledge of a self-knower.

The **fifth link** is that various sense organs eventually formed within living organisms, and the existence of sense organs then gave rise to the **sixth link**, which is that the sense organs of living sentient beings can make *contact* with objects and produce sensory perceptions or impressions of those phenomena that constitute a new type of Knowledge. Hence, first you have basic consciousness or sentience that develops, and then perceptual sense consciousness to join the cognitive mental processes by which the mind operates.

In response to the stimuli of those sensory impressions, the consciousness of a sentient being reacts by automatically producing pleasant, unpleasant or neutral *feelings or sensations*. These emotions or sensations are yet another form of Knowledge that constitutes the **seventh link** in the chain of dependent arising. They are a reflexive, non-deliberate type of mental activity that automatically arises within consciousness.

In terms of evolution, it might actually be that the formation of sensory organs was a prior necessity for the formation of consciousness within living organisms, otherwise mental "changes of state" (thoughts or mental fabrications) could never be generated. However, the swapping of the fifth and fourth links is irrelevant for the larger story of what is being conveyed.

Now, when you like a sensation or feeling/emotion that arises within your consciousness, this produces the **eighth link** of dependent arising, which is the arousal of a *desire or craving* to repeat those pleasant sensations. For instance, when you become hungry the desire or craving for food leads you to satisfy that hunger in order that you experience satiation. Everyday you eat in order to re-experience the comforting feeling of satiation that silences the agonies of hunger. You need the desire of hunger in order to survive.

In the causal chain of dependent arising that explains sentient life, we can say that the next **ninth link** in the chain is that mental *craving and desire* leads to *clinging or grasping* at (the fulfillment of) desires because we hold onto pleasant thoughts and sensations with *attachment*, and thus continually pursue them. Using the example of hunger again, once a living being experiences a pleasantry (such as the satisfaction of food) it then wants to hold onto the contentment of satiation and repeat that sensation regularly. During sex one wishes to hold onto pleasant sensations as long as possible. This produces a type of clinging, attachment, pursuit or grasping.

Consciousness prefers wholesome, pleasant (joyous or blissful) as well as neutral, equanimous, peaceful-tranquil states of mind over unpleasant, unwholesome, or negative mental states such as pain and suffering. Hence, craving, desire, greed or thirst are aimed at the pursuit of pleasant (comforting) sensations and feelings due to the elimination of suffering, and then we want to hold onto those pleasant experiences with clinging. Sentient beings therefore tend to run after and cling to pleasurable enjoyments such as sexual pleasure, emotional or physical bliss, beauty, music, and so on. They develop entire processes of behavior to serve desire and attachment. Detachment, on the other hand, helps you become situated in transcendence where you can subsequently attain release and then freedom from disturbing emotions or desires that might control you. Acceptance without clinging or rejection produces internal peace in the midst of the world, which then becomes liberation or freedom (*nirvana*).

Overall, in summary we see the development of a universe of formations, and then the eventual development of complex life in the universe that possesses the attribute of consciousness that can experience thoughts, sensory perceptions of the world, and generate emotions or feelings about those experiences. Sentient life is a transient set of processes that goes about pursuing its various survival-maintenance needs and other activities that also include running after pleasant sensations and avoiding unpleasant sensations. It *grasps* after experiences for gain, such as to fulfill needs such as *sustenance* or the desire for procreation (sex). It *clings* to or attaches to the achievement of objectives in order to sustain its living existence, and this *grasping, attachment* or *clinging* is the **ninth link** in the chain.

Shakyamuni Buddha said that desire, attraction and attachment for various mental factors was the cause of suffering and that getting rid of the vexations of desire and greed for various objects and mental states leads to the cessation of suffering. However, there will always be suffering in life. It cannot be totally eliminated regardless as to what sages say in order to motivate you to purify your animal tendencies and cultivate spiritual practice to attain peace. The real key is to learn how to handle pain, misery, suffering and agitation so that you can better eliminate it, minimize it, manage it, avoid it, ignore it, reinterpret (reframe) it, alter conditions so that it doesn't reappear for you in the future, etc. The target is well-being rather than the perfect elimination of suffering. While you should employ many strategies to deal with suffering, you should in life pursue well-being rather than the absence of suffering so that within well-being any remaining degree of suffering can be managed and tolerated.

This is one reason why individuals are encouraged to pursue value-based happiness rather than pleasure-based happiness in life, which is because individuals who pursue activities that hold meaning, significance and life purpose can forget any suffering they must bear in life while working to achieve those higher goals. Those activities – especially undertakings of service that improve the lives of others or help create a new and better world – make life worthwhile despite the suffering they entail to make them possible.

Thus there is the *existence* of sentient life in the universe – *living body-mind complexes* – that continuously sustain their lives by pursuing their various maintenance processes until death. This requires that they pursue desires. The overall process of living or beingness for sentient life as it experiences the world and transforms along the way is called its *life, existence* or *becoming*, which is the **tenth link** in the chain of dependent arising.

Living is a continuous process of always-new *becoming* or *transformation*. Sentient life is a living object that, unlike inanimate matter, possesses the wondrous attribute of consciousness that allows it to change its behavior (activity) according to circumstances, adapt to new conditions to sustain itself, and transform its properties or attributes over time. Sentient life during its existence experiences thoughts, perceptions and emotions and runs after blissful mental states (conditions) absent of suffering that are either peaceful/tranquil or actively pleasant in some way.

The implications of the interdependent arising that characterizes Shakti and which has produced life are that sentient life must learn to understand the universe's laws of cause and effect within these relationships in order to survive and prosper, which leads to a necessity for the development of knowledge, science, logic (rationality), wisdom and skillfulness. The implication of our existence arising from cause and effect interrelationships means that we must find our meaning in life through our actions and efforts aimed at specific aspirations and ideals, and *through our relationships* with larger unities such as our connectivity or belongingness with our family and ever larger groups of people united by common purpose. While autonomous, we are part of larger unities we can embrace that thereby help us transcend feelings of human alienation and isolation, and we can also embrace personal vows that will provide us with a sense of larger purpose, meaning and significance for our life. The implication of the fact that the universe is constantly changing is that we must always be learning, be *adaptable* in responding to new situations and adept at solving problems, and be willing to let go of clinging and change over time in order to survive. We must also refuse to freeze the forward march towards various types of positive growth and progress in society such as the development of new types of knowledge, greater opportunities for everyone, or justice and fairness that liberate individuals from oppression. Another implication of existence impermanence is that we need to strive for lifespan longevity, a continuity (of admirable personality characteristics, skills or attributes) across lives if such a thing is possible, and a continuity of strong growth, progress or improvement in human conditions that spans across generations (which helps to counteract entropy). The implication that the world does not exist in the way it appears to be means that we need to primarily rely on rational logic and our intellect rather than our emotions to make decisions and run our lives, and need to control our emotional minds so that they do not control us. The implication that happiness is a fleeting state of mind is that we need to pursue peace, meaning, purpose and significance in life instead of just short-term pleasurable states as our primary source of enjoyment or motivation. The implication that the universe is impure is that we need to beautify and improve/purify our living conditions to make them better. Impurity mandates that we need to develop rules of hygiene and cleanliness for daily living, create clean environments for habitation, and eat (clean) quality food because in a dirty world such factors are necessary for the survival of our bodies, their proper growth and the prosperity of our lives. The implication that entropy rules a universe of deterioration and ever increasing disorder is that we must strive to make conditions better not just *in the now* but *for the future* of our children and subsequent generations, which is by adorning the country with long-lasting improvements and working to bring out its magnificence. Nothing stands still so if we don't strive for growth and progress by improving conditions for ourselves and others then they are bound to decline. The implication that life is filled with suffering (due to our quality of knowingness) is that we should try to reduce the pain and suffering within our lives by becoming stronger and more resilient, learning to control our emotional mind, and by reducing the causes of suffering for ourselves and others. This once again leads to the need for making our circumstances and living conditions better and improving our own adaptability. The fact that we are not inherent souls or entities but composite dependent constructions having the same permanent real Self that eternally pervades all beings and existence implies that that there is no such real thing as a sentient being or own-entity receiving the fruits of their actions. Therefore we should reduce our desires, greed and attachments to the fruits of our own actions since there is no real being to receive them. We can certainly pursue pleasurable, enjoyable states to refresh ourselves now and then but for the greater good of ourselves and society we should also learn to become egoless at times and act with inner renunciation in selfless service that dedicates some personal efforts to improving the conditions of our close relationships and the world. While during life we should certainly pursue individual activities, aspirations and meaningful, significant purposes that reflect our own inner *dharma*, and while we should also certainly pursue pleasurable experiences, activities and emotions during life that produce mental states absent of suffering (*Kama*), we should also be willing to become devoted to certain higher causes, and take on sufferings to improve conditions for others while remaining stable and unaffected by the fleeting emotions of pain or pleasure they entail. It is through selfless, impartial, compassionate activities that are dedicated to the uplifting of mankind that humanity transcends its prior conditions and achieves a better body just as we attain a higher spiritual body through the discipline of spiritual efforts and self-cultivation practice. Through mental detachment from the fruits of our efforts and through persistent actions, unwavering in intent, that uplift society despite their difficulty we can through that selfless service find inner happiness within ourselves and move society forward. Therefore through kind acts of service we can maintain the prosperous continuity of society, elevate ourselves individually through consummate noble conduct, and exhibit proper activity that leads to liberating effects (that all will share in) rather than what is merely profitable or expeditious. Of course, you are free to arrive at your own differing conclusions as to the implications of the factors of life and existence. You can take each of these factors and arrive at different implications for human behavior, and the conclusions and emphasis you choose will build up an entirely different human culture.

So far we have simply explained the appearance of life within the universe, the evolution of consciousness and sense organs, and acknowledged their ability to produce perceptions of the world as well as thoughts and feelings in response to those sensations and perceptions. We also know that organisms will alter their behavior according to their desire to pursue pleasant sensations that they find attractive, wholesome, profitable or pleasurable for their lives. Desire consequently leads to some type of pursuit, clinging or attachment that may present a problem for living beings. Hence we have contact with objects that produces feelings, and then craving and grasping for pleasurable feelings, emotions and sensations. The *"nirvana"* of spiritual cultivation, on the other hand, is a peaceful state characterized by the extinguishment of (suffering-prone) craving and desire that are replaced by inner peace, tranquility and equanimity.

This briefly summarizes some of the mental activities of sentient organisms. They have consciousness and sensory perceptions of the world, can think and experience emotions due to possessing the attribute of consciousness, and are motivated by cravings and desires for positive experiences (some of which are necessary to sustain their life while some are for pleasure/entertainment) that can lead to clinging or attachments. They go about their lives revolving through these various states, and transform for better or worse during the process, which is called their "life" or "existence." You can guide the transformations that happen to you during life, which is called self-development or cultivation, but most people simply let changes happen to them.

In general sentient life, and certainly animal life, is preoccupied with two processes – *to find food and not to be eaten* so as to become food for others. They seek *resources* (for food or sustenance, medicine, prosperity, success, happiness, etc.) and *safety/protection* for their lives. Note that women often seek mates replete with money or power since they can then provide for them and protect them. Humans are social creatures that have banded together to live in peaceful, productive, collaborative and lawful communities in order to help ensure the supply chain of their food supply and protect themselves from worldly injustice, aggression upon their assets and belongings, oppression of their freedom, or outside attacks and exploitation by others, etcetera. This, too, is recognition of the individual's need for food/resources and safety/protection.

Groups, communities or societies eventually develop social rules for living together not only to ensure harmony but to establish fairness, justice and protect the rights of individuals within the group so that no one can oppress or exploit anyone else. Due to community living relationships, humans have developed the ethical values and virtues we have today that enable strangers to harmoniously live together in peaceful, cooperative and collaborative societies characterized by ethics and virtue. The laws of organization find that societies naturally develop into hierarchies of elites and commoners, or those who manage/lead and those who are lead, and societies develop laws, social forms and rules of fairness and justice so that people do not aggress upon others and so that the fortunate elites – who are subject to *craving, desire* and *greed* like all others – do not use their privilege, power and position to oppress the weak and take advantage of them, which is also a natural tendency. Hence the necessity for systems of checks and balances to restrain the powerful that we find in many societies.

Now, just as we explained the creation, appearance or birth of dancing, vibrating Shakti (*samsara*) from the pure, "empty" fundamental substratum of the universe, at this point we have to explain the birth of a specific sentient being (living organism) in the universe out of this entire matrix of interlinking conditions. This is called "birth," which is the **eleventh link** in the chain of dependent origination.

If we are speaking of a specific individual – you – then the eleventh link refers to the becoming of "rebirth" rather than simply "birth," and this difference is due to the existence of reincarnation. Birth comes with the fact of being entangled within cyclical existence. Reincarnation is a process managed by higher spiritual beings (enlightened Buddhas) who help guide the rebirth process (the recycling of lives) so that people's existence is not completely cut off at death (resulting in permanent annihilation or extinction) but sustained with some degree of continuity. The process of generating an independent spiritual body that is achieved through spiritual cultivation, on the other hand, is normally called "transformation" rather than "birth." However, you can also call it a "birth" achieved through the transformations caused by spiritual practice.

Entropy rules the universe so within the cosmos all phenomena are impermanent including life. Phenomena are all dependently arisen processes so they are all impermanent. They are conditional, which means they possess a nature that ceases; nothing but the primordial substratum has a permanent, changeless or independent (rather than conditional) own-nature. Since all conditional things decay, eventually a birth (living sentient being) will experience the deterioration of aging and then death, which are the **twelfth link** in the chain of dependent origination. Birth comes on the basis of consciousness, death comes when life has run its course, and extinction/annihilation comes from the elimination of that form.

As aging and death are inevitabilities, the major challenges for living beings during their existence cannot be limited to suffering alone. The big problem is the brevity of existence itself. Therefore the challenges in life are not just the elimination or avoidance of suffering but the prolongation of life, and the maintenance of the continuity of life itself (after death) so that it does not end in total annihilation upon death. Therefore, while sentient beings seek to avoid suffering and instead seek to experience happiness, well-being and meaning/purpose in its place, they must also pursue several other goals or activities during life as well. They need to cultivate methods that lead to *greater health and longevity and rejuvenation*, and to the persistence of consciousness after death if there is such a thing. There are some of the objectives of spiritual cultivation.

Here we come to the human condition, which is our condition. In terms of the universe we are living objects that possess the property of consciousness. We are best described as a *process* rather than as a being or living object, and our process is inseparably embedded within Shakti so that it belongs to Shakti but is capable of creative participation within its body. Specifically, we are a body-mind complex composed of energy and matter (simples such as atoms) and are conditionally defined through the interdependence of all other things in the universe such as energy fields, physical laws of nature, atomic qualities, the prior history of development, etcetera. As the body-mind entity that we are, we essentially have only two skills: *physical skills* and *cognitive skills*.

As an animal with consciousness that lives in social groups for the purpose of survival, the Great Learning required of our lives is that we learn how to master both our physical and cognitive skills and take them to their highest degrees of excellence. In particular, we have to learn how to use our consciousness correctly, effectively (skillfully) and optimally whenever possible. We need to learn how to manage the operations of our consciousness with excellence because consciousness creates our world, produces either suffering or well-being, and ultimately controls our behavior that produces either pain or the positive factors of prosperity, success, happiness and flourishing for our lives. All the events that we can experience in life are experienced through our body and its consciousness. Without consciousness we are the darkness of insentient matter or energy.

The Great Learning for our lives requires that we fully master our bodies and minds, and must cultivate their many abilities to their utmost stage of excellence. We therefore need to learn how to manage ourselves, our plans and our actions with wisdom, skillfulness and tact. During life we should pursue whatever goals, objectives and achievements that we want, and because of the great miraculous gift of consciousness should learn how to experience every moment of our life with full awareness and bliss. You want to experience mental states free of suffering (due to mastering calmness, detachment, desirelessness, dispassion, equanimity, peace, etcetera), but you should also want to experience an active *joie de vivre* during life and engage in various means of joyful enjoyment and self-expression. Life is not simply about existence. To say that life is only about a clear awareness of experience while absent of emotion experiences such as bliss, joy and other positive states makes it a robotic undertaking that is hardly worthwhile. However, you don't want to become mindless like the world of natural phenomena either. You want to embrace the life you have and enjoy it. The rewarding emotions or feeling states of life make it worthwhile and give it meaning, and yet the highest internal mental states entail the comfortable, calming bliss of internal peace, presence, tranquility, lightness, equanimity and flow although there are tremendously rewarding peak experience active states as well (joy, shine, glow, happiness, etcetera).

As to our body, which is our "lived space," we must cultivate its physical health, its fitness potential, its internal energy and ultimately train it to reach a point of natural ease and comfort. You want to always be feeling the blissful inner vitality of your body. You either want to forget the sensation of your physical body entirely because it is so healthy and comfortable, or cultivate its well-being to a stage where you feel a non-irritating subtle bliss in all its cells, which makes it feel especially comfortable but without that comfort occluding your internal clarity.

The Great Learning for your life is that you need to cultivate a mastery over your physical realm and psychological realm. You want to cultivate your mind so that you are always in states such as internal peace, clarity, presence, centeredness, lightness, flow (which is a type of samadhi or concentration state) or sunniness and shine, and always experiencing happiness or bliss in life. Life is existence (*sat*), your existence has consciousness (*chit*), and within that consciousness you want to experience *ananda* - physical and mental bliss, happiness, joy, peace, lightness, centeredness, presence, flow or however you wish to define an excellent state of non-irritating comfortable magnificence. This is the *sat-chit-ananda* of Hinduism.

In terms of cognitive skills to master, we are capable of *deliberate mental processes* that can be guided by our will such as thinking, reasoning, imagination, and the intellect. These mental abilities, and others such as concentration and focus, control our behavior, and these are all factors of consciousness we must learn to master for life.

To master our lives we must also master the *automatic processes* of our consciousness such as emotional feelings, mental states, moods and even afflictions that spontaneously arise in response to situations. Through devoted cultivation practice many automatic mental processes can be mastered or even reprogrammed, and you can also learn how to gain control over some autonomic physical processes of your body (temperature control, heart rate, muscle tone, etcetera) as well.

For the Great Learning of life, you basically have to master your *thinking mind* and *emotional mind*. These are your deliberate intellectual processes that are under voluntary control such as thinking and your automatic or reflexive processes of consciousness (such as your emotions, mental states and unwanted mental afflictions) that spontaneously arise within your mind. You want to be able to choose what you become emotional about and when you become emotional. You especially want to master your emotions by cultivating tranquility or equanimity, which is a balanced mind that is not easily shaken even by adversity, and dissolve any fetters of the mind such as incorrect mental algorithms that represent wrong perspectives or cause you to assume artificial limiting beliefs that hamper your development, your enjoyment of life or produce wrong activities.

These two mental aspects, as well as your physical body and behavior, should be the primary focus of your self-improvement (cultivation) work during life. They are what you should always be working on improving and taking to states of excellence. A living physical body together with its consciousness - which produce mental states, external behavior and material accomplishments - are what you must master during life. You need to master them by achieving a heightened level of performance excellence and self-governance.

To master our consciousness we must learn how to control many mental factors such as our attention, concentration, volition/willpower, and thinking. Ultimately our capabilities of deliberate consciousness - which include factors such as our thinking, wisdom (understanding) and decision-making - can be enhanced, improved, elevated or perfected through various types of education and training, and doing this is a primary requirement for life. We cannot remain feral humans but must elevate ourselves from the stage of being just animals to a stage of *humanity* (where we transcend our animal nature), and then to a stage of *nobility* (that expresses consummate conduct), *majesty* or *magnificence* (a greatness that far surpasses commonality) and then *spirituality* (where we can make great sacrifices for the benefit of others). We can only do this if we cultivate all our physical, mental and behavioral dimensions until they reach and abide in states of highest excellence.

For this to become possible we must train ourselves, and training requires that we correct ourselves when we diverge from ideal models and modes of thinking or behavior. This, in turn, requires that we be taught those ideal models or modes and then monitor and adjust our mind-stream and actions in real time when they deviate from the ideal patterns. To be able to do this, again in turn we must practice mindfulness and self-correction of our thoughts and behavior so that we are naturally practicing self-rectification all the time. This will enable us to overcome those parts of ourselves that hold us back from nearing our values and our higher potential.

This is how we can reduce imperfections in our thoughts and activities and reach towards the self-perfection of our body-mind vehicle. Only the witnessing practice of mindfulness (self-watchfulness) and self-rectification enable us to purify and elevate our various properties and processes to embody excellence and elegance or even majesty. When we have stubborn flaws and imperfections that require a stronger type of remedy than what mindfulness, introspective examination and wisdom-reasoning can do when we want to dissolve those problems at their roots - such as habits, ingrained mindsets or persistent types of bad emotional reactions - we must engage in entirely different training regimens to rectify those faults and imperfections. On the road of spirituality we're not just trying to get to normal (being non-faulty, non-errant, non-evil, non-sick) but to become exceptional.

Basically, starting from a child you want to learn *how to think better, feel better* and then *act better* for your life, and that striving to become better requires that you emulate models of perfection and engage in self-adjustment processes against those standards. You must *retrain yourself* to something higher and better when you find that your attributes are errant or sub-optimal. Everyone has imperfections so you must use various remedies to eliminate them and replace them with something better. As living beings with consciousness, we have the capability of *adaptability* that is necessary to maneuver within a world of changing impermanent conditions. We need to learn how to think better to improve our decision-making and act better (in new and improved ways) so as to create better conditions or circumstances for our lives, and we need to gain conscious control of all our mental processes so that we experience a more wholesome and enjoyable interior life of mental states and moods.

The principle of training is to *learn and put into practice methods that most reliably produce the highest levels of excellence*, and this requires that you develop excellent neurological (mental) patterns and programs through study and training practices as well as the normal process of environmental absorption. The ultimate goal is not just to always experience interior states of happiness and well-being but that your thinking and external behavior also become extremely skillful, tactful, kind, effective and perfectly appropriate for every situation (consummate). You want to program out the uncongenial aspects of yourself and perfect your behavior so that you exhibit consummate, compassionate, wise and skillful conduct of the highest excellence ("brightest virtue") and where your behavior ultimately exhibits kindness, elegance, grace, nobility, and elevation. Therefore you need to learn how to manage the operations of your consciousness with excellence, and bring your thought processes to a higher mode of operation because consciousness creates your world, creates either suffering or well-being and happiness within it, and ultimately controls your behavior, activities and their results.

As to our physical body, naturally we want to be as healthy as possible during life through proper diet, exercise and care. We want to have a sound mind and sound body. We want to be physically comfortable at all times (we want to feel physical bliss in every body cell or become so healthy that we don't notice our body feeling at all), and able to control our internal energy and other physical processes such as our breathing that in turn can be used to manage our mood, behavior and effectiveness during activities. We want to train our body to its maximum degree of fitness – maximizing its flexibility, agility, coordination, strength, endurance and speed – and we want to install within ourselves optimal reactive patterns for sports, self-defense, good conduct or other types of physical endeavors and aspirations. The body and its internal energy should become the servants of our mind, but they can only achieve elegance and refined gracefulness or poise through practice.

You want to cultivate a healthy body during life, and especially cultivate the purity, circulation and robustness of your internal energy even if you don't achieve enlightenment during this life. During life, the efforts you make to cultivate your Qi will produce definite degrees of progress, and those results will serve as a foundational base for enlightenment efforts in the afterlife (as a deva spirit) should you not succeed during this life. Enlightenment, as a necessity, entails cultivating the higher transcendental bodies inherent within your physical structure, and this requires that you cultivate your internal energy in various ways that purify its Yin and Yang components.

It is just a fact of the universe that we can split apart from living physical matter a set of different energies that reside within it and thereby unleash higher body vehicles that are copies of our original physical nature. In other words, a certain number of decompositions are inherent for physical matter and they can produce transcendental etheric copies of the original physical nature. To achieve enlightenment you must cultivate the internal vital energy of your physical body (Qi) until it can escape from the matrix of your physical body as an independent life form that is still tethered to your living physical nature, which begins the development of the *sambhogakaya* of enlightenment.

To do this you must follow a road of *gradual spiritual cultivation*, and the achievement requires the help of enlightened beings who have previously succeeded on the path, but who will not help you unless you are an ethical, virtuous being. Then out of your physical body you can cultivate an independent subtle body (that you normally only achieve upon death), out of your subtle body you can cultivate an independent Causal body, out of the Causal body you can cultivate an independent Supra-Causal body (the stage of the full Arhat enlightenment attainment that is the fourth dhyana) and out of the Supra-Causal body you can split out an Immanence body that is the equivalent of the Great Golden Arhat attainment. This is the spiritual path that mankind must tread. In Taoism this sequence is encapsulated within the phrase "Jing transforms into Qi, Qi transforms into Shen, Shen transform into Emptiness (the Supra-Causal Buddha light body), and you must break Emptiness to return to the Tao."

As conscious beings, a crucial aspect for life is not just learning how to use all the capabilities of the mind for survival purposes or safety needs (the prime directive of life is to survive), but learning how to use your mind (which begets thoughts and guides your actions) to also satisfy any needs for self-fulfillment because this is what makes life worthwhile. One goal is to learn how to use your mind to minimize your suffering in life by cultivating well-being, which requires you to learn how to think and act in optimal ways so that harmful states/conditions do not arise, either internally or externally; so that beneficial, beautific or "pure" states always arise instead; so that you can transform or cut off harmful states that arise or have already arisen; and so that you support any wholesome, beneficial states that are already existing to keep continuing.

You want to cultivate your consciousness so that you are not just calm, peaceful, clear and centered as a natural tendency but so that you regularly experience various positive or blissful states such as happiness, sunniness, shine, lightness, flow (which is a type of active samadhi or concentration state), presence, and are always experiencing happiness and joy in life. You want to cultivate your mind and your behavior to regularly experience various wholesome internal states such as these, both passive and active or *vibrant* states of consciousness. Those active, vibrant states of consciousness beyond the needs of survival require that man pursue roads of perfected behavior, ethical enjoyment, personal achievement, self-esteem, relationships and self-actualization that provide him with happiness, meaning, purpose and significance in life.

Thoughts and feelings are fleeting vibrations in consciousness connected with energy and internal biochemical reactions, and are essentially transient irritations of energy within our nervous tissues. These fleeting mind-stream elements can affect us substantially in either positive or negative ways, and so we must learn how to manage our mind-stream and reliably produce positive mental states rather than negative, painful or unwholesome mental states instead, and we must learn how to transform negative states into positive states at will. We must learn to manage consciousness so that it is not just pure or blissful, but so that it is skillful and effective because it enables us to produce what we want in the material and conscious realms. This is the basis of consummate conduct, which is perfectly appropriate for the situation at hand, skillfully leads to what we want with an optimal elegance, and is replete with bright or virtuous qualities that transcend our animal passions and propensities.

Therefore, through your actions, conduct and behavior you want to cultivate external conditions so that positive states can frequently arise for yourself (and others). You must therefore strive to improve the various circumstances you encounter in life by repairing unwholesome external conditions. You can replace them with what is better, and should make sure that wholesome admirable conditions are not destroyed but sustained or improved. Wherever you go, you want to improve conditions for both yourself, for others and for the possibility of a brighter future for society, never resting on the laurels of your past achievements. You want to seed the world to create a new and better now and tomorrow by accenting the good, promoting certain trends or activities to make it healthy or advance it, and by creating social, economic, cultural and other improvements along with a world of better circumstances as a legacy of your life and efforts.

As to the automatic processes of consciousness that you experience in your mind, they are like reflexes that mechanically arise without thinking. Many of the patterns for our automatic reflexes can be "purified" through retraining to produce superior mental and physical reactions, and as beings of consciousness we should train our consciousness to produce superior reflexive responses whenever and wherever possible.

Consciousness is the wish-fulfilling prize of the universe that lets us (sentient beings with higher consciousness) create or experience whatever we desire. We need to train/master consciousness (our cognitive machinery) so that we can fulfill our needs and desires in life and experience a bliss and joy of existence as well as meaning and purpose for our actions. Otherwise there is no point to existence. We want to live a life that has meaning and experience fulfillment, satisfaction, joy and bliss during our existence. In cultivation you therefore strive to learn the best ways of operating your consciousness for your greater benefit. You learn the best ways for handling yourself in the world such as by following the harmonious pathway of least resistance. The ancients basically told people how to use their minds and train their minds, but people don't understand their lessons or their importance. Our thought patterns can be trained, our cognitive skills can be developed, our emotional expressions can be elevated or controlled, control over our physical body and internal energy can be attained and perfected, and our mental states can be conquered and transformed into peaceful or active enjoyments at will.

Training is necessary for us to be able to attain these greater goals of life, which is the Great Learning of discovering the principles of cause and effect within Nature and the Great Learning of mastering our consciousness and behavior so that we can control ourselves and Nature (circumstances or conditions) to become, create and experience whatever we want. As a sentient being with the property of consciousness, you should maximize the capabilities of your consciousness and learn how to perfectly control it, such as learning how to think properly, change your mental states or moods at will, and ignore mental distractions such as emotional disturbances or unwanted afflictions and agitations that impair tranquil or beautiful mental conditions.

The Great Learning for our lives is learning to assume full control over our bodies and minds and behavior, to cultivate our bodies and consciousness and our behavior/actions to their utmost excellence, to pursue the goals and achievements we want during life, and to experience a life of significance with full awareness that often touches blissful, beneficial and joyous states of being. You want to cultivate yourself to the point where your psychological realm has been conquered and you are always in various comfortable/blissful states such as peace, clarity, egolessness, brightness, freshness, presence, flow, lightness, harmony, happiness, optimism, sunniness or shine, etcetera, and always experiencing a joy of life. You want to always be feeling the active inner vitality of your physical body and be experiencing a fulfilling joy of living through virtuous self-expression.

The Great Learning for life involves learning how to control our consciousness and maximize its capabilities. This includes such objectives as learning how to concentrate and ignore or subdue mental distractions, annoyances, emotional disturbances, agitations and excessive passions or cravings. Your mental apparatus is a dependent construction, and thus it is always conditionally mechanical or automatic to some degree beyond your control. What arises within your mind is not your fault because thoughts automatically appear without any effort on your part, but what you do with your mind-stream is your responsibility. Therefore you should learn how to control your thoughts and emotions once they arise. You are also the one who guides your own willpower to control their actions and behavior. The responsibility for controlling and perfecting these abilities rests in you and only in you.

Therefore, you should try to learn the highest and best ways of thinking, experiencing and behaving so that your deliberate thought-stream is predominantly filled with positive, skillful and enjoyable states of mind rather than negative experiences, and you need to learn the various techniques (such as mindfulness and self-correction) that enable you to break the momentum of your mind-stream (and your entrainment with it) so that you can change its contents and trajectory at will. You need to master the highest and best expedient means for altering or improving your states of consciousness so you can actualize the highest states of excellence. The ultimate goal is that you want to live life ethically and skillfully and fill it with wonderful experiences, enjoyments, and achievements so that you experience fulfillment, satisfaction and blissful states of mind rather than suffering and purposelessness.

So basically, the Great Learning for our lives is to assume full control over our bodies and minds (and behavior), cultivate the capabilities and status of our bodies and consciousness to their utmost excellence, formulate and then pursue particular goals and achievements we want, and to celebrate life with full awareness as a blissful experience. You want to cultivate to the point where your psychological realm has been conquered and you are always in a positive state of peace, vivid clarity, presence, lucidity, mental freshness, flow, lightness, compassion and kindness, wisdom, sunniness or shine, etc. and always experiencing great vigor along with a joyousness, happiness or blissful calmness in life. When not cultivating equanimity or tranquil states of mind you want to always be feeling a harmonious active inner vitality and you want to frequently experience a happy *joy de vivre* during fulfilling activities of self-expression.

In life you act to fulfill your physiological survival needs (food, water, clothes, shelter, sex, etc.) and security-protection issues that involve health, personal safety, emotional security, financial security and so forth. You also work to fulfill interpersonal needs such as desires for feelings of love, intimacy, friendship, connection or belongingness. As an individual being you seek feelings of mastery, competence, strength, accomplishment and self-esteem, and although you desire the freedom of independent autonomy where you *feel authentic in your life*, as a social animal you act to fulfill a need for feelings of status, respect, and recognition by groups of others by climbing dominance hierarchies. You act to satisfy your various internal promptings such as curiosity or the desire for novelty, and you often engage in creative activities such as the arts, sports, problem solving challenges and various forms of self-expression.

In life you are always working to actualize your goals and objectives, which are your accomplishments and attainments. You should be always working to change your circumstances for the better including your surrounding karmic conditions, life events or fate. As you experience life, you will grow in ways that transform your personality and perspectives (mindset), and you can work to beautify these aspects as well as master various skills and create stronger relationships for a better *this life* and *future life* since these attributes will carry through to your next incarnation. And, you might wisely decide to offer kind, compassionate, caring aid to others to help solve their current problems and transform the negative conditions of the world. This will not just make the world a better place for others *and yourself* but also make it possible that you might *inherit legacy improvements* in a subsequent incarnation. This also enables you to accumulate the merit necessary to earn a better subsequent incarnation such as the ability to enjoy those newly created beneficial conditions. One should never rest on their achievements in life but always pursue greater learning, skills, self-improvement and positive accomplishment, and you should try to achieve these objectives through the deliberate capabilities of consciousness that control your mind and behavior.

To summarize it a different way, the Great Learning for our lives is to assume full control over our bodies and minds and conduct, cultivate our bodies and consciousness and our behaviors to their utmost levels of capability and excellence, chart and pursue goals, achievements and experiences we want during life, and we should seek to experience life with full awareness and bliss. We need to cultivate to the point where our psychological realm has been conquered and we are always physically comfortable and mentally experiencing positive states like peace, calmness, vivid clarity, centeredness, presence, mental freshness, flow, lightness, happiness, elevation, sunniness or shine, and always experiencing a celebratory joy of life. Important during life is to learn how to control your mental state that is naturally peaceful and calm until you disturb it. Meditation practice helps us to retrieve the underlying natural peaceful, calm, tranquil or even happy state of our mind that lacks mental disturbances and pollution.

We can also cultivate states of egolessness and desirelessness that are extremely peaceful and calm but brilliant with vivid clarity, and more active states of bliss that are vibrantly engaging and fill life with more energy. This includes *peak experiences* that are deeply moving, exhilarating, elevating experiences – exciting, intense, oceanic moments of highest happiness and fulfillment – where your mental realm has opened up and you experience virility, vitality and advanced forms of perceiving reality. Such mental states are often triggered by pursuits in the arts, nature, sex, music, creative work, scientific discovery, sports, or religious worship. In those moments reality is often perceived with emotions such as wonder, awe, humility, reverence and feelings of goodness, beauty, truth, wholeness, uniqueness, self-sufficiency, perfection, completion, richness, effortlessness, playfulness and aliveness.

You are essentially the undying original nature, and with your body-mind that is the fundamental nature you can cultivate excellences in any direction you want. Being Shakti, you have the right to shape it in any direction you want as well as the right to shape your personality, mood, state of mind or *bhava* with a dominant note that is whatever you want, such as when you evoke certain positive emotions when in service to people who are essentially the same Self. There will be consequences to whatever you do. For life you must first handle survival issues, then improve the conditions of your life for yourself and others, and then cultivate your life to attain a higher existence in this and yet higher realms.

To do this, Buddhism says we must cultivate Wisdom-kaya, which means to continuously work at perfecting our knowledge, understanding, and wisdom (of cause and effect) so that we have better behavior. Wisdom-kaya involves honing the skillfulness and effectiveness of our actions and behaviors – honing our "accomplishment wisdom" – so that we can achieve/manifest whatever we want in reality.

Buddhism says that we should also cultivate Perfection-kaya in life, which means devoting ourselves to the yoga of self-development work to perfect not just our bodies and consciousness but their attributes such as our views and perspectives as well as our character and behavior. Perfection-kaya is a road of *self-discipline* and *self-perfection* that includes embracing the highest human values, ethics, virtues and morality. It involves striving to always exhibit skillful, noble, compassionate consummate conduct. Perfection-kaya includes the road of spiritual cultivation that entails cultivating our physical nature as well as developing the capabilities of our mind, behavior and our internal energy along with the ability to access and rest in the inherent purity or natural quietness of our mind. It also includes the ideal of making accomplishments in life with perfection.

Buddhism also says that we should always in life be practicing Compassion-kaya, or Karma Yoga, which is performing selfless deeds of kindness and various acts of service to benefit others. In the Hindu Ramakrishna Order the monks must not only engage in (1) meditation practice, (2) spiritual study, (3) devotional activities (prayer, chanting, ritualistic puja), but in (4) service activities too, which is Compassion-kaya. Service trains us to be helpful to others. Many Christian monastic traditions also emphasize the service aspect of spirituality foremost. We are social animals that must live together in groups, so group welfare is not only necessary for our survival but for our happiness and well-being. There needs to be a collective investment in society so that the individuals within it can thrive, flourish, prosper and have the conditions available to cultivate to enlightenment. Man finds purpose and meaning in life through his (social) relationships with others and his feelings of kinship, inclusiveness or belonging. Deeds of kindness such as charity exhibit a love for others, and such efforts should always be performed without any concern for personal recognition, rewards or benefit. Since there is no such true thing as a living being, there is no real being there to receive the rewards of merit. The only benefits one should expect to receive from acts of kindness and merit are positive emotions, the witnessing of happiness, and the reaching of a deeper understanding of life. However, these are receipts that money cannot buy.

Greek philosophy has advice to offer us as to the proper goals of human life as well. It says we must work to achieve *eudaimonia* (human flourishing and prosperity) to live a wise and good life of happiness and well-being, and this requires that we develop our reason as a nourishing quality. We must also cultivate personal *phronesis* (practical and moral wisdom), and *arête* (excellence or virtue) where you live up to your full potential of excellence, and where virtuous qualities and methods become your natural disposition rather than just a diluted light tendency.

In ancient Imperial Rome the *mos maiorum*, or set of Roman values, involved promoting the common good of the people, and so the Roman hero was someone who served the nation and sacrificed for others. While the Greeks stressed individual prowess (such as exhibited by Homeric heroes or Olympic champions) the ideal Roman hero was someone whose wisdom, courage, and self-sacrifice saved his country during a time of peril, which is the equivalent of the Bodhisattva hero.

Confucius said that we need to engage in self-cultivation, which is the art of becoming better (such as improving our thinking), and so during this life we should train to brighten our inherent virtues; love people and act in ways that beneficially help them and society (we become of service to others by enriching the world with benevolent activities); and continuously pursue these endeavors until we reach and reside in the highest levels of excellence. "Education" is formation of the self, and in Confucian education it is especially emphasized that you are to polish your virtues and abilities at learning, self-correction and performance (achievement). You must be careful in your thinking by becoming aware of your own thinking processes in order to assess yourself for self-correction. You must engage in proper conduct so as to live in a righteous way (propriety entails the way things should be done), and you should always treat others with humanness (benevolence, consideration, kindness, caring and compassion).

Christianity says we need to love other people, as was also emphasized by Confucius, and the pathway of Christian perfectionism prescribes that we unrelentingly perform good deeds on their behalf with all our might and by every possible means while devoting ourselves to the perfection of our character and other forms of self-improvement. It stresses that we should be cultivating our person as a whole and express ourselves through deeds of loving kindness, care and compassion that help others.

Hinduism says that during life it is proper that we pursue four goals or *Purusartha*. We are to pursue *Moksha* or liberation (the enlightenment of enjoying better mental states as well as the attainment of higher transcendental bodies). We are to pursue proper forms of *Kama* or joys, pleasures, amusements, benevolent emotions, desires, and wishes during life (so that life is neither boring nor stale, not simply a matter of survival, nor predominantly marked by suffering). We are to pursue *Artha* or a proper means of life (wealth, career, prosperity, success, livelihood, etc.) in order to reach and be in a state you want to be in. By engaging in proper *Artha* we can enjoy a virtuous livelihood and not be a burden by having to depend upon others for our existence. We are to pursue *Dharma* so that we can elevate our behavior and live harmoniously and cooperatively within society. To follow *Dharma* means to regulate our behavior so that we are in accord with ethical, moral, wise, compassionate, benevolent and virtuous ways, and the pathway of *Dharma* elevates our conduct and behavior so that we can peacefully live together with others in families and society.

As to Taoism, the instructions for human society and for your life are represented in the symbolism of the Three Divine Teachers, or the "Three Pure Ones." The first of the Three Pure Ones (Three Purities) is Yuanshi Tianwang who represents the absolute nature, original nature or fundamental essence since he is lord of the origin of things, lord of the primordial beginning. The second of the Three Purities is Shangqing, the Supreme Pure One who is also known as Lingbao Tianzun, "The Celestial

Worthy of the Numinous Treasure" who represents manifest existence and its evolution into various forms through the laws of nature, meaning the laws of cause and effect or dependent origination that rule all of causality. He is also called Jingbao, the "Treasure of the Laws of Nature" or "The Universally Honored One of Divinities and Treasures" since Shakti becomes differentiated into all sorts of forms, phenomena and functions that are here called divinities and treasures. Shangqing represents the entire field of manifestation, or Shakti-Creation, and everything within it are his treasures. The third of The Three Pure Ones is Taiqing - the Great Pure One or Grand Pure One – and the one most appropriate to us in terms of instructions for life. He is also known as "The Universally Honored One of Tao and Virtues" or "The Celestial Worthy of the Way and its Power" (Daode Tianzun). Through his title as Taishang Laozun he is known as the "Highest Elder Lord" or "Grand Supreme Elder Lord" to denote that he is the highest sentient aspect within the field of manifestation/Creation who serves as a teacher or leader of mankind. He represents an enlightened sage, which is your inherent potential if you cultivate spiritual practice. Pictures of Taiqing usually show him holding a fan to indicate that he has mastered the life-force energy that must be cultivated in order to attain the higher spiritual bodies of enlightenment. It also symbolizes power or mastery over the basic moving energy, *Prakriti* or Shakti aspect of Creation that includes the forces of the manifest cosmos. As animals with higher consciousness, we are charged with this task as well, which is to master or manage skillfully the various aspects of Shakti. Since we are to master cause and effect, religions that previously thwarted the development of science, math, innovation, invention and progress in various fields can clearly be seen as being in error. A fan also means that Taiqing can cause wind, meaning that he can create phenomena through his understanding of nature. Since he masters the laws of dependent origination and their manifestation, he is said to preach the Laws of Nature as well as how we should develop - how things are harmoniously "meant" to be. In conventional terms, because he is a sentient being with a mind that can form thoughts to know things he can develop understanding/wisdom that lets him gain control over phenomena, and this is the instruction for our lives. We are to grow by developing our consciousness and cognitive skills in various ways to gain control of nature, ourselves, and to make our lives better. This includes gaining control over ourselves and elevating our thinking, emotions and behavior – our virtues or perfections.

Active consciousness (knowing, knowledge or awareness) appears as a movement of energy and Taiqing represents the moving aspect of Creation as a sentient being who can manage its functions, properties and aspects, and thereby direct them however he wishes. Taiqing is also described as the educator who brings civilization, which is a task we are charged with, and is equated with the highest teaching. The highest teaching is disseminating civilizing influences throughout the world such as ethics in society, scientific and economic improvements, and the knowledge of the pathway to Tao (self-realization and the attainment of our higher spiritual bodies that take us out of the lower realms forever). As an educator who teaches or transmits, he represents gaining control over the forces of movement or transformation in the field of manifestation. But in which direction should we take things? He learns to master the transformations of phenomena and uses his knowledge of how to change things to make them better, thus enriching the world and human civilization in both the material and ethical, moral, cultural or spiritual spheres. We are advised to emulate Taiqing by becoming masters of our consciousness and external phenomena, and using them to elevate our personal lives and the conditions for society as well.

As a living, sentient body-mind complex, we are basically capable of deliberate acts of consciousness, and we also experience automatic processes that operate according to ingrained patterns. We must train these capabilities, and for our body we must cultivate its health and learn to master its movements, states and internal energy. Most important of all, its health and internal energy must be cultivated through purification practices in order that we become able to attain the spiritual bodies of enlightenment.

During the course of our lives we develop mental programs that control our mental states, thoughts, emotions and our will that guides/controls our actions. We need to install excellent mental programming (the patterning of consciousness) through a sustained effort that teaches us how to rest in mental stillness combined with training that installs new but optimal behavioral patterns or replaces any inferior programming that we have picked up through other forms of conditioning. Then we must monitor and adjust our consciousness in real time so that it produces elegant thoughts, mental states and behavior that embody excellence in regards to our highest models of behavior and achievement. We especially need to remain true to our sense of highest self rather than conform to inferior standards foisted upon us by society that encourage conformity to lower instincts or thinking. Instead one should follow the *ikigai* principle of becoming a sovereign, autonomous individual who devotes himself to pursuits he personally enjoys or that make life personally meaningful. We should strive to find our own voice and follow our own authentic aspirations in life so that we actualize our highest and best potentials, and direct ourselves towards everything that we want to become and are capable of becoming. We must become our authentic selves. We must be true to ourselves in our lives and say what we want to say and do what we want to do (as long as they are virtuous activities that do not infringe upon others' rights or hurt them). At the end of our lives we will not remember the time we spent in the office or in mowing the lawn, so you should "climb that mountain." By expressing your authentic true self you can access your inner vibrant, vitalizing energy that invigorates your whole being and the flourishing of your human spirit. You will achieve resilience along with a cheerful enjoyment of life when you genuinely feel internally alive and can continue to sense the feeling of being real, alive and creative even under adverse circumstances.

Basically, the fundamental way of the Great Learning of life is that we cultivate our minds, bodies and behavior to their highest octaves – thus vastly improving our cognitive and physical skills – and continuously pursue states of highest excellence in living. The goal is to cultivate the virtues and excellences of our body, mind and behavior; to not only make our virtues "illustrious," "bright" or magnificent but strongly manifest them in the world; to cultivate steady states of well-being (abundance, prosperity, success, health, happiness, peace, harmony, friendships, intimacy, comfort, joy and bliss) absent of suffering; to behave like your own authentic self to others and to eradicate selfishness by loving everyone and performing activities of merit that lead people to a better life; and to cultivate the spiritual path to enlightenment.

The fundamental way of the Great Learning is to always pursue such endeavors in life until we rest and reside in states of highest excellence, which includes the achievement of the deva enlightenment body. Through training and practice we must elevate our animal nature to human nature, human nature to noble or magnificent majestic conduct, and nobility to spirituality where one lives their life for others. In this way we earn heavenly merits even if we don't achieve the deva body from our cultivation efforts during this life.

We should make a Buddha or Bodhisattva vow to become a certain way (like a certain type of Buddha or Bodhisattva who will perform certain types of deeds and functions in the universe), and start performing good deeds and acts of merit in line with our vows. We should also try to perfect our character or personality by freeing it of faults, magnifying its qualities of greatness, ornamenting it with brilliant new virtues, and training ourselves to start performing actions in line with our highest ideals or aspirations. This effort is equivalent to transforming your basic core character or personality, which is typically denoted by your natal chart in astrology, and this takes effort. Nonetheless, that is the practice and process of cultivation.

We should try to transform our personality for the better in life via techniques like *watchfulness (mindfulness) and self-rectification practice* to correct our faults and cultivate various virtues (such as exemplified by the efforts of Liao Fan, Benjamin Franklin and Frank Bettger); *regular contemplative introspection and review practice* to spot or realize the underlying root causes of our errant attitudes and behaviors so that we can dissolve our problems, afflictions, or limiting beliefs at their roots and dissolve any psychological blockages standing in the way of cultivating virtues and betterment; *principal awareness* to impress virtuous emotions into our activities and inject them with higher ideals; *emulation* of individuals or ideal models who have talents, virtues or activities we admire; *bhava* attitude meditations and associated visualization practices to develop virtuous character traits; various other techniques (such as NLP, ACT and CBT) to help us *regularly emulate ideal models of behavior;* the *repetition of affirmations* to help us develop those traits, or the *repetition of prayers and/or mantras* to aid us in developing those traits and to help motivate us to perform in special ways; real world conduct *in line with those desired traits* to reinforce their development, especially acts of service that benefit others; studying the principles of good or *optimum behavior* or irreproachable conduct and incorporating them in oneself; *broadening yourself with culture* and restraining yourself with the principles of proper conduct (standards of proper behavior); a *regular schedule of repetitive disciplined training* to regulate our behavior towards self-perfection and help establish the new virtues we want; and by using various personality transformation techniques (such as CBT) to regularly work at incorporating ideal models of virtue and behavior into our psyche.

The purpose is not just to become "non-sick" or the normal state free of faults but to *cultivate the exceptional* through personal practice. At first you strive to get your head above the water but then you work at raising your head above the clouds. At first you try to restrain and then purify the errant tendencies or characteristics of your behavior and personality, but if you *go deep enough* it is like transforming your inherent personality characteristics as indicated by your astrological natal chart. You actually want to change your natal tendencies so that you don't have to continually police errant attributes and conduct because you don't have them anymore. You want to succeed at deep self-transformation in this very life - which is the crux of self-cultivation - rather than simply police yourself to be a certain way or just lightly alter your behavior/tendencies in a diluted, lukewarm fashion with hopes that you will inherit a new life with much stronger betterments.

You are trying to become the person you want to be, or the way you want to be just as you should try to become the specific type of Buddha you want to become. You should become the author of your own life, or one can say lives. As the famous actor Cary Grant once said, "You are just a bunch of molecules ("simples") until you know who you are." Therefore once you set a purpose for yourself you should start cultivating in that direction. Your personality determines your success or failure in life and whether people like you or not. You display your characteristics to the world through your personality and it can attract people to you or repulse them. For better or worse, it is how people recognize you and so your character determines your fate. It is under your control, is subject to your self-development efforts, and just as you can develop a talent or skill you can and should improve it to be whatever you want it to be in order to become the person you want to become and do what you want to do. You have an inherent natal personality inherited from past lives that develops according to influences such as your conditioning, but you can choose (to develop) your personality and you can choose your activities.

This is the path of spiritual practice. You work at changing your personality (your internal predispositions, attitudes and character traits) and behavior, developing virtues and excellences and wholesome qualities, doing good deeds for others ... and work at meditation practice and other spiritual exercises to purify your mind and attributes, and you also engage in internal energy exercises to start cultivating the deva body inherent within you.

We want to live life in the service of values. We want to be working at cultivating ourselves and our deeds and conduct so that we have the merit for achievement. We want to carry forward without interruption. We want to leave a legacy behind of golden footprints wherever we go. We want to cultivate virtuous, pure, consummate ways in ourselves, our conduct and activities, and use our personality and efforts to perform compassionate, kind, merciful deeds on behalf of others. This is cultivating *agape*, which is love that is an action.

Spiritual practice is not just about ourselves but about developing empathy and sympathy for others, and showing compassion in response is cultivating the vehicle of humanity. It is about compassionate action on behalf of the poor, oppressed and suffering, commitment to a life of service and sacrifice on behalf of individuals you know along with the larger human community, and having faith in working towards the possibility of a better world. Patanjali said, "When you are inspired by some great purpose, some extraordinary project, all your thoughts break their bonds, your mind transcends limitations, your consciousness expands in every direction, and you find yourself in a new, great, wonderful world."

At the same time we want to be cultivating the abilities and powers of consciousness to an excellence of perfection, the abilities and powers of our physical body to an incredible skillfulness, and the excellence of our behavior and accomplishments in the world. The ideal outcome is a sound mind and sound body where we regularly enjoy positive mental states and are in control of ourselves at all times.

There are mental states of well-being within reach of consciousness that are intrinsic to the nature of consciousness rather than being predicated on the contents of consciousness being one way or another, and we want to cultivate those natural states of peace and tranquility as well as more active states of bliss such as positivity and optimism, the joy of life, the bliss of feeling most alive, happiness, shine and flow etcetera. To achieve these states, which constitute a "positive mental attitude," we must tame the mind that is the creator of suffering, and especially learn to gain control of our emotions through detachment and other techniques. You must learn to control your emotional mind and mental attitudes because life is what you make it.

Cultivate your entire mind, body and behavior for this is the way to succeed. Enlightenment entails cultivating the most transcendental body possible that is oned with reality in the highest possible way, embraced in a larger unity of universal participation while preserving human autonomy and transcending all lower realms of existence. The highest possible spiritual body is considered a purified existence, synthesis and reintegration with the cosmos's highest possible level of beingness. This is considered *Moksha* or liberation or complete enlightenment – a return to as close to the original nature as you can go in terms of the beingness of transcendental body composition – because there is nowhere higher to go. The only achievements left are then to perfect the magnificence of your mind and its powers or capabilities (of thinking skills, moods, attitudes, etc.), improve the excellence of your body and its internal energies, ennoble your virtues and values that guide your conduct and strive to incorporate them into yet more skillful behavior (of your conduct, talents, activities, accomplishments, relationships, etc.), and cultivate tranquility, peacefulness, happiness, shine and lightness through the detachment of not taking yourself so seriously since you are a non-intrinsic being with illusory consciousness that can never truly know Shakti or your true nature. This realization should lead to detachment and the achievement of inner peace, tranquility and liberation from being controlled by your emotions and the passions. You can now pursue the science of happiness by cultivating greater wisdom for life, more positive mental states (both active and passive), more positive social relationships, more enjoyable activities, and by pursuing purposes that have great meaning for you in life.

To start attaining the higher transcendental bodies you must cultivate your character (ethics, virtue, morality, merit, etcetera) to deserve enlightenment because other beings must help you achieve it and they won't assist you in the arduous processes of transformation unless you are a virtuous individual. You must therefore cultivate mental and behavioral purity as "the way to Heaven," which means cultivating a core of virtues and values that you take as a moral compass throughout life, and you must also undertake the Yoga of inner energy work that is greatly assisted if you practice yoga, martial arts, rebounding, dance or athletics that require you to stretch your muscles completely and master your breathing and inner energy movements.

You have a mind and body for your existence – physical and cognitive skills – and so you must cultivate your mind, body and behavior to a higher level of perfection as the ideal.

Whether or not you achieve enlightenment during life, this is the pathway of spiritual cultivation and necessary human development within the field of Shakti.

ABOUT THE AUTHOR

William Bodri is the author of a number of books on spiritual cultivation. A related collection of books you might find useful, which would constitute the Yoga, Vajrayana and *neijia* or *nei-gong* paths to enlightenment, include:

Neijia Yoga
Nyasa Yoga
Buddha Yoga
Bodhisattva Yoga (forthcoming)
Meditation Case Studies
Color Me Confucius
The Mystical Path of Christian Theosis (Elijah John)
Visualization Power

The following books would also be helpful for the task of physical and spiritual transformation:

Culture, Country, City, Company, Person, Purpose, Passion, World
Detox Cleanse Your Body Quickly and Completely
Look Younger, Live Longer
Prevent and Reverse Atherosclerosis (Stanton Reed)
Super Cancer Fighters
Sport Visualization

Mr. Bodri is a self-supporting author who would be honored by your support of his work. You might appreciate his other books such as *Breakthrough Strategies of Wall Street Traders, Super Investing, Move Forward, Quick Fast Done, Husbands and Wives Were Connected in the Past, How to Create a Million Dollar Unique Selling Proposition*, and *High Yield Investments: Hard Assets and Asset Protection Strategies*.

www.ingramcontent.com/pod-product-compliance
Lightning Source LLC
Chambersburg PA
CBHW070519010526
44118CB00012B/1029